Economics After the Crisis

Economics After the Crisis is an introductory economics textbook, covering key topics in micro- and macroeconomics. However, this book differs from other introductory economics textbooks in the perspective it takes, and it incorporates issues that are presently underserved by existing textbooks on the market. This book offers an introduction to economics that takes into account criticisms of the orthodox approach, and which acknowledges the role that this largely Western approach has played in the current global financial and economic crisis.

A key feature of the book is its global approach: it offers examples from countries all over the world, including from developing and emerging economies. The chapters discuss all major economic topics, including: individuals and households; the behaviour of consumers; the behaviour of firms; markets; the role of the state; public goods and commons; labour markets; capital markets; the macroeconomic flow; economic growth; international trade; nature and environmental externalities; and poverty and well-being. Throughout, the book presents theoretical perspectives in which social structures, relatedness, uncertainty, and social norms provide key economic explanations, contrasting these with the idealised worldview of neoclassical economics.

Economics After the Crisis is designed for a one-semester introductory course in economics, primarily at undergraduate but also at postgraduate level, and is suitable for students from a range of disciplines. It will be of particular relevance to those students with an interest in developing economies.

Irene van Staveren is Professor of Pluralist Development Economics at the International Institute of Social Studies (ISS), Erasmus University Rotterdam, the Netherlands. She has been awarded the 2014 Lifetime Achievement Thomas Divine award by the Association of Social Economics.

Economics After the Crisis

An introduction to economics from a pluralist and global perspective

Irene van Staveren

LONDON AND NEW YORK

First published 2015
by Routledge
2 Park Square, Milton Park, Abingdon, Oxon OX14 4RN

and by Routledge
711 Third Avenue, New York, NY 10017

Routledge is an imprint of the Taylor & Francis Group, an informa business

© 2015 Irene van Staveren

The right of Irene van Staveren to be identified as author of this work has been asserted by her in accordance with the Copyright, Designs and Patents Act 1988.

All rights reserved. No part of this book may be reprinted or reproduced or utilised in any form or by any electronic, mechanical, or other means, now known or hereafter invented, including photocopying and recording, or in any information storage or retrieval system, without permission in writing from the publishers.

Trademark notice: Product or corporate names may be trademarks or registered trademarks, and are used only for identification and explanation without intent to infringe.

British Library Cataloguing in Publication Data
A catalogue record for this book is available from the British Library

Library of Congress Cataloging in Publication Data
Staveren, Irene van.
Economics after the crisis: an introduction to economics from a pluralist and global perspective / Irene van Staveren.
pages cm
1. Economics. I. Title.
HB171.5.S784 2014
330—dc23
2014025553

ISBN: 978-1-138-01611-8 (hbk)
ISBN: 978-1-138-01612-5 (pbk)
ISBN: 978-1-315-79396-2 (ebk)

Typeset in Times New Roman
by Swales & Willis Ltd, Exeter, Devon, UK

Printed and bound by CPI Group (UK) Ltd, Croydon, CR0 4YY

Contents

List of images	x
List of diagrams	xii
List of tables	xv
List of boxes	xvii
Acknowledgements	xviii

Introduction   1
Orthodox and heterodox economics 1
What went wrong with economics? 3
Heterodox economics 4
Signs of change 6
From orthodox and heterodox to pluralist economics 7
Approach of the book 7
Notes 9

1 Economics as a science   10
1.1 What is economics? 10
1.2 Social economics 15
1.3 Institutional economics 19
1.4 Post Keynesian economics 21
1.5 Neoclassical economics 23
1.6 Rationality 27
1.7 Power 28
1.8 Interesting sources 33
1.9 Glossary 33
Notes 35

2 Individuals and households   36
2.1 Individuals and agency 36
2.2 Households 37
2.3 Gender division of labour 41

2.4 Household production and bargaining 46
2.5 Social and institutional economics of household production 52
2.6 Neoclassical economics of household production 59
2.7 Interesting sources 62
2.8 Glossary 62
Note 63

3 Consumption 64

3.1 Consumer demand 64
3.2 Social economics of consumption 66
3.3 Institutional consumer theory 70
3.4 Post Keynesianism: consumption versus saving 71
3.5 Neoclassical theory of consumption 74
3.6 Externalities of consumption 80
3.7 Interesting sources 84
3.8 Glossary 84

4 Firms 87

4.1 Entrepreneurs, managers, and firms 87
4.2 Types of firms 89
4.3 Finance and accounting 95
4.4 Social economic and institutional approaches to management 99
4.5 The neoclassical approach to management 102
4.6 Post Keynesian theory of the firm 104
4.7 Neoclassical theory of the firm 108
4.8 Interesting sources 113
4.9 Glossary 114
Note 116

5 Markets 117

5.1 The market 117
5.2 Three critical theories about markets 118
5.3 Market types 121
5.4 Market failures 134
5.5 The failure of markets 140
5.6 Interesting sources 142
5.7 Glossary 142
Note 144

6 The state 145

6.1 The economic roles of the state 145
6.2 Social economic theory of the state 145
6.3 Institutional economics of the state 150

6.4 Post Keynesian economics of the state 153
6.5 Neoclassical economics of the state 157
6.6 Public finance 159
6.7 Interesting sources 166
6.8 Glossary 166
Notes 168

7 Public goods and commons   **169**
7.1 Domestic public goods 169
7.2 Theories of public goods 173
7.3 Global public goods 176
7.4 Governance and finance of global public goods 181
7.5 Commons 183
7.6 Interesting sources 187
7.7 Glossary 188
Note 188

8 Labour markets   **189**
8.1 Labour supply 189
8.2 Labour demand 198
8.3 Unemployment and wages 206
8.4 Interesting sources 217
8.5 Glossary 217
Notes 218

9 Financial markets   **219**
9.1 Introduction 219
9.2 Social economics 222
9.3 Institutional economics 226
9.4 Post Keynesian economics 235
9.5 Neoclassical economics 243
9.6 Interesting sources 248
9.7 Glossary 249
Notes 250

10 The macroeconomic flow   **251**
10.1 The macroeconomy 251
10.2 The embedded economy: social economics 255
10.3 Macro level institutions: institutional economics 259
10.4 The economy as an open system: Post Keynesian economics 262
10.5 The economy as a closed system: neoclassical economics 269
10.6 Interesting sources 275
10.7 Glossary 275

11 Money — 277

11.1 Money as a social relation: social economics 277
11.2 The central bank: institutional economics 285
11.3 Endogenous money: Post Keynesian economics 290
11.4 Money as neutral: neoclassical economics 299
11.5 Interesting sources 304
11.6 Glossary 304
Notes 305

12 Economic growth — 306

12.1 Introduction 306
12.2 Social economics of growth 309
12.3 Institutional economics of growth 314
12.4 Post Keynesian growth theory 319
12.5 Neoclassical growth theory 327
12.6 Interesting sources 334
12.7 Glossary 334
Notes 335

13 Nature — 336

13.1 The economics of nature 336
13.2 Social economics of nature 339
13.3 Institutional economics of nature 345
13.4 Post Keynesian economics of nature 352
13.5 Neoclassical economics of nature 357
13.6 Interesting sources 363
13.7 Glossary 363
Notes 364

14 International trade — 366

14.1 Introduction 366
14.2 Social economics of trade 371
14.3 Institutional economics of trade 373
14.4 Post Keynesian economics of trade 380
14.5 Neoclassical trade economics 382
14.6 Case study: NAFTA 388
14.7 Interesting sources 389
14.8 Glossary 389
Notes 391

15 Well-being and poverty **392**
  15.1 Introduction: the biases of GDP 392
  15.2 Social economics: multidimensional well-being and poverty 394
  15.3 Institutional economics: relative well-being and poverty 398
  15.4 Post Keynesian economics: the dynamics of wealth inequality 406
  15.5 Neoclassical economics: head counts and happiness 411
  15.6 Interesting sources 418
  15.7 Glossary 418
  Notes 418

  Annex: history of economic thought 420
  Family tree 420
  Contributions to economics from the Global South 429

  Index 432

Images

0.1	High hopes for a change in economics	2
1.1	MONIAC at Erasmus University Rotterdam	11
1.2	Nine key economists	14
1.3	Coffee and cake with a budget constraint and a behavioural constraint	21
1.4	Ice cream consumption and outside temperature	27
2.1	Golden container for a champion beer drinker	40
2.2	Non-stereotype occupations	44
2.3	Fairy-tale pony	55
3.1	Tesla electric car	72
3.2	Coffee and cake revised	80
4.1	Unilever head office in Rotterdam	88
4.2	Virgin airplane	90
4.3	Software firm Atlassian in Amsterdam	102
5.1	Unilever deodorants	125
5.2	Mobile phones for sale	127
5.3	Car mileage just before a mental limit	140
6.1	Toilet paper	148
6.2	Apple products	155
6.3	Street lighting	161
7.1	Park	175
7.2	Solar light	179
8.1	Elasticity	196
8.2	Textile factory	207
9.1	Rabobank office	230
9.2	Real estate in San Francisco	242
10.1	African and French traded products	261
10.2	Leakage effect	267
10.3	Equilibrium on skis	273
11.1	'In God We Trust' on a Dutch €2 coin	278
11.2	Argentinian peso pegged to the dollar	287
11.3	Financial trading	292
12.1	Kicking away the ladder	314
12.2	Assembled in China	317
12.3	Major currencies	331

13.1	Natural resource: wood	341
13.2	Renewable energy production in Germany	346
13.3	Earthquake damage in Groningen	351
14.1	Containerships from the Netherlands to Germany	375
14.2	Trade in coffee beans and cereals	385
15.1	Homeless man in Barcelona	399
15.2	We cannot all be winners	409
A1	Adam Smith	420
A2	David Ricardo	422
A3	Karl Marx	423
A4	Alfred Marshall	423
A5	Thorstein Veblen	424
A6	Joseph Schumpeter	425
A7	John Maynard Keynes	426
A8	Amartya Sen	427
A9	Elinor Ostrom	428
A10	Thandika Mkandawire	429
A11	Raul Prebisch	430
A12	Gita Sen	430

Diagrams

1.1	Gross National Happiness	13
1.2	Loss aversion	16
1.3	Institutional constraints	20
1.4	Consumer confidence in the USA 2004–2009	23
1.5	Utility function for beer and peanuts	24
1.6	Diminishing marginal utility	26
2.1a	Vladimir: production alone	49
2.1b	Olga: production alone	49
2.2a	Joint household with gender stereotype norms	51
2.2b	Joint household with gender equal norms	51
2.3	Joint household production maximisation	60
3.1	Opportunity sets of consumption	65
3.2	Engel curve	73
3.3	Individual demand curves and the market demand curve	74
3.4	Individual utility maximisation	78
3.5	Utility maximisation with changing prices	81
3.6	Individual demand function from a utility scheme	82
4.1	AIR FRANCE KLM share price development 2000–2008	92
4.2	Mondragon management model	94
4.3	Expansion frontier and finance frontier	106
4.4	Production function of pizzas	109
5.1	Monopoly	123
5.2	Oligopoly	126
5.3	Monopsony	129
5.4	Monopolistic competition, firm level	131
5.5	Perfect competition, firm level	133
5.6	Perfect competition, market level	133
6.1	Composition of tax revenue in Brazil, Latin America, and the OECD (2010)	164
7.1	Variations of public goods	171
7.2	The Laffer curve	176
7.3	Greenhouse gas emission growth	178
7.4	Variations of public goods including commons	184
8.1	Labour supply and employment	190
8.2	Determinants of labour supply	191

8.3	The discouraged worker effect in South Africa, 2013	194
8.4	The labour supply curve	197
8.5	Discrimination and inefficiency: labour market for truck drivers	199
8.6	Labour demand curve	206
8.7	Unemployment in the Post Keynesian perspective	212
8.8	Unemployment in the Post Keynesian perspective with increased labour demand	213
8.9	Labour market equilibrium in neoclassical theory	216
9.1	Historical US interest rates, 1955–2013	224
9.2	House foreclosures in the USA, September 2013	226
9.3	Trust in banks in the USA	235
9.4	Economic flow model of the real and monetary economy	236
9.5	US Financial Fragility Index	238
9.6	Financial cycle	239
9.7	Stock market value versus real value in the USA	240
9.8	Home prices and real values in the USA	240
9.9	The random walk of the EMH	244
9.10	Normal statistical distribution	245
9.11	Time to find your home key	246
10.1	Basic macroeconomic circular flow	255
10.2	Embedded macroeconomic flow	259
10.3	Institutional macroeconomic flow	262
10.4	Effective demand	265
10.5	Post Keynesian aggregate consumption function	266
10.6	Post Keynesian macroeconomic flow	270
10.7	Neoclassical macroeconomic equilibrium	272
10.8	Macroeconomic equilibrium with crop failure	274
10.9	Neoclassical macroeconomic flow	275
11.1	Gold reserves of the Reserve Bank of India in tonnes	278
11.2	Value of the bitcoin in US dollars since its introduction in February 2013	283
11.3	Inflation in India: the consumer price index	284
11.4	Exchange rate trends of the rupee	288
11.5	The money circuit	290
11.6	The Post Keynesian demand for money	293
11.7	The supply of money during boom and crisis	294
11.8	The neoclassical money market	300
12.1	Dependency ratios (%) for selected countries, 2012	307
12.2	Unadjusted labour share (%) in China, 1992–2008	312
12.3	The efficiency of land redistribution	313
12.4	Aggregate production function	328
12.5	Long run growth through shocks	329
12.6	New Growth production function	333
13.1	Global material use, 1900–2005	337
13.2a	Global sea level change	338
13.2b	Global CO_2 level change	338
13.3	Environmental pressure of road traffic in the Netherlands, 1980–2015	348
13.4	Trends in material intensity (MI) in the Asia-Pacific region	355

List of diagrams

13.5	Trends in domestic material consumption (DMC) in the Asia-Pacific region	356
13.6	Environmental Kuznets curve	357
13.7	Price development in the EU ETS	361
14.1	Trade ratios (EX + IM)/GDP, selected countries (%), 2012	368
14.2	Female labour share and manufacturing value added per worker	383
15.1	Tax revenue % of gross domestic product (GDP), 2006–2010	402
15.2	Conditional cash transfers in Latin America: reductions in the Gini coefficient	402
15.3a	Scatter plot of the Gender Equality Index (GEI) and formal gendered institutions in the Middle East and North Africa (MENA) region, 2010–2012	405
15.3b	Scatter plot of the Gender Equality Index (GEI) and informal gendered institutions in the Middle East and North Africa (MENA) region, 2010–2012	405
15.4	Capital/income ratio in Germany, France, and Britain, 1870–2010	407
15.5	The Kuznets curve	413
15.6	Production possibility frontier	415
15.7	Happiness of nations, 2012	417

Tables

1.1	Top competences scores of good leaders	17
1.2	Time use in the Netherlands in 2009	18
1.3	Rationality in the four economic theories	28
1.4	Market shares of the world's largest agro-businesses	30
2.1	Child labour, average hours per week for working children	37
2.2	Daily time use by women and men in six countries	43
2.3	Unpaid work and caring in Russia: hours per day (in Taganrog, 1997/1998)	46
2.4	Household bargaining power sources	48
2.5	World Values Study data for Russia on gender norms	50
2.6	Hours of leisure time in three household scenarios	52
2.7	Worldwide results of the ultimatum game	54
2.8	Suggested list of well-being dimensions for household bargaining partners	56
2.9	Evaluation of well-being outcomes: gender stereotype norm scenario	57
2.10	Evaluation of well-being outcomes: gender equal norm scenario	57
2.11	Pay-off matrix for well-being outcomes of household bargaining	58
2.12	Possible combinations of household production in neoclassical economics	61
3.1	Utility maximisation with two goods	76
3.2	Utility maximisation with two goods and their prices	77
4.1	Balance sheet	97
4.2	Profit and loss account	98
4.3	Variable cost of pizza production per evening	108
4.4	Total cost of pizza production per evening	110
4.5	Marginal cost of pizza production	110
4.6	Average costs of pizza production	111
4.7	Revenues and profits of pizza production per evening	112
4.8	Marginal cost and marginal revenue of pizza sales	113
5.1	Market institutions	119
6.1	Income inequality in Latin America, Gini coefficients	147
6.2	Deposit insurance in Brazil, 2011	153
6.3	Size of the state in the economy (% of GDP) across the world	157
6.4	Good governance indicator of business start-up costs (2013)	160
7.1	Official development assistance, % of GDP	180
7.2	Opportunity costs of global public goods, estimations in US$ billion	183
8.1	Net primary school enrolment rates in southern Africa (%)	191
8.2	Reasons given by nationals for being out of the labour force in United Arab Emirates (UAE), 2009	193

8.3	Contracts in the South African labour market, number of persons, last quarter 2013	202
8.4	Labour market institutions and their effects	202
8.5	Marginal revenue and marginal cost	204
8.6	Demand for labour	205
8.7	Unemployment rates for groups in South Africa, last quarter 2013	206
8.8	Minimum wages for domestic workers in South Africa, 2013	209
9.1	Bank balance sheet	220
9.2	US Balance of Payment (BoP) deficit, US$ million	237
10.1	Gross domestic product (GDP) growth rates for Japan, 1980–2012	252
10.2	Propensities to consume and save in Japan, 1980–2012	254
12.1	Annual economic growth rates in China (%), selected years	308
12.2	Country scores on the corruption index (0–100), selected countries, 2012	318
13.1	Ecological footprint: largest deficits and largest surpluses of bio-capacity	344
13.2	Top and bottom six countries on the Happy Planet Index, 2012	345
13.3	Drivers of change in domestic material consumption, Asia-Pacific region, 2000–2008 (%)	356
14.1	Composition of trade between Mercosur and EU (2012)	377
14.2	Historical import tariffs of developed countries	379
14.3.	Trade specialisation between Argentina and Brazil, 2012 (in US$ thousand)	385
14.4a	Autarky: production in kilograms	386
14.4b	Specialisation: production in kilograms	386
14.4c	Specialisation on comparative advantage and trade: consumption in kilograms	386
15.1	Human Development Index and performance, South Asia, 2012	395
15.2	Multidimensional poverty indicators	396
15.3	Multidimensional Poverty Index and indicators, South Asia, 2012	397
15.4	Regional disparities in human development in Thailand, 2014	403
15.5	Gender Equality Index (GEI) and gendered institutions in the Middle East and North Africa (MENA region), 2010–2012	404

Boxes

1.1	The story of Zhang Xin	32
2.1	Role model for family–work balance	43
2.2	Asymmetric information creating irrationality	55
4.1	The perverse effects of extrinsic motivation, such as money and status	101
6.1	Land titling in Bolivia	150
6.2	Brazilian incubators	156
6.3	Mexican debt crisis	165
7.1	Polio vaccination programme in Pakistan	170
7.2	World Social Forum	181
7.3	Common-pool resource management of irrigation systems	187
8.1	Labour unions in South Africa	215
9.1	The Dutch banker's oath	229
9.2	Nobel Memorial Prize winner Shiller on Nobel Memorial Prize winner Fama	231
9.3	London City banking blog	233
11.1	Local money on a large scale	281
11.2	The power of currency speculation	298
12.1	UN Economic, Social and Cultural Rights: a selection	310
12.2	Britain's early economic growth behind tariff barriers	315
12.3	The puzzle of China's weak financial institutions	318
12.4	China's economic growth	327
13.1	The 2013 Dutch National Energy Agreement	347
13.2	Dow Jones Sustainability Index	348
13.3	Pollution in poor countries is cheaper …	358
14.1	More gender inequality through Mercosur–EU trade	378
15.1	Better Life Index indicators	394
15.2	Poverty in the USA	400

Acknowledgements

> When a book really wants out, it will force itself to the light - regardless.
> William Least Heat-Moon, *Blue Highways*, 1982

I am very grateful for the support I received to write this textbook. First, thanks to Jos Mooij, the late Dean of the Institute of Social Studies, who enthusiastically supported my initiative to write this book for my introductory economics class. I wish she had lived to see the result and hear from the students how they experience the new course. Second, to my excellent research and editorial assistant Zahra Zarepour, who took care of the figures, tables, boxes, and permissions. Third, to my husband Eric Brinkhorst, who provided all the photographs in the book (except those for the history of economic thought), following up on often vague ideas which he turned into surprisingly good matches with images. Fourth, to the De Wit Fonds for providing funding which enabled me to commission the illustrations and pay other expenses. Fifth, to the team at Routledge, without whose trust and support this book would not be what it is now. Sixth, to Ben Fine, who kept me sharp with his relentless but fair feedback on a few draft chapters. Seventh, to all my colleagues to whom I said 'no' or 'later' over the past two years, for their patience until the writing was over. And last but not least, to all my students, who taught me what questions are relevant for a genuine pluralist economics course, and that diverse country context matters for learning.

Finally, I thank all the copyright holders who gave me permission to publish their artwork: Skylar Fein for the painting on the cover, Eric Brinkhorst for most of the photos, Getty Images for the picture of Keynes, *The Economist* and Jon Berkeley for a cover image, Gita Sen for her own photo, the London School of Economics (LSE) for a picture of Thandika Mkwandawire, UNCTAD for a picture of Raul Prebisch, Holger Motzkau for a picture of Elinor Ostrom, and SOHO China for a picture of Zhang Xin. The copyright holder of the image of Joseph Schumpeter is not known to the author.

The images of Smith, Ricardo, Marx, Marshall, and Amartya Sen are in public domain CC0 1.0 Universal Public Domain Dedication[1] and are not copyrighted.

Note

1 https://creativecommons.org/publicdomain/zero/1.0/

Introduction

This textbook fills a gap in the range of introductory economics textbooks that are available on the market. The gap refers to the lack of economics teaching that is critical of the orthodox approach, developed in Western countries. Also referring to this gap, the popular British economic magazine *The Economist* asked in July 2009, when the crisis was at its worst, what had gone wrong with economics. This was quite surprising coming from *The Economist*, because the magazine generally favours the orthodox approach to economic theory and policy, in particular free markets and neoliberal policy.

Orthodox and heterodox economics

When I studied economics, I only became gradually aware that I was being taught a particular theory, namely neoclassical economics. I remember my first discovery of the existence of Keynesian economics and its apparent disagreement with what I was being taught, when rumours went around that the professors on the eighth floor of the economics department and those on the other floors were not on speaking terms. Another instance of my growing awareness that one theory dominated my education, was when my favourite class, history of economic thought, was scheduled on Monday mornings at nine o'clock and was the only course for which we were not required to sit exams. Together with a friend, I read the chapters in our history of economics book that were skipped in class and we discovered the basic ideas of John Stuart Mill and Karl Marx. From there onwards, we became the outsiders among most of our fellow students, eventually doing our MA theses on unorthodox topics and using unorthodox methods, my friend in Mexico and myself in Indonesia.

I decided to apply to do a PhD in economics and wrote a proposal, partly inspired by the writings of development economist Amartya Sen. The rest of my inspiration came from my engagement with feminism, through which I learned about the gender division of labour and caring work. I realised that economics had several blind spots, of which ethics, power, and gender were only three. Then followed many rejections of my PhD research proposal by professors of economics. Nobody I approached was willing to be my supervisor – they advised me to study sociology, anthropology, political science, or gender studies. And when I found an interested professor abroad, I could not find the funding to study there. After 8 years, a Dutch professor of economics who had spent several years at universities in the USA returned home. He had interviewed Sen and had done unorthodox work related to ethics. We met at the same university where I had received my bachelor's and master's degrees, and he made me cry by simply listening to me and nodding intrigued on hearing my bold plans. I quit my job, did my PhD, and then was offered a job at the institute where I still work, with

Image 0.1 High hopes for a change in economics
Source: *The Economist*, 18 July 2009.

much pleasure and gratefulness for its openness to pluralism in economics: the International Institute of Social Studies, of Erasmus University Rotterdam. But for teaching, there was still no pluralist textbook and I increasingly felt this as severely constraining my teaching.

Even today, the most popular economic textbooks almost exclusively present the orthodox, that is, the *neoclassical economics* perspective, as the default theory of economics. They teach that economics is about choices under conditions of scarcity, simplifying human rationality, values, and complexities in the social and natural context. Popular textbooks rarely refer to other theories, and if they do, often only to concepts that have been adapted to fit neoclassical economics. There are very few introductory economics textbooks which give serious attention to a diversity of economic perspectives. Moreover, all available introductory textbooks, orthodox and heterodox, employ a dominant Western economy perspective. They take the US economy or that of a different developed economy as the standard.

What went wrong with economics?

Going back to the question asked by *The Economist* as to where it went wrong, there are various answers to this question and economists disagree about many of them. But a common understanding is that neoclassical economics has contributed to a self-fulfilling prophesy in economic behaviour with an unexpected and very serious side effect. And many economists agree that this is one of the causal factors behind the 2007 financial crisis in the developed world as well as the 1997 financial crisis in Asia. Moreover, the key policy response to the crisis by governments is *not* a neoclassical one but a Post Keynesian tool: increased public expenditures to stimulate economic recovery. Plus institutional reforms of banks and banking regulation. The self-fulfilling prophesy of neoclassical economics, which contributed to the crisis, has two dimensions. First, in neoclassical economics, all economic agents are supposed to act entirely independently and in their own self-interest (even when they do things for others). They are assumed to ask themselves all the time: *wiifm* (what's-in-it-for-me)? Second, neoclassical economics assumes that all economic agents rely on individual, probabilistic risk of gain and loss for each individual decision they make. At the macro level, neoclassical economists recognise that individual risk adds up to aggregate risk. But they ignore systemic risk. This is interlinked risk through social interaction within and between banks, households, firms, and the government. These linkages of risk reinforce individual risk so that aggregate risk becomes much larger than simply the adding up of your and my risk. Together, these two neoclassical economic assumptions which most textbooks teach – individual self-interest and independent risk – have resulted in economic models, business strategies, and policy advice that have increased risk levels in the financial sector worldwide. Moreover, the financial sector has partially shifted the downside risk to others through self-interested behaviour and inequalities of power: to the taxpayer, the unemployed, and the poor. The financial crisis and its aftermath had a variety of causes, and the self-fulfilling prophesy of the two key foundations of neoclassical economics were clearly part of it.

- Econometricians building complex models for maximising gains in financial trade, with automatic sales when asset prices reach certain levels. This was meant to control risk at the individual trading firm or bank level. But since many trading companies use similar models, an initial sudden decline in the stock exchange results in massive sales of assets, pushing asset prices down. In turn, this leads to further sales and further price declines, without any human decision-making process involved in weighing the quickly changing market dynamics. This cascade of banks and trading firms selling assets not only brings asset prices down very fast, it also creates unsustainable risk positions because all involved have to incur serious losses on their balance sheets, leading to insolvency and bankruptcies.
- Financial whizz kids packaging various mortgages together into new types of assets, which were traded as low risk. Nobody in the buying banks really understood these packages but traded them nevertheless because they seemed safe due to diversification and they were much in demand. However, their risk was not calculable. Also banks in developing countries bought these non-transparent assets, leading to bankruptcies in countries such as Nigeria. When the packaged assets (called MBS, mortgage backed securities) appeared not to be such safe investments after all, investors worldwide lost billions of dollars in the writing off of these non-transparent financial assets. Moreover, because they all had bought and sold them to each other, this resulted in interdependent risk positions, in which many investors were involved. And nobody is willing to buy these 'toxic assets' anymore.

- Consumers buying expensive houses with high mortgages with affordable short run pay-back conditions but unaffordable long run pay-back conditions if their incomes do not grow steadily. They assumed that their *wiifm* was basically a generous home loan, facilitated by the low interest rate policy of the US central bank. And since the loans were provided by regular mortgage institutions, consumers thought that these were reliable financial products. They often did not read the small print, which stated the worsening loan conditions over time. Or they believed that their incomes and home values would continue to grow steadily. They clearly did not suffer from insufficient information but from overly optimistic beliefs and misleading practices that had become common throughout US financial markets.
- Bankers selling MBS on the basis of a commission or bonus based on volume sold and not based on long run viability for their bank. The bonuses generated perverse incentives: many individual bankers, following *wiifm* reasoning, sold mortgages to as many clients as possible, also to customers who could not afford the increasing interest rates in the long run due to a weak employment position. The risky long run pay-back capability of clients was not factored into the *wiifm* reasoning of the bankers who sold these mortgages: the bonus was simply linked to the volumes they sold per year, not to pay-back risk in the long run. This has led to forced house sales with debts for consumers, and to high default rates on mortgages with subsequent losses for banks.
- Central bank regulators reducing regulation, under strong pressure by bank lobbyists, and relying increasingly on risk assessments by the market, assuming that if all clients and banks follow *wiifm* reasoning, they will serve their self-interest and hence keep total risk in check. This attitude by the key regulators of the financial sector appeared to shift too much confidence to the markets and to ignore systemic risk, which spiralled risk and the impact of uncertainty on financial markets to unsustainable heights. In the end, government debt increased enormously to save key banks. These were banks that were considered 'too-big-to-fail'. And that, in turn, fuelled the Euro crisis, through the interlinked risks between the US and European financial markets.

Heterodox economics

Although heterodox economists had warned about increasing instability, neoclassical economists were taken by surprise by the unfolding events. In the words of Alan Greenspan, the former Chair of the Federal Reserve Bank (the central bank of the USA) in a hearing of the US Congress in October 2008:

> Yes, I found a flaw . . . in the model that I perceived is the critical functioning structure that defines how the world works.[1]

He added that it was the crisis which made him realise that the model does not live up to what it is supposed to do, namely, providing reliable forecasts in a complex world:

> We have this extraordinarily complex global economy, which as everybody now realizes is very difficult to forecast in any considerable detail.

In a TV show in October 2013, Greenspan even made a plea for a capital reserve ratio for banks of at least 20 per cent. The EU only requires 3 per cent, although this is much disputed.

Of course, others, like the British economist Keynes who studied the 1929 financial crisis, had realised this long before him. Frederic Mishkin, a well-known professor at Columbia Business School and author of an American textbook on finance, also realised only after the crisis hit that his belief in rational and efficient markets was unjustified. In a neoclassical analysis of Iceland's economy, he had claimed that Iceland enjoyed financial stability, only 2.5 years before the financial meltdown of that country.[2]

Both Greenspan and Mishkin, as well as all other neoclassical economists, were taken by surprise by the crisis. And they said that no one could have seen it coming. This last claim is wrong. There were whistle blowers within the financial system whose warnings were dismissed. And there were heterodox financial economists who had warned of a crisis for 5 years. The online Real-World Economics network, with 11,000 members, has, in response to the 'we-could-not-know' claim, awarded the Revere Award to three economists who gave strong warnings of a serious crisis.[3] The winner was Steve Keen of the University of Western Sydney, Australia. He started a website in 2006 on the increasing debt problem in the USA and published monthly reports. The second prize was awarded to Nouriel Roubini of New York University. In the summer of 2005, he predicted that real home prices in the USA would fall by 30 per cent, and a year later he warned that this could trigger a crisis. The third prize went to Dean Baker, of the Centre for Economic and Policy Research in the USA. Already in August 2002 he warned of a housing bubble, and in 2004 he wrote in a paper:

> The fact that people are borrowing against their homes at a rapid rate (more than $750 billion in 2003) is more evidence of an unsustainable bubble. The ratio of mortgage debt to home equity is at record highs.[4]

In the meantime, the costs of the crisis to the US economy alone was estimated in 2013 by the US Government Accountability Office to be $US22 trillion.[5] This is equivalent to about 2 years of annual American gross domestic product (GDP) and is the amount lost in MBS and related assets – purely financial loss. But this figure excludes unemployment costs and other indirect costs, real economy losses. The actual expenditures on support for banks amount to 8 per cent of GDP, according to the IMF.[6] And for the world as a whole, the costs are even higher, with the Euro crisis, declines in world trade, and a crunch in lending. In 2009, the IMF estimated global bank losses alone were $US4 trillion, an amount that has increased every crisis year since.[7]

The Economist also hoped that the crisis would somehow move economic knowledge and teaching away from teaching that self-interest and risk spreading helps markets to flourish. *The Economist* hoped, as the cover image shows, that the crisis would automatically lead to a correction of economic theory and economic teaching. Unfortunately, more than 5 years after this cover image appeared, very little has changed in economics, even though heterodox economic theories have been around for longer than economics as an independent discipline has existed, and even though it is heterodox economic policies which have been implemented in reaction to the crisis.

The main difference of heterodox economics is that it does not share the neoclassical assumptions of individual self-interest, independent risk, market equilibrium, and independence of economic behaviour. Instead, heterodox theories assume that economic agents behave more like real-world men and women, interdependent and with a variety of motivations, in real-world contexts with fundamental uncertainty and interdependent risk, driven by social-level phenomena such as power, caring, status, beliefs, cooperation, and norms. This should inform economic teaching, as Robert Shiller, who was among those who predicted the crisis, has argued recently:

> For me, alternative views that must be incorporated in our teaching include those promoted by the other social sciences: psychology, sociology, political science, and anthropology. For me, maintaining a proper perspective on alternative views means also incorporating historical analysis. For me, too, we also must keep in view the fundamental importance of institutions - our established organizations, practices, laws - and remind our students that these must be taken into account before judging any economic model.[8]

Why has the crisis not led to a victory of heterodox economics over the orthodoxy? That is a good question. But if it was so easy that an economic crisis would simply change the supply of economic analysis and teaching, and that students would then simply adapt their demand to it, we would again assume markets would do what they are ideally supposed to do in neoclassical economics. We would still believe that market supply creates its own demand, resulting in an equilibrium in which everyone benefits from an allocation of scarce resources that is as efficient as possible. But the crisis has demonstrated clearly that markets often are not up to this task. Instead, neoclassical economics has suffered a blow, but yet remains dominant. Economists are just like people. They try to hold on to their worldview and put much effort into protecting their vested interests as academics, policy advisors, and teachers based on the skills they have acquired and invested in. And the teaching of neoclassical economics at universities in the developing world, with Western textbooks and professors with degrees obtained at Western universities, and supported with training courses by economists from the World Bank and IMF, limits the space for heterodox learning worldwide.

Signs of change

But there are signs that justify *The Economist*'s optimism that the crisis is helping to change the dominance of neoclassical economics teaching. The menu of economic policies has broadened in response to the crisis, and students demand information on this because they hear about it on the news. The curriculum of finance courses at prestigious business schools now pays more attention than before to the social responsibility of banks.[9] And in-depth heterodox economic studies on the causes of the crisis receive more attention than heterodox research did before the crisis. Heterodox economists, plus a few neoclassical economists who are looking for answers to the painfully revealed flaws in the dominant theory, have set up think tanks and networks to cooperate in research, providing policy advice, and teaching for an economy that is more stable, more equal, less wasteful, and contributing better to livelihoods for all. For example, the network IDEAS began in India as a forum for heterodox economists from the developing world. It was this forum which first pointed out the parallels between the US-originated financial crisis on the one hand and the earlier Asian financial crisis on the other. And the same forum has demonstrated the marked differences in IMF policies towards Asia then, which reinforced the enormous economic losses of income, jobs, and businesses, and IMF policy towards the USA and EU now, where the IMF supports state assistance for banks and accepts high government budget deficits in order to stimulate the economy.

The main demand for change in the economic curriculum comes from students. Before the crisis, groups of PhD students of economics had already raised critical questions about the dominance of neoclassical economics and mathematics in their education. This resulted in the Post-Autistic Economics Network, which later became the World Economics Association with its online newsletter *Real-World Economics Review*.[10] Since the crisis, many more initiatives have emerged all over the world. Students at the University of Manchester in the UK sent a petition to the Economics Department asking for more real-world economic skills training. They also set up the Post-Crash Economics initiative with a new course, which the university, however, decided not to accredit.[11] The International Student Initiative for Pluralism in Economics is a collaboration of many associations of economics students from more than 30 countries, including India, Brazil, Russia, Pakistan, the USA, and the Netherlands.[12] They published an open letter entitled 'Rethinking Economics'. The University of Pretoria, in South Africa, has set up an initiative called the 'Human Economy' at the Faculty of Humanities to contribute to a more human economics.[13] The Institute for New Economic Thinking (INET) supports a curriculum called 'CORE: Curriculum Open-access Resources in Economics',[14] which has, however, been criticised in turn for not being ambitious enough.[15]

From orthodox and heterodox to pluralist economics

The main strength of heterodox economics, that its analysis is closer to real-world people and contexts, is also considered a weakness, because it does not allow for neat, closed mathematical models with probabilistic economic predictions that so many economists seek. But neoclassical economics also has not lived up to this idealistic criterion for judging economic theories: it has been agreed that economic prediction is unattainable, as Greenspan acknowledged, since the economy is far too complex to be able to predict outcomes of prices and output. Heterodox economics was never much concerned with predictions and is more open-ended, accepting that economic reality is complex and uncertain. Heterodox economics takes a more realistic view of both human behaviour and social processes and structures, such as power, opportunism, short-sightedness, cooperation, and fairness. It does not reduce these complexities to neat mathematical models and mathematically calculable market equilibriums. Heterodox economists would rather be roughly right than precisely wrong. Explanation, rather than prediction, is the objective of science: trying to understand the world. This is what this textbook is about.

This is a textbook of pluralist economics and presents both heterodox and orthodox perspectives on the economy, showing their respective weaknesses and strengths and why these matter. Pluralism means good science. It allows space for competition between theories. But more importantly, pluralism creates the room for complementary explanations, which are context dependent. That is precisely why this book provides a wide diversity of context, with many real-world examples.

I hope that this approach will help you to understand the complexities, regularities, and challenges of the economic world around us.

Approach of the book

The book is designed for a one-semester introductory course in economics. The chapters discuss all major economic topics, in microeconomics and in macroeconomics. These topics will be presented from four different theoretical perspectives, beginning with the closer real-world theories, in which social structures, relatedness, uncertainty, and social norms provide key economic explanations. And at the end, the chapters present the idealised worldview of neoclassical economics on the topic, applicable to very specific, static, and stable situations.

The book is written for an international student audience doing an undergraduate or graduate degree in the social sciences or interdisciplinary studies. It is meant to provide a critical foundation of economic thought to enable students throughout the social sciences and interdisciplinary studies to link basic economic insights to political science, sociology, technical studies, and development studies. The global dimension has been expressed strongly through the global contextualisation of each chapter. All continents are represented in the book with the choice of country context steered by the topic. For example, the chapter on labour markets uses the context of South Africa, because that country has sizeable formal and informal labour markets, strong labour market institutions, and at the same time continued processes of exclusion and discrimination. Hence, that context provides a comprehensive learning background for a diversity of concepts and theories on labour markets. The book also uses the US context and the financial crisis that began there in 2007. This context helps understanding of the crisis, and also the diverse financial theories that explain the crisis.

Finally, I acknowledge that I have made many arbitrary choices in writing this book. Some countries are excluded although they offered equally suitable contexts to those selected. And each topic could only be treated in a limited way due to lack of space in an introductory textbook. Therefore, I selected what I like my own international students, who do an interdisciplinary MA degree in development studies, to learn in order to understand economic development processes. My choices have also necessarily been arbitrary regarding the theories I have included, perhaps the most fundamental selection process for this textbook. I have included neoclassical economics for the straightforward reason that it still is the dominant economic theory around. This is the case even after the crisis and despite *The Economist*'s hopes for a meltdown of neoclassical teaching. Of course, not all neoclassical economics has become superfluous – it has contributed valuable concepts and tools to economics, which are introduced in this book. I have included social economics because it is closest to sociology, the key discipline of the social sciences without which we would not be able to understand human behaviour and livelihoods. We cannot really understand economic behaviour and outcomes without paying attention to power, gender relations, and international social structures. Social economics includes behavioural economics, with its psychological insights and laboratory and field experiments. Institutional economics is included in the book because it has received increasing interest over time. I even think that it may become the most influential economic theory (yes this is a prediction, and not based on any model but simply on my experience and intuition as an academic economist). But more importantly, I have included institutional economics because economies worldwide are increasingly influenced and directed by human institutions, and much of economic policy is about institutional change. For example, preventing another serious financial crisis needs changes in laws, stricter regulation, more responsible habits and routines by financial professionals, and social norms directing consumers away from high-risk loans. Last but not least, I opted for the inclusion of Post Keynesian economics because of what Keynes' biographer has phrased so well: 'the return of the Master'[16] in the crisis responses by governments (increased expenditures), by central banks (re-regulation and a recognition of systemic risk) and by households (saving rather than spending due to increased uncertainties over livelihoods). Such responses were already explained by Keynes back in the 1930s.

Next to the four key theories reference will be made to Marxist economics and Austrian economics as well as feminist economics and ecological economics. But the core choice of theories consists of the four mentioned above which I consider the most influential economic theories today. The sequence in which these are discussed in each chapter is different from their order of presentation here. The theory that is closest to real-world economic behaviour is discussed first: social economics. Then follow institutional economics and Post Keynesian economics, and at the close of each chapter I will present the neoclassical perspective. Neoclassical theory will come at the end in recognition of its more abstract identity, closer to an idealised world of economic behaviour that fits mathematical properties of stability and an atomistic view of human beings. It relates to special cases of the real-world economy.

Now, let me say a few words on the use of the book. Most words printed in *italics* are keywords and are followed by a definition. You will also find these key terms listed at the end of each chapter (and at the end of the book in the index). Every chapter ends with suggestions of interesting sources either in print or on websites. The chapters do not include exercises or questions. Instead, students are invited to formulate questions about each chapter for each other. They could discuss possible answers, from different theoretical perspectives, among themselves, either in physical groups in or outside class, or through a virtual learning environment. Teachers may want to use these self-developed questions and discussion of answers as part of their grading, with individual or group grades. Finally, the book has an accompanying website with additional sources, both for teachers and students.

Notes

1 PBS Newshour Transcript. 23 October 2008. http://www.pbs.org/newshour/bb/business/july-dec08/crisishearing_10-23.html
2 Mishkin, F. and T. Herbertsson (2006) 'Financial Stability in Iceland'. Reykjavik: Iceland Chamber of Commerce.
3 http://rwer.wordpress.com/2010/05/13/keen-roubini-and-baker-win-revere-award-for-economics-2/
4 http://rwer.wordpress.com/?s=revere+award
5 'Financial Regulatory Reform: Financial Crisis Losses and Potential Impacts of the Dodd-Frank Act'. Washington, DC: US Government Accountability Office, 16 January 2013.
6 'Managing Capital Flows: What Tools to Use?'. IMF Staff Discussion Paper, Washington, DC: International Monetary Fund, 2011.
7 'Global Financial Stability Report'. Washington, DC: International Monetary Fund, April 2009.
8 Shiller, R. (2010) 'How Should the Financial Crisis Change How We Teach Economics?', *Journal of Economic Education*, 41(4), p. 407.
9 Palin, A., 'Financial Crisis forced Business Schools to change Curriculum', *Financial Times*, 23 June 2013.
10 http://www.worldeconomicsassociation.org/
11 http://www.post-crasheconomics.com/
12 http://www.isipe.net/
13 http://web.up.ac.za/default.asp?ipkCategoryID=15156&subid=15156&ipklookid=9&parentid=
14 http://core-econ.org/
15 http://www.hetecon.net/documents/The_prospects_for_a_new_economic_curriculum.pdf
16 Skidelsky, R. (2009) *Keynes: The Return of the Master*. London: Allen Lane.

1 Economics as a science

1.1 What is economics?

Economics only became an independent discipline around the year 1900. That was precisely when classical economics turned into neoclassical economics. Economists of those days tried to shape the new discipline along the lines of the natural sciences with the help of mathematics. They used the language of laws, mechanics, and equilibrium, as in physics, and they employed metaphors from biology, such as evolution and circulation of blood in the body. Image 1.1 shows a physics model of the economy, in which water flows represent the flow of resources and goods. Such a model was called a MONIAC (Monetary National Income Analogue Computer), and the one in the photos was a gift from the municipality of Rotterdam to Erasmus University Rotterdam in 1954.

1.1.1 Definition

There are many ordinary definitions of economics. Economics is said to be all about money. Or it is taken for granted that it studies markets and not other allocation domains as well. Or people assume that it analyses businesses and how they can maximise their profits. Others recognise a broader role for economics as studying the provisioning of the *oikos*, the classical Greek word for household: the oikos as the household of the state and communities.

Economists have often been characterised in not very flattering ways. A famous characterisation parallels the definition of a cynic by the 19th century Irish poet and novelist Oscar Wilde. This portrays economists as people who know the price of everything but the value of nothing . . . . This characterisation has a grain of truth, which is precisely why the Nobel Prize for economics was awarded much later than the original Nobel Prizes. And not from the legacy of Alfred Nobel, but initiated and financed by the Central Bank of Sweden as 'The Sveriges Riksbank Prize in Economic Sciences in Memory of Alfred Nobel', much to the dismay of the Nobel family who have distanced themselves from this additional 'Nobel Prize'. It took some time before economics was recognised as a real science, and it is still disputed by some as window dressing for supporting business interests over societal interests.

Most economists, including myself, make a distinction between neoclassical economics, followed by about 90 per cent of economists, and heterodox economics, a variety of other approaches, followed by the remaining 10 per cent. I was trained as a neoclassical economist and was given a very brief and incomplete overview of heterodoxy by two lecturers. These short insights stimulated me to study heterodox schools of thought by myself. Later, I sent a clumsy paper I had written as an activist researcher in my first job to Amartya Sen, whose work I greatly admired. To my surprise, I received a friendly and encouraging short

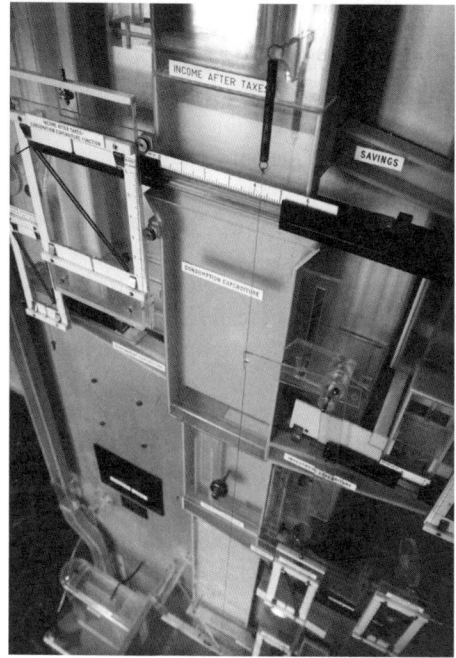 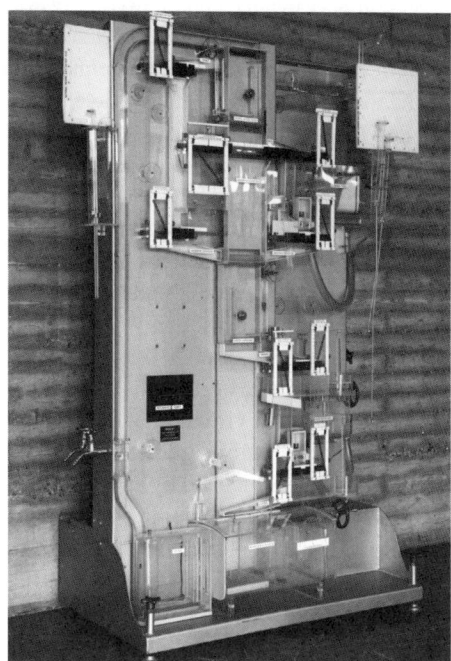

Image 1.1 MONIAC at Erasmus University Rotterdam

letter back. I did my PhD on the ethics hidden in economics. Now, I hold a professorship in Pluralist Development Economics at the International Institute of Social Studies of Erasmus University Rotterdam and teach students from all over the world about pluralist economics. This is what this book is about: a pluralist introduction to economics.

Despite the mathematisation that began in the 1950s, economics is part of the social sciences. It studies human behaviour in production, consumption, entrepreneurship, labour, investment, and distribution. This behaviour is not only located in markets but also occurs through economic agents' interactions with the state (in particular through paying taxes and receiving public services) and in communities – the community economy. So, economics is part of the social sciences and uses a plurality of theories and methods, both quantitative and qualitative, to explain a variety of economic behaviours in markets, the state, and communities. And for those who insist on a definition, here is one: *economics* is the study of how human beings interact for the provisioning of their livelihoods in markets, the state, and communities.

1.1.2 Purpose

What is the purpose of studying economics? The answer was formulated half a century ago by Joan Robinson, a well-known British economist working from the 1940s to the 1970s:

> The purpose of studying economics is not to acquire a set of ready-made answers to economic questions, but to learn how to avoid being deceived by economists.[1]

Is economics a means–ends study, analysing how people use certain means to achieve particular ends? Well, to some extent yes, because the means are not endless. Most of the means to provide for oneself and ones' dependents (children, the elderly) tend to be scarce. Not absolutely, but relatively. One would easily trade a scarce good like a diamond ring when lost in the desert and craving for water, while other goods seem abundant, such as clean air. But we make these goods scarce through pollution and waste. Scarcity is not an absolute but a *relative* limitedness of resources, influenced by economic agents. It is not an independent given, outside the agency of people. And therefore, economics goes beyond a means–ends study. That is because nothing is fixed. Scarcity, ends, and means are not fixed over time and space.

Innovation creates new means every day, from new ways of communication (remember how slow your first computer was and imagine how many additional features your cell phone will have in 5 years' time) to innovative forms of food production (for example, algae fields in the sea, a rich source of proteins), to new forms of power (the successful lobbying by industry for a newly created virtual market in pollution permits rather than regulation). Also the ends are not fixed. Nobody cared to save money for a smart phone before the new millennium. And who is not influenced by advertisements in her choice of coffee, jeans, or movies? While at the same time, some people choose to live less materialistic lives, valuing social time or a spiritual life over more consumer goods. Sometimes, a whole nation decides on such a shift, for example Bhutan, which has moved its system of National Accounts towards a broader system of National Happiness (see Diagram 1.1).

1.1.3 Values

There is one more concept key to the description of economics: efficiency. Efficiency is an ethical value, like equality and fairness. If you have to clean your house, you generally prefer to get it done as quickly as possible with the least effort, that is, efficiently. *Narrow efficiency* concerns the maximisation of output with the minimisation of input. But what is efficient at one level – cleaning your house in the shortest possible time and with minimal effort – may be inefficient at another level – using electricity for a vacuum cleaner leading to CO_2 emissions, and using chemical detergents, contributing to water pollution. So, efficiency can ideally only be assessed at the economy-wide level and even beyond, to include society and nature. This enlarges the definition: *broad efficiency* is the minimisation of waste throughout the economy or even society or the entire world. Just like scarcity, efficiency is manipulated by economic agents. For a company, firing workers may be efficient, but not for the economy as a whole, which sees itself confronted with rising unemployment. And, since means and ends are not fixed, efficiency has a dynamic meaning as well. So, investment may be costly now but makes production more efficient in the long run, for example through training workers or installing new software on office computers (and often through both).

Moreover, there are other economic values apart from efficiency, because economic processes go beyond simple means–ends relationships. These other values are important in themselves in social interaction, but may also have positive effects on efficiency. Such other values include fairness (if workers feel they are exploited they will not work diligently), trust (if a customer does not trust a supplier she will change shop), pride (which stimulates achievement), and equality (poor, unemployed people don't have the money to buy the products offered for sale by those who have the capital to produce them). In short, as John Maynard Keynes phrased it in 1938:

> Economics is essentially a moral science and not a natural science. That is to say, it employs introspection and judgments of value.[2]

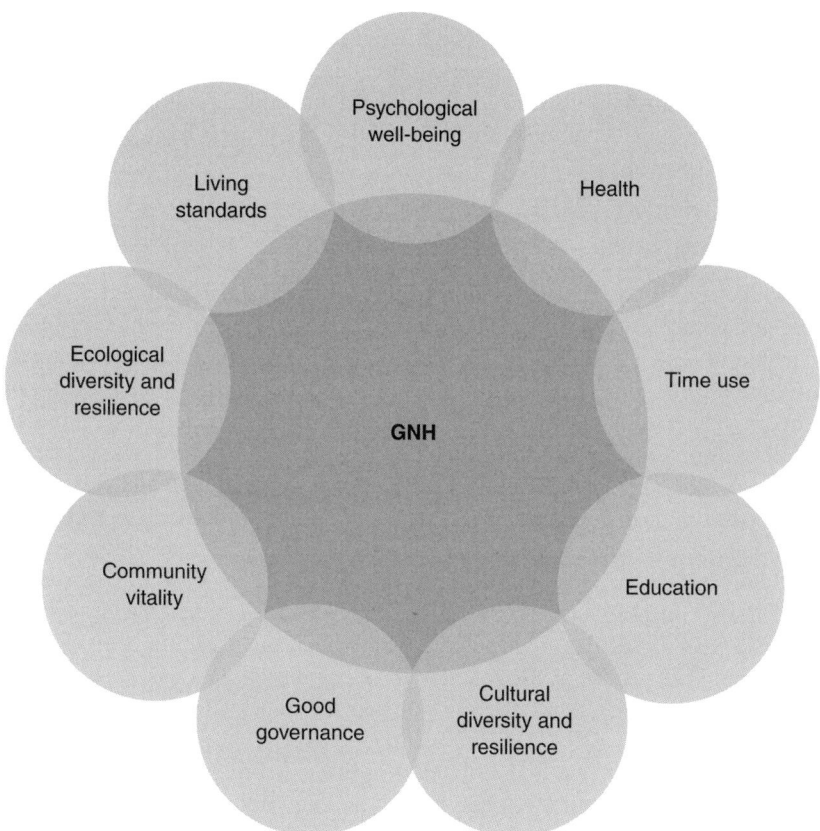

Diagram 1.1 Gross National Happiness

Source: Adapted by Zahra Zarepour from Ura, K., S. Alkire, T. Zangmo and K. Wangdi (2012) *A Short Guide to Gross National Happiness Index*. Thimphu, Bhutan: The Center for Bhutan Studies.

And yes, we use numbers, mathematics, and statistics, in addition to rhetoric, stories, case studies, and logic, to do economics. Economics has a peculiar place in the social sciences: it is both abstract and moral, both quantitative and qualitative, and concerned both with human means and ends as well as with material processes and money flows. This brings us to the third and last key ingredient of economics, next to scarcity and efficiency: money. Real world economies use money. Money is anything that allows its holder to purchase goods. But lots of economic interactions do not use money: regulation, economic rights, satisfaction with achievements, innovation, trust, and, of course, unpaid work. So, money is a dominant measure used in economics, but it is not the only measure of economic activity, and often not the most important measure. Money is not an end in itself but is a fungible means: money allocated to school fees can easily be diverted to buy a bargain of a car. And as a means of accumulation, money leads to a perverse effect, namely, that some mistake it for an end in itself. But empirical studies show that high incomes and wealth correlates only very weakly or not at all with firm sustainability, economic stability, human development, or happiness.

This textbook shows that economics is more than markets, money, and mathematics. This is illustrated by the contributions of the key economists in the history of economic thought. Their portraits are shown in Image 1.2. The annex to this book provides a brief overview of each of these economists' contributions. In addition to these nine key figures, the annex also features three contemporaneous economists from the Global South who have helped make economics a truly global science.

1.1.4 Pluralism

Pluralism refers to the conviction that a plurality of theoretical and methodological viewpoints is valuable and contributes to the advancement of science. Since present views may be false, it is sensible to have a plurality of views available. And different social contexts may require different explanations: it is not always a matter of theories being wrong or right, but more or less adequate to explain certain phenomena in certain contexts. Pluralism is therefore a matter of open minds and ensuring a variety of perspectives. It involves recognition of variation in real-world economies; of the economic lives of men and women; of people living in rich and in poor countries; and of the functioning of markets as well as of states and the community economy. This sounds self-evident, but since one theory and its methodology has come to dominate economics since the 1980s, the majority of economists have been trained in this single view – neoclassical economics. A recent survey among American economists with a PhD degree has demonstrated that the great majority of them accept key neoclassical assumptions as the foundation of economics as a whole: economic agents as utility maximisers, having unlimited wants, and the importance of mathematical modelling.[3]

Next to neoclassical economics, we find a plurality of other theories and methodologies, also referred to as heterodox economics. For any theory, we can only determine its value by comparing it to other theories, so that by using them we learn which one works best for which type of problem under which conditions. And perhaps we will find out that some theories are far less applicable to real-world situations than others, across a variety of contexts.

In this book, I present the four key economic theories, ranging from the broad, less precise, and more connected to the real world to the specific and more abstract: social economics, institutional economics, Post Keynesian economics and neoclassical economics. These four theories are very much alive today, with their own journals, associations, policy think tanks,

Image 1.2 Nine key economists

Sources: See Annex. Compilation: Zahra Zarepour, 2014.

conferences, and research groups. I have chosen this mix of theories because they offer, I think, a wide and representative range of economic pluralism at the introductory level.

1.2 Social economics

1.2.1 Embeddedness

The broadest of the four economic theories is social economics (sometimes referred to as socio-economics). Its name already indicates that it understands the economy as part of society and economics as related to sociology and social psychology in its analysis of human behaviour. We recognise this view of the embeddedness of the economy in society already in Adam Smith's work. But as a theory, it came into being only after World War II. Social economics acknowledges that there are moral, political, and cultural dimensions to economic behaviour. A major social economics insight is that communities and unpaid work play an important role in the economy. Even in the most developed economies, the number of unpaid work hours is not very different from the number of hours that people spend in labour markets.[4]

Another important contribution of social economics is the recognition that economic agents have a multitude of motivations and objectives, many of which are not material or self-interested. This is particularly contributed through the relatively new field of *behavioural economics*, which is an empirical approach to the study of the behaviour of economic agents under various conditions. Through field and laboratory experiments, games, and questionnaires, behavioural economists have discovered that economic agents often are risk averse, loss averse, select different options only because they are presented differently to them, are reluctant to learn from mistakes, and are generally satisfied with a 'good enough' choice. Diagram 1.2 illustrates loss aversion. It shows that people value a loss of an amount more than a gain of the same amount. The value on the curve, as measured on the y-axis, is lower for the gain (right-hand side of the curve) than it is for the loss (left-hand side of the curve). You can see this by comparing the vertical distances on the y-axis of the gain side with the loss side: the value of the loss is larger. . . .

1.2.2 Social economic rationality

The rationality question is answered in social economics, just as Smith did, with prudence in relation to intrinsic values, in particular freedom, justice, and care. In order to benefit from an exchange relationship, you need to find someone who wants what you have, or make, or do. Only *then* can you get what you want, either from this other person or from someone with the money you get in return. So, you need to make contact, show interest, listen, be flexible, generate trust, and be consistent, responsible, and fair. This allows you not only to make a transaction now, but also to develop an exchange relationship for future mutually beneficial transactions. Hence, what matters is a mutual recognition of shared values.

And for all three types of economic interactions – exchange, redistribution, and gift – social economists have discovered that many economic agents behave according to the logic of strong reciprocity. *Strong reciprocity* means that agents contribute resources to a joint activity when others do so as well even when there are no benefits to themselves or their kin, or future gains to be expected, or reputation gains, while they are prepared to punish free riders, at their own cost. This is how economic agents hold on to shared norms and keep others to these as well. So, rationality in social economics is defined as strong reciprocity.

16 *Economics as a science*

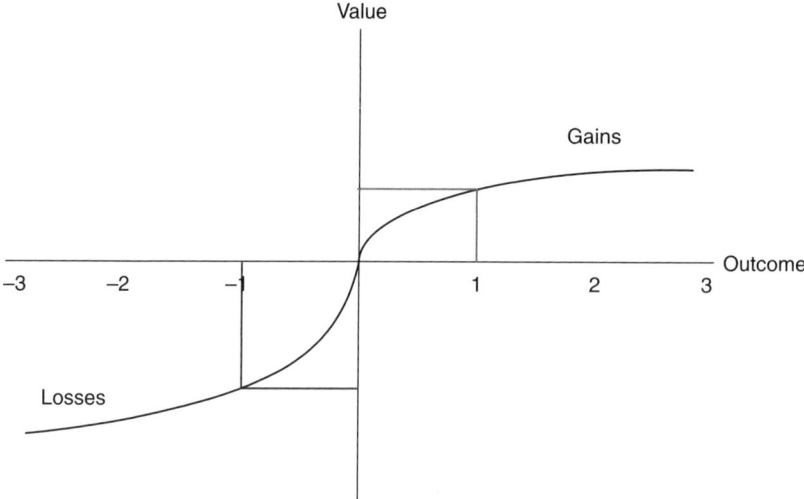

Diagram 1.2 Loss aversion

1.2.3 Virtues, social capital, and social cohesion

Social economics is influenced by *virtue ethics*, deriving from the ancient Greek philosopher Aristotle. This is a person-based ethics depending on social embeddedness of behaviour. Virtue ethics is not exclusively concerned with outcomes but with good behaviour in itself. Virtues cannot be traded off against one another, while conflicts can be solved, at least to some extent, by deliberation with others in private discussions and public debate. So, the businessman learns to become virtuous through his dealings with suppliers, investors, competitors, and clients. The famous theatre play 'Death of a Salesman' written by the American playwright Arthur Miller in 1949, shows what happens if a businessman ignores virtues in his tradings, but instead acts with arrogance, over-confidence, and lack of loyalty. Miller's businessman, Willy Loman, looses his clients, his earnings, the respect of his colleagues, and eventually the bond with his family. But he does not want to admit his failings to his best friend or to himself, he is too proud for that. He ends up committing suicide when he finally finds out that he failed as a businessman and as a human being.

Good leadership highlights the economic benefits of virtues. Good leaders are often characterised by their subordinates and peers as managers who keep a balance between performance-oriented traits and people-oriented traits. Performance orientation entails being strategic and decisive and showing self-confidence. People-orientation includes cooperativeness, showing responsibility, and being approachable. In the past, these two sets of characteristics for good leadership were labelled as 'hard' or 'masculine' versus 'soft' or 'feminine'. But recent empirical research indicates that female leaders more often manage to balance both sets of virtues than male leaders.

Table 1.1 shows survey data results for the year 2011 for more than 7,000 business leaders assessed by their peers (12.7 peers on average per male leader, 13.1 peers on average per female leader). The results indicate that both men and women display stereotype masculine and feminine leadership top competences. Overall, women scored better. Moreover, women scored statistically significantly better on 12 of the 16 top competences – both stereotype masculine and feminine competences. The result implies that good leadership involves high scores on both stereotype masculine and feminine competences. Apparently, gender stereotypes are meaningless for good leadership: the best male and female leaders in the world do not let themselves be influenced by such, still dominant, modes of thinking. But this does not imply that such stereotypes are not a hindrance to the careers of female managers at lower ranks: often, they experience less promotions than their male peers because of a masculine stereotyping of leadership in many organisational cultures.

Since the economy is a social process, the social virtues are even more important than the individual virtues in economic processes. That has been recognised lately by economists with the highly contested term '*social capital*'. This is defined as the value of the relationships between individuals and groups in society, which are valuable in their own right but often can have as a by-product economic costs or benefits. There are at least two types of social capital: *bonding social capital* with high within-group trust and interaction, and *bridging social capital*, also referred to as *social cohesion*. Social cohesion is the connectedness in a society, which is valuable in itself and helps to overcome the economic problems of transaction costs, free riding, and moral hazard. Bonding social capital tends to have positive effects at the individual level and group level but often has negative aggregate economic effects.

Table 1.1 Top competences scores of good leaders

Competence*	Men	Women	Gender difference**
Takes initiative	48	56	Yes
Practices self-development	48	55	Yes
Drives for results	48	54	Yes
Establishes stretch goals	49	53	Yes
Champions change	49	53	Yes
Solves problems and analyses issues	50	52	Yes
Communicates powerfully and prolifically	50	52	Yes
Innovates	50	51	No
Technical or professional expertise	50	51	No
Develops strategic perspective	51	49	Yes
Displays high integrity	48	55	Yes
Develops others	48	54	Yes
Inspires and motivates others	49	54	Yes
Builds relationships	49	54	Yes
Collaboration and teamwork	49	53	Yes
Connects the group to the outside world	50	51	No
Overall leadership effectiveness (49 items)	49	53	Yes

Source: Zenger, J. and J. Folkman, 'Are women better leaders than men?', *Harvard Business Review*, 15 March 2012.

*The first ten competences are masculine stereotypes (dark grey), while the next six competences are feminine stereotypes (pale grey).
**Statistically significant at the 1% level.

18 *Economics as a science*

Think about the mafia. This is because it limits economic interaction to insiders, thereby foregoing gains from trade with outsiders, and because of distrust of outsiders who may be exploited. Bridging social capital, or social cohesion, generally is related to both individual and aggregate economic benefits (because trust stimulates cooperation between people who do not know each other). So, it is only in a social economics perspective, recognising the intrinsic values of trust, collective action, and shared information and resources in relationships, that social capital and social cohesion become meaningful economic concepts. At the interpersonal level, the virtues that maintain and strengthen relationships are those of *caring*, which is work done by a caregiver for a care receiver, addressing the care receiver's needs. It is precisely those caring capabilities of economic agents that support the unpaid economy of housework, childcare, community work, unpaid services for sport clubs, voluntary labour in farm production, and unpaid home care for the sick and elderly.

Table 1.2 summarises how men and women allocate time for various activities in the Netherlands based on age groups in 2009. Significant differences in time allocation between men and women are evident, in particular, men spend about double the time on paid work. However, women spend about twice as much time as men on household chores and childcare.

A final key concern in social economics is power. Social economists recognise that *power* is ubiquitous, in markets, states, and in civil society and households. Social economists Samuel Bowles and Herbert Gintis have defined the *power* of B over A as B being capable of affecting A's actions to serve B's interests through threatening or imposing sanctions on A, while A lacks this capacity with respect to B. So, power in the economy is a case of asymmetric capacities. In the economy, A and B may be firms, households, individuals in households, non-profit organisations, labour unions, communities, or states. There are also more implicit

Table 1.2 Time use in the Netherlands in 2009

Time allocation per age group (%)	*20–24*	*25–34*	*35–44*	*45–54*	*55–64*	*Total*
Men						
Paid work	39.8	40.5	40.2	38.5	19.8	35.2
Household chores	9.4	12.0	11.8	13.7	17.5	13.6
Childcare	1.1	3.3	4.6	1.4	1.1	2.7
Voluntary work	0.1	1.2	1.3	2.3	2.9	1.9
Leisure	43.6	37.9	36.1	37.8	48.8	39.9
Personal time	73.9	73.2	74.0	74.3	77.9	74.8
Women						
Paid work	30.6	24.7	19.5	18.1	6.5	17.8
Household chores	19.2	20.4	25.6	27.3	28.5	25.3
Childcare	3.6	10.2	10.9	2.4	2.7	6.5
Voluntary work	0.6	1.2	1.7	2.3	4.2	2.3
Leisure	38.1	35.1	34.2	39.7	45.4	38.5
Personal time	76.0	76.5	76.1	78.2	80.6	77.7

Source: Ooms, I., J. Jonker and A.V.D. Torre (2009), *Werken en Weldoen*. Den Haag : Sociaal en Cultureel Planbureau.

forms of power, such as when B is able to divert A's wants with advertisements. Or when B is capable of stereotyping A into limited wants and A's agency becomes weak through reduced self-esteem, or when the options from which A feels she is able to choose become more limited, subjectively, even though objectively this is not the case. Such power in the economy is often hidden and not negotiated, in contrast to the bargaining between employers and trade unions for example. Moreover, power is not a separate concern in social economics but affects embeddedness, rationality, and social cohesion. Section 1.7 will discuss power in more detail.

1.3 Institutional economics

1.3.1 Formal and informal institutions

Institutional economics began around 1900 in the United States. This tradition, also referred to as old-institutionalism, regards markets as more than demand and supply meeting each other. Rather, this theory recognises that institutions matter too: they constrain or enable behaviour in a socially structured way. This may be through *formal institutions*, which are codified rules, regulations, and organisations, and through *informal institutions*, which are unwritten rules, beliefs, and rules of thumb. Hence, not only the state is an institution, but also the market is an institution. Whereas the state is a formal institution built on laws, rules, and organisations, the market is an informal institution, a practice of exchange on the basis of cooperation and mutual trust. Some institutions are asymmetric, referred to as *asymmetric institutions*, which means that they work out differently for different groups of economic agents. They tend to benefit one group over another. One set of asymmetric institutions is gendered institutions. For example, old boy networks which self-select male top managers and members of company boards, or inheritance laws in countries in which women inherit less land than men.

The foundation of institutional economics was laid by Thorstein Veblen. He already pointed out one of the major insights of institutional economics, namely that institutions that influence economic behaviour may cause inefficiencies. The market is an institution, shaped by the rules and routines of economic agents, and such informal institutions influence supply and demand through advertisement, innovation, and moral norms. As a consequence, markets are not automatically free, even when government regulation is absent. And markets are not necessarily efficient, because groups of economic agents may support institutions that are in their own benefit, at the cost of others. Moreover, institutional economics analyses not just institutions as influencing the economy, but also the changes in institutions caused by the economy. Technological change is a good example. Technology can change institutions, and through these institutions the behaviour of economic agents.

The ethical foundation behind some institutions is based on *deontological ethics*. This is an ethics concerned with rights, duties, and human dignity. It is a principle-based ethics and not concerned with outcomes. In economics, deontology is expressed in institutions in three ways. First, in the rules that shape markets and govern exchange contracts. This involves, among others things, property rights, money, courts of justice, accounting rules, and reliable information on prices. Second, deontology is expressed through the rights and rules that constrain economic agents in their choices. For example, it is not permissible to generate economic benefit by driving though a red traffic light or using slave labour. The third way is through socially shared norms, which influence behaviour informally. For example, taking

20 *Economics as a science*

the smaller glass from a tray with two glasses of beer. Not because utility maximisation is involved in the politeness of declining the large beer (you may be very thirsty and prefer to lessen that thirst over being polite), but because social norms require you to be polite – whether you like it or not, you simply have to do your social duty because it is the right thing to do, and you expect others to behave like this as well.

1.3.2 Institutional economic rationality

The rationality question is answered by institutional economists with reference to the social, legal, and cultural context, which determines what ends are legitimate and what ends are not legitimate to pursue. Acting too much out of synchronisation with what is deemed legitimate in a society, will sooner or later turn against an economic agent. The 'I' is considered to be part of 'we'. Rationality therefore is group dependent. So, the constraints from formal and informal institutions on behaviour are internalised. These constraints can be pictured as additional to budget constraint, which also limits one's options.

Diagram 1.3 shows how deontology imposes formal and informal constraints on consumption. The outer line is the original budget constraint for your consumption: €10. It represents all possible combinations of coffee and cake you can buy on a day, given your income and the

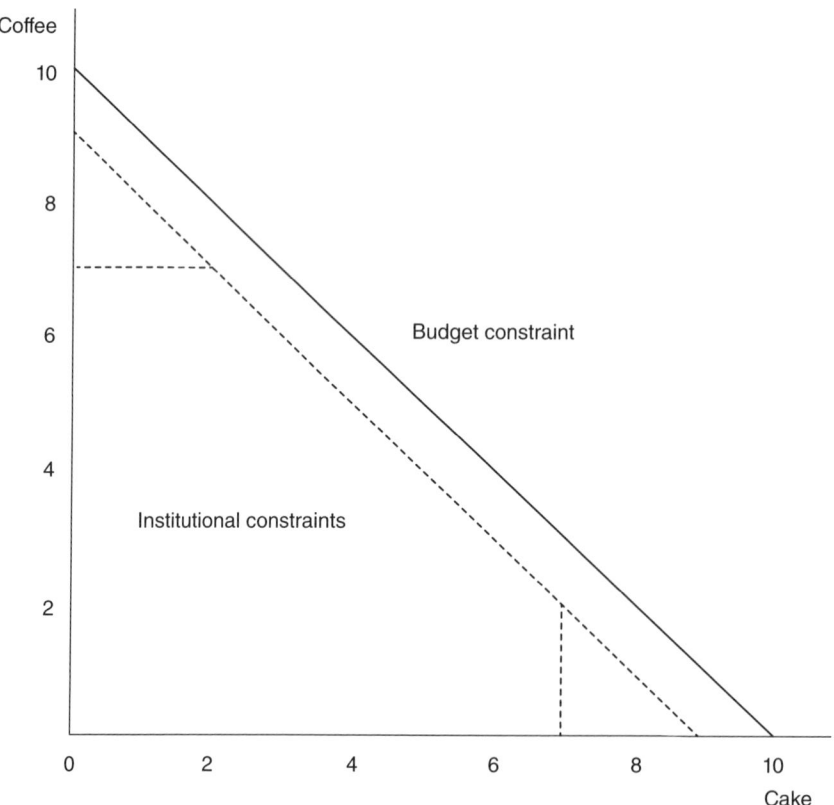

Diagram 1.3 Institutional constraints

prices of coffee and cake (€1 for each). So, you can buy ten cups of coffee and no cake, or ten pieces of cake and no coffee. Or you can buy five pieces of cake and five coffees or any other feasible combination. The inner line shows the budget constraint after an increase in the value added tax of 10 per cent imposed by your government (= €1). This tax is a formal constraint on your choice. This tax lowers all possible combinations of coffee and cake in the same way: it simply makes them more expensive, and with the same income, you can now buy less of each. So, the maximum you can now buy is nine coffees or nine cakes or any combination adding up to €9. The vertical and horizontal lines show an informal constraint on your choice, the following of a social norm. You have invited a friend over, and want to share coffee and cake with her. This means that less is left for you: you give two coffees and two cakes to your friend. As a consequence, you have only seven coffees or seven cakes (or a feasible combination) available for your own consumption.

1.4 Post Keynesian economics

1.4.1 Uncertainty and effective demand

Its name already indicates its inspirer, John Maynard Keynes, who lived in the first half of the 20th century. His ideas were further developed and complemented by others, among them Joan Robinson, mentioned earlier. The Post Keynesian approach to economics can be characterised by the recognition of uncertainty, internal dynamics, instability, effective demand, and the enabling role of the state in the economy. It recognises that markets do not automatically lead to the highest well-being, economic growth, or efficiency, but that markets have in-built shortcomings. One of these is a lack of *aggregate demand*. Aggregate demand is the total demand of all households, firms, the government, and the rest of the world (households,

Image 1.3 Coffee and cake with a budget constraint and a behavioural constraint

firms, and governments abroad). Low aggregate demand keeps the expectations of investors and producers low, and hence keeps demand for labour low. The resulting high unemployment keeps consumer demand low, due to limited purchasing power by households. This leaves the economy running at a low level of *capacity utilisation* – the extent of use of available resources – with low or even negative economic growth rates.

Another shortcoming of markets is recognised to lie in imperfections in competition, often caused by market power, through monopolies and oligopolies as well as collusion among firms, and lobbying or corruption to bend government regulation in favour of certain business interests. It was Joan Robinson who developed the model of monopsony, a market with only one buyer, such as a large employer being the only firm hiring labour in a region.

A third shortcoming of markets pointed out by Post Keynesians is that economic context is largely characterised by *uncertainty* – we simply do not know what may happen and how likely it is – rather than *risk*, for which we know the options and their probabilities. So, according to Post Keynesians, the economy is more like the unpredictability of the weather and nature than like the probability of the number of houses burnt down in a country per year. The weather is uncertain for everyone, and when a flood or earthquake occurs, it often results in very high damage costs. Therefore, many insurance companies do not offer insurance against floods and earthquakes. But insurance companies do offer fire insurance, because they can estimate, with a probability distribution based on historical statistics, what the chances are that a house will burn down. And when it does, the damage is often limited to a single house and does not affect many houses at the same time. So, whether a house will burn down is a risk. But whether an earthquake will occur is an uncertainty, with high damage costs. In the economy, Keynes argued, many investors unjustly assume a situation of risk rather than uncertainty, and often assume that risks are independent with relatively low damage costs if an event turns out not as hoped. In Post Keynesian theory, this assumption is considered to be false with evidence provided by financial crises.

1.4.2 Post Keynesian rationality

Post Keynesian economists also follow up on a Marxist idea, namely that of a distinction between classes. Post Keynesians have shown that an increase in the savings rate, which is a source for investment, emerges as soon as incomes grow: the higher the income level, the higher the share of savings and the lower the share of consumption. This insight implies not only that for investment to grow, incomes need to be stimulated first, but also that an increase in the incomes of the rich class will not result in much more consumer demand, whereas higher incomes for the poor class, who spend a much higher percentage of their income on consumer goods, will have a considerable positive effect on consumer demand. But consumer spending also depends on expectations. When households perceive much uncertainty about employment, they prefer to save rather than to spend. This is illustrated in Diagram 1.4 showing consumer confidence in the USA before and after the crisis.

Post Keynesian economics has particularly contributed, as Keynes has done himself, to the understanding of financial crises. This was enabled by the concept of *financial fragility*, which refers to the recognition that small shocks can lead to large crises. The strong inter-relatedness of banks, investment funds, rating agencies, stock markets, and government action, turns small changes into full blown crises, fuelled by speculation and herd behaviour. So, when the economic cycle moves upwards or downwards, this is not so much caused by self-interested decisions. Under conditions of uncertainty, it is often not so clear what actions serve one's

Economics as a science 23

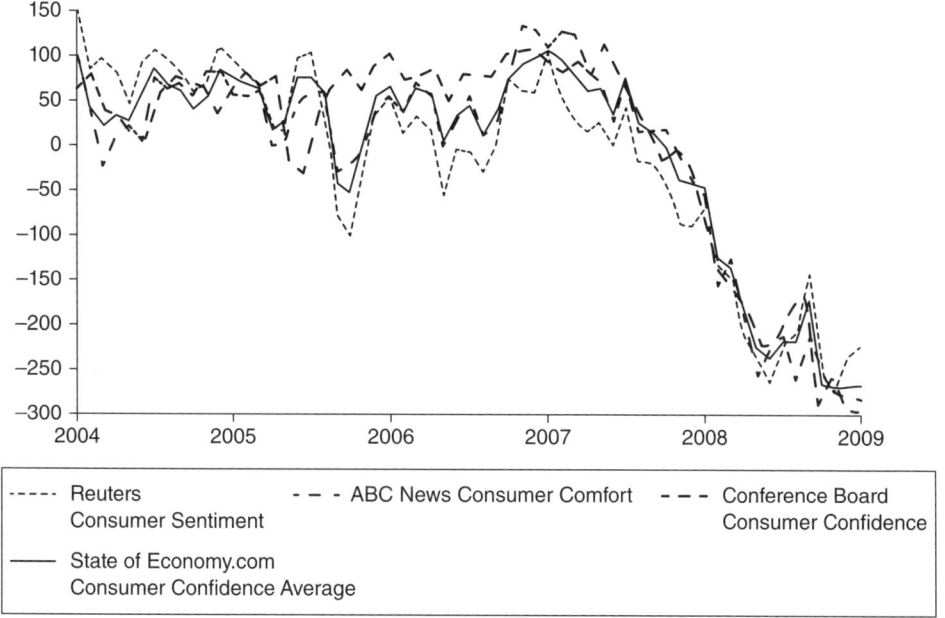

Diagram 1.4 Consumer confidence in the USA 2004–2009

Source: http://commons.wikimedia.org/wiki/File:Consumer_confidence_average_Jan_2009.png> (CC-BY-3.0 © Vlad.fridman).

interests best. In Post Keynesian economics, agents are very much aware of uncertainty and therefore act out of intuition, balancing profit-seeking with caution against loss.

1.5 Neoclassical economics

1.5.1 Utility and rationality

Neoclassical economic theory started with Alfred Marshall. I discuss this theory last, even though it is the dominant theory in economics worldwide. The reason that I discuss it last is because it is the most abstract economic theory. It consists of a set of eloquent but narrowly defined principles and assumptions, and thereby is developed for a stable, idealised economic context. This context is characterised by competitive markets (many suppliers, no market power) and perfect information, or at least, widely available information with known probabilities of possible events (risk, not uncertainty). Economic agents are assumed to pursue their self-interest with given preferences, all having some resource for which there is market demand. Their preferences are commensurable, meaning that they can be perfectly traded off against one another along a smoothly shaped utility function. This implies that rationality is defined by neoclassical economists with what's-in-it-for-me (*wiifm*), through the maximisation of an individual utility function.

A *utility function*, or *indifference curve*, is a curve with trade-offs of what contributes to economic agents' pleasure for given prices and income levels. It may also include non-material preferences, for example for social status or leisure time.

24 *Economics as a science*

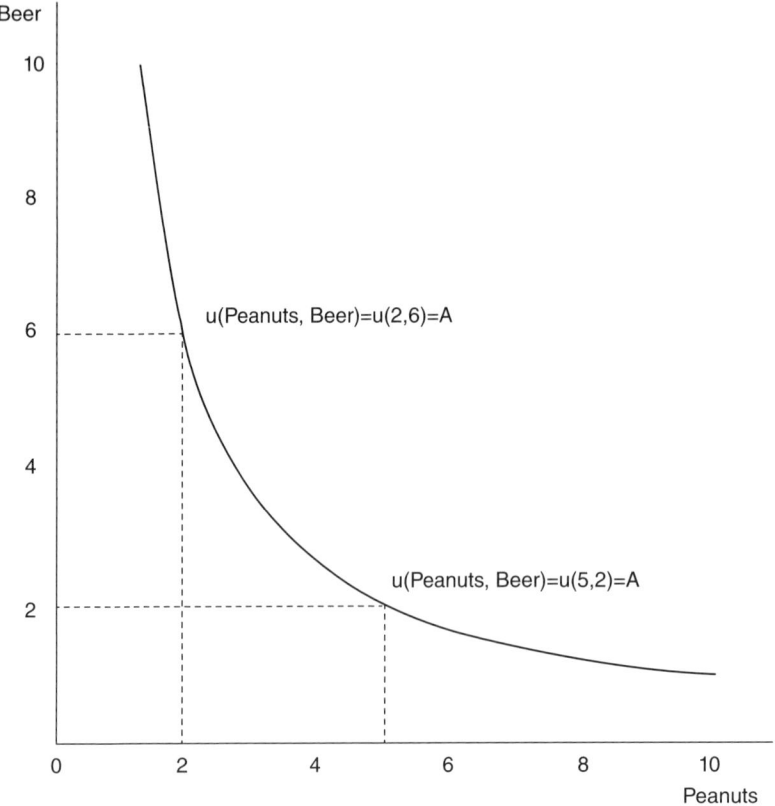

Diagram 1.5 Utility function for beer and peanuts

Diagram 1.5 shows a utility function, or indifference curve, for glasses of beer and bowls of peanuts. Beer is on the vertical axis (y) and peanuts on the horizontal axis (x). Wherever you are on the curve, your level of utility is the same: the level of A. This can be obtained with a combination of two bowls of nuts and six glasses of beer, or with five bowls of nuts and two glasses of beer – depending on whether you feel more thirsty or more hungry.

Trade-offs are also possible between material preferences, which are expressed in money, and *immaterial preferences*, which are expressed more directly on the pleasure/pain scale of a utility function. For example, the beer-lover may prefer to decline the offer of a big glass of beer and accept a small one in the presence of others, in order to show politeness. This will satisfy his preference for being regarded as a decent person by others, as someone who is willing to share. Now, in the social situation of being observed by others, he maximises his utility not by taking the biggest glass but by being polite, which gives him even more utility. So, he trades off beer against politeness on his utility function. Why? Perhaps it really gives him pleasure to follow the social norm. Or he dislikes receiving bad looks, and hence reduces the pain that he would feel in that case. Or he anticipates a decline in friendship if he does not abide by the social norm, so he is concerned with future utility from friendships. Or he knows that by showing politeness he will be building credits among his friends to ask for favours later if he needs them, a strategy to improve happiness in the future. Whatever the reason, this is irrelevant. What matters is the revealed preference of choosing politeness over more beer, because that is a choice which maximises utility.

The constraints to utility maximisation are twofold: prices and budgets on the one hand, and government regulation on the other. Economic agents are assumed to be rational in the sense that they prefer more utility over less utility. Economic agents trade off ends according to the *law of diminishing marginal utility*. This law states that for every additional unit of a good, the extra utility obtained decreases. This is shown in Diagram 1.6. The slope of the tangents at each point illustrates the marginal utility at that point, which is the extra utility gained from adding one unit of a resource. When you are thirsty, the first glass of water gives you more utility (0A) than the second one, which does not increase your satisfaction more than AB on the vertical axis. The third glass may not provide utility anymore: the curve becomes flat after point B. More water does not increase your utility. The same reasoning holds for the production side, where the law of diminishing marginal utility leads to an optimal mix of production factors. As soon as hiring an extra worker does not increase marginal utility anymore, an employer who wants to maximise profits will instead buy more capital goods (such as computers) or land (in the case of farming), assuming there is market demand for the extra production. So, the law of diminishing marginal utility is key to understanding demand and supply in markets, but only works under strict conditions of preference orderings, information, and full competition.

1.5.2 Equilibrium

The climax of neoclassical economic theory building was reached in the same period as MONIACs became popular. In 1954, Kenneth Arrow and Gerard Debreu delivered a famous mathematical proof of the existence of an efficient *general market equilibrium*. A *market equilibrium* is a situation in which supply meets demand so that all resources are fully employed and the economy functions at full capacity. For a general market equilibrium, this is the case for all markets in an economy. The proof shows that an efficient equilibrium exists in free markets with prices determined by the market values for every good. The equilibrium will arise if every economic agent maximises his or her utility with the initial availability of useful labour and the possession of some amount of every commodity. The proof is an eloquent piece of mathematics applied to an idealised free market with an almost communist assumption about the initial distribution of resources and goods: everybody must have sufficient labour and goods to exchange.

Later, neoclassical economics excluded this second assumption (was it too socialist?) by assuming that markets only involve agents with purchasing power, and not those without anything to exchange. However, this departure from the initial theory has an important implication for the efficiency of a market equilibrium. By excluding agents from markets who have no goods or labour power to exchange, the theory ignores that these agents have to find alternative ways to secure their livelihoods. Quite likely, they will become financially dependent upon the collective, which necessitates an active role of the state with taxation and subsidies to provide such people with a livelihood outside markets, or households must provide much unpaid time in community care for those unfortunate individuals who have no business on markets. In the minimal case, state action (taxation, regulation, redistribution) is necessary to prevent theft, chaos, and conflict. This fall-back function of the state and the community economy will affect the market equilibrium, requiring redistribution of resources. This pleads for the original, 1954 understanding of neoclassical market

26 *Economics as a science*

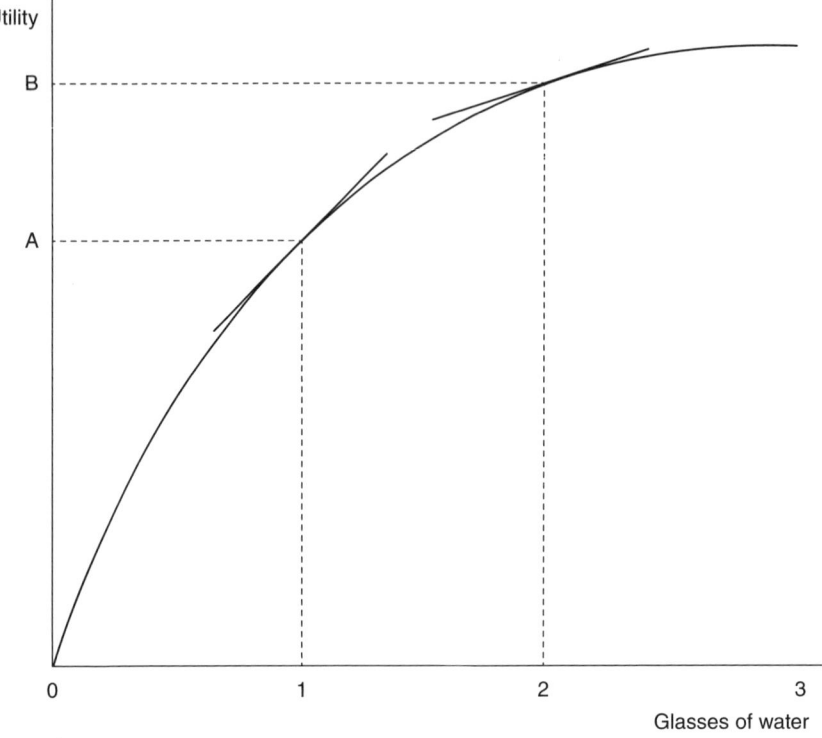

Diagram 1.6 Diminishing marginal utility

equilibrium, which requires everybody to have sufficient resources to participate effectively in market exchange.

Change in the neoclassical model is assumed to be *exogenous*: shocks are considered to be sudden external changes to a market equilibrium, such as from change in the weather, political crises, or economic policies. Neoclassical economics assumes that markets will quickly react to these shocks with adaptations in demand and supply, leading to a new equilibrium in the market with a new equilibrium price. A good example of exogenous change is the oil price shocks of the 1970s and 1980s. When OPEC countries formed a cartel and decided to increase the world oil price by reducing the supply of oil, markets quickly adapted with subsequent changes in the prices of petrol, electricity, airfares, and other goods. The new equilibrium settled at a higher price level with lower levels of the above-mentioned goods sold, at least temporarily, which led to an economic crisis in the 1980s.

1.5.3 Abstract theory for special cases

Since neoclassical economics is the most abstract theory of the four presented in this book, it is not always the most useful for explaining complex economic phenomena in the real world. It is powerful, for example, in explaining why firms relocate to low wage countries when labour costs are much higher in developed countries. While it is less useful in explaining why such relocation leads to sustained unemployment in the country of origin, where neoclassical economics assumes that labour is immediately re-allocated over other sectors. Or it helps to explain why and by how much demand for ice cream increases in summertime and decreases in wintertime. It may even calculate the increase in ice cream cones sold per degree Celsius increase in outside temperature. But it does not explain how advertising influences the demand for ice cream or a rumour about a bacteria in dairy products, or herd behaviour in certain age groups of consumers for a particular flavour of ice cream. So, neoclassical economic theory may provide adequate explanations for clearly defined, static, and independent market situations, with ideal circumstances in terms of information, preferences, rationality, balance of power, and stability. Such conditions are rare in the real world, and therefore, neoclassical economics refers to a special case where such conditions hold.

Despite this mismatch with the real world in many instances, neoclassical economists are much concerned with forecasting the economy: economic growth, inflation, budget deficits, trade volumes, and demand. Although forecasting models have become increasingly sophisticated, the forecasts often are incorrect, simply because future conditions are unknown, so they cannot be given probabilities based on past experiences.

1.6 Rationality

Each of the four theories has its own conceptualisation of rationality, a view of how economic agents make decisions that make sense to themselves and to others. Table 1.3 shows the four theoretical concepts of rationality in a matrix. The matrix has two axes: closed or open information base (columns) and self-referential or group-referential (rows). I will explain each of the four definitions of rationality.

In social economics, rationality is understood as prudence based on shared values. Hence, the reference is to the group, the community, in which values are shared. These values have intrinsic value, such as fairness, trustworthiness, and pride. But they are challenged and change over time and differ between communities: there is openness in values. Economic agents act relative to these values and are willing to defend them at a cost in their communities: strong reciprocity. So,

Image 1.4 Ice cream consumption and outside temperature

28 *Economics as a science*

we define social economic rationality as *strong reciprocity*. In institutional economics, rationality is understood at the group level, as 'I' as part of 'we'. It still leaves space for disagreement and change in group norms, but the group and its norms and values are the reference, they are considered as given. Hence, we define institutional economic rationality as *group-dependent rationality*. In Post Keynesian economics, rationality is understood to have a largely intuitive character. Keynes characterised it as *animal spirits*, a sudden urge to action, seeking profit or reducing loss. The uncertainty defines the open information base: the future is unknown. As a consequence, we define Post Keynesian rationality as *intuitive rationality*. Finally, neoclassical economics starts from a closed information base, with (near) perfect information about markets and conditions, and inner knowledge about one's subjective preferences and their ordering in a utility function. Rationality is completely self-referential, even though the well-being of others matters to economic agents, but only instrumentally so. This results in rationality defined as *individual utility maximisation*. Or, in plain language, what's-in-it-for-me: *wiifm*.

1.7 Power

In this book, we distinguish between power over resources, market power, the power vested in formal and informal institutions, and the market as a source of accumulation of power.

1.7.1 Power over resources

In capitalist economies, capital hires labour and not the other way around. This implies power of the first over the second, except in rare cases of labour scarcity, no immigration, and no opportunities for technological advancement. Another form of power over resources stems from the initial distribution of resources between and within countries: oil, fertile soil, minerals, water, and an educated population without deep social conflict. The colonial era disrupted this initial distribution of resources so much that even today developing countries suffer from its consequences. A third form of power over resources is much more taken for granted. It concerns unpaid labour and caring. This resource is largely available in households, but its supply is distributed very unevenly: women tend, historically, to provide much more unpaid labour and care than men. This leaves them less time available for paid work, and hence, for earning an income. Moreover, in paid labour, women receive lower wages than men, even with the same levels of education and work experience. These two gender inequalities together largely explain why female poverty worldwide is more widespread than male poverty.

1.7.2 Market power

Market power is the only form of power that is widely acknowledged among economists, independent of which theory they adhere to. This is because market power reduces choice

Table 1.3 Rationality in the four economic theories

	Open information base	*Closed information base*
Group-referential	Social economics: strong reciprocity	Institutional economics: group-dependent rationality
Self-referential	Post Keynesian economics: intuitive rationality	Neoclassical economics: individual utility maximisation (*wiifm*)

in the market, for competitors, new firms, and buyers. Market power undermines the market because it reduces supply or demand and thereby limits competition.

What is *market power*? It means that a supplier can influence the price level to his or her advantage or can prevent new entrants to the market. A free market consists of many suppliers, so that no one can set the price. This is also called a competitive market. If one supplier increases the price of his or her product, buyers turn away and the supplier quickly goes out of business. But if a supplier is the only supplier of a particular good, and therefore has a monopoly, she can set any prices she likes: consumers do not have the choice to move to a different supplier.

Less extreme forms of market power include an oligopoly, in which a few suppliers distribute the market among themselves, each with their own relatively high prices. And cartels, which are agreements between a few suppliers to determine the market price by selling less of the good they exclusively offer to the market. Think about the OPEC countries that formed a successful cartel in the 1970s and 1980s, strongly increasing world oil prices. Another form of market power is the creation of *entry barriers* for new firms, which are constraints put on newcomers by existing firms. An example of an entry barrier is a licence. For example, when taxi companies prevent new taxis entering the market by lobbying effectively to stop new licences being issued by the local government, and by selling existing licences at very high prices. Entry barriers keep supply relatively low and thereby create relative scarcity to the disadvantage of consumer choice and price levels. The benefits go to the existing firms in terms of higher sales.

The European Commission has a *competition policy*, a policy which prohibits mergers or acquisitions that would lead to a dominant market share by a single firm. This EU policy was enforced in the European market for deodorants in the year 2010, when the Dutch-British multinational Unilever wanted to buy parts of the American firm Sara Lee, another large producer of consumer goods. But with the deodorant produced by Sara Lee (Sanex) also coming in the hands of Unilever, almost all major brands of deodorants on the European market would have been supplied by only one firm. Unilever already produces four brands of deodorants, namely Axe, Dove, Impulse, and Rexona. With the addition of Sanex, Unilever would then have had the power to increase the price of each of its brands of deodorants, without having to fear that a competitor would lure away consumers by keeping the prices of other deodorants lower, simply because there were very few competitors left in the European deodorant market. The European consumer would be disadvantaged by this take-over of Sara Lee by Unilever, which is why the European Commission required Unilever to sell off the deodorant brand Sanex immediately after it bought the parts of Sara Lee it wanted to acquire.

Table 1.4 shows the market share of the top 10 seed and agrochemical companies. Just three companies account for more than half of the seed market worldwide and the world's largest seed company, Monsanto, has 27 per cent of market share. The increasing trend in market power of these companies is significant as the ten top seed companies had 57 per cent of market share in 2006, 49 per cent in 2004, and 37 per cent in 1996, while Monsanto's share of the seed market was 20 per cent in 2006 even though it did not appear on the 1996 list. A quick look at both lists reveals the close links between the seed and agrochemical markets. Five of the top six agrochemical companies appear on the list of largest seed companies, and BASF, which does not show up there, has long-term collaborations with BAYER CropScience and Monsanto.

Another form of market power consists of *asymmetric information*. This occurs when one party has more knowledge about the good to be exchanged than the other party. The standard example is of second-hand cars. Buyers often only find out the real quality of the car after having driven a few hundred kilometres, and not simply in a short test-ride. But by then the car has already been bought. . . .

Table 1.4 Market shares of the world's largest agro-businesses

World's top 10 seed companies

	Headquarters	Sales 2009 (US$ million)	Market share
Monsanto	USA	7,297	27%
DuPont	USA	4,641	17%
Syngenta	Switzerland	2,564	9%
Groupe Limagrain	France	1,252	5%
Land O'Lakes/Winfield	USA	1,100	4%
KWS SAAT AG	Germany	997	4%
Bayer CropScience	Germany	700	3%
Dow AgroSciences	USA	635	2%
Sakarta	Japan	491	2%
DLF-Trifolium	Denmark	385	1%
Total top 10		20,062	74%

World's top 10 agrochemical companies

	Headquarters	Sales 2009 (US$ million)	Market share
Syngenta	Switzerland	8,491	19%
Bayer CropScience	Germany	7,544	17%
BASF	Germany	5,007	11%
Monsanto	USA	4,427	10%
Dow AgroSciences	USA	3,902	9%
DuPont	USA	2,403	5%
Sumitomo Chemical	Japan	2,374	5%
Nufarm	Australia	2,082	5%
Makhteshim Agan	Israel	2,042	5%
Arysta LifeScience	Japan	1,196	3%
Total top 10		39,468	89%

Source: 'Who Will Control the Green Economy?', ETC group, 1 November 2011.

1.7.3 Asymmetric and dominant institutions

The third form of power in economics is through the institutions that enable or constrain the behaviour of agents in the economy. This occurs through *asymmetric institutions*: institutions that have different effects on different groups. The differential effect often hides power. For example, workers with migrant status may have less entitlement to pensions and unemployment benefits than regular workers in a country. This gives them a weaker bargaining position in the labour market of the host country as compared to nationals. Another example is the voting rules in the World Bank: countries that pay higher dues have more voting rights than countries that pay lower contributions. In practice, this means that the developed countries have more influence on World Bank policy than poor countries. There is no such asymmetry in voting rights for citizens in a democratic country: irrespective of the amount of income you earn or taxes you pay, you have an equal vote with everyone else in parliamentary elections. An example of an asymmetric informal institution in the economy is racial discrimination in the hiring of workers when job applicants of different ethnic backgrounds have similar levels of schooling and work experience. Asymmetric institutions generate power for one group over another, based upon discriminatory beliefs and prejudices expressed in unequal social norms.

Next to asymmetric institutions, are institutions that hold economic power simply through their historical or cultural dominance. For example, the programming codes for computer software developed by a software pioneer which have become the standard for all new software developments on the market. Without these basic codes, which are kept secret by the firm that initially developed them, competitors cannot develop software that runs on computers that have the dominant operating system. Think about the case of the firm Microsoft, which has power over software development because most computers in the world use Microsoft systems.

1.7.4 Market dogma

The market itself can also generate power in an economy, and hence, inequalities between groups in an economy. The market is the location of accumulation. *Accumulation* is defined as making money with money, directly or through production. Through labour markets, workers acquire and develop experience and expertise, which may earn them increasing incomes when they accumulate their human capital in response to labour demand. Through capital markets, investors accumulate financial capital through interest, dividend earnings, and profits made on trade in assets. Such accumulation tends to be stronger, the higher the starting position and the more demand for the skills or services provided, together with some luck. Moreover, when labour income becomes large, some of it can be invested in capital, so that accumulation can proceed faster through capital gains on top of labour earnings. Think about buying a house with money earned from labour, and selling it a few years later at a 50 per cent profit. Your labour income is much less likely to increase by 50 per cent in a few years' time than the value of your house.

Accumulation, therefore, already comes with inequality, even in markets without market power. Of course, it is possible for a factory girl to develop into a millionaire (see Box 1.1 for the story of Zhang Xin). Accumulation through markets, even when fully competitive, contributes to inequality in the following ways:

- Accumulation starts with a marketable initial resource, but as not everyone has such a resource, it excludes some agents from accumulation from the beginning.
- Accumulation requires market demand for the goods that one produces with that resource. However, for some goods demand is low and declining and substitution costs to shift to

the production of alternative goods may be high, so accumulation ends early for some agents because they have not been able to innovate on time or to adapt to shifts in demand.
- Accumulation depends partly on luck: some possible future events can be insured against, but many events are simply uncertain and cannot be mitigated; those with more resources are better able to get insurance, to diversify their portfolio, and to acquire expert advise to reduce the costs of possible mishaps; and through inheritance and privileged education by the already economically advantaged; luck is more on the side of those who have accumulated more than on the side of those who have accumulated less.

Box 1.1 The story of Zhang Xin

Zhang Xin (1965) was born in Beijing and received her economics degree from Cambridge University, UK. With her husband, she founded the real estate firm SOHO (Small Office Home Office), which became one of the largest in China and is listed on the Hong Kong Stock Exchange. She is the CEO and regarded as a young urban visionary, developing work spaces for the new Chinese entrepreneurs. Zhang Xin has won international prizes for her architectural innovation and has a passion for art. She is also a philanthropist, and engaged in education and poverty alleviation.

CC-BY-SA-3.0 © Sohochina/Wikimedia commons

The mission of SOHO China Foundation is to drive societal progress while promoting spiritual advancement. It is Zhang's aim, as she puts it, 'to advocate urbanism to the market, to create a neighborhood rather than just a compound.' — *Time Magazine*.

Source: http://eng.sohochina.com/about/en/zhangxin.html (accessed 1 May 2014).

Markets, therefore – even fully competitive markets – reinforce existing inequalities in resources, in supply and demand patterns, and in the ability to reduce risks and mitigate the costs of uncertainty. But this is not all. Those who are successful in accumulation will try to maintain their advantaged position, partly through developing market power (see section 1.7.2) and through creating or supporting dominant institutions that defend their interests (see section 1.7.3) through lobbying for example. Or they manage to forge asymmetric information situations in which they shift risks on to those less informed or on to the taxpayer. These accumulation-induced forms of strategic behaviour strengthen the market vis-à-vis the state and the community. Accumulation, hence, directly and indirectly increases the role of the market in the economy.

When markets become dominant in an economy, this comes with risks for the economy as a whole. Markets are inherently unstable mechanisms of allocation: they move along cycles. So, when markets become dominant, economies become less stable. The 2007 financial crisis is a good example of this. This instability is an important reason for keeping the market, state, and community economy in balance.

Finally, market dominance may turn citizens into market parties: consumers and investors. This leads to market-like behaviour in society as a whole. Taxpayers want to pay only those taxes from which they will benefit themselves. Hence, not for the municipal swimming pool if they don't have children taking swimming classes there, and not for bus services if they drive their own car, and not for development aid if they prefer to give privately to a development NGO for small-scale projects only. With such market thinking, contributors to a health care insurance fund want to pay only for the care they use themselves, undermining the capacity of the fund to insure a wide set of health care services for everybody. Citizens who increasingly experience market relationships and are addressed as customers rather than as citizens, may eventually ask themselves, also outside markets: *wiifm*?, thereby undermining community life and the collectiveness of the state.

1.8 Interesting sources

Christoforou, A. and J. B. Davis (eds) (2014) *Social Capital and Economics. Social Values, Power, and Social Identity*. London: Routledge.
Hodgson, G., U. Mäki and D. McCloskey (1992) 'Plea for a Pluralistic and Rigorous Economics', *American Economic Review* 82(2), p. xxv.
IDEAs Network: http://www.networkideas.org/
Inside Job. Documentary film on the financial crisis by Charles Ferguson. Sony Pictures Classics, 2011.
Nobel Prizes in economics: http://www.nobelprize.org/nobel_prizes/economics/
Peil, J. and I. van Staveren (eds) (2009) *Handbook of Economics and Ethics*. Cheltenham: Edward Elgar.
Reardon, J. (ed.) (2009) *The Handbook of Pluralist Economics Education*. London: Routledge.

1.9 Glossary

Accumulation   Making money with money, directly or through production

Aggregate demand   The total demand of all households, firms, the government, and the rest of the world (households, firms, and governments abroad)

Animal spirits   A sudden urge to action, seeking profit or reducing loss

Asymmetric information   When one party has more knowledge about the good to be exchanged than the other party

Asymmetric institutions   Institutions that have different effects on different groups

Behavioural economics   An empirical approach to the study of the behaviour of economic agents under various conditions

Bonding social capital   High within-group trust and interaction

Bridging social capital = **social cohesion**   High between-group trust and interaction

Broad efficiency   An economic evaluation criterion concerned with the minimisation of waste of resources

Capacity utilisation   The extent of the use of available resources

Caring   Work done by a caregiver for a care receiver, addressing the care receiver's needs

Competition policy   Policy which prohibits mergers or acquisitions that would lead to a dominant market share by a single firm

Deontological ethics   A principle-based ethics concerned with rights, duties, and human dignity

Economics   The study of how human beings interact for the provisioning of their livelihoods in markets, the state, and communities

Financial fragility   The recognition that small shocks in financial markets can lead to large crises

Formal institutions   Codified rules, regulations, and organisations

General market equilibrium   When in all markets supply equals demand without excess supply or excess demand and prices are determined for every good

Immaterial preferences   Preferences for intangible goods and services, social, cultural, and spiritual values

Informal institutions   Unwritten rules, beliefs, and rules of thumb

Law of diminishing marginal utility   For every additional unit of a good the extra utility obtained decreases

Marginal utility   The extra utility gained from adding one unit of a resource

Market equilibrium   A situation in which supply meets demand so that all resources are fully employed and the economy functions at full capacity

Market power   The influence of a supplier over the price level and/or over entry barriers for new entrants to the market

Money   Anything that allows its holder to purchase goods

Narrow efficiency   An economic evaluation criterion of the maximisation of output with the minimisation of input, or minimisation of waste

Oikos   The household of the state and communities

Pluralism   The conviction that a plurality of theoretical and methodological viewpoints is valuable and contributes to the advancement of science

Power   When B is capable of affecting A's actions to serve B's interests, through threatening or imposing sanctions on A, while A lacks this capacity with respect to B

Scarcity   A relative limitedness of resources, influenced by economic agents

Social capital   The value of relationships between individuals and groups, valuable in their own right, and often having as a by-product economic costs or benefits

Social cohesion   Connectedness in a society, which is valuable in itself and helps to overcome the economic problems of transaction costs, free riding, and moral hazard

Strong reciprocity   When agents contribute resources to a joint activity when others do so as well even when there are no benefits to themselves or their kin, or future gains to be expected, or reputation gains: they are prepared to punish free riders, at their own cost

Uncertainty versus risk   We simply do not know what may happen and how likely it is to occur versus known options and their probabilities

Utilitarianism   The ethics of the greatest happiness for the greatest number and concerned with maximisation of pleasure or happiness, and minimisation of pain

Utility function indifference curve   A curve with trade-offs of what contributes to economic agents' utility for given prices and income levels

Virtue ethics   Person-based ethics concerned with good behaviour in a social context of trial and error

Notes

1 Robinson, J. (1978) *Contributions to Modern Economics*. Oxford: Basil Blackwell, p. 75.
2 Written by J. M. Keynes in a letter to colleague Roy Harrod on 4 July 1938.
3 May, A. M., M. G. McGarvey and R. Whaples (2014) 'Are Disagreements among Male and Female Economists Marginal at Best? A Survey of AEA Members and Their Views on Economics and Economic Policy', *Contemporary Economic Policy*, 32(1), pp. 111–32.
4 In the Netherlands, people between 20 and 65 years of age spend on average 27 hours per week on paid work and 26 hours per week on unpaid work. For an overview of time use in the Netherlands, see Cloïn, M. (2009) *A Day with the Dutch – Time Use in the Netherlands and Fifteen other European Countries*. The Hague: SCP.

2 Individuals and households

2.1 Individuals and agency

The smallest unit of analysis in economics is the *economic agent*. This is an individual, but often a household or a firm. Through their interactions, economic agents (but you can also read households or firms) perform roles. The major economic roles are worker, employer, entrepreneur, consumer, producer, saver, tax payer, borrower, and investor. Of course, economic agents often take on several roles. For example, an economic agent has a job, cares for her elderly parents, brings home groceries that are paid from her salary, and saves some money at the end of the month in a bank account, which the bank lends out to someone else, while her employer puts a percentage of her gross salary aside as a contribution to the company pension fund, which is invested in bonds and shares across the world.

Economic agents make decisions and act upon these in an economically meaningful way. This implies that they have ends, in line with their values, and that they try to achieve these ends in a socially acceptable and efficient way. This requires *agency*, which means making autonomous choices and acting upon these. Without agency, people may be coerced, alienated, submissive, passive, or desirous to please. Economic agency implies that an individual has decision-making power over what he or she wants and how to achieve this, using available resources, and drawing upon *collective agency*, which is the agency of groups, and drawing on institutions through the social groups that he or she is part of.

Economists generally limit their use of agency to adults. But children also can be and often are economic agents: they have their own preferences which may differ from those of their parents, they consume, receive savings in their name, produce goods and services for the household and beyond, and invest in their human capital and wider economic capabilities. Children already engage in exchange at an early age through play, and have an understanding of the household economy. Therefore, children should not be ignored as agents, depending of course on their age.

Economic agency can be weaker or stronger, and individualistic or social, depending on internal factors (age, education, self-confidence) and external factors (information, collective action, uncertainty, social norms, and laws). Moreover, our agency involves rationality, as was explained in Chapter 1. But economic agents are just like people – we do not always act fully rationally. We try to be clear about our goals but sometimes have doubts about what we want. We do our best to allocate our time efficiently over all the roles we have and within these roles over all the tasks we do. But we are not robots and also like to spend time with friends. We forget things, our attention may be diverted to other things, we may feel tired or lazy, or fail to correctly estimate costs and benefits. And sometimes we don't even care much about such calculations.

This chapter will not include Post Keynesian theory. The reason is that it has a limited theoretical development of individuals and households. Two other theories will be combined, because they overlap in their analysis of individuals and the household: social economics and institutional economics. But first, the major concepts and major social norms will be introduced.

2.2 Households

2.2.1 Adults and children

An important group of which economic agents are members is the *household*, a small unit in which people live together in cooperation and conflict. The household is the smallest unit to which people belong, and which has a relatively fixed location, in which children are often raised and prepared for their adult economic roles. Of course, children may already have economic roles in childhood, ranging from helping with household tasks such as cleaning or caring for siblings, to responsible roles where they act upon their own agency, in farming, petty trade, as domestic servants, or as apprentices in handicraft production. Most parents invest in the education of their children by sending them to school, although more often for boys than for girls. And children learn skills by doing and develop social skills in various group settings. In fact, empirical research among children has shown that they, like adults, value work for status, skills, responsibility, and money. Table 2.1 shows a summary of paid and unpaid child labour experiences by children between 8 and 13 years of age in Africa and Asia, measured as the average hours per week those children spend working.

The majority of children between 8 and 13 years of age in Africa and Asia participate in housework, girls more often so than boys. In Africa, 8.5 per cent of children in this age bracket do unpaid work other than housework, and in Asia 1.5 per cent. A significant proportion of children between 8 and 13 years of age do paid work: 4 per cent of African children and 2.5 per cent of Asian children participate in paid work.

Households have five economic functions. The *economic household functions* are (1) reproduction, (2) joint production, (3) joint consumption, (4) income pooling, and (5) risk pooling. All five functions are imbued with power relations within, between, and external to households. Power is predominantly expressed in the age hierarchy and in the households' gender relations.

Table 2.1 Child labour, average hours per week for working children

		Paid work	House work	Unpaid work
Africa	Girls	12.9	16	7.5
	Boys	13.5	13	7.9
Asia	Girls	29.8	8	8
	Boys	37.8	6	14.5

Source: Adapted from Webbink, E. (2012) *Child Labor in the Developing World*. Nijmegen: Radboud University Nijmegen, PhD Thesis.

Note: The data are based on surveys among more than 165,000 children in 16 countries.

2.2.2 Reproduction

A major economic function of the household is the reproduction of the labour force. *Reproduction* is the unpaid caring for the current and future generation of labour and for others inside and outside the economy. It does so by giving birth to and raising children in a set of norms and values that prepare them for future economic roles, and by sending them to school. At the same time, the household also takes care of the daily recovery and support of its workers and entrepreneurs, by feeding them, clothing them, and listening to their stories, and perhaps by giving advise on the problems they experience in their economic roles. So, households reproduce the current and the future labour force, reproducing the human resources in the economy. Moreover, reproduction involves caring for others who are not participating in the economy, such as the sick, the handicapped, and the elderly.

The quantitative side of the reproduction of the labour force is the number of potential workers in the future. In ageing societies, this number is relatively low. An increasingly smaller labour force needs to finance a growing demand on pensions and health care. With a pension age maximised at 65 years and an increasing life expectancy, this may become an unsustainable burden for younger generations in ageing societies. The qualitative side of reproduction of the future labour force refers to human capabilities in a broad sense, well beyond the more limited notion of human capital. *Human capabilities* for the future labour force include not only formal schooling, but also social skills, social norms, and collective behaviour, which together support a worker's future chances of finding a job and being productive.

The reproduction of the labour force largely occurs through unpaid care giving. It involves years of parental care, helped by an enabling community and a supportive state, providing accessible and good quality education. Childcare and upbringing is generally the largest activity in the unpaid economy. It does have partial substitutes in the market and the state, but this is often limited to private or municipal crèches for a limited number of hours during weekdays. The bulk of the reproduction of the labour force occurs in households and wider communities, with a disproportionate number of unpaid hours spent by women.

2.2.3 Joint production

Households reap gains from joint production and joint consumption. For production, this is enabled by a *division of labour in the household* in which members specialise in different skills, unpaid work, and paid jobs. While one person specialises in earning an income through a paid job outside the household, another may specialise in childcare at home or studying for a university degree in addition to doing domestic tasks. Specialisation allows for more income earning and more total household production than is possible when people live alone. Moreover, households allow for complementary production processes. *Complementary production* occurs when households produce goods and services, which, together with goods and services obtained from the market or the state, provide for households' needs. For example, health care provided in a hospital can be complemented by unpaid home care for the patient after the operation by household members, who also administer the medication. The combination of paid and unpaid health care, when in balance with the patient's needs and care provider's skills, may be quite efficient. It saves the costs of paid health care through complementary home care and it supports the patient's healing through the love and affection received at home from family members and friends or volunteers.

2.2.4 Joint consumption

Also on the consumption side there are gains from joining activity in households as compared to individual consumption. These gains lie in the economies of scale and economies of scope of joint consumption. *Economies of scale in household consumption* are cost advantages due to an increasing scale of consumption. For durable consumer goods, economies of scale are reaped from the shared consumption of a single durable good. Sharing the fixed investment of a house among a group of people is cheaper than having individual houses per person. A similar economy of scale occurs for durable consumer goods such as a television and furniture, because their use can be shared. Even for some daily consumer goods it is possible to reap economies of scale in consumption. Groceries bought in larger quantities tend to be cheaper per portion than when bought in smaller packages, thanks to volume discounts.

Another form of gains from joint consumption is through *economies of scope*. This means that the enjoyment of consumption tends to be higher when shared with those you care about. It is often much nicer to have dinner with your family or fellow students than alone, or to watch the football game on TV with friends, so that afterwards you can discuss the results or celebrate your favourite team's victory. Joint consumption, hence, provides more than just cost advantages.

2.2.5 Income pooling

Next to joint production and joint consumption comes the question of income. Do households necessarily pool all income? Many households share a large part of the incomes earned by the members of the household. But often they do not share all the income. Household members tend to share the income that is necessary to sustain joint consumption, such as rent, energy and water, insurance, and groceries. The income used for personal expenditures is not always pooled. This means that those with higher earnings tend to have more money available for personal expenditures (clothing, drinking money, entertainment, gifts) than those who have low earnings.

Some households, for example in large parts of sub-Sahara Africa, do not pool income at all. There are two reasons for this. First, some of the households are polygamous. This means that the husband is expected to share some of his income between his wives (and his children), while the co-wives are expected to largely maintain themselves and their children and pay for the food that they prepare for their husband in turns. Husbands, therefore, derive a divide-and-rule power from their marital status, which wives cannot obtain. This is an asymmetric institution, as defined in Chapter 1, section 1.3.1. In reaction to this asymmetric institution, the co-wives often choose not to pool their income with their husband because it may end up supporting additional co-wives at the cost of the savings that are necessary to invest in schooling for their children or in expanding their own businesses. Second, non-pooling is a response to a lack of cooperation. Remember that households are also spaces of conflict. An increased contribution by one member to the common pool may result in a decline by another member, who then keeps more income for personal expenditures. Such uncooperative behaviour often leads to strategies of asymmetric information by household members: they conceal information from each other on the value of their individual earnings, assets, and savings. As a consequence, the household reaps lower benefits from joint production and consumption.

In order to reap the benefits of income pooling while at the same time enhancing cooperation, households can agree on symmetric institutions of registering expenditures. An example is a transparent book-keeping system with an in-built incentive to refrain from cheating. I found a striking example of this in the student house in which my son lives, in the town of Delft in the Netherlands. The ten students (five boys and five girls) who live there keep accounts of the beer consumption through an ingenious system. This consists of a set of ten plastic containers one painted gold – for the winner. They throw the caps of the bottles of beer they consume into their own name-tagged container, to be counted once per month for payment to the collective account for beer purchases. The golden container was invented to prevent dumping one's own cap in someone else's container: they have a monthly contest for the largest number of beer caps. The student with the highest number of beer caps in his or her container will receive the gold coloured container for the next month, as a reward for being the toughest drinker of the month, with the pride and bragging that comes with it.

The symmetric institution of the golden container discourages free riding. While the open placement of the ten containers in the kitchen, next to the refrigerator, encourages trust because everybody can check the number of beer caps in every container at any time of the day. The institution works as long as the students enjoy the fun of the contest as well as the

Image 2.1 Golden container for a champion beer drinker

bragging of being the toughest drinker of the house. As a mother I am concerned about the alcohol abuse that is stimulated by this institution, but as an economist I quite like the institutional innovation of transparent household financial management.

2.2.6 Risk pooling

Households are also units in which economic agents pool risk and counter the effects of uncertain negative events together. *Risk pooling* means reducing individual risk in a group by sharing resources and carrying out a division of labour, which makes the group flexible in responses to changes in the economic context. By sharing resources and carrying out a division of labour, households are able to better deal with the risks of unemployment, price increases, and changing returns to specialised skills than individuals. If one household member loses his job, another member may increase his hours supplied to the labour market to substitute for the lost income (this is called 'the added worker effect' and will be discussed in more detail in Chapter 8 on labour markets). When those with farming skills see their wages go down, other members of the household with information and communications technology (ICT) skills may see their wages go up, due to shifts in labour demand in the regional labour market. When the prices of food increase significantly, a household member with skills and time available may start a vegetable garden to substitute purchased vegetables and fruit with home production. Or when the government reduces health expenditures and clinics in rural areas close down and drugs become more expensive, rural household members may care themselves for sick family members, relying on traditional healers and unpaid caring labour in the household. So, households offer opportunities for risk pooling because of sharing resources and a division of labour. The fact that not everyone carries out the same task or job allows for some flexibility.

But over a longer period of time, specialisation may increase risks for some household members. In the case of divorce, the partner who specialises in unpaid childcare and domestic tasks will suddenly have lower pension rights and low potential earnings in the labour market (due to limited labour market experience) as compared to the partner who specialised in paid work. Those who specialise only in unpaid or low paid work, in childcare, and in domestic work, have a disadvantage in the long run if the household breaks up or the main breadwinner dies. So, specialisation helps to counter risks in the short run but may increase risks in the long run for household members specialising in unpaid work. Hence, Adam Smith's praise of the benefits of the division of labour was perhaps a bit too optimistic for the household – a blind spot because he spent most of his life living with his mother.

2.3 Gender division of labour

Gender refers to the socially and culturally constructed differences between men and women, with hierarchical meanings, often in favour of what is regarded as masculine. These differences are rooted in stereotype concepts that we also find in economics. These include rationality versus emotion, public versus private, competition versus cooperation, and paid work versus unpaid work. In these binary oppositions, the first one is in many societies labelled as 'masculine' and the second as 'feminine', which is why we call them *gender stereotypes*. Moreover, the first one often has higher social status than the second. Gender stereotypes create unequal and contested gender relations in society and the economy. In this section, I will discuss the major ways in which gender is expressed in economic behaviour in households.

2.3.1 Allocation of time

The members of a household (remember, we only refer to adults) have to decide how to spend their time between three alternative uses: paid work, unpaid work, and leisure time. Obviously, this choice menu is a simplification of real-life choices because we often combine activities. Some work is so enjoyable that it has a leisure component, while some paid work includes unpaid tasks, which are not expressed in a labour contract but which are generally assumed, by social norm, to be part of it. For example, overtime to get the work done, travelling, or maintaining social relationships with colleagues. In the example that I use here, I disregard such combinations and present a choice between paid work, unpaid work, and leisure time. Assuming that everyone needs 8 hours of sleep and 2 hours of personal care, there are 24 hours − 10 hours = 14 hours in a day left for the allocation of time.

Across the world there is a remarkable difference in the allocation of time between men and women. Whereas women, on average, spend most time on unpaid work, men, on average, spend more time on paid work. The total hours worked are higher, on average, for women, so that men generally have more leisure time available. This expresses a relatively universal *gender division of labour*. See Table 2.2 with a selection of data from time use surveys of 22 countries.

A strict gender division of labour constrains the choices of both women and men. Despite dominant gender norms of what is expected of a 'real man' and a 'good woman', many fathers like to spend more caring time with their children, and many women are frustrated by a high load of household chores. Besides, sharing the burden of running the household may strengthen cooperation in the household and provides more equal role models for children. But gender norms are resilient and are often internalised by men and women alike and so change only slowly. One way to change unequal gender norms is through role models.

Of course, much more than making role models visible needs to be done to change gender norms. Making gender institutions more symmetric also requires awareness campaigns and better enforcement of anti-gender discrimination laws.

Paid work has a higher status in almost every country because it provides not only income, and hence access to consumer goods, but also positions along a social hierarchy in firms, government organisations, and NGOs. The flipside of the social status of paid work is that unpaid work is generally valued less and is less visible. In addition, there is the suspicion that at least part of it is not work at all but leisure time.

For example, where does labour input end and consumption begin in preparing a cup of tea for oneself? Heating the water is clearly work, washing the teapot and the cups as well, and also bringing them into the room. But pouring the tea from the pot into the cup? Adding sugar and stirring? Is this work or consumption? Or does consumption only begin when you move the cup to your mouth? The solution in economics to this problem has been found in the *third-person criterion*: everything you can hire a third person to do for you is work, while other activities are consumption or leisure. This is, of course, a convention and not water-tight. Again there are overlaps between time allocations: enjoying consumption (leisure) can overlap with work. In fact, while I am writing this sentence, I am also enjoying a cup of tea. But, the third-person criterion at least gives us a rule of thumb (yes, this is a form of an institution) to distinguish paid work from leisure/consumption. You cannot hire someone to watch TV for you or to do your yoga and expect nevertheless to experience the same relaxing Zen feeling.

The gender division of labour has direct consequences for the gender division of income. It will come as no surprise that for every economy in the world, women's incomes are lower than men's incomes.

Table 2.2 Daily time use by women and men in six countries

	Australia	Brazil	Germany	Japan	Turkey	USA
Female						
Paid work and study	4:20	5:21	3:50	5:25	1:12	5:09
Unpaid work[1]	3:39	3:22	3:47	3:40	4:28	3:01
Childcare	1:21	0:36	0:37	0:33	0:48	0:59
Personal care[2]	10:24	10:14	10:47	10:46	10:58	10:08
Voluntary work	0:13	0:40	0:21	0:08	0:43	0:52
Social and events[3]	0:56	1:03	1:48	0:39	2:16	1:28
Leisure[4]	2:54	2:10	2:26	2:45	2:43	2:41
Male						
Paid work and study	7:28	7:59	6:07	9:32	6:02	7:20
Unpaid work	1:45	0:52	2:08	0:32	0:30	1:51
Childcare	0:26	0:06	0:11	0:04	0:10	0:22
Personal care	10:04	9:25	10:23	10:28	10:56	9:46
Voluntary work	0:08	0:16	0:18	0:08	0:32	0:46
Social and events	0:48	0:58	1:38	0:32	2:45	1:19
Leisure	3:10	2:20	3:08	2:41	3:04	2:58

Source: Fisher, K. and J. Robinson (2010) 'Daily Routines in 22 Countries: Diary Evidence of Average Daily Time Spent in Thirty Activities', Technical paper 2010-01. Oxford: Centre for Time Use Research at the University of Oxford.

Notes: Values shows hours:minutes of time per weekdays for men and women aged 18–46 except for Japan and Turkey where they were aged 15–46. Data for Australia, Japan, and Turkey were collected in 2006, for Brazil in 2001, for Germany in 2001–2002, and for the USA in 2003.

[1] Unpaid work includes cooking, housework, repairs, gardening, and shopping.
[2] Personal care includes sleep, meals, walking, and sport.
[3] Social and events include restaurants, pubs, parties, visits, and travel.
[4] Leisure includes relaxing, doing nothing, the internet, TV, radio, reading, and other hobbies

---

Box 2.1 Role model for family–work balance

Robert Polet, who was elected European businessman of the year in 2007 by the popular American business magazine *Forbes*, headed the luxury brand Gucci between 2004 and 2011. Throughout these years, managing 10,000 employees and a billion dollar international firm, he remained a family man. He switched off his Blackberry on Friday evening and switched it on again on Monday morning. He left early from his first international management meeting as the new CEO where he had just had laid out the new strategy, because he had promised his daughter to come to her birthday party on time. At the same time, Polet worked very hard and helped the company to develop and grow.

Source: http://money.cnn.com/2008/01/08/news/international/Gucci_Polet.fortune/

44 *Individuals and households*

Image 2.2 Non-stereotype occupations

Gender income inequality has six sources:

1 Less hours of paid work by women than men and more hours of unpaid work by women than men;
2 Average lower school enrolment rates for girls as compared to boys in many countries, particularly at secondary and tertiary level (but in some countries girls have higher enrolment rates);
3 Short periods of time out of the labour market due to maternity leave, and sometimes parental leave, taken largely by mothers (much less by fathers) when the child is young; this reduces labour market experience and (rightly or not) signals low ambition;
4 Concentration of women's employment in a limited number of sectors in the labour market, associated with women's work in the household: health care, education, and secretarial work. These jobs earn relatively low wages compared with jobs taken more often by men;
5 Asymmetric formal institutions, which give women limited rights to inheritance, individual ownership, and the freedom to buy and sell property in their own right;
6 Gendered beliefs about leadership, leading to very few women in top management positions in business, the civil service, and NGOs.

Finally, there is a reinforcing mechanism between the gender division of labour in the household on the one hand, and the gender division of paid labour in the labour market on the other. The lower average wages that women earn in the labour market reinforce the gender division of labour in the household because total household income will be higher if men specialise in paid work and women in unpaid work. This, then, is another explanation, next to the resilience of gender stereotypes, why the gender division of labour in households changes only very slowly.

2.3.2 Unpaid work and caring

Unpaid work and unpaid caring as part of unpaid work are important household tasks. The gendered patterns of unpaid work and caring have emerged in every society from prehistoric times due to the closeness of the biological function of childbearing and breastfeeding to the social-economic task of child raising and the domestic tasks of gathering and preparing food. Of course, men have the capabilities to also do these tasks, and many fathers are well-experienced in care giving and value these tasks highly. But once the social-economic tasks of domestic work and care were largely shifted to women, and paid work obtained an increasingly higher social status, it became difficult to redistribute unpaid work and caring more evenly between women and men. Stereotypes are powerful, and transmitted from one generation to another through traditional role models, images in schoolbooks and advertisements, and gendered expectations that parents have about the adult work life of their daughters and sons. These are reinforced by cultural practices, such as dowry payment by the parents of the bride to the parents of the groom upon marriage, and very early marriage of girls. And gender stereotypes are reinforced by social norms, such as beliefs that men make better leaders and are more suitable for technical jobs, while women have an innate inclination for social types of work and caring.

The economic value of unpaid work can be calculated by using the market price of the substitutes available on the market: ready-made meals, nurses, or tutors. Of course, this is only a symbolic exercise because the work remains unpaid. Using these calculations, economists have estimated the economic value of unpaid work to be between 40 per cent and 75 per cent of the value of all market production in an economy. So, the gross domestic product (GDP) of countries is actually much higher than national statistics indicate. This is particularly the case for developing countries that still rely heavily on agricultural labour in which much unpaid family labour is involved. In order to obtain a more realistic picture of the value of total production in a country, the UN statistical division has agreed that countries should estimate the amount of labour involved in unpaid family production on farms and multiply this by the average farm wage, and add this to GDP. However, if we add the imputed market value of all non-market production to GDP, countries simply have much higher GDP levels than before but without necessarily changing anything about the gender division of labour, the long-term inefficiency of specialisation, and the low productivity of unpaid work.

Rather than adding the imputed value of unpaid work to GDP, women's economic position would be served much better by taking some domestic work away from them and bringing their total hours of work down to the level of men's hours. For example, fetching drinking water or collecting firewood for cooking takes several hours every day in sub-Sahara Africa and rural Asia. If the government provided piped drinking water and helped people to make low cost solar cookers, this would free up time for women to earn their own income and for girls to go to school.

A special type of work, paid and unpaid, is *caring*: work done by a care giver for a care receiver, addressing the care receiver's needs. Care requires a relationship between care giver and care receiver. Many domestic tasks are not caring tasks: cleaning, shopping, laundry. Other domestic work is caring work: childcare, care for the frail elderly, and home care of a sick or handicapped family member. *Caring* involves a relationship between the care giver and care receiver and the value of caring goes beyond the imputed market value for a service provided and beyond actual wages for paid caring labour. Many unpaid caring work can also be done by a paid worker, and is indeed the case in nursing, childcare, elderly care, and is also part of many other jobs, such as teaching, coaching, and music therapy for example. What matters is the positive attention to the care receiver in a personal relationship, with a feedback loop to the care giver, developing and sustaining a personal relationship.

Moreover, caring provides an important contribution to social cohesion when it is done between (relative) strangers, because it enables and strengthens relationships between people, in which trust, cooperation, and collective action can develop. Table 2.3 shows the distribution of unpaid work and caring between men and women in a Russian village.

Table 2.3 Unpaid work and caring in Russia: hours per day (in Taganrog, 1997/1998)

	Women	Men
Gardening	0.38	0.55
Housework	4.53	1.14
Childcare	1.49	0.66
Total	6.40	2.35

Source: Löfmark, M.H. (2007) 'Gender and Time Allocation Differences in Taganrog, Russia', *International Journal of Time Use Research* 4(1), pp. 69–92, Table 1.

In conclusion, we can summarise the economic value of caring in three dimensions of what care does for the economy. Care:

- provides attentive, personalised services through personal relationships
- sustains personal relationships (which often contribute to people's life satisfaction)
- generates social cohesion (involving trust, networks, and collective action).

2.4 Household production and bargaining

Households are on both the supply side and the demand side of markets. They supply labour to the labour market, entrepreneurship to the production in firms, and savings to the financial markets. On the demand side, households demand consumer goods and services. Next to supply and demand on markets, households have an economic relationship with the state. They pay taxes and fees and they receive public goods and subsidies. Finally, households are small communities, which are part of larger communities in civil society, in which people provide for themselves and each other through gifts of unpaid work and caring, but also using coercion and cooperation.

This section will explain household bargaining as the major economic explanation of production, consumption, and the division of labour in households. This will be done through an extended example of a Russian couple forming a household and later having a baby. The next two sections elaborate the example from two theoretical perspectives: (1) social and institutional economics, and (2) neoclassical economics.

2.4.1 Household bargaining: concepts

Household bargaining concerns the continuous interactions between partners in a household in order to realise their individual and joint objectives of a sustainable livelihood for themselves and their dependents. This may involve more than two parties, adults as well as children, and same-sex households as well as heterosexual household settings. For reasons of simplicity, I will assume two adults in a heterosexual household setting.

To understand household bargaining we need to distinguish between what is bargained over, the sources of bargaining power, and the threat positions of both partners, where the household breaks up if the threat is enforced. So, what do members of a household bargain over? They bargain over the decision-making power over household income and household consumption, over mobility and the space for taking up opportunities, and over children's education and well-being. In some cases, often only implicitly, they bargain over the division of unpaid labour in the household.

The sources of bargaining power are located both inside and outside the household. They are resources, skills, and opportunities and include current income, assets such as land or a house, education, human capabilities, and the social networks in the community that one can draw upon (social capital), as well as support provided by the state (welfare benefits, social protection). Moreover, not only do absolute amounts of resources count, but also differences between the partners matter. For example, differences in age or education. Also, household members can bargain over the meaning of all these factors. For example, if men underestimate women's unpaid work and show disrespect for these tasks, women will not derive much bargaining power from their unpaid household contributions.

The exit option determines the threat point or fall-back position in the bargaining process. A *threat point* is the exit situation for a partner from a bargaining situation. It consists of the resources that one has individual command over when leaving the household. The resources that make up the exit option, and provide a credible threat in bargaining, are the same as those determining bargaining power, with the condition that they are individually owned and controlled and recognised as such by both partners in the household. So, a house that has been paid for partly by A's savings but is registered in the name of B as head of the household has provided bargaining power to A in the past because it enabled B to acquire the house. But once A's money is in the house and it is registered in B's name only, partner A will not be able to use the house as a threat point anymore: it is not an exit option for A but – legally – only for B. Only when the personal relationships are friendly and built on respect, can B be expected to share the value of the house with A when the household breaks up.

Income, wealth, social resources, and state support are not the only determinants of bargaining power. Another source of household bargaining power is *asymmetric institutions*. They favour one partner over the other in the household because of membership of a socially advantaged group. Asymmetric institutions are located outside the household, at the social level. And they function as a 'windfall gain' for the advantaged partner, who does not need to undertake any effort in acquiring this bargaining power. Asymmetric institutions therefore are an external source of bargaining power. Examples of asymmetric institutions are the social prohibition for lower caste people in India to take better jobs and gender norms which expect women to do all the unpaid housework. Table 2.4 shows the sources of household bargaining power, at three levels: individual, household, and institutions.

Research has shown that the bargaining power of asymmetric institutions can over-rule the bargaining power derived from resources. For example, when in the USA and Canada in the 1970s and 1980s divorce laws were changed to enable both women and men to initiate a no-fault divorce, women's bargaining power increased, even though women's incomes remained the same. While in Ethiopia, women who marry higher educated men, but who earn more income than their husbands, have less decision-making power when they live in ethnic groups in which gender norms are very asymmetric, as compared to women with less education or lower incomes than their husbands. So, when gender norms are very asymmetric, having more resources does not necessarily increase women's decision-making power. Instead, women are 'punished' for being more resourceful than their husbands, because they thereby challenge the social norm that their husband is the head of the household. These findings highlight how important it is to pay attention not only to income and other individual resources controlled by the individuals in a household. Institutions and the power asymmetries expressed by these may be equally important or even more influential when analysing well-being differences within households.

48 *Individuals and households*

Bargaining power is difficult to measure, but its outcomes can be measured more easily. There are two sets of outcomes: direct and indirect bargaining outcomes. The *direct bargaining outcomes* are the decision-making experiences of the partners in the household. These experiences can be measured by asking one or both partners to what extent they can decide alone, jointly, or not at all on major household decisions. For example, their time use in paid and unpaid work, or decisions on spending their own and joint income. The *indirect bargaining outcomes* concern the well-being of the household partners. This can be measured, for example, as health (for example through body mass index in the least developed countries), self-esteem (by asking partners about this), or the extent of domestic violence (either by asking partners or by counting police reports or hospital emergency aid reports on domestic violence in a community).

2.4.2 Household bargaining example: two scenarios of gender norms

Let us assume a young Russian couple, Vladimir and Olga, who live separately. Olga has a fixed contract with the local bus company as a bus driver. It is a low paid but steady job, earning her 200 roubles per hour. Vladimir works as a carpenter for a private construction company without a fixed contract. His hourly wages are 300 roubles. But the construction company does not always have work for him, so some weeks of the year he is unemployed. Hence, Vladimir earns more per hour than Olga but his annual income is less secure.

Vladimir produces his own furniture, for himself and to give to his friends, Olga, and their parents. Olga enjoys cooking and tries out wonderful dishes, even with the little money she can spend on ingredients. She often invites Vladimir for dinner. But Olga is not very good at carpentry, it takes her twice as long as Vladimir, and the results do not look so well. In turn, Vladimir never learned to cook, because his mother always did that for him. So, he takes a lot of time to produce a reasonable meal. In addition, both have to keep their houses clean and they both dislike this task and are equally efficient at it.

Diagrams 2.1a and 2.1b show the *household production possibility frontiers* for Vladimir and Olga for an average weekday. *Household production possibility frontier* is a curve which shows different combinations of goods that can be produced using the same work time. The possibility frontiers in Diagrams 2.1a and 2.1b indicate how much Vladimir and Olga could produce maximally on an average weekday if they did not form a household together but live separately, and still enjoy leisure time. To simplify matters, we will only look at weekdays and ignore weekends. The vertical axes in the diagrams show the income they each can earn and spend on market goods per day. Vladimir earns 300 roubles per hour × 8 hours = 2,400 roubles

Table 2.4 Household bargaining power sources

Individual level	Household level	Institutional level
Income	Difference in age	Unequal laws and regulations
Assets	Difference in education	Unequal social norms
Education	Difference in attitudes toward domestic violence	
Community support		
State support		

in a day. Olga earns 200 roubles per hour × 8 hours = 1,600 roubles in a day. The horizontal axes show their production of home goods: furniture, meals, and cleaning. But the home goods are produced without pay, so we have no money value for these goods. The home goods are not meant to be sold and there are no perfect market substitutes available. We therefore use a standard social economic value for the home goods, namely the time use involved. Vladimir spends 1 hour a day on carpentry and 2 hours a day on cooking. Olga spends 1 hour a day on cooking and 2 hours a day on carpentry. Each spends additionally 1 hour per day on cleaning.

Diagrams 2.1a and 2.1b show that Vladimir produces 2,400 roubles per day in market goods and Olga produces 1,600 roubles per day in market goods. Both spend 4 hours on home good production. In a day of 24 hours, first 8 hours for sleep and 2 hours for personal care have to be subtracted. This leaves 14 hours for paid work, unpaid work, and leisure time. From this we subtract 8 hours for paid work and 4 hours for unpaid work, which totals 12 hours of work. This leaves 14 hours – 12 hours of work = 2 hours of leisure time for each.

So, the only difference between Vladimir and Olga is 800 roubles of market goods production. But this ignores other possible differences. Perhaps Olga does not enjoy carpentry and prefers to have more income so that she can buy furniture instead. Or Vladimir hates carpentry but does it because his father expects him to do it as a family tradition. Moreover, Vladimir may have a less materialistic lifestyle than Olga and is able to save some income, whereas Olga may be rather unhappy with her income and the purchasing power she derives from it. So, household production and the efficiency of this is quite different from how people enjoy the products generated and how they perceive the meaning of their activities. Such more realistic social economic values of household production can only be analysed with extensive qualitative methods, using interviews, group discussions, or participatory observation rather than quantification of production in money and time.

Going back to our example, let us assume that Vladimir and Olga decide to live together in a bigger house. They have a baby after a year and call him Boris. Diagrams 2.2a and 2.2b show the joint household production and resulting leisure time for Vladimir and Olga together, after the birth of Boris, in two different scenarios. Diagram 2.2a shows the scenario of a gender stereotype social norm, according to which the mother works part-time and the father works full time, and all housework is done by the woman, and the furniture production, including the making of the baby's crib, is done by the man. Diagram 2.2b shows the scenario of a gender

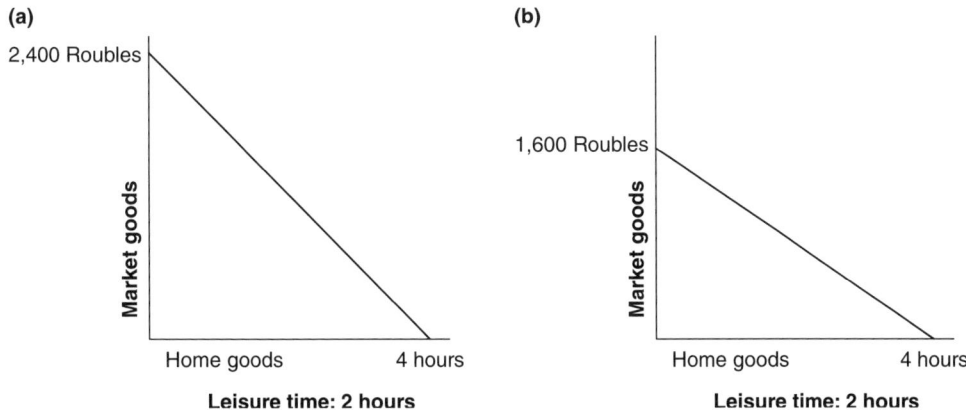

Diagram 2.1a Vladimir: production alone   *Diagram 2.1b* Olga: production alone

equal norm, referring to an equal distribution of total work and leisure time. This scenario also includes financial independence for both partners, determining a feasible threat point for both of them. Table 2.5 shows the dominant social norms about gender equality in Russia.

Diagram 2.2a shows the gender stereotype scenario. Vladimir works full time and earns 2,400 roubles per day, as in the single situation. Olga works part-time (50 per cent) and earns 800 roubles per day. This leads to a total value of market goods of 3,200 roubles for the household. For the home good production, the couple follows specialisation on the basis of dominant gender norms. In Russia, furniture production is regarded as a typical man's task, whereas cooking, cleaning, and childcare is generally regarded as a typical woman's task. This gender division of labour leads to efficiency gains simply because the social norms do not allow the other sex to acquire the skills to do the tasks of furniture production, household tasks, and childcare. Vladimir now only spends his unpaid time on furniture production, for two people (1 hour as before, due to economies of scale) and Olga spends 1 hour of unpaid time on cooking for both (also using economies of scale) plus 1 hour on cleaning and 5 hours on childcare. So, the total unpaid work time is 1 hour for Vladimir and 7 hours for Olga, which gives a total of 8 hours per day.

Table 2.5 World Values Study data for Russia on gender norms

In case of job scarcity, men should have more right to a job than women			
	1990	1995	2006
Agree	38%	47%	35%
Disagree	52%	38%	43%
Neither	5%	12%	19%
Don't know	5%	3%	3%

A woman has to have children to be fulfilled			
	1990	1995	2006
Not necessary	8%	16%	NA
Needs children	89%	78%	NA
Don't know	4%	6%	NA

Men make better political leaders than women do			
	1990	1995	2006
Agree	N.A.	54%	58%
Disagree	N.A.	36%	36%
Don't know	N.A.	10%	6%

Husband and wife should both contribute to income			
	1990	1995	2006
Agree	76%	85%	NA
Disagree	19%	12%	NA
Don't know	5%	3%	NA

Source: World Values Surveys, 2014. Compilation: Zahra Zarepour.

Individuals and households 51

Before, in the single situation and without a baby, unpaid work took up 4 plus 4 = 8 hours in total. In other words, there is an efficiency gain in a gender stereotype division of labour (even though they now have a baby). In the single situation, together they enjoyed 4 hours of leisure time. Living together, they enjoy a total of 8 hours of leisure time together. But this time is distributed unequally: 5 hours of leisure for Vladimir and 3 hours of leisure for Olga.

Diagram 2.2b shows the scenario with equal gender norms, with equal sharing of paid and unpaid work, resulting in equal leisure time. This is a very different gender norm based on

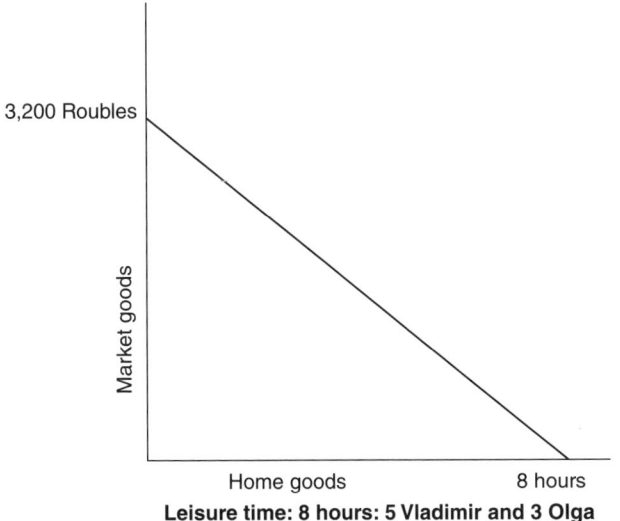

Diagram 2.2a Joint household with gender stereotype norms

Diagram 2.2b Joint household with gender equal norms

52 *Individuals and households*

mutual respect for each others' capabilities and fairness in burden sharing. The equal gender norm results in a different outcome for the household as compared to the gender stereotype scenario. Olga keeps her full-time job, so that total market good production is 4,000 roubles per day. Boris goes to a subsidised childcare institution, which is nearby. Vladimir continues furniture production alone and Olga continues cooking alone, because they both like it that way: a cooperative outcome. But they divide up the cleaning work and childcare. They do so according to the tasks they each are relatively good at. But because Olga has learned these tasks as a girl, living in a society in which the dominant gender norm requires girls and women to do cleaning work and help with childcare for their siblings, Vladimir spends more time on home good production. Hence, Olga takes on a few more tasks than Vladimir, so that they each spend an equal number of hours on cleaning and childcare. Total home good production takes 6 hours in this scenario: 1 hour furniture production by Vladimir, 1 hour cooking by Olga, and 2 hours cleaning and childcare for each of them. Vladimir and Olga together have 6 hours of leisure time, 3 hours each. But this is less than in the stereotype scenario, where total leisure time was 8 hours.

The lessons from Diagrams 2.1a, 2.1b, 2.2a, and 2.2b are threefold. First, joint household production leads to short-term efficiency gains: less time is spent on home good production and there is more leisure time in the household. Second, specialisation on the basis of stereotype gender norms may result in an unequal work burden between partners, with unequal outcomes for leisure time. Third, if production time is shared equally, leisure time is equal for both partners, but there may be some loss in efficiency, resulting in a decrease in total leisure time for the household as compared to the gender stereotype scenario. But household income is higher and both partners have a credible threat point (sufficient independent income). Table 2.6 summarises the leisure time outcomes for the different scenarios.

2.5 Social and institutional economics of household production

2.5.1 *Embeddedness of economic agents*

As explained in Chapter 1, social economics understands economic agents as embedded in society. This embeddedness both enables and constrains their agency. Socially embeddedness is enabling through:

- the *collective agency* of individuals as members of groups: this strengthens decision-making power, for example through farmer cooperatives and labour unions;
- the strength of *pro-social norms*, which are norms that facilitate interaction and have aggregate economic benefits, such as trust, fairness, and cooperation: this increases the frequency and distance of economic interactions;

Table 2.6 Hours of leisure time in three household scenarios

Single households			Stereotype gender norm			Equal gender norm		
Vladimir	Olga	Total	Vladimir	Olga	Total	Vladimir	Olga	Total
2	2	4	5	3	8	3	3	6

The constraints from social embeddedness, which social economists recognise, are:

- limited information about present and future prices, goods, needs, and conditions (*imperfect information*);
- limitations to the human capacity to process information, rank options, and select the best option (*bounded rationality*);
- limited power to control risks and uncertainties (vulnerability);
- institutions that limit options, gains, or self-awareness (laws, regulations, habits, routines, and social norms).

2.5.2 Fairness matters: ultimatum game results

Behavioural economic experiments in classrooms have demonstrated that rationality includes values and social norms, which influence decisions and outcomes. The ultimatum game is a good example. The *ultimatum game* is an experimental game in which two players interact to decide how to divide a sum of money that is given to them. The game is played with two players. The lecturer gives €10 to one of them, called the proposer. The proposer is free to distribute the amount between himself and the other, whom we call the receiver. They can both keep the money if the receiver accepts the proposed distribution. If, however, the receiver disagrees, all €10 have to be given back to the lecturer. The ultimatum game has been played hundreds of times, all over the world, including in isolated tribes in Africa, Asia, and South America (see Table 2.7). The average results are that the majority of the proposers offer around a 50/50 distribution (between 40 per cent and 60 per cent of the total amount). All receivers accept this distribution. But for those cases with a very unequal distribution offered, such as €9 to €1 or €8 to €2, the majority of receivers reject the distribution, even if the total amount to be distributed is not just a few euros but worth a months' salary. This is an interesting result from the perspective of rationality. The fact that a proposer offers an equal distribution is not necessarily altruistic: he may do this out of a fear that a low offer will be rejected and he will end up with nothing. So, an equal offer is perfectly rational to ensure that the deal is accepted and both get a positive some of money.

But the fact that receivers reject unequal offers is clearly not self-interested: if you are offered €2 and the alternative is nothing (rejecting a positive offer so that all €10 have to be returned to the lecturer), then €2 is better then none, isn't it? Nope. Most receivers punish the proposer for the unfair split, even at their own cost. This concern of real-world economic agents with fairness is a universal result of the ultimatum game. So here, rationality is concerned with reinforcing an important social norm and keeping others to it – a long-term perspective rather than a view limited to the current transaction. And this result is obtained in what is called one-shot games: where there is no further playing of the game anymore, hence, no gains to be reaped from 'teaching the other a lesson'. . . .

The ultimatum game teaches us two lessons. First, the majority of people act in a social way, conscious of being part of a group in which interests need to be balanced. Second, the majority of people are prepared to punish, even at their own cost, those who offer unfair deals. They enforce a group norm, namely, that given resources should be shared more or less equally in a group. This punishing behaviour, already mentioned in Chapter 1, is called *strong reciprocity*. This occurs when agents contribute resources to a joint activity when others do so as well even when there are no benefits to themselves or their kin, or future gains to be

54 *Individuals and households*

Table 2.7 Worldwide results of the ultimatum game

Country	Group	Mean offer (as a proportion %)	Rejection rate (%)
Peru	Machiguenga	26	4.8
Tanzania	Hadza (in big camps)	40	19.0
Tanzania	Hadza (in small camps)	27	28.0
Bolivia	Tsimane	37	0.0
Ecuador	Quichua	27	15.0
Ecuador	Achuar	42	0.0
Mongolia	Khazax	36	5.0
Chile	Mapuche	34	6.7
Zimbabwe	Unresettled villagers	41	10.0
Zimbabwe	Resettled villagers	45	7.0
Kenya	Orma	44	4.0
Paraguay	Ache	51	0.0

Source: Henrich, J., R. Boyd, S. Bowles, C. Camerer, E. Fehr, H. Gintis and R. McElreach (2001) 'In Search of Homo Economics: Behavioural Experiments in 15 Small-Scale Societies', *Economics and Social Behaviour*, 91(2), p. 74.

expected, or reputation gains: they are prepared to punish free riders, at their own cost. Strong reciprocity is clearly not self-interested, but also not altruistic: punishing at own cost benefits not a particular person in need, as is required for altruism, but it punishes free riders in a group. So, rationality understood as strong reciprocity is rationality understood as consistent behaviour in terms of goals, values, and social norms.

2.5.3 Satisficing

Institutional economics emphasises the fourth constraining factor mentioned under the social economic perspective: institutions that limit options, gains, or self-awareness (laws, regulations, habits, routines, and social norms). But for institutional economists, institutions are not only constraints but can also enable agency. For example, competition policy includes regulations limiting the market share of firms, while at the same time, such anti-trust law enables small new firms to enter the market. Similarly, a social norm, which ascribes unpaid housework to women and not to men, implies a time constraint for women's labour force participation but a windfall gain for men's labour force participation.

In institutional economics, rationality is not tied to maximisation but to satisfaction, to agreeing with 'good enough'. If we want a particular consumer good or insurance cover today, we should ideally compare all existing alternatives with their prices and characteristics, guarantee and service offerings, and estimated longevity. This is impossible. That is why we often are not *maximisers* of our goals but are simply *satisficing*: we compare just a few alternatives, and more often rely on the views and experiences of people around us. Perhaps we will only surf the internet for 20 minutes, or ask a friends and one family member what they have chosen when they were confronted with a similar consumer choice, and whether they are happy with their choice. We tend to act as satisficers because there is too much information freely available and our brains simply are not capable of processing that amount of information, and most of us don't like to spend much time on making choices.

Box 2.2 Asymmetric information creating irrationality

A real-life example of an individual market transaction shows that economic agents can act completely irrationally when there is asymmetric information about the quality of a good. A Dutch mother, Anja, had a sweet pony, called Sissy. Anja's children were growing up and she wanted the little horse to have new owners who would care for her and allow their small children to ride it. But it was a difficult time and there was an oversupply of horses in the Dutch province of Overijssel, where Anja lives. So, she offered Sissy for free on Facebook, through a notice at the local horse-riding club, and through mouth-to-mouth advertising, in July 2012. In April 2013 she had received not a single reaction, even though people could easily verify that the pony was sweet, adorable, and obedient.

Anja even received well-meant advise to bring Sissy to the butcher and earn at least €50 for the meat. But Anja wanted a good home for Sissy. She then decided to put the pony up for sale on a website specialising in the second-hand horse market. She offered it as a 'fairy tale pony' and now asked money: €250. To her surprise she received four replies within a week. She selected a potential buyer who immediately fell in love with Sissy, just like his twin daughters. They bought Sissy, paying the price without negotiation.

Source: Author's personal communication.

Image 2.3 Fairy-tale pony

56 *Individuals and households*

When the Dutch government privatised health insurance in 2006, health insurance providers who stepped into the newly created market offered an overwhelming variation of health insurance packages. But most people simply stayed with the same insurance company as before and often kept the same package as before. Were they irrational? The Dutch consumer association analysed the choice situation and discovered that an average Dutch consumer could choose between 10,000 different health package options. No wonder that people behaved like satisficers rather than maximisers – that was precisely the rational thing to do: if you were satisfied with your insurer and health care package, why change it for a few euros of possible gain, and why go for option X or Y or Z if you do not know the actual differences in health care experience? That is simply too much trouble for most people. Satisficing *is* rational, given the limitations of people's time, calculation capabilities, and values in life.

2.5.4 Back to the household bargaining example

A combined social and institutional economic perspective looks at the short-term and the long-term bargaining outcomes and context. This perspective takes into account the conflict dimension of the cooperative conflict inherent in household bargaining. It takes into account the fact that Olga has a steady job and Vladimir's job is insecure. And it includes the actual divorce rates in Russia, which are among the highest in the world. The statistics indicate that there is a 40–50 per cent probability that a young childless Russian couple with a median income will split up some time in the future.[1]

From this perspective, household bargaining is best modelled through a bargaining game with different pay-offs for each partner. In order to arrive at the numbers in the pay-off matrix, we first need to evaluate all the well-being effects of each scenario. Of course, this is a subjective evaluation. But potential effects and their values may be discussed in groups, such as a classroom, or social groups representative of each partner through social media, in order to seek convergence in evaluations. Groups can be divided according to sex (men's and women's groups: Do you see different well-being dimensions? Do you evaluate these differently for Olga and Vladimir?) or according to cultural background (regional origin, for example: Do some evaluate certain gender norms differently?). Table 2.8 is an example of a list of relevant well-being dimensions for both partners in the household bargaining process.

The two Tables 2.9 and 2.10 show examples of evaluations for the various well-being dimensions listed in Table 2.8 for Vladimir and Olga. They use a 4-point scale, with 0 indicating no

Table 2.8 Suggested list of well-being dimensions for household bargaining partners

Indicators:

- Big house
- Independent income
- Income security
- Live with child
- Tension with partner about norms
- Conflict with others about norms
- Leisure time
- Fairness in housework
- Average pay-off

Table 2.9 Evaluation of well-being outcomes: gender stereotype norm scenario

Indicator	Short term		Long term	
	Vladimir	Olga	Vladimir	Olga
Big house	3	3	2	0
Independent income	3	0	3	0
Income security	2	2	2	0
Live with child	3	3	0	3
Tension with partner about norms				
Conflict with others about norms				
Leisure time	3	1		
Fairness in housework	3	0		
Average pay-off	3	1	2	1

Table 2.10 Evaluation of well-being outcomes: gender equal norm scenario

Indicator	Short term		Long term	
	Vladimir	Olga	Vladimir	Olga
Big house	3	3	2	2
Independent income	3	3	3	3
Income security	3	3	2	3
Live with child	3	3	3	3
Tension with partner about norms	2	1		
Conflict with others about norms	1	0		
Leisure time	1	3		
Fairness in housework	1	3		
Average pay-off	2	2	3	3

value and 3 indicating the highest possible value. Think of the scale in qualitative terms, in which 0 refers to 'no advantage' or 'dissatisfied', and 3 is associated with 'very good' or 'very satisfied'. The first mentioned pay-off number (x) is for Vladimir, the second one (y) is for Olga. So, (3, 1) means that in that particular case, Vladimir gets 3 and Olga 1, hence, Vladimir is better off than Olga. Table 2.9 shows an evaluation of a number of relevant well-being indicators, on a 4-point scale, for each partner under the gender stereotype norm scenario.

Table 2.10 shows an evaluation of a number of relevant well-being indicators, on a 4-point scale, for each partner under the gender equal norm scenario.

The combined evaluation outcomes of Tables 2.9 and 2.10 are given in Table 2.11, a pay-off matrix. This shows the indirect bargaining outcomes: well-being outcomes in the short run and the long run. A *pay-off matrix* lists the payoffs for both partners under different scenarios. The totals of Table 2.9 appear in the first row of Table 2.11: (3, 1) in the short run and (2, 1) in the long run, with a total pay-off of 7. The totals of Table 2.10 appear in the second row of Table 2.11: (2, 2) in the short run and (3, 3) in the long run, with a total pay-off of 10.

58 *Individuals and households*

Table 2.11 Pay-off matrix for well-being outcomes of household bargaining*

	Short run	Long run	Total pay-off
Stereotype gender norm	3, 1	2, 1	7
Equal gender norm	2, 2	3, 3	10

*The pay-offs in each cell (x, y) have no units but simply refer to difference or sameness of bargaining outcomes. The first number (x) is for Vladimir, the second number (y) is for Olga

The pay-off matrix shown in Table 2.11 indicates that in the stereotype scenario, the household bargaining outcome will be 4 (3 + 1) in the short run and 3 (2 + 1) in the long run, which totals 7. For the equal scenario, the household outcome will also be 4 (2 + 2) in the short run, but 6 (3 + 3) in the long run. This totals 10 for the short and long run together. The total of short-term and long-term bargaining outcome in the equal scenario, hence, is higher than in the stereotype scenario, namely 10 instead of 7. This implies that for the household as a whole, following the gender equal norms for the production of market goods and home goods results in higher household well-being. This well-being combines short-term and long-term outcomes in market goods, home goods, stability of market goods, and threat points for financial independence in case of divorce.

So, the cooperative bargaining outcome, for the household as a whole, is the gender equal scenario. This is also the preferred scenario for Olga: both in the short run and in the long run, her pay-offs are higher than in the gender stereotype scenario. In the short run, the equal scenario gives her a pay-off of 2, versus 1 in the stereotype scenario. In the long run, the equal scenario gives her a pay-off of 3, versus 1 in the stereotype scenario.

But there is also conflict. Vladimir's pay-off is higher in the stereotype scenario than in the equal scenario in the short run. This is compensated for by a higher pay-off in the equal scenario in the long run. For him the total short-term and long-term pay-offs are the same for each scenario: in both cases the total pay-offs are 5 for Vladimir. However, in a context in which the stereotype gender norm dominates, it is more likely that Vladimir prefers the stereotype scenario. Because this does not require him to challenge the dominant norm and be confronted with resistance and perhaps ridicule or stigma when he deviates from the dominant gender norm. So, Vladimir is likely to prefer the stereotype scenario, whereas Olga will prefer the equal scenario.

How could Olga enforce the equal scenario (which, remember, is also the one with the highest household-level well-being)? Here is where bargaining comes in. For Vladimir, it means giving up 2 hours of leisure time. Olga may use her income as bargaining power, because Vladimir partly depends on Olga's earnings. But, of course, Olga equally depends on his income so this will not give her more bargaining power than Vladimir. Moreover, Olga's earnings are less than those of Vladimir, so she has more to lose from a separation than Vladimir: Vladimir has a stronger threat point.

Olga could also bring in the fact that the government provides subsidy for childcare in their neighbourhood, which makes childcare services affordable. Alternatively, Olga may use her social resources, bringing in the arguments used by some of her friends who also challenge traditional gender norms. Or perhaps point at a well-known Russian male role model for gender equality and caring fatherhood, to convince Vladimir that it is not against manhood to do housework and childcare. Moreover, she may remind Vladimir that childcare strengthens the

Individuals and households 59

bond with his son, and is a source of joy. If this all does not help, she may want to use her threat point of living on her own again. But this is not a credible threat anymore once she has given up her full-time job and has already moved to the gender stereotype scenario. A part-time job does not give sufficient income to live on her own. Vladimir knows this, but he also knows that he would no longer be able to afford the bigger house, and that he would have to pay childcare costs to Olga if she left. If he is rational, he would choose to spend 3 hours of unpaid work while keeping on living with Olga in the bigger house and enjoying her good cooking and being with his son. Finally, Olga may point out the long-term benefit for Vladimir of the equal scenario. Here, his insecure income will be supplemented with Olga's full-time secure income, instead of only a part-time secure income as in the stereotype scenario.

But perhaps Vladimir's bargaining position is not so rational at all, and merely rests on an emotional attachment to the internalised gender stereotype norm. . . .

But what if Olga's friends all follow the stereotype norm? And if Olga has internalised this norm so that she does not even think about challenging it? Or if Olga would like to challenge it but does not have the courage to bring this up? Or if she tried and experienced disapproval from her family and family-in-law. Hence, household bargaining will not always result in the optimal household production and distribution. The bargaining outcome depends on many factors, which are often inter-related and play out at the individual level, the interaction in the household and the social context with its gendered institutions.

The next section presents the same case from a different theoretical perspective, without the complex social context and with perfect substitution between market and home production.

2.6 Neoclassical economics of household production

2.6.1 The household bargaining example in neoclassical economics

The neoclassical perspective does not distinguish between short run and long run and focuses on maximising current production with the least time use – hence, it evaluates the household production in terms of efficiency in time use.

In the neoclassical theory of household production, home goods are valued in money terms. Moreover, the theory assumes that market goods and home goods can be substituted: there is always more paid work available, to produce market goods (no unemployment in the labour market). The imputed value of home goods is calculated through the opportunity costs of paid work – market good production. This method leads to different values for the production of home goods for Vladimir and Olga. This is because Olga needs to give up 200 roubles (=1 hour of market goods for her), whereas Vladimir needs to give up 300 roubles (=1 hour of market goods for him) for 1 hour of home good production. So, the *opportunity cost* – the value of the alternative forgone – of doing unpaid work is higher for Vladimir as compared to Olga.

This leads to an outcome, when Vladimir and Olga live together and have a baby, which maximises household production in money terms. Diagram 2.3 shows the possibility frontier in money terms with the maximum outcome: 5,200 roubles. Since Vladimir has a higher value of market goods, he specialises in the production of market goods, by doing 2 hours per day overtime. The 10 hours in the labour market earn him 3,000 roubles per day. However, he has a probability of 10 per cent of being out of work on any given day. This risk reduces his average earnings by 10 per cent, which is 300 roubles. This makes his average daily earnings

60 *Individuals and households*

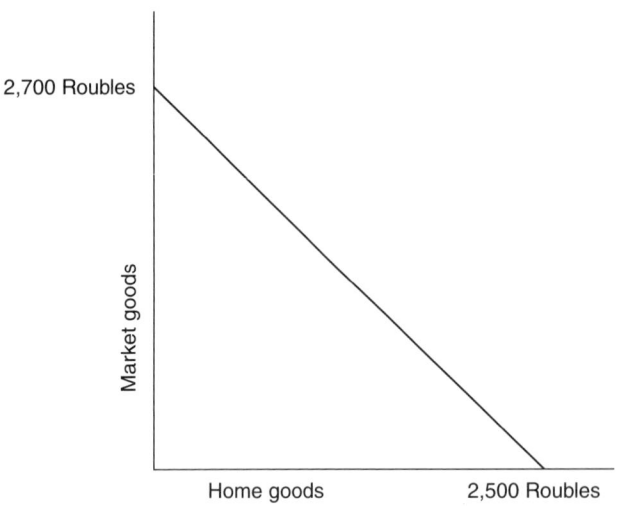

Diagram 2.3 Joint household production maximisation

3,000 − 300 = 2,700 roubles. His contribution to home goods is 1 hour of furniture production, valued at his opportunity costs of 300 roubles an hour. So, his total production in the household is 2,700 market goods plus 300 home goods = 3,000 roubles.

Olga now specialises in childcare (9 hours), cleaning (1 hour), and cooking (1 hour). The value of Olga's home production is 11 hours at 200 roubles per hour (her opportunity cost) = 2,200 roubles per day. The value of her market goods is zero, because she gave up her job when Boris was born. So, total household production is 3,000 by Vladimir and 2,200 by Olga, which totals 5,200 roubles. Although the specialisation on the basis of their opportunity costs leads to maximum household well-being – a cooperative outcome – Vladimir benefits more from this situation than Olga. First, Vladimir has a good threat point of 2,700 roubles per day of market goods, whereas Olga's threat point is 0 rouble. Second, the value of Olga's production is less than that of Vladimir: 2,200 versus 3,000 roubles. This gives Vladimir more bargaining power, derived from his higher money value contribution to the household. Third, the higher insecurity of Vladimir's income is compensated by overtime earnings, which earns money for days on which the construction firm does not operate. Overtime is always available in the neoclassical theory where the labour market always absorbs additional labour supplied. Fourth, Vladimir has an extra hour of leisure time (4 hours versus 3 hours for Olga).

Table 2.10 shows that the specialisation illustrated in Diagram 2.3 maximises household production. For these calculations we keep the leisure time of 7 hours for the household constant (the *ceteris paribus* assumption), with 4 hours of leisure time for Vladimir and 3 hours of leisure time for Olga. Table 2.12 shows three scenarios of market and home good production by the couple: a gender reverse distribution, a gender equal norm, and a gender stereotype norm.

In conclusion, the neoclassical theory of the household division of labour with opportunity costs of time shows that whatever the gender norms are, the partner earning the highest hourly wage rate should specialise in market goods and expand the number of hours of paid

Table 2.12 Possible combinations of household production in neoclassical economics

Scenarios	Vladimir			Olga			Total household
	Market goods	Home goods	Total Vladimir	Market goods	Home goods	Total Olga	
Gender reverse distribution	0	3,300	3,300	1,600	200	1,800	5,100
Gender equal norm	1,350	1,800	3,150	800	1,200	2,000	5,150
Gender stereotype norm	2,700	300	3,000	0	2,200	2,200	5,200

work. This maximises the money value of total household production. In our example this is 5,200 roubles, as compared to 50 roubles less in the equal scenario and 100 roubles less in the reversed specialisation scenario in which Vladimir specialises in home goods. Unless the productivity of a particular home good is much lower by the partner, so that the opportunity costs of the partner's time for that home good is higher. In our example, Vladimir is more efficient at producing furniture: he spends 1 hour while Olga spends 2 hours in furniture production. This takes 300 roubles of opportunity costs for Vladimir (1 hour × 300 roubles) against 400 roubles of opportunity costs for Olga (2 hours × 200 roubles). This is why it is more efficient if Vladimir produces the furniture and not Olga. The consequence of specialisation on the basis of opportunity costs is that the partner with the lowest hourly wage rate should specialise in the production of home goods and substitute paid work for unpaid work. And if that involves many hours of unpaid work (often the case because of its low capital intensity), that partner often has less leisure time.

In practice, in a world of gender stereotype norms, neoclassical theory justifies the persistence of unequal gender norms. Of course it is possible that Vladimir has a low paid job and Olga has a high paid job. In that case, the maximum household production would require Olga to specialise in market goods and Vladimir to specialise in home goods. But in the real world in which gender stereotypes about the gender division of labour are dominant (and not only in Russia), it is more likely that the household division of labour focusing entirely on (short-term) household production maximisation reinforces a traditional gender division of labour. Not simply because of gender unequal norms in the household, but also because of gender unequal norms outside the household, sustaining the disadvantaged labour market position of women with most women working in stereotype women's jobs, which earn low wages.

2.6.2 Comparing the two theories of household bargaining

When we compare the two household bargaining models, we see that the neoclassical model, focusing on cooperation, favours a gender stereotype division of labour. The social economics and institutional model, focusing on conflict, favours a gender equal norm for the division of labour. So, which bargaining outcome is obtained and perceived as optimal, depends on the theoretical perspective taken. What needs to be taken into account in this theory choice, is that the social economics/institutional household bargaining model takes more context into

62 *Individuals and households*

account, distinguishes between short-term and long-term outcomes, and recognises the less secure job of one of the partners. The neoclassical model focuses on a stable, short-term situation, assumes the absence of unemployment, and fully exploits the gender division of labour based on lower female wages in the labour market.

2.7 Interesting sources

Jacobsen, J. (2007) *The Economics of Gender*. Third Edition. Malden: Blackwell.
Santa Fe Institute research on human behaviour, institutions and social systems: http://www.santafe.edu/research/themes/human-behavior-institutions-and-social-systems/
Schwartz, B. (2004) *The Paradox of Choice. Why More is Less*. New York: HarperCollins.
Wood, W., and A. Eagly (2012) 'Biosocial construction of sex differences and similarities in behaviour', *Advances in Experimental Social Psychology*, 46, chapter 2.
World Values Surveys, containing data on social norms for various countries: http://www.worldvaluessurvey.org/wvs.jsp

2.8 Glossary

Agency   Making autonomous choices and acting upon these

Asymmetric institutions   Institutions that have different effects on different groups

Caring   Work done by a care giver for a care receiver, addressing the care receiver's needs

Ceteris paribus assumption   Keeping everything else constant

Collective agency   Agency of groups

Complementary production   When households produce goods and services which, together with goods and services obtained from the market or the state, provide for households needs

Direct bargaining outcomes   The decision-making experiences by the partners in the household

Division of labour in the household   Specialisation of household members in different skills, unpaid work, and paid jobs

Economic agent   An individual acting in relation to other persons, through exchange, redistribution, and sharing and gift giving

Economies of scale in household consumption   Cost advantages due to an increasing scale of consumption

Economies of scope   The experience that the enjoyment of consumption is higher when shared with those you care about

Gender   The socially and culturally constructed differences between men and women, with hierarchical meanings, often in favour of what is regarded as masculine

Gender stereotypes   The practice of labelling characteristics as either 'masculine' or 'feminine'

Household   A small unit in which people live together in cooperation and conflict

Household bargaining   The continuous interactions between partners in a household in order to realise their individual and joint objectives of a sustainable livelihood for themselves and their dependents

Household functions   Reproduction, joint production and consumption, and risk pooling

Household production possibility frontier   A curve, which shows different combinations of goods that can be produced using the same work time

Human capabilities for the future labour force   Formal schooling, social skills and norms, and collective behaviour

Indirect bargaining outcomes   The well-being of the household partners

Opportunity cost   The value of the alternative forgone

Pay-off matrix   Lists the payoffs for both partners under different scenarios

Pro-social norms   Norms that facilitate interaction and have aggregate economic benefits

Reproduction   Unpaid caring for the current and future generation of labour and for others inside and outside the economy

Risk pooling   Reducing individual risk in a group by sharing resources and carrying out a division of labour, which makes the group flexible in responses to changes in the economic context

Satisficing   Agents compare just a few alternatives to some extent, and more often rely on the views or experiences of people around them

Self-interest   An individual motivation purely directed at satisfying one's own interests

Strong reciprocity   When agents contribute resources to a joint activity when others do so as well even when there are no benefits to themselves or their kin, or future gains to be expected, or reputation gains: they are prepared to punish free riders, at their own cost

Third-person criterion   Everything you can hire a third person to do for you is work, while other activities are consumption or leisure

Threat point   Exit situation for a partner from a bargaining situation

Ultimatum game   An experimental game in which two players interact to decide how to divide a sum of money that is given to them

Utility maximisation   The maximisation of an individual, subjective utility function with a consistent ordering of all preferences

Note

1 This rate is calculated from a website with a divorce probability calculator. I calculated it for Olga, age 20, just married, no children, and a joint household income of around 800,000 roubles per year. See http://divorceprobability.com

3 Consumption

3.1 Consumer demand

3.1.1 Individual consumer demand

This chapter discusses consumer choices. Consumers express agency in consumer markets, under the agency constraints of incomplete information, limited capacity for processing information, risk, uncertainty, and institutions. There are three categories of goods that households demand: *final consumer goods*, for end use, *durable consumer goods*, for long-term use and to make domestic labour more efficient, and *intermediate consumer goods*, which are unfinished goods to which unpaid labour is added to produce final consumer goods. Households demand a variety of services, varying from entertainment (theatre, tourism) to financial services (health insurance, pension savings, and investment plans). The biggest consumer demand by households is for housing: this involves renting at a significant percentage of one's income. Or it involves buying a durable and non-movable good that is frequently worth several times a household's annual earnings, which often requires a loan (mortgage), generally varying between 25 per cent and 110 per cent of the house value, with a pay-back period of between 5 and 30 years.

Consumer demand in almost every economy in the world today requires purchasing power. In capitalist economies, which are in the majority in our world, purchasing power means money, either cash or in bank accounts. Without money, and hence, some source of income or wealth, one cannot exercise demand in a capitalist market. But not only income matters – prices matter too. Hence, what is relevant for a consumer is *real income*, which is the *purchasing power* of income, taking prices into account. The cost of a consumer good, however, is not simply the price paid for it and, hence, a subtraction of available purchasing power. The cost of a consumer good is also its *opportunity cost*: the value of the alternative forgone. When you buy jeans costing $75, you can't spend this money on shoes anymore. Credit reduces opportunity cost because it allows both goods to be bought with current income, with the bill shifted to the future.

Let us take for example the case of consumer demand without credit for a typical choice situation faced by youth in an urban lower-middle class setting in a capitalist economy. We analyse the choice between a pair of sneakers and healthy meals. The cost of a pair of sneakers may be $150 at first sight. But its real cost is that you now cannot purchase ten healthy meals worth $15 each for the rest of the month, risking vitamin deficiency and obesity. The budget constraint for a consumer (without credit) consists of income, wealth, and prices. Within this constraint, a consumer can buy any combination of goods he wants: this is called the opportunity set. Diagram 3.1 shows the opportunity set for a choice between two goods: sneakers and healthy meals. The shaded area is the opportunity set for the initial case: opportunity set 1. It allows for the purchase of one pair of sneakers or ten healthy meals, each totalling $150.

The top line shows a new budget constraint, after the price of a healthy meal has been reduced, due to a campaign by a new restaurant, by 33 per cent. A healthy meal is no longer $15 but $10. The new budget line implies that with $150 one can now buy 15 healthy meals instead of ten. The opportunity cost of a pair of sneakers has therefore increased from ten to 15 healthy meals. This is opportunity set 2. The dotted line shows a third new budget constraint, but in this case not due to a change in price but due to a change in income. Suppose now that income has increased by 50 per cent, from $150 to $225. This allows our consumer to buy one and a half pairs of sneakers (or look for a discount of the type 'second-pair-for-half-the-price') or to buy 15 healthy meals at the original price of $15 per meal. The new opportunity set, number 3, has expanded as compared to opportunity set 1 and set 2.

3.1.2 Consumption by the state and communities

Not all consumption is satisfied through market goods. Part of consumption is through the state and through the community economy. Government expenditure on goods and services for the population is referred to as government consumption. This formulation is a bit odd because obviously it is not the government consuming schools, public swimming pools, the judiciary system, and health clinics. But it is you and me consuming these goods and services, through the government. We distinguish two types of government consumption: social safety nets, for the deprived, and public goods for everyone. Public goods will be explained in Chapter 6 on the state and in more detail in a chapter of its own, Chapter 7. Here, I will

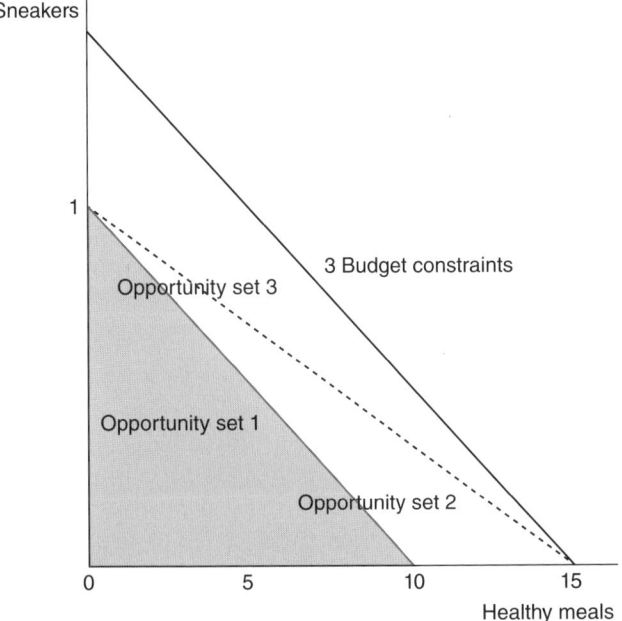

Diagram 3.1 Opportunity sets of consumption

explain the social safety net as a form of government consumption. A *social safety net* is a public service which provides social protection for the most disadvantaged in a society, to enable them to have a decent livelihood. There are two types of social safety nets: direct and indirect. Direct social safety nets concern the supply of consumer goods to address sudden needs, for example, disaster relief providing water, food, and tents, or food distribution during a famine. In developed economies, this type of safety net concerns some forms of public housing. Indirect social safety nets concern the redistribution of income to the poor, to enable them to buy necessary consumer goods. This is also referred to as income support, and ranges from conditional cash transfers to poor mothers if they send their children to school, to subsidies on public housing.

The third source of consumption, next to individuals/households and the state, are communities. They largely consume unpaid goods and services, produced in and by communities themselves. This consumption of unpaid goods and services may take place within households or between households. Think about informal childcare services, home care for the ill, or vegetable gardens. Some of the consumer goods in the community economy are intermediary goods, which are turned into final consumer goods with unpaid work in households, such as vegetables from a community garden which are turned into soup with unpaid labour.

3.2 Social economics of consumption

3.2.1 What we want

The agency of consumers is sometimes referred to as *consumer sovereignty*: in a perfect market, consumers determine what is produced, and hence, the economy produces exactly what people want. In the real world, however, consumer sovereignty is constrained in several ways. Social economics therefore rejects the idea of consumer sovereignty, and instead recognises various limitations. The most important constraints to consumer sovereignty are:

- advertising: whose preferences?
- social norms: what you should want
- market power: what the industry decides for you
- living standards: from needs to wants
- consumer credit: more than you want.

3.2.1.1 Advertising

Advertising does not just incidentally influence consumer choice, it was created to do just that. High-end market brands often spend around 50 per cent of total production costs on advertising. This is particularly the case for fashion, perfumes, and sports goods. Advertising has three functions, ranging from enabling consumer choice to constraining consumer choice. The first function is information. It is often through an advertisement that consumers are made aware of a particular product on the market. This helps them to list alternatives from which to choose. The second function of advertising is persuasion. Commercials try to persuade you to buy brand X rather than Y, or simply to buy more of X. Only when you are clearly aware of the tricks that are used in commercial persuasion, can this second function of advertising be helpful for making your choice in line with your wants, values, and budget. The third function of advertising goes beyond persuasion and concerns advocating a consumerist lifestyle.

Its messages promise happiness through consumption and status through materialism, and the advertisements offer luxury goods to satisfy these two wants.

Behavioural economics has provided interesting insights into this third function of advertising. It has discovered that consumers are sensitive to *framing*. This is the way that choices are being communicated to them. For example, urban youth visiting lounge bars across the world are more interested in vodka brands that present themselves as adventurous and stylish than brands than emphasise their quality and tradition, even if these latter brands have the same quality and taste and are cheaper. Economic agents also appear to dislike loss more than they prefer an equal amount of gain. This leads to the *status quo effect*: they would rather stay with their default option than shift to another one that claims to be cheaper but may have hidden costs or less coverage. This asymmetry in preferences for gain and loss also leads to the *endowment effect*. Economic agents tend to attach greater value to a good once they have obtained it. Commercial campaigns make use of this habit by offering products for free for a limited time period. By the end of the period, consumers who have tried it are willing to pay more for it than consumers who did not have the opportunity to try it out for free.

3.2.1.2 Social norms

Social norms are the way through which society sanctions certain consumer goods and lifestyles expressed by those goods. For example, among teenagers, being fashionable may be a strong social norm, urging kids to spend most of their money on brands that they see on TV, in magazines, and worn by their peers at school. Other social norms may warn against certain consumer goods. For example, African students' peer pressure against smoking, or religious norms supporting a vegetarian diet for Hindus. And we see subgroup styles, such as youth who deliberately go underdressed, rejecting industry-led fashion trends. Ironically, alternative brands respond to these alternative youth styles with, yet again, clothing, hairstyles, and music – but just different from the mainstream ones.

3.2.1.3 Market power

Some large firms have considerable market power on the supply side of the consumer market, when a small number or even a single firm dominates the market for a particular consumer product. This limits consumer choice, and it allows suppliers to circumvent strong competition and hence keep prices relatively high.

3.2.1.4 Living standards

Living standards have their own influence on consumer sovereignty, both at the low end and at the high end. They concern not only needs and wants, in a materialistic way, but also the meaning of these needs and wants. Living standards are culturally influenced and are therefore different between urban and rural areas and between countries. The Chinese government, for example, is implementing a large-scale migration project to move people from rural areas to cities because this will change their lifestyles. The Chinese government hopes that thereby, the domestic demand for modern consumer goods produced in China will increase and make the country less dependent upon exports. Only when the large domestic consumption potential is stimulated, will it result in increased demand for the consumer goods that Chinese manufacturing industry produces.

At the low end, living standards concern not so much wants but needs to survive. These involve a minimum consumption of calories per day (according to the World Health Organization (WHO) 2,000 calories for a woman and 2,500 calories for a man per day), plus clean drinking water, a minimum of clothing and housing, and access to health care. If an economic agent's income is not sufficient to cover these needs, this can lead to hunger, preventable diseases, and destitution. Hence, we talk about *absolute deprivation*, which is poverty below subsistence level. In such a situation, poor consumers can feel forced into desperate sales of their limited assets, such as land, jewellery, or their children's labour. Their consumption, at a very low level of living standards, does not contain much of a choice but satisfies current needs at the cost of future production capacity.

Less severe poverty, where consumers cannot afford to buy the goods that earn them full dignity in their communities, is referred to as *relative deprivation*. Adam Smith recognised this in his own Scottish urban environment of Glasgow in the 18th century. He noted that a labourer who could not afford leather shoes would not have the dignity that he deserved as a hard working citizen of those days in urban Scotland. So, absolute deprivation concerns inability to satisfy biological needs, while relative deprivation concerns inability to satisfy needs in relation to social standards of livelihoods.

At the high end, living standards are influenced more by lifestyle and therefore are more created by wants than by needs. Lifestyles come with particular consumer goods, from Tokyo teenage fashion to Los Angeles street gang outfits. With relatively limited budgets, such social-group induced wants may crowd out a healthy diet. For example, in downtown Manhattan neighbourhoods, some black kids from poor single parent households mirror the lifestyles of their sports heroes by saving their meagre earnings to buy the newest pair of sneakers, leaving only a few dollars a day for fast-food as the other lifestyle product they have come to want in their peer groups.

3.2.1.5 Consumer credit

Consumer credit breaks open the relationship between wants and values on the one hand and budget limitations on the other. Credit allows consumers to buy goods before they have earned enough income to afford them. But credit comes at a cost. In particular, credit cards carry high interest rates, which make buying on credit more expensive than consumers often realise. Consumption on credit may reach the point of insolvency and forced sales of home, car, and other durable consumer goods to pay off bank debt. But even if consumers had known the costs and risks involved beforehand, many of them would still not have resisted the temptations offered by advertisements, the nearby availability of consumer goods (also through online shops), and the sales tricks of credit line providers. Consumers tend to have a rather short time horizon and prefer satisfaction now over satisfaction later. At the same time, they have a very long time horizon for risk because they attach less importance to risks later than risks now. These are some lessons from behavioural economics for consumer theory. Section 3.6 will explain these insights.

3.2.2 Changing what we want

Consumer demand is, from the social economic perspective, strongly influenced by social norms. But social norms are not static. They vary over time and between groups in society. Two important social stratifications in consumption are class and the urban/rural distinction.

The consumption of white bread versus whole grain artisan bread is a good example of class norms regarding consumption. For example, in the UK, as well as in many other Western countries, the higher social classes ate white bread during most of the 20th century, because it was a sign of prosperity to eat bread that was refined and sweetened. The labour class ate wholegrain bread, heavy and nutritious, providing the energy for hard work. But in the 21st century we see a reversal of the social norms around bread consumption. Now, many British families recognise wholegrain bread as healthier than white bread. They have learned that it has less sugar and more fibre, and that it helps to prevent obesity and other welfare diseases and fits a sporty and healthy lifestyle. Moreover, they can afford to buy from organic stores and artisan bakeries, where this type of bread is sold, at prices double the price of plain white bread. Nowadays, it is the labour class in the UK which is the largest consumer of white bread. The earlier upper class norm is now dominant in the lower classes. Not because these consumers don't know about the health disadvantages of white bread, but because the social norm used to be a consumer ideal that remained unattainable for so long. And besides, the lower incomes of the labour class simply do not allow the daily consumption of artisan bread.

The other important social stratification of consumer behaviour is the urban/rural distinction. Cars in cities are more fancy but small, while in the countryside they are not always that fashionable but are certainly bigger. A similar difference is visible for food. Take Argentina, for example, the world's meat-eating champion. In the countryside, Argentinians eat large pieces of meat, preferably beef, twice a day. You may encounter some vegetables on your plate, when dining on the pampas, but only for decoration. In the cities, however, your plate will show a more balanced picture of brown, green, yellow, and red. There are even vegetarian restaurants in Buenos Aires and the ski resort of Bariloche.

Sometimes, we buy what we don't want because we cannot resist the temptation. Economic agents tend to have a rather short time horizon, which leads to the *immediacy effect*. They prefer a reward now over a bigger reward later. This means that they tend to suffer from *myopia* in their consumer choices. Even when they know their health will gain from drinking fewer sodas, they often cannot say 'no' to the big gulp containers of cola offered by the local fast-food outlet every day. Policy makers can help consumers stick to what they want with the help of *nudging*, which is the framing of choice situations towards a desirable default choice. For example, school canteens may change the order of food and place healthier food at the beginning and clearly within eyesight, and the less healthy food further away, as a contribution to fighting obesity among youth.

3.2.3 Strange goods and segmentation

Not all goods are normal goods. A *normal good* is a good for which demand increases when income increases. An *inferior good* is a good for which demand decreases when income increases. Think about low quality flip-flops produced by underpaid home workers in Cambodia, that wear out in a few weeks, as compared to well-designed sandals from recycled tires in quality controlled factories in Brazil which last for several seasons. As soon as the income of poor people rises, they may reduce their purchase of flip-flops and begin to buy better quality footwear. The flip-flops then become inferior goods for an increasing group of consumers.

A special type of inferior goods are *Giffen goods*, named after the Scottish 19th century economist Robert Giffen. People buy less of these when the price decreases and more when the price increases. The best-known example comes from Giffen himself and concerns staple food. Poor people tend to consume less of staple foods like potatoes, corn, rice, or cassava when the unit price goes down, because this allows them to buy some of the food they prefer more, namely vegetables and meat. This means that for a Giffen good, the demand curve is not downward sloping but upward sloping: the lower the price, the lower the demand, and the higher the price, the higher the demand.

In social economics, consumer demand by individual economic agents is not understood as neatly ordered and fixed. Therefore, this theory does not use mathematical methods to derive demand functions from preference orderings. Instead, social economics uses qualitative methods to understand differences in demand between groups of people and geographical locations. Or to understand changes in demand over time. This is done through segmentation of consumers. This happens vertically, along income groups, and horizontally, along socio-cultural groups. Examples of such horizontal segmentations are age groups – the grandparents of Vladimir and Olga have quite different preferences for food, clothing, and TV channels than the young couple themselves – and subcultures, such as fashionistas, rastafari, or skateboarders. Changes in demand by these segments over time are analysed by trend watchers but also through socio-cultural surveys which spot shifts in values, for example, from family-based, to individualistic, to peer group values, or from materialism towards new-age anti-materialism.

3.3 Institutional consumer theory

3.3.1 What is normal?

Some social norms of consumption are prescriptive social norms, giving strong directions to choices. This is particularly powerful when formalised into laws. For example, the requirement by the state to have health insurance or to wear a helmet on a motorbike. Or a prescriptive norm is a strong guidance because of membership of a group with strict norms. Think about traditional communities that have strict rules about the types of clothes men and women should wear. Other social norms are descriptive. Descriptive social norms simply register what the majority of people do. Economic agents register what 'is normal' by simply watching others. This may lead active members of an athletics club in Moscow to drink less alcohol and favour typical sports drinks instead because that is perceived to be the dominant social norm for a real sportsman.

But the influence of social norms on consumer behaviour is more complex than these examples suggest. There are often conflicting social norms and subcultures with their own lifestyles and social norms. And social norms are constantly challenged and change over time. That is why marketing firms continuously contact consumers to find out about their lifestyles, values, and preferences.

3.3.2 Affluenza

The fact that economic agents are social beings, and check on what others do, also leads to negative social patterns in consumer behaviour. One such pattern is an increased interest in expensive goods when economic agents see their income increase. This can be explained by the *Veblen effect*: the fact that some economic agents are willing to pay a higher price for a good which has a cheaper substitute that is quite similar. They may do this as a strategy to tackle the information and uncertainty problem: they assume that more expensive products are of higher quality than their cheaper substitutes. Of course, this assumption does not always hold, and suppliers of consumer goods can easily take advantage of this reasoning. They may offer two very similar products, one of which looks of higher quality and is more expensive. This will increase total revenue for a firm in a particular product class, as compared to the case where it had only one product on offer with the same characteristics of either the standard or the luxury item, which they could have sold at only one price. Another motivation behind the Veblen effect is status seeking through a *status good*. The function of status goods is that through their consumption, economic agents signal their status to each other. So, status goods are not only, and sometimes not at all, acquired because of their individual use value, but more for their social function. An example of a status good in Russia is a sports car purchased by midlife-crisis-suffering men who never really use it as a sports car (that is, driving at over 200 km per hour or participating in rally competitions), but simply cruise along Nevsky Prospect in St. Petersburg, to impress other men and hoping to attract the attention of young women.

Status goods stimulate high-price consumption, because all those consumers who are sensitive to these goods are in competition with each other for a higher rung on the status ladder. That is why the Veblen effect is also referred to as the grass-is-greener-at-the-Jones' effect. When a substantial group of consumers values status goods, and when an increasing number of people with lower incomes aspire to have such status goods when their incomes rise, there is a risk that individual economic agents and households become overly concerned with consumption, rather than also with saving and investment. Such a general focus on status good consumption not only pushes the economy out of balance, but also breeds a culture of consumerism, in which material standards become increasingly important in societies. In many developed countries as well as among elites of the developing world, this has led to consumer behaviour that can be called *affluenza*: too much consumption for a healthy economy, rather than too little, and of a kind that has negative unintended consequences.

Affluenza has *negative externalities*, unintended costs for a third party or society as a whole. The externalities of consumption are expressed both at the individual level and for society as a whole. Externalities at the individual level are addiction (how many pairs of fancy shoes are enough?) and health effects (obesity levels in the developed world are alarmingly high, while the fastest growth rates of obesity can be found in China and the Caribbean). Externalities at the societal level are lower health standards in the population (because of the aggregate individual health effects), pollution (sports cars produce higher levels of CO_2 per km than green cars) and environmental degradation (golf courses in desert areas crowd out water for agriculture and human consumption). Moreover, the Veblen effect reinforces itself in the absence of checks and balances. Such checks and balances can be provided by politics (taxation and regulation), in culture (providing a counterbalance of non-materialist values through art, sport, and community life), and by spirituality (by questioning materialism from the point of view of philosophical traditions, such as stoicism, or religious traditions emphasising the virtue of living a simple life). Hence, affluenza is an economic illness, with characteristics of an epidemic.

3.4 Post Keynesianism: consumption versus saving

In Post Keynesian economics, individual demand differentiation and change is not the focus of analysis, because Post Keynesian economists are concerned with the aggregate level demand and its changes. They rather look for patterns in demand, and explain rigidities in

72 Consumption

Image 3.1 Tesla electric car

these patterns. For Post Keynesians, segmentation according to income groups is more relevant than horizontal segmentation.

3.4.1 The Engel curve

The relationship between income levels and quantities consumed of a particular good is referred to as the *Engel curve*, named after the 19th century German economist Ernst Engel. The Engel curve shows that with increasing income, consumption of a particular good, or of all basic needs, will decline as a percentage of income (see Diagram 3.2). Richer consumers will spend an increasing share of their income on more luxurious goods, durable consumer goods such as a house, or on savings rather than consumption. If we plot the Engel curve in a diagram with income on the horizontal axis and the percentage of income spent on a particular good on the vertical axis, the Engel curve is downward sloping.

3.4.2 Propensities to consume and save

In Post Keynesian economics, it is the *propensity to consume* (c) which indicates the proportion of income (Y) spent on consumption (C). The remaining percentage of income goes to savings (S), because income is distributed over only two uses: consumption (C) and savings (S). In line with the logic of the Engel curve, Keynes stated that richer people, or owners of capital, tend to save more, and have a lower propensity to consume compared to poor people, or workers, who have a high propensity to consume. Of course, propensities refer to percentages and not absolute amounts. If a poor single mother spends 50 per cent of her budget on food and her budget is €800, she and her children consume €400 worth of food, whereas her

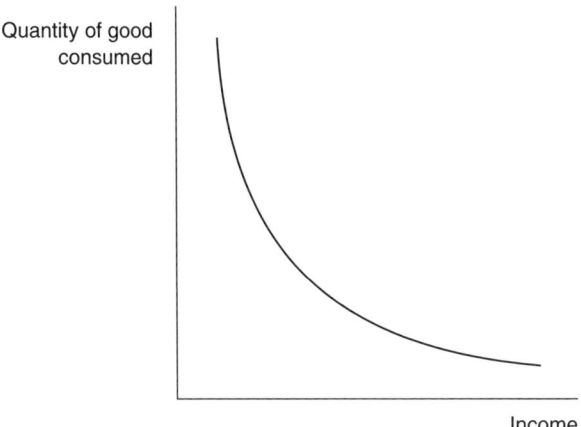

Diagram 3.2 Engel curve

boss, who spends only 10 per cent of her income on food, may consume €600 of food because she has an income of €6,000 per month. So, although the propensities to consume decline with rising income, the absolute amounts spent on consumption will generally not go down. This is because consumers with higher incomes tend to shift to the more luxury segments of a product category. For food, this means prepared food from the supermarket, exotic food from the delicatessen shop, and eating out in restaurants.

The *propensity to consume* (c) can be written in the following equation as the share of income (Y) going to consumption (C):

$$C = cY$$

The *propensity to save* (s) is its complement, namely the proportion of income saved (S):

$$S = sY$$

Together, income is distributed over consumption and savings:

$$Y = C + S$$

In other words:

$$Y = cY + sY$$

So, if income is 1,000 roubles and the propensity to consume is 0.8, then total consumption is $0.8 \times 1,000 = 800$ roubles. And, because $Y = C + S$, we can derive that total savings is 200 roubles, which is $Y - C$. This is $1,000 - 800 = 200$.

Finally, it follows that the propensity to save is 0.2, because $S = sY$, so $200 = 0.2 \times 1,000$. And also because the sum of the propensity to consume and the propensity to save is 1 (if we disregard borrowing, using the *ceteris paribus* assumption):

$$c + s = 1$$

Hence, if $c = 0.8$ and $c + s = 1$, then it follows that $s = 1 - 0.8 = 0.2$.

3.5 Neoclassical theory of consumption

3.5.1 Individual and market demand

In a purely material way, demand for a particular consumer good depends on its price level and the available budget. We tend to buy more of a good when it is cheap and when we have more income, and less of a good when it is expensive and when we have less income. This is the case for *normal goods*, the standard case in neoclassical economics. This results in a negative relationship between price (P) and quantity (Q), as Diagram 3.3 shows. When prices are high, quantities demanded are low, and the other way around. The result is a straight downward sloping demand curve (D_1) for, say, healthy meals bought per month. When the price is $35 per meal, our consumer buys none. However, at a price level of zero, she would like to have ten, and when a healthy meal costs $20, she would buy four per month.

Now, other consumers may feel differently about how much they are willing to pay for the same good. This leads to a variety of individual demand curves, each with its own shape, varying from steep (low demand) to flat (high demand) lines. In the diagram, these are the dotted demand curves D_1, D_2, and D_3. Together, the individual demand curves for a particular consumer good make up the market demand curve for that good (D). This curve indicates the quantity demanded in the market at the various possible price levels.

3.5.2 Price elasticity

Now we have established a relationship between quantity demanded and price through a demand curve, we can further analyse this relationship. This relationship is referred to as *price elasticity of demand*. It is the percentage change in the demand for a good in response to a percentage price change. This relationship determines the shape of the demand curve. In an equation:

$$e = \Delta D / \Delta P$$

in which e stands for elasticity, Δ for percentage change, D for demand, and P for price.

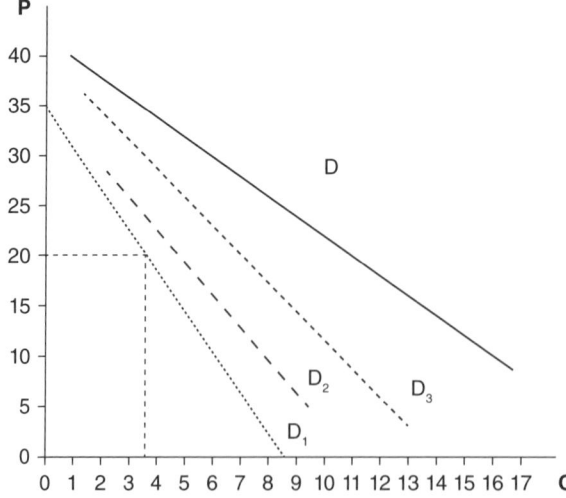

Diagram 3.3 Individual demand curves and the market demand curve

The change in demand can be negative or positive. For most goods the price elasticity of demand is negative: a price increase generally results in a decrease in the quantity demanded. An exception is Giffen goods, which have a positive price elasticity of demand. This is because a decrease in the price leads to a decrease in consumption, while a price increase results in higher consumption.

We distinguish between two outcomes of the elasticity of demand: inelastic and elastic. Inelasticity means that there is very little or no change in demand when the price goes up. This is expressed by a steep demand curve. In this case, the elasticity ranges between 0 and 1: a price increase of 1 per cent leads to a decrease in demand of less than 1 per cent. For change in a variable we use the Greek letter delta: Δ.

An example of an inelastic good is bread: when the bakery increases the price of bread by 10 per cent (so $\Delta P = +10$), its customers will probably not eat less bread but simply spend more money on their daily need for bread. They may perhaps become less careless and not leave bread around on the kitchen table, or feed it to the birds, so demand may decline by, say, 4 per cent (so $\Delta D = -4$). This results in an inelasticity (e) of -0.4 ($= -4/+10$). The other possible outcome of a price elasticity of demand is an elastic result, which means that the quantity demanded declines by more than the change in price. This case is expressed by a flat demand curve. An example is haircuts. When a hair salon charges 10 per cent more for a hair cut, it is likely that customers will go less often or will ask a family member or friend to cut their hair as an unpaid service. This will result in a decline in demand for haircuts by, say, 20 per cent. This results in a price elasticity (e) as follows: $\Delta D = -20$ and $\Delta P = +10$, so that $e = -20/+10 = -2$.

The extreme cases for price elasticity are: (1) perfectly inelastic demand, which is expressed by a vertical demand curve: demand does not react to price changes at all ($e = 0$); and (2) perfectly elastic demand, which is expressed as a horizontal demand curve: quantity demanded is extremely sensitive to price, hence, it has an elasticity of infinity ($e = \infty$).

Finally, neoclassical economics analyses the effects of price changes on the consumption of more than one good. Assume that we have two goods, X and Y. If the price of X falls, consumers may do two things. First, they may buy more of Y, even though the price of Y does not change, and less of X. This is the substitution effect and it results from a change in relative prices. More formally, the *substitution effect* is the reduction in demand for a good if the price of that good increases. Second, a price change in good X will change the income available for consumption, or the purchasing power, of both X and Y. So, consumers may buy more of X (as well as more of Y). The effect on demand for X is the income effect. More formally, the *income effect* is the reduction in demand for normal goods if the price of any good increases.

The total effect of a price change on consumption is the combined effect of the income and substitution effects. Substitution works only in one direction for normal goods: when a good becomes cheaper, consumers tend to buy more of it.

But the income effect can work both ways. When people have more purchasing power due to a price decrease, they may decide to buy more of any good – all goods or only one. This combined effect makes it difficult to predict consumer behaviour when the price of a particular good changes: demand may remain the same, may decline, or may go up.

3.5.3 Utility maximisation

In neoclassical economics, it is assumed that preferences are neatly ordered and rather fixed – per individual and over time. This assumption allows for a mathematical deriving of demand functions from individual preference orderings. Such preference orderings are called utility functions. Consumers are assumed to maximise their utility along a utility function, which is not a straight line but a curve, and therefore also called a utility curve. The *utility function* is a curve with trade-offs of what contributes to economic agents' utility for given prices and income levels. *Marginal utility* is the extra utility gained from adding one unit of a resource. This leads to the *law of diminishing marginal utility*: for every additional unit of a good, the extra utility obtained decreases.

Let's now move to a two-good situation, which is a simplified version of multi-good utility maximisation. Suppose you visit a café and want to have a coffee with apple pie. How much of each will maximise your utility? Well, that all depends on the marginal utility that each gives you. Table 3.1 shows you an example of the marginal utilities of coffee and apple pie per unit each. For simplicity we assume that each costs £2 per unit: £2 for a cup of coffee and £2 for a piece of apple pie.

Table 3.1 gives the marginal utilities for apple pie consumption. For coffee, I have added a list of marginal utilities with the same diminishing utility pattern, but different actual changes in utilities. Being a rational consumer, you want to spend your money wisely in the café, that is, in neoclassical language, you want to maximise your utility. This means that for every consumer decision, you will choose to buy that good that adds most to your utility. So, you start ordering coffee, not apple pie. Because a cup of coffee adds 6 utils, whereas a piece of apple pie adds only 5 utils to your happiness. If you have £2 left, you will order apple pie, because that adds 5 utils, whereas a second cup of coffee only adds 1 util. So, now you have gained the satisfaction of 6 + 5 = 11 utils. Suppose you find another £2 in your pocket – what will you order? Yes, indeed apple pie. Because a second piece of apple pie adds 1.5 utils, whereas a second cup of coffee adds only 1 util. So, now you have consumed one cup of coffee and two pieces of apple pie and gained 12.5 utils. Then you spot another £2 on the floor. What will you buy? Yes, a second cup of coffee to match your second piece of apple pie. This adds 1 util whereas a third piece of apple pie would only add 0.5 utils. So, now you have gained 13.5 utils from the consumption of two coffees and two pieces of apple pie.

The table shows that your utility can increase further if you have more money. If you had £4 more, you could have consumed even more. But the table shows that this would not add to your utility, because the marginal utility from a third cup of coffee and third piece of apple pie are negative. Your total utility would decline from 13.5 to 12.0 (because your utility would decline by 1 for coffee and 0.5 for pie). You maximise your utility from the consumption of two coffee and two pieces of apple pie – at least, for today, with 13.5 utils in the café, under your budget constraint of £8.

Now remember, we assumed for simplicity that the price of coffee and the price of a piece of apple pie were the same. But what if apple pie costs £4 and coffee £2? This brings prices into the analysis. And only when we know the prices can we maximise utility given our

Table 3.1 Utility maximisation with two goods

Number of units consumed	Marginal utility of apple pie	Marginal utility of coffee
0	–	–
1	5	6
2	1.5	1

budget constraint. If not, we would have a similar table for marginal utilities ranging from sailing in our luxury yacht or deep sea diving.... Again, we would probably add a bit of one and a bit of the other to maximise our holiday utility. But, well, if our budget does not allow such luxuries, we will never be able to maximise our holiday utility with only those two choices. So, we need to bring in the prices of each good for realistic utility maximisation under the constraints of given prices and budget. Suppose we visit the same café tomorrow, with £12 in our wallet. Unfortunately the discount on the apple pie is no longer available, so now it costs £4. The prices allow us to calculate marginal utility per £1. This gives us a revised table, Table 3.2. The added columns now give the marginal utility for each good per £1. Since the apple pie costs £4 per unit, we have to divide the marginal utility each time by 4. For coffee, which costs £2, we need to divide the marginal utility by 2.

Now, utility maximisation implies that we can spend our £12 by first buying a cup of coffee, then apple pie, then coffee again, and then apple pie again. This adds up to £12, our total budget. It gives us 6 + 5 + 1 + 2 = 14 utils of total satisfaction for £12. Any other combination would have given us fewer utils. For example, we could have bought one piece of apple pie (£4) and four cups of coffee (£8) with our budget of £12. But this would have given us 5 utils for the apple pie and 6 + 1 + 0.6 − 1 = 6.6 utils for the coffee. This would have made 5 + 6.6 = 11.6 utils in total, which is less than the 14 utils when we maximise our utility. In other words, we maximise utility when we consume a unit of a good, which gives us the highest marginal utility per money unit compared with the marginal utilities per money unit of all other available goods. Only when all marginal utilities per money unit are the same, have we maximised our utility, because it is not possible to improve our choice by choosing a last unit of a different good.

This brings us to the rule of utility maximisation: the marginal utility per money unit should be equal for each good:

$$\frac{MU_a}{P_a} = \frac{MU_b}{P_b} = \frac{MU_c}{P_c}$$

Diagram 3.4 gives a utility function on which we find the trade-off between the two goods, coffee and apple pie, and which is therefore also called an indifference curve. The indifference curve is convex-shaped. This is because at the ends, additional units of one of the goods will not bring as much utility as a more balanced combination, as we have seen above. An indifference curve represents all combinations of goods which are ranked equally by a consumer. So, on the left, with more apple pie and less coffee, you are equally as satisfied as on

Table 3.2 Utility maximisation with two goods and their prices

Number of units consumed	Marginal utility			
	Apple pie (£4 per unit)	Apple pie per £1	Coffee (£2 per unit)	Coffee per £1
0	–	–	–	–
1	5	1.25	6	3
2	2	0.5	1	0.5

78   *Consumption*

the right, where you consume more coffee and less apple pie. How do you find the maximum position on this graph? Well, then we need to plot in the budget constraint. This is a straight line indicating how much you can buy with the money you have available.

Let us assume that your budget is £12, coffee costs £2, and apple pie costs £4. This is shown in Diagram 3.4. The indifference curves have only one shape because this figure represents the preferences of a single consumer. The shape shows the particular combinations of coffee and apple pie between which the consumer is indifferent. But, not all these combinations are feasible with the available budget. Indifference curve B, the middle one, just touches the budget line at one point: any other point goes beyond the budget. So, two pieces of apple pie and two coffees are feasible (£12), but a choice further to the left on the indifference curve, with three pieces of apple pie and one cup of coffee is not feasible (£12 for apple pie plus £2 for coffee = £14). The same ratio of coffee and apple pie on a lower indifference curve, curve A, is feasible: 2.8 pieces of apple pie and 0.8 cups of coffee. But the café does not sell such broken units. Any point on curve C requires a higher budget – check for yourself. So, utility maximisation under the budget constraint and with given market prices results in point Umax, where the budget line touches the highest possible indifference curve. This gives you maximum possible utility, given the prices and your budget constraint.

Similar to the rule of utility maximisation given earlier, the graphical derivation of utility maximisation also has a formula. This can be seen from the diagram: the point Umax is exactly where the budget line touches the indifference curve (or in more detail: the highest possible indifference curve). This means, mathematically, that these two lines have the same slope at that point. The slope of the budget constraint is the ratio P_a/P_c of the price of the

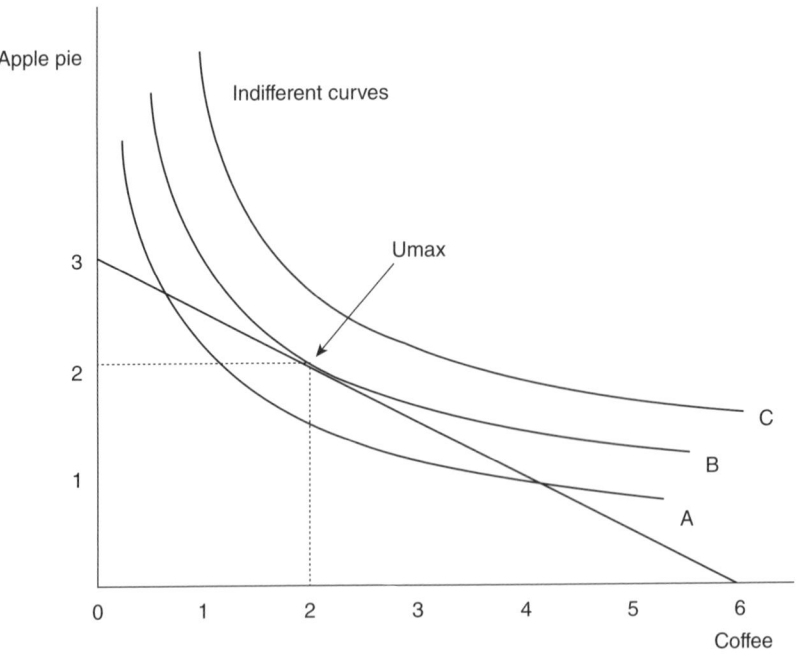

Diagram 3.4 Individual utility maximisation

good on the y-axis (price of apple pie = P_a) and the price of the good on the x-axis (price of coffee = P_c). The slope P_a/P_c is negative, because the budget constraint is downward sloping, from maximum possible consumption of apple pie to maximum possible consumption of coffee.

Slope of the budget constraint: $-P_a/P_c$

The slope has value = $-4/2 = -2$

The slope of the indifference curve varies along the curve: from steep on the left to flat on the right. At any point, the slope is the *marginal rate of substitution* between two goods: MRS A, C. This is the extra utility gained from an extra unit of the good on the y-axis (A) traded against a unit less of a good on the x-axis (C). We can see this in the diagram: the marginal rate of substitution on the left-hand side on the indifference curves is very high, because the consumer chooses to give up many cups of coffee to obtain more apple pie. On the right-hand side of the curves, the marginal rate of substitution between apple pie and coffee is very low: almost no pie and lots of coffee.

Slope of the indifference curve: $-\Delta A/\Delta C$

At point Umax, the slope of the indifference curve equals the slope of the budget constraint:

$$-P_a/P_c = -\Delta A/\Delta C$$

In other words, utility maximisation occurs when the marginal rate of substitution between two goods equals the price ratio of these goods. In our example, the price ratio, the slope of the budget constraint, is $4/2 = 2$. The marginal rate of substitution between the two goods at the point of utility maximisation is also 2: the marginal utility of apple pie is 2 and the marginal utility of coffee is 1. So the marginal rate of substitution is $2/1 = 2$.

3.5.4 Individual demand function

The final step in neoclassical consumption analysis is to derive the individual demand function for a good from the utility maximisation analysis. Remember, a demand function pictures the relationship between the price of a good and the quantity demanded of that good. If we know for two different prices how much a consumer wants to buy of a good, given this consumer's budget constraint, we will have two points in a diagram between which we can draw the demand curve. Suppose we want to find out the demand curve for apple pie for our consumer. From Diagram 3.4, we know that when the price of apple pie is £4, and everything else remains constant (thus, *ceteris paribus* the budget and the price of coffee and preferences), our consumer will buy two pieces of apple pie.

Now, suppose the price of apple pie reduces to £3. This shifts the budget constraint for apple pie outwards in Diagram 3.5, because with a budget of £12, our consumer can now buy four instead of three pieces of apple pie. The new budget constraint is the dotted line. It allows for a new maximum, B, point, which is where the new budget line and a higher indifference curve intersect. At this point, our consumer can have 2.5 pieces of apple pie and 2.3 cups of coffee. This gives higher utility than the earlier combination of two pieces of apple pie and two cups of coffee. Moreover, with this exercise of a price reduction in apple pie, we have now two combinations of price and quantity that our consumer demands: two pieces of apple pie at a price of £4 and 2.5 pieces of apple pie for the price of £3. In mathematical terms

80 *Consumption*

Image 3.2 Coffee and cake revised

for price and quantity (p, q), these points on the demand curve are point A (4, 2) and point B (3, 2.5). This allows for a straight demand line to be plotted in Diagram 3.5 between points A and B.

Diagram 3.6 shows the linear demand function of our consumer for apple pie, which simply connects the two points A and B from Diagram 3.5 but now in a diagram with the price and quantity of one good: apple pie.

3.6 Externalities of consumption

Negative externalities are the unintended negative side effects of consumption. Consumption has various positive and negative effects at the social level. Also, moderate consumer behaviour, and even the meagre consumption of the world's poorest, has wider social and environmental effects. Indeed, the externalities of consumer behaviour cut across the consumer behaviour of all income categories. This is reinforced by a capitalist mode of production, neoliberal policies, and globalisation. These are powerful, interlinked processes stimulating higher consumption with higher social and environmental costs due to cheap and easy global transport, and the internet and other media spreading middle-class consumerist lifestyles across the world.

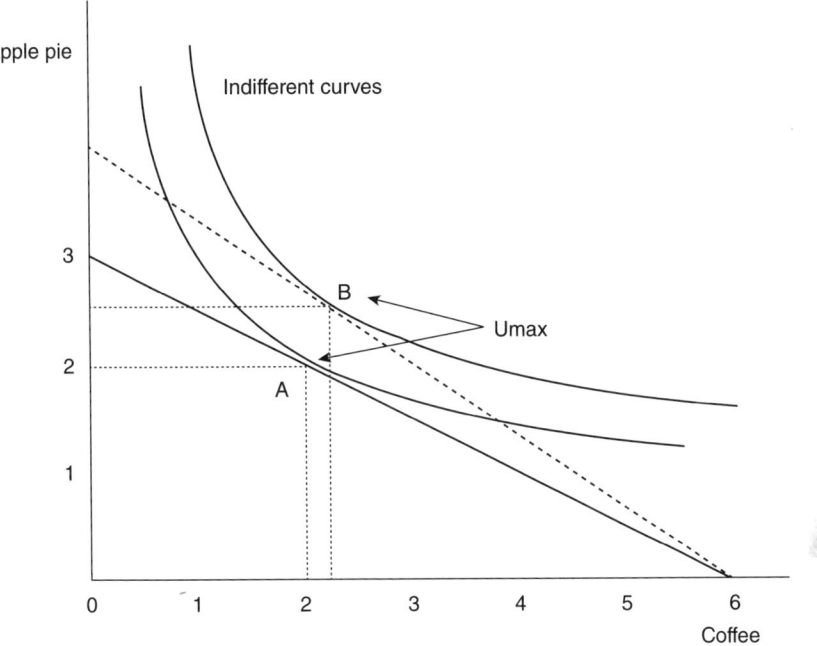

Diagram 3.5 Utility maximisation with changing prices

Examples of negative externalities of consumption range from oil spills from tankers or platforms in the oceans producing fuel for our cars, which destroy marine ecology and bird life, to lung cancer from smoking tobacco, to deforestation from wood collection by poor women in the Sahara region. Externalities are, as the definition makes clear, unintended – not intentional – consequences of behaviour. This implies that generally, consumers do not wish these negative effects to happen. Nevertheless, our consumer behaviour makes them happen, precisely because of the behavioural reasons mentioned above, as well as a few other reasons related to the supply side.

The next subsections will each discuss an externality of consumption.

3.6.1 No price attached to environment and society

The environment has no price tag. Nor does society, its values, and the relationships between people have a price. In a market-dominated economy, the absence of a price for a good receives an implicit meaning of 'not valuable', or at least 'not scarce'. When most of consumption is obtained through the market, in which a product's value is signalled through its market price, clean air and clear oceans are taken for granted – we do not pay for them. But they are being used as natural resources in the production of the goods we consume. And for which we pay too low a price because the environmental damage done to these natural resources is not included in the price. So, when we buy a pair of jeans, we pay for the cotton and labour and branding and transport costs, as well as the brand's profits. But we do not pay

82 Consumption

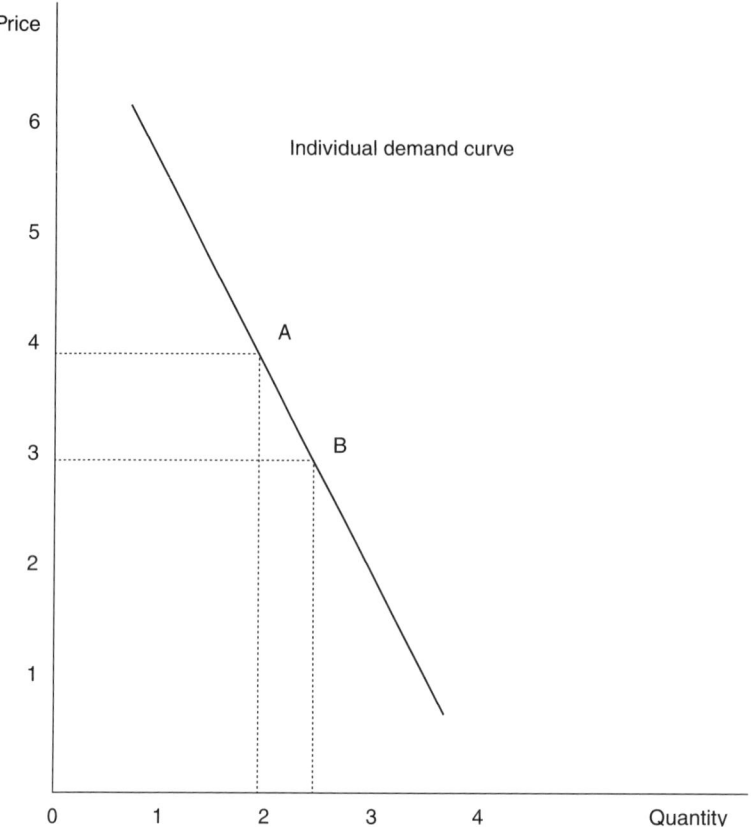

Diagram 3.6 Individual demand function from a utility scheme

for the waste of drinking water implied in the production of cotton, the world's most water-using crop. Because water is considered free. If the opportunity costs of this water use, calculated as the expenditures to keep the water supply at the level it was before cotton production expanded for jeans production, the sale price of a pair of jeans would be considerably higher. Now, the opportunity costs fall on society, and in particular on the communities of farmers living in areas where water is becoming increasingly scarce. So, agriculture and household drinking water collection becomes increasingly more expensive (think about irrigation systems) and time consuming (think about the further distances women and girls need to walk to fetch drinking water for their families).

3.6.2 Alternatives are too expensive: inconsistent pricing

The other side of the coin as regards environmental concerns is that consumer goods that do not affect the environment, or do so in a much more limited way, tend to be expensive. The price difference for the contents of a shopping trolley in an average supermarket and one filled in an organic food store can easily reach 25 per cent. That is because organic and fair trade products internalise at least some of the negative externalities in the final consumer good's price. Fair pay to farmers, abolition of child labour, and compensation for environmental damage each increase the cost price of a product. Moreover, the market share of fair trade and organic products is small, in most countries less than 5 per cent, which means that the scale of production is lower than for regular products. This keeps production costs per unit relatively high. This practice means that product pricing is inconsistent with societal values: whereas most people prefer a clean environment over a polluted one, and fair trade over exploitation, the prices of organic and fair trade products are higher and not lower than those of regular products.

3.6.3 Discouragement effect of individual behavioural change

When people are aware of negative externalities and are concerned about consumer behaviour leading to these effects, they may be willing to change their behaviour. The problem that many of us face is how effective our behavioural change will be. If we believe that others do not change their behaviour in the same way, or only very few, we tend to feel discouraged to make an effort because we will see very little or no effect of our behavioural change on total consumption. Hence, we see no effect on the externality. Indeed, economic agents perceive others who do not adapt their behaviour as *free riders*: those who do not make an effort to change their consumer choices, while benefitting from the gains of a better natural environment, through the efforts of others. Think about recycling behaviour, which requires an effort in sorting, storage, and trips to recycling points for various types of waste.

3.6.4 Myopia: distance between consumption and negative side effects

Another important problem with preventing externalities of consumer behaviour is myopia. There is often a distance in time or place between the benefits of consumption (for me, or now, or here) and the costs of it (for them, or later, or there). For example, it takes years before smoking translates into cancer. And my purchase of a pair of Levi's jeans today does not affect my water supply from the tap, but a farmer's water source for food production in Cameroon, a major cotton-producing country with low rainfall. And even when we know about these distance effects, through information provided in the media or awareness campaigns, we tend to forget these effects when we do our shopping because of myopia. This is reinforced by lack of adequate information to make responsible choices. There are a few green labels and fair trade labels, but it takes time and effort to find out what criteria they use for their buying practices and how they enforce their standards, and to find out where you can buy those products.

3.6.5 Framing and fragmented information

The complexity of external effects – their size, timing, location, impact – makes it difficult for consumers to make responsible consumer choices. Which car has least CO_2 per km? Perhaps an electric car? But how is the electricity generated – solar energy or coal power plant? And if I want to reduce my ecological footprint on Earth, is that possible without becoming some kind of freak, wearing self-knitted clothing, having a windmill in the back garden and solar panels on the roof, and bringing all my electronic devices to the shop for recycling? Unfortunately, green consumption too often receives unattractive framing. It is often considered as 'hippie' or radical or romantic, or all three together. Fortunately, there are examples of organic and fair trade brands that have managed to create a niche market with frames attractive to an increasing number of consumers. Think about fair trade and environmentally aware cosmetics brand The Body Shop, or the Tesla Roadster, a stylish electric sports car with extravagant wing-doors.

3.6.6 Say's Law: supply creates its own demand

In opposition to the notion of consumer sovereignty stands *Say's Law*, incorrectly named after the late 18th–19th century French economist Jean-Baptiste Say, who never formulated his ideas in this particular way. The law means that supply creates its own demand. So, consumers buy what is offered. Consumers' wants for goods that have little or no externalities will never translate into market demand, simply because it is inarticulate: you cannot demand a good that does not yet exist.

3.6.7 Materialism

The last reason for externalities to persist widely is the economic culture of materialism. Now, this is not entirely new. In the past there have always been societies in which material goods earned high status. Status goods have a function as a signal of status in the social hierarchy, even when such goods are being given away, as a signal of one's wealth. Because this reinforces one's place in the social hierarchy. Capitalist, globalised economies place an emphasis on materialism, which leads to a strengthening of the Veblen effect and its reinforcement over time through ever larger groups of people aspiring to higher consumption levels. Hence, the economies that most of us live in suffer from large externalities of consumption, which are difficult to remove without changes in social norms, stricter regulation, and a cultural or spiritual shift toward less materialist values.

3.7 Interesting sources

Behavioural Insights Team (BIT) of the UK government: https://www.gov.uk/government/organisations/behavioural-insights-team
Blog of the BIT: http://www.behaviouralinsights.co.uk/blog/
Fine, B. (2002) *The World of Consumption: The Material and Cultural Revisited*. London: *Routledge*.
Sunstein, C. and R. Thaler (2008) *Nudge: Improving Decisions about Health, Wealth, and Happiness*. New Haven: Yale University Press.

3.8 Glossary

Absolute deprivation   Poverty below subsistence level

Affluenza   Too much consumption for a healthy economy

Consumer sovereignty   The assumption that consumers determine what is produced, so that the economy produces exactly what people want

Durable consumer goods   Goods for long-term use

Endowment effect   The tendency of consumers to attach greater value to a good once they have obtained it

Engel curve   Curve which shows that with increasing incomes, consumption of a particular good, or all basic needs, declines as a percentage of income

Final consumer goods   Goods for end use

Framing   The way that choices are communicated to consumers

Giffen good   A good of which demand decreases when the price decreases

Immediacy effect = myopia   The tendency of consumers to prefer a reward now over a bigger reward later

Income effect   The reduction in demand for normal goods if the price of any good increases

Inferior good   A good of which demand decreases when income increases

Intermediate consumer goods   Unfinished goods to which households add their unpaid labour to produce final goods

Law of diminishing marginal utility   For every additional unit of a good, the extra utility obtained decreases

Marginal rate of substitution   The extra utility gained from an extra unit of one good traded against a unit less of another good

Marginal utility   The extra utility gained from adding one unit of a resource

Negative externality   An unintended cost for a third party or society as a whole

Normal good   A good of which demand increases when income increases

Nudging   The framing of choice situations towards a desirable default choice

Opportunity cost   The value of the alternative forgone

Price elasticity of demand   The percentage change in the demand for a good in response to a percentage price change

Propensity to consume   The proportion of income spent on consumption

Propensity to save   The proportion of income saved

Purchasing power = real income   What one can buy with one's income

Relative deprivation   When consumers cannot afford to buy the goods that earn them full dignity in their communities

Say's Law   The assumption that supply creates its own demand

Social safety net   A public service which provides social protection for the most disadvantaged in a society, to enable them to have a decent livelihood

Status good Goods that signal the (desired) social status of a consumer

Status quo effect The tendency of consumers to stay with their default option rather than shift to another one

Substitution effect The reduction in demand for a good if the price of that good increases

Utility function = indifference curve A curve with trade-offs of what contributes to an economic agent's utility for given prices and income levels

Veblen effect The tendency of some consumers to be willing to pay a higher price for a good which has a cheaper substitute that is quite similar

4 Firms

4.1 Entrepreneurs, managers, and firms

4.1.1 Entrepreneurs and managers

Firms are initiated by entrepreneurs. *Entrepreneurs* are risk-taking economic agents on the supply side of markets. Some entrepreneurs head their own firms, being owner and manager at the same time. Think about the British entrepreneur Anita Roddick of The Body Shop, who started in 1976 with just one shop in a niche market of socially and environmentally responsible cosmetics. She built a world-wide chain with 2,000 stores, which she headed for many years. Anita Roddick has been quoted as saying:

> Be courageous. It's one of the only places left uncrowded.

Other entrepreneurs have no capital of their own and are innovators who match the capital and production skills of others to their own innovative ideas to establish a firm. Here, the American software inventor Bill Gates is a good example. When he started Microsoft he was a student living on a meagre income. Again, other entrepreneurs are investors in a new market or they buy, reorganise, and then sell existing firms, while they often delegate the management of their firm to others. There are also poor entrepreneurs who survive at the margin. They are numerous and make up the majority of the working population in developing countries. These are self-employed entrepreneurs, without personnel, often operating with low capital and high labour time, sometimes outside the formally regulated and counted economy. In developed countries, we also find such entrepreneurs operating on the margin of profitability and livelihoods. We find them in the retail sector, as owners and family workers in shops, who find it difficult to compete against large chains such as supermarkets and clothing brands. And we find them in agriculture, where small-scale family farms struggle to survive in a sector with continuously increasing levels of scale and industrially operating national and international agribusinesses.

A firm is the continuation of initial entrepreneurship, which may be shaped and reshaped over time. For example, Unilever started in 1929 as a margarine producer in the city of Rotterdam and gradually turned into a Dutch-British multinational firm producing hundreds of household products in many countries across the world. The entrepreneurship of its initiators, the Dutchmen Anton van den Bergh and Samuel Jurgens, is still evident in the firm, and Unilever still produces margarine in Rotterdam.

A *manager* is an economic agent who is hired to lead an organisation. Management involves a complex coordination task. The coordination of a firm – management – is responsible for,

88 *Firms*

Image 4.1 Unilever head office in Rotterdam

and internally and externally accountable for: managing workers' motivation, accounting, production and its costs, price setting, marketing, sales, and last but not least, the relationship with consumers, capital providers, authorities, and civil society – in short, the firm's stakeholders.

4.1.2 Firms

Firms exist because innovation, investment, production, and sales can be done more efficiently and effectively through an organisation. This overcomes the transaction costs and uncertainties of doing each of these processes through market exchanges between a large number of individuals. *Transaction costs* are the costs involved in an exchange, not reflected in the price of the good exchanged. Moreover, firms can obtain economies of scale that individual contractors cannot. And, of course, firms try to develop market power in order to shift costs to others and to be able to influence prices and regulation to their advantage.

The particular objectives of firms vary, depending on the type of firm, the type of market, and stakeholder interests. *Stakeholders* are all parties that are affected by the operation of a firm. Generally, the overall objective of a firm is its continuation over time. Firms are not set up as short-term money machines, at least, not the large majority of them. If you want to get rich fast, you better learn to play poker very well, develop a skill like singing and join a TV talent show, or develop a unique low-cost-behind-your-desk technology such as an innovative app or web tool.

Firms require investment of capital and human resources, which expect returns, and these are generally earned over a long period of time. Moreover, the longer the time period, the higher the chances of success, through achieving intermediate objectives. The main intermediate objectives of firms are: sufficient profit, increase in market power, and growth. Other possible objectives include client satisfaction, innovation, societal change, and environmental care. Profit maximisation is often not listed as the number one objective by business owners and managers, except for publicly listed corporations, who thereby signal their attractiveness for investment to shareholders. In practice, firms steer toward reasonable, sufficient profits to satisfy the providers of capital and to enable growth.

The other intermediate objectives, that were mentioned already, are power and growth. These two are related. Market power improves the bargaining position of a firm, and hence, is a means and an end in one. Firms are concerned with keeping costs low, trying to set prices as high as possible in the market they operate in, and reducing production costs and transaction costs. This means that they will try to have power over their suppliers, which will allow them to force down the price of inputs. Growth helps in this, because the larger the firm, the more dependent suppliers are for the sales of their raw material on a big buyer in the market. Similarly, when a firm grows, it tends to outcompete some of its competitors and take over others, so that its market share increases. This implies that consumers have less choice and the firm can use its market power to keep prices higher than they would be if the firm was smaller and had more competitors. Finally, firms try to exert power over their employees. Growth also helps in this because when a firm becomes the largest employer in a region, workers have little choice other than to accept a job in that firm, even when wages and working conditions are bad.

In summary, firms exist because a hierarchical organisation overcomes transaction costs and uncertainties in the production process, and the objective of firms is continuation, conditional on sufficient profit, as well as power and growth, with possible additional objectives of serving various stakeholders' interests.

4.2 Types of firms

4.2.1 Small- and medium-sized enterprises

*SME*s, as small- and medium-sized enterprises are called, are the most prevalent type of firms worldwide. In the European Union, 99 per cent of all businesses are small or medium sized. They create the majority of employment in most countries in the world, and more jobs than multinationals or the public sector. Moreover, in the informal sector, SMEs are the only employer, and include many self-employed workers who work from home or on the street. The European Union has defined SMEs as firms with no more than 250 employees and an annual return of not more than €50 million and/or a balance sheet not exceeding €43 million. Other countries set 100 employees, or less, as the borderline between medium and large businesses. SMEs have unlimited personal liability, which implies that the owners have to pay back debts in case of bankruptcy. The obligation to pay back the firm's creditors applies also to all private assets of the owners (house, car, TV set, and savings for example). And in the case of marriage, the assets to be sold to pay back business debt may include those of the spouse as well.

The Finnish software developer Futurice was voted the best SME workplace in Europe in 2012 and 2013 in a European survey of 250,000 employees. Futurice has two offices in Finland, and offices in Germany and the UK, with a total of 140 employees. Its decision rule in product development is what Futurice calls '3 × 2': is the idea good for our clients, employees, and financial numbers (3)? And is this the case both now and in the future (2)? This decision rule is apparently so successful for employee satisfaction that it helped earn Futurice the first place in European SME ranking.

4.2.2 Large non-listed private enterprises

Large private enterprises have limited responsibility (abbreviated to 'Ltd'). This means that if they go bankrupt, the owner's private assets cannot be confiscated by the firm's creditors. Large, privately owned firms are increasingly rare. That is because in good times, investors offer large sums of money to the owners not only to benefit from returns on investments but also to reap the additional benefits of ownership. The owner is the *residual claimant* of a firm, the person receiving the remaining profit after all other production factors have been paid. This may involve large sums of money, making a firm attractive for acquisition by private equity funds and by publicly listed firms that can easily raise money through issuing new shares. In bad times, large private enterprises find it difficult to access the capital that is necessary for innovation or restructuring.

The initial owners are not always satisfied with a change in ownership: they lose influence not only to additional managers but also to thousands of unknown shareholders who expect high rates of profit every quarter. A good illustration of a large private enterprise that became publicly listed but was later bought back again by its initial owner is the UK-based Virgin Group Ltd. It is led by one of the world's most successful entrepreneurs, Richard Branson. He began his first business venture in 1968, soon started his own record label, later set up a low-cost airline, and now owns 200 other firms, including a more recent one offering space trips. The Virgin Group employs around 50,000 people in more than 30 countries. In 1986 Virgin was listed on the London Stock Exchange, and Richard Branson had to share management responsibility with a board. But he experienced this as unnecessarily constraining his creativity and decisions. Therefore, a year later, he bought all the shares back, so that in 1987 Virgin became private again. In 2011, annual revenue was £13 million, similar to the gross national product of countries such as Ivory Coast, Latvia, and Uruguay.

Image 4.2 Virgin airplane

4.2.3 Publicly listed firms

Publicly listed firms are not owned by an individual. Everybody who is interested and has the money available, can invest in the firm, and hence acquire partial ownership. The shares of ownership are traded on a *stock exchange*, the market for shares of stock of firms. The shareholders together own the firm. Their influence on the firm's policy and strategy, however, is limited. They largely vote with their feet: when shareholders are dissatisfied with a firm's performance, they simply sell their shares. If a firm's net worth becomes very low or negative, the most a shareholder can lose is that the shares she has bought become valueless: nobody wants to buy them anymore at any price. But she never risks her personal property as a shareholder.

Shareholders who hold a large part of a firm's shares generally claim influence over the firm's strategy and policy. They may even enforce decisions over mergers and change of management. Such large shareholders are often governments, families who have historical ties with a firm, or private equity firms whose interest is to buy cheap when a firm's performance is low, enforce reorganisation with the threat of withholding the necessary capital to survive, and then sell after a few years when the firm has become profitable again.

A well-known European publicly listed firm is AIR FRANCE KLM S.A. The abbreviation S.A. stands for 'Société Anonyme', which is the French label for anonymous society, which refers to the shares being owned by individuals and investment firms, and traded on a stock exchange. The two national airlines joined together in 2004, keeping their own brand names and remaining listed on both the Amsterdam stock exchange (KLM) and the Paris stock exchange (Air France). Revenue in 2011 was €24 billion and the joint venture employs 108,000 workers. In 2009, AIR FRANCE KLM acquired 25 per cent of the shares in Alitalia, which gives it an important say in the Italian airline market. The value of the shares has since moved between €37.95 per share at its highest point, just before the start of the financial crisis (May 2007), and €3.39 per share at its lowest point (in May 2012). The volume of trading in this company's shares has increased steadily. It rose from around 100,000 shares per month in 2004 up to 5 million shares per month in 2013. Diagram 4.1 shows the fluctuation in the share prices from month to month, between January 2000 and December 2008.

4.2.4 Multinational corporations

Multinational corporations are also called transnational corporations, *multinationals*, or MNCs. As their name indicates, MNCs have branches, or *subsidiaries*, in several countries. The main office is located in the country of origin, while the MNC's subsidiaries across the world are not just sales operations but contribute substantially to the corporation's objectives. They do so through designing a 'global assembly line' or a 'global workshop', in which different stages of the production process are located in different countries. This includes not only physical production, such as for Shell, which drills for oil in many countries. The globalisation of business activities also concerns design, marketing, sales, and financial operations. Multinational corporations follow not national but global strategies, selecting locations in countries either on the basis of minimising production costs, or on the basis of closeness to sales markets. To some extent, however, MNCs also set up subsidiaries that only exist on paper, which become financial-administrative hubs in 'tax havens', countries with low or zero profit tax or royalty tax, in order to minimise tax payment across their operations. This means that they organise their bookkeeping in such a way that low profits are reported in countries where profit tax is high, and that high profits are reported in countries where profit tax is low.

92 *Firms*

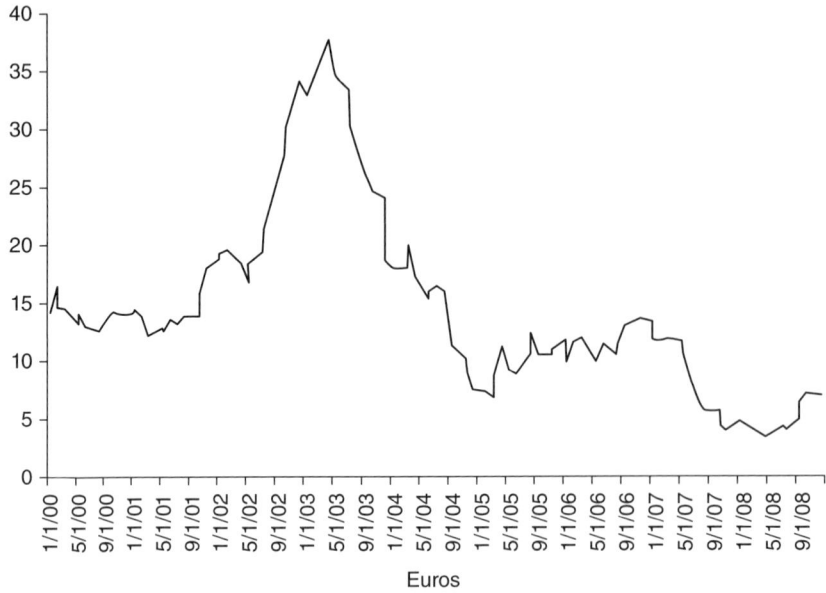

Diagram 4.1 AIR FRANCE KLM share price development 2000–2008

A well-known example of a multinational corporation is Unilever. It was established in 1929 and is listed on the Amsterdam, London, and New York stock exchanges. The corporation actually consist of two legal entities with separate stock exchange listings: Unilever NV and Unilever PLC. The abbreviation NV stand for 'Naamloze Vennootschap', which is the Dutch version of S.A. The abbreviation PLC is the English-language version: Public Limited Company. Unilever employs 173,000 workers worldwide. It is in the top three of the world's largest consumer goods companies and at least a quarter of all consumers in the world use Unilever products on a daily basis. Unilever is the corporation behind labels such as Lipton, Vaseline, Lux, Knorr, Hellmann's, and Ben & Jerry's. Some brands have different names in different countries, for example, Omo, its laundry powder and liquids, is also sold as Persil, Skip, Breeze, Ala, Wisk, Surf, and Rinso.

As it makes food products and household maintenance products, Unilever's major consumers are women. Since 2012, women have also become visible at the top of the firm: 40 per cent of its managers and a quarter of its board members are female, which makes Unilever a leader in female corporate leadership. Annual earnings are over €50 billion, with half of this amount being earned outside Europe and the USA. Unilever has hundreds of factories in Europe, the USA, Latin America, Africa, and Asia. Its production strategy is to produce close to its sales markets, because its products reach their consumers through dense local retail networks, including open-air market sellers in remote rural markets-under-the-tree.

4.2.5 Cooperative firms

Cooperative firms, or co-ops, are a special category because they can be small or big, national or multi-national, and profit or non-profit. They are special because they are not privately owned, not publicly listed, and not state owned. Cooperative firms are literally a cooperation of equals who are both its collective owners and capital providers, and its members, as either clients or producers. An example of a client cooperation is a cooperative bank: the clients provide the bank's capital, and profits are not paid out in dividends to anyone but are retained in the firm for investment in the capital stock, expansion of the business, and innovation of services and service delivery. Clients have a say in firm management, either directly through representatives on the board, or indirectly through an advisory role to the board.

An example of a producer cooperation is a dairy farmer's collective: the farmers invest in setting up a milk factory or other production unit, for example, with a single brand name, which helps them develop bargaining power vis-à-vis the large chain supermarkets to whom they sell their dairy products. The co-op organises its logistics, processing, and distribution, which creates important cost advantages as compared to doing this individually for each dairy farm. Hence, a production cooperative gains advantages both on the cost side and on the sales side.

The Spanish Mondragon company is one of the world's most famous cooperative firms. It is located in the Basque region in the north of Spain and consists of many cooperatives in the industrial, finance, retail, and knowledge sectors. It is the largest firm in the Basque region and the seventh largest in Spain. All cooperatives are united under the umbrella firm, the Mondragon Cooperation. It has 85,000 members who choose their managers and restrict executive pay to a maximum of 6.5 times the pay of the lowest-earning member per enterprise. In the area of finance, it includes the cooperative bank Caja Laboral, with branches in 77 countries and a total value of deposits of €25 billion. The management model of Mondragon puts people at the centre: its members, with their joint work projects and participative organisational structure. Its objectives are defined by cooperative principles, which in turn define its business strategy, aimed at top socio-economic performance. See, for the management model of Mondragon, Diagram 4.2.

4.2.6 Non-profit organisations

Non-profit organisations may be cooperatives, as indicated above, but are often associations or foundations. Think about a museum, sports club, or charity. Non-profit organisations, like most firms, require capital, labour, and material inputs, and are required by the state authorities to be registered and to produce annual reports. Even when they do not make profits, they are likely to pay taxes: labour taxes, value added taxes, and possibly other taxes (for example on their real estate). Non-profit organisations, as the name indicates, have a different objective than earning money. Earning sufficient returns is the major condition for serving their objectives. The objective generally reflects an ideal, such as humanitarian aid or nature conservation, or it has a more profane objective, such as preserving a family estate or enabling sport activities.

A well-known example of a non-profit organisation is MSF: Médecins Sans Frontières, or in English, Doctors Without Borders. MSF was created in 1971 in Paris and is now a movement with associations in 23 countries, operating in 60 countries. It was awarded the Nobel Peace Prize in 1999. Each of the associations operates independently and has a small office with staff engaged in fund raising and recruiting field staff for its operations. Doctors and other professionals are the members of the association and they do their work voluntarily (unpaid). The funding for its operations comes from 4.5 million private donations worldwide, not from governments. Even though MSF is not a for-profit firm and is not driven by shareholder interests, it does have to be competitive, because it competes with other humanitarian organisations, such as the Red Cross and Red Crescent, for donor funding. About 80 per cent

94 Firms

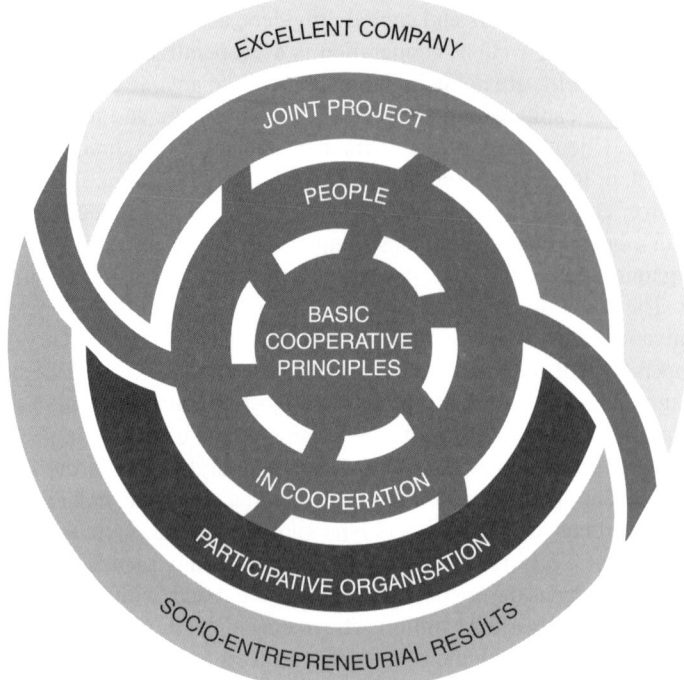

Diagram 4.2 Mondragon management model

of MSF funding is spent on humanitarian operations in the field. The other 20 per cent is spent on keeping the organisation running.

4.2.7 Public firms

State-owned enterprises, public firms, nationalised businesses – these are all names for firms that are 100 per cent in state hands. While such firms are managed like any other firm, their governance is different. The company board is appointed by the government. The reason for this political involvement is that a public firm's net profits and losses go into the treasury: the state's accounts. Parliament has democratic control over public firms. Some public firms have very little competition, because they operate as monopolies, for example when they operate a dam in a river to generate electricity, or when they are responsible for the land registration system or the railway infrastructure. Other public firms operate in a market with competitors. Nationalised banks, saved by states after a banking crisis, are such cases.

An example of a public firm is a state television and radio station. In the first decades of radio and TV, countries only had state-owned stations. However, private sector radio and TV stations were opened in most countries later on. In the UK, the BBC started in 1922 as the British Broadcasting Corporation and has 23,000 employees today. It is publicly funded through a fee paid by TV consumers and set annually by the British Government and approved by Parliament. In order to ensure press freedom, the BBC is governed not by the government and parliament but by an independent trust with 12 members who are appointed by the state after an open selection process. This trust operates as a company board.

4.3 Finance and accounting

In firms two flows are coordinated: a physical one, production; and a financial one, in money terms. Coordination of the financial cycle is achieved through the acquisition of capital and its management, which is reported through accounting systems. Before I explain the two basic accounting systems for firms, and costs and profits, let me first take you through the wide variety of sources for a firm's capital.

4.3.1 Sources of capital

4.3.1.1 Own capital and retained profits

When an entrepreneur has sufficient start-up capital, she will be able to start a firm with her own capital. Over time, when the firm is profitable, this capital can grow through retained profits. These, in turn, can be used for the replacement of old machines, expansion of buildings, research and development (R&D), and training workers. In this way, a firm is independent of capital markets. But growth is likely to be slow, because it takes time to accumulate sufficient capital through retained profits.

4.3.1.2 Bank loans

An important source of capital for firms is bank loans. In Europe, the financial needs of most companies are met by banks. Banks lend out money on the basis of a business plan and the reputation of a firm, and its *net worth* (assets minus liabilities), which provides *collateral* for the loan. This is a set of assets which a borrower owns as a security to obtain a loan. The interest rate paid on loans depends on the market rate in general and on the extent of risk, which banks expect to be attached to a particular loan. The higher the risk, the higher the interest rate that banks charge for their lending.

4.3.1.3 Private investment

There are various forms of private investment in firms. A firm may increase its capital by seeking partners who are willing to invest in the firm. Often, such a partner will get a seat on the board in order to have some control over how the investment will be used. Another form of private investment is through a *private equity fund*. These are firms in themselves, whose objective is to make money through short-term investment in other firms. After some time they hope to sell their shares at a higher value to make a profit on the deal. Finally, a third form of private investment is a combination of banking and investment, which is common in Islamic countries. It is therefore referred to as *Islamic banking*: banks do not just lend to a firm, but invest in it, and thereby become co-responsible for the use of the money: they share in the profits but also in eventual losses.

4.3.1.4 Bonds

Bonds are fixed-interest assets, tradable on a bond market or directly with the firm, which issues the bond, for a fixed period of time, often 10 years. A bond is therefore a loan, but not by a bank but by any member of the public. You and me, municipal governments, and sports clubs, anyone who has money available and does not want to run the risks of trading shares on a stock market can go for the safer option of bonds. Of course, bonds involve a risk: if the firm goes bankrupt, it may not or only partially pay back the value of the bond to you. But shares are much riskier: they do not earn dividend in years in which the firm makes a loss.

4.3.1.5 Equity: shares

The shares of a firm are financial assets which represent a partial ownership of a firm. So, shareholders are owners of the firm: collectively, they provide the firm's capital and thereby own the firm, as their property. A share entitles its holder to *dividend*, which is a share in a firm's profits over a year. So, if you have shares in AIR FRANCE KLM, for example, you will receive a dividend in proportion to the number of shares you have. If you own 1 per cent of all AIR FRANCE KLM shares, you are entitled to 1 per cent of the net profit available for dividend in a year. Shareholders buy and sell their shares on a stock market or stock exchange. As owners, they run the risk of losing their capital if the firm goes bankrupt, and in years when the firm does not make a profit, the dividend is zero.

4.3.1.6 Subsidies and tax benefits

Some financing of firms is not through financial markets but through subsidies from the state. Governments support businesses in various ways. They may provide business parks and export processing zones for factories, with all necessary infrastructure, which they rent out at a discount rate, below cost price, to attract firms. Hence, the rent includes a subsidy. Or, governments may give 'tax holidays' to foreign investors to attract them to invest in the creation of employment in the country. Other governments provide export subsidies or provide production cost subsidies to lower the market price of goods in their country. There are other types of business subsidies: for R&D, for training workers, and for investment in green technology. Such subsidies are additional finance for firms, and cheap finance because they do not need to be paid back.

4.3.1.7 Crowd funding

The last and most recent form of firm financing is *crowd funding*. This is a form of community financing through the internet, in which many small investors (sometimes only €10 is the minimum required investment) together finance a firm or an activity like the development of a new product. The crowd funders may be compensated with a variety of returns. For non-profit projects, such as the production of art for public space or nature conservation, the rate of return is simply the public good that has been created. For profitable projects, the rate of return may be vouchers for units of the end product or a share of the profits. Crowd funding is a flexible and horizontal form of financing, in which no individual investor can claim ownership and influence on the firm's operations. And there is often strong transparency due to detailed social media communication on the firm's use of the money. Without such transparency, people would not be willing to risk their money.

4.3.2 Accounting

All these above forms of financing require a system of accounting in a firm. For accountability not only to the providers of capital but to all stakeholders. The owners who provide the capital want to know how their money is being used; the workers want to know whether their remuneration is fair; potential investors want reassurance that the return on investment does not undermine long-term profitability; and the government wants to raise taxes from all taxable assets and activities of the firm. At the end of internal accounting processes, two main accounting results are presented by a firm: a balance sheet and a profit and loss account.

The *balance sheet* compares what a firm owns (assets) with what it owes (liabilities). If the difference is positive, the firm has a positive net worth, or equity. If the difference is negative, the firm has a negative net worth and has more debt than it can afford. This may be bearable in the short run but not in the long run. The solution to such a situation is either bankruptcy or a take-over by a firm interested in the potential embedded in its production, production process, labour force skills, market access, brand, or technique. Table 4.1 shows a balance sheet for a small company in Europe.

The balance sheet shows a list of assets on the left-hand side and a list of liabilities on the right-hand side. At the bottom of the right-hand side we see '*net worth*' (€130,000), which is the difference between the total assets on the left-hand side (€330,000) and the total liabilities on the right-hand side (€200,000):

Net worth = Assets − Liabilities

The *profit and loss account* shows how the result of the business operation in a year has been obtained. So, whereas the balance sheet gives an idea about the value of a firm, the profit and loss account shows the earnings and expenditures and the difference between the two, which is the firm's result (profit or loss). This is shown in Table 4.2.

4.3.3 Cost

The cost of a firm is what is paid for the production factors and input, plus other operation costs and marketing expenditures. The costs consist of a fixed and a variable part. *Fixed costs* are the costs of the firm even without producing a single unit: costs for land, buildings, machines, and contract labour. *Variable costs* increase with the number of units produced and concern the material inputs, flexible labour, energy use, and transport costs. Variable costs can be adapted in the short run, for example by substituting high quality for low quality inputs

Table 4.1 Balance sheet

Balance Sheet As of December 15, 2013				
Assets			*Liabilities*	
Cash at bank	170,000		Account payable	100,000
Accounts receivable	50,000		Sales taxes payable	40,000
Tangible assets	90,000		Accrued wages payable	60,000
Investment	20,000		**Total Liabilities**	**200,000**
Total Assets	**330,000**		Net Worth	130,000

Table 4.2 Profit and loss account

Profit and Loss account in 2013				
Net sale	120,000			
Cost of sales	(35,000)			
Gross profit		85,000		
Research and development	4,000			
Advertising and promotion	37,000			
Selling and administrative expenses	25,000			
Total expenses		(66,000)		
Profit before taxation			19,000	
Taxation			(10,450)	
Net Profit				**8,550**

or by energy saving measures. Fixed costs can only be changed in the long run, for example by selling or building a new production hall. Together, fixed costs and variable costs make up a firm's *total costs*.

From the total costs, we can calculate the marginal costs. *Marginal costs* are the extra costs when one additional unit of output is produced. Insight into the marginal cost structure of production helps decisions on whether the firm should produce more output (when marginal costs are low, an extra unit is cheaper than the sales price) or not (when marginal costs are high, an extra unit is more expensive than the sales price).

Two special cost concepts need to be mentioned. First, opportunity cost, which was defined in Chapter 2 as the value of the alternative forgone. For firms, opportunity costs are the benefits foregone by choosing a particular investment or production option. For example, if a private equity firm invests €100 million in a Finnish software company, it cannot invest that money in a French telecommunications company (and may regret this later when the return on investment in the latter company turns out to be higher). The other type of cost, which should be mentioned here, is an irrational type of cost accounting and involves *sunk costs*. These are the costs that have already been incurred and therefore should not be taken into account in a cost/benefit decision about the future. Nevertheless, people are tempted to do so out of spite or loss-aversion.

Suppose that you bought an entry ticket for your favourite artist at an open-air concert. The concert is tonight and it is raining. Now, although you hate rain, you may be tempted to go because you have paid for the ticket anyway. This is not rational, it is sunk cost accounting: the money you have paid in the past is irrelevant to your decision now: it is gone anyway. So, when deciding whether you want to go or not, you should only weigh the benefits of going (enjoying a live concert of your favourite artist) against the disadvantages of going (being wet to the bone all night).

Firms will try to minimise costs in order to survive competition and to satisfy consumers and stakeholders. One way to do this, and which at the same time serves their intermediate objectives of growth and obtaining market power, is through achieving *economies of scale*. These are cost advantages per unit due to an increased production size. The unit costs will decline with an expansion in production because the fixed costs will be distributed over a larger number of units produced, lowering the costs of each individual unit. This, of course, only works in the short run. Because in the long run, continuous increases in production will at some moment require an expansion of fixed costs, through acquiring more land, constructing new factories and offices, or adding more management layers.

4.3.4 Profit

Firms generally seek to make profits, sometimes as an end in itself, but more often as a condition so to continue over time and to achieve the intermediate objectives of growth and market power. There are different types of profits. *Commercial profit* is the positive difference from selling something for more than it costs to purchase it. This does not need to involve any production. *Business profit* is the residual of a business operation after all production factors and inputs have been paid. So, business profit (R) results from a production process and is the difference between total revenue (Y) and total costs (TC):

$$R = Y - TC$$

Total revenue is what a firm earns from selling its products at a particular price:

$$Y = P \times Q$$

in which P = price and Q = quantity.

The *profit rate* is the amount of profit divided by the value of capital goods owned. The profit rate, hence, is expressed as a percentage:

$$Y = R / K$$

in which r = profit rate, R = profit, and K = capital goods owned. Whereas r is expressed as a percentage, R and K are expressed in monetary units, for example, in euros or pounds.

4.4 Social economic and institutional approaches to management

4.4.1 Balancing stakeholder interests

In the broader economic view of management, the major role of a manager is to coordinate internal business processes and external stakeholder relationships, in order to optimise firm performance in the short run as well as in the long run. This role requires a continuous balancing of interests: of management itself, clients, workers, the providers of capital, the state, the local setting, and the natural environment. From a social economic and institutional perspective, the dominance of shareholders must be prevented, even in a capitalist economy, because it would shift the focus away from the long run to the short run.

Shareholders want to see short-term profits increase and are often not willing to accept one or more years of low profit to allow a firm to innovate and invest, or to train its workers in new techniques, or to adapt to greener technologies to reduce its ecological footprint. Shareholders would rather exchange the shares of such forward-looking firms for the shares of firms that are more oriented towards short-term profitability, with lower levels of investment and higher levels of profit allocated to dividends for shareholders. A capitalist economy therefore runs the risk of implosion: the undermining of its corporations not by an intervening state or angry activists, but by its own capital providers. . . .

Social economics describes two strategies that firms and governments use to prevent such an implosion. The first strategy is substantial government ownership of shares, to ensure stability among floating shareholders. Government shareholders are responsible for more objectives than just profitability, namely ensuring levels of employment, environmental responsibility, and investment in research and development to contribute to a country's competitiveness. Examples of government shareholders are the French and German governments who own substantial numbers of shares in car manufactures like Renault and Volkswagen. The second strategy is having labour union representatives on the supervisory boards of firms, to ensure that the firm's strategy takes the interests of workers into account, as a counter-balance to the interests of the shareholders. Countries that have labour representatives on supervisory boards are, for example, Germany and the Netherlands.

4.4.2 Motivation

What drives workers? Do they work only for the money? In the previous chapter, we discussed how this affects the agents' role as consumers. In this chapter we relate it to economic agents' role as workers. When we apply our general definition of agency from Chapter 2, to *workers' agency*, we can define the agency of a worker as making autonomous choices and acting upon these at work. This can be individual agency or collective agency, through trade unions or a workers' council. In their agency, economic agents act upon and re-enforce pro-social norms. Pro-social norms at work include trust, cooperation, mutual learning, fairness, and respect. But social economics also recognises power differences at work. Power is expressed through systems of meaning and through social groups at work. This goes beyond the distinction between owners and workers, and also includes groups such as managers, women and men, racial groups, and groups based on skills and expertise. Also, power may drive a wedge in teamwork: it may reinforce group thinking and us–them attitudes, which negatively affects labour productivity.

In social economics and institutional economics, a basic insight about motivation is that workers are satisficers and seek livelihood security through stable and fair pay. If they perceive their reward as unfair, they will try to punish their employer and seek help from a labour union or from the government who is responsible for enforcing labour laws. The easiest way to punish an employer is to reduce work effort. This can be done by reducing work hours (coming in late, leaving early, reporting ill), sabotage of machinery or the work atmosphere (arguments, sloppiness, carelessness), mobilising co-workers to go on strike (through labour unions), or simply slowing down the pace of work. For the employer, a reduction in work effort by employees means a reduction in labour productivity, and this implies a cost.

So, unfair pay – either through very large differences in pay between the top and the bottom, or through favouritism by management creating earning differences between workers with the same skills, or compared to the salaries paid at similar firms – is a demotivator and results in low work effort. The employer choosing to pay low wages shoots herself in the foot because it leads to a reduction in labour productivity. Moreover, when very low wages do not allow workers to obtain sufficient and nutritious food, to access health care, or to send their children to school, their labour productivity will also be adversely affected by their bad physical and psychological health, even when they try to keep up their work effort to prevent job loss. Hence unfair pay, whether relatively (compared to others) or absolutely (for minimum necessary livelihoods), reduces labour productivity.

In social and institutional economic theory, firms are seen as using two systems of worker motivation: top-down and bottom-up.

4.4.2.1 Top-down motivation: bureaucracy

A bureaucratic system of worker motivation is predictable and therefore provides security. Workers get promoted along a pre-defined trajectory within a firm – the internal labour market – on the basis of age and/or experience. This system does not necessarily promote the best workers to the positions in which they perform best: very good young workers may not want to wait until their fifties before getting promoted to management level, so they leave, while mediocre but diligent and patient workers get promoted, slowly but steadily, to the top, even when they have no leadership qualities. The bureaucratic system relies on rules that are generally regarded as fair, but which may in practice lead to the abuse of power by those higher up in the hierarchy if there are no democratic checks and balances. For example, through nepotism (friends or family of the boss being promoted faster) or a glass ceiling (women and ethnic minorities being promoted more slowly or being left behind on a 'mommy track' with less career opportunities).

4.4.2.2 Bottom-up motivation: intrinsic motivation

The system which relies on workers' own motivation is called intrinsic motivation. This system trusts that workers are self-motivated. This may sound idealistic but is quite in line with the findings on agency in behavioural economics, such as the ultimatum game that was discussed in Chapter 2.

Box 4.1 The perverse effects of extrinsic motivation, such as money and status

1. They can extinguish intrinsic motivation (see point 4 below).
2. They can diminish performance (people feel treated as money makers).
3. They can crush creativity (people focus on meeting quantitative targets).
4. They can crowd out good behaviour (by ignoring risk or client interest).
5. They can encourage cheating, shortcuts, and unethical behaviour (through myopia and the legitimisation of a narrow focus).
6. They can become addictive (meeting targets increases earnings, which is rewarding).
7. They can foster short-term thinking (ignoring more diffuse long-term goals which are not captured in the targets which must be met to achieve higher pay).

Source: Pink, D. (2009) *Drive - The Surprising Truth about What Motivates* Us. New York: Riverhead.

Research on intrinsic motivation has revealed that what really drives workers, once fair and secure pay is provided, are three elements: autonomy, mastery, and purpose. So, if workers are really treated as agents, having autonomy, and when they are given the space to learn and to give meaning to their work, having mastery, and when they find a purpose in their work that is larger than themselves, they will be strongly motivated. Many firms have now experimented with the system of intrinsic motivation, and have seen their labour productivity as well as employee satisfaction go up.

An example is Atlassian, a medium-scale software development firm with offices in Australia, the USA, and Europe. Important and commercially very successful innovations by Atlassian have not resulted from incentives or rules but from giving space to intrinsic motivation. First, Atlassian allows its software developers to use 20 per cent of their work time as they wish, to work on innovative ideas they chose themselves. They are also allowed, at least for some of this time, to do voluntary work for charities. Second, every quarter Atlassian organises a 24-hour event in which all employees are given complete freedom to work on anything they see as useful for the firm, with whoever they want to team up, as long as they do not work on their regular tasks. It starts on a Thursday after lunch and ends the next day at 4 pm with 3-minute pitches, drinks, and awards for the best innovation, voted for by all participants. The awards do not involve any money but consist of a champion shirt, a trophy, and the right to brag for the winning team. Atlassian calls it 'ShipIt days' and they do it because it fosters creativity, and allows employees to address software bugs, to realise radical ideas, and to have fun.[1]

4.5 The neoclassical approach to management

4.5.1 The principal–agent problem

The neoclassical major concern in management is the *principal–agent problem*: the potential gap between the interests of the principals (owners) who delegate tasks to agents, and the interests of the agents (managers). It may well be that the interests of the managers do not align with the

Image 4.3 Software firm Atlassian in Amsterdam

interests of the owners. For example, whereas managers have to balance the demands of customers (quality, price), workers (fair wages, acceptable working conditions), providers of capital (profit, loan pay-back), and society (regulation, 'license to operate'), the owners of a firm are mainly concerned with a return on their investment in the short-term and the long-term stability of the firm's performance. Or, managers may manipulate business accounts and give themselves high benefits at the cost of the firm's profitability, and hence, the principals' interests.

There are several solutions to the principal–agent problem. First, firms may have a supervisory board which checks on the operation of the executive board of a firm. Second, the owners may give extra rewards when managers ensure that the firm generates stable profit rates at the levels desired by the owners. This can be done either through a high fixed salary or through variable pay – a bonus – on top of a fixed salary. A *bonus* is a variable financial incentive which is tied to business performance, in particular profit: the higher the profit, the higher the bonus. This helps to explain the high levels of remuneration of top managers and executives at ever-diverging rates from shop floor earnings. Third, the owners may pay part of the managerial reward in the same units in which they themselves gain from the firm, namely in shares or stock options. *Shares* (or stocks) are partial ownership claims in a publicly listed firm, and *stock options* are future claims on shares, at a pre-set time, for example 2 or 5 years. This type of executive incentive realigns managerial interests very closely with shareholder interests, because the higher the firm's profits, the higher the dividend paid on stocks and the higher the share value of the firm on the stock exchange. This benefits both the owners of capital and the managers in exactly the same way.

The solutions to the principal–agent problem, however, generate another problem. This is the dominance of the interests of shareholders over the interests of all other stakeholders in the firm. When shareholders have managed to align the interests of the firm's executives and top managers with their own interests, who will take care of the interests of workers, consumers, creditors, and society? To state it crudely, for a shareholder, a share in a firm is just a means to reap return on investment (ROI), and if selling it and buying a share in a different firm will earn a higher ROI, a shareholder will often do this as soon as the shares of other firms look more promising. So, if a firm is concerned about the principal–agent problem and solves it by aligning managers' interests with shareholder interests, its focus becomes more and more short-term profit oriented.

4.5.2 Human resources management

The neoclassical perspective on workers' agency assumes that workers want to have maximum benefits at minimum effort. This view has resulted in labour management approaches of control and incentives, trying to bridge the supposed gap for employers between the expected worker effort on the one hand and the actual worker effort provided on the other hand. As a consequence, human resource management uses two systems of worker motivation: the stick and the carrot.

4.5.2.1 The stick: labour control

A system of control treats workers simply as inputs into a production process. Workers are reduced to their labour power and a system of control is geared towards maximum extraction of labour effort. In other words, a control system of work motivation consists of negative incentives ('sticks') to prevent low work effort. If workers do not perform up to a standard, their pay will be reduced or they will be fired. The more complex the task, the more difficult

104 *Firms*

to control workers. Moreover, the superior needs to be controlled in turn as well by managers higher up the system, and on and on. This can easily lead to a costly control system and a negative work atmosphere, of distrust and shirking.

4.5.2.2 The carrot: incentives

This system of worker motivation relies on monetary incentives through variable pay: not 'sticks' but 'carrots'. Variable pay may be a bonus at the end of the year, or a variable part of one's monthly earnings linked to a monthly measured performance indicator, or a piece rate through which more work effort immediately pays out in higher wages. The incentive system assumes, similarly to the control system, that workers have little work motivation of their own. It assumes that workers prefer not to work but have to in order to earn a livelihood. But rather than punishing low work effort, this system rewards high work effort. The incentive system therefore provides *extrinsic motivation* to workers: payment that is tied closely to performance.

But extrinsic motivation can undermine intrinsic motivation: when a worker feels only appreciated for certain outcomes of her work effort, but not for others that she herself and her co-workers value, she may feel treated like a money maker for her employer. This does not motivate in the long run and is likely to induce her to look for a job elsewhere that is more meaningful. It is precisely the reason why some ex-bankers sought new employment during the financial crisis in very different sectors, even with much lower pay: in education, health care, the arts, and charities. Another problem with the financial incentive system of worker motivation is that it tempts workers to play the system. This leads to perverse effects: benefits for the agent at cost of the principal (the firm or its owners).

4.6 Post Keynesian theory of the firm

4.6.1 Inputs and costs in the long term

Post Keynesians focus on the long run in their analysis of firm inputs and costs. The theory is concerned with dynamics. In the long run, fixed costs can change. This means that the most relevant type of cost for understanding the long-term cost structure is average costs. Remember from section 4.3 that average cost is the total cost per unit of output. The long-term cost strategy is then for firms to grow to the size where their average costs are relatively low, because that is where they can be competitive, at least, in terms of cost price. The long-term cost strategy also involves substitution of production factors. That is not possible in the short run, but in the long run, a firm can substitute labour for machines, or mechanical production for computerised production. Or it may decide to relocate to a different country where the cost of the major input is cheapest.

What matters for firm's cost and profit in the long run are the constraints on growth. In the Post Keynesian theory of the firm, the growth of a business has two types of constraints. First, finance constraints. Michael Kalecki's *principle of increasing risk* states that firms can and often want to borrow only limited amounts at a time. The more a firm borrows and the greater the amounts, the higher the risks, both actual and as perceived by investors. The principle of increasing risk attached to increased borrowing implies that increased finance can spur profits and growth, but not above a certain ratio, which is an expression of the *finance frontier*:

$r = g(1 - x)/sc$

where r = rate of profit, g = growth rate of the firm, x = external funding, and hence (1 − x) = internal funding, and sc = ratio of retained earnings to gross profit (total profit before taxes).

Let's take an example. Let us assume that Unilever, which has factories in east China, wants to expand to north and west China. It therefore needs to grow but also wants to generate a steady profit rate for its shareholders worldwide. What is its finance frontier? If it aims at a profit rate of 12 per cent, which is in line with its common annual profit margins, r = 12. And if shareholders expect to receive a total dividend of 60 per cent of the firm's gross profits, the remaining 40 per cent of gross profits is available for retained earnings: sc = 40. If the growth, g, that the multinational company plans in China is 20 per cent, then it means that the internal funding that it requires for this ambition is 1 − x and can be calculated from the finance frontier formula:

$r = g(1-x)/sc$

$12 = 20(1-x)/40$

$12 = \frac{20}{40}(1-x)$

$12 = \frac{1}{2}(1-x)$

$(1-x) = 24$

So, the internal funding necessary for the growth ambition and shareholder expectations is 24 per cent of total necessary funding. This means that external funding needs to be 76 per cent, as indicated by its finance frontier.

However, if the profits for this year are lower, say not 12 per cent but 6 per cent, the shareholders want a greater share of it, not 60 per cent but 80 per cent. This means that retained earnings will fall from 40 per cent in the example above to only 20 per cent in the case of lower profits. If we now fill in the formula of the finance frontier, we find that the new profit rate leads to r = 6 per cent and that the greater share of profits going to the shareholders leads to sc = 20 per cent. This leads to the following result:

$r = g(1 − x)/sc$

$6 = g(1 − x)/20$

$6 = (g \times 24)/20$

$6 = g \times 1.2$

$g = 5$

So, the growth rate that is possible with the lower profit rate, the shareholder expectations, and the available internal funding of 24 per cent is only 5 per cent. This means that the growth ambitions of 20 per cent by Unilever in the west and north of China cannot be realised in our example when profits are lower than the 12 per cent expected by the shareholders.

The second type of growth constraint that firms face according to the Post Keynesian theory of the firm concern *transaction costs* for coordination, in this case the management costs for oversight, and the risks involved when accessing foreign markets. For example, many Western and Japanese multinational firms who have entered China have incurred years of losses in their Chinese subsidiaries before they have finally become profitable. The Post Keynesian perspective summarises the costs for firm growth in the expansion frontier of a firm. The expansion frontier is the maximum profit that a firm can make for each possible growth rate. This is shown in Diagram 4.3. The diagram shows r, the rate of profit, on the vertical axis, and g, growth, on the horizontal axis. For completeness, the diagram also shows the finance frontier as explained above, which is a straight upward sloping line. The expansion frontier increases steeply, allowing a firm to grow fast to some point. But from that maximum onwards, the constraints start kicking in and growth becomes more difficult and costly. The maximum point R is where profit is maximised. From R to the right, the positive relationship between growth and profit turns into a negative relationship, also referred to as the *Penrose effect*, named after Edith Penrose, one of the first business economists, who described this effect in 1959. So after point R, more growth will not result in more profits.

Point G shows the point where growth is maximised: growth that is still possible given the firm's finance frontier. Different firms will choose different points: some firms will prefer point R, profit maximisation, which is a short-term strategy. Other firms will prefer point G, growth maximisation, which is a long-term strategy, and often involves an aggressive merger and take-over strategy. Most firms will choose a point between R and G, while firms that are less concerned with growth, profit, and market power will choose a point that is a bit left of R: a low-risk growth strategy. But point R and to the left of it is not without risk either: a well-performing firm growing slowly may become the target of a take-over by a firm with high growth ambitions . . . .

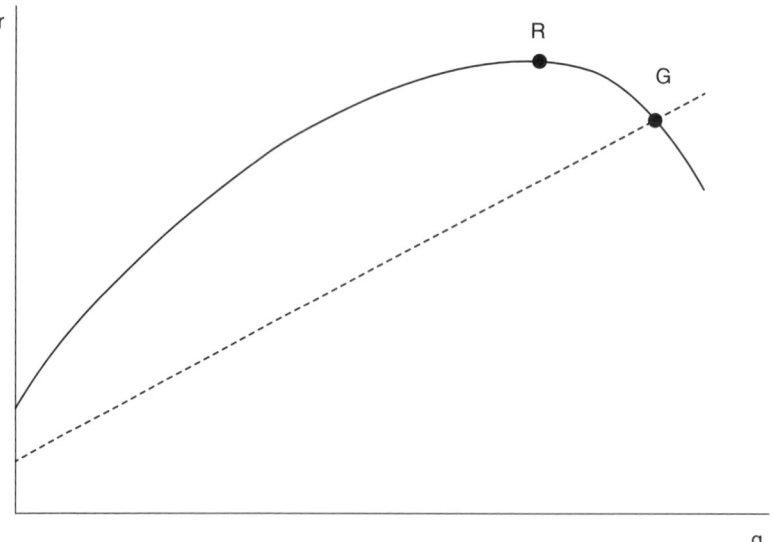

Diagram 4.3 Expansion frontier and finance frontier

Source: Lavoie, M. (2009) *Foundations of Post-Keynesian Economic Analysis*. Cheltenham: Edward Elgar, Figure 3.2.

4.6.2 Post Keynesian perspective of profit

In the Post Keynesian perspective, the price at which products are sold is not entirely determined by the market. That is because in the Post Keynesian perspective, most markets are not perfectly competitive but involve market power. And in the case of market power, firms have an influence over the price level, they have created room to set the price as they wish, generally a bit higher than the market price, to reap extra profit. We refer to this price-setting as *mark-up pricing*. This is the cost price plus a profit mark-up.

The mark-up is symbolised by k' (with ' pronounced as 'prime'). Why again symbol k? Because the mark-up is additional profit for the capitalists, not additional wages, so it is a source of excess profit. The mark-up is a percentage, which may range from only a few per cent, to more than double the production cost, depending on the competitiveness of the market in which a firm operates. This leads to the following price equation for the product price per unit (p), if we, for simplicity, only include wage costs (w) per unit of output (y):

$$p = k'(w/y)$$

In other words, the price equals the mark-up multiplied by the unit wage costs.

Let us now move to profits. The value of output, Y, is distributed over profit (R) and wages (W). So:

$$Y = R + W$$

We can rearrange the equation to define profits as the difference between output and wages, showing that the providers of capital are the *residual claimants* of a firm: they receive the total revenues after the wages have been paid:

$$R = Y - W$$

This gives us a variation of the earlier profit rate equation:

$$r = R/K = (Y - W)/K$$

The lower the wages paid to labour, the higher the profit for the capitalists. But who determines the adequate or fair labour share?

Remember that in a capitalist economy, capital hires labour and not the other way around. And because many labour markets are characterised by some rate of unemployment, capital is on the 'long side' of the market, with more bargaining power than labour to determine the wage rate. Labour is on the 'short side' of the market, with limited bargaining power. Thus, in a capitalist market economy, it is the capitalist firm's capital owners who determine the total wage sum, and hence, the amount of revenue left over as profit (normal profit and possibly more) for the capital owners. In the Post Keynesian and Marxist perspectives, profit is therefore labelled as *capitalist profit*, referring to the extraction of surplus profit from labour by capital.

When a capitalist economy is booming, and finds itself on an upturn in the economic cycle, shareholders expect profit rates of 15 per cent or even 20 per cent. In order to satisfy these expectations, firms must either further lower labour costs or increase the sales price for

108 Firms

consumers. Increasing prices will be the easier option. Reducing wages is difficult during a boom with an increased demand for labour. Hence, the profit earned by capital depends on the power relations and the general state of the economy in the Post Keynesian perspective. Profits cannot be calculated from the cost structure and market price.

4.7 Neoclassical theory of the firm

4.7.1 Inputs and costs in the short term

In neoclassical economics we can simplify the input–output process with a *production function*. This shows the relationship of inputs to outputs over a period of time. In the short run, fixed inputs create a capacity constraint on production expansion. Given this capacity limitation, how can the firm know which level of production (number of outputs) is most efficient for operating the business? Well, we first need to make an important assumption, namely, that whatever level of output is being produced in the short run, there is sufficient demand for the firm's output so that all its products will be sold. Obviously, in the real world, this assumption often does not hold.

Assume that your friend Roberto lives in Naples. He has a small pizzeria in an old narrow street, which he has rented for a year. He has no employees on a fixed contract. Hence, his only fixed input is the rent. His variable costs are pizza ingredients and the flexible labour of cooks and waiters (he is hiring students, on a daily basis, depending on the number of table reservations made and the season). Table 4.3 shows labour inputs, pizza outputs, and marginal returns for the short run, which in this example is an evening.

Table 4.3 shows that with more labour input (column 1), more output (column 2) is produced. The last column (3) shows that the marginal returns of the extra labour first increase (from 10 for one worker up to 18 for four workers), but then begin to decline: the fifth worker adds only 13 more pizzas to the output, whereas the fourth worker added 18. So, adding a fifth worker makes the marginal returns decline. Adding more workers further reduces the marginal returns to only five additional pizzas produced by adding a sixth worker. And worse, if Roberto hires student number 7, the marginal returns become negative: with seven workers, the restaurant personnel produce three pizzas less than they do with six workers. In column (2), you see that six workers produce 78 pizzas, whereas seven workers produce 75 pizzas. The reason for the negative marginal returns is not that student number 7 is lazy. But with

Table 4.3 Variable cost of pizza production per evening

(1) Input: labour (number of students)	(2) Output: pizzas	(3) Marginal return to labour input (pizzas)
0	0	–
1	10	10
2	24	14
3	42	18
4	60	18
5	73	13
6	78	5
7	75	−3

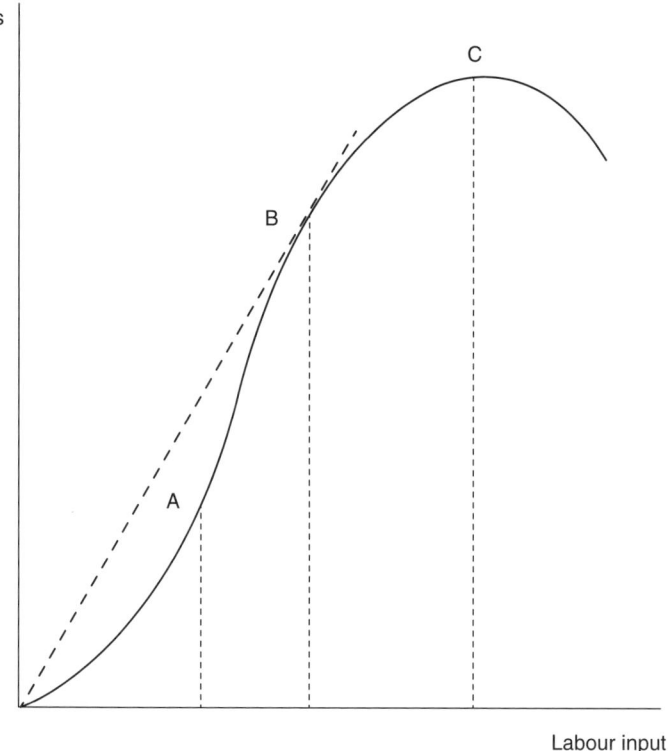

Diagram 4.4 Production function of pizzas

seven workers in a small restaurant, they all cannot move properly and further division of labour is impossible in the small space.

Diagram 4.4 shows the production function of pizzas for the variable input of labour. The shape of the production function is not a straight line or a smooth curve. Just like the marginal returns in column (3) of Table 4.3, they first move up quickly, then slowly, and then down. The shape of the production function shows what your friend Roberto already knew from experience on very busy evenings: endlessly increasing variable inputs will not necessarily result in endlessly increasing numbers of pizzas produced and sold. In the short run, we always run into capacity problems.

The shape of the production function shows the following changes from left to right:

- at a low level of production, an increase in inputs leads to a steep increase in outputs up to point A;
- from that point, the relationship becomes straight: more input leading to the same number of more output up to point B;
- from the second turning point, the production function levels off until more input does not result anymore in more output;
- after point C, adding more labour does not result in more pizzas produced, but actually in less pizzas.

Table 4.4 Total cost of pizza production per evening

(1) Input: labour (number of students)	(2) Output: pizzas	(3) Fixed cost (Euro)	(4) Variable labour cost (euro) = 25 euro × column (1)	(5) Total cost (euro) = column (3) + column (4)
0	0	20	0	20
1	10	20	25	45
2	24	20	50	70
3	40	20	75	95
4	60	20	100	120
5	73	20	125	145
6	78	20	150	170
7	75	20	175	195

In other words, the line can be broken up into four parts. The shape of the production function represents changes in marginal returns. Each part of the curve shows different marginal returns. They are referred to as:

- increasing returns: additional inputs lead to higher increases in outputs;
- constant returns: additional inputs lead to equivalent increases in outputs;
- diminishing returns: additional inputs lead to decreasing additions of outputs;
- negative returns: additional inputs lead to decreases in outputs.

Now let us add the cost dimension to the input structure: what are the costs of production in money terms? First, we need to add fixed costs to obtain total costs. Roberto's restaurant's fixed cost is the monthly rent. The amount is €600 per month. This is approximately €20 per evening, because the restaurant is open every day of the week. So, now we can add a column for fixed costs to Table 4.3, which is shown in Table 4.4. Let us again take only the labour input as variable input, and ignore the material inputs for the pizzas, for the sake of simplicity. The cost of labour is €25 per student per evening.

Roberto asks you for advice on how to maximise his earnings and minimise costs. The next table, Table 4.5 gives the marginal cost values for each additional unit of labour input.

Table 4.5 Marginal cost of pizza production

(1) Input: labour (number of students)	(2) Output: pizzas	(3) Fixed cost: rent (Euro)	(4) Variable labour cost (euro) = 25 euro × column (1)	(5) Total cost = column (3) + (4)	(6) Marginal cost = change column (5) / change column (2)
0	0	20	0	20	–
1	10	20	25	45	2.5
2	24	20	50	70	1.79
3	40	20	75	95	1.56
4	60	20	100	120	1.25
5	73	20	125	145	1.92
6	78	20	150	170	5.00
7	75	20	175	195	−8.33

Column (5) in the table teaches us what Roberto probably felt with his entrepreneurial instincts, but did not know exactly. It shows which number of workers creates how much extra cost per pizza. The results in the last column show that adding workers reduces marginal cost per pizza up to four workers (€1.25 per pizza). But more than four workers make the marginal costs per pizza go up. For five workers, the marginal costs become €1.92, and for six workers the marginal costs shoot up to €5.00 per pizza. The seventh worker is actually not adding value to Roberto's restaurant: the marginal costs are huge: €8.33 per pizza, and the big crew produces even less pizzas than the smaller crew of six (see column (2)). That is what the minus sign means: an absolute decline in production with additional workers added.

Now, assume that Roberto's firm operates in a perfectly competitive market: there is strong cost competition and no market power. In that case, the optimal level of production is when average cost is at its lowest point. See Table 4.6 for the calculation of average cost for the variable costs of labour.

The table shows that when five workers are hired, the average costs per pizza are minimised: €1.99 per pizza. For six workers, average costs are higher, namely €2.18 per pizza. This means, that the optimal production size, in terms of cost minimisation for Roberto's restaurant and all standard pizza restaurants in the centre of Naples, is five workers. But, of course, this would only be sensible advice for your friend if you could be pretty sure that he could sell 73 pizzas every evening (see column (2)).

4.7.2 Neoclassical perspective of profit

In neoclassical economics, the price of a product is determined by perfectly competitive market forces and cannot be influenced by any individual firm. And it assumes that markets are in equilibrium, without excess supply or demand: there is no long side and short side in the market. With these assumptions, it becomes possible to calculate the production level at which profits are maximised.

Going back to your friend's pizza restaurant in Naples, we should now add the revenues from the pizza sales to the table. The sales price of an average pizza is €6, because all other restaurants in the neighbourhood of similar quality charge the same price. If Roberto asked for more, he would lose customers. The sales price and quantity sold gives total revenue: $P \times Q = €6 \times$ number of pizzas sold.

Table 4.6 Average costs of pizza production

(1) Input: labour (number of students)	(2) Output: pizzas	(3) Fixed cost: rent (Euro)	(4) Variable labour cost (euro) = 25 euro × column (1)	(5) Total cost = column (3) + (4)	(6) Average cost = column (5) / column (2)
0	0	20	0	20	–
1	10	20	25	45	4.5
2	24	20	50	70	2.92
3	40	20	75	95	2.38
4	60	20	100	120	2.00
5	73	20	125	145	1.99
6	78	20	150	170	2.18
7	75	20	175	195	2.60

Table 4.7 Revenues and profits of pizza production per evening

(1) Input: labour (number of students)	(2) Output: pizzas	(3) Fixed cost: rent (Euro)	(4) Variable labour cost (euro) = 25 euro × column (1)	(5) Total cost = column (3) + (4)	(6) Total revenue (euro) = 6 euro × column (2)	(7) Profit (euro) = column (6) − column (5)
0	0	20	0	20	0	−20
1	10	20	25	45	60	15
2	24	20	50	70	144	74
3	40	20	75	95	240	145
4	60	20	100	120	360	240
5	73	20	125	145	438	293
6	78	20	150	170	468	298
7	75	20	175	195	450	255

Table 4.7 allows us to calculate profit (column 7): R = Y − TC. This is column (6) minus column (5). The result shows that with no workers producing pizzas, the profit is negative: −20. This is because the fixed costs keep running. For hiring one worker, who produces ten pizzas, the revenue is positive: €15. With six workers, profits are highest: €298 per evening. But with seven workers, this reduces to €255. So, is the profit maximisation point at six workers?

This can only be determined more precisely when we look at the marginal level. We need to compare *marginal revenues* (extra revenues with an extra worker) with *marginal costs* (extra costs with an extra worker). Because we need to know at which production level extra inputs no longer add to profit. This is when MC = MR: marginal costs equals marginal revenues.

Average revenue is revenue per unit (Yav). This is the same as the price per unit (P):

$$Yav = Y / Q = P \times Q / Q = P$$

Marginal revenue (Ymar) is the change in total revenue from an additional unit of output:

$$Ymar = \frac{\text{change in } Y}{\text{change in } Q} = \frac{\Delta Y}{\Delta Q}$$

In a perfectly competitive market, firms cannot influence the price. When P is given, Yav is given (which is the same as P). But Ymar is also given, because Ymar is also the same as the market price: the increase in revenues for one more unit sold is the price of this extra unit sold. So, in a perfectly competitive market the following equation results:

$$Yav = Ymar = P$$

In the case of your friend's restaurant, this is €6, the price of a pizza and hence the marginal revenue of each additional pizza sold. Which is also the same as the average revenue for each

Table 4.8 Marginal cost and marginal revenue of pizza sales

(1) Input: labour (number of students)	(2) Output: pizzas	(3) Marginal output	(4) Fixed cost: rent (euro)	(5) Variable labour cost* (euro)	(6) Total cost**	(7) Total revenue▫ (euro)	(8) Marginal cost▫▫	(9) Marginal revenue•
0	0	–	20	0	20	0	–	–
1	10	10	20	25	45	60	2.50	6
2	24	14	20	50	70	144	1.79	6
3	40	16	20	75	95	240	1.56	6
4	60	20	20	100	120	360	1.25	6
5	73	13	20	125	145	438	1.92	6
6	78	5	20	150	170	468	5.00	6
7	75	–3	20	175	195	450	–8.33	6

Notes:
* Variable labour cost = 25 euro × column (1)
** Total cost = column (4) + (5)
▫ Total revenue = 6 euro × column (2)
▫▫ Marginal cost = change in column (6) for each additional number of output in column (2)
• Marginal revenue = change in column (7) for each additional number of output in column (2)

pizza sold. Table 4.8 now shows columns for marginal revenue and marginal cost. This allows us to calculate the production size at which profit maximisation occurs. We know already that marginal revenue is the same as the market price. This is €6 and can be seen in column (9).

But we can also calculate it from the data of total revenue and quantity of pizzas produced. For the change from no production to ten pizzas (with one worker), revenue increases from 0 to 60. The quantity of pizzas increases from 0 to 10. So, the marginal revenue for the smallest production size is Ymar = $\Delta Y/\Delta Q$ = 60/10 = 6. For every increase in production, with every added worker, the result is the same. See, for example, the increase from four to five workers: $\Delta Y/\Delta Q$ = (438 – 360)/(73 – 60) = 78/13 = 6.

The table shows, when we compare the last two columns (8) and (9), where profit maximisation can be found. It is at the production level of MC = MR. This level is around six workers (MC = 5 for six workers, which comes closest to 6 of all numbers in column 8). But since you cannot hire part of a worker, and part-time work does not make much sense for only an evening, the profit maximising number of workers lies at six. So, the MC = MR equation for profit maximisation in a competitive market informs us that Roberto should hire six workers if he wants to maximise profits. At that level of personnel, he produces 78 pizzas.

Let us hope for Roberto that he is indeed going to sell all these pizzas every evening ....

4.8 Interesting sources

Crowd funding platform Kickstarter: https://www.kickstarter.com/
Penrose, E. (2009) *The Theory of the Growth of the Firm*. Fourth Edition. Oxford: Oxford University Press.
Pink, D. (2009), *Drive - The Surprising Truth about What Motivates Us*. New York: Riverhead.

4.9 Glossary

Average cost   The total cost per unit of output

Average revenue   The revenue per unit

Balance sheet   Compares what a firm owns (assets) with what it owes (liabilities) in a year

Bonds   Fixed-interest assets for a fixed period of time

Bonus   A variable financial incentive, which is tied to business performance

Business profit   The residual of a business operation after all production factors and inputs have been paid

Capitalist profit   The surplus profit from labour by capital

Collateral   Assets which a borrower provides as a security to obtain a loan

Commercial profit   The positive difference from selling something for more than it costs to purchase it

Cooperative firm   A cooperation of equals who are both its collective owners and capital providers, and its members, as either clients or producers

Crowd funding   Community financing through the internet, in which many small investors together finance a firm or project

Dividend   A proportion of a firm's profit as a reward for owning shares

Economic profit   Profit above normal profit

Economies of scale   Cost advantages per unit due to an increased production size, because the fixed costs will be distributed over a larger number of units produced

Entrepreneurs   Risk-taking economic agents on the supply side of markets

Finance frontier   Limitation of increased finance up to a certain ratio

Fixed costs   The costs of a firm even without producing a single unit

Gross profit   Total profit before taxes

Islamic banking   Investment by banks in a firm, thereby becoming co-responsible for the efficient and effective use of the money

Large private enterprises   Are privately owned and have limited responsibility

Manager   An economic agent who is hired to lead an organisation

Marginal costs   The extra costs when producing one additional unit of output

Marginal revenue   Extra revenue with an extra worker

Multinational corporations (MNCs)   Firms which have branches, or subsidiaries, in several countries

Net profit The amount of profit after taxes

Normal profit The profit necessary to satisfy the providers of capital

Opportunity cost The value of the alternative forgone

Penrose effect The positive relationship between growth and profit turns into a negative relationship beyond the point of profit maximisation

Principal–agent problem The potential gap between the interests of the principals (owners) who delegate tasks to agents, and the interests of the agents (managers)

Principle of increasing risk Firms only can and often want to borrow limited amounts at a time, otherwise their financing costs increase

Private equity fund A firm which earns money through short-term investment in other firms. After some time they hope to sell their shares at a higher value to make a profit

Production function The relationship of inputs to outputs over a period of time

Profit and loss account The result of the business operation in a year

Profit rate The amount of profit divided by the value of capital goods owned

Publicly listed firms Owned by shareholders who have partial ownership through shares which are traded on a stock exchange

Return on investment (ROI) Percentage earnings on the investment of capital

Self-employed entrepreneurs Have no personnel, operate with low capital and high labour time, and are sometimes outside the formally regulated and counted economy

Shares = stocks Partial ownership claims of a publicly listed firm

SME (small- and medium-sized enterprise) Firm with only one worker (self-employed) up to hundred or more

Stakeholders All parties that are affected by the operation of a firm: suppliers, customers, workers, providers of capital, the government, society, and the natural environment

Stock exchange The market for shares of stock of firms

Stock options Future claims on shares, at a pre-set time, for example 2 or 5 years

Subsidiaries Branches of a multinational firm in various countries

Sunk costs The costs that have been incurred in the past and which therefore should not be taken into account in a cost/benefit decision about the future

Total costs The sum total of fixed costs and variable costs

Transaction costs Costs involved in an exchange, not reflected in the price of the good exchanged

Residual claimant The person receiving the remaining profits after all other production factors have been paid

Variable costs Costs, which increase with the number of units produced

Workers' agency Making autonomous choices and acting upon these at work, individually or collectively

Note

1 For information about the firm Atlassian, see: https://www.atlassian.com/. The case of Atlassian is also mentioned in the book *Drive* by Daniel Pink.

5 Markets

5.1 The market

5.1.1 Plaza of exchange

The market is the best-known economic institution. It is used as a location of exchange, as a *plaza*, as well as for the act of exchange, for trading or *quid pro quo* in Latin. In the past, markets were located in physical spaces of exchange: town squares, oases in the desert, quays in ports, trading route crossing places, and warehouses. Today, markets exist increasingly without a physical location, through the internet. Think about eBay, electronic financial trading, payments though apps, and online shops.

The *market* can be defined as the interaction of the supply and demand of goods and services through exchange. But it is only one of three economic domains and stands in close relationship with the state and communities. It is the focus of analysis in economics because it is the only one of the three economic domains whose function is exclusively economic. States and communities have other roles in society, but markets do not have roles other than their economic role.

Exchange may be through barter trade or through money. *Barter* is exchange of a good for another good, while *monetary exchange* is exchange of a good for money. And only when there are more parties than one supplier and one buyer, does competition come in. So, markets only begin to perform their full role in an economy when exchange occurs amidst multiple suppliers and buyers, so that competition arises for the best deals. And such fully developed markets are the ideal types analysed in neoclassical economics. Then, it almost is as if markets are neutral mechanisms bringing supply and demand together, leading automatically to a price level and amount of goods exchanged against that price.

5.1.2 Morality and efficiency of markets

Markets are not morally neutral. There are many laws against certain market exchanges. Think about slavery. Or bribery. Or paying someone to sit your economics exam for you (even a voluntary gift from your sister to do this for you will not be allowed). There are also goods and services that have been traded on markets for a long time even when social norms reject this. Think about prostitution and child labour. They are often morally condemned but nevertheless there is demand and supply on markets for sexual services and the labour of even young children.

New markets emerge in response to new coordination problems, even when many people think that a particular market solution is immoral. For example, rich patients are being given increasing opportunities, for extra payment, to reduce their waiting times to see a doctor. This makes the waiting time for the poor even longer, because the rich buy themselves places at the top of the waiting list or in the front row in the hospital. Moreover, some wealthy health market customers even buy themselves out of waiting completely by hiring a 'row-sitter', whom they pay a small amount and replace when it is their turn. Or they pay a high fixed monthly fee to their doctor who has only few patients and is available almost instantly when needed. But in countries where there is a limited supply of doctors, this creates even longer waiting lists for middle-class and poor patients who cannot afford to pay such high fees for an almost private doctor. This example shows that a market solution is in the interest of those who have the necessary purchasing power, but can be a disadvantage for the majority of clients. We call this a zero-sum game: one wins, another one loses. This goes against the basic logic of a free market, where both parties have a net gain from an exchange.

Should such new market solutions be prohibited? Or should rich clients have the right to get better health care access when they are willing to pay for it? And is it really efficient? When relatively healthy patients reduce the access of the least healthy, the health statistics are not likely to improve. Life expectancy will increase faster when diseases from which the poor suffer most (malaria, diarrhoea, tuberculosis) can be cured and prevented, because these contribute more to high mortality rates than diseases from which the rich suffer: the rich die on average at a later age. Hence, from an economy-wide perspective, new markets to reduce the opportunity costs of the rich in obtaining health care are not efficient.

5.2 Three critical theories about markets

5.2.1 Social economics and markets: embeddedness

Social economic theory recognises the market as embedded in society, as shaped by social norms and reflecting social structures. Without rights and fairness, markets cannot function very well. They would soon be captured by those who abuse their power to enforce very uneven gains from trade. This, in turn, would discourage others to engage in market transactions, so that markets would be controlled by other systems such as feudalism, colonialism, slavery, and autarky.

The ideal market is based on free exchange. And free exchange is not ethically neutral: freedom is an ethical value and not a natural given. Moreover, as we have seen, markets are never completely free: they involve formal and informal institutions, regulation, and social norms, even if they seem to be free. So, markets have a degree of freedom, which may be limited or wide. And freedom is an ethical value. So, how then have markets ethical substance? This happens in three ways: through a feasible no-trade option, discrimination and regulation, and the endogeneity of demand and supply.

5.2.1.1 Feasible no-trade option

First, free exchange requires freedom to exchange: each party on a market, on the supply side and on the demand side, needs to be free to decide whether they want to engage in trade or not. They should not be forced into an exchange. This means that they should have a feasible no-trade option. A *feasible no-trade option* is that without engaging in an exchange, each party is still able to survive, to have access to a livelihood. So, for example, a poor Tuareg nomad without savings who is denied access to land for his cattle to graze due to privatisation has no freedom to exchange. In order to feed himself and his family, this pastoralist nomad wandering with his cattle in the Sahara desert will have no other option than to sell his cattle in order to earn some cash to buy food. This is a desperate sale: it brings a gain in the short run but a severe loss in the long run, because he exchanges his stock of capital, the basis for his livelihood. In the long run, the exchange deprives him of his dignity, his freedom, and his livelihood as a pastoralist. He will soon end up with nothing to exchange anymore. So, free exchange requires a feasible no-trade option in order to be genuinely free, not only in the short run, but also in the long run.

5.2.1.2 Discrimination and regulation

Second, free exchange implies that exchange is not constrained by limitations set on quantities, price, and non-relevant characteristics of the goods to be exchanged (discrimination). However, real-world markets often do have such constraints. These fall into two categories: discrimination and regulation. Discrimination often originates from norms in communities, sometimes reinforced by state regulation or lack of enforcement of regulation. Real-world markets are never completely free from regulation and constraining norms. Regulation is the responsibility of the state and implies limitations on prices (maximum or minimum prices or a range), or on quantities (quota to be traded), or conditions on minimum quality (for example of food and medicine). In neoclassical economics, which emphasises these types of limitations to free exchange, they are referred to as market distortions.

5.2.1.3 Endogeneity of demand and supply

Demand and supply are not neutral givens themselves. They are created, manipulated, and psychologically biased. So, both demand and supply are not exogenous but *endogenous*. This means that demand and supply are influenced in the market process itself and not outside it (exogenous). Moreover, supply and demand are not independent of each other. Supply generates demand, through advertisements, group pressure, and status goods. Whereas demand generates supply, through showing niches to entrepreneurs and stimulating innovation to address needs and wants. When demand and supply influence each other, the market mechanism is not neutral. There is no invisible hand generating the quantity transacted and the price at which this happens.

5.2.2 Institutional economics of markets

Markets were defined as processes of exchange embedded in particular formal and informal institutions. In this section, I will discuss these market institutions further. The formal institutions of markets are various types of regulation. The informal market institutions are social norms of many kinds (pro-social and anti-social). Table 5.1 shows the types of market institutions that are most influential.

Table 5.1 Market institutions

	Enabling institutions	*Disabling institutions*
Formal institutions	Property rights; equal opportunity laws	Distortions
Informal institutions	Pro-social norms	Discrimination

120   Markets

5.2.2.1 Enabling formal market institutions

Enabling formal market institutions are rights and laws, which concern property rights and equal opportunities in markets. They require an effective judicial system and fairness in socio-economic laws. For example, market parties should be able to go to court in case of disputes over contracts. And labour laws and social laws should provide basic social protection to workers and their families with a feasible no-trade option.

5.2.2.2 Disabling formal market institutions

Disabling formal market institutions are referred to as *distortions*. These are regulations which do not support markets but rather constrain them. Necessary distortions of markets are numerous. They not only serve to protect nature and society from negative externalities of markets, through environmental regulation and pension premiums to be paid by employers for their employees, for example. They also serve to protect markets against their own potentially negative effects, in particular instability. That is why financial markets must be regulated by Central Banks and market authorities. Markets are powerful drivers of well-being, but at the same time potentially destructive, as the latest financial crisis has shown. Unnecessary distortions are, unfortunately, also ubiquitous. They often hide group interests, depending on which side of the market has more power. They are all asymmetric institutions because they benefit one group over another. And they are often institutionalised in formal rules.

5.2.2.3 Enabling informal market institutions

Enabling informal market institutions consist of pro-social norms. In particular the pro-social norms which support exchange: trust and cooperation. Without such pro-social norms, markets will not function very well, as Adam Smith noted in his book *The Theory of Moral Sentiments*. Every culture has its own informal market institutions. For example, in the Sahara, before you engage in bargaining over a price, both parties first need to enquire extensively about each other's well-being, the health of family members, and other personal matters. Simply starting an exchange and mentioning a price will be regarded as rude. This will damage the exchange: you will not make the best bargain or the exchange will not even happen.

5.2.2.4 Disabling informal market institutions

Disabling informal market institutions come down to various forms of discrimination. Just like unnecessary distortions, they are asymmetric institutions: they benefit one group over another in the market process. Discrimination occurs on the basis of discriminating social norms, in particular on the demand side of markets. Discrimination, hence, reflects anti-social norms, because they marginalise, exclude, or exploit one group in the market as compared to other groups. In this way, markets tend to reinforce existing social inequalities. So when a society has anti-social norms about certain groups, it is very likely that these disadvantaged groups (migrants, ethnic minorities, women) will face discrimination in labour markets, credit markets, and other markets.

5.2.3 Post Keynesian economics of the market: traverse and equilibrium

A *static market* is a market situation in the short run, in which the determinants of demand and supply do not change. This means that there is a fixed supply function and a fixed demand

Markets 121

function, with an intersection, which is referred to as *equilibrium*. This is the intersection between supply and demand at which a particular quantity is transacted at a particular price. For example, on the tomato market in Ouagadougou, the capital of the sub-Saharan country of Burkina Faso, 50,000 kg of tomatoes are traded at a market price of 1,000 West African francs, or CFA, per kilogram. This is approximately US$2 per kilogram. The market price of 1,000 CFA is the exchange value of tomatoes on markets in Ouagadougou on a particular day in 2013 given the quantity traded.

With lower supply or higher demand, the market price would probably have been higher. Next year, or even the next day, the market equilibrium may be different. For example, tomatoes may sell at a lower quantity at a higher price. This is because the determinants of supply may change due to the season: production costs go up when farmers need to provide extra water, through irrigation or manually, of their tomato plants. This will shift their supply function to the right: they want to earn more from selling the same quantity as before, in order to cover their costs. The new equilibrium may be only 40,000 kg sold at the higher price of 1,200 CFA per kg. As a consequence, Burkinabe consumers with the lowest purchasing power now have no tomatoes because they can no longer afford them. They will probably find a substitute, either a different vegetable that is cheaper, or tomatoes from their own vegetable garden. Or they simply postpone buying tomatoes until supply increases and prices come down again.

In this example, we assumed that every day or month, the tomato market in Ouagadougou starts anew and achieves a new equilibrium. But this is, of course, not how it really works for the farmers and consumers in Burkina Faso's capital. They experience the market not as a series of short-term periods but as a continuum. This is precisely what Keynes meant with his notion of *traverse*: markets are not jumping from one equilibrium to another but are continuously on the move. An equilibrium period never lasts long because there are continuously changing conditions. Therefore markets are most of the time in traverse: on the move. Markets experience changes along the demand and supply functions, depending on the choices of consumers at every point in time, and on the supply choices of producers and traders. In addition, market conditions change continually. Demand factors change and supply factors change as well. From the Post Keynesian perspective, they change because of *endogenous* factors. That is, factors inherent in the economic process, such as insecurity, routines, advertisements, the general economic climate, consumer confidence, investment opportunities, etc.

From the neoclassical perspective, demand and supply determinants do not change continually, they are regarded as *exogenous*. This means a change due to an outside shock to a market. This may be a natural shock (rain, drought, disaster), a financial shock (banking crisis), a policy-induced shock (currency devaluation), or a societal shock (political change, legal changes, trade unions striking). This is an important difference between economic theories of market dynamics.

5.3 Market types

5.3.1 Monopoly

A *monopoly market* has only one seller. This firm sells to all buyers. Moreover, the buyers have no alternative, because the good offered has no close substitute. A substitute can only be obtained at some cost and difficulty, for example, because there is only one supplier in the area, a local monopoly. Think about power plants, which often supply a whole region with energy. The neighbouring power plant may not necessarily be owned by the same firm, but when it supplies a different region, energy consumers of each region have no choice but to buy the energy supplied by their own regional power supplier.

Also, a monopoly has barriers to entry in order to prevent new firms producing the same good. These may be technical or legal barriers, as discussed earlier in the case of oligopolistic markets. But monopolies also use strategies to deliberately create entry barriers. There are two types of such deliberately created entry barriers. First, monopolies may engage in *exclusionary practices*: putting pressure on suppliers not to sell the same input to other firms. This may be the case, for example, for some rare mineral resources necessary for the production of particular electronic devices. This practice would make it difficult or more costly for potential competitors to obtain the necessary input for competing with the product of the monopoly. Another strategy is *dumping*: temporarily selling products below cost price to price competitors out of the market. Of course, this requires the dumping firm to have sufficient financial reserves.

A monopoly market has no competition and often uses strategies to keep it that way. Without competition a market does not really seem to be a market. But there is exchange: between one seller and many buyers, which still makes a monopoly a market. The market price is the seller's price: a monopoly is a price maker, and decides the sales price, only limited by the purchasing power and preferences of customers. This leads to higher prices and profits and lower quantities sold as compared to most other market types. Partly this is because of the opportunity to reap extra profits. Partly it is due to inefficiencies, which can continue because there is no incentive, from a competitor's lower prices, to produce more cost-effectively.

There will always be monopolies because of technical and legal barriers to entry. Or a firm producing a variety of products may have a monopoly, or near-monopoly, in one product market but not in others. Such a firm is the US agricultural biotech firm Monsanto, which has developed and patented a genetically engineered herbicide-resistant soybean, of which it is the only producer in the world. The genetically manipulated soybean is immune to a weed killer which helps to increase food production. But the patented seeds are expensive and can only be bought from Monsanto. So, many farmers in Africa cannot afford to buy the seed. And due to the monopoly position, which the firm has acquired through long fights and law suits against its previous competitor DuPont, there is no alternative weed killer-resistant soybean available on the market. Hence, the Monsanto's monopoly of genetically modified soybeans resistant to weed killers can only contribute to food security in developing countries such as in Africa, at high cost. Most poor farmers cannot afford to buy Monsanto's seeds. If governments want to help, they need to provide subsidies to the farmers, at a cost to the taxpayer and other government expenditures, for example on health and education.

Other monopolies, which affect African consumers, positively or negatively, are based in Africa itself. For example in railways, airlines, and energy supply. Air Burkina has a monopoly on domestic flights in Burkina Faso, just like many other national airlines on the continent. The railway company Sitarail received a long-term concession for its exclusive operations in the country. And oil is supplied by a state owned monopoly in Burkina Faso, which imports refined oil. This allowed the government to smoothen price increases in 2007 and 2008 for Burkinabe consumers. In that case, the state monopoly created a price benefit for consumers, instead of a price disadvantage, because it was a state-owned monopoly with a social objective: to keep prices reasonable for consumers.

There are two types of solutions to make monopolies operate more efficiently and set consumer prices lower: privatisation and benchmarking.

5.3.1.1 Privatisation

The government could break up a public monopoly by privatising it. *Privatisation* is the sale of a public firm to market parties. Sometimes, this strategy is not deliberate but emerges out of technological change. This the case all over the world with the mobile phone revolution: the entry into the market of various mobile phone operators eventually broke up national and regional telecommunication monopolies in fixed line phone services in many countries.

Today, many monopolies have been privatised. However, if the privatised company remains a monopoly, consumers are often worse off because there is no democratic control over a private firm. Whereas in the case of a state-owned monopoly, the parliament has democratic control over the firm's behaviour and governance.

5.3.1.2 Benchmarking

One solution is to simulate a market in the case of a series of local monopolies through benchmarks. *Benchmarking* is an artificial competition policy with targets or rankings which governments use to force more efficiency from public organisations. The state can provide incentives for those local monopolies which achieve certain performance indicators for cost reduction, quality improvement, or client satisfaction, for example. An example of such an incentive policy is that the government will only allow a price increase or tax relief for a public firm if performance indicators meet a certain benchmark. This benchmark may involve a 10 per cent increase in client satisfaction for the national railways, for example, or research output within the top 10 per cent of best-performing universities of the world.

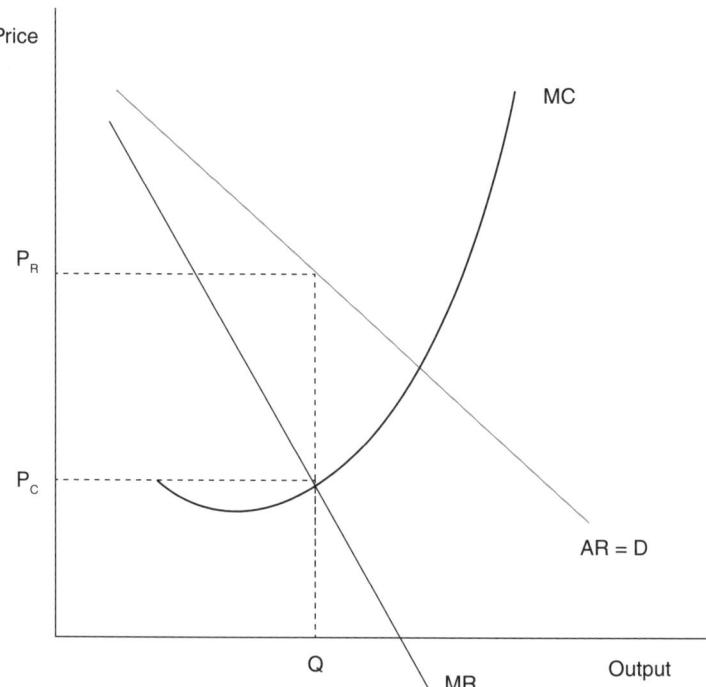

Diagram 5.1 Monopoly

Diagram 5.1 shows a picture of a monopoly market. The cost curve shown is the marginal cost curve (MC). The market power over the price is shown in the demand curve (D), which is average revenue (AR), and higher than the marginal revenue curve (MR). Hence, monopolist firms charge higher prices than necessary to pay all production factors: they earn surplus profit. If they had operated in a competitive market, they would have sold quantity Q at price P_C. But in a monopoly, firms can sell the same quantity at price P_R.

5.3.2 Oligopoly

Oligopolistic markets are not competitive markets and they dominate national economies and the world economy. Competition is small because *oligopolistic markets* are markets which are dominated by a few large sellers. They are the focus of analysis in Post Keynesian economics. Entry into an oligopolistic market is difficult for new suppliers, either because it is costly, or because it is technically demanding. *Entry barriers* are mechanisms which prevent newcomers entering a market. They can be technical or legal.

Technical entry barriers stem from high start-up costs due to large economies of scale or high fixed costs. For example, physical internet infrastructure in remote areas requires huge amounts of fibre-optic cables involving high investment cost. Or existing suppliers are so big that they reap maximum economies of scale, allowing for low product prices and high marketing budgets, against which a small newcomer cannot compete. Think about the world's major brands of deodorants, which are produced by only a few large firms, in particular Procter & Gamble and Unilever. No new firm can realistically compete in the deodorant market, unless it introduces a mould-breaking new type of deodorant for which consumers are willing to pay significantly more than for their regular brand.

Legal entry barriers to markets with a few large sellers are laws made to prevent competition with a state-owned enterprise. For example, it is generally prohibited for more than one firm to produce coins and banknotes for the Central Bank. Other forms of legal entry barriers, not related to state-owned firms, are copyrights and patents, which grant private firms the right to be the sole supplier of goods under a particular copyright or patent, at least for a period of time.

Oligopolistic markets have three to ten large firms. Some oligopolistic markets have only two sellers (think about Pepsi Coke and Coca Cola) and therefore are also called *duopolistic*. Products in oligopolistic markets may be either homogeneous or heterogeneous. The two coke firms claim substantial difference of taste between their soda drinks, but blind consumer tests often show no difference. So, coke seems to be heterogeneous and is claimed to be so, but for most consumers it is a homogeneous product.

As a consequence of characteristics of the oligopolistic market, oligopolistic firms have influence over their prices. But not completely, because their competitors are likely to react to price changes. This may even lead to price wars. For example between large supermarket chains which lower the prices of certain products in reaction to price reductions by competitors, a process which may go on for weeks until one gives up when profit margins become too small or negative. Indeed, price wars are a competitive strategy that oligopolistic firms use to price competitors out of the market and hence strengthen their market power. But for consumers a price war is beneficial, at least until it ends and price levels go back to where they were before the main competitor was driven into bankruptcy. Some oligopolistic markets have price leaders: if that firm increases or lowers its price, other firms will follow. A *price leader* is an established firm and often the largest in the market. Price leadership helps to stabilise

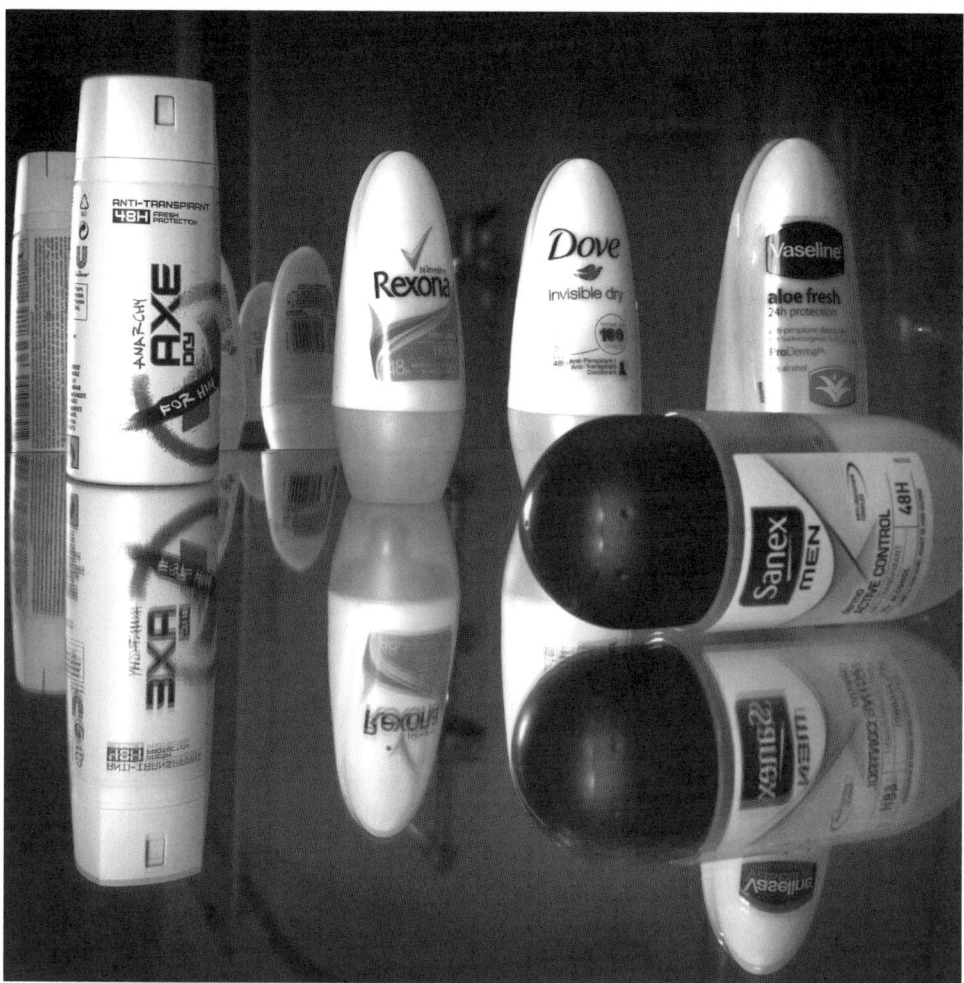

Image 5.1 Unilever deodorants

price levels in oligopolistic markets and prevent price wars. It is an informal institution which sometimes emerges in an oligopolistic market.

Oligopolistic firms not only compete through prices but also through product differentiation and advertisement. Oligopolistic firms spend a relatively large share of their production cost on marketing. Well-known sports brands, for example, all sell similar trainers and running shirts and baseball caps. But they spend up to half of total costs on TV commercials and advertisements in glossy magazines and sponsorship of major league sports clubs to strengthen the visibility of their own brand vis-à-vis competitor brands. This in itself is a competitive process: which brand has most air-time on TV and radio or the best-located billboards in town?

Diagram 5.2 shows an oligopolistic market. Compare it with the monopoly market shown in Diagram 5.1. You will note that it is a variation of it. Next to the marginal cost curve (MC),

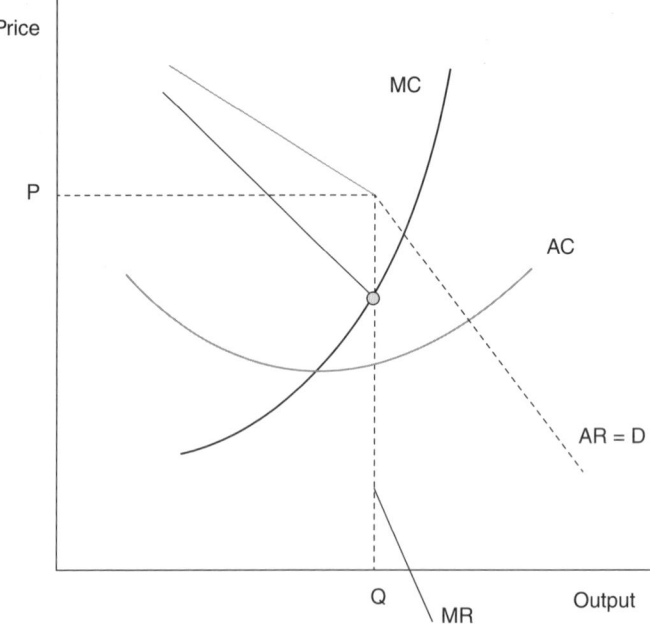

Diagram 5.2 Oligopoly

it includes the average cost curve (AC). The main characteristic of the oligopoly diagram is the kinked demand curve. The discontinuous space indicates the interdependency of firms in an oligopolistic market. When a firm increases its price, the others will not follow and hence customers will switch to a different brand. So, the upper part of the demand curve is very price elastic. But when a firm reduces its price, the other firms will follow. This makes demand less elastic.

Collusion is cooperation among competitors to set the market price. It is also known as price fixing. Collusion may be done through a secret formal agreement or only informally, simply by trusting that no firm will start to lower prices. But also the formal agreement has no other power than the trust that the firms' top management has in it. In most countries in the world, collusion is illegal. That is because it goes against the interests of consumers, keeping prices high and generating high profit margins not through fair competition but rather by excluding the competitive process of markets.

Cartels go further than collusion. A *cartel* is an organisation of large producers with the objective of eliminating price competition. Most countries prohibit cartels, but since there is no world government to enforce this, international cartels exist. The best-known cartel is OPEC, the Organization of Petroleum Exporting Countries, largely based in the Middle East. The first impact this cartel had was in the 1970s and 1980s when on two separate occasions all members supported a significant price increase at the cost of the consumer. Thereby, they also increased the input prices of almost all industries in oil importing countries across the world. The cartel created oil price shocks. In the following decade OPEC was less influential, partly because its members disagreed on their strategy, and partly because non-members became increasingly important oil or natural gas producers and exporters.

Image 5.2 Mobile phones for sale

A clear example of an oligopolistic market is mobile phone services. Every country has only a few suppliers in this market. And all products are quite similar: phoning, texting, and internet services. It is just the individual packages and prices that differ, and sometimes the quality of help-desk services in case of problems. There is probably no continent where the introduction of mobile phone technology has improved telecommunications and reduced prices as much as in Africa. In the fixed phone line era, up to the 1990s, most phone companies in Africa were monopolies and state-owned. They were renowned for bad service, high prices, and long waiting lists for a connection. In some African countries, it took several years before a consumer could get a phone connection to their home.

Today, a much larger share of the African population has a phone than in the era of fixed landlines: three quarters of Africans had mobile phone access around 2012. Africa is the largest growth market for mobile phone services and has more subscribers than Latin America. Even poor Africans own mobile phones, which is an important economic tool because it gives them access to the market prices of the crops they grow, weather forecasts to plan their agricultural activities, and access to networks of producers, suppliers, and buyers to coordinate their trading. Moreover, smart phone services are being adapted to Africa with cheap phones and tailor-made apps and web services in a wide variety of African languages. Financial services for money transfers and savings are a major popular service in Africa. An example is M-Pesa, which derives from the Swahili word for money. In Nigeria, a new low-cost phone from a South Korean producer now offers a dictionary in the Yoruba language and a movie app for watching the latest Nollywood films.

Every African country now has three to five mobile phone operators. This is a typical oligopolistic market with much advertising effort, regular price wars, and fast movement of product differentiation through the introduction of innovative phones and services. Overall in Africa, prices for mobile phone services decreased on average by 18 per cent between 2010 and 2011. So, in this market and at this time, oligopolistic competition favours consumers in terms of price decreases. Experts on the mobile phone market in Africa expect that the market will lead to more mergers and acquisitions of African mobile phone operators, because in this market only the largest companies are likely to survive the fierce competition.

In Burkina Faso, for example, 10 million of its 17 million inhabitants owned a mobile phone in 2012. The market penetration of fixed lines in this West African country is less than 1 per cent, but for mobile phones it is over 50 per cent (these are proportions of the potential market of private consumers and firms together). The Burkinese market is divided between three large firms: Telmob (51 per cent owned by Maroc Telecom), Airtel (100 per cent owned by Bharti Airtel, from India), and Telecel Faso (owned by Planor Afrique, a Burkinese firm).[1] As long as these firms compete with each other on price, this will continue to benefit the Burkinabe consumer. But if a merger results in the three suppliers reducing to two or only one, or if the three companies collude and agree on price, this would lead to higher prices over time.

5.3.3 Monopsony

A *monopsony market* is a market with only one buyer. For example, when there is only one firm in an area hiring labour, such as a mining company with an exclusive concession to operate in a particular region. Or the army being the only buyer of certain intelligence equipment, prohibiting its producer from selling it to the armies of other countries. This type of market is characterised by strong market power, just like a monopoly market. But now, the power is not on the seller's side but on the buyer's side. Just like a monopoly, a monopsony firm has strong influence over the price level. The monopsony buyer will tend to offer a low price for the good that it buys, relying on the low bargaining power of the sellers, who have no alternative buyer to go to with their resources, such as labour or a primary product.

The good may be homogeneous (for example, low-skilled labour) or heterogeneous (for example, high-tech military devices). And monopsony has entry barriers. These may be legal, as is the case for military equipment where a country's ministry of defence will buy only under the condition that there will be no other buyers. Or there may be deliberately created entry barriers for new buyers. Such strategies may include successful lobbying for regulation which protects the future of the single licence provided to the monopsonist. Or the monopsonist will provide its suppliers with credit in exchange for inputs, which will prevent them from seeking alternative buyers, and lock them in to an even stronger economic tie. This is supply-chain power.

Policies to balance the market power of a single buyer would stimulate potential buyers to enter the market by reducing deliberately created entry barriers for new buyers. For example, a government may set up an auction to sell buyer's licences, under the condition that each buyer can only obtain one licence with a maximum of, say, 25 per cent of the market. But a monopsony buyer is likely to be a powerful firm which will try to protect its interests through lobbying or even stronger, illegal, practices. This is of course the mirror-image of the strategies of monopolist firms.

Diagram 5.3 shows a monopsony market. Supply equals average cost (S = AC). The demand curve is the marginal revenue product (MRP). It is the demand curve that matters most here, because monopsonists have market power as the only buyers in the market. When

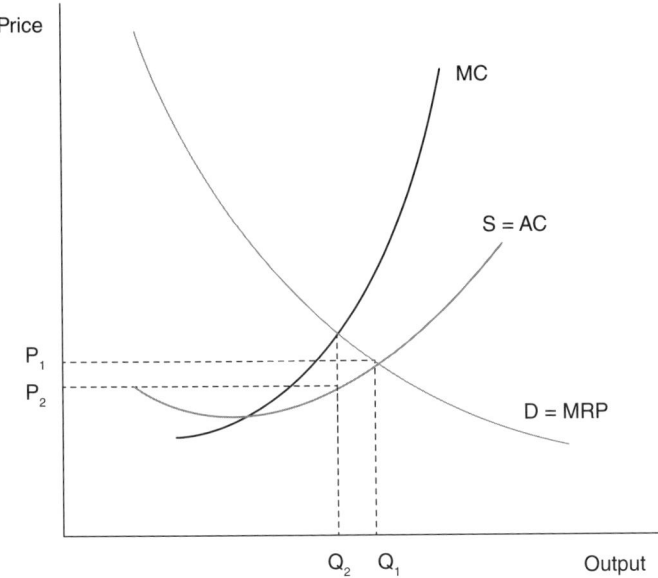

Diagram 5.3 Monopsony

they buy less, from Q_1 to Q_2, they even pay less, from P_1 down to P_2 (at the intersection of the supply curve, $S = AC$).

A real-world example of monopsony is the cotton market in sub-Saharan Africa, in particular in Benin, Burkina Faso, Chad, and Mali. The cotton is produced in these countries by small-scale farmers who sell their raw cotton to a single buyer. Africa's share of global cotton exports has increased over the past few decades, while Africa's share of the export of other agricultural products has fallen. This means that cotton is both a means to reduce rural poverty and a source of export revenue in sub-Saharan Africa. In Benin and Burkina Faso, cotton provides half of the merchandise export revenue. Therefore, it is nicknamed 'white gold'. Cotton production is very input-intensive. And since the small-scale farmers are poor, they rely on credit to buy inputs. Now, the buyers of the cotton provide the farmers at the beginning of the season with inputs on credit, which is paid off at the end of the season with part of the production sales of the cotton, bought by the monopsonist.

This dependence on input credit provided by the cotton buyer leads to vertical integration, turning the cotton buyer effectively into a monopsonist for many farmers. The semi-state cotton buying organisations are not necessarily inefficient – they actually have been evaluated as quite efficient in the four countries mentioned. But with the steep decline in world cotton prices in the early 2000s, they began to subsidise cotton prices for farmers, which is a burden on the already weak government budgets in the region. However, the alternative, to allow private buyers to take over the role of the semi-state organisation, is likely to reduce cotton production, because then the price subsidy will disappear. New private buyers will only come in if they can make a net profit. But when world market prices go down, farmers are less willing to grow cotton, and are likely to shift to other products. So, the cotton buyers are likely to remain semi-state firms.

In 2010 and 2011, world market prices for cotton increased enormously, with a price increase of around 400 per cent. The farmers, however, only received a relatively small part of this because the semi-state buyers had already agreed to sell the cotton for export at the lower prices that they obtained 6 months previously. So, only with sustained higher prices, a shift from monopsony (a single state buyer) to more competition (several private buyers) could be efficient without hurting farmers.

It is not easy for a small African country to bargain over prices with powerful multinational companies. Some of the semi-state monopsonists even have representatives of these international textile and clothing industries on their boards. This reduces the bargaining power of the African countries' cotton sellers in the world market, because it is in the interest of the international textile industry to pay low prices for the cotton they buy. This practice shows that Burkina Faso's farmers and their neighbouring cotton producers in the region may be better off with full-state monopsonists buying their cotton and selling on the world market when prices are highest, than with privatisation and international integration of the export of cotton in private or semi-state organisations.

5.3.4 Monopolistic competition

A large number of firms in the world operate under the market type of monopolistic competition. This market is a mix between perfect competition and a monopolistic market. *Monopolistic competition* is characterised by a large number of sellers and buyers and low entry barriers. So, just as in perfect competitive markets, the firms are relatively small so they do not have market power from dominating the market, and new sellers can enter the market all the time. The goods are heterogeneous, which means that they are differentiated. They distinguish themselves from each other by quality, design, style, taste, and social-psychological dimensions, such as status, masculinity, authenticity, or religious connotation. This heterogeneity of goods in monopolistic competition implies that firms make intensive use of marketing tools to signal the characteristics of their products to consumers. Hence, this type of market is not limited to price competition, but also uses advertisements and other forms of non-price competition to compete. The variety of products are to a large extent substitutes – if you cannot afford a hand-crafted silver bracelet, you can opt for a brandless standard one produced by the dozen. Each firm will try to create a monopoly for its product, emphasising its unique characteristics (even though in reality differences may be small). This is precisely why advertisements in such markets are so ubiquitous and expensive.

Another competitive strategy is to find a better location than other suppliers. For example, locating one's ice cream stall near the cinema exit or beach entry. Firms in monopolistically competitive markets have some control over prices. The more known and posh or fashionable a firm's brand has become, the higher the prices consumers are willing to pay for such brands. In particular at the top end of monopolistic competition markets, prices may be extremely high, as for hand-made watches, which easily command tens of thousands of dollars.

Diagram 5.4 shows monopolistic competition for firms in the long run. With new entrants, there will be more firms competing. This pushes down the demand curves (D) for each individual firm and hence their marginal revenue (MR).

An example of a market with monopolistic competition is provided by local art markets in tourist attractions around the world. For example, along the beaches of many tourist destinations or in old city centre bazaars. Artists or their traders sell leather ware, jewellery, paintings, sculptures, clothing, and other artefacts that are a mixture of local cultural tradition and

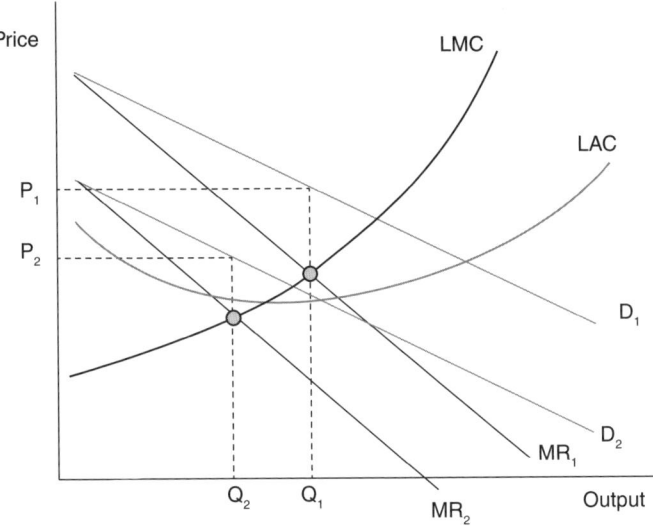

Diagram 5.4 Monopolistic competition, firm level

individual artists' skills and design. The sellers are numerous, even to the extent that tourists become tired of the many attempts to persuade them to buy. But there are also plenty of buyers, with new groups of tourists arriving every week. Sellers try to signal their products by advertising by mouth as well as by distinguishing their products by colour, material, and design from the rest. Moreover, they all try to find the best location to get near the tourists.

This shows that monopolistic competition is a market form where the winners can stand out, both in sales and in price levels. Think about famous pop music stars or football players. The top performers in these professions earn many times the income of average singers or players. That is why these specific monopolistic competition markets are referred to as 'winner-takes-all' markets.

5.3.5 Perfect competition

The ideal market form, in which price and quantity occur as if arranged by an invisible hand, is a market with perfect competition. It is this type of market which is the focus of neoclassical economics analysis. Obviously, such markets are rare. A *perfectly competitive market* has many suppliers and many buyers, low entry barriers, and the good exchanged is a *homogeneous good*. This is a normal good which has standard characteristics and individual items cannot really be distinguished from each other. Examples of homogeneous goods are crude oil, electricity, drinking water, and rice: buyers cannot select on the basis of quality, nutrition, taste, or other characteristics because these are simply the same for every individual item.

So, for perfect competition you need many sellers and many buyers and a homogeneous good. Such a market is a market where none of the sellers or buyers have market power. No single seller or buyer can influence the price level: they are all *price takers*. If one seller raised the price, all customers would flee to other sellers and the seller would not be able to trade anything. However, if one seller reduced the price, he would attract all buyers and be sold out immediately. In order to prevent loss of sales, the other sellers will quickly follow the price reduction set in motion by one seller. So, competition is entirely on the basis of price. This characteristic of a perfectly competitive market leads to low profit margins for sellers and low prices for consumers. Hence, it is a market form which particularly benefits consumers, because price competition keeps prices as low as possible. And, as a consequence, these markets are relatively efficient markets: there is no extra profit, nor waste of resources in inefficient production processes, because that would raise costs and eliminate profits. So, a perfectly competitive market seems the best for everyone: low prices, low waste of resources, and reasonable but not high profits.

Ideally, low consumer prices and effective production cost structures will also continue over time because perfectly competitive markets have no or very low entry barriers: new sellers can relatively easily enter the market. Think about eBay: registration is cheap and easy for a new seller. You can simply offer your old bicycle or too small winter coat for sale this evening. New entrants will come to a perfectly competitive market as soon as the profit margins become higher than in other markets, due to cost reductions. Such cost reductions may occur through innovations in the production process, cheaper material inputs, or higher labour productivity.

Whatever the source of cost reductions, they will increase the profit margin and therefore attract new sellers. This will increase competition even more, because if the demand remains the same, more sellers now need to compete with each other for the same demand. So, their returns are under pressure and they are likely to look for further cuts in their costs so as to lower prices, attract more consumers, and retain profit margins. This will push the least efficient suppliers out of the market: they can no longer compete. Hence, also in the long run, a perfectly competitive market is advantageous for consumers: the low entry barriers ensure continued price competition.

Diagram 5.5 shows a perfectly competitive market situation for a single firm in the short run. Each firm is a price taker, which turns the market demand curve (D), which equals marginal revenue (MR), horizontal. The supply curve (S = MC) is the marginal cost curve. Diagram 5.6 shows the situation at the market level in the long run.

An example of a perfectly competitive market is a local street market for tomatoes in Africa. The market women selling tomatoes are many, they sit in rows on the local open-air markets and along several streets in town. Their clients, also largely women, are many too. They walk along and look, feel, and bargain in order to get the best deal. Because of strong competition and a homogeneous good, sellers cannot distinguish themselves through their tomatoes, which are more or less the same (apart from some differences in ripeness and size). So, they draw attention to their stalls with their bargaining skills and social capital, trying to establish relationships with clients to ensure a fixed stream of the same buyers every week. While from the buyers' perspective, on such a competitive market, they compare the price of the tomatoes offered by various sellers before they make their choice. Perhaps they will negotiate with more than one supplier, in order to try to force the price down, trying to get a discount and playing the game of bargaining. Often, an exchange in such a situation, in which both seller and buyer feel they have struck a good bargain, is closed with a handshake or a smile and a joke and friendly goodbyes.

But even a market of perfect competition is not really guided by an invisible hand. It is regulated to some extent. For example, the sellers have to obtain a licence from the city administration, and are required to clean up at the end of the day under threat of a fine. And there are social norms. Customers receive bad looks or even angry reactions when they touch

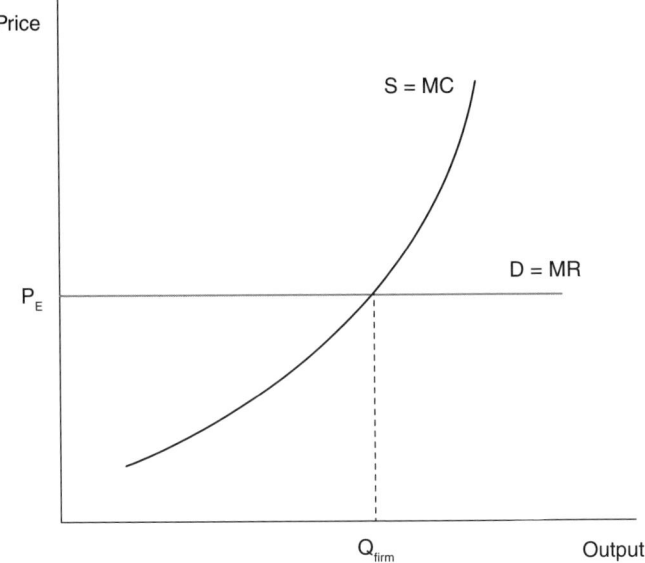

Diagram 5.5 Perfect competition, firm level

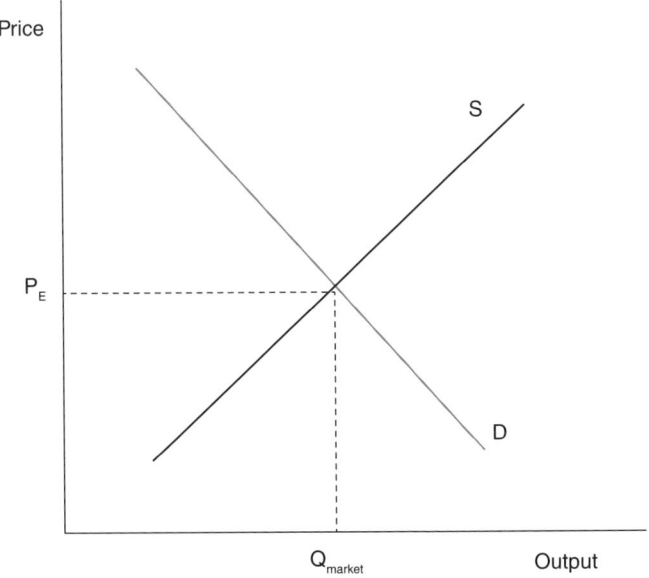

Diagram 5.6 Perfect competition, market level

the tomatoes too much, or bargain too harshly, going beyond the implicit rules of the game. Some sellers may try to speak badly about newcomers to the market in order to protect their trade, or they may engage in collective action against the municipality in order to get a better location, with more shade or further away from a rubbish dump that attracts flies to their tomatoes.

Moreover, perfectly competitive markets are never perfect because the factors of skills, luck, and accumulation will always lead to some sellers obtaining some power over the market conditions. For example, a few market women in Ouagadougou may sell not only tomatoes but also other products, and hire sellers to do the actual sales for them. They may over time obtain a dominant position in the main open air fruit market and derive from this the bargaining power to get the best locations and lower costs for licences. This will further increase their net earnings (through more sales and lower costs), which could lead them to become exclusive suppliers of high quality tomatoes to local expensive restaurants and hotels. Such exclusive contracts allow them to demand higher prices, in exchange for quality guarantees. This, in turn, gives them access to high purchasing power buyers, which gives them more opportunities . . . . So, even if at one moment in time a market comes close to the conditions of perfect competition, over time, the process of accumulation, as Marx predicted, will always result in some power imbalances, to the benefit of one or a few market parties. So, a perfectly competitive market is an ideal type of market, which hardly exists or persists in real world economies.

5.4 Market failures

Markets are very influential economic institutions. But they do have weaknesses. In this section, I will discuss market failures, indicating instances in which markets do not deliver what they are supposed to: an efficient allocation of resources, thereby generating well-being. We define *market failures* as inefficient or harmful outcomes of relatively competitive markets. I will distinguish here four sources of market failure:

- public goods
- externalities
- segmentation
- imperfect information.

5.4.1 Public goods

Public goods are goods for which no one can technically be excluded from enjoying their benefits. Examples are military defence and streetlights. Even if you are a pacifist you enjoy the benefits of the fact that the army of the country in which you live protects its borders against attacks from foreign armies. And everyone benefits from the streetlights when on a road at night, whether they are residents and have paid their local taxes or are just visitors from another town.

This impossibility of excluding people from the benefits of a good is the reason why there are no private suppliers of such goods. The private suppliers would not be able to sell the good to individual users and receive the money value for it, and hence, they would not be able to make a profit. More technically: there is a market failure justifying a public good when the private returns on investment are zero or small, and the social returns are positive and higher than the private returns.

If there is a democratic majority and minority rights are protected, there is no economic problem in publicly funding the supply of certain goods and services with the tax collected from the constituency. Of course, this is a challenge in countries with common practices of corruption, large bureaucracies, and slow adaptations to increased demand. This may lead to inefficient state-run organisations with low quality public good supply. An example is the bad drinking water services in various fast-growing African cities such as Lagos in Nigeria. Most households in Lagos do not have an individual connection to piped water. Poor households pay from 10 per cent to 100 per cent more for drinking water than middle-income households who have a connection to piped water. The poor have to buy water from private vendors or make use of illegal taps on makeshift pipes that sometimes are contaminated with sewage. So, providing public goods to everyone is not an easy task in many countries.

Chapters 6 and 7 will go much deeper into the topic of public goods.

5.4.2 Externalities

A potentially more serious market failure are externalities, in particular negative externalities. *Externalities* occur when private costs and benefits are different from the social costs and benefits of an exchange. A *negative externality* is an unintended cost for a third party or society as a whole. An example of a negative externality for a third party is noise, as an unintended cost for the neighbour of a family having a loud birthday party in their garden. An example of a negative externality for society as a whole is global warming. The total of all human production, transportation, and consumption activity has been acknowledged to be a major contributor to global warming. This is a cost for all of us, even for all living creatures on our planet. But not intended by anyone. The fact that your energy use generates CO_2, which in turn contributes to global warming is not your intention. It is a negative externality of your consumer behaviour.

A *positive externality* is an unintended benefit for a third party (silence) or society as a whole (education). An example of a positive externality for a third party is a furniture shopping mall. When you want to buy a new sofa, you do not need to go around the town to the various suppliers, as the suppliers have located next to each other to facilitate consumers. This saves time and transportation costs for you. An example of a positive externality for society as a whole is education. There are various positive side effects of having an educated population. Educated mothers have less children and healthier children. Moreover, a higher educated population generates more productivity and innovation.

Positive externalities are clearly not a problematic form of market failure. The more the better, isn't it? But this does not imply that no policy is needed. If education has social benefits which exceed its private benefits (more knowledge and higher earning potential), then policy makers may want to stimulate the population to achieve higher levels of education. This is precisely why education is subsidised in so many countries.

Negative externalities are a real problem. They reduce well-being, in the short run or in the long run, for a small or a large group of people, or even for nature or the earth as a whole. There are four policy options to deal with negative externalities.

5.4.2.1 Introducing a price

First, the parties could bargain over a price for the removal of the externality. Take the example of the noisy birthday party at your neighbours. If you offered them a sufficient amount of

136   Markets

money to lower the volume of their music and call in their children who are playing outside, this would solve the market failure: you would get rid of the noise, by paying a price for silence, and your neighbours would be paid for the loss of comfort in expressing their joy. This is a market solution: solving a market failure by introducing another market, in this case for the externality. The disadvantage is that it involves a corruption of values. Isn't it just a matter of decency to respect your neighbour's right to sufficient quiet so that at least they can sleep or read a book? And how far should we go with this market solution? Would it be alright to pay your other neighbours who regularly beat their children to reduce the beating so that the kids no longer scream so loudly?

5.4.2.2 Internalisation of the external costs

A second solution to negative externalities is *internalising the costs*, including the external costs in the final product price. For example the premium that you are forced to pay in some countries when buying a new car, for the recycling costs of your car at the end of its life-cycle. Of course, this partial solution does not cover the environmental and health costs of the air pollution caused by the use of fuel in cars.

5.4.2.3 Regulation

A third solution to negative externalities is regulation: prohibiting a certain level of externalities, which forces its producers to reduce this level. Think about a maximum level of pollution allowed for heavy industries, above which firms have to pay a fine or are threatened with closure.

5.4.2.4 Systemic reorganisation

A fourth solution is at the systemic level. An example is over-fishing in Lake Victoria, Africa's largest fresh-water resource bordered by Kenya, Tanzania, and Uganda. These countries have agreed on a set of policy measures and monitoring to prevent trading in undersized fish. This includes standards for the minimum sizes of traded fish (tilapia and Nile perch), the minimum size of mazes of fishing nets, and restrictions on the use of nets and other fishing methods. This systemic level solution goes beyond regulation, and includes awareness raising among the local population, fair trade labelling of fish to generate more eco-friendly demand from international buyers, and the stimulation of alternative income earning sources for people living along Lake Victoria's shores.

Negative externalities of consumption were discussed in Chapter 3. Negative environmental externalities will be discussed in Chapter 7 when we examine global public goods, and in Chapter 13 where we will consider the relationship between the economy and nature.

5.4.3 Segmentation

Segmentation is a form of market failure based on social norms. Even in perfectly competitive markets, social norms may generate market segmentation. *Segmentation* is the division of markets over distinct segments, each with their own price levels. The social norms underlying segmentation are often of a discriminatory character. Take for example the labour market. Immigrants are often constrained to low-end jobs. Women often do typically 'pink collar' jobs, for example as nurses, primary school teachers, and secretaries, whereas men often do 'blue collar' and 'white collar' jobs, ranging from train drivers and carpenters to pilots and CEOs of multinationals. But entrepreneurs may also discriminate among themselves. New entrants, immigrants, lower-class entrepreneurs, or those belonging to minority groups may be excluded from the most beneficial business locations and business associations.

Segmentation is a market failure because it leads to inefficiencies. It leads to allocation of labour and other inputs on the basis of prejudice rather than relevant economic features such as quality. If tomato sellers are successful in keeping some groups of tomato sellers out of the central market place where middle-class women do their shopping, they can keep the prices artificially high because they keep part of the competition out. This means that the consumers pay more for their tomatoes than they would have done with more competition between suppliers of tomatoes in the market hall. This is inefficient. Hence, segmentation creates unearned benefits for some, at a cost to others, with as a consequence, higher prices for consumers.

Another form of segmentation is cherry picking by firms entering markets with high cost segments or with low purchasing power segments. *Cherry picking* is the process by which firms only serve those segments of the market where costs or risks are low or where buyers have higher purchasing power. In this way, they reduce average costs and risk. Markets with high cost segments are, for example, remote rural areas. It is costly to transport goods and services there, so some goods and services will simply not reach consumers in those places. That is why in remote villages throughout Africa, it is very costly to get access to the internet or to drugs for rare diseases, for example. Pharmacies will deliver drugs to rural hospitals and even small-scale clinics and dispensaries, but only for the most common drugs, and not for those for rare diseases. Similarly, specialised medical operations will only be available in urban areas.

Markets with low purchasing power segments are, for example, microcredit markets. Microcredit institutions tend to provide credit not to the poorest segments of societies but to those just above that level, who have already demonstrated that they have earning potential, signalling good pay-back rates. The problem with such segmentation is that large groups of consumers and investors are not served, which is an inefficient allocation of resources, excluding groups from the market. This kind of cherry picking (serving the presumably most profitable borrowers) leads in Africa to the exclusion of illiterate landless farmers, migrants, and women entrepreneurs from most credit schemes. The most entrepreneurial among these groups, with good business plans in their minds, have no choice but to obtain loans from private money lenders in their villages, who charge up to ten times higher interest rates than microcredit institutions. This makes their production costs unnecessarily high, which makes it difficult to compete with entrepreneurs who obtain credit through microcredit programmes. Therefore, segmentation in credit markets is not only unfair but also inefficient: it disadvantages the most entrepreneurial poor, who, despite strong limitations, manage to innovate, produce, and find markets for their products.

Policy measures against segmentation are threefold.

5.4.3.1 Regulation

The state may intervene with regulation: a strict enforcement of anti-discrimination laws. In our example, this means equal access to and pricing of licences for tomato sellers, and equal access for all groups of sellers to the best places in the central market hall. And access to microcredit programmes for all entrepreneurs. But this is often not enough, because social norms can be very strong. Hence, discriminatory practices may continue, and the practices by advantaged sellers may affect consumer behaviour, because consumers are made to believe that the tomatoes offered by immigrants are of low quality. Or loan officers in microcredit programmes may not believe in the feasibility of the business plans of the poorest clients because they are illiterate or speak a different language.

5.4.3.2 Changing social norms

That is why a second type of policy measures is often needed to address the market failure of segmentation. These are policies concerning the underlying social norms: awareness raising. A change in such norms requires awareness campaigns, education, and trust between social groups. These are long-term policies investing in fairness and social cohesion in societies, which require role models provided by political leaders and social responsibility shown by policy makers and firms.

5.4.3.3 Public service delivery

Third, an additional policy against cherry picking would be to supplement the private suppliers with a public supplier to serve the disadvantaged. But since the private suppliers already serve the richer segments (therefore the name cherry picking), the public supplier will be left with the high-cost and high-risk category of clients, which have low purchasing power and few savings. As a consequence, it is likely that the private firms will be profitable but the public firm will not. This is a drain on public resources – the government budget. In order to prevent the public firm from suffering losses, a better option would be to take over the entire market rather than only the bottom segment.

In this way, the public firm could use the strategy of *cross-subsidisation*. This is compensating for losses made on lower end segments with profits made on higher end segments. Alternatively, the government could force the private firms to do this, rather than step in as a public supplier. This could be done by attaching conditions on serving all market segments to the granting of business licences or any type of support. Indeed, this is being done in the field of microcredit in developing countries. Private lenders of small amounts of credit are increasingly required by governments and international donors to take up poor clients, and to make up eventual losses with profits made on less poor clients.

5.4.4 Imperfect information

The market failure of imperfect information is perhaps the most ubiquitous, simply because there is no perfect information in any market. And you need to spend time on getting more information, and sometimes you even need to spend money on getting access to information. In a market, sellers and buyers will often have *asymmetric information*: when one party has more knowledge about the good to be exchanged than the other party. And sellers are likely to share only the information that will increase the value of their property and not information that decreases its value. Or similarly, a real estate representative will keep the information asymmetry in place – it is her job to sell property at the maximum possible price, to satisfy her selling clients. So, asymmetric information tends to benefit one party at the cost of the other party in a market transaction. This creates a bias in the division of the gains from trade.

This bias may sometimes be so big that one party will actually not have gained at all from the exchange. Asymmetric information has two clear problems: adverse selection and moral hazard.

5.4.4.1 Adverse selection

At the market level, this may lead to *adverse selection*: when exchanges occur on the basis of incomplete or asymmetric information. When this concerns not just one individual exchange but is systematic, adverse selection becomes a problem. A famous example of asymmetric information leading to adverse selection is given by George Akerlof, a Nobel Prize winner, concerning the second-hand car market. Sellers know the quality of their car, buyers do not. Let us assume that half of the second-hand cars in Dar es Salaam are good and half of them are bad. And that a good second-hand Toyota is worth US$5,000 but a bad one only US$2,500. In Tanzanian shillings (TZS), this is about 10 million TZS for a good 10-year-old Toyota and 5 million TZS for a low quality Toyota. Over time, the buyers of second-hand cars find that they have a large chance of buying a bad car, and pay too much if they assume it is a good car. The sellers of good cars will find it more difficult to sell their cars at a good price, because buyers begin to fear asymmetric information. They are afraid they will get stuck with a bad car. Hence, sellers of good cars are less likely to sell their car in an unregulated car market, but rather will try to exchange it for a new car at an official car dealer and pay the difference as estimated by the experts of the car dealer. At the same time, the unregulated car market attracts more sellers of bad cars, who still hope to convince clients that their car is a good one. The buyers who do not want to go to an official car dealer but prefer the cheaper unregulated second-hand car market, will bargain strongly to prevent paying too much. In the long run, the unregulated second-hand car market will have low prices and bad quality cars only.

So, assume you are a starting entrepreneur in Tanzania and want to buy a 10-year-old Toyota on the second-hand market in Dar es Salaam. What to do? Well, if you have no expert knowledge about cars, your best option would be to play safe and buy it from an official Toyota dealer with a quality guarantee system. If you cannot afford this, you can hope to be lucky in the unregulated second-hand car market. But only when you have expert knowledge of cars or bring a friend whom you can trust and has such knowledge. Oh, and do not forget that cars are cheaper when their mileage has just passed a round number as compared to when they are just below such a limit: you will be able to save thousands of shillings when going for a 102,486 mileage car as compared to a similar car with 98,973 miles on the clock . . . .

A policy measure to reduce information asymmetry is to require sellers to include an information sheet about their products and services and potential risks. For example, a list of the possible side effects of certain drugs. But the quality of the information depends entirely on the supplier, so this may still allow for information asymmetries. Another policy measure would be an independent agency providing relevant information. For example an agency providing quality certificates. In the second-hand car market, this is often an official car dealer. The prices of the second-hand cars are higher than for the cars offered without a certificate. But this higher price covers the reduction of risk of buying a bad car.

5.4.4.2 Moral hazard

A final problem of incomplete information is *moral hazard*. This means taking risks when the costs are borne by others. This is, for example, the case with insurance. If your house burns

Image 5.3 Car mileage just before a mental limit

down because you smoke in bed, or because you left candles burning next to the curtains with the windows open, your careless behaviour causes high expenses for the insurance company. Moral hazard can even go a step further, towards deliberate deception. For example, claiming for a lost camera from a travel insurance company when it had not been stolen at all. Insurance firms therefore require responsible behaviour (such as smoke detectors in your house for fire insurance) and certified documentation (such as a declaration of theft signed by a police officer, which takes you time to get). And insurance companies often require an amount of own risk, to be paid by clients themselves, to discourage false claims. Nevertheless, many forms of moral hazard cannot be prevented. Entrepreneurs may make wrong investments with their credit and banks may engage in speculation and risky investments trusting that the government will save the bank when in trouble.

Market failures are not exceptions but are common features of many markets that we are engaged in every day. In some cases, policies by firms (self-regulation) or the government (regulation, taxation, and subsidies) help to reduce market failures. But in other cases there is not much to be done. We have to live with the imperfections of markets, as long as markets, even with these imperfections, still make net contributions to well-being.

5.5 The failure of markets

There are more fundamental problems with markets than just market failures. This is the case when there are failures of markets even when the invisible hand works properly. In those cases, the invisible hand seems to be accompanied by an invisible foot, which kicks at the very fundamentals of markets: the underlying values of freedom and equality, their enabling formal and informal institutions, and the efficiency they are supposed to generate in the allocation of scarce resources. We speak of a *failure of markets* when markets, which function properly, nevertheless do not provide a net increase in aggregate well-being. In those instances, markets are no longer the best solution to allocation problems, and we need to consider the state or the community economy to allocate resources for a particular good or service. The failure of markets happens along two paths: exclusion of needs without purchasing power and the crowding out of pro-social norms.

5.5.1 Inherent asymmetries and exclusion of needs

Markets have inherent inequalities which tend to get worse over time when not corrected. For production, capital owners hire labour power and not the other way around. Moreover, labour power can be substituted for capital through innovation and technical progress. This makes labour more dependent on capital than the other way around. This is a fundamental asymmetry of markets.

Markets also follow cycles, with long periods of economic downturn and recession. During such periods, aggregate demand is limited because of uncertainty, leading to low consumer confidence, more savings, and less goods bought. As a consequence, employers do not hire more labour, even when the wage level goes down as they simply cannot sell the additional products produced by the extra workers. This leads to unemployment in the labour market, even when in product markets supply meets demand.

Remember also that markets respond not to any need but only to needs that are backed up by purchasing power. This leaves many needs unmet by markets. But economic agents are human beings who need to survive, with food, clothing, and shelter. If they cannot serve those needs on markets, due to lack of resources to exchange, or lack of demand for the resources they have, even when they are willing to supply these at below-market prices, they will be *de facto* excluded from markets. Remember from Chapter 3 where we explained *absolute deprivation* as poverty below subsistence level. The absolute poor will have no other option than desperate sales of their limited assets. This is a short-term strategy of survival through markets. But it undermines their productive capacity in the long run. Hence, there will always be groups that become dependent upon the state and communities. Serving their needs requires taxation and redistribution by the state, and gifts of care in communities.

Moreover, if the needs of these groups of people are not being met by markets, state redistribution, or community care, this will inevitably lead to social unrest, conflict, crime, and perhaps violence and war. This reaction by the excluded can turn out to be more costly than providing everyone with the resources to satisfy minimum livelihoods on markets. Exclusion of the poor is inefficient because it causes damage to an economy's resources. Or it leads to early deaths. An example is the co-existence of hunger due to lack of purchasing power, on the one hand, and grain-fed pigs and cows producing meat for those with a lot of purchasing power, on the other. This practice of markets seeking purchasing power, irrespective of human needs, destroys human well-being in a very fundamental way: on a day-to-day basis, thousands of people die due to a lack of sufficient or sufficiently nutritious food. At the same time, we see long-lasting social conflict or civil wars in areas where large groups are excluded from the gains of markets.

5.5.2 When exchange crowds out pro-social norms

Markets rely on enabling pro-social norms, as we have seen earlier in this chapter. Without these norms, markets cannot expand, they will stay at low levels of supply and demand, and will undermine even the exchange that is still occurring. Fairness in rewards from markets, trust between supply and demand, and equal participation in markets all enhance the efficient allocation of resources. But when social cohesion is undermined when markets are allowed to increase inequalities, and when competition makes use of unfair means, the very social norms on which markets are based will be undermined.

Moreover, the more dominant the market, with its individualistic competition values, becomes in an economy, the less community interaction there is to sustain social values. And weak states run the risk that they will be captured by the interests of dominant market parties. One example is that an increasing dominance of markets vis-à-vis communities and the state allows for rent-seeking by dominant market parties. *Rent-seeking* is the increase of one's share of wealth without contributing to this wealth, through lobbying or bribes. Another example is that markets are created in domains that affect human rights. Not so long ago this was through slavery. Today, we see child labour by very young children and bonded labour by whole families who are forced to pay off their debts, or their ancestor's debts, through unpaid labour for the creditor.

In conclusion, markets are not perfect, even when they work well to bring supply and demand together and when market failures are solved. Markets generate and increase inequality, involve social costs, and undermine the very social norms on which they flourish. Therefore, well-functioning economies need to find a balance between the market, the state, and community economies. Not only for reasons of fairness, but also for reasons of efficiency and effectiveness.

5.6 Interesting sources

M-Pesa, the mobile wallet in Africa: http://www.vodafone.com/content/index/about/about-us/money_transfer.html

Sandel, M. (2012) *What Money Can't Buy: The Moral Limits of Markets*. London: Allen Lane.

5.7 Glossary

Absolute deprivation   Poverty below subsistence level

Adverse selection   When exchanges occur on the basis of incomplete or asymmetric information

Asymmetric information   When one party has more knowledge about the good to be exchanged than the other party

Barter   Exchange of a good for another good

Benchmarking   An artificial competition policy with targets or rankings, which governments use to force more efficiency from public organisations

Cartel   An organisation of large producers with the objective of eliminating price competition

Cherry picking   The process by which firms only serve those segments of the market where costs or risks are low or where buyers have higher purchasing power

Collusion   Cooperation among competitors to set the market price

Cross-subsidisation   Compensating losses made on lower end segments with profits made on higher end segments

Distortions   Regulations which do not support markets but rather constrain them

Dumping   Temporarily selling products below cost price to price competitors out of the market

Duopoly   A market with two sellers

Endogenous change   The characteristic of an economic variable as influenced in the market process itself and not outside it (exogenous)

Endogenous factors   Factors inherent in the economic process, such as insecurity, routines, advertisements, the general economic climate, consumer confidence, investment opportunities, etc.

Entry barriers   Mechanisms which prevent newcomers entering a market

Equilibrium   The intersection between supply and demand at which a particular quantity is transacted at a particular price

Exclusionary practices   Putting pressure on suppliers not to sell the same input to other firms

Exogenous change   A change in an economic variable due to an outside shock to a market

Externality   When private costs and benefits are different from the social costs and benefits of an exchange

Failure of markets   When markets which function properly nevertheless do not provide a net increase in aggregate well-being

Feasible no-trade option   That without engaging in an exchange, each party is still able to survive, to have access to a livelihood

Homogeneous good   A normal good, which has standard characteristics and individual items cannot really be distinguished from each other

Internalising costs   Including external costs in the final product price

Market   The interaction of supply and demand of goods and services through exchange

Market demand   The relationship between price and quantity demanded of a particular good

Market failure   Inefficient or harmful outcomes of relatively competitive markets

Market supply   The relationship between price and quantity supplied of a particular good

Monetary exchange   Exchange of a good for money

Monopolistic competition   A large number of sellers and buyers and low entry barriers

Monopoly   A market with only one seller

Monopsony   A market with only one buyer

Moral hazard   Taking risks when the costs are borne by others

Negative externality   An unintended cost for a third party or society as a whole

Oligopolistic markets   Markets which are dominated by a few large sellers

Perfect competition   Many suppliers and many buyers, low entry barriers, and the good exchanged is a *homogeneous good*

Positive externality   An unintended benefit for a third party or society as a whole

Price leader   An established firm and often the largest in an oligopolistic market, which has the power to set the market price

Price taker   No single seller or buyer can influence the price level

Privatisation   The sale of a public firm to market parties

Public goods   Goods for which no one can technically be excluded from enjoying their benefits

Rent-seeking   The increase of one's share of wealth without contributing to this wealth, through lobbying or bribes

Segmentation   The division of markets over distinct segments, each with their own price levels

Static market   A market situation in the short run, in which the determinants of demand and supply do not change

Traverse   Process in which markets are not jumping from one equilibrium to another, but are continuously on the move

Note

1 Data from African Mobile Observatory, 2011. Also see http://www.budde.com.au/Research/Burkina-Faso-Telecoms-Mobile-and-Broadband.html

6 The state

6.1 The economic roles of the state

The state has five economic roles. Together, these roles enable, regulate, stimulate, and stabilise markets. But the state also interacts, in enabling and disabling ways, with the community economy of households, non-profit organisations, and networks of people. So, the state is one of three economic domains, in addition to the market and the community economy. At the same time, the state is the economic domain setting and protecting the rules of the game for the economy as a whole. The five economic roles of the state are as follows: (1) ensuring property rights; (2) implementing policies for equal opportunities and to address market failures; (3) redistribution; (4) ensuring stability and economic stimulation; and (5) supply of public goods.

Each theory has its own view about these roles, the policy instruments to carry out these roles, and the types of failures of these roles and instruments. Not only the market suffers from failures. Governments can also have failures. *Government failure* occurs when the government does not effectively carry out its economic roles.

6.2 Social economic theory of the state

6.2.1 Equal opportunities

In social economics, the state and society are understood as closely intertwined: both the market and the state are seen as embedded in society with a continuous interaction between the three. Moreover, social economists emphasise the third economic domain, of the community economy, with its own economic role of providing unpaid services, sharing resources, networking and cooperation, and trust building within and between communities. Hence, the state is only one of three domains in the social economic perspective, and not the basis of the other two. The basis of the economy is society at large with its communal relationships, as Adam Smith described in his book *The Theory of Moral Sentiments*, well before he wrote his foundational work on economics, *The Wealth of Nations*. According to this book and social economists, the alpha and omega of the economy is not the state or the market, but the community economy. The state therefore has a responsibility towards society, which is expressed in particular through its roles of public goods provider, protector of equal opportunities in markets, and redistributor, to support society.

Equal opportunities require social policies. Equal opportunity policies concern education and a wider set of human development policies, which provide people with access to food, health care, and social security (emergency food programs, pensions, health insurance, disability insurance). These policies ensure that economic agents have real choices in markets, through a feasible no-trade option in the case that there is no demand for the labour power they have on offer.

6.2.2 Redistribution

Redistribution is the deliberate shifting of resources and rewards from one social group to another. For example land, income, and access to public services. Redistribution is both a means and an end in itself in social economics. It is a means to ensure equal participation in and benefits from markets and to prevent market power emerging. And redistribution is an end in itself because the human dignity of disadvantaged groups is endangered if there is too much inequality.

The border between redistribution as a means and as an end in itself is vague. That is because when economic agents are treated with dignity, their participation in markets and as users of public services becomes more effective. The persistence of inequalities without adjustment may lead to social conflict and hence to costs. Think about the public outrage at firms where top managers annually receive large increases in their earnings while the factory workers do not. The outrage is particularly strong when the firm's performance is poor and when lower-level workers are fired for cost-saving reasons.

Indeed, redistribution helps to make and keep markets as efficient as possible. For example, land redistribution in Latin America is likely to increase food production and entails a more efficient use of agricultural land as compared to large-scale landownership and landless peasants. This, in turn, may help to reduce the pressure on tropical rainforests and illegal logging and burning, and coca growing for the illegal drugs trade.

Latin America is known for its relatively high income inequality as compared to other regions in the world. Since the election of democratic governments on the continent since the 1990s, Latin American states have made serious efforts at redistribution. The result has been that over the decade 2000–2010, inequality has declined in most Latin American countries.[1] This has contributed importantly to the reduction in poverty. The major reason for the decline in inequality was redistribution. First, directly, through government transfers of tax money to poor households. Second, indirectly through rising minimum wages and state support for stronger labour unions and state action opposing discrimination against ethnic minorities and women. Interestingly, these results were achieved not only in countries with high economic growth over this decade (such as Argentina), but also in countries with moderate growth (such as Brazil). Moreover, the redistribution programmes appeared to be not expensive, as they constituted only a small part of total social expenditures. This recent Latin American experience indicates that redistribution can contribute to lower inequality and poverty without constraining economic growth.

An important measure of inequality is the Gini coefficient, named after the Italian economist Corrado Gini who published a paper describing his measure in 1912. The *Gini coefficient* is a measure of income inequality based on the income shares of each percentile of households in the income distribution. So, if every 1 per cent of the total population earns 1 per cent of the income, income distribution is fully equal. This gives a Gini coefficient of 0. But when 1 per cent of the population earns all the income and the other 99 per cent receives nothing, the Gini coefficient stands at 1. So, the higher the Gini coefficient, the higher the inequality. Table 6.1 shows the Gini coefficients for Latin America for five recent years, and a comparison with the OECD average.

Table 6.1 Income inequality in Latin America, Gini coefficients

	2000	2007	2008	2009	2010
Argentina	51.11	47.37	46.26	46.13	44.49
Bolivia	62.78	57.44	56.29	N.A.	N.A.
Brazil	N.A.	55.89	55.07	54.69	N.A.
Chile	55.26	N.A.	N.A.	52.06	N.A.
Colombia	58.68	58.88	57.23	56.67	55.91
Costa Rica	46.53	49.25	48.87	50.73	N.A.
Dominican	52.01	48.69	49	48.86	47.2
Ecuador	56.59	54.31	50.62	49.43	49.26
Guatemala	54.28	N.A.	N.A.	N.A.	N.A.
Honduras	N.A.	56.16	61.33	56.95	N.A.
Mexico	51.87	N.A.	48.28	N.A.	47.16
Panama	N.A.	N.A.	N.A.	52.03	51.92
Paraguay	N.A.	53.31	52.05	51.04	52.42
Peru	50.75	51.65	48.95	49.05	48.14
Uruguay	44.39	47.63	46.27	46.28	45.32
Venezuela	N.A.	N.A.	N.A.	N.A.	N.A.
Average	53.11	52.78	51.69	51.16	49.09
Average OECD	31.23	30.89	30.05	30.44	30.53

Sources: World Bank and OECD Statistics.

6.2.3 Public goods

Chapter 5 already explained public goods. The state is the supplier of public goods. This may be the national state, for example for national defence, the police, and national highways. Or regional governments, for example for the maintenance of canals or regional airports. Or municipal governments, for example for the supply of business parks, garbage collection, or street lighting.

When we look at the history of public goods, we see first a tendency away from charity and church towards the state. Many public goods, in particular social public goods, used to be provided by the community economy. The provision of health care and education used to be the job of monasteries and churches and a few private charities, up to the 19th century in most countries of the world. Then, the state gradually took over these tasks, so that at the end of the 20th century all countries had state schools and state hospitals, often next to private education and health care facilities and a continuation of community-provided services. But in the 1980s the state role in the economy began to decline again. Privatisation and technological developments led to the market taking over some public goods: from telecommunications, water supply, energy supply and railways, to postal services, universities, and health care.

This retreat by the state from public goods provisioning since the 1980s has also affected a special type of public goods, namely merit goods. *Merit goods* are goods supplied by the state because they are regarded as desirable for everyone. Because market prices are too high to make the desirable goods accessible for everyone at sufficient quality. Think about playgrounds for children in disadvantaged neighbourhoods, or free wifi in public spaces in cities, or vaccination programs. Over time we see public support increasing for some merit goods and decreasing for others. What a merit good is apparently changes over time. In Norway, cities offer free air pumps for bicycles. In Argentina, municipalities throughout the country have built barbeques with picnic tables alongside roads. While Norwegian cities are bike-friendly and so the pumps

148 *The state*

cater for a real need, Argentinians go out for a typical Argentinian *asado* at the weekend with their families and friends on a *parilla* at the road-side. The pumps and barbeque facilities not only are a collectively financed service for citizens, but also help to prevent negative externalities: of left bikes that may be stolen in Norway and of forest fires in Argentina.

6.2.4 Regulation: price controls

A well-known type of regulation, which has the objective of creating equal opportunities, is *price controls*. This means that the market price is allowed to move only within a restricted range or is completely fixed. For example for house rents, the price of train tickets, or the price of basic food items. Or, the price boundaries are set by the government together with other agents in a bargaining process, for example a minimum wage in the labour market. This is often the result of a *tri-partite bargaining process* between the government, labour unions, and employers' representatives.

Price controls can be upwards, preventing the market price going above a certain level. An example is the price of basic necessities that many governments have tied to a maximum in order to ensure affordable livelihoods for the poor. In Venezuela this has resulted in government-controlled prices for milk, coffee, and other basic consumer items under the government of the popular president Hugo Chavez up to his death in 2013. These items then became scarce in supermarkets because the suppliers were not earning the profit margins on the sales of these products that they used to do before the price controls. In the spring of 2013, toilet paper could no longer be found in the supermarkets. The supply of toilet paper by Venezuelan factories had gone down, due both to the maximum price that the government had set below the market price, and to the lack of imported paper for the production process because the government had also put controls on obtaining foreign exchange. And without dollars, Venezuelan firms cannot buy toilet paper abroad.

Image 6.1 Toilet paper

Other price controls may be not upwards but downwards, preventing the price going below a certain level. A well-known example is the minimum wage. Employers are not allowed to hire workers at wage levels below this legal minimum, even when some categories of workers are willing to work for lower pay. Again the reason is protection of the poor, in this case low-wage earners. A minimum wage helps workers earn a decent wage, also referred to as a living wage, sufficient for a decent standard of living. Ensuring decent wages is a key policy theme in social economics, connecting human dignity with rewards for labour productivity.

6.2.5 Government failure: low tax revenue

The social economics of the state is concerned with the social consequences of government failure. The key to this is low tax revenue. Because without sufficient public resources, governments cannot provide sufficient public goods, enforce equal opportunity policies, or provide sufficient social protection through income redistribution. There are three reasons for low tax revenue:

- a limited tax base
- a regressive tax system
- tax evasion.

The *tax base* is the number of economic agents from which taxes are raised. The narrower its definition and the more exceptions granted by the government, the smaller the tax base. Obviously, you can collect more profit taxes if you lower the threshold for the size of firms or the amount of profits to be taxed. A *regressive tax* system collects relatively more taxes from the poor than from the rich. The problem is that, even when the rich pay absolutely more tax than the poor, this constrains the total tax revenue, simply because the poor don't have as much taxable income as the rich. That is why social economists favour a *progressive tax* system, which collects relatively and absolutely more taxes from the rich as compared to the poor. The stronger shoulders carry the highest tax burden, out of fairness (an end in itself) and out of efficiency (a means for an effective tax system). A progressive tax system has increasing tax rates with increasing incomes, and more tax exemptions for the poor than for the rich. Tax evasion is the non-payment or insufficient payment of taxes due. This is due to weak enforcement by the government of its tax collection, and to strategic behaviour by high-income households and multinational firms which relocate their money or residences to other countries with lower tax rates.

6.2.6 The state and the community economy

Social economics is the only one of four theories describing the relationship between the state and the community economy. The key characteristic of this relationship is that the former requires the social capital that is generated by the latter, for its tax morale and the prevention of free riding on public goods. Only when economic agents trust each other and the institutions of the state, are they willing to pay taxes and play by the rules. And only when economic agents feel responsible for the public services that their government provides, will they restrain themselves from free riding, such as running illegal electricity cables to their houses or illegal waste dumping by their businesses. The other side of this relationship is that

150   *The state*

the state needs to deserve this trust and responsible behaviour by not engaging in corruption and not allowing tax evasion.

Hence, in the social economic theory of the state, the state depends partially for its effectiveness in carrying out its roles on the community economy. This brings us full circle back to the role of the state in the economy in social economics: the economic role of the state is first and foremost to serve the community economy.

6.3 Institutional economics of the state

In institutional economics, the state lays the foundation for the market. It does so with a set of formal institutions, ranging from property rights, to equal opportunity rules, to regulation against market failures. Without a state, markets do not function, in the institutional perspective. There will, of course, be some individual exchange transactions in the absence of a state, as they have existed since humanity began. But individual *ad hoc* exchanges are not yet markets, with a reliable money system, a reasonable stability of supply and demand, and informative prices. Markets require formal institutions, set up by an authority beyond the market parties. Moreover, institutional economists recognise that the state can enable, fund, and cooperate with private sector parties in order to innovate in sectors, industries, and technologies. So, in institutional economics, in the beginning was the state. . . .

Box 6.1 Land titling in Bolivia

From 2003 to 2008, Bolivia's National Agrarian Reform Institute successfully implemented the Bolivia Land Titling Program in order to develop the property registration system. Some 470,000 hectares containing more than 25,000 properties were registered at an affordable cost for farmers. This program helped farmers to obtain secure property rights with the full benefits of holding land assets, including receiving loans. And it improved access to the land market. This program was an important step in a country where access to land is a critical political issue and the major cause of rural inequality.

Moreover, in coca-growing regions like Chapare, this program has contributed to a broader program in Bolivia combating narcotics: within 4 years, the area of legal agriculture increased by 33 per cent and exports of bananas, an important local product, expanded significantly. This economic and social progress, and improvements in the infrastructure of rural areas, in addition to the beautiful countryside, is promising for the local tourist industry.

Sources: USAID websites http://www.usaid.gov/sites/default/files/success/files/ss_bo_title.pdf and http://www.usaidltpr.com/bolivia-land-titling-program

---

6.3.1 Property rights

Property rights are rights to control, benefit from, and transfer property. They may be formal, guaranteed by a judicial system, or informal, acknowledged in a social group. Basic property rights concern the recognition of ownership of land, capital, and material goods, as well as the property rights of intellectual goods, such as inventions and artistic creations. If you are not the legal or socially recognised owner of a good, you cannot exchange it against money or another good, because the owner of the good you want in exchange is not sure that the good you offer will become his or her property after the exchange.

Property rights can be of diverse character: individual or joint (for example owned by a family) or owned not by persons but by institutions (firms or a foundation). These rights may be written down in contracts and registered at a land registry (land, buildings) or in a state-controlled inventory (patents). Or property rights may not be codified but socially recognised and monitored, through oral communication and rituals. In that case, the relevant social group, such as a tribe or a neighbourhood in a modern city, will be the guardians of the property right. In many countries, common land ownership is still applied among indigenous peoples, which does not allow for sales to third parties. Other property rights may be individual but are not yet codified. Think about a house that has been built by the labour of the couple who live in it. Upon separation, both are entitled to the house, and probably an equal split of the value upon sale is fair, if both put in the same amount of work and effort and money for the construction materials. Without codification of the joint ownership, the distribution of the value of the house when the couple separates may lead to conflict.

In Brazil, large land administration projects over several decades have ensured property rights to over a million hectares of land for 55,000 farmers. In Guatemala, 3,000 properties of rural land were titled. Women and men obtained titles in their own names. The registered land titles not only allow for the sale of land but also provide land security for their owners, who are likely to invest more in the quality of their land. This, in turn, stimulates higher yields, which contributes to regional food security. Moreover, for female farmers, land titles ensure their continued access to land, even when their marriage breaks down or their husband sells the land registered under his name.

Without clearly defined, generally agreed property rights, and a reliable judicial system to enforce these rights, markets will experience high transaction costs when exchanging property from one person or organisation to another. *Transaction costs* are costs involved in an exchange, not reflected in the price of the good exchanged. Transaction costs are inefficient: they increase the costs of obtaining a good through market exchange. Moreover, when transaction costs become too high, they will prevent exchanges occurring. That is precisely why the government also set up the formal institution of money, by installing a Central Bank and exercising its right as the sole supplier of bank notes and coins. This helps to reduce transaction costs in the economy, as compared to barter or a variation of privately issued monies existing side-by-side.

6.3.2 Regulation through formal institutions

Economic laws reflect the political situation of a country. With more neoliberal governments, countries often abolish laws and regulations that are considered to interfere too much in markets. And with more socially oriented governments, countries often adopt new laws for regulating markets. At the same time, there is a process over time in which countries gradually increase social protection and curb extreme inequalities in accumulation.

Laws require effective enforcement, in particular when activities are very profitable for certain groups. A good example is the illegal production of cocaine. Colombia is the main supplier of cocaine in the world, with the most important consumer markets being in the USA and Europe. The value of the illicit international trade in cocaine has been estimated as the third largest in the world after arms and oil. Cocaine trade is very profitable: the street value in the USA of a kilo of cocaine is between ten and fifty times the production cost. Of course, illegal transport and bribes add to the costs, while the risk of being caught by the police entails another cost. But which other product has profit margins of more than 500 per cent? So, the drug trade is not likely to disappear, even with strong regulation at all stages of the value chain, from land use to street corner coke dealers.

The most developed countries of Latin America, such as Brazil, Chile, Costa Rica, and Uruguay, have an impressive record of strong state institutions. The congresses in these countries appear to be quite effective in the policy making process, there is relatively high judicial independence, and these states have a strong civil service capacity. This implies that the economic role of the state in these countries is relatively efficient.

6.3.3 Government failure: government capture

The institutional economics view of the state emphasises the problem of *government capture*. This is when businesses and their representatives, such as sector-wide associations and lobbyists, manage to bend formal institutions, market regulation, and fiscal policy to serve their own interests. Government capture is more likely in case of a weak state and when there are dominant market parties, such as a powerful employers' association, a dominant lobby group, or a large firm which can threaten to relocate to a foreign destination. Government capture of institutions happens through influence on decision making about institutional reform. For example, changes in property rights through land reform. In Latin America, the continent with the most unequal land distribution and very powerful large landowners, lobbying by large landowners has held up reform measures for decades in many areas.

Government capture takes place through rent-seeking and moral hazard.

6.3.3.1 Rent-seeking

Rent-seeking is the increasing of one's share of wealth without contributing to this wealth, through lobbying or bribes. For example, lobbying for investment subsidies in agriculture by large landowners, even though they have the resources to invest by themselves and there is sufficient labour supply to work the land with lower levels of capital intensity.

An example of rent-seeking as a government failure is the public procurement policy of the government of Paraguay, in South America. Due to its high earnings from a power project with an enormous dam, it has a large pool of resources making up 50 per cent of all tax revenue.[2] An important share of these revenues is used to buy services from private firms. The firms are supposed to compete with each other in a fair procurement process with transparent rules and effective enforcement, to obtain contracts for delivery of services and goods to the state. However, some firms become favoured in this process because they share part of the budget they receive for their services with some public officials managing the procurement process, and who by-pass the formal legal arrangements for public procurement. Moreover, most of the rent-seeking activities by the favoured firms occurs through the resale of imported goods by the private sector to the government at much higher prices. This leads to extra profits, at a cost to tax-payers. This practice not only represents a serious form of corruption, but also implies serious inefficiency in the allocation of public resources in the economy of Paraguay.

6.3.3.2 Moral hazard

Moral hazard is defined as taking risks when the costs are borne by others. For example, banks providing high-risk loans when the government provides deposit insurance to all account holders.

A *deposit insurance* is a guarantee, up to a maximum amount, of savings in bank accounts. When loans are paid off, the banks reap the benefits. But when the borrowers do not pay back their loans, it is the tax-payer who pays the bill, not the banks. The moral hazard is that the banks only have the upside of the risk but not the downside.

Deposit insurance is not only provided in the developed world; middle-income countries also provide this to bank account holders in order to strengthen consumer confidence in banks. In Latin America, Brazil has a deposit insurance system in place. Table 6.2 gives an overview of the amounts of money held by insured deposit holders in the year 2011. As you can see, up to 175 million clients, and 1.3 billion reais were involved.[3]

6.4 Post Keynesian economics of the state

The market generates economic cycles, with growth and sometimes long and severe recessions. Post Keynesian economics views the state as a offering a solution to the disadvantages of such cycles. The state can provide stability for and stimulation of the economy through macroeconomic policy. In Post Keynesian economics, the state is potentially a positive force that could improve the overall economic performance of firms and households. Keynes rejected the view of *self-adjusting markets* that would automatically lead to a full-employment equilibrium with low inflation. Instead, he argued that an economy could be stuck at high levels of unemployment. So, Post Keynesians are in favour of the state taking on the role of director of the economy. They see this role of director in two forms: dampening the economic cycle and the developmental state.

6.4.1 Anti-cyclical budget and subsidies

If the government does nothing, economic cycles result in a *cyclical budget deficit*: when the economic cycle is low, the government budget deficit is high, and when the cycle is at the top, the budget deficit turns into a budget surplus. Hence, the government's expenditures should be complementary to consumer expenditures and business investment, according to Keynes: when firms invest little and households buy little, the government should spend more. This

Table 6.2 Deposit insurance in Brazil, 2011

Bracket	Clients		Amount	
Real (R$)	Number	%	Real (R$ Million)	%
under 5,000	155,254,271	88.83	67,772	5.09
5,000 to 20,000	12,179,991	6.97	122,382	9.19
20,000 to 40,000	3,456,804	1.98	96,936	7.28
40,000 to 70,000	1,759,101	1.01	92,715	6.96
more than 70,000	2,132,893	1.22	952,003	71.48
Total	174,783,060	100	1,331,808	100

Source: Fundo Garantidor de Creditos, http://www.fgc.org.br/libs/download_arquivo.php?ci_arquivo=145

view results in the policy advice for an *anti-cyclical budget*: deficits when the economic cycle is low and surpluses when the cycle is high.

Some of government expenditures and revenues entail *automatic stabilisers*. These are parts of spending and taxes which smoothen the economic cycle automatically. They are built into the economic system through the government's tax and expenditure structures, which lead to automatic increases or decreases in government expenditures (G) and tax revenue (T) when the economy moves along the economic cycle. When an economy is in a downturn, tax revenue goes down by itself. There are more unemployed people, and those who keep their jobs may earn less income, so that together they pay less tax. Also some businesses will close down while others will make less profits or even losses, which leads to lower profit taxes paid by firms as well. So, without any planning or decision making, during an economic downturn, tax revenue also goes down. This enables consumers and firms to sustain, at least to some extent, their levels of consumer spending and investment. And that is necessary to keep aggregate demand going.

On the government spending side, a similar automatic process occurs. When the economy is in a downturn, more people will be eligible for social welfare, whether it is unemployment benefits in developed countries or food aid or public work schemes in developing countries. More people are in need of social support, and, unless the government puts a cap on its support programmes, this will increase these people's disposable incomes, which they will use for consumer expenditures. Again, this keeps aggregate demand higher than it otherwise would be in a downturn. Of course, this leads to higher government expenditures, so the budget deficit will go up: G – T will increase. And that is precisely the mechanism behind automatic stabilisers: they automatically increase the difference between G and T: the automatic increase in the budget deficit helps to stabilise the economy: it makes the low stage of the economic cycle less deep and its duration shorter.

In order to calculate the extent to which government spending stimulates the economy, Keynes developed the concept of the *multiplier*. This is an accelerator on aggregate demand through an initial injection and its stimulating effects on other demand variables. It is called a multiplier because the effect on output is generally larger than the extra amount spent (the increase in G, or ΔG). That is because the increase in government spending is likely to increase jobs, and the additional workers will spend some of their income on consumption. And that extra consumer spending will also increase output (GDP). So, for an increase in G of, say, 200 billion pesos, and a multiplier of 3, GDP will grow by 600 billion pesos. In the macroeconomic section of this book, I will show you how the size of the multiplier can be calculated.

Higher government expenditures can be implemented through subsidies to firms and households, to encourage their investments. Think about subsidies for solar panels on the roofs of factories and houses. Or think about a newly created state investment fund for scholarships for third level education. Such government investments kill two birds with one stone. They increase aggregate demand in the economy by filling the investment gap left by firms and households. This reduces the downturn in the economic cycle. And it helps to finance public goods, thereby fulfilling certain unfulfilled needs in the economy or reducing negative externalities.

6.4.2 The developmental state

A *developmental state* is a state which guides the market on a long-term economic development path with subsidies, investments, and risk absorption for firms. This entrepreneurial role turns the state into a funder of new technology and risk-financer for key investment activities. The role of the developmental state has been ignored for a long time. Recent research has shown that the state can play a crucial role in development. Not only in countries like China, which is largely a state-led market economy under a communist regime, but also in highly capitalist countries, such as the USA. A recent study has shown how important the state has been and still is for US innovation. It has demonstrated, for example, that much of Apple's success depends on state innovations and state grants for R&D in the ICT sector.

> All the technologies which make the iPhone 'smart' are also state funded: the internet, wireless networks, GPS, microelectronics, touch screen displays, and the latest voice-activated SIRI personal assistant.[4]

The developmental state, or *entrepreneurial state*,[5] turns the state into a major agent in the economy, stimulating activity in the private sector, which goes above and beyond its role of enabling and regulating markets. An example is the government of Brazil, which carries out its developmental role through various mechanisms. One is the state investment bank (BNDES).[6] It is run by experts in innovation, in particular in the biotechnology and green technology sectors. The development bank particularly invests when an innovation is in the testing phase and approval is being sought from the relevant authorities. It invests both in traditional Brazilian large-scale industries, such as the aircraft and automobile industries, and in small-scale new sectors and firms, such as in the ICT sector and green technologies. Despite the high innovation risks it takes, the Brazilian development bank is profitable. Another tool that the Brazilian government uses for its developmental role are local *incubators*: spaces for start-up firms with

Image 6.2 Apple products

156 *The state*

close connections to research institutions, finance, and business advice. The Brazilian government has increased its budget for R&D so that it now equals that of China as a share of GDP.

Box 6.2 Brazilian incubators

Brazil pioneered the implementation of business incubation programmes in Latin America in the 1980s with five technological foundations for the transfer of technology from universities to the production sector. The first Brazilian incubators consolidated in 1987 in Rio de Janeiro. In the same year, the Brazilian Association of Science Parks and Business Incubators (ANPROTEC) was created. In 2009 Brazil had 400 operating incubators, predominantly located in the most developed states. Their main objectives are to provide incentives for entrepreneurs, and encourage regional economic development, job creation, and technological development. The incubators tend to concentrate on information and communication technology, agribusiness, electro-electronics, mechanics/biotechnology, and services. These areas reflect the priority segments in the Brazilian national policy for development.

In general, local governments provide the incubator infrastructure. The state government, through state research agencies, provides innovation-driven grants targeted at specific types of firms and sectors. The state also regulates the functioning of the incubated firms, through the licensing of installations or the registration of products by the Brazilian National Health Surveillance Agency (ANVISA). Another role of the state is as buyer of products and services provided by incubated start-ups, especially at the local level, for low R&D-intensive outputs.

Source: Corradi, A. (2013) *Critical Learning Episodes in the Evolution of Business Start-Up: Business Incubators in South-Eastern Brazil*. The Hague: Institute of Social Studies of Erasmus-Rotterdam University, PhD dissertation.

The state's role in economic development stimulates innovation-led growth and can ensure that growth is inclusive. The state provides public venture capital precisely where private venture capital does not want to risk entering uncertain areas of innovation. For example, Google's algorithm was developed by the state. In the USA, private venture capital only followed public venture capital 15–20 years later, according to the study referred to above.[7] These findings do not accord with the common dichotomous belief that the state is rigid and the market is entrepreneurial. Instead, the state's developmental role includes entrepreneurship. Often, private firms benefit from the state's innovations and subsidies without any compensation. In addition, firms lobby for lower taxes. US pharmaceutical industries have already managed to get tax reductions for their laboratories, multinational firms make use of foreign tax havens to reduce their tax payments, and they downsize their R&D spending, relying on state-funded university research. As institutional economics has explained, these are forms of moral hazard and rent-seeking by firms.

6.4.3 The paradox of the strong state

Empirical research on the developmental state in OECD countries, the Asian tiger economies, China, and some Latin American countries, shows that for markets to grow at high rates, the state should be strong, not weak. And even more so when successful firms, with state support, try to capture state investments through moral hazard and rent-seeking without paying back sufficiently to the state and the domestic economy. This leads to the paradox of the strong state: the more dominant the role of the market, the stronger (but not necessarily the bigger) the state should be. A strong state is necessary in order to ensure that the market functions optimally. And given the inherent tendencies of markets to exclude needs without purchasing power, to reinforce inequalities through accumulation, and to accumulate market power by dominant firms, a bigger market needs a stronger state to keep the invisible foot in check. Not just to prevent the kicking at the markets' foundations, like property rights and equal opportunity laws, but also to prevent the invisible foot kicking the distribution of the market's benefits towards ever increasing inequalities.

The paradox of the strong state often leads to confusion. Those supporting free markets fear that a stronger state automatically leads to a bigger state at the cost of the functioning of the market. There is a widely held belief that the state is necessarily rigid and inefficient and that markets are necessarily flexible and automatically result in efficient outcomes. Against this belief, it is insightful to quote Joan Robinson again, whom I also quoted in the introductory chapter:[8]

> It is a popular error that bureaucracy is less flexible than private enterprise. It may be so in detail, but when large-scale adaptations have to be made, central control is far more flexible. It may take two months to get an answer to a letter from a government department, but it takes twenty years for an industry under private enterprise to readjust itself to a fall in demand.

6.5 Neoclassical economics of the state

The neoclassical view of the state is a minimalist state, or a night-watch state. The reason is that, compared with individual agents in the market, the state can never oversee all the complex decisions being made in the economy. It is therefore better, according to neoclassical economists, to rely on the rationality of each individual party in the market, who takes every

Table 6.3 Size of the state in the economy (% of GDP) across the world

	1981–1990	*1991–2000*	*2001–2005*	*2006–2012*
Geographical classification				
East Asia & Pacific	13.9	14.4	16.0	16.4
Middle East & North Africa	23.8	21.8	17.8	16.2
Euro area	20.1	20.1	20.3	21.2
Sub-Saharan Africa	16.0	15.9	15.1	16.5
North America	16.4	15.4	15.4	16.4
Latin America & Caribbean	11.1	14.1	14.5	15.0
Income classification*				
Low income	10.2	10.1	10.4	10.7
Lower middle income	11.9	11.4	11.1	11.4
Upper middle income	13.0	14.8	14.8	14.6
High income	17.6	17.3	17.7	18.5
The world	16.7	16.7	17.0	17.7

Source: World Bank.

158 *The state*

opportunity to make profitable investments out of available resources. So, the complement of the rather negative view of the state by neoclassical economists is quite an optimistic view of the self-regulating power of the market. Table 6.3 shows the size of the state in economies across the world. The data in the table show that the euro-zone and high-income countries have the largest state role in their economies.

The economic role of the state in neoclassical economics is therefore limited to three activities:

- enforcement of property rights (as in institutional theory);
- preventing market power by dominant firms through enforcing competition (as in social economics);
- creating new markets with new property rights to address market failures.

Market failures often require the state to step in where the market has failed. The neoclassical response to market failures is the creation of new markets through a combination of privatisation (remember the telecommunications example in Chapter 5), infrastructural investment (such as a business park or seaport), and its own demand for goods and services (think about defence supplies or hiring primary school teachers). Think about privatisation, shifting property rights from the state to the private sector, or land titling of communal land, creating individual codified property rights and land markets for the exchange of titled land.

Some market failures can only be addressed by public goods. For those public goods, neoclassical economics is concerned about the problem of free riding. *Free riding* means that people make use of public goods without contributing to their costs, through fees or tax payment. For example taking a ride with a public bus company without buying a ticket. Free riding is another reason for supporting a minimalist state by neoclassical economists.

6.5.1 Price distortions

Remember that neoclassical economics assumes that markets result in equilibrium and remain there until a shock occurs, and that in equilibrium supply meets all demand. From this perspective, price regulation has negative side effects on the quantity exchanged in the market. The lower the price of food, enforced with a maximum price, the less farmers will produce because they will earn less than before from selling food. They may rather prefer to grow export crops, such as coffee or tobacco, which earn a higher return on their labour and land investment. As a consequence, food production may go down with the implementation of maximum food prices. That makes the policy of a maximum price rather ineffective: the poor now still have limited access to food. Not because it is too expensive, but because there is not much food available. That creates long lines of customers in front of shops, waiting for food to become available. This explains the lack of coffee, tea, and toilet paper in Venezuelan supermarkets. Hence, neoclassical economics regards price regulation as price distortion, which make markets inefficient and pro-poor policies ineffective.

Is price regulation necessarily inefficient? Not so. It depends on the type of market. For the labour market with an over-supply of labour, a minimum wage is also a price distortion. Neoclassical economists argue that the higher the minimum wage, the more expensive labour becomes for firms. Hence, the more likely that firms will hire undocumented immigrants at below-minimum wages, or that they will substitute some of their labour force for capital goods, for example by mechanisation. This results in less demand for labour, and hence, contributes to unemployment. Hence, again ineffectiveness and inefficiency due to a price distortion.

But this result is not a necessary outcome. With a maximum sales price, producers will try to minimise production costs so that they will keep a similar profit margin as before the regulation. And a minimum price for inputs will similarly stimulate producers to cut their costs and to benefit from increased productivity generating the more valuable input.

Moreover, consumers are likely to buy more of products with a price ceiling, because they have become cheaper. This increases the volume sold, which allows for economies of scale, and hence further declines in production costs. In the case of minimum wages, the more expensive labour force now tends to be more productive, encouraged by higher wages, so that producers suffer no net cost disadvantages of a minimum wage above the market wage. Why? Because with higher wages, the workers' opportunity costs of losing their jobs have become higher. And the higher value for their work, in particular when it is regarded as fair by the workers themselves, contributes to work motivation. So, the negative view of price regulation as distortions in neoclassical economics may be justified in some cases but is not always supported by real-world situations.

6.5.2 Good governance

Even a minimalist state needs to perform its roles adequately. Recent developments in neoclassical economics have pointed at the effectiveness of states to support the functioning of markets. This is referred to as *good governance*. There are even statistics for good governance at the country level. These measures include the number of days it takes to get through the bureaucracy to set up a business and the extent of economic freedom from regulation for firms. Table 6.4 shows data for the bureaucracy involved in setting up a business for selected countries across the world. The advantage of such indicators of good governance is that you can compare some dimensions of the efficiency of the state's economic role between countries. The limitation of measuring good governance only as the state's role in supporting markets, is that it excludes other important dimensions of good governance. For example, the available measures do not address the effectiveness and efficiency of the state's role in redistribution, social service delivery, poverty reduction, or economic stability.

6.6 Public finance

The state's finances are referred to as *public finance*. This concerns the revenues and expenditures by the state. The policy concerning the government's revenues and expenditures is called *fiscal policy*. From the government's perspective, there is a balance in public finance when tax revenues equal expenditures. In symbols: a *balanced budget* implies that T = G. When there is a *budget deficit*, G is bigger than T, and when the government runs a *budget surplus*, T is bigger than G. From the perspective of an individual, there is before-tax income and after-tax income. After-tax income (Yd) is called *disposable income* or *net income*: income (Y) after taxes (T). In symbols: Yd = Y − T. This means that disposable income is income after taxes are deducted.

Public debt is the total of accumulated budget deficits minus surpluses over time. Every country has public debt. For some countries, the amount of public debt is even higher than the value of GDP. There is no evidence that debt levels of 100 per cent of GDP have a negative effect on the economy. But high public debt can become a burden on public finances because of the interest payments that need to be paid annually to the creditors.

Table 6.4 Good governance indicator of business start-up costs (2013)

	Starting a business			
	Rank	Procedures (number)	Time (days)	Cost (% of GNI* per capita)
Armenia	6	2	4	1.1
China	158	13	33	2
Indonesia	175	10	48	20.5
Thailand	91	4	27.5	6.7
Egypt	50	7	8	9.7
Iran	107	8	16	3.1
Kuwait	152	12	32	1.1
UAE	37	6	8	6.4
Bangladesh	74	7	10.5	19.9
India	179	12	27	47.3
Austria	138	8	25	4.8
Bulgaria	65	4	18	1
Germany	111	9	14.5	4.7
Italy	90	6	6	14.2
Netherlands	14	4	4	5.2
Ethiopia	166	9	15	100.1
Kenya	134	10	32	38.2
Nigeria	122	8	28	58.3
Rwanda	9	2	2	4.4
Canada	2	1	5	0.4
United States	20	6	5	1.5
Bolivia	180	15	49	71.6
Brazil	123	13	107.5	4.6
Mexico	48	6	6	19.7

*Note: GNI, gross national income.

Sources: Int'l Finance Cooperation (IFC) of World Bank, http://www.doingbusiness.org/data/exploretopics/starting-a-business, Heritage Foundation http://www.heritage.org/index/ranking.

Assume that a country has a debt of 100 per cent of GDP, meaning that the amount of public debt equals the value of GDP. And let us also assume that the interest on that debt is 5 per cent per year. This means that every year, an amount worth 5 per cent of GDP needs to be paid by the government to its creditors. Now suppose that total government expenditures are 25 per cent of GDP, the interest payment on the public debt then amounts to 20 per cent of all government spending (5 per cent of GDP out of a portion of 25 per cent of GDP is one fifth: 5/25 = 1/5 = 0.20). And that is only interest payment, without paying back any of the debt. The implication for public finance is that only 80 per cent of government expenditures remains available for all other government spending categories. And when the debt is to other countries, it needs to be paid back in foreign currency, which can only be earned through exports.

Government expenditures consist of three main categories:

- government consumption and investment
- transfer payments
- interest and debt payments.

6.6.1 Government consumption and investment

Government consumption is the actual running expenditures by the state: the salaries of civil servants, subsidies for firms and NGOs, road maintenance, annual expenditures for the operation of the national defence forces, the police, and the judicial and other legal systems. They can all be found in the budgets of individual government sectors, such as of the Ministry of Justice, the Ministry of Public Administration, and the Ministry of Finance and Planning. *Government investment* concerns the long-term expenditures for development: schools, hospitals, street lighting, military aircraft, laboratories, and other R&D expenditures. These budget items can also be found in sector budgets.

6.6.2 Transfer payments

Transfer payments is the category of expenditures for social policy, such as social security and social safety nets. Part of such expenditures is arranged not through tax payment but through contributions to social security funds. *Social security* is an additional tax system, but with earmarked expenditures for social protection. You can think of social security contributions for pensions. These contributions should not be used by the government to finance gaps in teachers salaries or the road maintenance budget, for example. These two systems together, taxes and social security contributions, make up all resources for the transfers by the state.

In Europe, North America as well as the most developed countries of Latin America (such as Argentina, Brazil, Chile, Costa Rica, and Mexico), transfer payments began taking shape in the 1950s and 1960s. By then, these Latin American countries had rapidly expanded public education, public health care, and state-run pension systems. However, these often did not reach the poorest segments of the population. Social policy and social security was oriented towards the urban middle class and urban and rural upper class. That is why, despite an

Image 6.3 Street lighting

expansion in social policy and accompanying transfer payments, high levels of inequality and poverty persisted in Latin America for several decades.

For example in Argentina, democratic governments in the 1940s and 1950s managed to provide pension coverage for 70 per cent of the population. This was rare in Latin America in those days. But the military dictatorships of the 1970s and 1980s eliminated employers' contributions, and in the 1990s, neoliberal policy reforms led to partial privatisation of the pension system. These changes, together with free riding through widespread evasion of pension contributions, were responsible for the fact that in the decades afterwards, Argentinian pension benefits declined and became less and less a reliable form of social security for the Argentinian elderly.

As we have seen, Brazil is one of the world's most unequal countries. Surprisingly, its taxation and government expenditures are quite high, more at the level of European welfare states than of a middle-income country. And higher than for the USA: Brazil's tax revenue is more than 30 per cent of GDP, whereas the United States' tax revenue is less than 30 per cent of GDP.[9] But much of the Brazilian tax revenue that is reserved for social spending is spent on people in the higher income brackets: on pensions for retired civil servants and unemployment benefits for formal sector workers. However, many Brazilians work in the informal economy and are not entitled to such social security. Among the other categories of spending, we have seen that debt payments take a considerable share of the Brazilian government budget.

6.6.3 Interest and debt payments

Interest and debt payments are government expenditures to pay back debt and the interest on the debt. These payments are to the holders of government debt, which are households, firms, and investment funds (including pension funds), as well as lenders in other countries, including international development agencies and governments. For the payment of debt to foreign debt holders, a country must earn foreign currency. *Debt service* is debt and interest payments as a percentage of a country's export earnings. Debt service uses foreign currency earnings to pay back foreign holders of public debt, such as the World Bank, foreign commercial banks, international investment funds, and foreign governments. Latin American countries traditionally rank high in debt service. Brazil's debt service stands at around 20 per cent, whereas Mexico's debt service is about 10 per cent.[10]

This means that 20 per cent of the foreign exchange earned from exports flows directly back to foreign countries and international institutions to pay off Brazil's public debt.

6.6.4 Tax revenue

Next to government expenditures (G), there is tax revenue (T). These have varied sources:

- income and profit taxes
- value added taxes (VAT)
- import taxes
- fees.

An additional category that is technically not a tax but in practice functions like a tax is *social security* contributions, as mentioned above. Employees and employers in the formal economy pay social security contributions for pensions, health care, and disability insurance.

In Latin America, tax revenue is below the world average as a percentage of GDP. The only exception is Brazil, as we have seen above, which has tax revenue at the level of OECD countries. When we look at the break-down in types of taxes, Latin America appears to have very low levels of income taxes, in particular personal income taxes. Those taxes only begin at quite high levels of earned income, and have many deductions and exemptions. As a percentage of GDP, personal taxation is almost five times higher in OECD countries, starting at much lower levels of earned income relative to the median income (that is the income which 50 per cent of the households find themselves below and 50 per cent above). In contrast, *value added tax* (VAT), for simplicity equated with sales tax here, is a tax levied on consumer products. This contributes a higher share in Latin America: on average 37 per cent of GDP. For Brazil, Diagram 6.1 shows the break-down of taxes for the year 2010, as compared to other Latin American countries and OECD countries. The diagram shows that income and profit taxes are relatively low (21.2 and 2.7: 24 per cent), the social security contributions are at the level of developed countries (26 per cent), and the highest tax revenue is from VAT (9.1 and 3.7: 43 per cent).

The tax structure of Brazil is quite representative of developing countries. Most taxes come from sales taxes and not from incomes and profits. This means that most taxes are not progressive but *regressive taxes*: they do not tax most those with the highest incomes. On the contrary, the poor pay the same tax on food, transport, clothing, and medicine as the rich, while the rich often have ways to evade such taxes through owning foreign houses and other forms of tax evasion. Sales taxes are regressive taxes: they place a relatively high burden on the poor, because there are no tax deductions and exemptions for sales tax. Income and profit taxes are *progressive taxes*: the strongest shoulders bear the heaviest tax burdens. When income is low or firms make losses, they pay low or no taxes on their earnings. Only higher incomes and positive business profits are taxed.

6.6.5 Bonds

Most governments run a budget deficit most of the time. This means that $G - T < 0$. They spend more than they earn in tax revenues. The budget deficit needs to be financed in order to be able to pay the higher expenditures. One of the ways is for the Ministry of Finance, also referred to as the Treasury, to issue government bonds. *Bonds* are government papers sold in a bond market which entitle their holders to a fixed amount of interest over a fixed time period (often 10 years), after which the original amount will be paid back. So, by selling bonds, the government receives money with which it can finance its deficit. You can regard a bond as a loan to the government, but as a tradable loan: you can buy and sell bonds on exchange markets.

Who buys bonds? Bonds are mainly bought by large investment funds seeking low-risk assets to invest in. For example pension funds. Other buyers of government bonds are banks and wealthy individuals. And some not so wealthy people who like to invest in order to try to reap higher returns on investment than the interest rate they would earn on a savings account in a bank. John Maynard Keynes was an example of such a moderate earning but not wealthy private investor. He enjoyed speculating on the London stock exchange, buying and selling financial assets, including British government bonds.

Are government bonds low-risk assets? Yes and no. Yes, because, unlike a firm, a state cannot go bankrupt. A country has an enormous amount of resources: natural resources, its infrastructure and housing stock, the value of its firms, and most importantly, its human resources. This enormous wealth gives the confidence to investors that lending to a government is relatively safe. But economic history has shown that bonds can become almost

164 *The state*

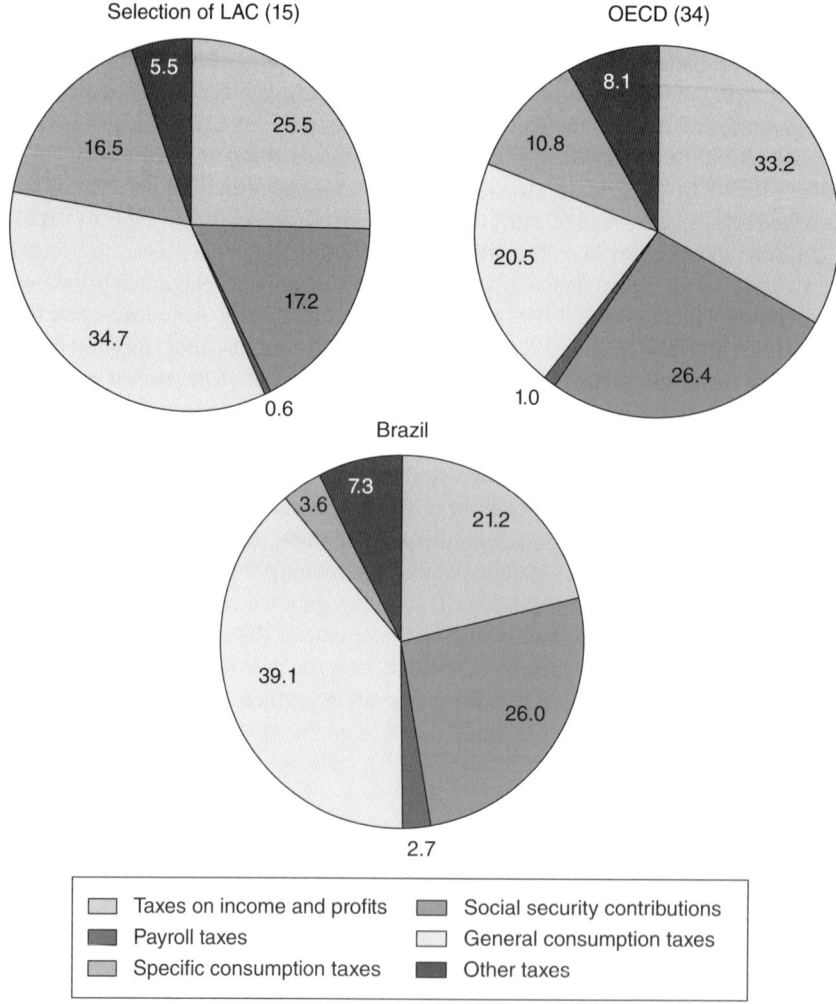

Diagram 6.1 Composition of tax revenue in Brazil, Latin America, and the OECD (2010)

LAC, Latin American countries.

Source: http://www.oecd.org/ctp/tax-global/Brazil%20country%20note_EN_final.pdf

valueless when government debt becomes so high that a government is no longer able to pay it back. Or when investors fear that they may never get their money back and begin selling their bonds on a second-hand market for much lower prices than their initial value, in order to get at least some value in return for their investment. In 1982 Mexico was the first country in the world to announce to its debtors that it could no longer pay off its debt. The *debt ratio* had become unbearable: the public debt as a percentage of GDP. Technically, the country was not bankrupt, but practically it was because the government was no longer able to get loans to pay its civil servants, pay for other expenditures and service its debt: nobody in the world wanted to provide loans to the Mexican government anymore, and the bonds and other loans that had been provided in the past to the government were traded at low values on second-hand bond markets. They were reduced to the status of *junk bonds*: low-rated but high-interest yielding bonds in which speculators invest in order to reap high returns on investment in the short run.

Most of the Mexican debt in 1982 was foreign debt: to foreign banks, governments of developed counties, and the World Bank. The additional problem of foreign debt is that it needs to be paid back in foreign currency, mainly dollars, euros, and pounds. But Mexico was spending most of the foreign currency that it earned from exports on paying for imported goods. It did not have sufficient foreign exchange earnings to pay foreign creditors.

Mexico could only obtain emergency loans from the IMF and loans to restructure its economy from the World Bank on the condition that it would implement so-called *Structural Adjustment Programmes* (SAPs). These are macroeconomic reform programmes which reduce government expenditures and expand markets, through expenditure cuts, privatisation of public firms, and the liberalisation of several markets. SAPs resulted in Mexico and later in other countries suffering from high debt with declines in GDP, high unemployment, and rising poverty. Only in the 1990s, did Mexico climb out of its debt crisis. But at high social and economic cost. And, as critics had argued from the beginning, with many unnecessary costs, because the privatisation of public firms and services and the cut-backs on social expenditures had caused more poverty and increasing inequality.

Are there alternatives to structural adjustment? Yes, although there is no magic bullet, as can be seen from the fact that every year other countries experience debt problems, even members of the European Union, and they have their own type of adjustment programmes with serious cut-backs in government expenditures.

Box 6.3 Mexican debt crisis

In the 10 years leading up to Mexico's debt crisis, public debt increased more than tenfold, from US$4 billion to over US$40 billion. Foreign debt rose to 50 per cent of GDP. Mexico's oil export revenue also increased steadily, so that it earned dollars to pay back the debt. But in 1981 oil reserves appeared smaller than expected and the interest rates on foreign debt increased, while inflation rose to 100 per cent. In 1982 the Mexican Central Bank decided to let the value of the peso depreciate by 40 per cent against the dollar. Moreover, wages increased to keep up with inflation, so that the largest private firm defaulted on its foreign debt, which suddenly had become 40 per cent higher in peso terms. The peso then lost another 30 per cent against the dollar. This induced capital flight by rich Mexican households and medium and large-sized firms, drawing away the necessary domestic sources of finance.

The crisis was met in 1982 by debt restructuring and loans from the USA, the IMF, commercial banks, and others, with US$15 billion. The conditions – the Structural Adjustment Programme – were severe, requiring lower subsidies, tighter money supply, curbing of wage increases, and increasing interest rates in the hope that would keep the remaining capital of the rich from fleeing the country. As a consequence, GDP fell by 10 per cent over 2 years. Whereas capital could freely move out, migrants were increasingly stopped at the US border. The structural adjustment was borne by the poorest half of the population, with lower incomes, more unpaid time to make-up for reduced public services, and higher interest rates on their loans.

Sources:https://www.imf.org/external/pubs/ft/history/2001/ch07.pdf and https://www.utexas.edu/lbj/uscir/binpapers/v3c-2alba.pdf

An alternative policy in a debt crisis concerns debt restructuring, which means cancelling part of the debt (also called debt forgiveness) and refinancing other parts of the debt at favourable terms (at low or zero interest rates). This is similar to what happens when private firms run into financial problems: they go bankrupt, in which case their debt is cancelled, or they are offered debt restructuring by their biggest lenders who thereby enable the firm to survive and generate future earnings.

6.6.6 Public debt

Why do governments run budget deficits and accumulate debt? Isn't that unwise compared to one's household finances? If you as an individual, or the household you are a part of, regularly run a deficit, and pay off your old loans with new loans, your bank and your friends are likely to refuse to lend you more money one day. But for a government, which represents a country, it is not the same. There are sound economic reasons for public debt. First, governments have generally a good financial standing in financial markets. This allows the state to borrow at favourable interest rates. Second, government borrowing is often for long periods and new loans can be used to pay off old loans. And old loans were taken out in the money values of long ago. Over time, inflation reduces the value of the money. So the value of a million reais 10 years ago is much less today, due to inflation. Moreover, GDP generally grows over time. So, the government budget is likely to have grown as well, and the old loan as a percentage of today's budget is much less than it was when the loan was taken out.

The combination of these two macroeconomic tendencies – inflation and GDP growth – means that today, the debt of a loan from 10 years ago is relatively cheap to pay off: the payment capacity has increased as government revenue has increased relative to GDP, and the value of the loan in today's money value is lower than it was 10 years ago due to inflation. Second, government expenditures have an important economic and social function. So, in times when tax revenues are disappointing, the only way to sustain government expenditures is through running a deficit, and hence, borrowing money.

6.7 Interesting sources

Smith, A. [1759] *The Theory of Moral Sentiments*. Indianapolis: Liberty Fund, 1984.
Smith, A. [1776] *An Inquiry into the Nature and Causes of the Wealth of Nations*. Indianapolis: Liberty Fund, 1981.

6.8 Glossary

Anti-cyclical budget   Budget with deficits when the economic cycle is low and surpluses when the cycle is high

Anti-trust agency   Government agency which detects and punishes cartels

Automatic stabilisers   Those parts of spending and taxes which smoothen the economic cycle automatically

Balanced budget   When government revenues equal expenditures (T = G)

Bonds   Fixed-interest assets for a fixed period of time

Budget deficit When government expenditures are bigger than revenues (G > T)

Budget surplus When government expenditures are smaller than revenues (G < T)

Cyclical budget deficit When the economic cycle is low, the government budget deficit is high, and when the cycle is at the top, the budget deficit turns into a budget surplus

Debt ratio Public debt as percentage of GDP

Debt service Debt and interest payment as a percentage of a country's export earnings

Deposit insurance A guarantee, up to a maximum amount, of savings on bank accounts

Developmental state A state which guides the market on a long-term economic development path with subsidies, investments, and risk absorption for firms

Disposable income net income Income after taxes

Fiscal policy The policy concerning the governments' revenues and expenditures

Free riding Making use of public goods without contributing to their costs through fees or tax payment

Gini coefficient A measure of income inequality based on the income shares of each percentile of households in the income distribution

Government capture When business lobbying manages to bend formal institutions, market regulation, and fiscal policy to serve business interests

Government consumption The actual running expenditures by the state

Government failure When the government does not effectively carry out its economic roles

Government investment The long-term expenditures by the state for development

Incubators Spaces for start-up firms with close connection to research institutions, finance, and business advice

Interest and debt payments Government expenditures to pay back debt and the interest on the debt

Junk bonds Low-rated but high-interest yielding bonds in which speculators invest in order to reap high returns on investment in the short run

Merit goods Goods supplied by the state because they are regarded as desirable for everyone

Moral hazard Taking risks when the costs are borne by others

Multiplier An accelerator on aggregate demand through an initial injection and its stimulating effects on other demand variables

Price controls The market price is allowed to move only within a restricted range or is completely fixed

Progressive taxes Taxation in which the rich pay absolutely and relatively more tax than the poor due to increasing tariffs with income

Property rights   Rights to control, benefit from, and transfer property

Public debt   The total of accumulated budget deficits minus surpluses over time

Public finance   The revenues and expenditures by the state

Redistribution   The deliberate shift of resources and rewards from one social group to another

Regressive taxes   Taxation in which the poor pay relatively more than the rich

Rent-seeking   The increase of one's share of wealth without contributing to this wealth, through lobbying or bribes

Self-adjusting markets   Markets which automatically lead to a full-employment equilibrium and low inflation

Social security   An additional tax system, but with earmarked expenditures for social protection

Structural Adjustment Programmes (SAPs)   Macroeconomic reform programmes which reduce government expenditures and expand markets, through expenditure cuts, privatisation of public firms, and the liberalisation of several markets

Tax base   The number of economic agents from which taxes are raised

Transaction costs   Costs involved in an exchange, not reflected in the price of the good exchanged

Transfer payments   The public expenditures on social policy, such as social security and social safety nets

Tri-partite bargaining process   Bargaining over labour conditions between the government, labour unions, and employers' representatives

Value added tax (VAT)   A tax levied on consumer products

Notes

1. See for the complete study: Lustig, N., L. Lopez-Calva and E. Ortiz-Juarez (2013) 'Declining Inequality in Latin America in the 2000s: The Cases of Argentina, Brazil, and Mexico', *World Development*, 44, pp. 129–41.
2. See for the full paper: http://idei.fr/doc/wp/2011/wp_idei_661.pdf
3. See data in: http://www.fgc.org.br/libs/download_arquivo.php?ci_arquivo=145
4. Mazzucato, M. (2013) *The Entrepreneurial State*. London: Anthem Press, p. 188.
5. See the source in note 4.
6. See, for a detailed evaluation of BNDES: Hochstetler, K. and A. Montero (2013) 'The Renewed Developmental State: The National Development Bank and the Brazil Model', *Journal of Development Studies*, 49(11), pp. 1484–99.
7. See the source in note 4.
8. I thank Mariana Mazzucato for including this quote in her book *The Entrepreneurial State* (London: Anthem Press, 2013, p. vi). The quote is from Robinson, J. (1987) 'Obstacles to Full Employment', in: *Contributions to Modern Economics*. New York: Academic Press, p. 27.
9. http://www.oecd.org/ctp/tax-global/Brazil%20country%20note_EN_final.pdf
10. World Development Indicators, World Bank.

7 Public goods and commons

7.1 Domestic public goods

This chapter elaborates on the public goods sections of Chapters 5 and 6. It will also discuss the financing of public goods, and therefore will also follow up on the public finance part of Chapter 6. Why do we need an extra chapter on public goods? There are two reasons. First, public goods, and their use and financing, are a key government policy tool. They allow for redistribution (whether or not redistribution actually happens), they address major market failures, and they are a tool for government investment and stimulation of the economy. So, through public goods, the state has a key tool for economic development as well as for social development. The second reason is that in addition to domestic public goods, there are global public goods. But without a global state, how are these provided and funded? This chapter will discuss three global public goods and explain their characteristics and challenges from an economic perspective.

Finally, this chapter introduces the notion of commons and common-pool resources. These are a variation on public goods: they are collective goods, not financed and supplied by the state. Commons are used, owned, preserved, or protected by collectives, not individuals. Think about nature reserves, cultural heritage, and joint agricultural land.

7.1.1 Types of public goods

We distinguish between three types of public goods: public goods, merit goods, and club goods.

7.1.1.1 Public goods

Public goods are goods which no one can technically be excluded from enjoying. They cannot be provided by the market or by communities. Markets fail to provide these goods because the benefits cannot be collected by the provider of the goods, or only at high cost, which makes private supply unprofitable. Think about public defence, the judicial system, or a lighthouse. And communities fail to provide these goods because they lack the financial and human resources to do so. Public goods have a certain non-rivalry and non-excludability. Non-rivalry means that consumption by the one does not preclude consumption by another. When one ship is warned of a dangerous coastline in thick fog by a lighthouse, the next ship sailing by is also warned: the consumption of the light by the first ship does not preclude any next ship from consuming the same light as a warning. Non-excludability means that it is not possible to exclude someone from enjoying the good unless that economic agent pays for it. You may be a pacifist and be against weapons, but you nevertheless enjoy the border protection of your country by the army. You are not excluded from this protection. So, public goods are characterised by non-rivalry and non-excludability.

The state supplies public goods and has no competitor. This creates three challenges:

1   Public goods may be supplied through monopolies, which are likely to be inefficient (high cost, high prices). For national defence to be effective against foreign threats, we do not need rival armies to compete with each other for border protection, but a single, well-structured, and hierarchically managed army under the command of a single senior officer.
2   Public goods may trigger free riding behaviour by consumers, which is inefficient (low revenues). A free rider is an economic agent who enjoys a good without paying for it. This payment may be a tax contribution or a user fee. Think about littering in a nature reserve park or taking a bus ride without buying a ticket.
3   Public goods may have limited public financing due to low national income or because of high income inequality, so that the rich organise club goods or buy private goods for themselves and so don't want to contribute to certain public goods. In this way, only the households with the least purchasing power will make use of the particular public good, but have limited means to complement the public funding with user fees. This affects the quality of the public good.

7.1.1.2 Merit goods

Merit goods may be provided by the market and communities, but then will only serve part of the population. Others may be excluded, and this entails a social cost. Merit goods are often not non-rival and non-excludable. But although they can technically be provided by the market, they are nevertheless provided by the state. *Merit goods*, as their name indicates, are goods supplied by the state because they are regarded as desirable for everyone. Think about free vaccination programs. They serve the population as a whole and thereby are effective in preventing epidemics. But if the market were to provide vaccination programs, only a section of the population would be willing and able to afford them, leaving a substantial risk of contamination by those not receiving such preventive health care services.

Box 7.1 Polio vaccination programme in Pakistan

Pakistan is one of three countries in the world where polio is still endemic. Every year, fifty to hundred new cases are reported. The central government has regular vaccination campaigns where health care teams travel to remote areas to give the oral vaccination to children. In every country of the world, vaccination is considered by a large majority of the population to be a merit good. Also in Pakistan. But a minority of violent Taliban groups boycott the campaigns. That is why the medical teams require police protection. However, several teams have been attacked by bombs and guns, while some other teams have been kidnapped. Early in 2014, twelve security guards who were escorting a polio vaccination team were killed near the city of Peshawar.

Source: *The Guardian*, 2 March 2014.

7.1.1.3 Club goods

Club goods are non-rival but only accessible for members, hence, they are excludable. Only members of a tennis club can play on the tennis courts. Only licence holders are allowed to go hunting deer or elephants. Club goods can be provided by the state, for example through hunting licences, or by communities, for example through sports clubs. At the same time, a community-provided club good may be supplied through a firm, often a non-profit firm, for example by a non-profit association or a cooperative. So, a *club good* is supplied by a club, either literally by a community association, or by a virtual club consisting of all holders of a particular licence, such as a fishing or hunting licence.

Both public goods and merit goods may be produced by private firms or public firms. Think about vaccines: they may be produced by a state laboratory, or by the pharmaceutical industry and then bought by the state for distribution. The same applies for defence supplies, such as a naval ship: this may be built by a private shipyard, and bought by the state for its navy. Some public goods, paradoxically, are at the same time considered to be private goods. This is the case, for example, with public housing and public education. When the municipality provides housing for people with low incomes, the renters pay a rent and are legally considered the occupants of the apartment, with their constitutional rights to privacy. They rent a home on the housing market – it is just a deliberately segmented market with public housing supplied to low-income groups only.

So, public goods are always supplied by the state, but not necessarily produced by the state or consumed in a collective manner. There are degrees to which we can label a good as a public good. This requires two axes: the extent of rivalry and the extent of excludability of a good. See Diagram 7.1. The closer to the origin of the diagram, the purer a public good: non-rival and non-excludable. The further away from the origin and the closer to the upper right-hand side of the diagram, the more a good is a private good, such as jeans or a bicycle or a fashion magazine.

The degrees of rivalry that co-exist with non-excludability imply externalities. Remember that externalities imply costs or benefits to others. When a good is rival, but at the same time others cannot be excluded from consuming it, it will often trigger surplus demand. An example is traffic jams on public roads. Use of the road is non-excludable: any driver can use it, even when she does not pay taxes, for example because she is a foreign tourist. But when

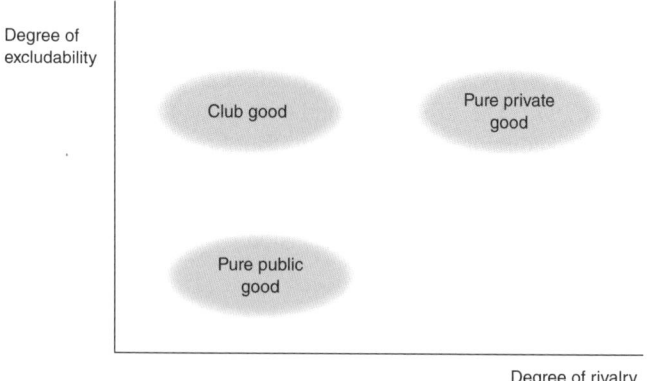

Diagram 7.1 Variations of public goods

172 *Public goods and commons*

traffic becomes more congested during rush hours, there are many rivals on the road, each of them trying to get enough space to get to work or home. This results in a negative externality, namely waste of time in traffic jams and pollution caused by a multitude of cars producing CO_2 and particulate matter. The extent of rivalry on a road varies by time of day. At midnight, there is often no rivalry, whereas at mid-day there may be some rivalry but not as much as during rush hour. So, externalities arise in the case of goods that are not pure public goods: they are non-excludable but not purely non-rival.

7.1.2 Financing domestic public goods

Domestic public goods are financed through various types of tax revenue and social insurance systems, sometimes complemented with fees. This occurs at the national and local level. Let me give three examples of public goods financing.

7.1.2.1 Predominantly tax financed: primary education

Primary education is largely financed by tax revenue. This is often from a national/federal or state-level tax base. This includes the general tax revenue, which is a combination of income taxes, profit taxes, value added taxes, property taxes, import taxes, etc. The national/federal or state budget will allocate part of this general tax revenue to primary education, both to its investment costs (schools, teacher training institutions) and to its consumption costs (salaries, school supplies, electricity bills). In addition, schools may require fees, but these are often low and/or means-tested, or only for additional services which are voluntary such as transport, school meals, and sports activities. When the fees become a substantive share of primary education financing, the public good shifts towards becoming a private good and may exclude lower income households from sending their children to school.

7.1.2.2 Predominantly social insurance financed: pensions

Some countries have a public pension system in addition to a private pension system. The public pension system may be financed not through taxation but through social insurance. This means that during their working life workers contribute part of their income (often supplemented with a contribution from their employers) to the public pension fund. This pension fund, hence, consists of accumulated contributions plus the net returns (profits minus losses) on investment of these contributions in bonds and other financial assets. By the time an individual worker retires, he is entitled to a pension from this fund, relative to his contributions but also subject to the size of the fund. The size of the fund at the time that a particular individual retires depends on inflation and returns on investment. But financial crises may result in negative net investment earnings for the fund, while inflation reduces its purchasing power. The advantage of financing pensions through social security rather than taxation is that the general tax revenue will not be burdened by increased pension demands during economic downturns and when the population is ageing.

7.1.2.3 Predominantly fee financed: a fast highway

An example of a predominantly fee-financed public good is a new highway that does not replace an existing road and train connection but provides a complementary connection that is faster. For example, through including a tunnel or bridge to pass quickly over a lake or through a mountain. Although the construction costs will be pre-financed through tax money, recovery of the costs occurs entirely or largely through a fee: a toll road. In this way, the tax money invested will be earned back over time so that the net costs for the treasury will be zero. This use of a fee will not necessarily exclude low-income groups because they still have the option of using the toll-free existing road (but that will mean a longer travelling time) or the train. In addition, the user fee is also a disincentive to use the toll road, in particular at busy times when traffic jams reduce the time gained as compared to the existing road. So, the fees also help to reduce the negative externality of traffic jams, and may, at rush hours, induce some commuters to choose the train rather than the car.

7.2 Theories of public goods

7.2.1 Social economics of public goods

In social economics, social norms and group pressure are understood to keep free riding behaviour in check. That is why many people who take a train buy a ticket even if the risk of being caught without a ticket is small and a cost–benefit calculation would show that the annually accumulated fines would be less than the expenditures saved from free riding over a year. Hence, group norms help prevent over-use and under-funding. For a problem on the supply side of a public good, namely low quality of service due to a monopoly, social economics also has a solution. This policy only works when there are multiple units of supply, such as schools and hospitals. The policy is benchmarking, which I already introduced in Chapter 5. *Benchmarking* was defined as an artificial competition policy with targets or rankings, which governments use to force more efficiency from public organisations.

For example, primary education is not supplied through one big school, but through a large number of public schools spread throughout the country. There may be quality differences between public schools, which result in more and less preferred schools. By rating and publicising the quality of individual primary schools, policy makers can provide incentives for the best performing schools. For example, more general funding or higher teacher salaries. This simulates competition between schools to achieve better quality. Benchmarking thereby enforces an efficient use of public educational resources: it forces schools to generate the highest possible performance within a given budget. Schools which under-perform will see their budgets decline and will eventually have to close down or restructure. This will increase the average quality of primary schooling in a municipality, province, or country.

7.2.2 Institutional economics of public goods

Institutional economists recognise that in large communities, such as modern cities, social norms and social control may not work effectively to prevent free riding. That is why they see a need for institutions to prevent free riding. Such institutions may be found in subscriptions and member cards, which reduce the transaction costs for consumers paying a fee every time they make use of the public good. Such institutions are a win–win solution: they reduce free riding, and hence crowd-in payment for a public service, and they reduce the time users need to get access to the public service. That is the reason why a yearly bus card is cheaper than the sum of single day cards over a year.

174 *Public goods and commons*

7.2.3 Post Keynesian economics of public goods

The opportunity cost method applied to public goods gives estimations of two types of costs. First, it gives estimations of the externalities if a particular public good is not provided, for instance clean water. Water pollution costs include health losses, production losses, loss in enjoyment of nature, and various feedback effects between water systems and economic and social systems. Second, the opportunity cost method results in estimations of what the delivery of the particular good will cost. So, what would be the costs of stopping pollution of a river? Think about compensation paid by a firm to a community, clean-up costs, and the price of new filter technology, as well as immaterial consumption, such as sailing a boat or enjoying kayak holidays on the river.

Comparing these two types of costs – the externalities of doing nothing and the provisioning of the public good – will indicate whether the costs of providing a public good will be lower than the costs of not providing it. If this is the case, the public good should be provided, because then the opportunity costs of doing nothing would be higher. Also the uncertainties involved in continued pollution for future generations and the ecological system should be taken into account. Hence, the Post Keynesian policy tool of opportunity costs calculation goes beyond simple cost–benefit analysis: it also includes the recognition of uncertainties involved in doing nothing.

7.2.4 Neoclassical economics of public goods

Neoclassical economics has no solution to free riding because it follows from the neoclassical *wiifm* reasoning. It is in the self-interest of an economic agent to free ride on a publicly provided good, so economic agents are actually assumed to be free riders . . . . However, neoclassical economists also recognise the need for some public goods. But they reject most merit goods and those public goods that are further away from pure public goods, as located close to the origin in Diagram 7.1. In neoclassical economics, public goods are considered a necessary evil, they are only accepted when the market cannot provide them when there is a large demand for them and preferably positive externalities. This is a major reason why neoclassical economists favour a small state. When a theory assumes that all economic agents are self-interested and concerned with the maximisation of their own individual utility, public goods beyond the minimum deemed necessary are considered a waste of resources and an unnecessary restriction of freedom through the taxation that is necessary to finance not only the public good but also the cost of free riding behaviour.

To determine the minimum necessary amount of public goods and their funding, neoclassical economics uses its key tool of optimisation. The optimum level of public funding for a good is where the sum of each individual's marginal willingness to pay equals the marginal cost of providing the good. How is the willingness to pay calculated? Ideally, this is derived from a survey among all people potentially affected by a public good, or a sample of that population. Such a survey asks individuals how much money they would be willing to pay if a particular public good were provided.

Let us take, for example, a park. Some people would be willing to pay $100 per year to be able to enjoy having a park nearby. Others would not be interested and would not be willing to pay, or to only a small amount, say not more than $5 per year. Other stakeholders, such as local businesses, may also be willing to pay for the park, perhaps because it would increase the demand for their products (think about a local ice cream vendor). From this

Image 7.1 Park

survey information, it should be possible to calculate the marginal willingness to pay for a public good: the amount that people, on average, would be willing to pay for an additional unit of the public good – such as an additional square metre of park. The municipality can now determine the optimal size of the park, namely, that number of square metres at which the marginal willingness to pay is equal to the marginal cost of the last added square metre. When the costs of the last added square metre equals the willingness to pay for an additional square metre of park, that will be the optimal size of the park. For example, if a park was to be 100 by 100 metres (1 hectare), the willingness to pay for an extra square metre may be $500 per year, while the costs of realising that extra square metre of park may also be $500 per year. For additional square metres of park, the willingness to pay declines and will be below the cost price. So, a park of 1 hectare would be the optimal size of the public good, from a neoclassical perspective.

However, this willingness to pay method of calculating the optimum size of a public good has several flaws. First, people may say they are willing to pay certain amounts, but they may not be prepared to do so when that translates into higher municipal taxes or a user fee. Second, the same space may have opportunity costs: without a park, the 10,000 square metres could have contributed to more parking space, a student hostel, or a community-driven permanent flea market. Third, a park may have hidden social benefits, which people forget to take into account. It may contribute to social cohesion and become a venue for major sports events, for example. Or simply reduce the amount of dog excrement on the pavements and youth hanging around on the streets.

A financing problem may arise when the actual costs of providing the public good requires an amount of tax revenue to which some economic agents will react with tax evasion. This constitutes free rider behaviour. The more agents evade tax payment, the lower the tax revenue and the more difficult it is to finance the public good. Tax evasion occurs when agents move to a different jurisdiction with lower taxes, when they make use of tax havens where they register their tax base (income, profit, or property), or when they do not fully declare their earnings and assets. The higher the tax rate, the more economic agents are likely to evade tax payment. So, a very high tax rate is inefficient: with a lower tax rate more economic

176 *Public goods and commons*

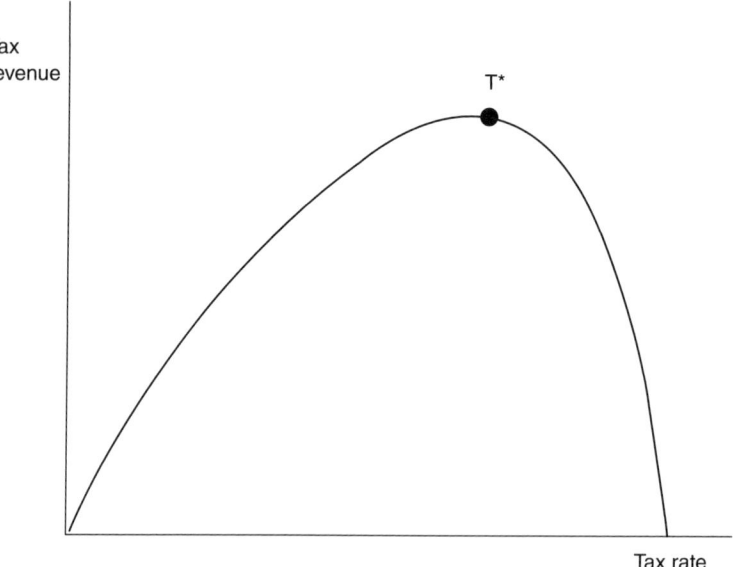

Diagram 7.2 The Laffer curve

agents are willing to pay their taxes. Diagram 7.2 shows the relationship between tax rate and tax revenue: the Laffer curve, named after the American economist Arthur Laffer.

For the tax rate at point T*, the tax revenue is maximum. Beyond that point, tax rates increase but the revenue will decrease. This is inefficient. So, the tax rate should lie at T* or a bit to the left of it, depending also on the extent to which a government is able to enforce taxation (and hence punish free riders).

What if the Laffer curve is so flat that optimum tax revenue is not sufficient to finance the public good? Here the collective *wiifm* argument comes in: internalisation of positive externalities. When the rich recognise that it is in their interest that certain public goods are supplied even though only the poor and middle class will make use of them, they are more likely to contribute to the public good. For example, public primary education contributes to a more productive labour force, a healthier population with less infectious diseases, and lower fertility rates in countries with high population growth. These are positive externalities, which benefit the rich just as much as the poor. For this collective *wiifm* argument to work, a strong state is needed, with the power of persuasion.

7.3 Global public goods

The public goods discussed above concern the domestic level – either nationally or locally. Domestic public goods range from national defence and national coverage of primary education to public swimming pools and street-lighting provided by local government. But at the world level there is also a need for public goods which have a cross-border character: their benefits accrue to countries, people, sometimes over generations, and the earth. When they are not provided, the costs affect everyone everywhere. Hence, we define *global public goods* as goods from which countries, people, and generations benefit. The major challenge of global public goods as compared to domestic public goods is that there is no world government to provide them. Before I tackle this challenge, let us first review three major global public goods and the opportunity costs of not providing them.

7.3.1 End global warming

The Intergovernmental Panel on Climate Change (IPCC) is a scientific UN body which was set up in 1988 to assess the state of knowledge on climate change and its potential environmental and socio-economic impacts on a global scale. The panel has reported five times up to 2014. The conclusion of every new report has resulted in a higher level of confidence that climate change is caused by human behaviour, in particular economic behaviour. Therefore, climate change is a clear global externality, and stopping this externality requires a global public good. While there is increasing certainty that humans are the cause of global warming, there is still much uncertainty about which policy measures would stop the trend and how long it would take. There is also uncertainty about how trends and policy measures interact: do they counter each other's effects or rather reinforce them? See Diagram 7.3 for greenhouse emission growth up to 2010. It shows a strong increase over time, with faster growth in more recent years, in particular for upper-middle-income countries.

You will notice from IPCC reports how important the role of uncertainty is in countering the trend of global warming. This is why policy would be best informed by a Post Keynesian perspective, which recognises the important role of uncertainty in economic behaviour. Ending global warming, as a public good, would therefore require Post Keynesian ingredients: government investment, automatic stabilisers, and prevention of contagion.

Government investment is necessary as a complement to private investment in green technology and energy saving. Think about subsidies for solar panels and sun-heated boilers on buildings, the construction of public wind energy parks and solar energy parks, and the public funding of R&D for green technology. Automatic stabilisers should increase such investments when the world economy is growing faster, because faster GDP growth causes faster greenhouse gas emission growth. And green investments can decrease when the world economy is in a downturn or growing slowly, when pollution growth will also stabilise. This could be realised if countries agreed upon a fixed percentage of their GDP being invested in the transition towards a green economy. So, *automatic green stabilisers* are public green investments which are pro-cyclical: going up when the economy is growing fast, and going down when the economy is stagnating or contracting. Finally, the prevention of a shift of emissions from one region to another requires agreement on and enforcement of thresholds everywhere. For example for the maximum of greenhouse emissions per country as a ratio of its GDP.

A problem for a globally accepted agreement on a reduction in greenhouse emissions is fairness. The most polluting countries are those that have contributed in the past most to global warming. So, why should emerging economies now be restricted in their increasing levels of emissions? Moreover, the developed countries have more financial resources and know-how to reduce emissions and to make the transition to a greener economy. Next to fairness, the effectiveness of a global public good to end global warming requires the participation of all countries. So, for the global public good to be effective, it needs to be inclusive and fair.

7.3.2 End poverty

Poverty is not only an individual bad, affecting many millions of people in the Global South, as well as several millions of people in the North. There are significant negative externalities

178 Public goods and commons

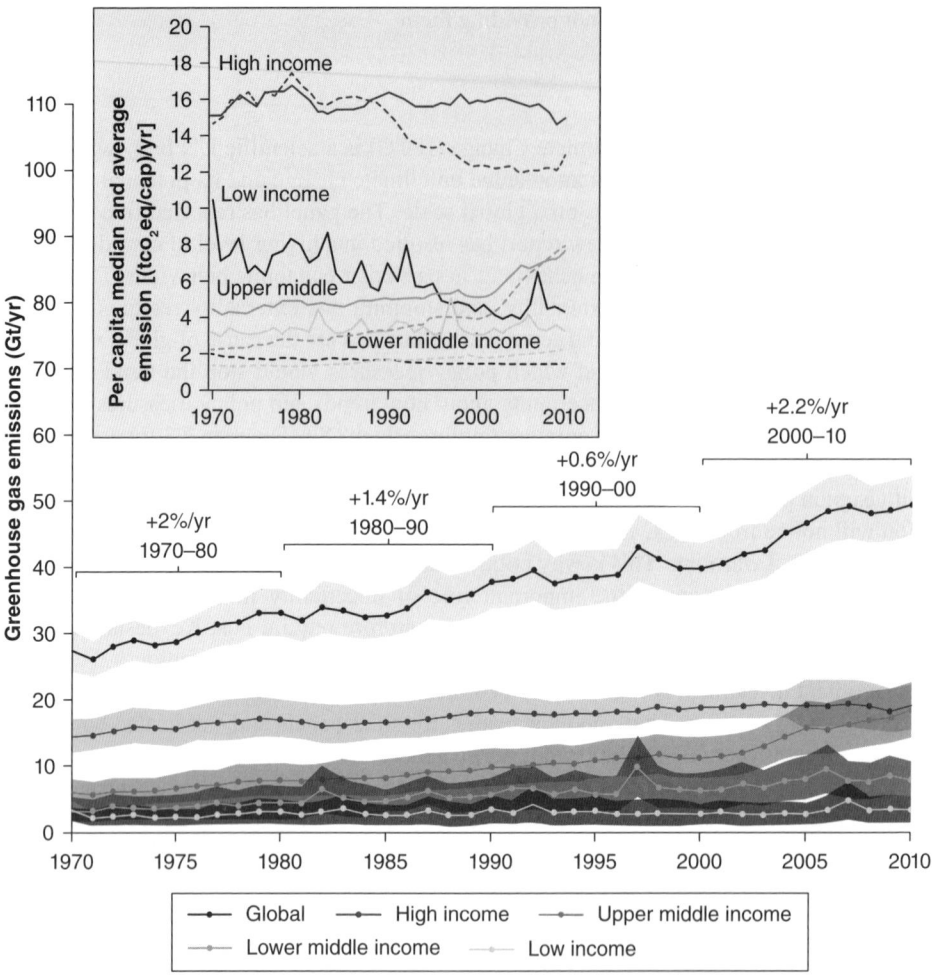

Diagram 7.3 Greenhouse gas emission growth

Main figure shows world total (top line) and growth rates per decade, as well as the high, low, upper middle, and lower middle income countries. Insert shows trends in annual per capita mean (solid lines) and median (dotted lines) greenhouse gas emissions by region 1970–2010 in tonnes of CO_2 (tonnes/capita/year).

Source: IPCC report 2014 available at http://report.mitigation2014.org/drafts/final-draft-postplenary/ipcc_wg3_ar5_final-draft_postplenary_chapter1.pdf

of poverty at a global level. These externalities would justify treating poverty not only as a national evil but also as a global evil. A first global externality is international migration. This implies transportation and relocation costs for the migrants themselves, often financed through a loan from family members. The sending countries may suffer from a *brain drain*. This is the loss of well-educated participants in the labour force to migration. Brain drain is particularly costly in terms of public human resource investment, when the best educated leave the country. This is a loss of human capital for their labour markets. When migrants

Image 7.2 Solar light

have small children, their moving away without their children implies a gap in childcare, which is often filled by communities. This implies an extra burden of unpaid work, often for elderly women, the children's grandmothers.

The externalities also concern the receiving countries. The receiving countries have not always sufficient absorption capacity in their labour markets, housing markets, and social protection systems for immigrants. This creates social tension. On the other hand, immigrants may help to ease shortages in the labour markets of receiving countries and help keep wage costs from increasing above levels at which countries can no longer compete.

A second negative externality of global poverty is inequality. This affects human dignity and human rights. And it may lead to tensions, which result in violence through political support for fundamentalism, violent uprisings, and perhaps even terrorist attacks by groups who are and feel marginalised and excluded. So, poverty and the inequality inherent in it can result in large social costs to society.

A third negative externality of global poverty is apparent through the demand for different types of goods and services. Whereas the rich can consume up to the level they want, and use the remainder of their income and wealth for savings, wasteful consumption of status goods, and speculation, the poor are not even able to satisfy their basic needs. With a more equal income distribution, it is likely that average consumption per person would increase worldwide: the rich would spend less on speculation and status goods, while the poor would be able, at least so some extent, to provide themselves with sufficient livelihoods.

What do public goods which address the problem of global poverty look like? They take the form of global-level agreements. This is a formal institutional solution. For the period 2000–2015, the UN, World Bank, IMF, and OECD agreed upon the Millennium Development Goals (MDGs). These goals included a reduction in global poverty by 50 per cent, as well as goals for universal primary and secondary education, a reduction in child mortality, and other poverty-reduction goals. Statistics have indicated that the MDGs have been achieved in quite a number of developing counties. But not everywhere. A number of developing countries have not yet met the goals.

The public good financing involved in realising the MDGs is quite traditional: official development assistance (ODA) for the receiving country's government budgets for social expenditures (mainly education and health care). Developed countries have agreed to give 0.7 per cent or more of their GDP for development aid. But the majority of donor countries do not achieve this target. Table 7.1 shows the ODA shares for all OECD countries.

Table 7.1 Official development assistance, % of GDP

	2007	2008	2009	2010	2011	2012
Australia	0.47	0.48	0.45	0.48	0.51	0.53
Austria	0.62	0.53	0.36	0.38	0.31	0.32
Belgium	0.56	0.61	0.68	0.77	0.64	0.54
Canada	0.37	0.41	0.38	0.41	0.38	0.38
Denmark	1.39	1.30	1.38	1.33	1.26	1.19
Finland	0.56	0.58	0.70	0.74	0.68	0.66
France	0.50	0.49	0.59	0.61	0.55	0.53
Germany	0.44	0.46	0.42	0.44	0.42	0.40
Iceland	0.31	0.36	0.34	0.27	0.21	0.22
Italy	0.23	0.24	0.17	0.16	0.21	0.14
Japan	0.25	0.28	0.26	0.28	0.25	0.24
Korea	0.05	0.07	0.08	0.09	0.09	0.11
Netherlands	0.99	0.98	0.96	0.98	0.88	0.82
New Zealand	0.31	0.34	0.32	0.29	0.30	0.29
Norway	1.75	1.48	1.94	1.77	1.55	1.44
Spain	0.38	0.44	0.45	0.43	0.28	0.15
Sweden	1.38	1.39	1.56	1.37	1.42	1.33
Switzerland	0.70	0.69	0.78	0.71	0.75	0.76
United Kingdom	0.39	0.48	0.56	0.65	0.63	0.61
United States	0.16	0.19	0.21	0.21	0.20	0.19

Source: OECD statistics.

7.3.3. Reduce financial instability

Financial stability is a public good. As I have pointed out in the introduction to this book, the costs of the 2007 financial crisis were high, first in the USA, then in Europe, and finally everywhere else as it spread through trade contraction and toxic assets.

In contrast to many other public goods, the global public good of financial stability does not require funding. The service implied in financial stability can be delivered through regulation and institutional reform. I will briefly discuss two parallel forms that this global public good currently takes. First, the Basel Committee, which is the global governance institution of Central Banks. Since the 2007 financial crisis, the committee has come up with stricter regulation which requires, among other things, that commercial banks should have higher capital reserves than they had previously. However, critics argue that the new threshold is still much too low. Second, the EU stability fund which was created during the euro crisis in 2012, to provide financial support to governments of member states in case of a sovereign debt problem (unsustainable budget deficits and public debt of a government). Again, critics argue that the fund will be insufficient to prevent the problems plaguing the European Union's finances because of the absence of EU level taxation.

An effective public good to counter the effects of financial instability would need to achieve more than the Basel Committee and EU can deliver. It requires change at the institutional level, both nationally and internationally. Global financial institutions that one could think of are a global central bank, a global single currency, global taxation, and a global budget. Of course, this is not feasible, at least not in the short or medium term.

7.4 Governance and finance of global public goods

The major challenge of supplying global public goods is the fact that there is no world government to provide them and no global tax revenue to fund them. This is precisely the reason why civil society protests against global externalities and the lack of global public goods. Think about protests at meetings of the World Bank and IMF, or the World Social Forum, which is a large gathering of a wide variety of civil society organisations regularly meeting in different countries. This forum, together with other civil society initiatives, is a good example of civic action on a world scale, where civil society demands global public goods.

Box 7.2 World Social Forum

The first World Social Forum (WFS) was held in 2001 in Brazil by the leading members of the global movements for social and economic justice. It was a response to the World Economic Forum of rich countries, which takes place every year in Davos, Switzerland. Tunisia hosted the 2013 WFS. The following topics were the subject of challenging discussions and decisions:

Responsible agriculture investment: The trends in agriculture investment in different regions of the world, the domination by corporate interests, and the exclusion of those who are most affected by food insecurity from policy making.

(continued)

(continued)

> *Strategise the Post-2015 Development Agenda (MDG deadline) and Rio+20 (UN Conference on Sustainable Development):* The general consensus was to put the poverty and environment agendas together in a single framework in order to go beyond the neo-liberal conceptualisation of development and to have an integrated holistic approach to address finance, the economy, and the environment.
>
> *Sustainable agriculture, food and energy sovereignty:* possible policies and actions to support small-scale food production and initiatives for building a global movement for sustainable agriculture. Importantly, the impact of biofuels on food sovereignty was discussed.
>
> Sources: http://www.globalpolicy.org/conferences/30733-world-social-forum.html and http://www.cidse.org/content/articles/rethinking-development/world-social-forum-2013/world-social-forum-2013-in-tunis-the-transition-to-democracy-and-beyond.html

Does the absence of a global government mean that there will be no global public goods at all until we have a world government? No, fortunately not. There are several ways to deliver and finance global public goods, albeit not as effectively as domestic public goods.

7.4.1 Institutional economics of global public goods

It is institutional economics which describes and explains the institutional arrangements that are currently discussed and implemented for the governance and financing of global public goods.

First, we have global governance institutions which help to address cross-border problems. These include the United Nations and its various organisations, influential regional organisations such as the OECD, EU, and NATO, and *ad hoc* coalitions among the world's largest economies in the shape of the G8, G20, and other G variations. These also include the informal World Economic Forum and World Social Forum. These global governance institutions have their own policy instruments. These include treaties and agreements, which define the rights and duties of countries vis-à-vis each other. And they include two parallel funding systems: development cooperation, consisting of transfers from developed to developing countries, and global and regional public banks, providing below market price funding (at low or even zero interest rates) for national governments in times of crisis and restructuring. And, importantly, they have the power of collective action and persuasion.

Second, international law provides the legal institutions to force the internalisation or compensation of negative externalities caused by states, firms, and households of a nation to other nations. This includes global-level international law, for instance concerning the use of territorial waters and the resources in and under these waters. And it includes regional-level law, such as in the case of European Union legislation, in which 'Brussels' requires EU member states to provide certain public goods for European citizens.

Third, there are attempts to generate global taxation contributing to a global fund from which global public goods could be financed, controlled by an independent group of experts and with appropriate mechanisms of transparency and international control. The major proposal for a global tax is a financial transactions tax (FTT), a low tax (less than 0.1 per cent) on every cross-border financial transaction. But the major problem in implementing an FTT is

Table 7.2 Opportunity costs of global public goods, estimations in US$ billion.

		International financial stability	Reducing the excessive disease burden	Climate stability	Peace and security	Total
Cost	Inaction	50	1138	780	358	2326
	Corrective action	0.3	93	125	71	289.3

Source: Kaul, I., P. Conceição, K. Le Goulven and R. U. Mendoza (2003) *Providing Global Public Goods*. Oxford: Oxford University Press, p. 159.

the chance that some countries would not participate and hence attract many financial transactions to their own territories. This would make the taxation ineffective, and worse, deprive all other countries from benefitting from financial trading.

7.4.2 Post Keynesian economics of global public goods

When we apply the opportunity cost method to some major global public goods, estimations of the costs of their provisioning and the costs of their absence show that these diverge widely. In general, the costs of the absence of these types of public goods are several times the costs of providing these goods. Hence, the opportunity method provides a justification for delivering such global public goods. Table 7.2 shows rough estimations of the opportunity costs for four global public goods.

Estimating the opportunity costs of global public goods is one thing. Getting the goods financed is another. Even when the cost of providing is substantially lower than the cost of doing nothing, the provisioning of global public goods will not automatically occur, precisely because of the lack of a world government, with global taxation and spending powers, as we have seen earlier.

So how then can global public goods be financed? The problem of financing global public goods through ODA and development related international funds, as is currently the case, is that aid is diverted away from domestic public goods in low income countries towards public goods that are also in the interest of developed countries. That is why global public good would require funding that is *additional* to ODA. This can be done in three ways.

First, through international treaties with adequate budgets from national taxation. These could be treaties on reducing pollution or overfishing, for example. These require earmarked funding above and beyond ODA. Second, financing the elimination of negative cross-border externalities by national entities. These may be governments but also firms. This is a decentralised way of financing those public goods that are the source of a nationally identifiable externality. Such as a chemical factory causing pollution in an international river. Obviously, the source and size of international externalities are not always clear, and hence, the question of who should pay, how much, and to whom is often not answered. The third source of funding global public goods would be a global fund from a global tax, such as the FTT in financial markets as discussed earlier.

7.5 Commons

Commons are a variation on public goods: they are collective goods, often referred to as common-pool resources (CPR) since the seminal work by Elinor Ostrom on CPR. They are

184 *Public goods and commons*

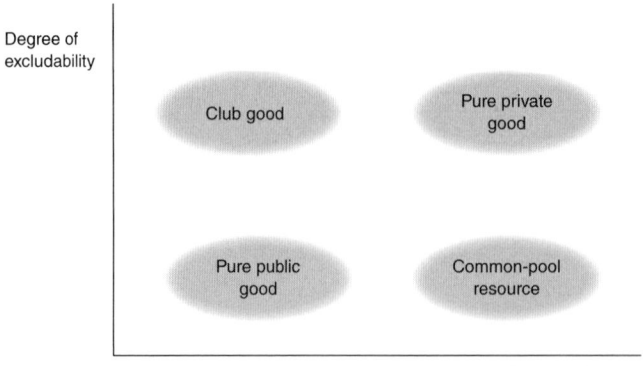

Diagram 7.4 Variations of public goods including commons

public not in the sense of supplied by the state, but public in a societal sense: they are used, owned, preserved, or protected by local collectives and not by individuals. These collectives are generally a local community. Hence, *common-pool resources* can be defined as collective goods used, owned, preserved, or protected by local collectives, often communities. Commons include concretely defined jointly owned land, buildings, and cultural heritage, as well as not clearly defined natural areas with or without rights of access and use-rights. Hence commons range from a neighbourhood-owned playground to a protected cultural heritage maintained by indigenous peoples, to vast forests and natural wildlife reserves governed by its inhabitants. Diagram 7.4 adds commons to the typology of the public goods Diagram 7.1.

7.5.1 Types of commons

We can distinguish between two types of commons: natural and social. *Natural commons* are the earth's environmental heritage: water, air, organic and non-organic material, biodiversity, and genetic variability. They are not necessarily used as resources by human beings. They may either be ignored by people (but at the same time affected by negative externalities such as pollution) or they may be valued and protected by human beings, rather than being used as resources as inputs in economic processes. Natural commons are recognised to be valuable in their own right, as the fundament of 'system earth', so to speak. They are our common heritage, and that of future generations, and of Earth itself: they are not owned by people. This recognition turns the environmental heritage into commons. Without this recognition, it is just nature. Natural commons will be discussed further in Chapter 13 on the environment, where I will introduce ecological economics.

Social commons are quite different from natural commons. *Social commons* can be regarded as shared social resources governed through forms of common governance. The resources are varied: they include environmental resources, cultural resources, and social resources. As noted, the environment features both in natural and social commons. But it does so in a very different way. In natural commons, the environment is not turned into a resource, whereas in social commons it is turned into a resource.

The economist who is famous for her research on commons is Elinor Ostrom. She received the Nobel Prize for it and she is briefly described in the annex of this book. The theoretical framework for the analysis of common-pool resources is a particular field of institutional economics, referred to as the institutional analysis and development framework (IAD). It emphasises that institutions emerge, or develop, from the bottom up in communities, through locally developed rules and a learning process through which these rules become more effective over time.

7.5.2 Institutional theory of common-pool resources

The recognition of common-pool resources brought the role of communities back into economics, in addition to markets and states. Moreover, acknowledgement of the key role of communities in the governance of some goods has made clear that property rights exist in more variations than just the individual (in markets) and the collective (in the state).

Communities have for centuries managed, to varying degrees of success, common-pool resources. From grazing land to irrigation systems, and from large forests to monasteries. The social dilemma around common-pool resources is very complex and uncertain. This is partly due to their biophysical conditions, and partly due to the high degree of rivalry in the use of common-pool resources combined with low possibilities to exclude people from their use. Hence, common-pool resources suffer from a high risk of resource depletion and destruction. Nevertheless, the world has numerous examples of successful local governance of common-pool resources. Detailed empirical studies have revealed how local communities across the world have succeeded or failed in the governance of common-pool resources.

Analysis of common-pool resource governance first requires examination of a so-called action situation around a common-pool resource:

- Who are the agents?
- What are their roles?
- What set of allowable actions do they have?
- What are the potential behavioural outcomes?
- How much control do individuals have?
- What information is available?
- What are the costs and benefits of actions and outcomes?

Action situations are not only influenced by exogenous variables about biophysical conditions and key characteristics of the community, but also depend on the rules that communities design. These rules don't start from scratch. They build on the social norms already available in a community. For example, norms of fairness, merit, and punishment of free riders.

Remember, rules are institutions, and when not defined by the state but emerging in communities, they are informal institutions. Working rules for common-pool resource management are the set of rules to which participants would make reference if asked to explain and justify their actions to fellow participants. Rules that are not top-down and exogenous, but emerging from local communities are not fixed but dynamic: they change over time in response to changes in the biophysical conditions of a resource and to changes in the community and its values. Such rule-changing reflects learning: people change rules because they learn from mistakes and adapt to changing circumstances. Effective translation of learning into changes in rules leads to more effective rules, and hence, to better common-pool resource governance.

But rules should not change too often or too rapidly. Rules only function when they have shared meanings in a community. This implies that when rules change over time, through a process of learning, the shared meanings of these rules also need to change in order to ensure that the new rules continue to govern the actions of all agents involved in an effective way. Ostrom has distinguished seven types of working rules:

- boundary rules: who is a legitimate participant?
- position rules: who has specific governance roles?
- scope rules: what are the understandings of authorised and forbidden locations and actions?
- choice rules: what tools are allowed for harvesting and how is this monitored?
- aggregation rules: what are the understandings of the choice of harvesting activities?
- information rules: what information must be kept secret and what must be made public?
- payoff rules: what are the sanctions for breaking rules and how are these enforced?

7.5.3 Social economic theory of common-pool resources

A complementary theory of commons, also part of Ostrom's detailed study of common-pool resources, has its roots in social economics. When communities come up with a set of working rules that they agree on and have shared meanings, another social process is necessary to make the community governance work. That is the generation of trust: trust in others and being trusted by others in the community. This helps to establish the reciprocity that is necessary for the norms to work. With trust in others, participants will behave as strong reciprocators. Remember from Chapter 1 that social economic rationality is understood as *strong reciprocity*, which involves punishment of free riders, at own cost. But trust does not start from zero. Like rules, it builds on the values and social norms already available in communities. And it develops slowly, step-by-step when through continuous interaction a community is built and reciprocity emerges. If, however, trust is low, the governance will fail. No rules, however well negotiated and designed from the bottom up, will be able to function without the trust that is necessary for the reciprocal behaviour to put the working rules into practice.

Local communities who collectively govern a common-pool resource can suffer from the problem of free riding by outsiders. But free riding in such a governance context becomes costly due to local-level monitoring and sanctions. And the higher the proportion of people in a community with a commitment to the shared norm of resource maintenance and with the willingness to punish free riders, the more costly and difficult it becomes for free riders to abuse the common-pool resource. Or, in terms of behavioural economics, the higher the proportion of conditional co-operators in a community, the more effective the community governance system becomes and the lower the free riding. But it is continuously challenged when modernisation, migration, and tourism increase the number of outsiders in the community.

Finally, outcomes of the community governance process need to be evaluated according to various criteria which are valued in the community. These often include efficiency, accountability, equity, and sustainability. The more satisfactory the outcomes are, and are assessed as such by participants, the more successful the common-pool resource management is perceived by the community and the more likely it will continue over time.

> **Box 7.3 Common-pool resource management of irrigation systems**
>
> A study of 74 farmer-managed irrigation systems in the Chitwan valley in Nepal has shown that the self-management of common-pool resources can be very effective. This was due to three informal institutions:
>
> - a group history of organising
> - the willingness of some individuals to assume leadership
> - investment of time and energy in making, testing, fine-tuning, interpreting, monitoring, and enforcing rules.
>
> Moreover, the effectiveness of the self-management of irrigation systems appeared not to be affected by ethnic diversity, but it was less effective in groups with more income inequality.
>
> Source: http://www.indiana.edu/~workshop/colloquia/materials/papers/regmi_paper.pdf

7.5.4 Neoclassical theory of common-pool resources

The neoclassical approach assumes that individual self-interest will eventually destroy common-pool resources. This view is also known as 'the tragedy of the commons'.[1] It stems from the assumption of individual self-interested behaviour, the *wiifm* attitude of *Homo economicus*. It leads to free riding and hence to the depletion of a common-pool resource rather than its maintenance and shared use over a long period of time.

The neoclassical policy toward the tragedy of the commons is to divide the common resources into individual parts with individual property rights. This will ensure that individual owners will manage their part of the resource properly, through investments which will reap individual returns. However, as we have seen in the classification of common-pool resources, it is difficult to exclude others from their use. Dividing up a forest or lake, for example, requires enormous costs in policing by every individual owner to prevent trespassing and resource extraction by others. Moreover, the individual owners may also try to extract resources from their neighbours. So, free riding cannot be effectively stopped with individual property rights. Hence, a public good problem arises due to a market failure of stopping free riding.

The solution to this market failure, still in neoclassical economic theory, is then regulation by the state into a public good. However, this does not ensure maintenance of the common either, because of the risk of government failure. The more complex the situation, the more likely that the top-down approach of government governance – through a public good – will fail. That is because common-pool resources are by definition complex resources, which are impossible to manage when external controls and enforcement are exclusively relied on. Maintaining the public good through the state may become increasingly expensive.

7.6 Interesting sources

Digital library of the commons: http://dlc.dlib.indiana.edu/dlc/contentguidelines

7.7 Glossary

Automatic green stabilisers   Public green investments which are pro-cyclical

Benchmarking   An artificial competition policy with targets or rankings, which governments use to force more efficiency from public organisations

Brain drain   The loss of well-educated participants in the labour force to migration

Club goods   Non-rival and excludable goods supplied by a real or virtual club

Common-pool resources   Collective goods used, owned, preserved, or protected by local collectives, often communities

Global public goods   Goods from which countries, people, and generations benefit

Merit goods   Goods supplied by the state because they are regarded as desirable for everyone

Natural commons   The earth's environmental heritage

Public goods   Goods which no one can technically be excluded from enjoying

Social commons   Shared social resources governed through forms of common governance

Strong reciprocity   When agents contribute resources to a joint activity when others do so as well even when there are no benefits to themselves or their kin, or future gains to be expected, or reputation gains: they are prepared to punish free riders, at their own cost

Note

1 This was the title of a study by Garrett Hardin published in 1968 in *Science*.

8 Labour markets

8.1 Labour supply

Labour markets provide a special input into production, namely labour power. Obviously, labour power cannot be disconnected from the human beings that have this power. Therefore, the use and reward of labour power is even more embedded in the social relations of power asymmetries and cooperation than is the case for other factors of production. Human labour power is also referred to as *human capital*, which is a production factor consisting of skills, experience, and capacities. This is a limited concept, reducing human labour power to a capital-like production factor, as if it were a container of human resources to be used similarly to financial capital. *Human capability* is a more appropriate term and refers to the skills and capabilities of human beings which can be transferred through labour into productive activity. This can be done in endless ways: paid and unpaid, with dedication or automated, highly productive or wasteful, and under a wide variety of conditions impacting on the productivity of labour.

The supply of labour to the labour market is related to population size, education, social protection, and social norms, including gender norms. But let us start with some definitions. The *population of working age* is directly derived from the population size and its age distribution: it is the number of people between 15 and 65 years of age. This is an agreed international age bracket, although some countries allow, or have in practice, children working below the age of 15 and elderly people working over the age of 65. Although from the 1960s onwards, retirement age has been set at 65 years in many countries (in some countries at 60 years for women), recently some countries have diverged from this. The Netherlands now has a retirement age of 67 in response to the ageing of the Dutch population.

Within the working age population, some people do paid work, others want to do paid work but do not have a job, while still others do not want to do paid work (but want to study or travel or care for children) or are unable to do paid work (due to illness or being imprisoned, for example). Hence, the labour force is smaller than the working age population. The *labour force* consists of everyone between 15 and 65 years of age who is willing and able to work. But not everybody in the labour force has a job. The labour force can be divided into those employed and those unemployed. Employed are those with a job, and unemployed are those who are trying but cannot find employment. These statistical categories are pictured in Diagram 8.1.

190 Labour markets

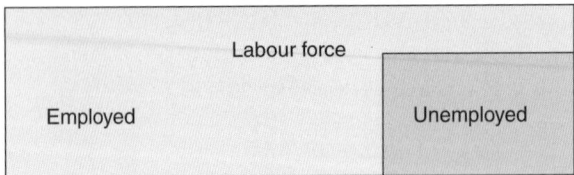

Diagram 8.1 Labour supply and employment

8.1.1 Social economics: labour as a produced input

The production factor of labour (labour power) is a produced production factor. Unlike land and natural resources, which are exogenous. Labour is therefore an endogenous production factor, quite similar to physical capital, which is also a produced production factor. Whereas capital is produced by a combination of material inputs and labour power, labour is produced largely by labour. Labour is produced from childhood onwards through family care, education, and peer groups. It is produced through a long-term process of learning and socialisation. Moreover, labour is also being cared for in families and peer groups, and often continues to learn new capabilities and skills while participating in the labour market. This is the short-term production of labour, on a day-to-day basis. These two forms of producing labour in the long run and the short run are referred to as *reproduction*. This is the unpaid caring for the current and future generation of labour and for others inside and outside the economy.

Reproduction of the labour force is strongly influenced by class and gender. Children born in high-class families tend to receive higher quality formal education, are socialised into the norms and social networks of the elite, and tend to be healthier and less exposed to child labour. In many countries, girls have lower school enrolment rates than boys, which give them lower levels of formal human capabilities when they enter the labour market. However, some countries have lower enrolment rates for boys. For example Lesotho, where cultural traditions keep boys from secondary school in order to herd cattle in the fields as part of the transition ritual to become men. Table 8.1 shows the net primary school enrolment rates (corrected for drop-outs) for countries in southern Africa. More than half of the children out of school worldwide are in Africa.

Gender norms influence access to, length of, and type of education for boys and girls, and also their ambitions and opportunities. Many societies have different expectations for boys (such as full-time breadwinners) and girls (such as full-time mothers and homemakers). These gendered expectations lead, on average, to disadvantaged preparation for participation in and benefit from labour markets for girls.

While we consider labour supply as endogenous, it is not a constant factor linearly related to population size. Labour supply from the social economic perspective also varies according to social norms, gender relations, and social policy, in addition to changes in population size. And social policy refers both to education and to social protection. Moreover, behind these factors is modernisation, which progresses over time, although with periods of fast and slow progress, and in some countries even reversals. These determinants of labour supply are presented in Diagram 8.2.

Table 8.1 Net primary school enrolment rates in southern Africa (%)

		2000	2003	2006	2009	2012
Angola	Boys	N.A.	N.A.	N.A.	91.8	N.A.
	Girls	N.A.	N.A.	N.A.	80.6	N.A.
Botswana	Boys	79.0	81.3	83.0	83.3	N.A.
	Girls	82.4	84.3	84.6	84.4	N.A.
Lesotho	Boys	76.6	77.6	75.1	74.4	80.1
	Girls	83.9	83.7	79.7	78.8	83.2
Mozambique	Boys	61.5	N.A.	83.2	91.2	88.6
	Girls	49.9	N.A.	76.3	85.8	83.9
Namibia	Boys	85.4	86.9	83.3	84.2	86.4
	Girls	90.0	91.7	87.9	87.6	89.0
South Africa	Boys	90.5	91.2	90.6	89.6	85.6
	Girls	89.9	90.4	89.0	88.6	84.4
Swaziland	Boys	71.5	71.9	81.8	N.A.	N.A.
	Girls	72.7	73.3	82.5	N.A.	N.A.
Zambia	Boys	71.9	N.A.	91.9	90.1	93.0
	Girls	69.5	N.A.	93.8	90.9	94.4
Zimbabwe	Boys	84.7	82.1	N.A.	N.A.	N.A.
	Girls	84.9	83.5	N.A.	N.A.	N.A.

Source: World Bank, World Development Indicators.

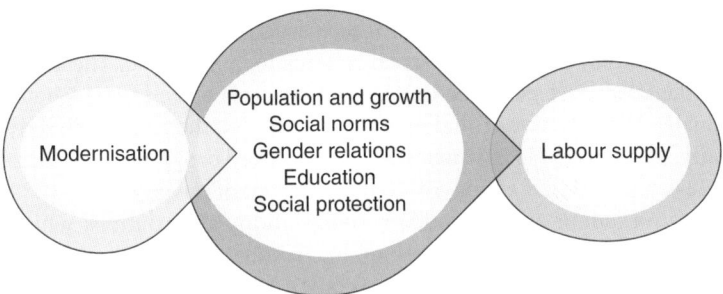

Diagram 8.2 Determinants of labour supply

Modernisation affects labour supply through all five factors shown in Diagram 8.2. For example, demographically through population size, and socially through gender equality leading to more women earning an income. The *demographic transition* is a shift from high mortality and high birth rates to low mortality and low birth rates. Parents will choose less children with higher investments in health and education per child. This generates demand for more education and better health care. But this is not necessarily the case for girls. Rather, modernisation of gender norms often includes a social ideal of the housewife who 'does not need' to work, and can fully specialise in bringing up the children and homemaking. This is a large unpaid female investment in reproduction, complemented by full-time male paid employment as breadwinner. But modernisation can also change social norms towards individualism, materialism, and self-realisation. Modernisation may in that case result in more gender equality, stimulating women's labour force participation.

192 *Labour markets*

8.1.2 Institutional economics: constraints to labour supply

Labour supply is not free. It is constrained by both formal and informal institutions. So, with the same population size, countries differ in the size of their labour force. Not only because of the social economic factors discussed above (social norms, gender relations, modernisation, and social policy). But also because of laws and routines. Some of the labour supply institutions will be asymmetric.

Formal constraints to labour supply are imposed by laws and regulations concerning education and social protection. Laws and regulations regarding education may require children to be in school up to a certain age and to gain a qualification for a wide variety of jobs. The higher the age limit and the stronger the requirement for qualifications, the smaller the labour supply among the younger working age population. Because these formal institutions provide an incentive to stay longer in school.

Social protection policies protect the unemployed against loss of income due to unemployment. These policies provide social benefits, often in money or food coupons, either on an individual basis or also for dependants of the unemployed. Such social support may have an unintended consequence, namely, less willingness to supply labour as soon as labour demand goes up. This negative effect of social protection on labour supply is reinforced when the beneficiaries in addition to a single benefit are also eligible for additional social support. This may include a subsidy on housing rent, reduced health care fees and subsidised health insurance, and exemptions from school-related expenditures for their children. These social benefits together create a welfare poverty trap.

A *welfare poverty trap* is the situation of being unable to escape poverty because of dependence on state benefits, which are reduced by the same amount as any income earned. As a consequence, the stock of unemployed labour force participants contains a core of people who remain unemployed and dependent on social benefits for a long time. The longer this time period, the more depleted these people's diplomas and skills become for the labour market and hence, the smaller their chance of finding employment. So, the welfare poverty trap creates, unintentionally, a vicious cycle in which some unemployed people become long-term unemployed and are less likely to find employment and grow out of poverty.

Informal constraints on labour supply concern social norms and routines which discourage groups of people from becoming part of the labour force. The major group affected by such informal constraints are women. Women's labour supply is influenced by asymmetric informal institutions concerning stereotype roles for men and women in households and society. The asymmetric informal institutions reducing women's labour supply include the following:

1 Low school enrolment of girls at all levels of education due to parental views that girls should become full-time mothers and care givers in the household and that this does not require formal skills;
2 High school drop-out in secondary education due to early marriage and teenage pregnancy;
3 Specialisation in social-cultural subjects in education, with relatively low labour market value, by girls and specialisation in technical and mathematical tracks in education, with relatively high labour market value, by boys;
4 Gender division of labour in households with men specialising in paid work and women specialising in unpaid work;

Table 8.2 Reasons given by nationals for being out of the labour force in United Arab Emirates (UAE), 2009

	UAE nationals (%)
Receiving non-work income	11
Unwilling to work	6
Early retirement	70
Disability	12
Other	1
All reasons	100

Source: Kherfi, S. (2012) 'Unemployment and Labor Market Participation of UAE Youth'. Workshop Discussion Paper for the workshop on the social-economic situation of middle east youth on the eve of the Arab Spring, Beirut, 8–9 December 2012. Available at http://www.shababinclusion.org/files/1893_file_kherfiuae.pdf

5   Women's stronger time and locational constrains for paid work as compared to men due to limited mobility with continuous caring responsibilities in the household;
6   The widely shared practice among men not to take up parental leave and among women to make use of parental leave, which leads to temporary disengagement of women with the labour market.

Finally, economies provide the dominant class with the wealth that allows them to earn an income through rents rather than through labour. An example is the large rentier class in oil-rich Arab countries, which have low labour supply rates for both women and men. The labour force in these counties includes a large proportion of immigrants. In the United Arab Emirates, for example, the labour force participation rate for Emiratis (that is, nationals of the UAE) is less than 50 per cent, whereas for immigrants it is over 80 per cent. Table 8.2 shows the reasons behind the low labour supply among Arab nationals in the United Arab Emirates.

8.1.3 Post Keynesian economics: endogenous labour supply

In Post Keynesian economics, labour supply is seen as endogenous, as it is in social economics. But not only from a social-economic perspective of the economy, but also from a perspective of markets. The three key concepts in the Post Keynesian perspective on labour supply are: the discouraged worker effect, underemployment, and the added worker effect.

8.1.3.1 Discouraged worker effect

The *discouraged worker effect* is the withdrawal of those workers from the labour force who have no confidence that they will find employment. The effect occurs after a long period of unemployment, often coinciding with a recession. This shows the endogenous character of the discouraged worker effect: it increases when the economic cycle is low. Where do these workers go to? Well, they will either retire early, or go back to school to obtain additional qualifications, or they report ill and become dependent on state social protection or the care of their families.

In South Africa, the group of discouraged workers is around 13 per cent of the labour force, according to the 2013 Statistics South Africa labour force survey.[1] The consequence for labour statistics of the discouraged worker effect is that the size of the labour force shrinks.

194 *Labour markets*

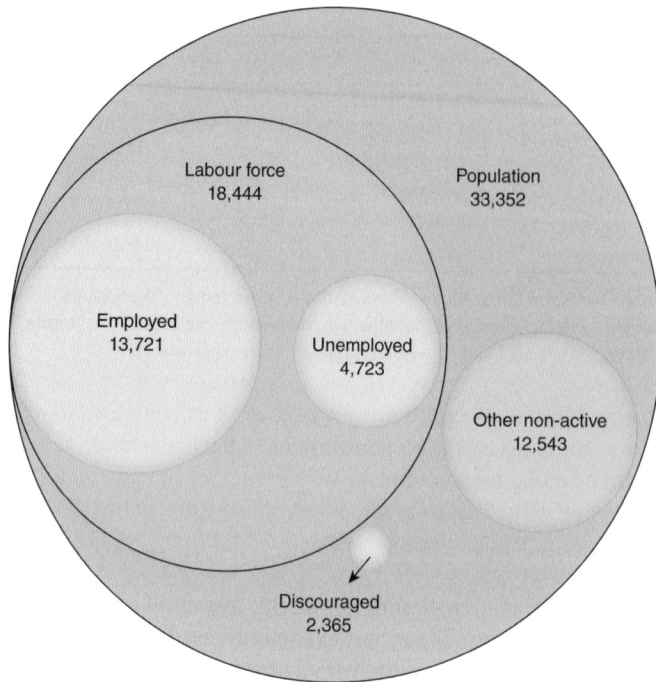

Diagram 8.3 The discouraged worker effect in South Africa, 2013
Source: http://www.statssa.gov.za/publications/statsabout.asp?PPN=P0211&SCH

Remember that the labour force consists of those working age people who are *willing* and able to work. But discouraged workers have given up looking for a job out of frustration. Hence, they are no longer willing to work. So, the discouraged worker effect artificially reduces the *unemployment rate*, which is the percentage of those in the labour force who have no employment. An example with labour market statistics from South Africa illustrates this in Diagram 8.3.

8.1.3.2 Underemployment

Underemployment is the situation in which a worker has employment but for less hours of effective work time than desired. In developed countries, underemployment often refers to seasonal employment and flexible hour contracts where actual hours are less than the worker desires. Think about temporary substitute jobs for teachers, replacing teachers on the days that they are ill, or harvesting jobs in agriculture. In developing countries, underemployment is widespread in the informal economy.

The *informal economy* is that part of the economy which is undercounted, under-registered, and undervalued. The informal economy consists of many self-employed workers who have long working days but very low productivity due to limited demand for their products and services. For example, self-employed workers may work 12 hours a day in a food stall, but have only 10 clients per day for the vegetables they sell. If each client spends 3 rand, the productivity of a day is 30 rand in gross sales, which is 2.50 rand per hour, which is very small. The earnings from a long day of work are barely enough to feed and cloth oneself, let alone provide for adequate housing, save for a business investment, and provide for family members. Moreover, the 10 clients could be served in an hour. The other 11 hours spent at the food stall is waiting time.

Underemployment is endogenous because it refers to a structural low demand for labour, either expressed through high flexibility (less than full-time contracts) or expressed through informality (no contracts or reliable sales at all). Only when the demand for labour structurally changes towards stable higher levels, will underemployment decline. With underemployment, the unemployment statistics under-report actual unemployment rates. Just like the case of the discouraged worker effect, but now not because people drop out of the labour force, but because they keep the status of 'employed' although for much of the time they are not working but waiting.

8.1.3.3 Added worker effect

The third and last endogenous labour supply concept is the added worker effect, which occurs at the household level. The *added worker effect* is the increased labour supply by household members as a response to reduced hours of paid work or earnings per hour of other household members. The logic behind the added worker effect is the desire of households to keep their income level constant, or at least, not to allow a decline. So, a decline in income by one household member leads to an attempt by another member of the household to compensate for this with increased labour force participation. Here, the endogeneity is very clear: increased unemployment rates and/or a decline in wages will induce household members to supply additional labour to the labour market. Again, this effect occurs during a recession in response to lower purchasing power at the household level.

Often, but not always, the added worker is female. In that case, the traditional gender division of labour is broken: women will enter the labour market or, if they had already done so with part-time work, will increase their hours of work to full time. But not necessarily with the same job – they may engage in multiple part-time jobs. Statistically, the added worker effect leads to an increase in labour force participation. But not all the additional labour supplied will find employment. Therefore, it is likely that the added worker effect will also contribute to an increased unemployment rate.

8.1.4 Neoclassical economics: opportunity costs

In the neoclassical perspective, labour supply is ultimately determined by population size. All the social, cultural, and psychological factors taken into account in the three theories discussed above are assumed to be reflected in the opportunity costs of paid labour in neoclassical economics. Workers decide whether they will supply labour and if so, how many hours they will supply, based on the opportunity costs of paid work. The *opportunity costs of paid work* is the wage rate: the higher the wage rate, the higher the opportunity costs of not having a job. This means that with low wages, neoclassical economics predicts that people prefer to enjoy leisure time and perhaps engage in unpaid work, rather than doing paid work. Of course, this is only feasible when there are other means of subsistence, the so-called no-trade alternative that we discussed in Chapter 1. For most workers, their labour power is the only resource they have, and hence, they will not see leisure time as a feasible alternative to paid work. Instead, they will regard paid work as the preferred alternative over poverty and dependence on others.

196 *Labour markets*

For the higher range of wages and in welfare states, the neoclassical perspective uses the twin concepts of substitution effect and income effect, as we have seen earlier in Chapter 3. In labour supply, the income and substitution effect go in different directions. At high levels of wages, every additional hour supplied will earn significantly higher income. This means that leisure time has a high price: forgoing the extra income has high opportunity costs. So, the substitution effect of high wages will lead to more hours worked: an increase in labour supply. But high wages also imply high income obtained from all the hours worked already.

So, why work additional hours? A high income can buy many goods and services, including leisure time by simply working less hours. So, the income effect of high wages will lead to no additional hours or even to less hours worked, because the high income allows one to enjoy more leisure time. The total effect of high and increasing wages on labour supply depends on the relative size of the substitution effect (more hours) and income effect (less hours). When the income effect is larger, the total effect of a wage increase on labour supply will be negative: a reduction in the hours supplied.

Another consequence of the neoclassical focus on the wage rate as indicator of opportunity cost is that female labour supply is explained as much more wage-elastic than male labour supply. Neoclassical labour market economics predicts that the higher the female wages, the stronger the reaction of the female labour supply. Indeed, statistics from developed countries confirm that this is the case. Men's labour supply is much less responsive to higher wages, because men already have high labour supply. Women's supply is more responsive to wages because for them, the opportunity costs of unpaid work time (in particular childcare) are more important. This also helps to explain why childcare opportunities and childcare subsidies in developed countries have a positive effect on female labour supply.

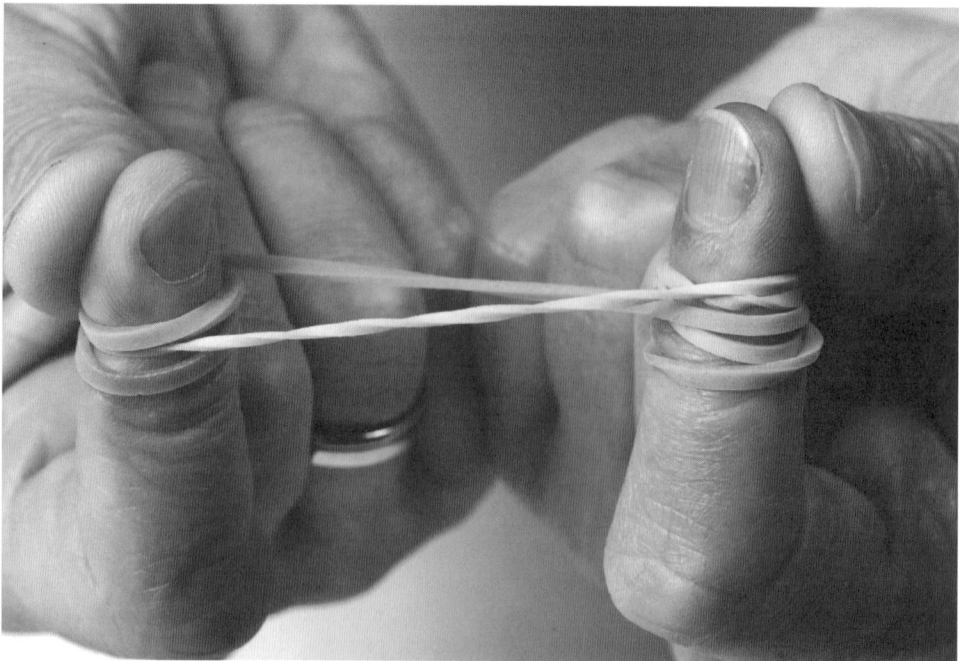

Image 8.1 Elasticity

Male wage elasticity is very small, close to zero. This means that men's labour supply hardly varies with the wage rate: they supply their labour irrespective of the market wage. Female wage elasticity in developed countries varies between 0.2 and 0.6. This means that on average, women's labour supply increases by 40 per cent when wages double. But, just like for men, women's wage elasticity is below 1, so their labour supply is also inelastic. One reason for this average wage elasticity of women of around 40 per cent is that in many societies, due to a traditional gender division of labour, more hours of paid work for women implies that part of the earned income from those hours must be spent on childcare and domestic help, formally or informally. So, only when wages increase sufficiently, will women with childcare responsibilities find it affordable to supply more hours to the labour market.

8.1.5 The labour supply curve

Each of the four theories has a different view of the shape of the labour supply curve. This is because in a labour market diagram, we have only two axes: a horizontal axis for the amount of labour supplied, and a vertical axes for the wage rate to which this supply is related. But all the theories acknowledge that more factors than the wage rate determine labour supply, and most theories state that these other factors are likely to be more important. Moreover, most workers need to earn a minimum income for their livelihoods and that of their dependants (unless they receive financial support). And they face a choice between paid work, unpaid work, and leisure time, while a healthy life requires a minimum of leisure time, and the caring needs of a household and community require a minimum of unpaid work time. So, the number of hours available for paid work is not so flexible. This is precisely what is reflected in the inelasticity of labour supply. This results in a rather vertically shaped and backward-bending labour supply curve, as shown in Diagram 8.4.

The diagram shows that labour supply is concentrated around the number of hours per day that is culturally accepted and socially desirable. Only when wages are very low, will workers supply more hours in order to compensate for low hourly earnings. Here, we also see the

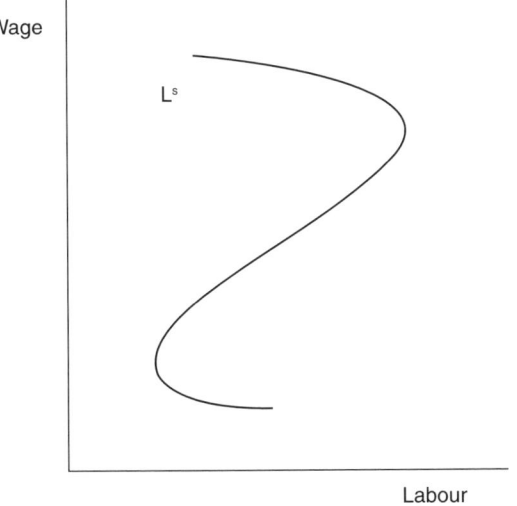

Diagram 8.4 The labour supply curve

discouraged worker effect for the labour market as a whole: at low wages, more household members are likely to supply labour to the labour market. In the higher wage range (the upper part of the diagram), we see the backward-bending part of the labour supply curve. This reflects widespread individual preferences as well as the social norm that when wages are high, people are less willing to give up leisure time and more likely to hire services to substitute for their unpaid work (such as childcare), simply because they earn enough to live well.

So, the labour supply curve is flat at low wages, positive at medium wages, and flat again but backwards at high wages. For developing countries, many workers will find themselves on the lower flat part of the curve, where wages are low and work hours are long, often through underemployment. The high-earning upper class finds itself on the upper flat part of the curve, where additional earnings per hour contribute more to a reduction in hours than to an increase in hours: the income effect is bigger than the substitution effect. This will be visible in early retirement, more leisure time, and a reduction in paid hours per week.

8.2 Labour demand

8.2.1 Social economics: segmented labour markets

Like any market, the labour market is segmented. *Labour market segmentation* is the categorisation of labour according to social norms and practices. We distinguish two types of segmentation: horizontal and vertical segmentation.

Horizontal segmentation is the differentiation of labour according to social groups and stereotypes. For example, whereas we find African Americans in all ranks of the US labour market, they tend to be concentrated in the less well-paid positions, largely in service industries in the public and private sector. White Americans are more evenly spread over the occupational ladder, with a dominance in managerial positions as well as in manufacturing jobs with strong labour union representation. Like ethnicity, gender is also a horizontal force in labour market segmentation. Gender differences in labour supply, through women largely being educated in social fields like teaching, health care, and personal services, and men largely being educated in the sciences, technical fields, and high-skilled manufacturing jobs, are reinforced by similarly stereotyped labour demand. It is difficult for a man to find a job as a birth assistant, for example, and not easy for a woman to be employed as a car mechanic.

Horizontal segmentation reinforces itself through crowding. *Job crowding* is the concentration of a social group in a small number of occupations. This leads to downward pressure on the wages in those occupations. With, on average, not more than twice as many men as women in the labour force, the small number of occupations taken by women are more crowded than the large number of occupations taken by men. If 75 per cent of women in the labour market find themselves in only four occupations (such as teacher, nurse, secretary, and shop assistant), whereas 75 per cent of men are spread over twenty occupations, there is more competition in the four stereotype women's occupations (the 'pink' jobs) than in the twenty occupations in which men dominate (the 'blue' jobs). With more competition, wages are pushed down. This leads to average lower wages for women as compared to men.

Vertical segmentation refers to invisible barriers between better paid, higher status, and more secure jobs and those that are low paid, low status, and flexible. When this occurs within a firm, it is referred to as the glass ceiling. But more generally in the economy, the distinction between better and worse jobs is largely between the formal economy on the one hand, and the informal economy on the other.

Once labour markets are segmented, labour demand limits itself to the stereotype categories, and segmentation becomes a self-fulfilling prophesy. This makes it very difficult to break segmentation: even with increased labour supply that is non-stereotype, such as African Americans graduating from business schools and women with skills training in mechanics, there will not automatically be more hiring outside the traditional stereotypes. The reason for this is discrimination.

Labour market discrimination is the disadvantaging of some groups in the labour market on the basis of ethnicity, age, gender, religion, sexual orientation, or disability. When people are equally qualified in terms of education and work experience, they should have equal opportunities. This is not only fair but also efficient. Employers who discriminate against certain social groups reduce the pool of potential workers in their firm, and hence, they limit the human capability potential of their workforce. This may negatively affect labour productivity, teamwork, innovation, and leadership in a firm. Diagram 8.5 shows how this happens.

When the individuals who supply their labour do not have equal opportunities in the labour market, they suffer from discrimination. Labour market discrimination ranges from explicit forms of discrimination ('we do not hire blacks here') to implicit forms of discrimination (recruitment of new managers through current managers' social networks). Moreover, labour market discrimination occurs along three dimensions of labour demand:

1   hiring: discrimination in access to employment
2   promotion: the glass ceiling
3   remuneration: wage discrimination.

Diagram 8.5 shows the distribution of labour demand for truck drivers. The columns are for male and female truck drivers. The rows distinguish between the higher skilled and the lower skilled drivers. The shaded cell (left-hand upper corner) indicates those who have already been hired as truck drivers. Now suppose that there is more trade with neighbouring countries and hence more demand for road transport. This leads to an increased demand for truck drivers. Who will be hired, do you think?

Employers would be acting rationally if they first hired all high-skilled drivers before hiring low-skilled drivers. In practice, however, segmentation often results in only men being hired for stereotype masculine jobs. As the diagram shows, there are more male than female

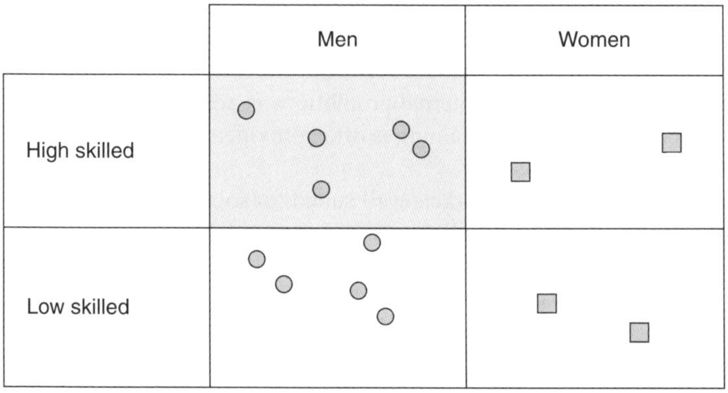

Diagram 8.5 Discrimination and inefficiency: labour market for truck drivers

drivers in the market for truck drivers. This is because of the gender stereotyping of truck driving as a typical masculine profession. Very few girls will enter this profession. But those who do, will have made an extra effort to get access to the training and to overcome their marginal position. Just like men, some women turn out to be very good drivers, others not. The diagram shows that by hiring low-skilled men, employers forego having the high-skilled women in their workforce, which is an inefficient choice. Simply because low-skilled workers are less productive than high-skilled workers.

Why would employers discriminate in hiring and promotion if this is inefficient? There are two possible explanations. First, employers may prefer to hire similar workers, to have a homogeneous workforce. This maybe because they fear unrest in the existing workforce due to 'strange' newcomers. This preference for homogeneity is not so much aimed against the outsiders as to protect the status quo and the insiders. It is a form of prejudice.

A second explanation for discrimination is stereotyping of the skills that are necessary for the job. This stereotyping may be so strong that employers hold on to the belief that the outsider group simply cannot have the required skills (despite proven ability through education and/or work experience). This stereotyping matches the stereotyping on the supply side of the labour market and thereby makes the social norms that underlie the stereotyping strong and difficult to change.

When we do see a change in stereotype social norms, this may be only partial, for example resulting in a more detailed and subtle level of stereotyping. For truck driving, this may be a distinction between small package delivery to homes, which requires communicative skills, and long-haul truck driving with heavy loads, which requires several days away from home. The first may become open for women, and the second even more restricted to men.

8.2.2 Institutions of labour demand

Institutional economics explains the demand for labour in terms of institutions, which can either encourage or constrain labour demand. The relevant institutions of labour demand are internal labour markets, contracts, and labour rights. I will discuss each of these.

8.2.2.1 Internal labour markets

Internal labour markets are labour markets located within firms. These employers recruit for junior positions, often through traineeships. Higher level positions along the job ladder are filled largely through internal promotion and transfers between different branches or foreign subsidiaries of the same firm. This process of internal promotions is accompanied by firm-specific training and job-specific training. This training is often provided within the firm and either on-the-job or as separate training courses.

These characteristics make internal labour markets well suited for socialisation into a particular firm culture, which may be relatively closed. In combination with regulations that prohibit ex-employees from using their firm-specific knowledge elsewhere for a certain period of time, this generates a dedicated workforce. Examples of such internal labour markets are the hierarchies in the judicial system and large multinational firms. Such firms tend to have relatively advantageous employment benefits, such as a generous pension system and health care package, childcare provisions, and sometimes even housing and sports facilities, but only for their core workers, selected for the internal labour market system.

Internal labour markets are also a solution to the asymmetric information problem in hiring personnel. By hiring them at a low level, employers get to know their employees and can better select who will be promoted to what level after some time. Without internal labour markets, employers are likely to solve the asymmetric information problem with *statistical discrimination*. This is the disadvantaging of individuals on the basis of the group average of a particular characteristic. In labour markets, this often results in gender discrimination, simply because women can get pregnant and men not. Even women who are very productive when also mothers, or who have grown-up children, don't want children, or cannot have children for medical reasons, will all be treated as having the same 'risk' for the employer, namely taking maternity leave or choosing to work less hours after childbirth. So, women as a group suffer from statistical discrimination in labour markets.

8.2.2.2 Contracts

Contracts are labour demand institutions because they are offered by employers and not by employees: they are demand-side located and defined. We distinguish five types of contracts (see Table 8.3):

1   *Fixed contracts for an indefinite period of time.* This type of contract is decreasing in importance all over the world. It is typical for public sector jobs at all levels and managerial jobs in the private sector. Such contracts are difficult to break by employers, due to high legal protection. Employees can fight any breach of the contract (such as termination or lower pay) in a labour court.
2   *Fixed contracts for a fixed period of time.* This type of contract lies between the first and the third type of contract. It has the benefits of a fixed contract, namely agreed pay and various employment benefits. But it has the disadvantages of flexible contracts, namely no job security after the fixed employment period.
3   *Flexible contracts.* Many employment contracts in the world are flexible and their share is increasing. This implies that the number of hours is not fixed and may vary from week to week. Often the hourly wage rate is agreed, but benefits (such as maternity leave and pension rights) are often excluded or very limited.
4   *Commercial contracts.* This type of contract is also on the increase and is not an employment contract with the firm one works for. Instead, it is a service contract with that firm, or a flexible employment contract with an employment agency, which sells the worker's service in a triangular employment relationship.
5   *No contracts.* The most disadvantaged category concerns the complete absence of labour contracts. This category encompasses the great majority of informal economy employment including self-employment. But the absence of a written contract does not necessarily imply any absence of mutual obligations between employer and employee. The employee is generally expected to show up for work as soon as there is work. And the employer is expected to take care of a worker who is sick or has a work-related accident. For the self-employed, reliable relationships with buyers may substitute to some extent for a contract.

8.2.2.3 Labour rights

The third relevant labour demand institution is labour rights. *Labour rights* are entitlements to a set of rights for employed and unemployed workers. These rights can be defined at the firm level

202 Labour markets

Table 8.3 Contracts in the South African labour market, number of persons, last quarter 2013

Contract type		Women (×1,000)	Men (×1,000)	Total (×1,000)
Formalities	Written contract	4,166	5,226	9,392
	Verbal contract	1,098	1,179	2,277
Time	Limited duration	748	893	1,641
	Permanent nature	3,228	4,120	7,348
	Unspecified	1,289	1,391	2,680
Total		5,264	6,405	11,669

Source: http://www.statssa.gov.za/publications/statsabout.asp?PPN=P0211&SCH

and national level. Many labour rights, which are set down in national laws and enforced through the labour inspectorate of ministries of labour and labour courts, have been agreed upon at the international level. The United Nations body responsible for international agreements on labour rights is the ILO: the International Labour Organization, based in Geneva. It is a tripartite body, which means that it consists of three constituencies: representatives of labour (labour unions), representatives of employers (employers' associations), and representatives of the state (delegates of ministries of labour). The first ILO convention was adopted in 1919 and concerned the restriction of hours of work in industry. It was a response to practices in the then-industrialised countries of the world (North America and Europe) with extremely long workdays and absence of rest days. In 1998, the ILO defined a core set of labour standards, which it seeks to achieve in every country across the world, in the public and private sector, in the formal and informal economy, and for all social groups. It is referred to as the Declaration on Fundamental Principles and Rights at Work. This declaration commits member states to respect and promote principles and rights in four categories, whether or not they have ratified the relevant labour conventions. These categories are: freedom of association, the elimination of forced labour, the abolition of child labour, and the elimination of discrimination in respect of employment and occupation.

Labour market institutions may work out more to the benefit of workers as a whole or only certain groups, or they may work out more to the benefit of employers, with disadvantages for (groups of) workers. This is shown in Table 8.4.

8.2.3 Post Keynesian economics: labour demand as derived demand

The Post Keynesian perspective always starts from a macroeconomic viewpoint, as you will know by now. For labour demand, it asks the question: how much labour will be demanded by employers over the economic cycle? The answer to the question is: low labour demand

Table 8.4 Labour market institutions and their effects

Type of institution	Workers	Employers
Internal labour market	Positive for insiders; negative for outsiders	Positive (socialisation)
Labour rights	Positive (fairness)	Negative (costly)
Flexibilisation	Negative (insecurity)	Positive (adaptation to market changes)
Discrimination	Negative (constrained access)	Negative (inefficient)

when the cycle is low and high labour demand when the cycle is high. This means that labour demand is considered as *derived demand* in Post Keynesian theory: the demand for labour depends on the aggregate demand in the economy. When aggregate demand (AD) in the economy (demand for all goods and services and investment) is high, there will also be high demand for labour, in order to produce all the goods and services that are demanded in the economy and abroad (export goods). Similarly, when AD is low, as in an economic downturn or crisis, the demand for labour will also be low. Firms will downsize and fire workers and they will want to sell their stocks first before hiring more workers.

What is so special about the theory of labour demand as derived demand, is that labour demand is low during a downturn, even when wages decline, and even when individual workers are willing to work for lower than market wages. How is that possible?

Let us assume an open-air fruit market in Cape Town right after the harvest season. Unless the harvest was destroyed by bad weather conditions, we can expect a high supply of fresh apples. Consumers may be interested in buying more apples now than a month earlier when only some remaining, small, and dried-up apples from last year were available. But even when they all buy twice as much this month as the previous month, there will still be more fresh apples available, in particular if the harvest was exceptionally good. It is then quite likely that a price discount ('two kilos for the price of one') will induce consumers to buy more apples than they planned. And it is quite likely that they will do so, because it is a bargain. They will buy extra apples and save a few for later, give them away, make apple chutney, or bake a pie. So, when the sellers in the market lower the price of apples, consumers are likely to buy more and perhaps eat less pears and oranges: a substitution effect.

But this process does not occur in the labour market when the economy is in a downturn of the economic cycle. Unemployed workers who offer to work for firms for less than the market wage will not be employed. Worse, many existing workers with employment will be fired. The reason is that the labour market is an input market for the production process – labour power is a production factor. And when firms cannot sell all the products they make, they will slow down production. No matter how low the wage offers of workers are. . . .

And there is another reason why labour demand is not closely related to wages. It is in the interest of employers for there to be a certain level of unemployment. This gives them bargaining power over wages, also in times when the economic cycle is high: it allows for a labour reserve to be hired from a segmented labour market without having to raise all wages due to shortages. Workers functioning as folding chairs.

8.2.4 Neoclassical economics: productivity and wages

The neoclassical perspective focuses on the contribution that workers make to maximising profit. This contribution consists of two parts: work effort and output produced per unit of work effort. And it has a cost in the form of wages. Hence, a firm that seeks profit maximisation will try to:

- increase work effort
- increase labour efficiency
- reduce wages.

Remember from Chapter 4 that we showed how neoclassical economics calculates the point of profit maximisation for a firm, with the accompanying optimal level of workers. We used

204 Labour markets

Table 8.5 Marginal revenue and marginal cost

(1) Input: labour (number of students)	(2) Output: pizzas	(3) Marginal output	(4) Fixed cost: rent (€)	(5) Variable labour cost (€) = €25 × column (1)	(6) Total cost = column (4) + (5)	(7) Total revenue (euro) = €6 × column (2)	(8) Marginal cost*	(9) Marginal revenue**
0	0	–	20	0	20	0	–	–
1	10	10	20	25	45	60	2.50	6
2	24	14	20	50	70	144	1.79	6
3	40	16	20	75	95	240	1.56	6
4	60	20	20	100	120	360	1.25	6
5	73	13	20	125	145	438	1.92	6
6	78	5	20	150	170	468	5.00	6
7	75	-3	20	175	195	450	-8.33	6

*Marginal cost = change in column (6) (=25) for each additional number of output (2).
**Marginal revenue = change in column (7) for each additional number of output (2).

the example of Roberto's pizza restaurant. Now, there is a different way to get at the same outcome of the number of workers hired in the short run in a fully competitive market (where every additional unit of output will be sold because of the assumption of Say's Law: supply creates its own demand). This method centres around the *value of the marginal product of labour*. This is the value of additional output generated by employing one additional unit of labour. Let us revisit Table 4.8 in Chapter 4, which is here called Table 8.5.

What level of employment maximises profit for Roberto? Remember that the additional cost of hiring another student in the restaurant is the wage rate, which is €25 (W = 25). And what does Roberto get in return for hiring an additional student? He gets the extra number of pizzas produced, multiplied by the price of these pizzas: the marginal product of labour (MPL) multiplied by the price per pizza (P). The outcome of this multiplication is called the value of the marginal product of labour (VMPL):

$$VMPL = MPL \times P$$

So, how many workers should Roberto hire? Well, more workers as long as the value of the marginal product of labour is higher than the wage rate (which, remember, is the marginal cost of labour). At which number of workers is that no longer the case? In order to answer this question we need to make a new table. Table 8.6 will help us determine the labour demand when Roberto maximises profit.

The new Table 8.6 will copy columns (1) and (2) for number of workers and output produced. Column (3) gives the price per unit of output = P = the price of a pizza = €6. Remember in Chapter 4 this was also called marginal revenue (MR). Column (4) is the old column (3) and presents the marginal product of labour (MPL), which is the additional output produced with an additional unit of labour. Column (5) gives the value of the marginal product of labour (VMPL), which is the product of column (3) and column (4). Column (6) gives the wage rate (W).

Table 8.6 allows us to determine optimal employment for Roberto's restaurant, namely where VMPL equals W, or is slightly above it. There is no exact match, but for six students, VMPL comes closest to the wage rate: VMPL = 30 with six workers while W = 25. For five

Table 8.6 Demand for labour

(1) L	(2) Output	(3) P	(4) MPL	(5) VMPL	(6) W
0	0	6	–	–	25
1	10	6	10	60	25
2	24	6	14	84	25
3	40	6	16	96	25
4	60	6	20	120	25
5	73	6	13	78	25
6	78	6	5	30	25
7	75	6	–3	–18	25

Note: L, labour; MPL, marginal product of labour; P, price per unit of output; VMPL, value of the marginal product of labour; W, wage rate.

workers, VMPL if 78, and so is well above W and hence more workers can be hired. For seven workers, VMPL becomes negative, so there is no positive value anymore. Hence, the optimum employment in Roberto's restaurant is six workers.

Remember that this is exactly the same number of workers required for profit maximisation, as we calculated in Chapter 4. It is just a different way of calculating the optimisation problem for Roberto. Now, we approached it from the perspective of labour demand. In conclusion, in the neoclassical perspective, labour demand is determined by the wage rate and the value of the marginal product of labour, which in turn is the product of the price of the output and the marginal product of labour. This is an optimisation problem that can be solved with the fixed numbers given by a perfectly competitive market in which the sales price is constant and the wage rate is constant, and the productivity of every individual worker is assumed homogeneous, and every additional number of output will be sold.

8.2.5 Labour demand function

Just as the labour supply function in an aggregate labour market diagram is not a straight line, so the labour demand function does not have a predictable shape either. What do we know about its shape?

1 Labour demand increases with more aggregate demand in the economy and more purchasing power of consumers → higher wages, higher demand;
2 Labour demand decreases with higher wages because it makes labour more costly → higher wages, lower demand;
3 Labour demand varies per segment of the labour market, partly depending on the economic performance per sector and partly depending on social norms including discrimination → aggregate labour demand may be little related to wages due to the importance of social factors.

This leads to a labour demand curve which is quite independent of the wage rate, because the positive and negative effects of wages on demand may very well net each other out. This results in an almost vertical labour demand curve as shown in Diagram 8.6. The location of this curve determines the level of employment.

206 *Labour markets*

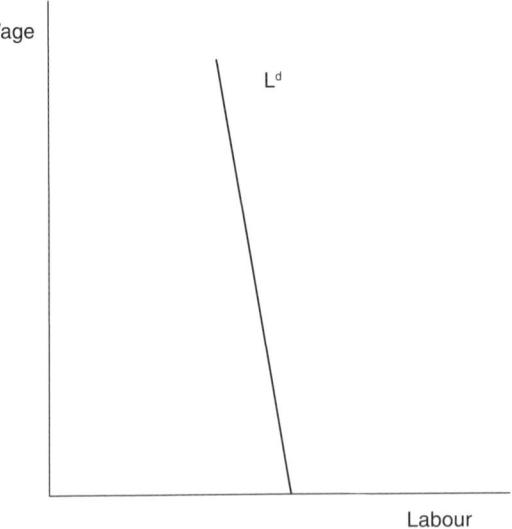

Diagram 8.6 Labour demand curve

8.3 Unemployment and wages

The *unemployment rate* is the proportion of unemployed people as a percentage of the labour force, as defined in section 8.1. Unemployment rates can also be calculated for groups, such as young workers, women, or ethnic groups. Table 8.7 shows the various unemployment rates in South Africa in 2013.

8.3.1 Social economics: structural unemployment and wage inequality

In social economics labour markets are acknowledged to be segmented, as we have seen earlier. This implies discrimination in hiring and promotion. As a consequence, it also leads to segmentation among the unemployed. We distinguish three categories of unemployed: temporary unemployed, structural unemployed, and the labour reserve. Each of these categories consists of very different social groups.

Table 8.7 Unemployment rates for groups in South Africa, last quarter 2013

		Unemployment rate
Racial	Black workers	29%
	Coloured workers	25%
	Indian/Asian workers	13%
	White workers	6%
Sex	Women	28%
	Men	23%
Total		26%

Source: http://www.statssa.gov.za/publications/statsabout.asp?PPN=P0211&SCH

8.3.1.1 Temporary unemployed

The *temporary unemployed* consist of those in the labour force who are between jobs. They generally have high chances of finding employment. Hence, their unemployment status will generally be short and not problematic. When the economy is in a recession, some of these will experience longer spells of unemployment and may decide to obtain additional training to improve their chances of finding work. The category of the temporary unemployed is the least problematic because with an improvement in the economic cycle the large majority will succeed in finding a job again.

8.3.1.2 Structural unemployed

The category of the *structurally unemployed* is more problematic. Structural unemployment is long term and is a consequence of structural changes in the economy. For example, the textile industry shifting from high-wage to low-wage countries. This means that textile workers in the origin countries will not be able to find employment again in the textile sector because the sector has moved abroad. Another driving force is mechanisation. Firms which replace workers with machines and computers, will fire workers and hire smaller numbers of higher skilled workers to replace them. Due to segmented labour markets, workers who can no longer find employment due to structural economic change will remain long-term unemployed.

8.3.1.3 Labour reserve

Finally, the category of the *labour reserve*. This is the category of additional workers when economies are at the height of their economic cycle, who are hired when labour markets

Image 8.2 Textile factory

experience scarcity. When not needed, most of them drop out of the labour force, in particular women – the folding chairs as mentioned already in section 8.2.3. But some of them keep searching for a job but often without success due to their low social status: no support from labour unions and little protection by contracts or by the state.

8.3.2 Wage inequality

In social economics, wages are considered not only as a reward for labour effort, but also as the means of subsistence. Low wages are a concern because they constrain people's livelihoods. When wages are very low, this may even lead to child labour and exploitation because households seek to maintain minimum necessary livelihoods. That is why in social economics, a decent wage, or a living wage, is crucial. How do we determine the level of a decent wage? This is contextual. Adam Smith pointed out in his foundational book *The Wealth of Nations* that there is no absolute rate for a decent wage, but that it is determined by the social norms of dignity in a society. In his society it meant that a Scottish urban worker should earn enough to be able to afford leather shoes.

Wage inequality is related to low wages, because when low wages are increased, for example through a minimum wage or government benefits, this will raise the threshold and thereby reduce the gap with higher wages. Hence, decent wages reduce wage inequality. Inequality in hourly wages is expressed along the same lines as those leading to labour market segmentation. Workers in disadvantaged sectors and marginalised positions along the job ladder also earn low wages. Wage inequality can have two causes: (1) differences in human capital (or broader human capabilities), such as level and type of education, work experience, and health, and (2) discrimination.

A solution to the first type of wage inequality is better education accessible for everyone and better health care and other well-being improving policies for children and adults. A solution to wage discrimination is more difficult. Almost every country in the world already has formal institutions in place to prevent wage discrimination: laws about equal wages for equal work, a labour inspectorate to enforce this law, a labour court for complaints, and labour unions who have this on their agendas in their bargaining with employers. Nevertheless, wage discrimination is widespread, both in developing and in developed countries. For example, wage discrimination against women. Many studies have shown that about half of all wage differences between men and women in the labour markets across the world can be explained by lower levels of female education and less work experience by women as compared to men. But the other half of the gender wage inequality cannot be explained. Women with the same qualifications as men and the same work experience earn on average lower wages than men. Everywhere. This discriminatory part of wage inequality is responsible for the wages of women being about 10–20 per cent lower than those of men. How is that possible?

There are at least three explanations for the persistence of wage discrimination.

8.3.2.1 Compensating wage differentials

In this explanation, lower wages are assumed to be compensated with non-wage benefits, such as a pleasant work environment, good working conditions, social status, or high job satisfaction. An example concerns the wages for nurses and truck drivers. In many countries, nurses have higher levels of education but nevertheless earn lower wages than truck drivers. The difference is explained with compensating wage differentials: more social status, higher job satisfaction, and a more pleasant work environment for nurses as compared to truck drivers.

Is this a universal and adequate explanation? What about the benefits of being a truck driver? No high-status bosses looking over your shoulders all the time and the possibility of playing loud music at work, the freedom to pause when you like (although increasingly restricted by GPS tracking), and no emotional pressure from crying family members or patients begging you for more painkillers.

8.3.2.2 Gender division of labour

A second explanation for wage discrimination is the gender division of labour. The gender division of labour in the household restricts women's work experience and training opportunities due to long hours of unpaid work and care giving. Together with segmentation in labour markets, the gender division of labour in the labour market builds on the gender division of labour in the household.

8.3.2.3 Job crowding

A third explanation for wage discrimination is job crowding in the labour market, mentioned in section 8.1.1. As a consequence of labour market segmentation, disadvantaged groups crowd into a smaller number of occupations than the rest of the labour market, with a downward pressure on their wages.

8.3.3 Institutional economics: minimum wages and efficiency wages

A major labour market institution, which we have not yet discussed, is minimum wages. Most countries in the world have minimum wage laws. But the way these are applied varies. Some countries have only minimum wages for the pubic sector, while other countries have minimum wages agreed for the economy as a whole or differentiated per economic sector or for urban versus rural areas. What matters most about minimum wages is that they should be effective. That means that they are set at a level above the market wage that would prevail without the minimum wage. So, a minimum wage of 5 rand per hour when the lowest paid workers already earn 7 rand per hour is not an effective minimum wage. But if it was set at 8 rand per hour it would be effective, because low wage earners would then begin to earn a higher wage and hence bring home more income. So, a minimum wage, when effective, increases low-income earners' wages and incomes.

In South Africa, minimum wages were introduced in 1999 and have since expanded to include more and more low-earning sectors of the economy. The rates distinguish between rural areas and urban areas, and between number of hours worked per week. The level of the minimum wage is determined by the Minister of Labour on an annual basis. For example, for domestic workers, the minimum wage for 2013 is given in Table 8.8.

Table 8.8 Minimum wages for domestic workers in South Africa, 2013

	Minimum wage per hour (rand)	
	Urban areas	Rural areas
27 Hours per week or more	8.95	7.95
27 Hours per week or less	10.48	9.03

Source: mywage.co.za

210 *Labour markets*

So, a minimum wage is enabling for workers who are already employed because it supports their livelihoods. It also helps to reduce income inequality. But is a minimum wage also enabling for the unemployed? If a country provides unemployment benefits and when these are legally set at a certain proportion of the minimum wage, then the unemployed also benefit directly from a minimum wage. They will enjoy higher social protection.

But what about the labour-cost increase for firms? It may well lead to a reduction in demand for labour, and hence, to more unemployment. In the short run, a minimum wage increases production costs and hence may reduce the competitiveness of firms. Their products will become too expensive and they may lose out in competition with firms in other regions or countries that do not have a minimum wage or where it is set at a lower level. In the long run, employers do not suffer much because they will simply adjust the capital/labour ratio in their firm: they will replace labour with capital if they find the labour costs becoming too high relative to labour productivity.

But this is a static story – it leaves out labour market dynamics. And it ignores the fact that labour markets are not perfectly competitive markets but are characterised by segmentation, asymmetric power (of capital over labour), labour demand as a derived demand, and different types of contracts. Because of these characteristics of labour markets, the effect of minimum wages on unemployment may in fact be . . . nothing.

Moreover, the wage cost increase for employers may be compensated for by a productivity increase by the workers. This dynamic effect is referred to as the efficiency wage theory. *Efficiency wages* are above market wages, which trigger positive externalities in labour effort. The theory of efficiency wages not only applies to minimum wages, but also to other wage increases. It is part of institutional economics because the theory draws on various formal and informal institutions to explain a positive effect of wage increases for workers, the unemployed, and employers.

Why would efficiency wages have positive employment effects? There are five reasons.

8.3.3.1 Only few workers earn the minimum wage

First, possible increases in unemployment tend to be limited in the case of minimum wages, because only a part of the labour force works at low wages. So, even if there are negative effects on unemployment, they are likely to be small.

8.3.3.2 Capability and motivation improvement

Second, a major positive effect is on the capabilities of workers through improved health (nutrition, health care), education and training opportunities, and dignity. This directly improves the labour productivity of workers. When workers suffer from malnutrition, anaemia, low weight, and non-treated infections, their physical capabilities for work are constrained. With limited education and training, their capabilities are underdeveloped and hence their skills to produce more productively. In addition, when they feel exploited and powerless to increase their wages despite additional work effort, their mental health and dignity may be affected through demotivation and alienation. They lose creativity, team spirit, and loyalty, which leads to a constraint on their psychological capabilities for work.

8.3.3.3 Lower labour conflict

A third positive effect of efficiency wages is that they prevent labour unrest and conflict through strikes, riots, and obstruction of workplaces. This leads to work days lost and may even result in material costs for firms. So, efficiency wages help to prevent costs related to labour unrest.

8.3.3.4 Prevention of race to the bottom

A fourth positive effect of efficiency wages is that they prevent a race to the bottom in labour markets with a large oversupply of labour (unemployment, underemployment, and discouraged labour reserve). Strong competition among the unemployed to bid wages downwards leads to a vicious circle of low wages, the added worker effect in households resulting in even more labour supply, and possibly child labour. This will kick in reductions in labour productivity due to low health and undermined dignity, as discussed in section 8.3.2.2.

8.3.3.5 Strengthens intrinsic motivation

A fifth and last reason for a positive effect of efficiency wages on work effort is that a higher wage rate is motivating in itself, not only because it increases the cost of losing one's job (opportunity costs). But more importantly because it is part of what we referred to in Chapter 4: the intrinsic motivation of workers, leading to higher productivity when they are satisfied with their wage rate and do not need to bother about it.

Do these positive externalities prevent unemployment rising as a consequence of higher wages? Many studies suggest that unemployment is not affected by minimum wages or other wage increases. The reason is increased productivity. The higher productivity compensates for the increase in wage costs and therefore the product will not become more expensive. Hence, there is no negative effect on sales, and so no change is needed in the demand for labour. Moreover, when workers earn higher incomes, they will also have more purchasing power to allow them buy more products. This creates a virtuous circle of higher wages – higher consumer spending – higher production levels – space for higher wages.

Obviously these dynamic effects are context dependent. Empirical studies therefore show varying results of minimum wages. What matters for labour market policy concerning minimum wages and wage increases is that such policies should ensure that the institutional context is conducive to generating the positive externalities listed here. In a context of conflict and high inflation, for example, the efficiency wage effects are less likely to emerge.

8.3.4 Post Keynesian economics: involuntary unemployment

The Post Keynesian analysis of unemployment directly follows from the Post Keynesian analysis of labour demand as derived from aggregate demand in the economy. If the demand for labour is constrained by low aggregate demand, and the economy is stuck at a level well below full capacity, not all labour supplied will be hired. Hence, there will be unemployment. Not because those who are not hired are not productive enough, or want higher wages than offered to them. But because their labour is not needed, since the products that could be produced with their labour cannot be sold. That is why in Post Keynesian theory, unemployment is involuntary unemployment.

How are wages formed in this theory? Technically, the wage rate for every segment of the labour market is where the demand curve and the supply curve intersect. In Diagram 8.7 we use the demand and supply curves presented in section 8.4. We now combine the labour supply and labour demand curve into a single diagram. This allows us to find the market wage rate and unemployment level for one particular segment in the labour market.

212 *Labour markets*

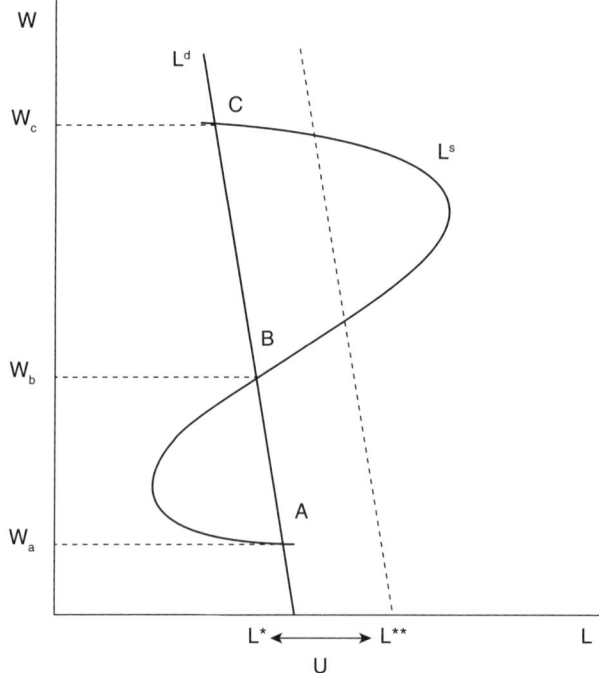

Diagram 8.7 Unemployment in the Post Keynesian perspective

Diagram 8.7 shows that the labour demand function has three points of intersection with the labour supply function (A, B, and C). Because of the almost vertical labour demand curve, the equilibrium level of employment, L*, is almost the same for all three equilibriums (we distinguish them as L^*_a, L^*_b, and L^*_c but due to lack of space in the diagram these labels are not included). There is slightly more employment at point A (L^*_a) than at point B (L^*_b) and slightly more at point B than at point C (L^*_c). In other words, the level of employment is less at higher wage rates. But full employment occurs along the labour demand curve labelled L**. This is the labour demand curve for full capacity. The difference between L** and L* at each equilibrium point is unemployment (U).

At point A, the labour market is at a low wage level equilibrium: wage W_a. Here, the labour supply curve is downward sloping, because wages are around or below subsistence level: people need to work more hours to survive and more household members supply their labour. There is no unemployment for this group of low wage earners because everybody who is able to work is working (also those under 15 and over 65 years of age), although often they are underemployed.

At point B, the intersection of the labour demand function is at a higher wage level, W_b. This is where the labour supply curve begins to slope upwards. So, when people supply their labour partly in response to higher wages, around equilibrium point B, they work at decent wages and supply less labour when wages go down and more labour when wages go up. Here is where the opportunity costs of work kick in, and more wages make leisure time more

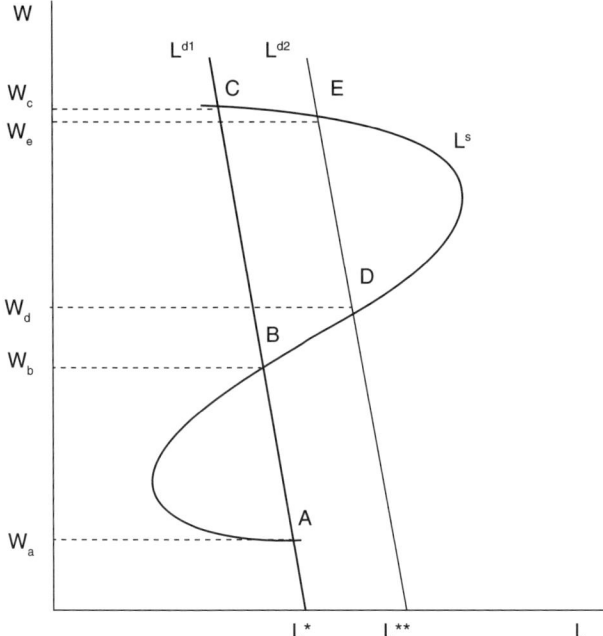

Diagram 8.8 Unemployment in the Post Keynesian perspective with increased labour demand

expensive, so that on average people decide to substitute paid work time for leisure time. And with the income earned they may reduce some of their unpaid work time by purchasing household durable goods (washing machines, refrigerators) or by hiring domestic help (cleaning, repair work).

The third equilibrium, C, occurs at a high wage level, W_c. This happens at the backward bending part of the labour supply curve, where households earn more than enough livelihood and begin to value leisure time more than additional income. Hence, with higher wages, labour supply goes down: less hours per person and/or less household members supplying paid labour. Also, the high income earned allows for a reduction in unpaid work time, by buying more expensive household durable goods (microwaves, dishwashers, cars) and hiring more domestic services or buying ready-made food.

Now, suppose that the economy is booming, with relatively high aggregate demand and hence, high demand for labour. This leads to a shift in the labour demand curve to the right (from L^{d1} to L^{d2}) and the new labour market equilibrium is at the level of L^{**} of employment. This is the level of full employment, hence, there is no unemployment anymore. We see this in Diagram 8.8.

The new labour demand curve shows two intersections with the supply curve: D and E. Both equilibriums have a higher employment level than before, a shift to the right from L^* to L^{**}. In equilibrium D, with wage rate W_d, there is more employment than before at a higher wage rate than with both W_a and W_b. This is because labour is becoming relatively scarce and the opportunity costs of leisure time increase.

In equilibrium E, with wage rate W_e, we also see an expansion of employment to L** as compared to the old equilibrium in the top wage sector, C. But we see a small decline in the equilibrium wage rate from W_c to W_e.

The reason for this small difference is that at such high wage levels, people generally prefer to do more unpaid work and spend more leisure time than do many hours of paid work. But when there is a decline in those high wages, they like to keep their level of high income, so as to afford a luxurious standard of living. As a consequence, they will supply more labour hours per individual and/or per household.

Which equilibrium will occur with the original and with the new labour demand curve? We do not know. This depends on which segment workers are in on the labour supply curve: at the bottom where they earn more or less subsistence wages, in the middle where they earn decent wages, or at the top where they have high wages and enough income to reduce hours of work to enjoy more leisure time and/or do more unpaid work.

These equilibriums are not stable. And labour supply and labour demand are inter-related through aggregate demand: those employed will spend their income on goods that workers need to produce. . . . So, a shift in one curve will induce a shift in the other. Hence, the equilibriums A, B, C, D, and E shown in Diagram 8.8 are ideal states. Real world labour markets are dynamic, so that the level of employment depends on the level of aggregate demand (which shifts continuously) and the wage level depends on the bargaining power of labour vis-à-vis capital.

Remember that capital – employers – hire labour and not the other way around. The only pattern of wages that the diagram shows is that with increased labour demand (a shift of the labour demand curve to the right), wages tend to go up for those at the bottom and in the middle of the wage ladder. This concerns the great majority of workers. At the macro level, this pattern is expressed through the ratio of labour income over capital income. When the economy is on an upward path along the economic cycle, we expect an increase in the labour share of income and a decline in the capital share of income, due to the higher demand for labour, which will push up wages. Data from the USA, however, indicate that since the 1960s, the labour share of income has declined, with a temporary and small increase in the 1990s. We see a particularly steep decline since 2000. In the USA, labour share of income has declined from around 70 per cent in the 1980s to around 63 per cent in 2007.[2] So, even though we have seen movements in the economic cycle between 1960 and today, with periods of high economic growth and tight labour markets, labour share has on average declined, not only in the USA but in many countries.

This decline in the labour share shows that the wage rate in the various segments of the labour market is more a consequence of the bargaining power of labour vis-à-vis capital in a context of labour market flexibilisation, technological advancement, and trade liberalisation, than explainable by labour demand and labour supply forces. So, the Post Keynesian explanation of wage rates, just like the explanation of unemployment, refers to aggregate demand in the economy as a whole, which determines the bargaining power of labour vis-à-vis capital.

How can the bargaining power of labour be strengthened so that wages will increase vis-à-vis capital earnings? The answer is through the organisation of labour. This happens in labour unions, in workers' cooperatives, and in self-organising groups of the self-employed.

Box 8.1 Labour unions in South Africa

Labour unions in South Africa played an important role in the struggle against apartheid. In 1994 new legislation was introduced that regulated the rights of labour unions and collective bargaining. The Labour Relations Act, 1995 and the Basic Conditions of Employment Act, 1997 drastically changed the basis of labour relations in the country.

There are four main labour union federations, of which COSATU or the Congress of South African Trade Unions, is the largest, with 21 affiliated unions representing some 1.9 million workers. COSATU also forms a formal tripartite alliance with the largest political party, the African National Congress (ANC) together with the South African Communist Party. The other three main federations are FEDUSA (with 20 unions representing 515,000 workers), NACTU (with 22 unions representing almost 400,000 workers), and CONSAWU (with 20 unions representing 290,000 members). In addition there are some 14 smaller federations and 100 independent labour unions. Together all these unions represent about 24 per cent of all workers in the formal sector.

These unions are responsible for the annual increase in salary for 30 per cent of workers. The remainder either try to negotiate individually (10 per cent) or cannot negotiate at all. Outside the formal sector, the organisation of workers and own account workers is weak and attempts to organise, for example street vendors, have failed (there was SEWU –the Self Employed Women's Union—between 1994 and 2004). A notable exception is the independent labour union for farmworkers Sikhula Sonke, which organises (seasonal) workers – especially women – in the Western Cape around issues of the workplace (wages, working conditions) but also 'domestic' issues like school drop-out rates of children and gender-based violence.

Sources: Schiphorst, F. B. (2011) 'Defending Vulnerable Workers in South Africa After the Crisis: What Role for COSATU?', in: van Bergeijk, P., A. de Haan and R. van der Hoeven (eds), A Crisis of Capitalism? A Crisis of Development! Cheltenham: Edward Elgar, pp. 215–30; Statistics South Africa, Department of Labour (2014), Alphabetical List of Registered Trade Unions in South Africa for May 2014. Pretoria: Department of Labour.

8.3.5 Neoclassical economics: voluntary unemployment

Neoclassical labour market theory assumes a positively sloping labour supply function, where higher wages lead to a substitution of paid work with leisure time. And it assumes a downward sloping labour demand function, where additional labour is characterised by a decline in the marginal productivity of labour, and hence, in the value of the marginal product of labour. Together these curves lead to a stable labour market equilibrium with an equilibrium level of employment and an equilibrium wage rate. This equilibrium level of employment is precisely at the level of full employment: there is no involuntary unemployment. That is because employers will hire additional workers assuming that they will be able to sell what these additional workers produce. So, the only brake on hiring workers is the law of diminishing marginal returns: they will stop hiring when their fixed stock of capital no longer allows for the hiring of more workers in order to add value as compared to the costs of these workers.

Hence, in the neoclassical labour market perspective, unemployment can only arise when some of those who supply their labour are not willing to work for the going wage rate. That is

216   Labour markets

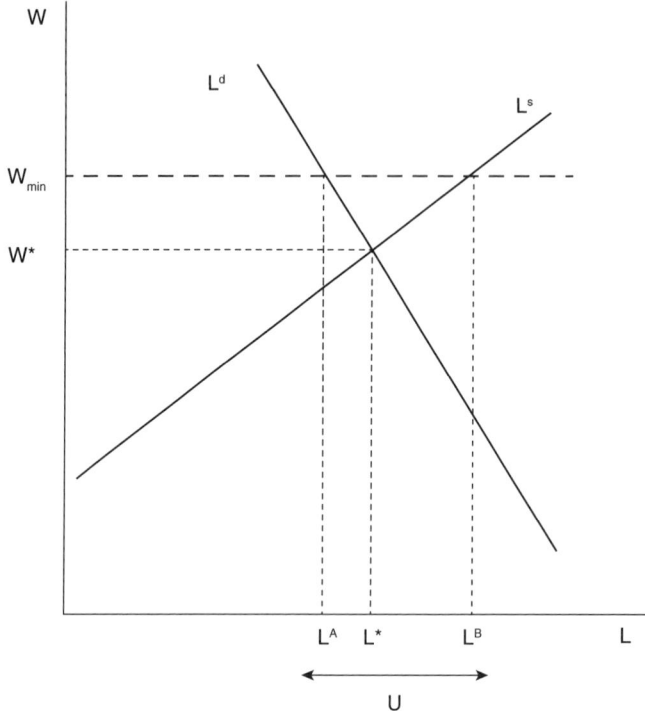

Diagram 8.9 Labour market equilibrium in neoclassical theory

why in neoclassical theory, unemployment is regarded as voluntary: these people could find work if only they would accept market level wages. But if there is regulation of the labour market by the state, there is a possibility of unemployment of the involuntary type. Diagram 8.9 shows how a minimum wage can lead to unemployment in the neoclassical perspective.

The equilibrium level of employment, L*, with wage rate W*, shows that there is no unemployment. At wage rate W*, everybody who supplies labour is hired.

Let us now introduce a minimum wage, W_{min}. At this wage level, there is no equilibrium in the labour market anymore: the supply and demand curves do not intersect. Instead, labour demand is at level L^A and labour supply is at level L^B. The difference is unemployment:

$$L^B - L^A = U$$

How can this unemployment be solved? Reducing or eliminating the minimum wage is obviously a solution. And it is often advocated by neoclassical economists. But then we are back in the starting position with low wages. An alternative would be an increase in the labour demand function. That is, a shift to the right, until it meets the labour supply function at the minimum wage, W_{min}. That would increase employment up to the level of full employment at the minimum wage, at the level of L^B. How could that shift of labour demand happen?

In neoclassical economics the policy answer is flexibilisation of the labour market. That is, fewer fixed contracts, more flexible contracts, and flexible contracts with varying number of hours per week. This would allow firms to hire more workers when they need to, without running the risk of having contracted workers that they do not need at times when their sales lag behind their expectations. So, more flexibility in reducing the number of workers and hours per workers would stimulate more hiring when employers can afford this. This may indeed help to reduce unemployment. But probably not sufficiently. Moreover, flexibilisation undermines the working of efficiency wages: worker's productivity depends largely on their motivation and dignity. With less job security, less loyalty to employers, and no perspective of wage increases, motivation is not stimulated. This may keep the labour market stuck at low wages.

8.4 Interesting sources

International Labour Organisation: www.ilo.org

Wage Indicator: if you want to check how your wage compares to others in your country you can fill in an online survey and find out through the Wage Indicator website for your own country: http://www.wageindicator.org/main

8.5 Glossary

Added worker effect   The increased labour supply response by household members to reduced hours of unpaid work or earnings per hour of other household members

Compensating wage differentials   Lower wages are compensated for with other benefits, such as a pleasant work environment, good working conditions, social status, or high job satisfaction

Demographic transition   A shift from high mortality and high birth rates to low mortality and low birth rates

Derived demand   The demand for labour depends on the aggregate demand in the economy

Discouraged worker effect   The withdrawal of those workers from the labour force who have no confidence that they will find employment

Efficiency wages   Above market wages which trigger positive externalities

Horizontal segmentation   The distinction of labour according to social groups and stereotypes

Human capital   A production factor consisting of skills, experience, and capacities

Human capability   The skills and capabilities of human beings which can be transferred through labour into productive activity

ILO (International Labour Organization)   The UN tripartite organisation of governments, employer associations, and labour unions

Informal economy   That part of the economy which is undercounted, under-registered, and undervalued

Internal labour markets   Labour markets located within firms

Job crowding   The concentration of a social group in a small number of occupations

Labour force Everyone between 15 and 65 years of age who is willing and able to work

Labour market segmentation The categorisation of labour according to social norms and practices

Labour rights Entitlements to a set of rights for employed and unemployed workers

Opportunity costs of paid work The wage rate: the higher the wage rate, the higher the opportunity costs of not having a job

Population of working age The number of people between 15 and 65 years of age

Reproduction Unpaid caring for the current and future generation of labour and for others inside and outside the economy

Statistical discrimination Disadvantaging individuals on the basis of the group average of a particular characteristic

Structurally unemployed Unemployed people with a disadvantaged position who are the first to lose their jobs and who suffer from limited job protection by labour unions or fixed contracts

Temporary unemployed Those in the labour force who are between jobs

Underemployment The situation in which a worker has employment but for less hours of effective work time than desired

Unemployment rate The percentage of those in the labour force who have no employment

Value of the marginal product of labour The value of additional output generated by employing one additional unit of labour

Vertical segmentation The invisible barriers between better paid, higher status, and more secure jobs and those that are low paid, low status, and flexible

Welfare poverty trap The situation of being unable to escape poverty because of being dependent on state benefits which are reduced by the same amount as any extra income gained

Notes

1 See: http://www.statssa.gov.za/publications/statsabout.asp?PPN=P0211&SCH=
2 http://www.clevelandfed.org/research/commentary/2012/2012-13.cfm and http://www.brookings.edu/~/media/Projects/BPEA/Fall%202013/2013b_elsby_labor_share.pdf and http://economix.blogs.nytimes.com/2013/09/09/why-labors-share-of-income-is-falling/?_r=0

9 Financial markets

9.1 Introduction

This chapter explains financial markets in the context of the United States of America. The USA has the most advanced financial sector in the world, where the latest trends in financial innovation often begin. And it is the country where the financial crisis originated in 2007 with underperforming subprime mortgages, which led to bank and household insolvency (origin at the national level) and in 2008 with the bankruptcy of the Lehman Brothers investment bank, which led to a cascade of insolvency problems in banks worldwide as well as to international macroeconomic effects (transmission of the crisis to the international level).

Banks are financial institutions which take savings deposits, provide credit, and create and trade financial assets. This gives them two central roles in the economy. The first role is that banks are intermediaries between the monetary and the real economy: they enable investments to be made beyond the amount that firms and households have available from savings and retained profits. In other words, they allow higher investment in the economy than would be possible without banks, through the creation of debt. This leads us to the second role of banks. Banks create money by giving credit because the credit they create is more than the savings they obtain, through a *leverage ratio*: the number of times that a dollar of savings or equity is lent out. Hence, the more credit extended by banks, the more money available in the economy and the higher the level of private debt.

We distinguish two types of banks and a combination of these two:

- retail banks: serving households, firms, and the government
- investment banks: serving corporations, financial institutions, and the government
- universal banks: large banks which are a combination of retail and investment banks.

The main *assets* that banks have (use of funds) are:

- cash: banknotes, coins, gold
- loans to customers: mortgages, consumer loans, business credit
- loans and deposits to other banks: interbank lending
- *securities*: tradable financial assets including stocks, bonds, and debt
- *derivatives*: asset-backed securities which allow for speculation through futures, options, and swaps
- *futures*: agreements to buy or sell a particular security on a fixed date at a fixed price

- *options*: contracts that entitle the holder to buy or sell an underlying asset at a given price and before the expiry date
- *call options*: entitle the holder to buy the underlying assets
- *put options*: gives the holder the right to sell assets
- *repurchase agreements* (repo): short-term trade in securities with a promise to repurchase in the future at a set price
- *swaps*: exchange of streams of payments between two parties, typically in order to reduce interest rate or currency risk.

The main *liabilities* that banks have (source of funds) are:

- *equity capital*: capital provided by shareholders through stock
- customer deposits: bank accounts with money owned by customers
- borrowing and deposits from other banks: interbank borrowing
- repurchase agreements: idem as above
- long-term borrowing: borrowing for more than a year
- derivatives: idem as above.

A bank's balance sheet looks as shown in Table 9.1. On the left are the assets (use of funds) and on the right are the liabilities (source of funds). Some items appear on both left and right. These concern transactions within the financial sector not with the real economy. These are referred to as money market transactions and securitisation, including derivatives. The transactions with the real economy concern loans and deposits and equity (stock held by the bank's shareholders). A special type of securities is mortgage-backed securities (MBS). An MBS is backed by a mortgage pool as collateral. Investors receive payments derived from the interest and principal of the underlying mortgages.

How do banks earn their income? For centuries, banks have been making money from customers in two ways. One is through fees for financial services, the other is through the difference in the interest rate charged for loans and the interest rate paid on saving deposits. There are three types of banking fees:

- hourly fee for financial advice: this is a fee which pays for the time spent by a financial professional giving a customer financial advice;
- fixed rate administration fee: this is the costs you pay for the administration of your bank account and for financial transfers and services, such as a bank card;
- percentage of earnings on a profitable transaction: this is a fee charged by investment banks for their deal making for large corporations and financial institutions, such as issuing new stock or organising mergers.

Table 9.1 Bank balance sheet

Assets	Liabilities
Cash	Equity capital
Loans to customers	Customer deposits
Loans and deposits to other banks	Borrowing and deposits from other banks
Repurchase agreements	Repurchase agreements
Securities	Long-term borrowing
Derivatives	Derivatives

For standard banking services to consumers, fees are easily comparable, so competition between banks keeps the fees in check. That is why banks use a second and often more important earnings model in addition to fees. This model relies on the differences in interest paid (to you on your deposits) and interest received (from you on your credit card debt or mortgage). The difference between these two provides gross earnings for the bank and is called spread. A *spread* is the difference between two prices of a financial asset or between two interest rates. This amount needs to be corrected for risk: the riskier an investment is for a bank (that is, a loan to you as a student or to your big spender friend), the higher the interest charged to you. This extra interest charged is meant to cover the higher risk that the bank bears in case you (or your friend) don't pay back the loan (when your friend loses his job or when you quit your studies and become a hardworking but low earning poet).

The gross earnings of a bank (Yb) consist of the amount of interest paid by customers and received by the bank (i^c_b) minus the amount of interest paid by the bank and received by the customers (i^b_c), the spread. Below, I show these gross earnings from interest rate differences, the spread, in an equation:

$$Yb = i^c_b - i^b_c$$

The net earnings of the bank is the same equation but corrected for the interest risk premium (i_{rp}), to account for the risk which the bank bears in case the loan is not paid back. This risk premium is based on past experience. But when past experience is limited in time or to a particular group of borrowers, banks construct the risk premium on the basis of a subjective estimation. This estimation is made on the basis of optimistic or pessimistic beliefs about the economic prospects of a particular market and social group.

How is the risk premium calculated? Let us assume that in the past, 2 per cent of the car loans by a bank were not paid back. This is the past experience approach to calculating the risk premium. Or the bank's risk managers expect that the current market trends in car values and household incomes for their major client group will result in a 2 per cent default on car loans. This is the subjective estimation approach to calculating the risk premium. In both cases, the expectation is that 2 per cent of the future car loans will not be paid back by the borrowers. This means that 100 per cent of all borrowers who take out car loans will pay extra interest in order to cover the losses of these 2 per cent defaults. Simply because it is not known beforehand which customers will default. If that was known beforehand, these 2 per cent of customers would not have obtained a car loan in the first place.

Assuming that a car loan is on average US$10,000 and that a particular bank has a portfolio of 3,000 car loans, the amount of the risk premium to be covered by all borrowers is:

1. the total amount lent out: US$10,000 × 3,000 borrowers = US$30 million
2. 2 per cent defaults: 0.02 × US$30 million = US$600,000 lost on the car loans
3. distribution of this amount of default risk over 3,000 borrowers: US$600,000/3,000 = US$200 average risk premium per borrower
4. calculation of this amount in terms of extra interest rate:
    a. assume an annual interest rate of 8 per cent for a car loan without a risk premium
    b. assume the loan is for 2 years and needs to be paid back fully in this period
    c. interest of 8 per cent for an average car loan of US$10,000 is income for the bank of 0.08 × US$10,000 = US$800 per year

d   the risk premium of US$200 over the total car loan is US$100 per year (US$200 divided by 2 years: 200/2 = US$100)
e   and US$100 per year is 1 per cent of the total loan of US$10,000: 0.01 × US$10,000 = US$100
f   conclusion: the annual interest rate of 8 per cent will be increased for all car loan takers by 1 per cent so that the total annual interest rate they pay on their car loan will be 9 per cent.

For the bank, this means that net earnings from interest differences will be corrected with the risk premium, which seems like an additional earning for the bank but is not: it is the cost of the risk of loan default. But, this risk is entirely born by the borrowers: the risk is not subtracted from the bank's profits.

$$Yb - i_{rp} = \left(i_b^c + i_{rp}\right) - i_c^b$$

So, the borrower pays the risk premium (i_{rp}) as an additional interest rate, which makes total interest rate paid on a loan $i_b^c + i_{rp}$. The bank's earnings minus the risk premium (which is paid by the customers) is $Yb - i_{rp}$. Hence, the net income of the bank is not negatively affected by the risk premium: the customers pay this cost, not the bank. Gross income for the bank (Yb) equals net income (Yn). This is shown when we subtract i_{rp} from the left hand side and the right hand side of the previous equation:

$$Yb = Ybn = i_b^c - i_c^b$$

9.2 Social economics

9.2.1 Segmentation of financial services

Financial markets are, like labour markets, segmented markets. This segmentation is tied to capital accumulation: small deposits earn low interest rates and small consumer loans carry high interest rates. Small here is not beautiful but costly. Costly for the consumer through low interest earnings and high financing costs. Small loans and deposits are also costly for banks due to relatively high transaction costs per earned unit of income. In order for banks to still provide financial services to consumers with small purses, they shift the transaction costs to the consumer. These transaction costs include a variety of real and potential costs. Real costs concern administrative costs: the more loan transactions for every US$1 million lent out by a bank, the higher the administrative costs. Potential costs refer to risk: the risk of the bank not being paid back. This is the risk premium as discussed in section 9.1 (i_{rp}). The smaller the loans and the smaller the income of households or firms, the higher the risk for the bank that it will lose money due to limited time for monitoring individual loans and the limited pay-back capacity of the borrowers.

Banks shift the real and potential transaction costs of lending to households and firms because the banking market is far from a competitive market. It is rather an oligopolistic market with a few large banks dominating the market for deposits, consumer loans, and business loans to small and medium enterprises (SMEs), through their many branches and ownership of local banks. Only when customers have bargaining power equivalent to that of the banks, can they force banks to share the risk premium evenly. In that case, going back to the example of a car loan in section 9.1, the interest rate charged would not be 9 per cent but 8.5 per cent and the bank would absorb the other half of the US$100 annual risk premium: 50 per cent × 100 = US$50 per year. But, as is the case with individual workers in the labour market, bank customers lack such bargaining power vis-à-vis firms. Hence, customers pay higher interest rates on their loans because the bank transfers the risk premium for loans entirely to the customers. In other words, customers pay the full price for other customers' defaults and the bank becomes risk free.

In a segmented financial market, the distribution of the risk premium is not necessarily equal among all types of borrowers. Banks charge lower risk premiums to social groups which have statistically lower risks of a loan default, while they charge higher risk premiums to groups which have statistically higher risks of default. This means, going back to our example, that more economically stable and wealthy social groups may pay 8 per cent on a car loan, while less stable and poorer groups may pay 9 per cent on a car loan. How are these interest rates for different social groups determined by banks?

Mostly, on the basis of geographical location, of particular neighbourhoods characterised by particular average levels of income, education, and likelihood of unemployment. Often, disadvantaged neighbourhoods with these characteristics in the USA have relatively more ethnic minorities and single parent households. Indeed, if we look at income development among social groups in the USA before and since the crisis, we find that women's wages lag behind men's wages and black and Latino workers earn lower wages than white workers.

Hence, banks' strategies to vary the risk premium between social groups on the basis of geographical statistical averages implies indirect discrimination. This is called, just as in labour economics, *statistical discrimination*: disadvantaging individuals on the basis of the group average of a particular characteristic, like income or unemployment rate. This is unfair for individuals belonging to those groups but performing better than the average characteristics.

9.2.2 Financialisation

Up to the 1990s, banks earned their income largely through the two earnings models mentioned in section 9.1: fees for services and spreads of interest rates. From the 1990s onwards, the era of neoliberal policies and globalisation, banks shifted to a third earnings model, which boosted banks' balance sheets. This consists of financial trading for profit. This trading in financial assets is the most basic earnings model of capitalism, already explained by Marx: making money with money. But no longer through the intermediary of commodities, but directly, from money to money:

$$M - M' - M'' - M'''$$

In the 1990s and up to the financial crisis, an increasing number of financial assets were invented and subsequently traded. This process is referred to as financialisation. *Financialisation* can be defined as the increase in the quantity, velocity, and complexity of financial assets in the economy. Even a manufacturing firm like General Motors has vastly expanded its financial activities and earned 66 per cent of its profits in 2004 from its financial activities rather than from selling cars.[1] During the crisis it had to be saved by the US government because not only car sales but also the value of its financial assets had collapsed.

224 *Financial markets*

For the economy as a whole, financialisation means than an increasing share of economic activity consists of borrowing and lending money, developing financial products, and trading in a wide variety of securities and derivatives, at costs of material goods and personal services, such as food, computers, cars, or hairdressing. This is paralleled by increasing income inequality, as we will see in more detail in Chapter 15.

9.2.3 High liquidity

The combination of segmentation, market power by banks, financialisation, and increased income inequality is only one set of causal mechanisms behind the 2007/2008 financial crisis. Another driving force was the response by governments to the increasing income inequality in underserved segments of financial services markets. The US government responded in two ways to the increasing income inequality. First, the Central Bank of the United States, called the Federal Reserve Bank, better known as the Fed, kept the interest rates it charges to commercial banks very low. The Fed interest rates had been around 1 per cent since the beginning of the new millennium up to 2013 at least (except for 2004). This means that commercial banks could borrow money from the Fed at very low cost. Compare this with the Fed interest rate in 1981 when it was 20 per cent. This monetary policy (of which more details in a later chapter) of low interest rates helped to make home loans affordable for low-income households. Diagram 9.1 shows Fed interest rates from 1955 to 2013.

Another US government response to increasing income inequality was through two private but state-supported mortgage institutions, lending at low interest rates to low-income households. These two institutions are the Federal National Mortgage Association, nicknamed Fannie Mae, and the Federal Home Loan Mortgage Corporation, nicknamed Freddie Mac. Government protection includes access to a direct credit line with the US Treasury. Fannie

Diagram 9.1 Historical US interest rates, 1955–2013

Source: Federal Reserve historical data available at http://www.federalreserve.gov/releases/h15/data.htm#fn1

Mae and Freddie Mac buy mortgages from commercial banks, and, due to the US government funding, have been able to do this for millions of households.

These two US government policies – low interest rates and government-supported mortgage institutions – helped to ease the purchasing power constraints on low-income households by providing them with access to low-interest mortgages. This not only enabled them to become homeowners. The mortgages also allowed low-income households to take on an increasing amount of borrowing against the expected increase in the values of their homes. The additional credit obtained through additional mortgages enabled households to keep consumer spending up to the levels of the 1980s and early 1990s despite a growing income gap. And it helped to pay for health care bills and school fees. And to keep up, at least a little bit, with the Joneses – the households who earned increasingly higher incomes. Hence, borrowing became a way out of the negative purchasing power effects of increasing income inequality. More than half of the loans to low-income households were not used to acquire a new house but to access cash from loans based on an expected increase in the future value of the house.

The commercial banks and other mortgage lenders paralleled this government strategy by providing an increasing number of mortgages at initial low interest rates targeting low-income households. How could the bank make a profit out of these loans, given the low interest rates and high-risk premium for the low-income segment of the mortgage market? Well, in two ways. First, they offered low interest only for a short period of time, say 2 years out of a period of 20 years. This is referred to as *teaser rates*. Second, they could often sell the mortgages to Fannie Mae and Freddie Mac. In turn these two mortgage institutions were able to attract foreign investors because the US government funding line gave them a very solid credit rating in international financial markets: the risk of bankruptcy of Fannie Mae and Freddie Mac was very small given the state's financial back-up. Moreover, housing prices had been increasing steadily since the 1980s, so the risk of default of the mortgages themselves was expected to be very small: if a borrower could no longer pay back, the bank would sell the house and still make a profit. There seemed to be no downside risk involved in the increasing number and value of home loans provided in the United States since the 1990s.

Back to the low-income households in the USA who were given access to low-interest mortgages to become homeowners. Let me first define the term *subprime loans*. These are loans to people with a relatively high risk of pay-back problems, which is therefore compensated for with increasing interest rates over time and unfavourable loan conditions. Examples of such unfavourable conditions are a steep increase in the interest rate after an initial period of low interest rates, high administration fees, or high penalties for late payment, all disguised in technical language written in small print in the mortgage contract. The households are more likely to be black, Latino, and headed by a woman. They are often desperate for credit due to low wages, unemployment, single parenthood, and uninsured health care costs. Black and Latino borrowers were twice as likely to receive subprime loans as white borrowers. Low-income neighbourhoods in US cities saw continued growth of subprime lending even when household incomes in these neighbourhoods declined from 2002 onwards. Single women's home ownership doubled in 20 years. Subprime loans constituted 25 per cent of all home loans in the USA.[2]

The households targeted for subprime loans had low bargaining power. They desperately need cash in order to maintain their livelihoods in an environment with increasing income inequality. The home loans that they were offered seemed a solution to their financial problems. But borrowers seem to have had an incorrect understanding of the expected value of the subprime loans because of the market power of the banks. This market power includes asymmetric information about loan conditions, a widely shared belief in increasing housing prices,

226 *Financial markets*

and optimism about unemployment risk. The consequences for the borrowers were that they lost money and many of them also lost their homes. First, they paid a very high price for their loans due to fees, penalties for late paybacks, and increased interest rates after an initial teaser rate. Second, they lost their homes due to foreclosures. A *foreclosure* of a mortgaged house occurs when the bank appropriates the house when the owner can no longer afford to repay the loan. Diagram 9.2 shows the regional distribution of foreclosures in the US in 2013.

In conclusion, the social economic theory of financial markets explains costs and benefits of financialisation from the perspective of long-term trends and structures in financial markets. This approach explains first how the downside of financial risk is systematically shifted to the weakest parties in financial transactions and, second, how this leads to loan defaults, a major trigger of financial crises.

9.3 Institutional economics

An institutional perspective of financial markets looks beyond supply and demand. It focuses on the behaviour and underlying rules, norms, and beliefs of the agents in financial markets. We can distinguish three types of institutions in financial markets:

- formal institutions of the government
- formal institutions of private sector self-regulation
- informal institutions dominating financial sector behaviour as a whole.

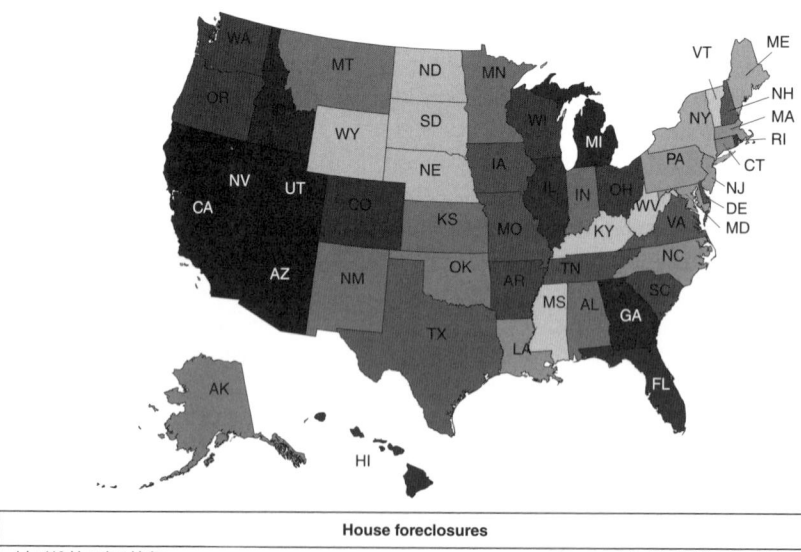

Diagram 9.2 House foreclosures in the USA, September 2013

Source: http://www.fbi.gov/stats-services/publications/mortgage-fraud-2010

Each type of institution influencing financial behaviour can do so in an enabling way (financial stability, efficiency, effectiveness) or a disabling way (perverse effects, inefficiency, harm to the real economy, and reduction of well-being). This section will review each type of institution in the financial sector and will explain how they have contributed to the crisis and its international spread.

9.3.1 Formal government institutions

Financial markets have steadily become globalised and are now the most globalised market worldwide. The only government-like institution constraining the operations of financial markets at the international level is the Bank for International Settlements (BIS) based in Basel (Switzerland). This bank was set up in 1930 as a response to the 1929 stock market crash in the USA. Regulation of the financial sector by BIS is negotiated by the Basel Committee on Banking Supervision. This committee consists of representatives of Central Banks and develops rules for global banking supervision, to be implemented by national and regional Central Banks. Up to the financial crisis, the global financial economy operated under the rules of what was referred to as 'Basel II'. However, the crisis brought the Central Bankers together with a shared urgency that new and stricter rules were necessary to prevent another such crisis, and 'Basel III' was developed with the following requirements:

- *Leverage ratio* of at least 3 per cent. This means that every dollar owned by the bank can be lent out 33 times. Many economists agree that 3 per cent is still too low. With a leverage ratio of 10 per cent, a bank can still lend each dollar out 10 times. Various European banks had leverage ratios of around 3 per cent when the crisis broke and went bankrupt or were saved by the state.
- Common equity capital of 4.5 per cent (previously 2 per cent). This means that banks need to have 4.5 per cent of their own assets as a percentage of all assets, with weights for different risk levels of types of assets. But the risk-weighting is a subjective matter and left to the banks themselves.
- For systemically important banks (the too-big-to-fail banks) an additional 1–2.5 per cent common equity capital ratio. However, 5 years after Lehman Brothers went bankrupt, most systemically important banks were not yet able to achieve these additional ratios.

These rules are implemented by national and regional Central Banks who have the freedom to make them more detailed or stricter. A *Central Bank* is the banking institution supervising all banks in a country (or in a region such as the European Monetary Union). The Central Bank of the United States is the Fed, as mentioned earlier. While Basel III regulates banking supervision in terms of shock absorption, risk management, and governance, Central Banks have a wider role. They are a lender of last resort and play a crucial role in addressing problems during a financial crisis.

After the 1929 financial crisis, the Fed implemented strict regulation to prevent such a serious crisis happening again. The core of this regulation was a split between investment banking and retail banking through the Glass-Steagall Act of 1933. So, universal banks were prohibited: a bank was either a retail bank or an investment bank but not both. Retail banks were not allowed to trade in securities (which entails speculation), while investment banks were not allowed to take deposits. The Act proved effective for 70 years: between 1929 and 2007 the USA did not experience a systemic banking crisis, although it did have several relatively small financial crises. In the 1980s and 1990s, with neoliberal policies dominating the US economy, the banking lobby managed to get the Glass-Steagall Act repealed. This happened in 1999.

From then onwards, US banks increased quickly in size, combing retail and investment banking at a new, unprecedented level of universal banking. This fast growth of banks was enabled by computerised trading, the globalisation of finance, and the invention of new financial tools in securitisation. In less than 10 years this resulted in too-big-to-fail banks in the USA and in various European countries (Iceland, UK, Luxemburg, France, Germany, and the Netherlands). So, the Fed has effectively reduced banking regulation since the late 1990s. As explained later by Alan Greenspan, president of the Fed in the years just before the crisis, this deregulation was driven by a widely shared belief in the market's independent power to bring financial stability, efficiency for banks and their clients, and effectiveness in supporting the real economy.

Crisis control by the Fed has resulted in re-regulation since 2008. But this differs from the 1930s regulation in two major ways.

9.3.1.1 More rules with less impact

The replacement of the Glass-Steagall Act with the much weaker Dodd-Frank Act in 2010 met with strong resistance from banks. This resistance, through fierce lobbying, has resulted in a watering-down of the new supervision law and many exceptions. As a consequence, the Dodd-Frank Act has over 30,000 pages. Glass-Steagall needed no more than 37 pages with much stricter implications for banking back in 1933.

9.3.1.2 Bail-outs of too-big-to-fail banks

Although Lehman Brothers, a major investment bank, was not saved by the government, other major US banks received strong financial support through a policy called quantitative easing (QE). Since 2008, the Fed has set the interest rate close to zero to encourage lending by banks to the real economy: firms and households. The *QE policy*, which has been applied for several years since the crisis, permits the Fed to buy over-valued assets from banks to help them get rid of these on their balance sheets. The money, which the banks receive in return, is supposed to stimulate the economy through loans to firms and households. However, in practice, banks are very reluctant to lend out money.

9.3.2 Private sector self-regulation

The banking sector, in addition to having to comply with government regulation, also has its own formal regulation. In particular, through the institution of credit rating agencies and through advisory committees on interbank lending interest rates. Some banks go further and set up an ethics committee in order to learn from ethical dilemmas or they introduce a code of conduct for its bankers. Dutch banks have agreed among themselves on a banker's oath (see Box 9.1).

> **Box 9.1 The Dutch banker's oath**
>
> I swear/promise that I will exercise my function properly and carefully.
>
> I swear/promise that I will duly weigh all the interests involved in the enterprise, i.e. those of the clients, the shareholders, the employees and the society in which the enterprise is active.
>
> I swear/promise that in this weighing I will focus on the client's interest and that I will inform the client to the best of my ability.
>
> I swear/promise that I will act in accordance with the laws, regulations and codes of conduct which apply to me.
>
> I swear/promise that I will observe secrecy about anything to which I have been entrusted.
>
> I swear/promise that I will not abuse my knowledge.
>
> I swear/promise that I will maintain an open and verifiable attitude and I know my responsibility towards society.
>
> I swear/promise that I will perform to the best of my abilities to maintain and promote confidence in the financial services sector.
>
> So help me God!/This I declare and promise!
>
> Source: http://www.nibc.com/investor-relations/dutch-banking-code/bankers-oath.html

Credit rating agencies address the asymmetric information problem in financial transactions. Individual deposit holders and investors, firms, and even professional traders and banks themselves lack information about the solvency of a bank, the creditworthiness of a country's government, and the value of packaged securities.

The two major credit rating agencies (Moody's and Standard & Poor's, both US-based) rate countries, banks, and certain financial products on the basis of a mix of fundamental financial information and expert knowledge (which includes intuition and expectations). The top rating is triple A (AAA) and the bottom one is referred to as junk status. Before the crisis, the agencies gave triple A ratings to the USA as a country, to US banks, and to new financial products such as derivatives. Lehman Brothers, for example had a triple A rating when it went bankrupt, and the securities containing subprime mortgages (MBS) also received triple A ratings from the rating agencies. The crisis has demonstrated that these ratings were flawed both for the USA and for many European counties, as the Icelandic crisis and the euro crisis have demonstrated. The major reasons for the failings of the credit rating agencies are dependence on fees paid by the institutions they rate, an erosion of rating standards, and the oligopolistic market structure of rating agencies, with only two firms dominating the market and a small third one. Without their rosy assessments, the subprime mortgages and their packaging in larger securities would not have seen the huge trade volumes between banks and investors. Thanks to favourable ratings, the mortgage backed securities market became the world's biggest securities market in the world.

230 *Financial markets*

A second formal institution of self-regulation in the sector is the committee which determines the interbank lending rates. The major interbank lending rate is called Libor, the London Interbank Offered Rate, which is the basis not only of the interest rates banks charge each other but also of the thousands of interests rates which bank charge their clients: from loans to small firms to mortgages. This formal institution also appeared to fail as was shown with the Libor scandal. The selective group of highly respected large banks which jointly determine the Libor, appeared to have committed fraud by manipulating the interest rate to their own advantage. In 2013, the European Committee imposed fines of over US$1 billion on eight participating banks. Among these were Citigroup, Deutsche Bank, and JP Morgan. The Dutch Rabobank received a €774 million fine from the American authorities, and the Swiss UBS a €1.2 billion fine. On top of that, the EU imposed another €1.7 billion worth of fines for the same crime on several banks.

Self-regulation of the sector through various institutions has clearly failed. The question is whether a revision of these institutions will prove sufficiently effective or whether the state must take over their roles. The European Commission plans to set up a European state-owned credit rating agency which may be less dependent upon large financial interests than private sector agencies.

9.3.3 Informal institutions

The major informal institution underlying financial sector behaviour concerns the perception of the condition and movement of financial markets, including real asset markets. This perception can be understood as a widely shared belief in the growth and stability of asset markets. Developments in financial economics since the 1920s led to a theoretically supported belief that financial risk could be more or less eliminated, and that economic growth in the real sector of the economy is reflected in ever increasing values in asset markets, ranging from the stock exchange to derivatives, to the housing market.

Image 9.1 Rabobank office

Where did this belief come from and why was it so strong? There are two answers, which mutually reinforce each other: academic legitimisation and organisational culture. These two factors are discussed below.

9.3.3.1 Academic legitimisation of efficient financial markets

The economic theory claiming that financial markets are efficient, spreading risk and reflecting real economic value, took root in the 1920s. The world's first financial economist, Irvin Fisher, became its earliest and highly respected supporter. On 15 October 1929, just 2 weeks before the New York Stock Exchange (NYSE) crash, he claimed in *The New York Times* that stock prices had reached 'what looks like a permanently high plateau'. In order to benefit from his theoretical insights, he had invested large amounts of money, partly borrowed from his wealthy family-in-law. On Black Monday, 28 October, Fisher lost all his wealth and endangered that of his sister-in-law. Nevertheless, the theory further developed in the 1940s.

When the NYSE crashed again in October 1987, finance professor Eugene Fama claimed this demonstrated the truth of the efficient market hypothesis, rather than its defeat. He stated that, apparently, the financial markets quickly absorbed new information about lower business values in the real economy, leading to a sudden decline in stock prices. But what he failed to explain is what this information was and why it came so suddenly.

Moreover, the stock exchange recovered quickly and again it was unclear on what information this was based. Why would real business values change so dramatically? Fama would receive the 2013 Nobel Memorial Prize in Economics, together with Shiller and a third economist, for his work on efficient markets. Box 9.2 contains a quote by Shiller on why he thinks that he shared this prize with his opponent.

Box 9.2 Nobel Memorial Prize winner Shiller on Nobel Memorial Prize winner Fama

'Professor Fama is the father of the modern efficient-markets theory, which says financial prices efficiently incorporate all available information and are in that sense perfect. In contrast, I have argued that the theory makes little sense, except in fairly trivial ways. Of course, prices reflect available information. But they are far from perfect. Along with like-minded colleagues and former students, I emphasize the enormous role played in markets by human error, as documented in a now-established literature called behavioral finance. (. . . .) It's interesting that Professor Fama is also the intellectual father and major adviser of an investment company that has, by many accounts, been beating the market. The company, Dimensional Fund Advisors (D.F.A.), has impressed investors with its performance so much that its assets under management have grown to $296 billion, as of Aug. 31 [2013]. So, how does D.F.A. reconcile the successes with Professor Fama's efficient-markets theory? The D.F.A. Web site refers to the "dimensions" of investing, reflecting the name of the company. First on the list of dimensions are "size" (the stock returns of small companies tend to do better) and "value" (low-priced companies tend to have better returns as well).

(continued)

(continued)

(. . . .) Now, many of us are accustomed to describing these size and value anomalies as reflecting market inefficiencies, or investor errors. (. . . .) D.F.A., and Professor Fama, use different language, referring to "risk premia." Professor Fama avoids theories that describe these risk premia as even possibly reflecting irrational behavior, and I think he's wrong about that.

(. . . .) He doubts the existence of any bubble before this crisis, and his philosophy would have let banks fail at the beginning of it.'

Source: *The New York Times*, 26 October 2013. Available at http://www.nytimes.com/2013/10/27/business/sharing-nobel-honors-and-agreeing-to-disagree.html?_r=0

In the 1990s, colleagues of Eugene Fama developed a financial model of stock pricing and began to use it in an investment fund called Long Term Capital Management (LTCM). As long as financial markets remained stable, they made good profits, with very high leverage ratios. The fund quickly grew larger, with many investors trusting the academic backing of its investment strategy. But the 1997 Asian financial crisis and the 1998 rouble crisis resulted in high losses. LTCM had to close down. And yet, the theory of efficient financial markets, by then called the efficient market hypothesis, continued to receive support: in academia, among investors, from politicians, and even among regulators. Justification for this belief was found largely in the technical advancement of financial markets: very fast communication through computers and the internet and sophisticated financial models used by banks and investment funds to inform their buying and sales decisions. In addition, deregulation increased international trade in securities and derivatives, and more effective macroeconomic policies also supported the trust in stable financial markets.

Reaction to the crisis by politicians, regulators, bankers, and most economic scholars, was therefore one of widely shared disbelief. The former Fed chairman, Alan Greenspan, admitted to the 2008 hearing before the US Congress that he was shocked that his confidence in the efficiency of financial markets was proven to be false. Until then he had trusted that financial markets knew best: they spread risk, gathered information, and reflected real economic value. Greenspan responded to the hearing as follows:[3] 'Yes, I found a flaw . . . in the model that I perceived is the critical functioning structure that defines how the world works'. He also stated that it was the crisis which made him realise that the model does not do what it is supposed to do, namely, provide reliable forecasts in a complex world: 'We have this extraordinarily complex global economy, which as everybody now realises is very difficult to forecast in any considerable detail'. It therefore came as a surprise that the 2013 Nobel Memorial Prize in Economics was awarded not only to Robert Shiller, who saw the crisis coming, but also to Eugene Fama, one of the architects of the efficient market hypothesis. This points at the resilience of the theory: first after the 1929 crash, then after the 1987 crash, and yet again after the 2007 crisis.

9.3.3.2 A culture of hubris

The Greek word *hubris* refers to extreme pride, arrogance, and over-confidence. When a culture is characterised by hubris, it cherishes grand objectives and is overly optimistic about achieving these. In the financial sector, these objectives concern profit and the steady increase in wealth, ignoring risk and uncertainty and the common-sense analysis of dissenters. For an insight into banking culture in the years following the beginning of the crisis, see Box 9.3 with excerpts from the London City blog by anthropologist Joris Luyendijk.

Box 9.3 London City banking blog

'A few years into my first job at an investment bank I made more in a year than my father in 25 (. . . .) London investment banks do everything to make you as productive and focused on making money as possible. There's a dentist in the building, a doctor (. . . .) I found out that my investment bank often hired two people for one role, to see who'd survive (. . . .) Banks divide up the world in a matrix; by product and by country (. . . .) There was always at least one person on whose toes I stepped. "Where does an 800lb gorilla sit? Answer: wherever he wants to sit." This summarizes an investment bank pretty well. A newcomer is the opposite of an 800lb gorilla. You have to fight your way in. Nobody has time. Nobody cares who you are. But you have been brought in with "a budget". This is the money you have to make for the bank or out you go.

(. . . .) Investment banks are a bunch of pockets. You belong to one and your revenue goes into that pocket's joint bonus pool. Who gets what? That's far more subjective than in private banking. Some people bring in a lot but aren't good at the office politics. They may end up with less than they deserve (. . . .) A major factor with bonuses in fixed-income is net present value (NPV) off P&L [profits and losses]. The sort of instruments we were selling ran over many years. NPV means you calculate the total revenue for your bank over those years and the total number goes to your P&L for that year. Obviously if you can book the NPV off future revenue of the next seven years in one go, that's a huge number. This is one of the reasons why bonuses shot up the way they did in fixed-income.

(. . . .) Now you can see how NPV could make people aggressive. No longer do you need to maintain a relationship with a client over many years. Sell them one product and bang you're there. Compare again to private banking. I've got a client and every year this client decides to stay with my bank, we pocket a 1% management fee. See how that breeds a different culture? (. . . .) What surprises me most, five years after the crisis? How everyone is again pontificating about the future like there never was a crisis that demonstrated just how little we know.'

Source: Luyendijk, J., *The Guardian*, 19 September 2013. Available at http://www.theguardian.com/commentisfree/joris-luyendijk-banking-blog

---

Organisational culture is the collection of values and norms in an organisation that control the way people interact with each other and with stakeholders outside the organisation. Since the 1990s, the dominant banking culture has developed increasingly separately from the rest of the economy and society. Banks operated increasingly as untouchable and self-sufficient, with salaries well above those for comparable professions, extravagant bonuses for the top performers and for financial traders, and disdain for clients. Investment bank Goldman Sachs, for example, developed from a respectable partnership in which the partners owning the bank kept each others' risk taking in check, to a publicly listed large corporation in which the top considered itself 'Masters of the Universe' and clients were referred to as 'Muppets'. The dominant banking culture did not focus anymore on serving the interests of clients. Because the traditional earnings models based on interest spreads and fees had been consciously shifted by bank managers, financial regulators, and investment funds and trading firms, to a financial trading earnings model. This turned into a self-supporting earnings model depending little on client satisfaction and client interests: banks made money through creating, selling, and buying newly constructed and ever more complex market assets. So, the culture of banks shifted away from serving clients and investing in the real economy, to boosting asset markets, deriving high earnings from these, and generously rewarding employees, managers, and shareholders for their contribution to this.

A common feature of a closed, self-sufficient organisational culture is that there is no space for dissenters. The top only listens to voices which confirm its own views. As a consequence, whistle blowers were marginalised. Their warnings were not taken seriously or were regarded as threatening the new earnings model. Dissidents did not fit into the culture of hubris – they spoiled the party. In 1997, Brooksley Born, Chair of the US Commodity Futures Trading Commission called on Congress to regulate derivatives. Orange County, California, went bankrupt due to derivatives trading. Ten years later, a large social housing organisation in the Netherlands, Vestia, lost millions of euros due to unregulated derivatives trading. In 2006 it was Sheila Bair, chair of the US Federal Deposit Insurance Corporation, who warned about non-performing mortgages. Well before the crisis, an increasing share of subprime mortgages suffered pay-back problems, and houses were taken over by banks. But the trade in MBS continued unregulated. Also in 2006, Madelyn Antoncic, risk manager at Lehman Brothers, warned that the risk levels at her bank were too high. She was ignored and the bank continued to trade at very high leverage levels.

All three whistle blowers, leading figures in the financial sector, were sidelined. In addition to these whistle blowers, various academics also warned about an approaching crisis. In 2010, some 2500 members of the forerunner of the global movement of critical economists called the World Economics Association, voted for the economist who best forecast the 2007 financial crisis. The winner was Steve Keen (University of Western Sydney, Australia) who warned in 2006 about high and increasing levels of debt in the US economy and an emerging crisis. The second place went to Nouriel Roubini (New York University) and third place to Dean Baker (US Center for Economic and Policy Research). While Robert Shiller (Yale University and co-winner of the previously mentioned 2013 Nobel Memorial Prize in Economics) began warning in 2000 about a housing bubble. In 2005, 2006, and 2007 his warnings became more and more specific, stating that there was a high risk of falling prices, rising default and foreclosures, serious trouble in financial markets, and a possibly worldwide recession. All these predictions came true. I will use Shiller's extensive explanation in the next section as part of the Post Keynesian perspective on finance.

It took a crisis to shake up the culture of hubris, but a set of serious reforms are required to really do away with the remnants of this culture. The culture is still there, as shown by the strong lobbying against re-regulation and the watering down of the Dodd-Frank Act. And the fact that since the crisis only banks, as institutions, have had to pay fines, while in the USA none of the leaders responsible have been brought to justice, and the sector, even while receiving financial support from taxpayers, still pays above average incomes. This resilience of the culture of hubris explains society's ever-decreasing trust in banks. Diagram 9.3 shows

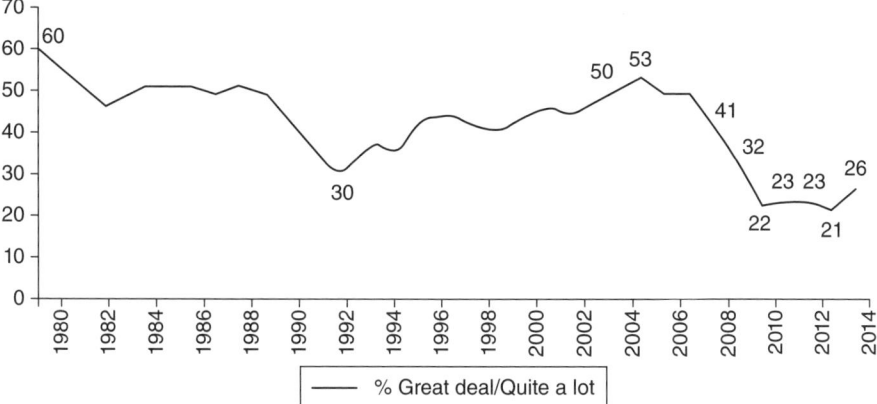

Diagram 9.3 Trust in banks in the USA

Source: Gallup, available at http://www.gallup.com/poll/163073/americans-confidence-banks-first-time-years.aspx

the changes in trust in banks in the USA from the late 1970s onwards. Trust was at its height at 60 per cent in 1979, moved down to 49 per cent in 2006, and then declined steeply to an all-time low of only 21 per cent in 2012.

The institutional perspective explains financial behaviour as based not so much on demand and supply forces and prices reflecting real value information, but on deregulation, a widely shared belief in efficient markets, and a culture of hubris. These three sets of institutional factors help explain the 2007 financial crisis, its global reach, and the inadequate reform of the financial sector almost a decade later.

9.4 Post Keynesian economics

The Post Keynesian analysis of financial markets is based on recognition of the economy as consisting of two distinct but interlinked sectors: the monetary and the real economy. This enables analysis of two characteristics. The first is fragility, first put forward as a hypothesis by Minsky assuming increasing volatility of financial markets with their expansion. The second process is herd behaviour leading to speculative bubbles.

9.4.1 Stock-flow model

At the economy-wide level, the real economy and the monetary economy are distinct but interconnected. The connection between the monetary and the real economy is most easily illustrated with a simplified flow model of the economy (see Diagram 9.4). Here, we introduce only two economic sectors: the real sector and the financial sector. The real sector consists of households, firms, and the government. The financial sector is referred to as the FIRE sector: it consists of Finance, Insurance, and Real Estate.

Diagram 9.4 illustrates the relationship between the monetary economy, through the FIRE sector, and the real economy. The flows from the real economy to the monetary economy

236 Financial markets

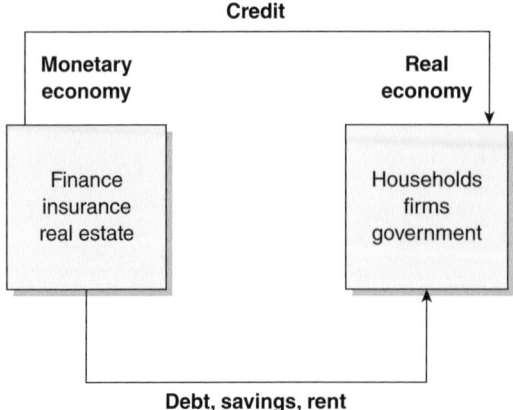

Diagram 9.4 Economic flow model of the real and monetary economy

consist of savings, rent paid on financial assets, and debt servicing. For example, savings deposits, interest payments on loans, and fees on financial services. The flow from the monetary economy to the real economy is credit. This model enables the financial deepening of an economy to be measured. This can be calculated as the growth in debt versus the growth in GDP.

9.4.2 Financial fragility

The key economist in Post Keynesian financial market analysis was not Keynes but another thinker in the same tradition: Hyman Minsky. He recognised that financial markets, more than any other market, are inherently fragile. Financial fragility is the increasing volatility of financial markets as they expand. Fragility occurs because there is no direct and transparent relationship with value in the real economy. For example, equity values reflect not only the actual value of a firm, when sold today, but also future value, as the future stream of dividends. Moreover, equity value may include non-tangible assets of a firm which cannot be found on the firm's balance sheet. These include the reputation of a brand and indirect subsidies from the state, such as bailouts. And more, the inherent fragility of financial markets cannot be corrected by policies because of uncertainty. This key feature of financial markets makes them unpredictable and makes it impossible for strategies of spreading risk to overcome fragility. Because risk and uncertainty are two very different things. The first can be calculated through probabilities and can be insured against. The second not: we simply do not know. So, when markets are basically uncertain, no risk strategy will be able to change that. It was Hyman Minsky who stated that financial markets are the most fragile of all markets.

9.4.2.1 Financialisation with globalisation

Financial fragility is enhanced when financial markets become bigger relative to the real economy, with larger quantities of financial assets traded. Remember that in social economics this is referred to as financialisation. Since the time that Minsky claimed that financial markets are more fragile than other markets, and explained that policies cannot completely

Table 9.2 US Balance of Payment (BoP) deficit, US$ million

	1996–2000	2001–2005	2006–2010	2011	2012	2013
BoP deficit	239,529	548,455	604,863	457,725	440,417	379,278

Source: OECD statistics.

change this, financial markets have expanded enormously. Both in width and in depth. The width of financial markets has increased through globalisation and the increasing interconnectedness of financial firms through national and international bank branches and internationally operating investment funds. But also through the international flow of capital away from countries with a surplus, towards countries with a deficit on the current account of the Balance of Payment.

The USA has a large and long-term Balance of Payment deficit, as shown in Table 9.2, while some other countries, such as the Netherlands and China, have large and long-term surpluses. These countries' surpluses are partly due to the fact that they export more to the USA than they import from the USA, and partly due to excess savings that are not invested in these counties but seek investment opportunities in quickly expanding financial markets abroad. Hence, in addition to access to the cheap credit enabled through a low Fed interest rate to commercial banks, US financial markets have also been flooded with capital coming in from abroad, seeking returns on investment in a deepening financial derivatives market. This point leads to the next driving force behind increasing financial fragility.

9.4.2.2 Increasing financial depth

The increase in depth of the financial sector in the USA implies an increasing share of the economy is being financed by a wide variety of increasingly complex and packaged financial assets. This led to an enormous increase in securitisation, a strategy widely used for spreading risk. *Securitisation* is the pooling of tradable financial assets in order to balance risk. The idea was simple: the larger the financial markets, the higher the total risk, but when this risk is spread through a wide variety of financial instruments throughout the system, a loss in one type of assets will not affect other investment portfolios. This strategy was part and parcel of the efficient market hypothesis.

A major type of asset that banks have created for securitisation are *mortgage backed securities* (MBS). These are packaged assets consisting of pieces of different mortgages, high risk and low risk. They were perceived by traders as low risk, which led to a flourishing market in MBS. Also internationally the triple A-rated MBS attracted demand among investors and traders, which explains why the crisis quickly expanded to the rest of the world after 2008. The worldwide derivatives market is estimated to be around 20 per cent of world GDP. European banks and investment funds appeared to have bought MBS on a large scale, even though as they later admitted, they had no idea what was actually in these packaged securities, relying entirely on their generous ratings by the oligopolistic rating agencies. In fact, the invisible mix of underlying assets often appeared to be biased towards high-risk mortgages, which led to the nickname for MBS, after their collapse, of 'toxic assets'.

But securitisation and its international expansion appeared not to be an effective risk spreading strategy. On the contrary, the enormous size of this type of new asset market increased the level of systemic risk in the economy. *Systemic risk* is the level of risk not of individual assets or investment portfolios, but of a system as a whole, due to the interdependence of the risks of assets and portfolios. The result for financial markets was expressed in higher levels of volatility. Diagram 9.5 illustrates how financial volatility, which is a measure of fragility, increased before and after the crisis.

Hence, due to globalisation and financialisation, since the 1980s fragility has become a more important feature of the economy. Why was this ignored so often? Because macroeconomic models of the economy, as used by government agencies, banks, and academic economists, did not include the monetary sector – the FIRE sector. The models assumed that the FIRE sector was only enabling the real economy so it did not need to be modelled itself: only the investment into the real economy was modelled as a result of financial market outcomes. But the absence of the FIRE sector in macroeconomic models appeared to hide the source of economic fragility, namely accumulating debt and systemic risk due to its spread throughout the world economy, and the fundamental uncertainty of financial market movements because of the high volume of trade in these securities. If the FIRE sector had been taken into account, through macroeconomic accounting models showing flows of credit and debt between the monetary and the real sectors of the economy, belief in efficient markets would not have been sustained.

Stock-flow models, or accounting models, can trace the extent to which debt grows faster than the economy as a whole and the extent to which debt is absorbed as productive investment in the real economy, or in excess of this, leading to wealth creation and thereby feeding back into the FIRE sector. These models are able to explain unsustainable debt building up and therefore explain financial bubbles.

9.4.3 Herd behaviour and bubbles

A third feature of Post Keynesian financial market analysis is the recognition of *bubbles and bursts*: the tops and bottoms of cycles in financial markets with over-valuation of assets and sudden corrections through steep price declines. The bubble phase occurs with the building up of over-valuation: when asset prices are actually higher than their underlying real value.

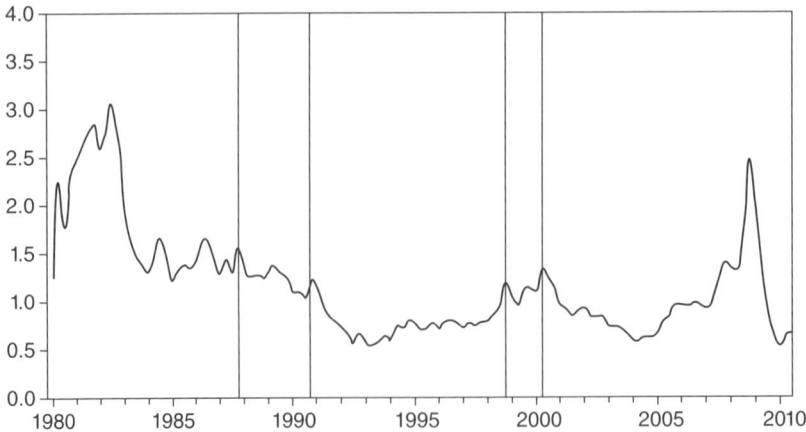

Diagram 9.5 US Financial Fragility Index

Source: Bagliano, F. C. and C. Morana (2014) 'Determinants of US Financial Fragility Conditions', *Research in International Business and Finance*, 30, pp. 377–92.

The opposite happens when the market collapses, when the bubble bursts: a sudden correction of asset prices too close to their real values, and sometimes over-shooting to levels below the real value of the underlying assets. Diagram 9.6 shows a financial cycle.

The three major financial bubbles leading up to the financial crisis were the stock market bubble, the housing bubble, and the bubble in derivatives, in particular MBS. Whereas Steve Keen and Robert Shiller saw the housing bubble and stock market bubble coming, and Brooksley Born and Madelyn Antoncic signalled a bubble building up in derivatives, it is Post Keynesians who provide a general explanation for this phenomenon. Behavioural economics, in particular through Shiller, has provided the behavioural details.

Let us first look at the stock market bubble. Diagrams 9.7 and 9.8 are from Robert Shiller.[4] Diagram 9.7 does not show the Dow Jones index, because that includes only 30 stocks. Instead, it uses a wider stock exchange index for 500 firms. The lower line represents the real value of these 500 businesses listed on the NYSE, measured as their annual earnings. The upper line represents the stock value of these firms. The diagram indicates that until the end of the 1980s, stock prices more or less reflected real value. There were a few exceptions: 1929, the early 1970s (oil price shocks), and a small spike and decline in 1987 with a quick recovery. After 1990, a strong disconnect emerges between real value and stock prices. Here we see a huge bubble building up until 2000, a burst (the dot-com crisis of 2001), and again a bubble, which burst in 2007. This is followed by strong volatility in stock prices, much stronger than in the underlying business earnings.

The housing market in the USA and elsewhere is believed to have a strong upward trend. This belief is justified with reference to underlying real factors. Housing prices involve increasingly scarce land (on which houses, offices, public utilities, and factories, are built) and population growth and a preference for smaller households take care of a continuously

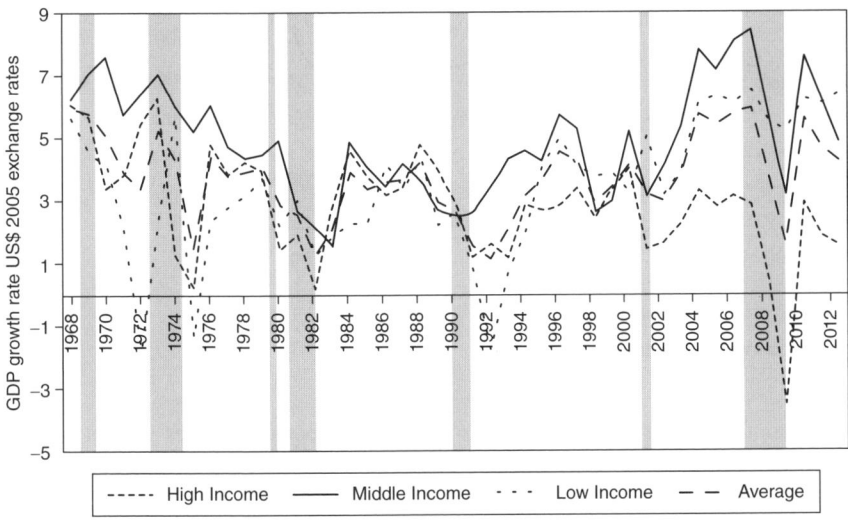

Diagram 9.6 Financial cycle

Note: The shading shows the recession dates announced by NBER, available at http://www.nber.org/cycles/cyclesmain.html

Source: Ikeda, E. PhD Draft Design Seminar, Institute of Social Studies, The Hague, 2012.

240 *Financial markets*

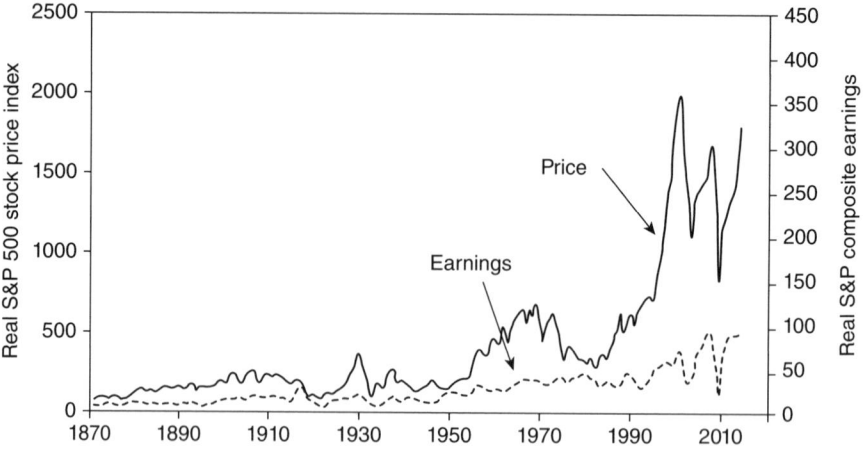

Diagram 9.7 Stock market value versus real value in the USA

Note: S&P, Standard & Poor's.

Source: http://www.irrationalexuberance.com/

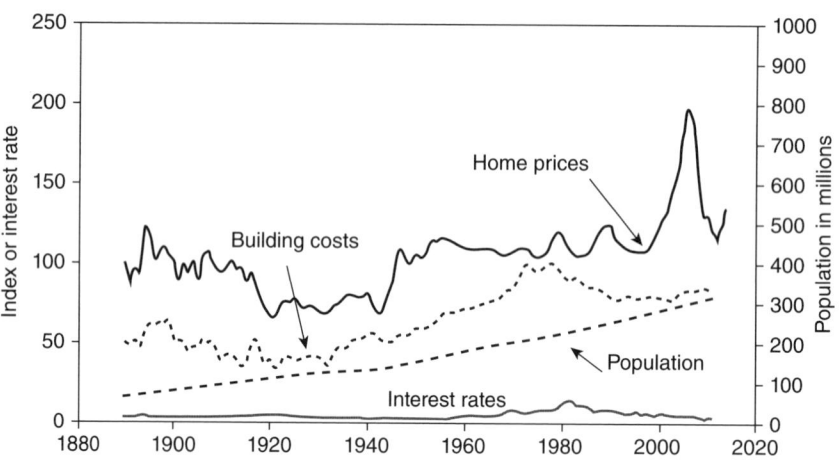

Diagram 9.8 Home prices and real values in the USA

Source: http://www.irrationalexuberance.com/

increasing demand for houses. But history has shown that housing prices do not always increase. However, people like to forget such episodes. Because the fundamentals behind the housing price increase seem so logical: increasing scarcity.

Shiller was worried by the statistics. Diagram 9.8 demonstrates why. The diagram shows four lines over a 130-year period. The bottom line shows interest rates, showing very little volatility. The line above shows a steady increase in population, at a linear rate. The next line represents building costs, showing volatility but always lower than the housing price level and housing price volatility. The upper line shows that home prices are more volatile than any of the three underlying curves. Moreover, it shows, contrary to the common belief up to 2007, that housing prices sometimes decline, as they did in the Great Depression following the 1929 crisis. From 2000 onwards, housing prices increased steeply – until the burst just before the subprime crisis, in 2005.

Keynes described the behaviour of investors underlying these bubbles and bursts as *herd behaviour*. This is a collective over-confidence driving prices further up above their real values, and a collective panic bringing prices down below their real values. Keynes labelled such intuitive behaviour at the individual level as *animal spirits*: a sudden urge to action, seeking profit or reducing loss.

The main behavioural economic explanations for this behaviour in relation to the 2007 financial crisis were suggested by Shiller according to the following factors: confidence, anchors for the market, and tellable stories.

9.4.3.1 Confidence

Confidence in markets easily turns into over-confidence when markets show a strong upward trend. Stock market investors come to believe that stocks are the best investment and nothing can go wrong in the long run. Homeowners taking out additional mortgages come to believe that the value of their house will only increase due to increasing scarcity of land, population growth, rising building costs, and declining household size. And financial traders wanted to believe the high ratings for derivatives, while relying on others' beliefs in this when selling those they packaged themselves with relatively more subprime mortgages and keeping those they made with relatively fewer subprime mortgages. Shiller has conducted regular surveys among wealthy individuals about their perception of markets. The responses indicate that in 2000, some 97 per cent of respondents agreed that stock markets are the best investment. His questions about real estate value resulted in different but comparable responses in different US cities. When asked if real estate was the best investment, 90 per cent of his respondents in San Francisco agreed and 74 per cent in Milwaukee.

The bubbles, hence, were both a cause and a consequence of over-confidence. Optimism, high expectations, and a disbelief in a downturn together fed a bubble. Partly naively, partly opportunistically, reinforcing the extreme optimism, and hoping to benefit from further price increases before stepping out and selling at high profit.

But when some investors become suspicious and begin selling, others are likely to doubt as well and also sell. This then triggers a large sale of assets, bringing prices down suddenly. For the stock market, this means a steep drop in stock values. For the housing market, it implies foreclosures of houses where the mortgage value exceeds the market value of the house and its owners can no longer afford to pay the mortgages they have taken out and which over time have more and more disadvantageous conditions and higher interest rates. This, then, also triggered the third bubble to burst: a steep decline in the trading prices of MBS. The derivatives market for these toxic assets simply dried up with a huge supply and zero demand. As a consequence, the value of these assets on bank balances was suddenly much less than they were in the books, resulting in huge losses.

9.4.3.2 Anchors

Another behavioural economics explanation behind bubbles concerns psychological anchors for the market. Quantitative anchors are round and convenient numbers which investors use as

242 *Financial markets*

Image 9.2 Real estate in San Francisco

reference points for their decision making. Often, these are entirely unconscious. For example, relatively often a crash happens on a Monday. This was the case in 1929, in 1987, and when Lehman Brothers filed for bankruptcy in 2008. The turn of the millennium also presented such a quantitative anchor: stock markets rose steeply up to 2000, reflecting a widely shared optimism that the new millennium would mark a new era of unprecedented prosperity. Only when the threshold had been reached, did realism kick in and stock market prices were corrected.

9.4.3.3 Stories

The third behavioural characteristic explaining bubbles is story telling: people like to communicate mouth-to-mouth and are influenced by such communication. A basic psychological insight is that when people regularly communicate verbally they begin to think along similar lines. Moreover, people easily accept a majority view, adjusting their own views to that of those around them. This leads to herd-like behaviour through simulation of others' behaviour. This happens very easily because personal communication includes emotions. This enables behaviour to diverge from rational deliberation and to simply move with the crowd. This was confirmed in Shiller's surveys where he asked how people had learned about and talked about the stock market crash of 1987. Individual investors talked to seven other people about the crash on the same day, whereas professional investors talked to 20 others about it on the same day. Despite the fact that it was already on the radio and TV news. Spoken communication appears to be key in investor communication, and apparently more appealing than information transmitted through the media.

So, the Post Keynesian explanation of financial markets combines financial fragility, financialisation, and psychological processes, to explain volatility and crises. The theory cannot predict the momentum and size of crises due to uncertainty. But Post Keynesian economics has shown that it is able to warn of bubbles before they burst, which is the closest an economic theory can come to real-time understanding of economic practices.

9.5 Neoclassical economics

9.5.1. The efficient market hypothesis

The dominant theory in financial economics for decades has been what ultimately became known, by the 1980s, as the EMH: the *efficient market hypothesis*. As explained above, Eugene Fama was one of its architects. The *EMH* states that free financial markets will virtually eliminate risk because all available information about the assets traded is immediately translated into asset prices. So, high-risk products have a high-risk premium and low-risk products have a low-risk premium, in the words of this theory, so that the opportunities and risks of all assets are reflected in their prices. The discounting of risk in asset prices is assumed to be immediate and without systematic error. *Systematic error* means that there is a pattern in the errors made, a connectedness between the underlying causes of errors. The EMH assumes instead that all errors are random. *Random error* means that the volatility in prices is caused by independent, exogenous factors. Of course the theory acknowledges that there are errors in asset pricing: nobody can have perfect information about the market. If that were possible, we would all be rich and able to buy low and sell high. Although . . . if everybody could do this, nobody would become rich, because we all would seize this opportunity at the same time.

This insight is nicely phrased in an economists joke: two economists are walking along the street. 'Hey, there's a $20 note on the ground', says one economist to the other. 'No, that can't be possible', replies the second, 'because if it was, it would already have been picked up by someone else'. So, the EMH states that nobody can outsmart the market because all relevant information is already included in asset prices. All opportunities for arbitrage (making a profit out of buying low and selling high) are at every moment already taken up through the large amount of trading going on.

The investment advice that followed from the EMH is therefore: 'do not try to beat the market'. But invest in index funds, which perform at the market average. So that you, as an individual not having all the relevant information available at all times at zero cost, will not perform below the market average. Indeed, index funds have risen strongly since the 1980s during the time the EMH has firmly established itself. The EMH can be visualised in a diagram showing two tendencies:

244 *Financial markets*

- a straight upward sloping line indicating a steady increase in the average underlying real value of asset prices, along with economic growth;
- random points around the straight line, which represent the actual asset prices, which diverges from the underlying real value but only slightly and not in any systematic way.

Diagram 9.9 shows that asset values are seen as taking a random walk around a steady upward sloping line of real and increasing asset values.

Statistically, randomness can be understood as a normal distribution. So, the volatility of asset prices is, in the EMH, regarded as having a normal statistical distribution (the 'bell curve'). This means that the great majority of price movements up and down is close to the mean, which is the supposedly real value of an asset, shown by the straight line. Stronger price fluctuations, further away from the mean, are much less frequent. These are found at the ends of the bell curve in Diagram 9.10 (left: large negative price movements; right: large positive price movements).

The EMH allows for small changes in the value of assets, reflected for example in daily movements of the Dow Jones index, as Diagram 9.9. shows. But the theory claims that financial markets will no longer be subjected to sudden large fluctuations. Because in a normal distribution of price changes, large fluctuations are very rare. The EMH adherents therefore ignore the possibility of large price fluctuations and focus on the random walk of small, random price fluctuations.

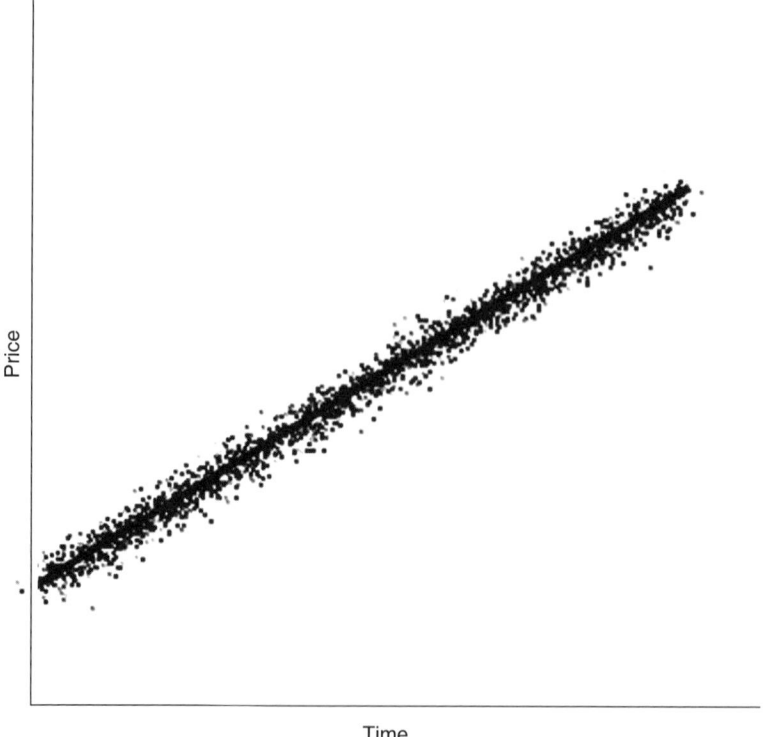

Diagram 9.9 The random walk of the EMH

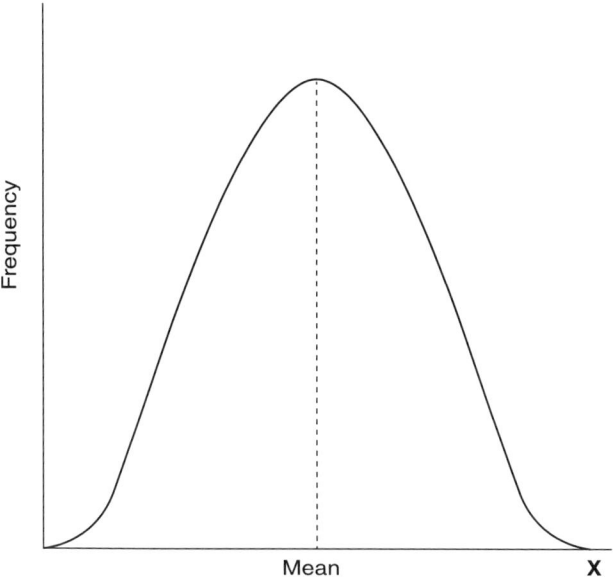

Diagram 9.10 Normal statistical distribution

The 2007 financial crisis has proved the EMH is wrong. Although some economists still try to save the theory by making adjustments to it, the majority of neoclassical economists now mostly agree that the theory is flawed. Because the crisis has shown that widely dispersed risk does not necessarily reduce risk at the systemic level. And that asset prices were influenced by the over-positive ratings by rating agencies and by opportunistic financial traders not disclosing the toxicity of MBS. And that, perhaps, there was too much unwarranted optimism in the market. . . .

So what are the neoclassical explanations for the crisis? These are twofold and will be discussed in the next two subsections: ignoring tail events and market failures.

9.5.2 *Fat tails*

The EMH assumed that financial risk is normally distributed, with the tail ends of the bell curve sloping towards zero. But the 2007 crisis, and, with hindsight earlier crises also, has shown that there are abnormal events which happen not often but more than once in the lifetime of a generation. This has led to the insight that the normal distribution perhaps does not tend towards zero but has fat tails. That is, at the extremes, the likelihood of price movements very far away from the mean occur more often than assumed under the EMH.

But it is more likely that financial volatility is not normally distributed. This insight has resulted in new research into fat tails. The empirical research on asset price fluctuations suggests that relatively frequent, strong price fluctuations have an effect on the distribution of asset prices. Hence, fat tails are not normal but influence the distribution itself. . . . This is not unusual.

246 *Financial markets*

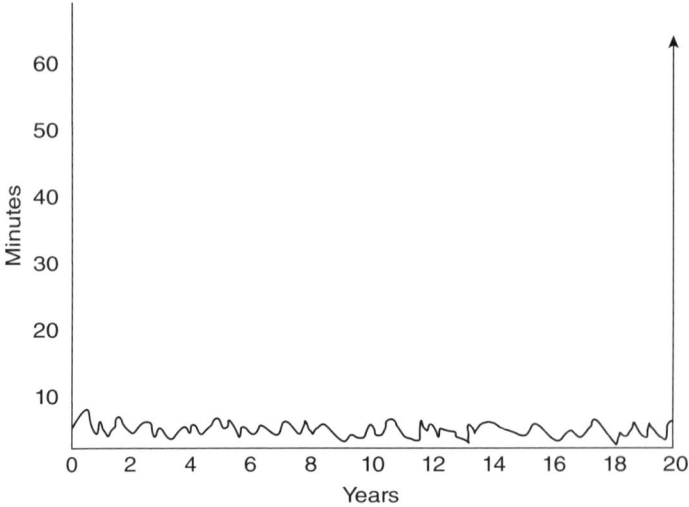

Diagram 9.11 Time to find your home key

In daily life, there are many surprising events that we do not expected. Think about losing your house key. For 20 years you always knew where it was. Everyday, every hour, except for a few times when you forgot and had to look for it. But you always found it again. And suddenly it is no longer where you thought it was, and after searching you cannot find your key anywhere. You realise that you must have lost it on the way home. This event is pictured in Diagram 9.11: the time it has taken you to find your key over the past 20 years.

Back to the financial crisis. While analysts simply focused on the Dow Jones index and may have become a bit nervous due to its volatility and steep increase leading up to the crisis, they should have been worrying about the accumulating debt through mechanisms never experienced before. Mechanisms which the EMH scholars had claimed were not in the realm of the uncertain but in the safer realm of risk, and, due to the spread of risk throughout the system, cancelled each other out so that average risk disappeared.

The critique from statistics, pointing out that financial markets are more about uncertainty than risk and that extreme events are more likely to happen than we thought, is a serious criticism of the EMH. It goes well beyond neoclassical theory, because there are not just fat tails in a normal distribution, but fat tails influence the distribution of prices itself, so that it is not normally distributed around a mean. Hence, price fluctuations are endogenous and not calculable with risk but are in the domain of uncertainty.

9.5.3 Market failures

In Chapter 5, I discussed markets and the commonly agreed failures of markets. The market failure that neoclassical economics is primarily concerned with is government interference in free markets through regulation (leading to distortions in the neoclassical view) and public goods. But the 2007 financial crisis and the two decades preceding it clearly show the crisis was not due to such a market failure. Regulation diminished over this period, rather than increased. Financial markets became freer, not more regulated, almost all banks were private and not public institutions, while the rating agencies were private sector firms. So, what market failures could help explain the crisis? There are two other candidates: moral hazard and asymmetric information. The first has become known as the too-big-to-fail problem, and the second as the rating agencies problem. I will discuss each of these below.

9.5.3.1 Moral hazard: too-big-to-fail

Banks perform a key dual role in the economy, as intermediaries between the monetary and the real economy and as creators of money, through debt. Without banks, economies would function under serious financial constraints. But should banks grow bigger all the time? Is there a natural limit in the capitalist system to bank size?

If banks were entirely independent capitalist firms, they would probably be smaller than the world's largest banks are today. Banks are not entirely independent capitalist firms. Precisely because of their key functions in the economy, creating money and even controlling the payment infrastructure, banks receive implicit subsidies from the state. This is not a fiction. The crisis has shown that governments were prepared to save banks from bankruptcy through nationalisation (Black Rock, ABN AMRO bank, and to a large extent the insurance company American International Group (AIG) where the US government bought 60 per cent of the stock) and through providing huge loans to give them capital where their own capital buffers had evaporated (for example Citibank and ING). Why did governments do this, at severe cost to taxpayers?

Because these banks had become too big to fail. If they were allowed to go bankrupt, even with basic protection of savings accounts up to a certain amount, this would have caused much harm to the real economy. Firms would have to pay back loans long before their maturity, and as many of them would not be able to do this, they would go bankrupt. Households would have to sell their homes in order to pay back their mortgages, but the housing market would not be able to cope with the additional supply due to a severe lack of demand for houses: the average sale period of a house has increased dramatically since the crisis. I have had my house in Rotterdam up for sale for over 2 years, but it does not look like the market is improving very much. And, finally, deposit holders with amounts above the threshold set under the deposit guarantee system would lose their money. Hence they would lose their collateral for taking loans, their sources for investment, their pensions, and their working capital.

So, the big banks in trouble were saved by the state. And the banks knew this all the time. This is the moral hazard: the fact that the large banks knew that they would be saved by the state if they were to suffer high losses. As a consequence, they took very high risks: they were only benefitting from the upside (high profits) but not suffering from the downside (bankruptcies) of risk. This spurred their growth through expanding their balance sheet with derivatives and other securities, mergers with smaller banks, acquisitions of insurance companies, and setting up their own hedge funds.

9.5.3.2 Asymmetric information: rating agencies

The financial whizz kids in banks and other financial institutions who packaged mortgages into collateralised securities, knew very well what they were doing. They knew exactly the types of mortgages and the default risks of these in the package. But the packaging made this information disappear to outsiders: the product was non-transparent. Why did the credit rating agencies assess these assets so favourably? First, due to the non-transparency they had to estimate, which involves random error. Second, they were paid by the issuers of the securities. So, they rated them favourably in order to keep their well-paying clients – the banks. This is clearly a case of a perverse incentive: the fee-based system in which rating agencies were paid by the institutions whose assets were rated creates a dependence relationship with unreliable ratings. Simply as a consequence of *wiifm* rationality.

The underlying individual mortgages themselves also suffered from asymmetric information. Because the households taking on subprime mortgages were not properly informed about the disadvantageous loan conditions over the time period of the mortgage. These were mentioned in section 9.2 as increasing interest rates, high penalties for late payback, and high administration costs. This asymmetry in information about the loan conditions created a stronger demand for subprime mortgages than was justified by the actual loan conditions. As a consequence, household debt has become larger than it would have been without asymmetric information.

The problem of asymmetric information has been aggravated by another market failure, namely perverse incentives. Remember from Chapter 4 that the neoclassical solution to the principal–agent problem was to align the incentives of the agents with the interests of the principals. In business remuneration, this was done through giving managers stock options and bonuses dependent upon targets for returns, profits, and the firm's stock price. This solution to the principal–agent problem has been widely applied in the financial sector since the 1980s. From bonuses and stock options for CEOs to variable pay dependent upon sales profit on derivatives, to bonuses for mortgage sales staff in poor neighbourhoods in US towns depending on the number of mortgages they sold. These incentives provided a huge stimulus to the sales of subprime mortgages, to the trade in MBS, and to the shift in the earnings model of banks away from customer services towards trading profits. In reaction, and thanks to strong societal protests, the European Union has fixed the maximum annual bankers bonuses at 100 per cent from 2015 onwards.

In conclusion, neoclassical economists have recognised the failure of the efficient market hypothesis, pointing at fat tails and market failures. But they have not yet provided an alternative financial theory to replace the EMH. That would require a fundamental theoretical shift away from risk towards uncertainty, from exogenous financial shocks to endogenous volatility, and from a belief that *wiifm* reasoning by investors and traders will keep markets in balance to a recognition of rationality.

9.6 Interesting sources

Documentary film about a German ex-investment banker: 'Master of the Universe', directed by Marc Bauder (Germany/Austria), 2013.
Financial terminology: website of the *Financial Times*, lexicon page: http://lexicon.ft.com/
Scott, B. (2013) *The Heretic's Guide to Global Finance - Hacking the Future of Money*. London: Pluto Press.
Shiller, R. (2005) *Irrational Exuberance*. Second edition. New York: Broadway Books.
van Bergeijk, P., A. de Haan and R. van der Hoeven (eds) (2011) *The Financial Crisis and Developing Countries. A Global Multidisciplinary Perspective*. Cheltenham: Edward Elgar.

9.7 Glossary

Animal spirits   A sudden urge to action, seeking profit or reducing loss

Banks   Financial institutions which take savings deposits, provide credit, and create and trade financial assets

Bubbles and bursts   The tops and bottoms of cycles in financial markets of over-valuation of assets and sudden corrections through steep price declines

Central Bank   The banking supervision institution of all banks in a country

Derivatives   Asset-backed securities which allow for speculation through futures, options, and swaps

Efficient market hypothesis (EMH)   Theory which states that free financial markets will virtually eliminate risk because all available information about the assets traded is immediately translated into asset prices

Equity capital   Capital provided by shareholders through stock

Financialisation   The increase in the quantity, velocity, and complexity of financial assets in the economy

Foreclosure   When the bank appropriates the house when the owner can no longer afford to repay the loan

Futures   Agreements to buy or sell a particular security on a fixed date at a fixed price

Herd behaviour   Collective over-confidence driving prices further up above their real values, and a collective panic bringing prices down below their real values

Hubris   Greek word for extreme pride, arrogance, and over-confidence

Leverage ratio   The number of times that a dollar of savings or equity is lent out

Mortgage backed securities (MBS)   Packaged assets consisting of pieces of different mortgages

Options   Contracts that entitle the holder to buy (call option) or sell (put option) an underlying asset at a given price and before the expiry date

Organisational culture   The collection of values and norms in an organisation that control the way people interact with each other and with stakeholders outside the organisation

Quantitative easing (QE)   The Central Bank buying over-valued assets from banks to help them reduce these on their balance sheets

Random error   Volatility is caused by independent, exogenous factors

Repurchase agreement (repo)   Short-term trade in securities with a promise to repurchase in the future at a set price

Securities   Tradable financial assets including stocks, bonds, and debt

Securitisation   The pooling of tradable financial assets in order to balance risk

Spread   The difference between two prices of a financial asset or between two interest rates

Statistical discrimination   Disadvantaging individuals on the basis of the group average of a particular characteristic (see also Chapter 8)

Subprime loans   Loans to people with a relatively high risk of pay-back problems, and therefore compensated for with increasing interest rates over time and unfavourable loan conditions

Swap   Exchange of streams of payments between two parties, typically in order to reduce interest rate or currency risk

Systematic error   A pattern in the errors made, a connectedness between the underlying causes of errors

Systemic risk   The level of risk of a system as a whole, due to the interdependence of risks of assets and portfolios

Teaser rates   Low interest rates on loans for a short period of time

Notes

1 Hakim, D., 'Detroit Profits Most from Loans, Not Cars', *The New York Times*, 22 July 2004. Available at http://www.nytimes.com/2004/07/22/business/detroit-profits-most-from-loans-not-cars.html
2 The figures and more information can be found in Dymski, G., J. Hernandez and L. Mohanty (2013) 'Race, Gender, Power, and the US Subprime Mortgage and Foreclosure Crisis: a Meso Analysis', *Feminist Economics*, 19(3), pp. 124–51.
3 PBS Newshour Transcript, 23 October, 2008. Available at http://www.pbs.org/newshour/bb/business/july-dec08/crisishearing_10-23.html
4 See up-to-date information on Robert Shiller's website giving background data on his book *Irrational Exuberance*: http://www.irrationalexuberance.com/index.htm

10 The macroeconomic flow

10.1 The macroeconomy

Macroeconomics is the study of the aggregate level of the economy – the macroeconomy. The macro level of the economy is the economy as a whole, often measured at a national scale. But it may also be studied at a regional level or on a world scale. It includes the aggregate levels of economic variables such as total consumption, total investment, government expenditures, and exports and imports. In other words, the aggregate behaviour of households, firms, and the state. But the macro level also includes non-behavioural aggregates, such as the general price level, the government budget deficit, and the unemployment rate. The most widely used (but imperfect) macroeconomic variable is *gross domestic product* (GDP). This is the aggregation of all market transactions and government expenditures. The market transactions include domestic consumption of goods and services, the value added to intermediate products by industry, the export of resources, private investments, and public services as if they were sold on the market. However, the measurement of GDP has various shortcomings – these will be discussed in the final chapter, where alternative measures of aggregate well-being will also be presented.

For now, let us keep in mind that GDP measures the money value, at market prices or cost price of government services, of all paid goods and services in an economy. Hence, the GDP measure of the macroeconomy excludes all unpaid production and services which are provided by society and nature.

10.1.1 Aggregate demand and aggregate supply

At the macro level, we speak of *aggregate supply* (AS) and *aggregate demand* (AD). AS and AD are the supply and demand of all households, firms, the government, and the rest of the world (households, firms, and governments abroad). Together, AS and AD determine the aggregate level of output in an economy, also labelled as Y and measured as GDP. Where AS equals AD, we have *macroeconomic equilibrium*. This is the situation in which there is no excess demand or excess supply in any product market in the economy. These markets include consumer goods, intermediate goods, and investment goods.

It is important to note that macroeconomic equilibrium does *not* necessarily imply the absence of excess demand or excess supply in the labour market. Macroeconomic equilibrium can co-exist with unemployment. When all goods produced are actually bought, this does not necessarily mean that all labour supplied is hired. It may well be that the economy functions below its maximum capacity, so that some factories, offices, and labour power remain unemployed. In other words, the economy may operate below full capacity.

10.1.2 The macroeconomic equation

AS = aggregate supply = Y = output produced. But not all of this will necessarily be sold: some goods and services will remain unsold, and hence, remain in stock.

AD = aggregate demand = expenditures on output. These are expenditures by households (consumption: C), firms (investments: I), the government (net public expenditures: G), and expenditures by the rest of the world (exports: EX) minus expenditures in the domestic economy on imported goods (imports: IM).

These symbols can be used for the *macroeconomic equation*. This represents the situation where AS (output) = AD (demand for output):

$$Y = C + I + G + EX - IM$$

Or, with net government expenditures more explicitly:

$$Y = C + I + (G - T) + EX - IM$$

Comparing the two equations above, there is possible confusion about the meaning of G. The first macroeconomic equation above uses G to refer to the net result of (G − T), or net government expenditures. The second equation uses G to refer to total government expenditures, from which tax revenue still needs to be subtracted. In order to prevent such confusion, we generally refer to G as the net government expenditures, as in the first macroeconomic equation.

An increase in aggregate output, Y, as compared to the previous year, implies economic growth: an increase in GDP. Obviously, countries do not always exhibit economic growth. Sometimes they do not grow at all, or their GDP declines. See, for example, the variation in GDP growth rates for Japan over the past few decades shown in Table 10.1.

Table 10.1 Gross domestic product (GDP) growth rates for Japan, 1980–2012

Year	Annual growth rate (%)	Year	Annual growth rate (%)
1980	2.82	1997	1.60
1981	4.18	1998	−2.00
1982	3.38	1999	−0.20
1983	3.06	2000	2.26
1984	4.46	2001	0.36
1985	6.33	2002	0.29
1986	2.83	2003	1.69
1987	4.11	2004	2.36
1988	7.15	2005	1.30
1989	5.37	2006	1.69
1990	5.57	2007	2.19
1991	3.32	2008	−1.04
1992	0.82	2009	−5.53
1993	0.17	2010	4.65
1994	0.86	2011	−0.57
1995	1.94	2012	1.96
1996	2.61	2013	1.54

Sources: World Bank and International Monetary Fund.

The general pattern of growth and decline in an economy is referred to as the business cycle, or better, the *economic cycle*. Cycles have occurred throughout history. Hundreds of economic booms and crises have been documented in Europe, Asia, and the American continent. They are measured as changes in GDP, but underlying this measure are changes in the size of AS and/or AD, leading to different levels of Y: the intersection of the AS and AD curves. And, as said above, any level of Y, the macroeconomic equilibrium, may co-exist with any level of employment, and hence, with unemployment.

The shape of the aggregate demand and supply curves depends on the economic theory. Two of the four theories that we discuss in this book include detailed analysis of the macroeconomic level, and they have opposite interpretations of the shape of the aggregate demand function. Post Keynesian economics draws the AD curve with a positive slope (like the AS curve) in the space of output and employment. Hence, the more demand, the more output, and the more employment, because AD increases capacity utilisation in the economy. So, an economy functions more closely to full employment with higher levels of aggregate demand.

Neoclassical economics draws the AD curve with a negative slope (as in neoclassical individual market analyses for normal goods) in the space of output and the overall price level. Therefore, in the neoclassical perspective, more AD will also increase output but push up the general price level. This is very similar to a neoclassical micro level picture of demand: the demand for labour or for a normal good is also downward sloping in the space of quantity and price. The diagrams for the macroeconomic equilibrium in the Post Keynesian and neoclassical perspective will be discussed in sections 10.4 and 10.5.

The macroeconomic equation has its underlying subequations. The major one is for consumption. Consumption (C) depends partly on income (Y) – the more money you have the more you can spend: cY.

The higher Y, the higher C through c. Think about c as a proportion, it is always above zero and often, but not necessarily, below 1. c is called the *propensity to consume*, the proportion of income spent on consumption. If c is 0.8, it means that you consume 80 per cent of your income: $C = 0.8Y$. So, if you earn 1,600 yen per month and $c = 0.8$, then you consume $0.8 \times 1,600 = 1,280$ yen per month out of your income. If c is 1.0 you consume all of your income: $C = 1Y$. If your income is only 400 yen, you need all of it to survive and hence you consume: $C = cY$ is $1.0 \times 400 = 400$ yen consumer expenditures per month.

But not all of your consumption depends on your income. A basic part of consumption is what we call *autonomous consumption*, a constant of consumption for minimum survival, not dependent on income: C^*.

So, even if you earn no income you will consume (eat, cloth, lodge). You can finance this through your savings, by receiving gifts, or through a government welfare benefit. So, autonomous consumption, C^*, does not depend on your income. The consumption function, hence, consists of a fixed part, C^*, and a variable part, cY:

$$C = C^* + cY$$

But what happens to the rest of the income? The income that you do not consume? This part of income is saved: S. This leads to a simple definition:

$$Y = C + S$$

254 *The macroeconomic flow*

So, if you consume 80 per cent of your income, you automatically save 20 per cent. And if you consume 100 per cent of your income, you save nothing. This indicates that we can re-write the income definition as follows:

$$S = Y - C$$

This equation states it even more clearly: savings are what is left of income after consumption. The savings function does not have an autonomous part, as the C* in the consumption function. You simply save what you do not consume. This leads to the following savings function, with the propensity to save, s, the proportion of income that is saved:

$$S = sY$$

Now, given the fact that your income is only used on consumption and saving, the propensity to consume and the propensity to save add up to 1. Together, they use 100 per cent of your income:

$$c + s = 1$$

If you use 80 per cent of your income for consumption (c = 0.8), this implies by definition that you save the other 20 per cent of your income. Hence: s = 0.2. Because c + s = 1, so, 0.8 + 0.2 = 1.

Alternatively, if you are very wealthy and put a lot of savings aside for luxurious holidays and speculation on the Tokyo stock exchange, your propensity to consume may be only 0.25 and your propensity to save 0.75. The variation in the propensities to consume and save for Japan are given in Table 10.2.

Table 10.2 Propensities to consume and save in Japan, 1980–2012

Year	Propensity to consume	Propensity to save	Year	Propensity to consume	Propensity to save
1980	0.69	0.31	1997	0.71	0.29
1981	0.68	0.32	1998	0.72	0.28
1982	0.70	0.30	1999	0.74	0.26
1983	0.71	0.29	2000	0.73	0.27
1984	0.70	0.30	2001	0.75	0.25
1985	0.69	0.31	2002	0.76	0.24
1986	0.68	0.32	2003	0.76	0.24
1987	0.69	0.31	2004	0.76	0.24
1988	0.67	0.33	2005	0.76	0.24
1989	0.67	0.33	2006	0.76	0.24
1990	0.67	0.33	2007	0.75	0.25
1991	0.66	0.34	2008	0.77	0.23
1992	0.67	0.33	2009	0.80	0.20
1993	0.69	0.31	2010	0.79	0.21
1994	0.70	0.30	2011	0.81	0.19
1995	0.71	0.29	2012	0.81	0.19
1996	0.71	0.29	2013	NA	NA

Source: World Bank database.

10.1.3 The macroeconomic circular flow

The *macroeconomic flow*, or *circular flow*, is a metaphor of the macroeconomy as a circular flow system, in which households, firms, and the government are connected through flows of goods and flows of money as shown in Diagram 10.1. Remember from the first chapter that economists have long used a flow metaphor for the economy. They even constructed a machine – the MONIAC – to illustrate the flow mechanism, using water to symbolise the flows of money and goods in an economy as pictured in Chapter 1.

The circular flow diagram shows three agents: households, the government, and firms. You will learn in this chapter that each theory extends the circular flow diagram in a different way. The simple version of the circular flow diagram shows two flows, in opposite directions. Flows of goods and services (including labour power), and flows of money as payments for goods and services or as tax payments for the financing of public goods. For the government, there are two flows with *transfer payments*, the public expenditures on social policy, such as social security and social safety nets. Net government expenditures is G–T. Diagram 10.1 shows six flows:

- L^S = labour supply from households to firms;
- C = spending on consumer goods from firms by households;
- Y = income earned by households from firms (wages and profits);
- C = consumer goods from firms to households;
- G–T = transfer payments between the government and households: the difference between government expenditure (G) and taxes paid by households (T);
- G–T = transfer payments between the government and firms: the difference between government expenditure (G) and taxes paid by firms (T).

10.2 The embedded economy: social economics

Social economics perceives the economy as part of society and human life generally. This means that the economy is seen as embedded in society and nature. This *embeddedness* means that the economy as a whole, at the aggregate level, is only a part of wider society and nature and is therefore strongly influenced by society and nature. It is not the case that social relations, politics, and culture are part of the economy, but rather the other way around: society and nature are the larger systems, and the economy takes part in these, and is embedded in these larger systems.

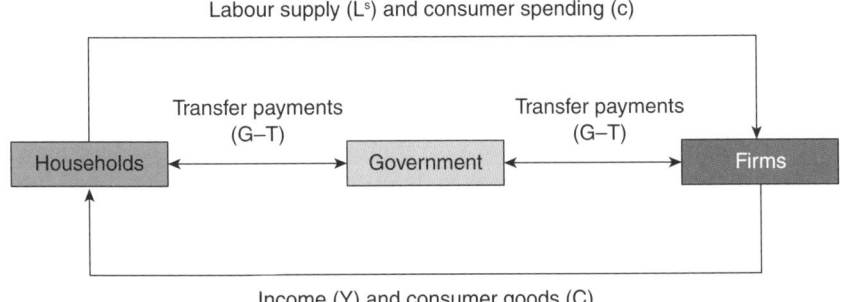

Diagram 10.1 Basic macroeconomic circular flow

10.2.1 Embedded in society

The embeddedness of the economic system in society implies two things for the circular flow. First, every economic agent and economic relationship is affected by social influences, such as power, values, beliefs, and cooperation. Second, the economy has an additional sector, called the community economy, of unpaid work and caring. Below, I will discuss the social embeddedness of households, the government, and firms, and I will discuss the role of the community economy.

10.2.1.1 Households

The relationships within households are primarily social, and only secondarily economic. This shows, for example, in the gender division of labour and the extent to which households are nuclear or extended families. Economic roles and flows of goods and resources in households are derived from the social relationships in households. Also, the economic relationships of households with the rest of the economy, particularly the market and the government, are built on underlying social relationships between these agents. This leads to a social contract. A *social contract* is a society-wide agreement about rights and duties and the distribution of the costs and benefits of social and economic behaviour. It includes social protection and investment in new generations, and governs which transactions occur in the market, the state, and the community economy. For example, labour relations between individuals and firms are embedded in a social contract and go well beyond an agreement about wages and benefits. Labour relations also involve social security, differences in bargaining power between labour and capital, and silent agreements about the extent of tolerable discrimination, for example.

Another example of how the social contract of a society influences the behaviour of households in the economy is through consumer behaviour. The consumer relationships of households are governed by a combination of free choice to move between suppliers of goods and services ('exit'), consumer power through collective action influencing price and quality of goods ('voice'), and the social bonds developed in social groups with particular firms and their brands and in the community economy ('loyalty'). So different social contracts will emphasise different modes of consumer relationships: exit, voice, and loyalty. Neoliberal societies are likely to give priority to the exit relationship, stimulating consumers to make cost–benefit calculations and change health insurance, energy supplier, or cell phone company regularly. Small-scale societies with strong bonding social capital are more likely to emphasise the loyalty relationship, with strong bonds between consumers and suppliers, perhaps through a dominance of cooperative firms or an extensive community economy.

Different societies will have different social contracts, so that the embedded economic relationships will be affected differently by social relations in each society. In the macroeconomic flow, the social embeddedness of households has two major implications for macroeconomic variables. First, for labour supply, as already explained in Chapter 8. Household members need to survive and hence will supply additional labour when the economy is in a downturn of the economic cycle: the added worker effect. This increases labour supply, but with unemployment and a decline in wages in an economic downturn, this often does not result in an increase in household income. So, more labour will be supplied without additional labour income as a return flow. This is indicated in the embedded flow Diagram 10.1 as L^s. The second implication of the social embeddedness of households is that households will reduce their consumer expenditures in bad economic times. They do so partly by increasing their unpaid workload, providing unpaid services. They supply unpaid work within the same household and to other households. This implies an increase in unpaid work time from the household to the community economy: L^{up}. And in return, households enjoy the consumption of unpaid services: C^{up}.

10.2.1.2 Firms

Although firm relations are largely exchange relations in markets, they are not immune to social influences. That is because supply and demand relationships are decided upon and carried out by humans in their role as economic agents. Firms hire labour power, which is governed by a society's social contract as was explained above. Firms also demand resources, require governance, and supply intermediate and final products. Society's norms and values influence which resources can be legitimately used. For example, for energy, some societies use nuclear power plants and others do not. Also the governance of firms is largely determined by social relationships and varies from very hierarchical to more horizontal forms of governance, and varies between independent competing entities to strongly interconnected firms through the social networks of board members.

Finally, the supply of goods is also socially influenced. Social norms determine which goods are considered legitimate to be traded, and which goods should not be left to the market and commercial firms but to non-profit firms, the state, or civil society. These social influences on the market and firm behaviour are not easily quantified in macroeconomic variables. But various studies have shown that pro-social norms have a positive effect on AD because they tend to reduce transaction costs.

10.2.1.3 Government

The social relations of the government influencing economic behaviour are twofold. On the one hand these relationships are political and a formal expression of social values, and on the other they are purely social and often informal. The political relationships determine the extent of taxation and regulation that a society finds acceptable. They determine the role of the government in the economy in general. The social relationships are expressed in how households and firms interact on a day-to-day basis with the government. This includes corruption and discrimination in terms of contracts, payments, and access of labour supply to public sector jobs and access of households to public services. Hence, this is how the government's representatives act in the economy, following the dominant culture of state interactions.

In terms of macroeconomic variables, the political and social relationships of the government are likely to affect the role of the government in the economy. With political effectiveness, democratic control, and effective public service delivery, the role of government is relatively larger in an economy because of the political and social support for it. Hence, transfer payments are likely to be larger: more tax revenues and more public expenditures in the economy. This is shown in an increase of transfer payments: G.

Together, society strongly influences the economic behaviour of households, firms, and the government. That is what social embeddedness of the economy means.

10.2.1.4 Community economy

Social economics explicitly recognises the key role of the community economy in the macroeconomic flow. Therefore, it is included as an additional sector, with its own agency centred

258 *The macroeconomic flow*

on loyalty rather than exit and voice. In the embedded economy, this sector receives unpaid labour from households and delivers services to households. Also, this sector is responsible for caring for nature. This concerns unpaid work from households, through the community economy to nature. And in return, nature provides environmental services through the community economy back to households. These flows are pictured as follows. One flow between households and the community economy, L^{up}, and unpaid services in return, C^{up}. The other unpaid flow is between households and nature, through environmental services from nature, C^{up}, and unpaid work to nature, L^{up}.

10.2.2 Embedded in nature

Social economics recognises the economy as embedded not only in society but also in nature. Nature is the wider system in which society and the economy are embedded. The embeddedness of the economy in nature involves two relationships. The first is about resource use and concerns a flow from nature to the economy. The second is about environmental damage, such as pollution, and concerns a flow from the economy to nature. However, not as a two-way relationship between two independent entities, the economy and nature, but as a two-way relationship between the economy and nature in which the economy is embedded in nature. So, nature comes first and enables the economic system to function. Why?

Because nature provides all the material inputs that go into production. Of course, human labour transforms these inputs, but they originate in nature: from grain to bread and from iron ore to steel. Even labour supply and the human capital underlying it, derives from nature through human reproduction. Without an economy, nature would still function as it has done for millions of years. Without nature, the economy would come to a standstill. By understanding the relationship as an embedded one, social economics emphasises that the relationship should not be broken.

This implies that nature's ability to serve the economy and society should not be undermined by excessive resource use or too much damage. The long-term functioning of the economy and society therefore require limits on resource use and pollution. This is precisely the definition of sustainable development which was formulated in the 1987 UN report on sustainable development, *Our Common Future*. This report defines *sustainable development* as development that meets the needs of the present without compromising the ability of future generations to meet their own needs. This is a social economic definition of sustainable development because it puts people's needs at the centre, while putting limits on the economy's use of nature.

The caring behaviour of economic agents vis-à-vis nature is captured, as was already explained above, as a flow of unpaid work from the community economy to nature, L^{up}. There is also a return flow, which consists of environmental services, such as enjoying walks in parks or the countryside, listening to bird song, or watching the sun set: the consumption of environmental services: C^{up}.

10.2.3 The embedded macroeconomic flow

The social economic perspective of economic embeddedness is shown in Diagram 10.2 as three interlocking systems: the wider natural system (nature), in which the social system is embedded (society), in which the economic system is embedded.

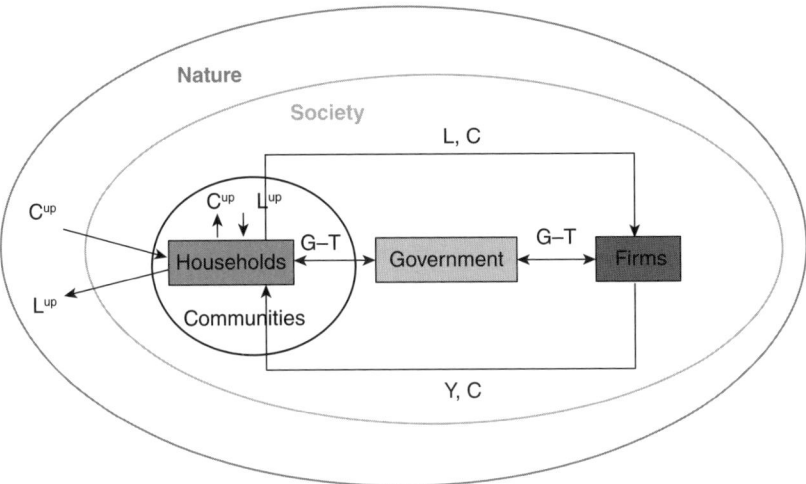

Diagram 10.2 Embedded macroeconomic flow

The embedded macroeconomic flow of social economics is particularly useful for a comparative analysis of different economic systems. It helps to explain differences between, for example, welfare states and more market dominant economies, or between communist economies and hunter-gatherer societies. The differences are explained with reference to differences in societies (including politics and culture) and natural conditions (ecological conditions, natural resources, climate). The embedded macroeconomic flow also enables the analysis of the community economy at the macroeconomic level. It helps to answer questions about how big the community economy is, and what its relationship is with firms, households, the government, and nature.

10.3 Macro level institutions: institutional economics

In previous chapters, we focused on the effects of institutions on the behaviour of individuals, households, and firms. In this section, we focus on how institutions affect the macroeconomic level, other than through the sum of micro decisions. In other words, institutional macroeconomics recognises that some institutions mediate behaviour at the meso level, in between micro and macro, or directly at the aggregate level. Institutional economics orders institutions from macro to micro, in which the most aggregate level is the world level, affecting trade and investment flows between countries. Therefore, the circular flow diagram for the institutional economic theory explicitly includes the rest of the world (symbolised as RoW).

10.3.1 Macro institutions and macroeconomic variables

What are the major macroeconomy institutions? These are formal and informal institutions which affect the relative size and stability of macroeconomic variables. What are the main macroeconomic variables and how are they related? Macro level institutions influence the relative size and stability of Y through AD. Let us consider the influence of macro level institutions on each of the macroeconomic variables that make up AD.

10.3.1.1 Consumption

Formal institutions may constrain the consumption function by increasing taxes by law. Remember, consumption is partly autonomous and partly from income. This is of course out of net income (Yd, or in short Y) after taxes, also called *disposable income* (Y = Yg – T). So, the higher income taxes, the less income available for consumption:

$$C = C^* + c(Y_g - T) = C^* + cY$$

Formal institutions may also enhance the consumption function by lowering taxes and providing social security and welfare benefits. In that case, net income, or disposable income, becomes higher and hence you can consume more. Informal institutions may influence the consumption function due to cultural values such as immaterialism or solidarity. This may increase savings or equalise consumption across population groups.

Informal institutions may enhance the consumption function through a culture of borrowing, with increasing social acceptance of household debt. This may even lead to consumption levels above income levels: C > Y. This is possible when C* increases strongly due to increasing consumption standards. Or it is made possible by a very high propensity to consume, c > 1, because of the use of savings and assets as collateral (like a house) for borrowing or the use of credit lines based on regular income. Of course, a value of c higher than 1 implies a negative propensity to save: dissaving and borrowing. So, when c = 1.3, this means that s = −0.3. Remember that c + s = 1, so that 1.3 − 0.3 = 1.

In other words, consumption, which is 30 per cent higher than income implies that savings decline by 30 per cent of income. At the aggregate, households, as a whole, borrow more than they earn, so that debt is 30 per cent of income. *Debt* is precisely the opposite of saving, it is dissaving. So, a debt of 30 per cent of income is the same as negative saving. Institutions reflecting a materialist culture with short consumption horizons ('I want it now') are likely to become increasingly indebted. This is pictured in the institutional macroeconomic flow as increased C and decreased S.

10.3.1.2 Investment

Formal institutions may enhance investment (I), for example by a low Central Bank interest rate. But formal institutions can also constrain investment, for example by capital reserve controls requiring higher levels of equity capital or minimum investment periods from foreign investors. This implies that formal institutions from the government to firms can either increase I or decrease I.

Informal institutions can constrain investment by contributing to negative expectations about returns, hence a negative investment confidence. The opposite is also possible, optimism about future returns, and hence investor optimism (or even over-confidence, which may lead to bubbles in asset markets).

10.3.1.3 Government transfers

Formal institutions can constrain the net government transfers (expenditures minus revenue) by strict budgeting rules for example. Other formal institutions may enable net government

Image 10.1 African and French traded products

expenditures, in particular automatic stabilisers in the budget. For example when the total sum of unemployment benefits increases in times of economic crisis. Informal institutions may also affect government transfers. Think about corruption, which reduces the effectiveness of public services, or, conversely, a high tax morale, which increases government revenues.

10.3.1.4 Exports and imports

Formal institutions can also affect exports. For example the exchange rate or export taxes which influence the price that economic agents abroad need to pay for your country's products. Informal institutions also affect the size of exports. This may be due to language barriers for example: former French colonies in Africa tend to trade more with each other and with France than with former English colonies and the UK.

10.3.2 The institutional macroeconomic flow

Diagram 10.3 shows the institutional macroeconomic flow. It includes the rest of the world (RoW), but more importantly, formal and informal institutions. Formal institutions (FI) are laws and regulations, and hence flow from the government sector to firms and households and the RoW. Informal institutions concern social norms and have a two-way relationship with every sector: households, firms, the government, and RoW.

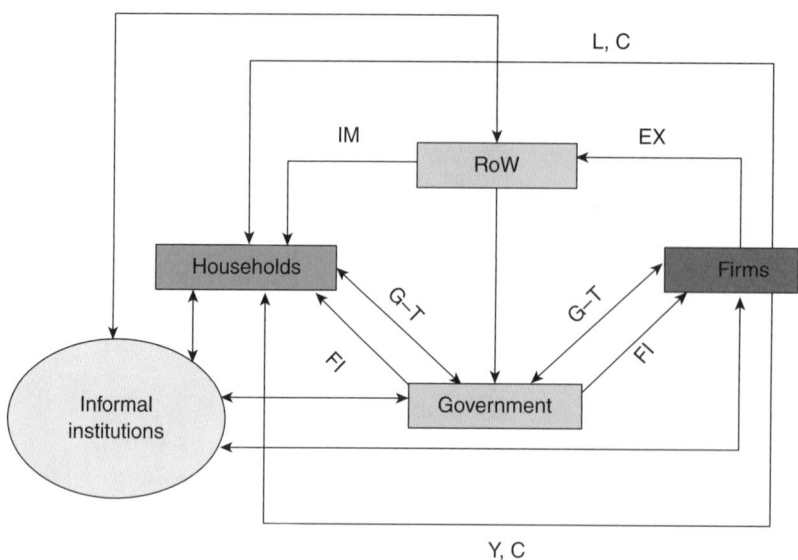

Diagram 10.3 Institutional macroeconomic flow

10.4 The economy as an open system: Post Keynesian economics

The major contribution of Post Keynesian economics is in macroeconomics. Keynes rejected the old classical assumption that the macro level is the sum of all micro-level behaviour. Instead, he argued that there is a fallacy of composition at the macro level. The *fallacy of composition* is the wrong assumption that the aggregate is the sum of the parts. What makes sense at the level of individual households or firms does not necessarily make sense for the economy as a whole. Macroeconomic variables are not necessarily a summing up of micro-level variables. The reason is that, in the economic process, interactions take place which interfere with a simple aggregation of micro-behaviour to macro-behaviour. The sum is bigger than the parts.

Keynes has demonstrated various cases of the fallacy of composition. The two best known are herd behaviour in financial markets and the paradox of thrift in households. Herd behaviour, as we have seen in the previous chapter, is the non-rational following of others' behaviour in markets, either in selling or buying assets, which leads to bubbles and bursts. The paradox of thrift refers to the contradictory phenomenon of savings as wise at the micro level (to keep resources for a rainy day) and as unwise at the macro level (because it lowers aggregate consumption), lowering aggregate demand, and hence, the level of GDP. The *paradox of thrift* is therefore defined as the virtue of saving at the individual level to counter uncertainty, and the vice of saving at the aggregate level because it reduces aggregate demand. So, at the micro level, more saving helps to balance livelihoods during a downturn in the economic cycle, whereas at the macro level, more aggregate saving reduces AD and keeps the economy at a low level of the economic cycle, due to lower consumer expenditures.

Remember another key ingredient of Post Keynesian economics: uncertainty. This leads to prices not reflecting real values, to volatility, and to expectations that may be optimistic or pessimistic, and driving investments below or towards full capacity utilisation of an economy's resources.

As a consequence of the combination of uncertainty and the fallacy of composition, macroeconomic equilibrium does not necessarily imply that an economy operates at full capacity with full employment. When firms decide not to invest but to sell their stocks first, and when households decide to consume less and to save more, production will be suboptimal, and unemployment will result. The economy does not automatically tend towards a desired outcome of full employment and no waste of resources. It simply balances where demand equals the supply of goods, at whatever level of output this is the case. This is what is meant by the economy as an open system: it does not necessarily arrive at a stable equilibrium with all resources being used, but it is dynamic, responding to confidence, expectations, and social dynamics of imitation, which drives economic cycles. *Open system economics* is the study of the economy in which there is no automatic balance between savings and investments, and hence, where macroeconomic equilibrium does not automatically eliminate excess supply in the markets for production factors.

10.4.1 Open system dynamics

Keynes developed his insights from studying the 1929 financial crisis and the subsequent Great Depression of the 1930s. He found out that despite macroeconomic equilibrium in product markets (AS = AD), an economy may suffer from unemployment. Because employment depends on the level of aggregate demand (AD) and not on an equilibrium between AS and AD. It is the size of aggregate demand in the economy (the sum of C, I, G, and EX – IM) which determines capacity utilisation, which in turn determines the demand for labour. Only when AD is located at a sufficiently high level, will it be able to absorb all labour supplied in the economy. In other words, macroeconomic equilibrium does not imply equilibrium in the labour market (absence of excess demand or excess supply). See Diagram 10.4, which will be explained below.

Does AS not have any role to play in this? No, not in the view of Keynes. Because the driving force for aggregate supply is investment, which is the only way in which potential production capacity can be expanded. And investment is part of AD: so, investment helps to increase employment and GDP through the demand side of the economy. On the supply side, the amount actually invested and leading to additional production depends on savings available in the economy, expectations about future sales, and the extent to which banks are willing to lend out money. Hence, investment will go up when more savings are available and there is optimism about the development of aggregate demand by firms, and optimism by banks about the risk of lending out money. According to Keynes, the level of investment does *not* depend on the interest rate, which is the price of investment. Isn't this inconsistent? If the demand for apples depends on the price of apples, why doesn't the demand for investment depend on the price of investment? Good question.

Keynes gave the answer: because investment requires savings, and savings depend on income. This was explained in section 10.1: both C and S depend on income. And the more you consume, the less you save, and the other way around. So, it is the level of income, Y, which determines savings, and not the level of the interest rate. Of course, the interest rate plays some role, but a minor role, namely in enabling credit. But what is more important for the amount of credit available in an economy is expectations about the future. When entrepreneurs do not expect sales to increase, they will not take out credit to invest, however low the interest rate at which they can borrow is. In 2014, the interest rate is historically low in the USA and Europe, as it has been for many years in Japan. But low demand and pessimistic expectations imply high savings combined with low consumption and low investment.

So, in Post Keynesian economics, savings equal the level of investment in an economy not through the level of the interest rate but through the level of income. The higher income, the more savings and the more optimistic expectations about the future, and hence, investments. This creates a virtuous circle in the economic flow:

- households consume more ($\uparrow$C) and save more ($\uparrow$S) absolutely (because of $\uparrow$Y);
- households save more relative to consumption ($\uparrow$S > $\uparrow$C), because the higher the income ($\uparrow$Y) the lower the propensity to consume ($\downarrow$c) and the higher the propensity to save ($\uparrow$s);
- firms will invest more because more savings become available ($\uparrow$S = >$\uparrow$I);
- firms will invest more because they become more optimistic about the future when incomes grow: they expect households to consume even more ($\uparrow$C = >$\uparrow$I).

It is precisely because of the typical macroeconomic phenomena, driven by non-rational motivations and the paradox of thrift, that the circular flow in Post Keynesian theory is understood as an open system. Not as a closed system, which after a shock quickly comes to equilibrium, but as a system in which relationships do not necessarily tend to equilibrium. Open systems may experience long-term non-equilibrium and may even lead to chaos, due to spiralling upward or downward dynamics. That is exactly why Post Keynesian economics can explain cycles, with its booms and bursts. These are instances in which the system is moving away from an equilibrium, possibly into chaos, of bank-runs, government insolvency, bankruptcies, and sky-high levels of unemployment.

10.4.2 Aggregate demand with a positive slope

In the Post Keynesian perspective, the AS can function either at its maximum level of capacity utilisation (cu^{max}), or below this level ($<cu^{max}$). Below this level there is excess capacity, not only in the use of capital goods and land but also in the use of labour. This implies that labour demand is insufficient to generate full employment. Full employment is indicated as N^{max}, when unemployment is zero: U = 0. So, when capacity utilisation in the economy is less than its maximum (cu < cu^{max}), unemployment is the result (U > 0).

That is why in the Post Keynesian perspective, the diagram for macroeconomic equilibrium is not pictured in a space of income and price level, but in the space of income and employment, or in the space of income and capacity utilisation. And, it is not really an equilibrium in the sense of an absence of excess supply or excess demand throughout the economy. Therefore, Post Keynesians do not refer to the intersection between AS and AD as an equilibrium, but give it the more appropriate name of effective demand. *Effective demand* is the intersection between aggregate supply and aggregate demand in an economy, which determines the level of output and employment. Diagram 10.4 shows the Post Keynesian macroeconomic diagram with effective demand in the income–employment space. The intersection where AS = AD shows equilibrium output (Y*) and employment (N*), which may be below full capacity utilisation and below full employment.

The diagram shows that both AD and AS are upward sloping, AS because more production requires more labour. In fact, the aggregate supply function describes the relationship between expected earnings by firms and the labour they want to hire for that expected level of earnings. So, more expected earnings increases production, and this requires hiring more labour. As a consequence, an increase in AS leads to an increase in employment (assuming that labour supply remains unaffected of course – a *ceteris paribus* assumption).

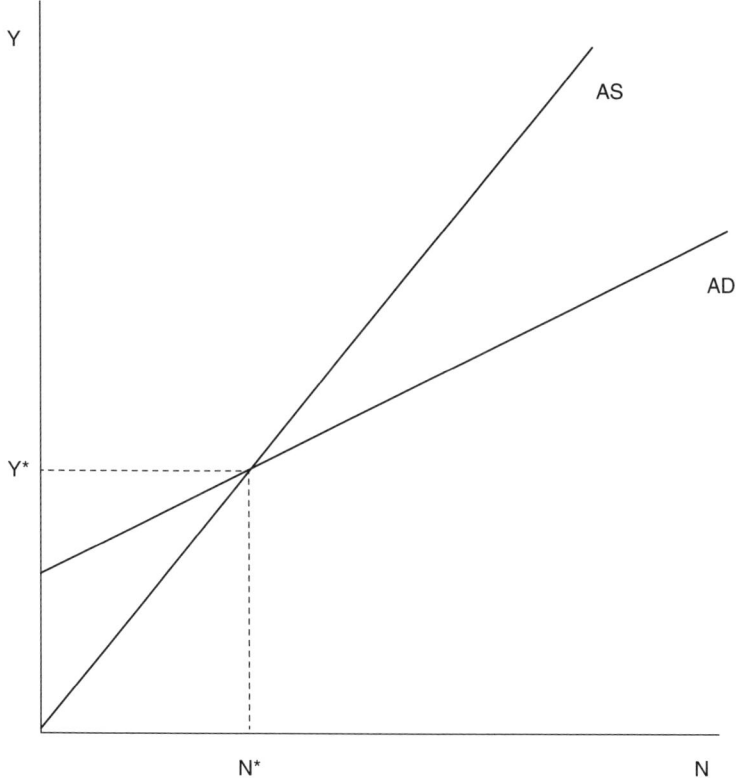

Diagram 10.4 Effective demand

AD slopes upward because more expenditures in the economy requires more income and more income can only be produced with hiring more labour. Again, this stimulates employment. But the slope of the AD curve is less steep than the slope of the AS curve. Why?

The difference in slope between the AS curve and the AD curve means that for every increase in income of a fixed amount, the employment effect on the demand side (AD) is larger than on the supply side (AS). The reason is that on the supply side, there are no endogenous effects between supply and employment: hiring labour simply contributes to higher output. But on the demand side, there are endogenous effects between demand and employment: more labour employed means not only that this is coupled with more investment by firms (you need to have more machines, computers, office space, or land to put more labour to work). But also that more employment means more wage earnings, and hence, more consumer spending, in the aggregate. That is because now more households have wage earners. Moreover, the more employment, the higher the tax revenue from labour income for the government (T). This allows for more government expenditures (G). So, through the AD curve, more income generates more employment than through the AS curve.

Since consumption accounts for the largest part of aggregate demand, let us analyse the Post Keynesian consumption function at the aggregate level more closely. Diagram 10.5 shows the aggregate consumption function in the space of income (Y) and consumption (C).

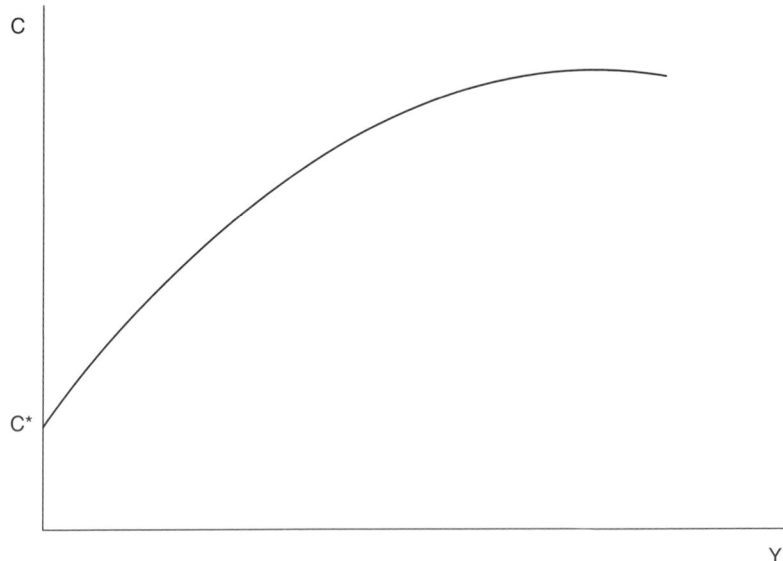

Diagram 10.5 Post Keynesian aggregate consumption function

The diagram shows that consumption is never zero. The minimum level is C*, the autonomous consumption: the level that people consume, irrespective of their income level. The next observation is that the line is not linear. Indeed, the relationship between consumption and income is not linear: cY varies over the level of income. We can distinguish three components of the relationship between Y and C. The part closest to the y-axis is where consumption levels are low: people spend most or all of their income on consumption, sometimes even more. At this part, the propensity to consume, c, is 0.8 or more. Halfway along the curve, at intermediate levels of income, people begin saving money. They consume more than they save, hence c lies in between, say, 0.5 and 0.8. In other words, they save between 20 per cent and 50 per cent of their income. The last part of the curve, on the right, is where people earn high incomes. This part reflects the richest households in an economy's income distribution. This group can afford to save just as much as they consume or even more: c will be below 0.5.

The important insight from the above aggregate consumption function is that an increase in income is likely to lead to a proportionate, or almost proportionate, increase in consumption for poor households, but to a much smaller increase in consumption by rich households. Apparently, the extent to which aggregate demand helps an economy to grow or to move out of an economic downturn depends partly on whether economic policy benefits the poor (big effect on AD) or the rich (small effect on AD). This brings us to the last key feature of Post Keynesian macroeconomics, namely leakages and injections, which can be analysed with multiplier effects.

10.4.3 Multiplier effects

Let us go back to Diagram 10.4, showing effective demand in the Y–N space. We have seen that for a given increase in income, aggregate demand generates more jobs than aggregate

Image 10.2 Leakage effect

supply. Now, the reverse is also true. For a given increase in employment, aggregate supply generates much more output than aggregate demand. That is because the additional fixed amount of labour hired contributes directly to output (AS). But a fixed amount of additional jobs is weakened in its effect on demand (AD). This weakening is caused by leakages in the circular flow.

Macroeconomic leakages are non-consumption uses of income, which reduce aggregate demand. There are three leakages: savings, taxes, and imports.

1   *Savings leakage*: When additional income for labour or capital is not spent on consumption but is added to savings (S).

2   *Taxation leakage*: When additional income is taxed away to reduce government debt, so that it is not spent on consumption or on government expenditures (T).
3   *Import leakage*: When additional income is spent on imports instead of domestically produced goods (IM).

Macroeconomic leakages make macroeconomic policies less effective. For example, the government may want to stimulate economic growth by lowering its budget deficit through higher taxes. This policy could signal 'sound public finances' to international financial markets, attracting foreign investors. This would increase I in the long run with more foreign investments. But the increased taxes will decrease C in the short run. Because more taxation will lower the disposable income of households, and hence, their consumer expenditures. This will decrease AD in the short run. Whether that will be compensated for by higher investments, from foreign sources, in the long run, is uncertain, because foreign investment depends on more factors than 'sound public finance'. It also depends, for example, on social-economic stability and effective property rights.

Next to leakages, the macroeconomic flow also includes injections. *Macroeconomic injection* is a stimulus to aggregate demand through I, G, or EX. The two major injections are through government expenditures (G) and investment (I). If the government increases its expenditures (remember, we refer to net expenditures, so taxes remain the same), we will see in the aggregate demand function that G increases, *ceteris paribus*: ↑G. This will have a direct positive effect on Y through AD, which can be seen from the macroeconomic equation:

$$Y = C + I + G + EX - IM$$

But there is also an indirect effect of ↑G, namely through the employment created through G, increasing income and in turn increasing consumer expenditures: ↑C. And if ↑G is spent on stimulation of the export sector, it may also boost exports: ↑EX. And on and on until the effects become zero over time. This will take a few rounds of effects, because when C and/or EX increase, the government will earn more tax revenues (sales tax or profit tax from exporting firms), and hence, can further increase G without creating a budget deficit. The higher government expenditures will again generate more C and/or more EX, and so on, and so on, but smaller than the first time due to leakages. Until the initial effect has worked out. By adding up all the direct and indirect effects we get what we call a multiplier effect. A *multiplier* is an accelerator on aggregate demand through an initial injection and its stimulating effects on other demand variables.

In addition to the government multiplier (through G), we have the investment multiplier (through I). This multiplier could be triggered by a decrease in the interest rate set by the Central Bank. This makes investment cheaper, *ceteris paribus*, because it makes borrowing cheaper. So, a lower interest rate functions as an injection to aggregate demand, stimulating investment: ↑I. There are also indirect effects here. Increased investment will lead to more jobs, and hence to more labour income. This will stimulate consumption: ↑C. It may also result in higher profit taxes due to more sales by firms that have invested, and more income tax from the additional income earnings, which will allow an increase in net government expenditures: ↑G. After several rounds of such effects, which become smaller over time due to leakages, we can calculate the investment multiplier: the total affect of an increase in investment on aggregate demand, and hence, on Y.

10.4.3.1 Calculation of the multiplier

The multiplier is the total effect on output of multiple rounds of effects of an injection in aggregate demand, through consumer expenditures. So, what is crucial is how much of their income consumers spend on buying goods. This is reflected in the propensity to consume. The higher c, the higher the multiplier effect. There is a simple formula to calculate the total effect:

$$\text{Multiplier} = \frac{\text{Injection}}{1-c}$$

So, let us assume that c = 0.6 and that the injection is an increase in G of 100 billion yen. This leads to an increase in Japanese output of 250 billion yen:

$$\Delta Y = \frac{100}{1-0.6} = \frac{100}{0.4} = 250$$

In other words, the multiplier is 2.5 because an injection in G of 100 billion yen results in an increase of output (Y) of 250 billion yen, which is 2.5 times bigger than the injection.

Now what if the propensity to consume was not 0.6 but less, say 0.5? Then the Japanese economy has a lower multiplier:

$$\Delta Y = \frac{100}{1-0.5} = \frac{100}{0.5} = 200$$

Now, the multiplier is 2.0 instead of 2.5. This example illustrates how important aggregate demand is in Post Keynesian analysis, and how important consumer expenditure, as part of aggregate demand, is for the economy and economic growth and macroeconomic policy.

10.4.4 The open system circular flow

The open system circular flow, or the Post Keynesian macroeconomic flow, includes the FIRE sector (remember from Chapter 9: Finance, Investment, Real Estate). This sector mediates savings (S) and investments (I), but also directly generates financial investments (I). The open systems character is expressed by leakages and injections. These are included in the flows. Leakages can be found for S, T, and IM. Injections can be found for I, G, and EX. The open system circular flow is shown in Diagram 10.6.

10.5 The economy as a closed system: neoclassical economics

Neoclassical economics is closed systems economics. It assumes that equilibrium is the normal state of an economy and disequilibrium is only a short temporary stage, caused by an outside shock to the economy. In jargon: there is always macroeconomic equilibrium, and exogenous shocks move an economy briefly out of equilibrium, but they are rare and not cyclical but random. So, AS = AD. But does this always imply full employment?

270 *The macroeconomic flow*

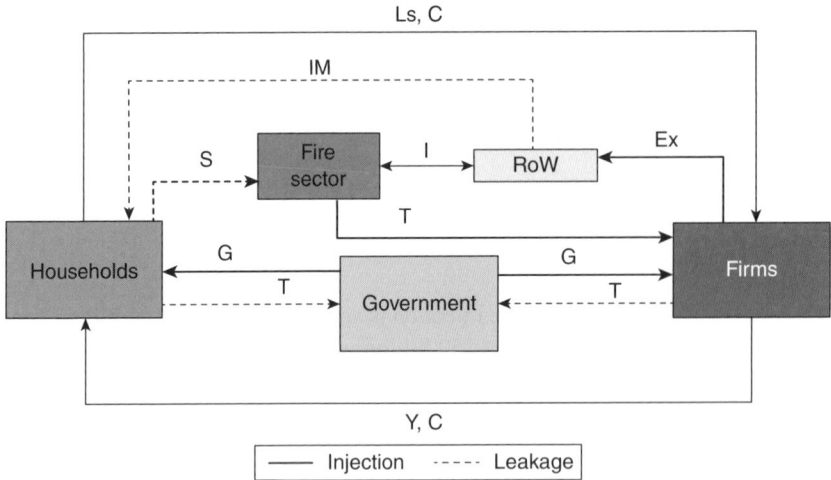

Diagram 10.6 Post Keynesian macroeconomic flow

Yes, if markets are free and fully competitive, there is no uncertainty, and no fallacy of composition, macroeconomic equilibrium implies full use of resources in an economy: no excess supply or excess demand for resources, just like on the goods market. The general price level in an economy is where AS equals AD, the macroeconomic equilibrium. At the same time, prices in other markets adjust until there is equilibrium without excess supply or excess demand. The wage rate makes L^s and L^d equal at full employment in the labour market. The interest rate makes S and I equal in the financial market with no excess demand or excess supply of credit. And, finally, the exchange rate makes EX and IM equal in the international goods market, with no deficit or surplus on the Balance of Payment with the rest of the world.

Of course, the real economies in which we live hardly ever show zero or close to zero unemployment rates. So, neoclassical economists agree that macroeconomic equilibrium in reality does not necessarily imply full employment. But this is attributed to distortions of the labour market: if the labour market was free, without any regulation, wages would be allowed to go down until firms would hire all labour supplied. In contrast to Post Keynesian economics, aggregate demand imposes no constraints on the demand for labour: all goods supplied are bought, and hence, all labour to produce this is hired.

And what about equilibrium in the financial market? As in the product market (flexible goods prices) and the labour market (flexible wages), flexible interest rates ensure market clearing between savings and investments. Suppose that entrepreneurs want to invest more than savings in the system allow. And let us assume, for the moment, that foreign investment is prohibited. In that case, the interest rate would increase due to scarcity of credit: firms would bid up against one another to get loans, and offer higher interest rates than their competitors for the same loans. The increased interest rate in financial markets would then in turn trigger households to save more money: when they can earn higher interest rates on their savings accounts, the average household is likely to choose to consume less and to save more, in order to reap extra income. This is assumed to be a quick adjustment process so that any disequilibrium is quickly solved by an adjustment in the interest rate. In this case, an increase in the interest rate up to the point that the level of desired investment equals the level of obtained savings (S = I).

Hence, the neoclassical macroeconomic flow predicts a quick adjustment of all markets, without distortions from regulation, social norms, or mis-pricing. It is self-contained, in that every market clears simply through adjustments in the price level. When labour becomes cheaper, more workers will be hired and less workers will want to work, so the demand and supply of labour get pushed to equilibrium through lower wages. The same is the case for higher wages: when more people get better training and firms invest in more complex techniques for which they want to hire better educated workers, workers demand higher wages and firms are willing to hire these more expensive better educated workers because they are more productive than lower educated workers. Again, the supply and demand of labour will be pushed to equilibrium by the price level. The wage increase stops when the marginal productivity of the last hired worker is equal to the wage rate (remember from Chapter 8).

The neoclassical macroeconomic flow is called a closed system because, without any interference from the government, all markets will tend towards equilibrium and no market will suffer from excess demand or excess supply. The rest of the world is included for international analysis, but a world-economy level neoclassical analysis is not substantively different from a national economy analysis: both are studied as closed systems.

10.5.1 Aggregate demand and aggregate supply

Diagram 10.7 shows the neoclassical picture of macroeconomic equilibrium, with AS and AD.

The diagram shows a standard neoclassical market, but now at the aggregate level. Supply (AS) has an upward slope and demand (AD) has a downward slope. The intersection of AS and AD expresses macroeconomic equilibrium: equilibrium output (Y*) and the equilibrium aggregate price level (P*). This also coincides with full employment if there are no distortions in the labour market. So, when AS = AD, there will be full employment ($L^s = L^d$), through the adjustment of wages, which removes excess demand or excess supply.

This model can only reflect economic reality when an economy is at or near the top of a cycle. That is because at that point, Y increases, investment (I) grows, and consumption (C) increases. For the rest of the time, when the economy is not at or near the top of a cycle, the neoclassical model does not coincide with full employment. In the neoclassical model, savings and investments are always in equilibrium because of adjustment to the interest rate. The market interest rate depends on the basic interest rate set by the Central Bank. The lower this interest rate is, the lower market interest rates will be, and vice versa. So, when investment is lower than savings, banks like to lend out money because they need to earn from credits in order to pay interest on savings accounts. Hence, banks will offer lower interest rates for credit. Also, as we have seen in the previous chapter, banks lend to each other and sell and buy all kinds of interest-related products such as mortgage-backed securities. The interest rate for all these financial products is related to the basic interest rate set by the Central Bank. Hence, the Central Bank will reduce its interest rates in order to help investment increase through credit, to match the amount of savings available. At the same time, savings will decline as a response to the lower interest rate, because it will become less attractive to save

272 *The macroeconomic flow*

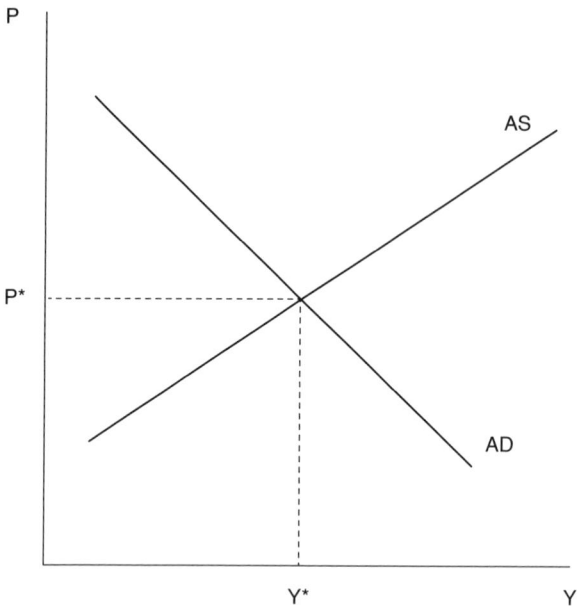

Diagram 10.7 Neoclassical macroeconomic equilibrium

when households earn lower interest on their savings accounts. This is how adjustments in the interest rate bring equilibrium to investments and savings (S = I), from both the investment side and the savings side.

10.5.2 Macroeconomic change: shocks

The macroeconomic equilibrium in a closed system will only be disturbed by *shocks*, which are exogenous changes to the economy. Why? Because an equilibrium-tending system will absorb all available information at any time into buy and sell decisions. So, if investors know beforehand that interest rates are going to go up, they will offset the decreasing effect of such a increasing interest rate on investment by quickly investing before the increase occurs. But due to the assumption of perfect information, every investor would know this, so that actually, there is no shock to be noticed. There is just continued and very quick adaptation of supply and demand on the investment market, between savings and loans, so that every time an equilibrium results. So, only real shocks, that is, random, unpredictable shocks, will disturb an open system. Just as the meteorite that hit the Earth millions of years ago killed the dinosaurs but allowed the rest of life to eventually find a new equilibrium, a shock to the economy will bring a sudden change but allow the system to find a new equilibrium afterwards. Although with a possible loss, whether dinosaurs, deaths from hunger, or discouraged workers. But in a closed system it will never lead to chaos – the system will adapt and find a new equilibrium.

For example, assume that due to extreme weather conditions, half of the crops are destroyed. This means the domestic food supply is halved. In an economy without exports and imports,

Image 10.3 Equilibrium on skis

the excess demand on the food market will be solved by a quick increase in domestic food prices. This will reduce the demand for food by those who do not have sufficient purchasing power. Poor people will simply eat less, throw away less food, or buy cheaper food. And they may borrow money to buy food now, and pay back the loan in the future. Rich people will just buy and waste the same amount as before but will now spend more money on food. Any remaining gap in food consumption, for the poorest households who cannot afford to buy domestically grown food at the higher prices, may be closed through imported food from countries that have not suffered bad weather. The government may decide to pay for this and to distribute the food among the poor to prevent them from starving. So, consumer expenditures will be higher and imports will be also higher.

The new equilibrium will settle at a lower level of domestically grown food transacted at higher prices, and a higher level of imports. If the increase in C is higher than the increase in IM, then the bad weather and low yield will result in higher national income – isn't that ironic? But if the spending on imported food exceeds the higher spending on domestic food, the national income will decline: remember that import has a negative sign in the macroeconomic equation.

But now we cannot compare current income with income in a previous year, because not only volumes but also prices have changed. In fact, the increased consumer expenditures imply lower food volumes, not higher. Production has declined and not increased. The major effect is a price increase in the food market, driving up the general price level in the economy. As a consequence, the increased income simply reflects a price increase and not at all an increase in output. This is shown in Diagram 10.8, which shows, as before, AS and AD in the P–Y space.

274 *The macroeconomic flow*

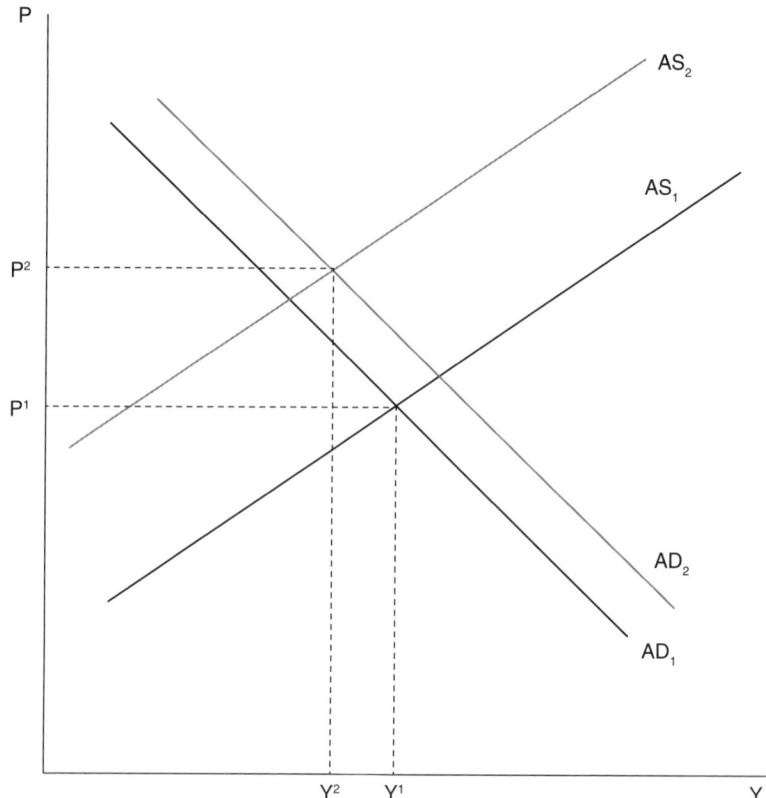

Diagram 10.8 Macroeconomic equilibrium with crop failure

The diagram shows the starting position as in Diagram 10.7 with equilibrium Y^1, P^1. Now, production will decline due to the lower food yields: AS shifts to the left (AS_2). And consumer expenditures increase due to the higher food prices. This increase in C shifts the AD curve to the right (AD_2). The new equilibrium, Y^2, P^2 (intersection of AD_2 and AS_2), has a higher price level P and a lower output level Y. We can conclude that the bad harvest has caused national income to grow but that this reflects not output growth but increased prices.

This result is also referred to as inflation: the price level in the economy has increased. So, you can have inflation in an economy which suggests that the economy is growing (higher national income) but actually may hide stagnation or even income decline because it consist largely or completely of an increase in the general price level. This shows the importance of distinguishing *real economic effects* (corrected for price changes) from *nominal economic effects* (expressed in current prices).

10.5.3 The closed systems flow

The closed systems flow, or the neoclassical macroeconomic flow, includes RoW and nature, but not the FIRE sector, society and its institutions, and communities. Nature has input arrows: to firms and households, in the form of resources and environmental services. See Diagram 10.9.

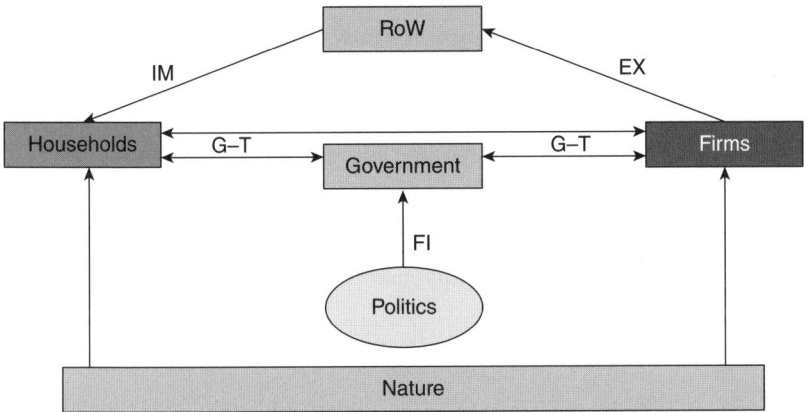

Diagram 10.9 Neoclassical macroeconomic flow

10.6 Interesting sources

Keen, S. (2001) *Debunking Economics – The Naked Emperor of the Social Sciences.* Annandale: Pluto Press.
Macroeconomic flow visualiser: http://econviz.org/macroeconomic-circular-flow-visualizer/

10.7 Glossary

Aggregate demand (AD)   The total demand of all households, firms, the government, and the rest of the world (households, firms, and governments abroad)

Aggregate supply (AS)   The total supply by all households, firms, the government, and the rest of the world (households, firms, and governments abroad)

Autonomous consumption   A constant of consumption for minimum survival, not dependent on income

Debt   The opposite of saving, it is dissaving

Disposable income = net income   Income after taxes

Economic cycle   General pattern of growth and decline in an economy

Effective demand   The intersection between aggregate supply and aggregate demand in an economy, which determines the level of output and employment

Embeddedness   The understanding that the economy as a whole, at the aggregate level, is only a part of wider society and nature and is therefore strongly influenced by society and nature

Fallacy of composition   The wrong assumption that the aggregate is the sum of the parts

Gross domestic product (GDP)   The aggregation of all market transactions and government expenditures

Macroeconomic equation $Y = C + I + G + EX - IM$

Macroeconomic equilibrium The situation in which there is no excess demand or excess supply in any product market in the economy

Macroeconomic flow = circular flow Metaphor of the macroeconomy as a circular flow system, in which households, firms, and the government are connected through flows of goods and flows of money

Macroeconomic injection A stimulus to aggregate demand through I, G, or EX

Macroeconomic leakage Non-consumption uses of income, which reduce aggregate demand

Macroeconomics The study of the aggregate level of the economy, the macroeconomy

Multiplier An accelerator on aggregate demand through an initial injection and its stimulating effects on other demand variables

Nominal economic effects Economic variable changes expressed in current prices

Open system economics The study of the economy in which there is no automatic balance between savings and investments, and hence, where macroeconomic equilibrium does not automatically eliminate excess supply in the markets for production factors

Paradox of thrift The virtue of saving at the individual level to counter uncertainty, and the vice of saving at the aggregate level because it reduces aggregate demand

Propensity to consume The proportion of income spent on consumption

Propensity to save The proportion of income saved

Real economic effects Economic variable changes corrected for price changes

Shocks Exogenous changes to the economy

Social contract A society-wide agreement about rights and duties and the distribution of costs and benefits of social and economic behaviour

Sustainable development Development that meets the needs of the present without compromising the ability of future generations to meet their own needs

Transfer payments The public expenditures on social policy, such as social security and social safety nets

11 Money

11.1 Money as a social relation: social economics

11.1.1 Money as a matter of trust

Social economics recognises strongly that money is a social relation. Money probably originated before it was required to facilitate market exchange, because money was already needed to solve the oldest human conflicts, namely conflicts over property and harm. Money was in the first place a unit of account to settle debts, debt as guilt: one was liable or indebted to someone else due to theft or other harm done.

Money has no intrinsic value. The money in a modern economy is not based on gold or bank reserves or any guarantee by the state. It is not based on any material foundation of precious metals, or on a state institution that guarantees its value. Money is a silent agreement in a community built on trust. Money has economic value as long as people are willing to give and accept this trust. Some bank notes and coins in different countries across the world even refer to the help of God when this need for mutual trust is recognised. The Dutch €2 coin has the inscription 'God Zij Met Ons' (God Be With Us), following a tradition of having this inscription on Dutch guilders going back to the Republic of the United Seven Provinces that existed between the 16th and 18th centuries. In 1957, the USA followed with the inscription 'In God We Trust' on all dollar notes.

Up to the end of the 20th century, the world's money systems were backed by gold, which was called the *gold standard*. But since then, economies have expanded so quickly that the required gold reserves could not keep up with the global expansion of money. Also, keeping 100 per cent reserves of gold for all money in circulation became a very costly activity for Central Banks. So, in the 1970s the world changed to a money system without a gold standard. However, Central Banks increase their gold reserves when the volatility of exchange rates and capital flows increase.

Central Banks still keep some gold reserves, because this helps them to sell reserves in times of need and to buy reserves in times of prosperity: gold reserves allow Central Banks to buy in international currency markets foreign currency or their own currency. Diagram 11.1 shows the increase in the gold reserves of the Reserve Bank of India in 2010.

Money is anything that allows its holder to purchase goods. Money has four functions: it is a (1) unit of account, (2) means of exchange, (3) store of value, and (4) means of accumulation. The first function of money is as a unit of account. Money comes in a fixed set of denominations. This allows for a fixed unit of account: something costs Rs 1, Rs 10, Rs 50, or Rs 30,023. Money allows values to be counted and stocks and flows of money to be evaluated

278 *Money*

Image 11.1 'In God We Trust' on a Dutch €2 coin

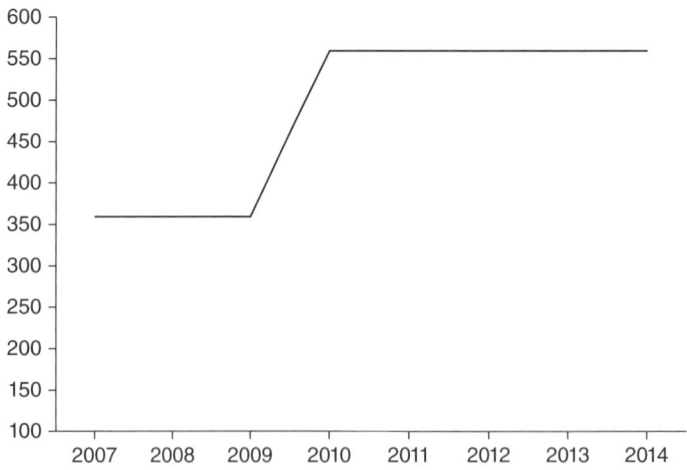

Diagram 11.1 Gold reserves of the Reserve Bank of India in tonnes

Sources: World Bank and World Gold Council, available at http://www.gold.org/reserve-asset-management/statistics

through accounting. The second function of money is as a unit of exchange. Obviously, this makes economic life much easier. Rather than dragging your home-made lentil soup or naan bread to the next village to exchange it for a new sari, and where you would need to find a seller of saris with an appetite for your soup or naan, you simply sell the food in your own village to whoever wants to buy it. And with the money earned, you go to your favourite sari seller in the next village and choose your size and colour, even when this sari seller does not like lentil soup. The third function of money is that it also serves as a store of value. Unlike soup or naan, it does not rot or evaporate as days go by. So, you can keep money for a long time – in your wallet, under the mattress, or in your bank account. The fourth function of money is that it enables accumulation in a capitalist economy. This was expressed by Marx as the sequence of money (M) and commodities (C), which begins and ends with money: M – C – M'. The beginning of the exchange chain is money through debt, which an entrepreneur invests. Then there is a process of exchange in commodities. Also the end of the chain is money, but now through profit for the entrepreneur.

When money depends on trust, it may also lose trust. *Monetary institutions* are organisations, regulations, and social norms which together guarantee the functioning of a monetary system. When economic agents lose trust in a particular bank, they are afraid that the money that they have in their checking account and savings account will no longer be accessible to them, because the bank has lent it all out or even lost it. This fear creates a bank run, to make the money liquid. *Liquid money* means that money is shifted from deposits to immediately accessible forms of money. The problem, however, is that banks use leverage for the money they take in on deposits, so that they cannot fulfil the desire for liquidity of all their deposit holders. *Leverage* means that banks lend out several times what they take in.

When trust breaks down and a bank run is in full flow, many economic agents will not be able to withdraw their money, or to transfer it to accounts at other banks. This may result in bankruptcy, which is the result of a self-fulfilling prophesy: when people are no longer confident that their money is safe in a particular bank, they will create that bank's failure by withdrawing their money.

Another way in which money is a social relation is that it is created through debt. As was explained in the chapter on financial markets, money is created by commercial banks through their lending activity. Banks not only lend out what they actually have – their equity capital – they also lend out what they deposit or borrow from others, using leverage based on their reputation, risk management, and implicit state guarantees. So, banks simply create money by lending it out against an IOU ('I Owe You'), creating money. So, money is created through debt: economic agents take a loan and enter into a debt relation with a bank.

This leads to a puzzling macroeconomic implication, namely: if all money enters the economy as debt, how then can this be paid back with interest? Where does the money to pay the interest come from? At the micro level, one pays back with the profits from an investment. But for the economy as a whole there is no other source of money than again . . . debt. This means that the economy needs to grow and to continuously issue new money, through debt, on and on and on.

So, money is a social relation of trust and debt. Sometimes the two come together, and money plays a beneficial role in the economy. While at other times, one of the two is out of balance (low trust or high indebtedness). And sometimes, both are out of balance. In which case, there is a financial crisis.

11.1.2 Money systems

As long as money has existed, individuals and communities have developed alternative monies to the state-based money system regulated by a Central Bank. The reasons are all embedded in social relations: distrust, social exclusion from the dominant monetary system, inequality, and dissatisfaction with asymmetric information. We distinguish three monetary systems: fiat money, local money, and virtual money.

11.1.2.1 Fiat money in a monetary union

Standard money as we know it – yen, pesos, and rupees – is fiduciary money, as explained above, and authorised by the state. This we call *fiat money*. The notes and coins are not only supplied by the state (and may be produced by a private firm with an excusive contract with the state), but they are also regulated by the Central Bank, a state institution. They are accepted as legal tender throughout a nation and they are accepted in international currency markets for exchange with other currencies. Fiat money is also the currency in which a government's budget deficit is denominated and it is the currency in which the government requires taxes to be paid.

Until the eurozone crisis of 2010–2013, many economists thought that the above features of state-based money were sufficient for a stable and trustworthy monetary system in a monetary union of countries. But the euro crisis has proven otherwise. The euro was introduced digitally in 1999 and physically in 2002. Today, 18 EU member countries have the euro as their fiat money. They form the European Monetary Union (EMU) coordinated by the European Central Bank. The euro has fluctuated quite a lot in value, from US$0.83 for €1 in 2000 to US$1.60 for €1 in 2008. That is a value increase of almost 100 per cent. It all went well for the euro for a decade.

But then, triggered by the financial crisis in the USA, the eurozone got into trouble, with strong volatility in its exchange rate. Trust in the euro began to weaken due to high private debt in the eurozone, several banking crises throughout the EMU as a result of toxic assets bought from US banks, and a structural imbalance between eurozone countries in the North and in the South of Europe. For example, Spain and Portugal have small budget deficits and small government debt compared to countries such as Germany and the Netherlands. But they suffer from low productivity and low competitiveness, leading to trade deficits, whereas the countries in the North benefit from a trade surplus. Obviously, in a single country such imbalances cannot happen. The EMU clearly had not turned the eurozone in a euro-state. Before the euro was introduced, this was already considered a significant risk by various critical economists.[1]

The euro crisis has taught us an important lesson about the social relation of money: fiat money requires a state to perform *all* state economic roles. But the EMU did not have all these roles. There was agreement between the member states to stick to a maximum public debt (60 per cent of GDP) and a maximum budget deficit (3 per cent of GDP). But without any enforcement by a central government, this agreement appeared to be weak. And much more was not arranged beforehand. Individual member countries remained sovereign over their own banks and taxation, and they issued their own national government bonds. The European Central Bank's task was too limited, concerned with the prevention of inflation in the eurozone. But it had no oversight function for all banks in Europe. And there is no overall European government operating with a single budget, pan-European taxation, and euro-bonds to finance European budget deficits. When a country finds itself in deep economic crisis, such as Greece and Cyprus, it no longer has available the policy tool of currency devaluation: these countries are part of the euro and do not have their own currencies anymore – their drachma and pounds are gone.

A *currency devaluation* is a value reduction in one's currency vis-à-vis foreign currencies, which makes one's export products cheaper. This helps a country to earn more money from exports, and hence to boost aggregate demand. The opposite is a *currency revaluation*, which is an increase in one's currency value vis-à-vis foreign currencies, which makes one's imports cheaper.

11.1.2.2 Local money

There are several forms of local money that function in parallel with fiat money. In contrast to fiat money, local currencies do not come into existence through debt. Instead, community members first need to sell a good or provide a service from which they can earn community currency. Then they can buy goods and services themselves and then the local currency begins to circulate. Another major difference from fiat money is that local currencies don't earn interest, so saving is discouraged. Instead, community currencies are meant to stimulate the circular economic flow, paying for the production of goods and services, relying on the resources available in a community, in particular idle labour resources. Therefore, such local money systems are also referred to as local employment trading systems (LETS).

So, local currencies don't create debt and don't earn interest and they are managed locally, outside the fiat money system, by a community. This does not imply that the state has no role at all. Many local currencies are actually supported by local governments and sometimes are initiated by local governments. The most famous example is the local currency initiated by the city of Curitiba in Brazil. The local currency system developed out of poverty. The city had grown quickly in the 1960s and 1970s, with large favelas where the poor live. Garbage became a serious problem, because the city's collection system could not access the small dirt streets in the favelas. The city surroundings are very fertile and hence, the city has large supplies of fresh fruit. Moreover, the city has a modern bus system, which was under-used, because the poor, who most need bus transportation, could not afford to buy bus tickets. The mayor of Curitiba, Jaime Lerner, found a solution to this mismatch in supply and demand of the city's resources in a local currency system. He placed garbage containers around the favelas and gave people local money for collected and sorted garbage for recycling and processing. This local currency, plastic chips, served as payment on the buses in Curitiba. This allowed the inhabitants of the favelas to seek employment in the city. And it allowed school children to go to school and to purchase fruit and school supplies. Interestingly, the wider community began to accept the local currency as means of payment as well. So, the chips, which initially functioned only as bus tickets, now became more widely accepted by shop owners in Curitiba because they trusted that they themselves could pay with them. Eventually, 70 per cent of the households of Curitiba participated, so that nearly a million bus tickets were used and 11,000 tonnes of garbage were collected.[2]

Box 11.1 Local money on a large scale

In Argentina, an environmental community organisation decided to print their own money to facilitate exchanges among 25 neighbours in a Buenos Aires suburb in 1995. The experiment helped the first participants to get to know their neighbours better and increase their income by trading with others. Membership grew quickly by word of mouth and after a while other groups replicated the scheme locally across the

(continued)

(continued)

city. By 2000 there were 4,500 groups across Argentina trading goods and services using local or regional community currencies. Participants used their community currencies to buy and sell groceries, second-hand clothes and shoes, handicrafts, bicycles, and even livestock, in addition to services like legal counselling, training, personal care, and even holiday packages.

Community money allowed the 6 million participants to survive the worst economic crisis in the country's history (1999–2001) by adding the equivalent of 1.5 minimum salaries in kind on average per household. It saved some local businesses from bankruptcy and was even accepted to pay for municipal taxes in arrears. The initiative has shrunk markedly since then as a result of the burden of sustaining the scheme, the launch of various social welfare subsidies, and the recovery of the regular economy.

Source: Gomez, G., based on her PhD thesis: *Making Markets. The Institutional Rise and Decline of the Argentine Red de Trueque*. The Hague: Institute of Social Studies, 2008.

11.1.2.3 Virtual money

A recent alternative to both fiat money and local money is money that is completely separate from a nation state or a community of people bound together on the basis of geography, class, or political unity. This alternative money exists only virtually and is disembedded money. The currency is digital and traded on the internet. The value of virtual money is determined only through its supply and demand on a few internet markets. Assuming that no one manipulates the currency, and its value is indeed the result of moment-to-moment buy and sell transactions, it is a transparent currency.

There is no monetary policy behind it, no Central Bank regulation, no government influence, and no local interests. The flip-side of this disembeddedness is volatility. It is like a language without a country: virtual money is homeless. An example of virtual money is the bitcoin. You can obtain bitcoins only through the internet. The value of the bitcoin at the moment I am writing this sentence is US$824.60 or €603.90 for one bitcoin (see Diagram 11.2).[3] But it fluctuates strongly and nobody really knows why. . . .

11.1.2.4 Inflation as social relation

Inflation is a general increase in absolute prices. The opposite is *deflation*, which is a general decrease in absolute prices. This seems an entirely monetary phenomenon and not affecting the real economy. But that is only the case in an exceptional situation, where all prices of all resources and goods increase simultaneously and at the same rate. In real life, we often experience price hikes of a single product (like oil) or a bubble in a particular asset (like real estate). And often, an increase in the prices of basic needs is not (sufficiently) compensated for by an increase in purchasing power (such as wages or pensions). So, inflation is not entirely a monetary phenomenon, it affects the real economy. It lowers purchasing power and it shifts demand away from more expensive goods to cheaper substitutes.

Moreover, inflation affects social groups differently. Those with savings and who have lent out money are disadvantaged by inflation because their savings become worth less and less and by the time the loan is paid back, the amount will be much less in value than it was

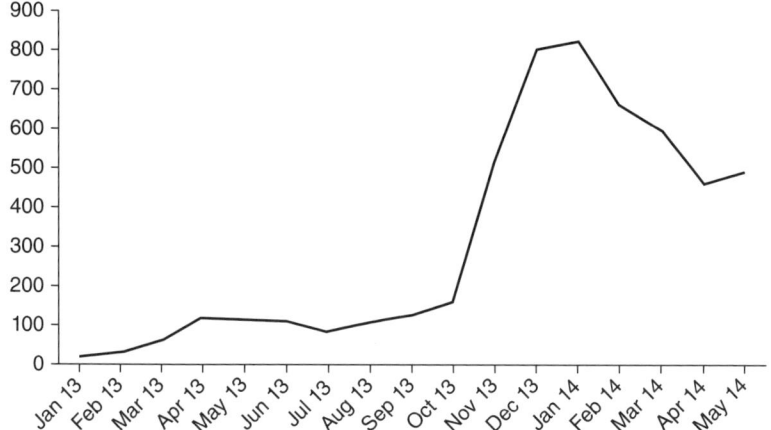

Diagram 11.2 Value of the bitcoin in US dollars since its introduction in February 2013
Source: https://bitcointalk.org/index.php?topic=322058.0

at the time it was lent out. Also, those paid in fixed amounts (think of pensions) or wages without indexation, also lose money. The opposite is the case for those who have debts. In that case, inflation is a blessing. First, the interest paid, if it is a fixed interest rate, becomes smaller and smaller in real terms.

Rs 100 of interest to be paid now represents much less value today than Rs 100 to be paid in interest 10 years ago if the inflation rate over 10 years was 5 per cent each year. Second, the total amount of the loan decreases in value. So, by the time you need to pay it back, the amount's value in real terms has decreased. A debt of Rs 1,000 last year is only worth Rs 500 this year if the inflation rate is 100 per cent. And the interest you need to pay on the full amount of, say, 5 per cent is Rs 50. But the real value of that amount is also worth half. And since almost every economy runs on some level of inflation, at least a few percentage points per year, having a long-term debt, like governments and home-owners do, is not such a big deal over time. Hence, a little bit of inflation does not hurt the economy – it enables debt repayment. And this, as was explained above, is necessary for economies to continue functioning smoothly with their fiat money systems.

How do we calculate inflation? This is the nominal price of a good corrected for the price increase. So, if today you pay Rs 150 for a sari and a year ago you paid Rs 135 for the same sari, the inflation is:

$$\frac{(150-135)}{135} =$$
$$\frac{15}{135} = 0.11$$

We use percentages for inflation, so the result needs to be multiplied by 100 per cent to give the inflation rate:

$$0.11 \times 100\% = 11\%$$

284 *Money*

But how to calculate the inflation rate of not just one item but of, on average, all your expenditures as a consumer? Now, the statistical office in your country is able to help, by providing you with the consumer price index. For every country this concerns the price changes in a basket of standard consumer products. The *consumer price index* (CPI) is a number compared to a base year at which the number is fixed at 100. So, a CPI of 121 means that consumer prices have increased by 21 per cent since the base year. If the base year was last year, this points to a relatively high inflation rate of 21 per cent. But if the base year was 7 years ago, then the accumulated inflation of 21 per cent over 7 years is only 3 per cent on average annually.

With the help of the CPI statistics, it is fairly easy to calculate inflation for any period of time you want: per month, per year, or from February 2012 up to November 2013, for example. Let us do precisely this, with help of the CPI data of India in Diagram 11.3.

In February 2012, the CPI for India was 199 (rounded off), and in November 2013 it had reached 243, the highest since 1960. How much more expensive has life become for the average Indian over this almost 2-year period? Again, we subtract the latter index from the former, divide by the earlier one and multiply by 100 per cent:

$$\frac{(243-199)}{199}$$
$$=\frac{44}{199}$$
$$=0.22 \times 100\% = 22\%$$

The consumer basket from which the CPI is calculated differs from country to country – again an indication that inflation is a social relation. For example, for India, it will include saris and lentil soup and chai and rent, whereas for Russia it will include also rent and chai, but instead of saris and lentil soup most likely winter coats and borsch.

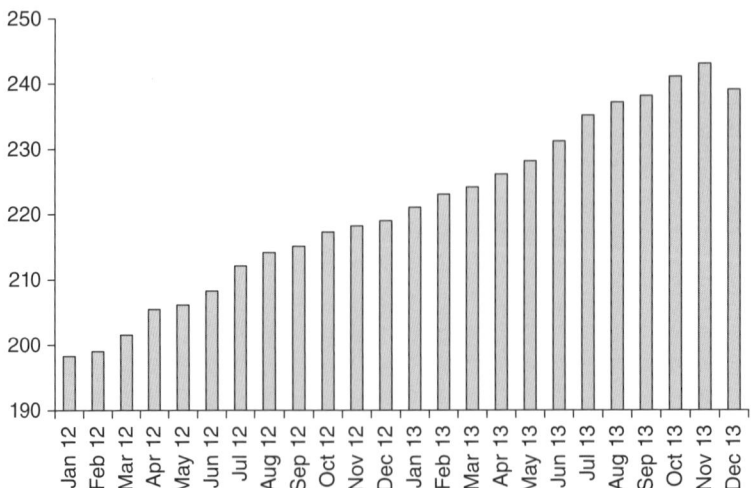

Diagram 11.3 Inflation in India: the consumer price index

Source: http://www.tradingeconomics.com/india/consumer-price-index-cpi

The examples above indicate that inflation makes consumer goods more expensive without providing any quality improvement. They simply become more expensive over time. If your income also increased by the same amount over time, this would not be such a problem. That is why labour unions bargain for inflation compensation in times of relatively high inflation. When they do this consistently and have negotiated a clause about compensation for inflation in wage payments in labour contracts, we refer to this as wage indexation. But, obviously indexation can only be realised under favourable conditions for labour:

- low unemployment, so there is a relative scarcity of labour for firms;
- government backing of labour contracts through tripartite wage bargaining (labour unions, employers' associations, and the government).

If the inflation rate is 8 per cent and your wages are indexed to 5 per cent inflation, what happens to the purchasing power of your wages? In that case, indexation is insufficient. You still suffer from price increases in the goods you buy: 8% − 5% = 3%. But this is a little bit better than for your grandparents whose pensions may not be indexed at all: they experience the full 8 per cent inflation.

11.2 The Central Bank: institutional economics

The institutional economics of money is concerned with the formal and informal institutions in money systems. The previous section, reviewing the social economics perspective of money and prices, described the informal institutions of money by explaining money as a social relation concerning trust and debt. In this section we will therefore only focus on the main formal monetary institution and its role and instruments, which are to some extent institutions of their own: the Central Bank.

11.2.1 The Central Bank's roles and instruments

The Central Bank is an independent government institution which is responsible for the money system. The roles of the Central Bank are diverse and concerned with money, price levels, bank supervision, and the state of the financial sector. Below I list the seven roles of Central Banks, which are to:

- Issue money (the mint role);
- Stabilise the domestic price level (prevent high inflation);
- Stimulate investment (and for some Central Banks, also to stimulate employment);
- Stabilise the currency level (prevent large increases or decreases in the exchange rate);
- Control the commercial banks and other financial institutions (insurance firms, pension funds);
- Regulate the financial sector (rule setting and enforcement);
- Lender of last resort.

Let us go through these roles one-by-one with help of the Indian Central Bank, called the Reserve Bank of India (RBI), which was set up in 1934, before independence. This example allows us to learn about the instruments that Central Banks have to perform their roles. Note that the Indian Central Bank has four local boards, located in Mumbai, Calcutta, Chennai, and New Delhi, which help the national-level bank carry out its functions.

11.2.1.1 Issue money

Fiat money is issued by Central Banks. They control the design, denominations, and minting of money. For India, the Reserve Bank controls the issuing of all rupees and paise (Rs 1 consists of 100 paise). RBI owns two mints which produce notes and coins, one in West Bengal and one in the state of Karnataka. But in 1996 and 1997, production was less than the banks needed for their lending operations, so the RBI had to import foreign-printed bank notes. This may sound strange, but some countries do not have their own mint for the production of their fiat money. They import all their banknotes and coins from a foreign producer.

11.2.1.2 Stabilise the domestic price level

Inflation, as we have seen above, may have benefits for some groups, but has disadvantages for other groups and negative externalities for the economy as a whole. Hence, Central Banks are responsible for preventing high inflation. This raises two questions: When do we consider inflation to be high? And how can inflation be prevented and controlled?

Some countries experience spells of negative inflation rates: deflation. For example, in December 2013, the monthly deflation rate in Greece reached 3 per cent. Many countries have experienced spells of high inflation. Some even more than a 1,000 per cent per year. Very high inflation is called *hyperinflation*. Zimbabwe has experienced hyperinflation since the 1980s. As a reaction to the fast reduction in the value of the Zimbabwean dollar, the Central Bank of Zimbabwe once issued a denomination of 100 trillion Zimbabwean dollars. This was necessary to enable day-to-day monetary exchange when the prices of ordinary goods like food were expressed in millions. And quite recently, in 2007, inflation in Zimbabwe was estimated by the IMF to be 100,000 per cent.

But what about countries which experience annual inflation rates in the range of 5–20 per cent? India's inflation rate over the year 2013 was 9 per cent. But its economic growth was also high, at around 5 per cent. From a development economics perspective, it is generally agreed that inflation rates of 10 or even up to 20 per cent are not harmful for the economy. Instead, moderate inflation rates may support poverty reduction because they help reduce debt burdens and enable investment through relatively cheap credit, which contributes to employment growth. What matters, of course, is that credit is invested in sectors which indeed create jobs and services for the poor, such as agricultural processing, infrastructure, and public service delivery in education and health care.

11.2.1.3 Stimulate investment and thereby employment

The Central Bank can help the government to improve the economy by stimulating investment. The interest rate is the major policy tool: the lower the interest rate at which banks can borrow from the Central Bank, the cheaper the loan, and the more likely firms and households will borrow from banks for investments (and consumption, which also stimulates the economy but in the short run only). This, in turn, will help to create new jobs: employment.

But there is a second policy tool for economic stimulation: open market operations. *Open market operations* refer to the Central Bank's buying and selling of government bonds and bank assets. Central Banks buy government bonds, and thereby provide the government with loans to close a budget deficit. Also, when banks are in trouble and in need of liquidity, Central Banks can buy some of their assets, in particular those assets which private parties in financial markets do not want to buy. This purchase of risky bank assets by a Central Bank provides the banks with money for lending out to households and firms. In the financial year 2012, RBI conducted five open market operations. Together, these operations by the Reserve Bank of India financed 12 per cent of all Indian government bonds for that financial year.

11.2.1.4 Stabilise the currency

Every country in the world needs to exchange its currency for other currencies in order to pay for its imports, to invest abroad, and to keep reserves in the Central Bank. Some currencies are easily convertible on foreign exchange markets (abbreviated to FOREX). The dollar and the euro are examples of fully convertible currencies on FOREX. Other currencies have restrictions on their convertibility set by their Central Banks. The Indian rupee is such a currency with limited convertibility. This means that the outflow of rupees is regulated, to prevent sudden large outflows of rupees from the country for foreign investment instead of domestic investment, or for currency speculation. At the same time, the inflow of foreign currency is restricted. This means that foreign investors require permission before they can invest in India. Restrictions on the inflow and outflow of capital are generally referred to as *capital account controls*.

Next to differences in capital account controls and convertibility, countries can choose between two exchange rate regimes: fixed and flexible. A *fixed exchange rate regime* means that the value of a currency is fixed to that of another currency. For example, Argentina pegged its peso for some time to the US dollar until this was untenable due to strong imbalances in

Image 11.2 Argentinian peso pegged to the dollar

the economy. A fixed exchange rate requires the Central Bank to take a strong role in maintaining the fixed rate in a currency market changing daily. For example, when Argentinian exports increase, foreign traders will increase their demand for pesos in order to be able to pay their Argentinian suppliers. This increased demand for pesos will push up the value of the peso, which is, however, not allowed in a fixed exchange rate system. Hence, the Central Bank of Argentina needs to balance the increased demand for pesos with an equal increase in its supply. It will do this partly by buying foreign currency, for example dollars, and paying in pesos. As long as there are no large changes in imports and exports and in international capital flows to and from a country, this is not a problem for a Central Bank. But as soon as there are sudden imbalances in the economy vis-à-vis other countries, the Central Bank may run out of reserves. In that case, it will no longer be able to keep the fixed exchange rate. This happened in Argentina in December 2001. The Central Bank released the peg to the dollar and the peso's value plunged.

A *flexible exchange rate* regime means that the value of a currency is determined by supply and demand for the currency on the currency market. The advantage for a Central Bank of a flexible exchange rate regime is that it does not require high reserves to support a fixed value. But the disadvantage is that it has little control over the exchange rate. There is only some control over the exchange rate: with its reserves, a Central Bank can buy its currency to support its exchange rate, or sell it to prevent too much increase in its value. For this there are two other terms available: appreciation and depreciation. *Depreciation* is the market-induced decrease in a currency's value, while *appreciation* is the market-induced increase in a currency's value.

India has a partial flexible exchange rate, which fluctuates to some extent. But the RBI intervenes in the rate with its reserves to prevent too much volatility in the value of the rupee. Diagram 11.4 shows the exchange rate of the rupee over a period of 4 years, against the dollar,

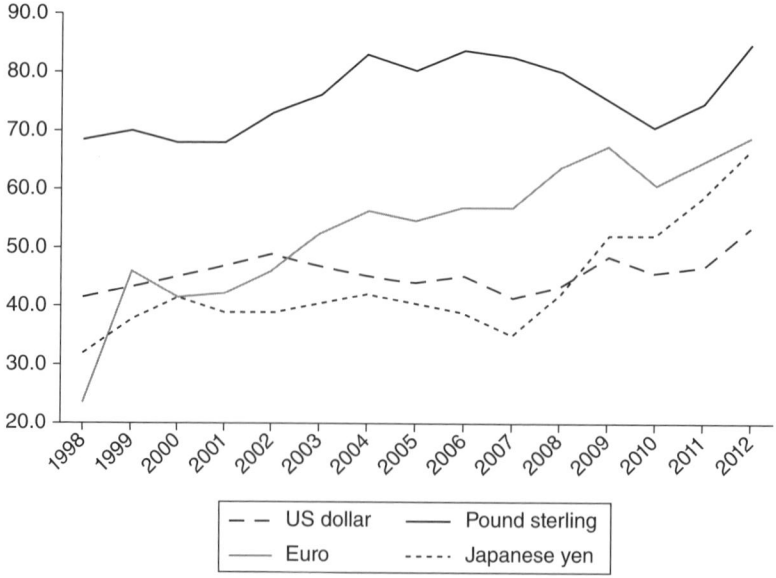

Diagram 11.4 Exchange rate trends of the rupee

Source: Reserve Bank of India.

euro, pound, and yen. The diagram shows that, despite an increase in the value of the rupee at the beginning of the financial crisis in 2007, it has suffered a decline since 1998 against all major currencies. This implies that the rupee has become cheaper over time.

11.2.1.5 Control of financial institutions

All banks, insurance companies, and pension funds are under the oversight of the Central Bank. All banks require a banking licence from the Central Bank. Furthermore, the Central Bank checks the accounts of all banks and other financial institutions. The financial crisis has shown that this oversight role of Central Banks was weak in the USA and Europe. Central Banks were not aware of the high-risk positions their domestic commercial banks had taken in toxic assets consisting of US subprime mortgages, and of the high share of government bonds of countries with very weak economies, such as Greece and Cyprus, but also Portugal and Spain.

Moreover, the Central Banks had long given up control over financial products and bonuses. This had provided commercial banks and investment firms with the room to create and trade in non-transparent high-risk financial products such as derivatives, and to pay their top managers extraordinary bonuses. The 2007 financial crisis has roused Central Banks worldwide to perform their oversight role again as they had done before the liberalisation of the 1980s. The Icelandic internet bank Icesave, which attracted savings abroad through offering above average interest rates, went bankrupt and hundreds of thousands clients in the Netherlands and the UK lost their money. But if the Bank of England and De Nederlandsche Bank had taken their control function more seriously, they would never have allowed Icesave on their markets in the first place. The parent company, Landsbanki, had taken extreme high-risk positions in Iceland, which turned into bankruptcy in 2008. Now, the EMU has agreed upon centralisation of the oversight of all major banks in the eurozone. In addition, the European Central Bank is setting up a reserve fund for failing banks at the European level and a single rule-book with uniform rules for resolution of banking crises in the EMU.

11.2.1.6 Regulation of the financial sector

Another role that was neglected in the three decades before the current financial crisis was regulation. The regulation imposed after the 1929 crisis has been gradually undone since the 1980s under the influence of the widespread belief among Central Bankers, academic economists, and politicians in the efficient market hypothesis (EMH), as was discussed in Chapter 9. Now, regulation of the financial sector has made a new start with the Basel III agreement at the international level and stricter regulation by national Central Banks.

Interestingly, India was hardly affected by the 2007 financial crisis. The major reason for this lies in the strong regulation of banks and other financial institutions in India and its control of international capital flows. The strict regulation involves quite a bit of bureaucracy, but it prevents the build up of huge asset bubbles, and too strong in- and out-flows of foreign capital, and non-transparent derivatives.

11.2.1.7 Lender of last resort

A Central Bank is a lender of last resort. This means that a bank or a government which cannot borrow money anywhere else, can borrow from the Central Bank. If, of course, its means allow this without causing price instability at the domestic price level or in the currency. Banks regularly borrow from the Central Bank, and when there is distrust due to a crisis, banks do not want to lend out to each other anymore, so they all go to the Central Bank to obtain loans, and sometimes also to put money in a savings account in the Central Bank from which they can earn interest. By playing the role of lender of last resort, Central Banks can help stop a bank run and prevent bankruptcies. This provides monetary stability in an economy.

11.3 Endogenous money: Post Keynesian economics

The Post Keynesian perspective follows closely on Keynes' insight that money is not neutral, an insight that is also followed in social economics, as was made clear above. Money matters for the real economy, not only for the monetary economy. We have also seen this in the previous chapter, in the Post Keynesian circular economic flow. This includes the financial sector not as neutral but as having real economic impacts because money enters the economy as debt. But Post Keynesian theory goes further than social economics. With money having real impacts and since money in our modern economies is fiduciary, money has a crucial role in the economy because changes in the stocks of this fiduciary economic means can severely harm investment, employment, consumption, savings, and incomes.

The increase and decrease in money supply in the economy is driven by the amount of credit lent out by the commercial banks. The situation is shown in the money circuit in Diagram 11.5, in which we see that credit is a flow variable and money is a stock variable. You need to read the diagram clockwise and start with the bank providing credit to a firm. With this credit, the firm invests in additional productive capacity, for which it hires additional workers to put the investment to use. Hence, the credit allows more workers to be hired and more wages to be paid out than before. These workers, in turn, will spend most of their wages in buying goods from firms (in this example the same firm, for simplicity), from which the firm will earn money to pay back the loan. The loan given by the bank has increased money supply in the economy. The pay back of the loan has decreased the money supply in the economy. The other transactions in the circuit: investment, wages, and consumption, do not affect money supply (M^s) directly, but they enable the loan to be paid back eventually. The diagram makes it clear that M^s changes not due to any Central Bank activity or Ministry of Finance decision, but through the lending activity by commercial banks.

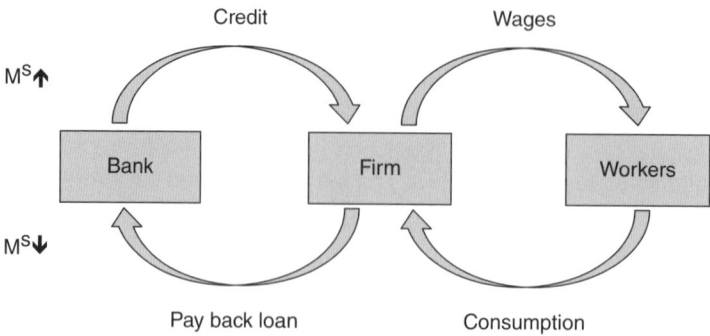

Diagram 11.5 The money circuit

Money   291

The recognition by Post Keynesians that money is endogenous leads to a paradoxical policy position on money. On the one hand, Post Keynesians stress the responsibility of the Central Bank to stabilise prices (domestic price level and exchange rates). On the other hand, they recognise the limited policy space that Central Banks have to ensure such price stability. This paradox will be explained in the three subsections below.

11.3.1 Demand and supply of money

The demand for money in an economy should not be confused with the demand for credit. Credit is used for investment (and sometimes for durable consumer goods). This is a real economy activity, as you will remember from the macroeconomic equation, which includes I, investment. Credit is a flow variable which comes and goes because credit is lent out and paid back. Money is a stock variable, which is an amount available in the economy, which grows or shrinks. Another way to think about credit and money is that money is a monetary variable which enables credit. When an entrepreneur takes a loan from a bank, she will receive money in her bank account, which she can transfer electronically or withdraw in cash to pay for her investment. For this entrepreneur there seems little difference between the credit and the cash. But for the macroeconomic level there is a crucial difference, because the amount of money available in the economy will increase the stock of money, whereas the credit increases aggregate demand and thereby generates economic growth. So, let us not mix up money with credit, or bank account funds with investments enabled with it.

Post Keynesians distinguish three motives behind the demand for money (M^d): (1) the transaction motive, (2) the precautionary motive, and (3) the speculative motive.

11.3.1.1 Transaction motive (M^d_{tr})

Transaction money is the money required for exchange and redistribution in the real economy. This is the demand for money for expected expenditures: to buy goods, to pay bills, to pay taxes, and to pay wages to workers and interest to the providers of capital. It also includes demand by the rest of the world for our money when they import our goods, hence, to pay for our exports. Obviously, we do not want to be paid in foreign currencies because our domestic shops generally do not accept these.

11.3.1.2 Precautionary motive (M^d_{pr})

Precautionary money is the money people like to keep aside, as liquidity. This is the demand for money, which is for unexpected expenditures. During upswings of the economic cycle, there is optimism and people feel less uncertainty, which results in low demand for money for precautionary reasons. Economic agents rather like to ride the wave of investment and income growth by spending rather than hoarding. With more uncertainty, they become more cautious and want to put money aside for a rainy day.

11.3.1.3 Speculative motive (M^d_{sp})

Speculative money is the money people use for both real investments (in production) and monetary investments (in financial assets). This is the demand for money, which seeks profit from asset price differences and increases in asset values. The majority of money demanded

Image 11.3 Financial trading

from the speculative motive is for investments in financial assets and not in the real economy, in particular short-run asset trading.

Diagram 11.6 shows the three motives for the demand for money. The diagram pictures a relationship between the interest rate (on the vertical axis) and the quantity of money available in the economy (on the horizontal axis). Both the demand for transactions and for liquidity (precautionary motive) are vertical lines. This means that economic agents demand money for these two motives irrespective of the interest rate. They simply want an amount of money for precautionary reasons and they require an amount of money to buy goods and services and to pay taxes. Whether the interest rate is high or low, does not matter for these two types of demand for money. But the demand for money from the speculative motive is pictured as a convex curve. It is downward sloping with a steep upward slope at high interest rates. This means that at high interest rates, the demand for speculative money is very low. At the other end of the curve we see a rather flat part. This implies that at low interest rates, there is high demand for money with which to speculate.

The supply of money (we limit ourselves here to fiat money) is the monopoly of the Central Bank, as we have seen above. The money supplied will enter the economy through bank credits and will increase the stock of money (M). The interesting thing about money demand and money supply in Post Keynesian theory is that they do not nicely generate an equilibrium in the money market. That is because the supply of and demand for money are not independent of each other. In Post Keynesian theory, the supply of money is explained as determined by the demand for money. Because money enters the real economy through credit, and banks create this through IOUs, as we have seen in the financial chapter: the demand for credit creates credit, and hence, the money which enables it. And for the cash needed to fill your deposit account – money – the Central Bank simply supplies what the commercial banks need

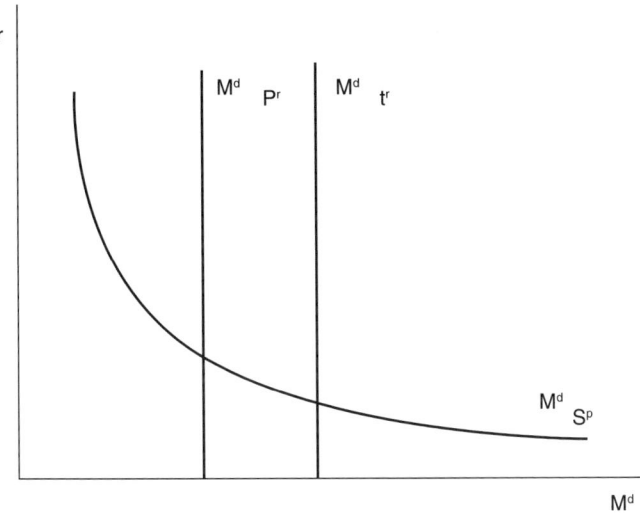

Diagram 11.6 The Post Keynesian demand for money

to transfer. For that supply to run smoothly, there is a gradual increase in money circulating in the economy, partly to supply new money to catch up with economic growth, and partly money replacing old money – torn notes, scratched coins, and money lost in fires or forgotten under an old mattress.

The shape of the money supply is not stable according to the Post Keynesian perspective. When there is high liquidity in the market, with increasing debt driving asset bubbles, money supply is virtually unlimited. Money supply grows at a *conventional interest rate*, which is an interest rate which investors find reasonable given expected inflation and perceived risks. The conventional interest rate will be around the rate set by the Central Bank for bank borrowing, the default rate. But this has a bandwidth, which determines the reasonableness perceived by the investors: the conventional rate. Small changes in this interest rate will not affect the supply of money as long as it moves within the subjective bandwidth. This leads to a horizontal money supply curve (M^s) in the Diagram 11.7, which can move up and down depending on the conventional interest rate, but will remain flat as long as it moves up and down within the bandwidth of reasonableness.

In a financial crisis, liquidity dries up and banks do not like to lend out money anymore. They need to fill the gaps in their reserves and they distrust each other and do not provide credit to each other anymore. They also reduce lending to the public because in a crisis the pay-back capacity of many customers reduces. This leads to an almost vertical money supply curve during a financial crisis, as pictured in Diagram 11.7: the money supply is fixed in response to the transaction motive and precautionary motive of the demand for money, while the demand for money from the speculation motive is close to zero. The money supply curve is almost vertical because whatever the interest rate, the supply remains more or less fixed by the banks. In most cases, however, the money supply curve will lie somewhere in between a horizontal and a vertical line, and may be linear or curved – we simply do not know due to its dependence on money demand and the three different motives behind the demand for money.

294 *Money*

In Diagram 11.7, the horizontal curve represents money supply during a boom in the economy, when there is high liquidity. It therefore is referred to as M^s_{liq}. The vertical curve represents money supply during a downturn, when there is no liquidity anymore, referred to as M^s_{nonliq}.

Now, I have discussed one part of the paradox: the Central Bank cannot determine the supply of money because the commercial banks, through their lending decisions, actually generate the money supply. However, this is not the whole story. Inflation and the need for its control also play their part.

11.3.2 Inflation as cost price increases

In the Post Keynesian perspective, inflation is not caused by too much money supply by the Central Bank. Simply because Central Banks do not have much control over the money supply. Therefore, the interest rate set by the Central Bank is of limited use to influence the money supply: part of the money is demanded and supplied because of the transaction motive and the precautionary motive, which are not dependent on the level of the interest rate. And the rest of the money supply responds to the speculative motive, which only weakly relates to the interest rate because investors do not change their behaviour around the conventional interest rate, as we have just seen above. So, only large changes in the interest rate by the Central Bank will be able to influence money supply, and even then only the speculative part of it. Moreover, when the interest rate is already very low, further declines are impossible, which completes the paralysation of the interest rate as a tool for monetary policy. In 2014, the Central Bank interest rates were around zero in various countries.

In the Post Keynesian perspective, inflation is caused by cost price increases. This is because prices of goods and services consist of costs plus a mark-up for profit, as we have seen in Chapter 4. Two major sources of costs in the prices of goods are labour cost and the costs of resources. Sudden increases in the prices of crucial resources, such as oil, will drive

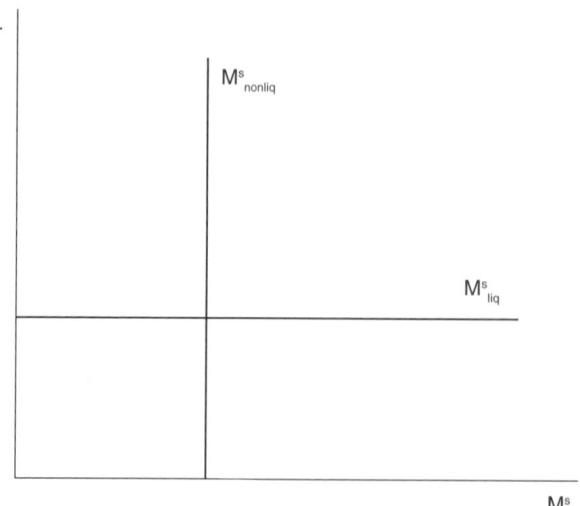

Diagram 11.7 The supply of money during boom and crisis

up the cost price of many products. Wage increases will also drive up the prices of many goods, in particular labour-intensive goods, such as low-tech manufacturing products and all types of services. But this is not always the case.

Higher wages do not necessarily increase the unit cost price of goods, because when labour productivity increases at the same rate as wages, the production cost per unit remains the same. Hence, the cost price will remain unchanged and with a given mark-up the product price will also remain unchanged. Wage increases will only cause inflation when they are higher than the increase in labour productivity. This is shown with the Post Keynesian price equation that we used earlier in Chapter 4. In Post Keynesian economics, a product price consists of a mark-up above the production cost (for simplicity we include only labour costs):

$$p = k'(w/y)$$

in which p is the sales price of a good, k' is the mark-up for profit, w is the money wage rate per unit produced, and y is the output produced per worker (= labour productivity).

If we assume that k' is constant, then the price (p) will increase if the wage rate (w) increases faster than labour productivity (y). For example, if wages increase by 10 per cent and labour productivity increases by only 5 per cent, then the price will have to increase by 10%/5% = 2%. If not, the mark-up will decline and hence, profits will be lower.

We can also write this equation in terms of changes in the variables, using the delta sign we have used before (Δ). This turns the ratio into a difference:

$$\Delta P = \Delta w - \Delta y$$

So, prices will increase in line with the difference between the wage increase and the productivity increase. When the wage rate increases more than labour productivity, prices will increase, because the difference of w − y will be positive. But when the wage rate increases less than productivity, or remains stable, prices will decline, because the difference of w − y will be zero or negative.

Let us run through an example for wage cost inflation. Assume that the large Indian producer of bicycles, Hero Cycles, has managed to increase labour productivity thanks to better training of its workers. But that this induces the labour union to demand higher wages. Early in 2014 they are in the midst of negotiations.

Indeed, Hero Cycles is the largest producer of bikes in India and its market share is 50 per cent. Hero is a strong brand, with 100 million Hero bicycles sold annually in India and an expanding export market.

The Hero Neon boys bicycle sells in 2014 at a price of Rs 3,000 (p = 3,000). The actual average wages of the bicycle factory workers early in 2014 are around Rs 1,636 per day (w = 1,636). The labour productivity can be derived from the new factory in Bihar, which plans to produce 1 million bikes per year with 650 workers. That is 1,538 bikes produced per worker per year. Assuming 240 working days in a year, this results in a labour productivity of 6.4 bikes per worker per day (y = 6.4).

So, we can fill in the price equation:

$$p = k'(w/y)$$

$$3{,}000 = k'\left(\frac{1{,}636}{6.4}\right) = k'(256)$$

Rearranging, this will give k':

$$k' = \frac{3{,}000}{256} = 11.7$$

Hence, the mark-up for every bicycle sold is 11.7 times the labour cost. So, the sales price of Rs 3,000 consists of the following two components: wages and profits (the mark-up):

Wages per bicycle = Rs 256
Profits per bicycle = Rs 3,000 – Rs 256 = Rs 2,744

This amount of profits sounds huge. But remember, for reasons of simplicity we left out the costs of capital to produce the bikes (factory, machines) and resources going into the bikes (steel, rubber, plastic, paint).

Now, if wages increase faster than productivity, the price of the Neon boys bicycle will increase, if k' remains the same to cover capital cost, material cost, and profit. Assume that the foreseen increase in productivity will boost bike production per worker per day from 6.4 to 7. This is 9 per cent so that $\Delta y = 0.09$. The new daily wage rate that the unions manage to negotiate is an increase from Rs 1,636 per day to Rs 2,000. This is a wage rise of 22 per cent so that $\Delta w = 0.22$. This allows us to calculate the price increase for a Neon boys bike:

$$\Delta P = \Delta w - \Delta y$$
$$\Delta P = 0.22 - 0.09 = 0.13$$

Hence, the bicycle price will increase by 13 per cent. This makes the new sales price for the Neon boys bike Rs 3,390. Remember that the inflation rate in India was around 10 per cent in 2013, so a price increase for a bicycle of 13 per cent does not seem extraordinary at all.

When the cause of inflation is cost increases, the solution to inflation should be found in limiting sudden increases in cost prices and preventing wages from growing faster than productivity. Central Banks have two types of Post Keynesian monetary policy: stabilisation and open market operations.

11.3.2.1 Ensuring a stable financial environment

A stable financial environment prevents the money supply curve, through the commercial banks, from moving strongly between the two extreme positions of horizontal (unlimited money supply) and vertical (severely constrained money supply). An important tool for this type of policy is transparency about the Central Bank's views, current behaviour, and future plans. This is done through communications from the Central Bank, often from its president. But it can also use additional instruments, such as strict control of banks and clear and consistent regulation.

11.3.2.2 Open market operations

The second Post Keynesian type of broad monetary policy is within the policy range of the Central Bank. Open market operations (OMO) are the buying and selling of bonds and other assets by the Central Bank, as was explained in section 11.2.1. It may buy directly from the Treasury in the case of newly issued bonds, or it may buy existing bonds from banks. During an economic downturn, when the money supply curve is almost vertical, OMO enables the Central Bank to provide banks with the liquidity they need to provide credit. Moreover, through OMO, the Central Bank can stimulate national development banks to invest in the necessary supply-side economic infrastructure. In fact, OMO can help development banks to invest in public infrastructure such as roads, ports, water and sanitation, education, and business development programs.

11.3.3 Capital flows driving exchange rates

Post Keynesian economics recognises that most of the trade in currencies is not to finance international trade in goods and services but to finance international capital flows. Hence, the value of a currency depends more on capital flows to and from a country than on trade. Currency prices – from rupee to euro and from yen to peso – are largely a consequence of the decisions of international investors, in particular regarding short-term capital flows for speculative purposes. Millions of international speculative actions generate large demand and supply of currencies, which determines the exchange rate of many currencies, from minute to minute.

Capital flows are registered on the capital account of the Balance of Payments. The *Balance of Payments* is the account of a country's transactions with the rest of the world. The *capital account* is that part of the Balance of Payments which registers capital inflows and outflows. When this account is positive, there is a net capital inflow: more capital flows in than out of the country. This implies that there is more demand for a country's currency than supply for it in the capital markets. This net positive demand for a currency will drive up its value: an appreciation of the exchange rate. When the capital account is negative, there is a net capital outflow: more capital leaves the country than enters it. This implies that there is more supply of the currency than demand for it, which pushes down its value: a depreciation of the exchange rate.

International capital flows consist of two parts which are described below.

11.3.3.1 Long-term investments (foreign direct investments)

Foreign direct investments, or FDI in short, is direct investment by firms in productive activities in other countries. Hence, these are investments in the real economy, in the productive capacity of factories, offices, agriculture, or services industries, or in non-profit sectors such as health and education. They include the building of factories, transfer of technology, and investment in machines and ICT, and in health and education. FDI comes in two categories: investments in existing productive capacity, called mergers and acquisitions, and investments in new productive capacity, called greenfield investments. Mergers and acquisitions are joint ventures by two companies, while acquisitions are take-overs. A major Indian firm which has taken over key Western firms, is Tata Steel, which has bought steel factories in the UK,

Belgium, Germany, the Netherlands, and France. This makes Tata the second largest steel company in Europe, superseding two centuries of European dominance in the steel sector on the continent.

11.3.3.2 Short-term investments (portfolio investments)

The large majority of international capital flows consist of *portfolio investments*. These are investments in financial assets and include investments in real estate, banks, insurance companies, and foreign bonds and equity, as well as trade in currencies, securities, and derivatives, and speculation in commodities such as oil and food. Speculation involves large volumes of money traded in the short run, sometimes just for a few minutes. Hence, the absolute amount of money flowing across the globe is enormous. But since most transactions are finalised in a very short time, the net effect of all these flows is much less: it consists of the differences, over a whole year, between all the inflows and all the outflows of speculative capital for each country.

What matters for the capital account is the net flows. But what matters for currency values, and hence, their exchange rates, are the flows themselves, which can suddenly push exchange rates up or down, due to the buying or selling of large volumes of financial assets, in order to try to gain from a small price difference over time or vis-à-vis a market elsewhere around the globe.

It is the animal spirit of speculators, as Keynes described it, which is responsible for price formation in capital markets, which is equally the case at the international level, and hence, influences exchange rates. This explains the last part of the paradox of Central Bank policy. When the exchange rate is moved by large capital flows in and out of the country, the Central Bank's reserves (own currency, foreign currencies, and gold) are often not large enough to compensate for pressures on the currency.

Box 11.2 The power of currency speculation

In the UK, 16 September 1992 has become known as Black Wednesday. It was the day on which the Hungarian-American private equity investor, George Soros, cashed in on a speculation against the British pound sterling with a US$10 billion bet. The pound was overvalued vis-à-vis other currencies and Soros expected a further decline in its value. By going short against the pound, which means borrowing a large amount and selling it again, while actually buying the amount after some time when the value has collapsed, he actually created a self-fulfilling prophesy: his large amount of pounds sold (before actually buying them) brought the value of the pound down further. This forced the Bank of England to support the value of the falling pound with its reserves after a crash on Black Wednesday. Soros was successful and earned almost US$1 billion with his speculative act.

Source: Briody, D. (2003) *The Iron Triangle: Inside the Secret World of the Carlyle Group*. Hoboken: John Wiley & Sons.

What policy option is left for the Central Bank vis-à-vis such large capital flows destabilising the exchange rate? The Post Keynesian policy prescription is simple, relatively effective, but constraining for international investors: capital account controls. *Capital account controls* are restrictions on the inflow and/or the outflow of capital, as I have explained already in section 11.2.1. Such restrictions imply time costs and money costs, which thereby significantly reduce the flow of speculative capital. So, a small tax or waiting time before invested capital may be repatriated will discourage the most risk-seeking and fast moving capital flows.

India is among the few countries in the world which has capital account controls. This policy helped India to insulate itself from the 1997 Asian financial crisis, when all the other countries in the region, except China, did not have capital account controls and suffered sudden large outflows of capital. The large capital outflows in the other South Asian countries generated a cascade of bank and firm bankruptcies in 1997, declines in GDP of up to 10 per cent or more, crashes on the local stock exchanges, and reductions in exchange rates of 50 per cent or more. India's capital account controls protected the country from this fate. The Indian capital account controls consist of various quantitative restrictions, which are implemented by the RBI:[4]

- limits on cash and transfers made by individuals in India to other countries;
- limits on foreign direct investments by Indian firms;
- limits on the size of foreign direct investment and portfolio equity investment by foreigners in Indian firms;
- limits on the size of loans taken out by Indian firms in other countries and a minimum term of 3 years per loan;
- limits on foreign investments in Indian government and private sector bonds;
- limits on currency speculation in India (but leading to offshore currency speculation in rupees).

In conclusion, Post Keynesian theory regards price instability as a real threat which can never be controlled fully, but which can be addressed to some extent by a wide range of monetary and complementary policies.

11.4 Money as neutral: neoclassical economics

In the neoclassical perspective, money is neutral. This means that the role of money in the economy is as a lubricant, enabling economic transactions but not affecting the real economy. The effects of money remain limited to the monetary economy, having effects only on price levels and price changes. Of course, neoclassical economists agree that money enters the real economy and performs its functions there. And they agree with the three other schools of thought, that money enters the real economy through bank credits. The major difference with the other theories is that neoclassical economists see a key role for the Central Bank in determining the money supply. Money supply and demand are independent of each other in the neoclassical view, with money supply controlled completely by the Central Bank.

11.4.1 Monetarism

The neoclassical theory of money and inflation is called monetarism. *Monetarism* is the theory which claims that money is neutral so that a change in the money supply by the Central Bank will only change the price level in the economy and not have any real effects.

300 *Money*

The monetary equation explains price changes from changes in the money supply, which do not match changes in economic growth. So, inflation is zero as long as the money supply grows at the same pace as GDP. But as soon as the money supply grows faster than the paid economy, there will be inflation. For deflation it is the reverse. In that case, the money supply grows more slowly than the growth of the paid economy. The monetary equation is shown below:

$$\Delta p = \Delta m - \Delta y$$

in which p = the price level, m = the money supply, and y = economic growth. It clearly shows that the change in the price level (p) is a result of a difference in the change in the money supply (m) and the change in economic growth (y). There is no inflation or deflation when money supply nicely follows economic growth.

The policy implication of monetarism is that inflation will be kept low when the money supply does not or hardly exceeds economic growth. But how to control the money supply in neoclassical economics? In the neoclassical perspective, this is done by the Central Bank. It fixes the money supply at a desired level. Hence, the money supply curve is vertical. Hence, the Central Bank needs to have quite a good estimation of the level of economic growth in any given year. That is one of the reasons why prediction is deemed so important in neoclassical economics.

The neoclassical money market consists of a declining demand for money, as is the case in the Post Keynesian perspective when the demand for money is dominated by the speculation motive. Diagram 11.8 of the neoclassical money market with the interest rate on the vertical axis and money on the horizontal axis, shows the equilibrium i* at the point where the declining demand function intersects the vertical supply function.

There is equilibrium in the money market when the demand for money equals money supply. Since the money supply curve is vertical, equilibrium necessarily occurs exactly at the

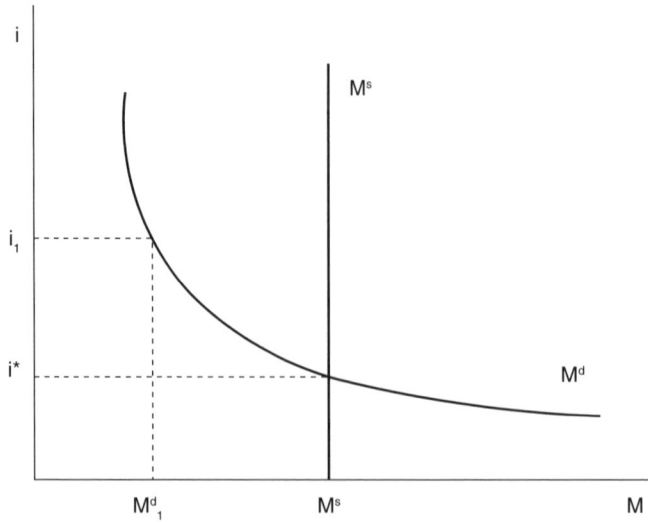

Diagram 11.8 The neoclassical money market

level of money supplied by the Central Bank. Depending on the level of inflation, the Central Bank can shift its money supply curve to the left (less money supply, pushing the price level (p) down) or to the right (more money supply, pushing the price level (p) up).

If the market interest rate lies above i*, the equilibrium rate, there is excess money supply, and hence, inflation. For example, at i_1, the size of the excess money supply is $M^s - M^d_1$. How will the money market tend to equilibrium? This will be driven by a decline in the interest rate, which is a policy variable of the Central Bank. So, the Central Bank will lower the default interest rate to the point where demand for money will expand up to the size of the money supply (M^s). This decline in the default interest rate, passed on by banks through their lending rates, will make credit cheaper for households and firms. At the same time, a lower interest rate will induce households and firms to reduce their savings, because the returns on these decline. Instead, they will invest in government bonds, which are regarded as just as low risk as savings accounts. When the market interest rate is low, the value of bonds tends to increase: economic agents will transfer money from savings to bonds. This satisfies the speculation motive of money demand, which in the neoclassical perspective is the dominant motive for the demand for money. The higher demand for bonds will increase the demand for money: households and firms will use savings and may even borrow, to invest in bonds. This represents a move along the money demand curve to the right: towards lower interest rates (i) and an expansion of the demand for money (M^d). Until the demand for money hits the supply curve and the money market settles in equilibrium (M^s).

A similar dynamic occurs in the case of an excess demand for money, which takes place on the demand curve to the right of the money supply curve. Now, try yourself to reason what the dynamics in that case will be: the Central Bank will . . . households and firms will therefore . . . and this will represent a move along the demand curve to. . . .

Why do bond prices move in the opposite direction to the interest rate? That is a good question. Remember why we have bonds in the first place. Government bonds represent government debt, which is sold for fixed terms and issued at fixed interest rates. So, when the government sold government paper, a bond, 5 years ago at a higher interest rate than the market rate is today, many economic agents like to own such a bond to reap the higher fixed interest rate. They therefore express an increased demand for bonds on the (second-hand) bond market. This increase in demand for bonds will drive up bond prices: you have to pay more for obtaining a bond than the original buyer had to pay for it 5 years ago. But today, economic agents are willing to do this, because the alternative (opportunity costs!) is to keep money in a savings account where it earns low interest. . . . of course, the additional demand for bonds will end when the price for bonds, their value, becomes so high that the accumulated future higher interest rates to be earned on a bond equal the cost price of the bond.

This leads us to a final neoclassical concept related to money and bonds: the crowding out effect of government borrowing. The government is a large economic agent, and the budget deficit is large compared to the budget deficits of households or the credit needs of firms. *Crowding out* is the absorption of available credit in the market by the government, at the cost of credit available for households and firms. Moreover, such a large borrower as the government can drive up interest rates with its high demand for credit. Bonds are almost always in high demand because they are considered low risk investments: countries are not supposed to go bankrupt. So, the more banks, firms, and households buy government bonds, the less money is invested in the private sector of the real economy through bank credit and other loans, to boost investment (I) and consumption (C). Going back to the macroeconomic equation, crowding out may help to increase government expenditures (G) but it may at the same time constrain C and I. . . .

Whereas in the Post Keynesian perspective, government borrowing may stimulate the economy through an expansion of G, government borrowing in the neoclassical perspective may see this increase in G being compensated for by a brake on the growth of C and I through the crowding out effect. This can only be solved when there are international capital flows, providing foreign buyers of bonds and foreign suppliers of investment.

11.4.2 Free capital flows

Neoclassical economics regards markets as relatively perfect, with prices as the adjusting mechanism, also at the international level. This is also the case for international capital flows. In fact, neoclassical economics studies international capital flows as if there is a single world market for finance, which is, indeed increasingly the case in the current era of financial globalisation. Money moves within seconds across the globe, representing supply and demand in one global financial market.

The exchange rate is determined, in the neoclassical perspective, primarily by the trade in goods and services, and to a lesser extent by capital flows. Net exports (EX − IM > 0) increase demand for our currency, and the exchange rate will appreciate. Net imports (Ex − IM < 0) decrease the demand for our currency, and the exchange rate will depreciate. Capital flows are regarded as a consequence of trade imbalances in neoclassical economics. If exports and imports do not balance, but there are net exports or net imports on the current account, the difference will be either compensated for by an adjustment of reserves or an adjustment of the flows on the capital account of the Balance of Payments.

For example, India has had for many years a trade deficit with the rest of the world (RoW). Major exports are textiles and major imports are energy, but the value of imports is higher than the value of exports. Hence, for India's trade with the RoW: IM > EX, which is a trade deficit. Let us assume that the size of India's trade deficit in a particular year is US$10 billion. Here are the two ways to finance this in the neoclassical perspective.

11.4.2.1 Adjustment of reserves

In order to finance the higher imports, India needs to have more foreign currencies than it earns with its imports. So, there is a gap. For this reason, Central Banks keep reserves of foreign currency. So, the Reserve Bank of India (RBI) will sell dollars from its reserves so that importers can buy these with their rupees to finance imports from the USA and other countries. The disadvantage of this policy is that the reserves of the Central Bank will reduce and may eventually be depleted if the deficit on the current account persists.

11.4.2.2 Capital inflows

In order to finance the deficit on the current account (more imports than exports), India can attract foreign capital to generate an equally large surplus on its capital account. This capital inflow will provide the foreign currency needed to pay for the net imports. So, India needs to find buyers for its financial assets: bonds, real estate, and securities, but it could also look for investors for the real economy through FDI. We already saw that India has a set of capital account controls which limit such capital inflows. So, here the disadvantage is that the capital account controls reduce the flexibility of the capital account as an equilibrating mechanism for imbalances on the current account.

Now, what if the two tools to finance a trade deficit on the current account of the Balance of Payment are insufficient to finance a trade deficit? Then there is always an emergency tool available, namely, a currency depreciation or devaluation. In that case, the Central Bank stops selling reserves and allows the exchange rate to adjust downwards due to lower demand for rupees than supply of rupees (depreciation), or the Central Bank announces a new fixed exchange rate which is lower than the previous one (devaluation), to the level at which there will be more exports and less imports.

The Balance of Payment is always in equilibrium, if not through trade, then through the capital account or changes in the reserves, and if that does not help, then through an adjustment of the exchange rate. In the neoclassical perspective, hence, trade is the driving force of (dis)equilibrium, the rest only follows to balance this. Balance of Payment equilibrium is when the total balance value is zero. This can be shown in an equation:

$$BoP = current\ account + capital\ account + reserve = 0$$

If this does not add up to zero, then an adjustment in the exchange rate becomes inevitable: if foreign sellers of goods do not get paid in their currency and investors of their country are not interested in owning assets in your country, and your Central Bank has run out of reserves, there is no other option but to make your currency cheaper so that your consumers buy fewer goods abroad and foreigners want to buy more goods in your country.

The problems in the real world are that such adjustments do not happen smoothly and that they require real economy adjustments, affecting economic growth, employment, and the relative incomes of labour and capital. The major problem lies in the capital account, where adjustments not only react to imbalances of the current account (that is, in exports and imports of goods), but also to returns on investments from capital invested abroad, determined by foreign interest rates and perceived risk. High interest rates and perceived low risk may attract large inflows of capital. These then cause imbalances of their own if changes in the interest rate do not help to bring the in-and-out flows of capital into equilibrium with the current account.

An illustration of such a mismatch of capital flows with the interest rate was shown right after the Asian financial crisis of 1997. The countries affected needed Balance of Payment support from the IMF because the crisis had resulted in a large net capital outflow. Foreign investors were withdrawing their capital from Asia because they had lost their trust in these economies: the bubble burst. The IMF was willing to provide financial support to the affected governments, under the condition that these governments' Central Banks increased the default interest rate substantially. The Central Banks of these countries did so – they had no other option. The neoclassical assumption of the IMF economists was that a significant increase in the interest rates in the affected counties would attract foreign investors again, and soon revert the outflows to inflows. But that did not happen. Even though the interest rates were increased by up to 10–15 per cent, Western capital did not return. Why not?

Because the perceived risk was too high in the eyes of Western investors. They had lost considerable amounts of money in Asia. Now, they would rather invest in their home countries, or Latin America and Africa, against lower interest rates, than risk their money again in Asia.

The experience of the Asian financial crisis showed that the neoclassical view of price adjustment is too optimistic for international capital markets. Whatever the interest rate, foreign investors do not want to invest in countries they consider unstable. And the high-interest policy came at high cost as well: it meant debt holders were unable to pay off their debts at such high interest rates. As a consequence, many banks and businesses went bankrupt – not because of the crisis but because of the post-crisis policy. Joseph Stiglitz, Nobel Prize winner in 2001 and chief economist of the World Bank during the Asian crisis, was forced to collaborate with the IMF to help solve the crisis. He disagreed strongly with the IMF policy requirement but could not change the minds of the IMF economists. Stiglitz resigned and wrote a book about his experiences.[5]

11.5 Interesting sources

Skidelsky, R. and E. Skidelsky (2012) *How Much is Enough? Money and the Good Life*. New York: Other Press.
Stiglitz, J. (2002) *Globalization and its Discontents*. New York: Norton.

11.6 Glossary

Appreciation   The market-induced increase in a currency's value

Balance of Payments (BoP)   The account of a country's transactions with the rest of the world

Capital account   Part of the Balance of Payments which registers capital inflows and outflows

Capital account controls   Restrictions on the inflow and outflow of capital

Consumer price index (CPI)   Index number of the average price level of a basket of standard consumer products, relative to a base year with value 100

Conventional interest rate   An interest rate which investors find reasonable given expected inflation and perceived risks

Crowding out   The absorption of available credit in the market by the government, at the cost of credit available for households and firms

Currency devaluation   A value reduction in one's currency vis-à-vis foreign currencies

Currency revaluation   A value increase in one's currency vis-à-vis foreign currencies

Deflation   A general decrease in absolute prices

Depreciation   The market-induced decrease in a currency's value

Fiat money = fiduciary money   Authorised and monitored by the state

Fixed exchange rate regime   When the value of a currency is fixed to that of another currency

Flexible exchange rate regime   When the value of a currency is determined by supply and demand for the currency in the currency market

Foreign direct investment (FDI)   Direct investment by firms in productive activities in other countries

Gold standard   Money system in which all money is backed by gold

Hyperinflation   Very high inflation rates

Inflation   A general increase in absolute prices

Liquid money   Immediately accessible forms of money

Monetarism   The theory which claims that money is neutral so that a change in the money supply will only change the price level in the economy and not have any real effects

Monetary institutions   Organisations, regulations, and social norms, which together guarantee the functioning of a monetary system

Money   Anything that allows its holder to purchase goods

Open market operations (OMO)   Central Bank buying and selling of government bonds and bank assets

Portfolio investments   Investments in financial funds and assets

Wage indexation   Automatic compensation of wages with the inflation rate

Notes

1. In 1997, I was one of the economists, still a PhD student, in the Netherlands who signed a petition against the introduction of the euro under the weak conditions that were then proposed, and later agreed. For those who read Dutch: http://www.volkskrant.nl/vk/nl/2680/Economie/archief/article/detail/486508/1997/02/13/Met-deze-EMU-kiest-Europa-verkeerde-weg.dhtml
2. For more information on this case as well as on community currencies more generally, visit the website of Bernard Lietaer: http://www.lietaer.com/2010/09/the-story-of-curitiba-in-brazil/
3. For the website with the moment-to-moment exchange rate of the bitcoin, see http://preev.com/btc/eur
4. For details, see http://www.nber.org/chapters/c0162.pdf
5. Stiglitz, J. (2002) *Globalization and its Discontents*. New York: Norton.

12 Economic growth

12.1 Introduction

12.1.1 Do we need growth?

Economic growth is a major macroeconomic concern for both economists and policy makers. *Economic growth* is defined as the increase in gross domestic product (GDP). Negative growth is a decline in GDP. There are three main reasons why economic growth is considered to be so important: (1) population growth, (2) distributional conflict, and (3) poverty.

12.1.1.1 Population growth

The first reason is population growth: with a growing population, zero economic growth would imply a reduction in well-being per capita (we use the Latin word *capita* for head when we refer to growth per inhabitant). In other words, economic growth should be at least as high as population growth in order for there not to be individual declines in economic development. In particular for developing countries, this is an important reason for economic growth because many developing countries experience high fertility rates. In contrast, some European countries experience the problem of an ageing population. This creates a high *dependency ratio*, which is the ratio of people outside the labour force, over the working population who earn the income to provide for both groups:

$$\text{Dependency ratio} = \frac{(\text{population} < 15 \text{ years}) + (\text{population} > 64 \text{ years})}{\text{population } 15-64 \text{ years}}$$

An increasing share of elderly people in the population and a low birth rate imply that a shrinking working population needs to earn the income and provide the unpaid care for an increasing elderly population. For such countries, economic growth helps to overcome the problem, because economic growth ensures increasing incomes, which are necessary when the share of the population earning incomes declines. So the paradox is that both for countries with high population growth and for countries with zero population growth, economic growth is a solution for their demographic problems. It prevents declining per capita incomes in the case of high population growth and it expands the sum of income available for redistribution to an increasing number of non-earning elderly people.

Diagram 12.1 shows the dependency ratios of selected countries. The dependency ratio varies from just below 20 per cent to a bit over 100 per cent. The higher the ratio, the higher the burden on the working age population to provide for the livelihoods of the children and/or

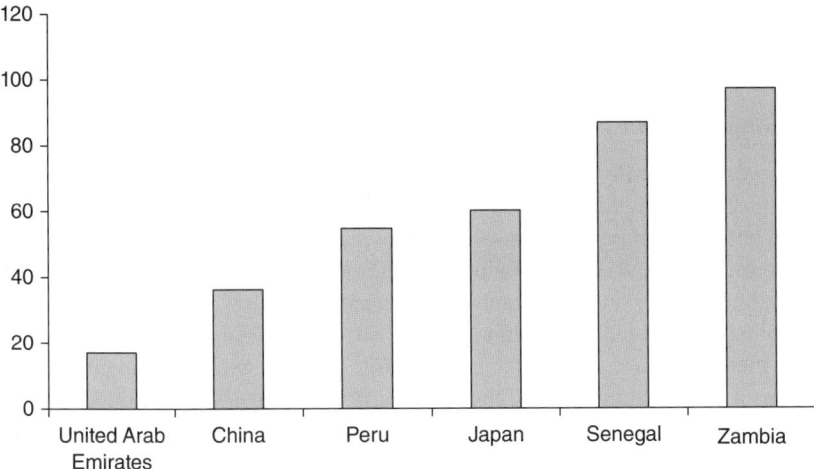

Diagram 12.1 Dependency ratios (%) for selected countries, 2012
Source: Compiled by the author from Databank, World Bank.

the elderly. The dependency ratios are very low for countries with large labour forces, such as the United Arab Emirates (17 per cent) (migrant labour) and China (36 per cent) (population growth in the past combined with low birth rates for a generation). And they are very high for many sub-Saharan African countries, such as Senegal (87 per cent) and Zambia (97 per cent), due to high birth rates and low life expectancy (often well below 64 years).

12.1.1.2 Distributional conflict

The second reason why economic growth is helpful is that it reduces potential conflict over the distribution of economic benefits and gives individuals a sense of progression, even if they do not improve their position relative to others. If social policy improves the position of a disadvantaged group, economic growth provides the possibility to finance this from an expansion of output. This reduces potential conflict as compared to the situation of redistribution from a fixed amount of output away from other groups. Moreover, individuals and families like to see progress in their economic position over time as a reward for their investment in schooling, work experience, and increased labour productivity. If they do not manage to improve their relative position vis-à-vis others, economic growth can at least provide them with progress in their own position over time.

12.1.1.3 Poverty

The third justification for the widespread concern among economists and policy makers with economic growth is the fact that many people in the world live in poverty – about 1 billion people. An increase in GDP and particularly in GDP per capita (so, higher GDP growth than population growth) provides the resources for more jobs and income for the poor and more public good provisioning in social sectors by the state. Obviously, poverty reduction also depends on how growth is distributed over the population. Several countries, such as Pakistan

308 *Economic growth*

and Ethiopia, have seen good growth rates over a decade or more, but slow improvements in poverty reduction and human development. Growth is clearly not sufficient for poverty reduction. I will examine this subject in greater depth in the final chapter of the book.

12.1.2 Measuring economic growth

Economic growth is generally used as the only measure to assess the improvement in well-being in a country. Not CO_2 emissions, not mortality rates, and not survey results concerning feeling happy, but the increase in the gross domestic product is generally considered to be the key variable to measure how our well-being increases or decreases. GDP is a statistical name for what we defined earlier, in the chapter on macroeconomic flow, as Y: total output, which in turn is equalled by total income in an economy. So, GDP = Y = all paid production transacted through markets, hence, all income earned. Note that this excludes unpaid services and nature. GDP, as a statistical measure of the well-being of nations, was introduced in 1934 by the Russian-American economist Simon Kuznets to the US Congress. It has since been used throughout the world and was codified in the unified System of National Accounts agreed upon by the United Nations. This allows cross-country comparison of GDP levels as well as GDP growth rates. But GDP is a narrow measure of well-being. Other measures of well-being will be introduced and discussed in the chapters on nature and on poverty. Here, we will limit ourselves to GDP as the dominant measure of economic growth.

There are two widely used GDP growth measures. Both can be positive (growth) or negative (economic decline) and both can be measured for a year, a quarter, or a multi-year period. First, the GDP growth rate. This is measured as the percentage growth in GDP of a country: $(GDP_{year1} - GDP_{year0}) / GDP_{year0}$. Or in economic symbols, with Y for GDP and t for time period: $(Y_{t1} - Y_{t0}) / Y_{t0}$. The resulting percentage shows the increase (or decrease) in the size of a country's paid economy. For example, the first column in Table 12.1 shows the annual growth rates for China for every 10 years in the period 1961–2010.

Second, the GDP per capita growth rate. This is the GDP growth minus the population growth rate. The second column of Table 12.1 gives the population growth rates for China. The third column shows GDP per capita growth rates, which is the difference between the first and the second columns. When you check this, be aware that the statistics are not fully reliable, in particularly not for the earlier years. This leads to the following equation for per capita growth:

GDP per capita growth = GDP growth – population growth

For example, in the year 2000: GDP per capita growth = 8.4 – 0.8 = 7.6%.

Table 12.1 Annual economic growth rates in China (%), selected years

Year	GDP growth	Population growth	GDP per capita growth
1961	−27.1	−1.0	−26.4
1970	19.4	2.7	16.2
1980	7.8	1.3	6.5
1990	3.8	1.5	2.3
2000	8.4	0.8	7.6
2010	10.4	0.5	9.9

Source: Compiled by the author from the World Bank DataBank.

12.1.3 The determinants of economic growth

What causes growth? In other words, what are the determinants of growth? All theories agree that these are the production factors in an economy. This is explained in the growth equation. The *growth equation* explains the determinants of economic growth. Growth is referred to as GDP growth, as ΔY, or simply as g.

Economic growth is determined by an increase in size and/or efficiency of the use of production factors in an economy. These fall into three categories: capital including land (K), labour (L), and other (X). Each theory has a different interpretation of X, the other variables behind economic growth. Mathematically, the growth equation can be written as follows:

$$(Y_{t1} - Y_{t0})/Y_{t0} = \Delta Y = g = f(K, L, X)$$

The rest of this chapter will explain how each economic theory interprets this equation.

12.2 Social economics of growth

12.2.1 Why quality and values matter

Economic growth has never had much importance in social economics. There are three reasons for this. First, in social economics the quality of growth matters more than its quantity. Growth of what? Growth for whom? Second, social economists strongly disagree with the dominant measure of growth as GDP and its variations. They acknowledge the importance of the community economy, or unpaid economy, which is excluded from this measure, and they emphasise that the substantial size of the community economy shows how biased GDP is. And negative externalities, both social and environmental, need to be subtracted from GDP in order to come up with a more reliable measure of well-being based on market transactions. Third, social economists see the efficiency of resource use, enabling growth, as inextricably related to the equity of resource use, the access to resources for all groups in an economy.

Despite this criticism, there are social economists who analyse growth. They do so from a broad perspective. In particular, including social relationships and ethical values. They point at social values which could be conducive to growth, often referred to as *social cohesion*. This is the connectedness in a society, which is valuable in itself and helps to overcome economic problems of transaction costs, free riding, and moral hazard. These pro-social values also enable collective action and the provisioning of club goods in communities.

Measuring social cohesion, however, is recognised as being very difficult. Social economists agree that uni-dimensional measures, such as a survey question asking whether people in general trust other people, are inadequate. This is because they do not capture the complexity of social connectedness necessary for civic engagement and for the emergence, spread, and continuation of pro-social norms throughout an economy. The perfect measure for social cohesion does not exist, because social cohesion is a contextual matter, and its meaning varies with culture, time periods, and types of economies. An example of two measures that try to capture at least part of social cohesion can be found in the Indices of Social Development database.[1] This database contains a set of six indices, each consisting of about twenty indicators which try to capture social inclusion and social cohesion in societies.

12.2.2 Inclusive growth

The social economic view of growth is *inclusive growth*. This can be defined as economic growth of which the benefits extend to all social groups. Hence, it concerns the social quality of growth. Inclusive growth may also include a concern with the natural environment, trying to do justice to the intrinsic values of nature. Chinese economic growth is currently making a major shift towards environmentally inclusive growth in response to the large negative externalities of economic activity on nature.[2] Air pollution is so severe that it causes 100,000 deaths each year, while the Yellow River is severely polluted over one third of its length, leading to dying fish and human health problems. Now, regulation for polluting industries has become stricter, while China has quickly turned into the world's largest producer of solar energy panels.

The reasoning behind inclusive growth is both social and economic. The social justification for inclusive growth is founded upon a human rights perspective, as part of the UN social and economic rights, namely that human dignity requires that everyone benefits from the well-being effects of economic growth.

Box 12.1 UN Economic, Social and Cultural Rights: a selection

Article 1

1. All peoples have the right of self-determination. By virtue of that right they freely determine their political status and freely pursue their economic, social and cultural development.
2. All peoples may, for their own ends, freely dispose of their natural wealth and resources without prejudice to any obligations arising out of international economic co-operation, based upon the principle of mutual benefit, and international law. In no case may a people be deprived of its own means of subsistence.

Article 2

1. Each State Party to the present Covenant undertakes to take steps, individually and through international assistance and co-operation, especially economic and technical, to the maximum of its available resources, with a view to achieving progressively the full realization of the rights recognized in the present Covenant by all appropriate means, including particularly the adoption of legislative measures.
2. The States Parties to the present Covenant undertake to guarantee that the rights enunciated in the present Covenant will be exercised without discrimination of any kind as to race, colour, sex, language, religion, political or other opinion, national or social origin, property, birth or other status.

Article 7

The States Parties to the present Covenant recognize the right of everyone to the enjoyment of just and favourable conditions of work which ensure, in particular:

(a) Remuneration which provides all workers, as a minimum, with:
  (i) fair wages and equal remuneration for work of equal value without distinction of any kind, in particular women being guaranteed conditions of work not inferior to those enjoyed by men, with equal pay for equal work;
  (ii) a decent living for themselves and their families in accordance with the provisions of the present Covenant.

Article 11

1 The States Parties to the present Covenant recognize the right of everyone to an adequate standard of living for himself and his family, including adequate food, clothing and housing, and to the continuous improvement of living conditions. The States Parties will take appropriate steps to ensure the realization of this right, recognizing to this effect the essential importance of international co-operation based on free consent.

Source: Excerpts from the United Nations International Covenant on Economic, Social and Cultural Rights (entry into force: 3 January 1976): http://www.ohchr.org/EN/ProfessionalInterest/Pages/CESCR.aspx

The economic justification for inclusive growth is twofold. The first reason is that social conflict undermines social cohesion, creating distrust and lack of cooperation. This often reflects unequal distributions of growth, with an elite benefitting from growth while the majority of the population benefits much less or not at all. Social conflict creates social cost, such as strikes and shirking, which in turns reduce growth. The second reason for aiming at inclusive growth is that equality in access to and control over resources improves capacity utilisation in the economy. More labour employed, more wasteland used, and more human capital used in paid and unpaid productive activities, results in less waste and more resource use. For human resources, the minimisation of waste also implies that labour needs to be valued and paid according to its contribution, in order to support both intrinsic and extrinsic motivation. So, when the poor and the socially marginalised, such as ethnic minorities, women, and immigrants, are given access to resources, and control over these resources, and their contributions are valued and paid accordingly, growth will be enhanced according to social economic theory. Inclusion crowds-in production and productivity.

Let me elaborate on these two dimensions of inclusive growth. First, the social conflict dimension, which undermines social cohesion. When growth is accompanied by rising inequalities, or when growth does not remove existing inequalities, it is likely that social conflict will emerge. For example when vertical inequalities between capital and labour increase. In China, growth is distributed increasingly unequally between capital and labour. Diagram 12.2 shows the steady decline in the labour share of income between 1992 and 2008 in China, and hence, the increase in the capital share of income. The labour share of income declines in this period of high economic growth from 64 per cent to 47 per cent of total income. Although China is still a communist nation, from 2005 onwards, capitalists have benefited more from China's economic growth than labourers. The question is how long this trend can continue without affecting growth itself.

312 *Economic growth*

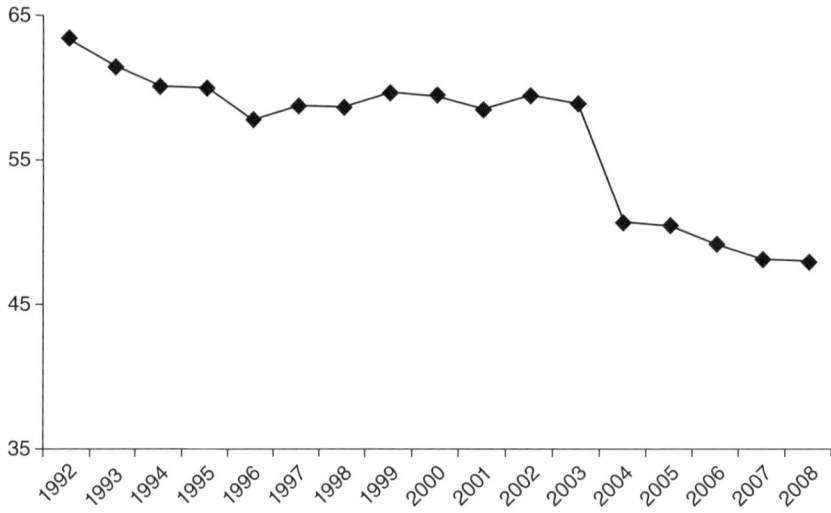

Diagram 12.2 Unadjusted labour share (%) in China, 1992–2008

Notes: The unadjusted wage share is calculated as the total labour compensation of employees divided by value added. The sudden change between 2003 and 2004 likely reflects an adjustment to data; nonetheless, it does not change the direction of the trend.

Source: ILO (2013) 'Global Wage Report 2012/13: Wages and Equitable Growth'. Geneva: International Labour Office.

The declining labour share of income has led to an increase in social unrest in China, in particular labour protest and strikes. Since 2010, China has experienced an increasing number of strikes, from Honda and IBM factories to domestic employers. The labour protests concern not only higher wages but also social and political rights. The strikes involve opportunity costs for the affected firms (they cannot produce output) and regularly push labour costs up in an *ad hoc* way (sudden increases in wages and benefits as a response), affecting China's international position as a low-labour cost manufacturer. This social unrest may affect China's export growth, which forms an important part of its GDP growth.

The second economic dimension of inclusive growth, the equal access to resources dimension, involves both vertical inequality, between classes, and horizontal inequality, across society, such as along the lines of age and gender. Let me give an example for each. First, inequality in access to land, a vertical inequality between the landowning class and the landless class. Empirical studies in South Africa and Brazil, two countries with very unequal land ownership, have shown that much land owned by big landowners is not used. It simply confers status on its owners and provides political power. As soon as this land is redistributed to poor landless farmers, it will be used for the production of food crops (to feed the families who work the land) and cash crops (to sell and earn an income). This increases total production and contributes to economic growth. Moreover, the land that is being used by the big landowners is often worked with relatively more machines than labour power. The reason is not that farm labour is too expensive but that agricultural capital goods are too cheap, thanks to the lobbying activities of the big landowners. They manage, through their political power, to obtain capital subsidies and tax breaks for acquiring machines. So, they over-invest in capital goods and replace labour more than they would have done without their powerful position of large landownership and strong policy influence.[3] Hence, biased agricultural subsidies

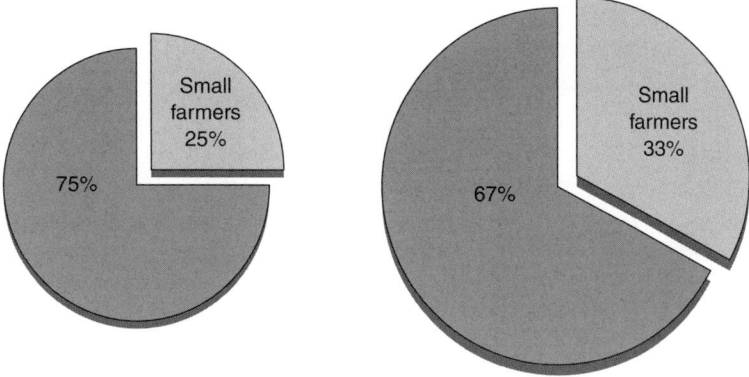

Diagram 12.3 The efficiency of land redistribution

also contribute to unemployment. Diagram 12.3 shows how land redistribution (more land to small farmers) contributes to efficiency (more output with the same land and labour): the second pie has not only a larger share for small farmers but is also bigger.

The second example is about a horizontal inequality, namely gender discrimination. Here, the analysis concerns the comparison of low-growth regions with high-growth regions in the world and the gender gaps in education and employment in these regions. In the Middle East and North Africa, as well as in South Asia, girls' school enrolment rates are much lower than boys' school enrolment rates. Moreover, adult women's employment rates are much lower than adult men's employment rates. These two gender gaps in education and employment represent lower access to and control over resources for women as compared to men. When comparing these gaps to the situation in East Asia, a region with higher average economic growth rates (4 per cent annually compared with 2 per cent annually in the Middle East and North Africa), we find that the gender gaps in education and employment are much smaller in East Asia.

Econometric analysis has shown that the larger gender gaps in the Middle East, North Africa, and South Asia are responsible for a substantial proportion of the lower economic growth rates between 1960 and 2000 in these regions. Between 0.1 and 1.7 percentage points lower growth. And they had 2 per cent growth, so less gender inequality could have increased growth from 2.0 to rates between 2.1 and 3.7 per cent. The gender inequality in education and employment in the Middle East and North Africa, hence, implies a substantial loss of economic growth.

The social economic theory of growth is based on the insight that equity and efficiency are not trade-offs but that the first is a necessary condition for the second. So, the social economic growth equation contains measures of equity: inclusion and equality. This implies that the variable X in the standard growth equation consists of measures of inclusion, for example inclusion of minorities and women in the labour market. Moreover, the other two variables, K and L, will be included not only in terms of size but also in terms of distribution, to measure the extent of inequality, such as inequality in agricultural land distribution and inequality in wages paid to men and women and to different ethnic groups for the same work.

$$\Delta Y = g = f(K, \text{inequality of } K, L, \text{inequality of } L, X)$$

in which K = capital, L = labour, and X = social cohesion, such as inclusion of minorities, gender equality, or intergroup cohesion.

Image 12.1 Kicking away the ladder

12.3 Institutional economics of growth

12.3.1 Formal institutions of growth

Detailed historical research of how rich nations became rich has revealed that they all used similar strategies, from Britain in the 18th century and the USA in the 19th century, to Japan, Korea, and Taiwan in the 20th century. They are referred to as *developmental states*, which was already explained in Chapter 6. These are states which guide the market on a long-term economic development path with subsidies, investments, and risk absorption for firms. They all used a mix of strategies that are based on three types of institutions: redistribution, state intervention, and trade protection. Box 12.2 provides an illustration for Britain in the period 1721 (under King George I) to 1846 (repeal of the Corn Laws, abolishing many import tariffs).

> **Box 12.2 Britain's early economic growth behind tariff barriers**
>
> 'First, import duties on raw materials used for manufactures were lowered, or even altogether dropped. Second, duty drawbacks on imported raw materials for exported manufacturers were increased. Third, export duties on most manufactures were abolished. Fourth, duties on imported foreign manufactured goods were raised. Fifth, export subsidies (then called "bounties") were extended to new export items such as silk products and gunpowder, whereas the existing export subsidies to sailcloth and refined sugar were increased. Sixth, regulation was introduced to control the quality of manufactured products, especially textile products, so that unscrupulous manufacturers would not damage the reputation of British products in foreign markets.'
>
> Source: Chang, H.-J. (2007) 'Kicking Away the Ladder: The "Real" History of Free Trade', in: Shaikh, A. (ed.), *Globalization and the Myths of Free Trade*. London: Routledge, p. 27.

Of course, developmental states differ widely in economic structure. Some rely on tourism (for example Greece and Mauritius), others on financial services (for example Luxembourg and the Cayman Islands), and still others on manufacturing (South Korea, Taiwan, and Brazil). Developmental states also differ widely in their governance structures and politics. They include democratic and authoritarian states and are federal states, republics, and kingdoms. But they all rely on a mix of the three types of growth institutions. Below, I list the ten most common growth institutions, as they have been implemented by developmental states.

12.3.1.1 State-owned firms beyond public good production

These include firms in key sectors such as energy, basic chemicals, and agricultural processing industries. These sectors are necessary for further economic development. If private firms do not emerge, or only foreign companies with their own interests, public firms need to fill the gap in these sectors.

12.3.1.2 State-owned banks and development banks

These are required to finance the development of domestic economic sectors in manufacturing, infrastructure, and services. This helps to prevent dependence on foreign investment and multinational companies. For example, all South Korean banks were state owned when high economic growth took off in the 1970s. In China, banks are still state owned.

12.3.1.3 Land reform and income redistribution

Forty years ago, South Korea and the Philippines had very similar economic structures with the same level of GDP per capita. Their GDP per capita incomes were closest to each other in 1969: US$242 per year for the Philippines and US$237 per year for South Korea. Since then, South Korea has carried out substantive land reform programmes and implemented progressive taxes to finance accessible and good quality education and health care. This has resulted in much higher economic growth in South Korea compared to the Philippines. In

2012, GDP per capita in South Korea was seven times that of the Philippines: US$32,000 versus US$4,400.

12.3.1.4 Widely accessible and good quality free education at all levels

If the Middle East and North Africa had the girls' school enrolment rates of South Asia, their economic growth rates would have been much higher, as we have seen in section 12.2. A similar effect occurs for quality improvements in education.

12.3.1.5 Good quality health care and sanitation

A healthier workforce generates higher labour productivity, even with low-capital intensity. Simply because people have less sick days and are in better physical condition, while better nutrition provides more energy to sustain high levels of work effort, whether physical or mental.

12.3.1.6 Industrial policy including subsidies for selected growth sectors

The market suffers from many failures, in particular at low levels of economic development. Mauritius is a good example: it used to be a low-growth sugar plantation economy until the Mauritian government forced a shift to textile manufacturing, which also led to other manufacturing activities. And when international competition from low-wage countries reduced earnings in this sector, the government forced yet another transition. Now the economy has been pushed to luxury tourism, with yet other spin-off activities such as financial services.

12.3.1.7 Initially labour-intensive production, later capital/technology catch-up

Only when the labour reserve is usefully employed, will firms experience rising wages and be stimulated to become more efficient. This enables both income growth among the poor and international competitiveness. China seems to have entered this phase now, with labour shortages in its export processing zones, forcing factories to pay wage increases of up to 50 per cent.

12.3.1.8 Capital account controls and selective FDI

When countries strictly control foreign inflows and outflows of capital, they prevent the importation of foreign financial crises and prevent sudden outflows of capital. We have already seen this in the chapter on money. The Asian Tiger economies followed this policy in the 1970s and 1980s, but abandoned it in the 1990s under the global wave of neoliberal policies. However, with the 1997 Asian financial crisis, they paid a high price for this decision and lost several years of economic growth. Indonesia, for example, experienced a reduction in GDP of 13.5 per cent and 10 years after the crisis investments had still not returned to their pre-crisis levels.

12.3.1.9 Infant industry protection

All those counties that have now developed used to have high import tariffs to protect their infant industries. But they required through the World Trade Organization, World Bank, and IMF, developing countries to lower their tariffs. This is what the Korean development economist Ha-Joon Chang calls 'kicking away the ladder'.

Economic growth 317

Image 12.2 Assembled in China

12.3.1.10 Rule of law, even with high corruption

Economic growth requires stability. Rule of law helps to create such stability. Interestingly, this does not necessarily imply low levels of corruption or limited bureaucracy. Various tiger economies score high on the corruption index, while there is extensive bureaucracy in China and India.

12.3.2 Informal institutions of growth

The early work on informal institutions of growth was influenced by a major sociological study on economic growth. It dates back to the year 1905, when sociologist Max Weber posed his hypothesis of a 'Protestant ethic' as the main driver of economic growth in North-West Europe and the USA. He attributed the economic successes of those days of countries like Germany, England, Switzerland, the Netherlands, and Scandinavia to the dominance of Protestantism and its Calvinist values in these regions. He argued that the central values of hard work, the rejection of luxury spending, and high savings, fuelled economic growth. Whereas, in his view, Catholic nations had lower labour productivity standards and a weaker savings culture. In recent decades, not much empirical support has been found for this hypothesis. For example,

Table 12.2 Country scores on the corruption index (0–100), selected countries, 2012

Country	Score
Denmark	100
Singapore	97
China	39
India	35
Afghanistan	2
Somalia	0

Source: Worldwide Governance Indicators, World Bank: http://info.worldbank.org/governance/wgi/index.aspx#home

China is not Protestant but has been the world's growth champion for three decades. And Ireland, a Catholic country, was the fastest growing European country in the 1990s, nicknamed the Celtic Tiger. Apparently, other informal institutions play a role in enabling growth.

Today, institutional economists have found that not so much religion but rather pro-social norms such as trust and honesty are positively correlated with growth. But there is much debate about the actual indicators and their measurement of the relevant pro-social norms. And it is still unclear what the direction of causality is: do pro-social norms promote growth, or does growth enable the emergence and consolidation of such norms? The same ambiguity appears in the empirical literature on normative formal institutions of growth, such as the rule of law and democracy. Also here, it may well be the case that growth comes first, and the solidification of pro-social norms in rules and laws follows. . . .

What does emerge from the institutional growth literature is that there can be a trade-off between formal and informal institutions of growth. So, countries with a strong rule of law but a lot of corruption and clientelism can still have relatively high economic growth, for example several tiger economies and baby tigers such as Thailand and Indonesia. See for corruption rankings of countries Table 12.2 (0 means very corrupt, 100 means not corrupt at all). The reason is found in strongly bonding social capital with inter-personal norms of trust. Alternatively, countries with a weak rule of law may attract foreign investors to their natural resources, such as Angola.

Box 12.3 The puzzle of China's weak financial institutions

China's creditor rights are very limited. Secured creditors are not paid first in a bankruptcy and there is no legally required minimum capital ratio for Chinese firms. Rule of law is limited, while the corruption score is very high. Moreover, Chinese banks have a high percentage of non-performing loans, well over 10 per cent. This is only tenable due to increasing tax revenue following high growth: the state-owned banks can access funds from the Treasury, to compensate for the losses. Despite these weak formal institutions of property rights and investment, the Chinese private sector is growing at high speed. This is only possible when the weak formal institutions are balanced by strong informal institutions based on personal relationships: bonding social capital.

Source: Allen, F., J. Qian and M. Qian (2005) 'Law, Finance and Economic Growth in China', *Journal of Financial Economics*, 77, pp. 57–116.

For all the above reasons, the formal and informal institutions of growth do not lead to an unambiguous institutional growth equation. But institutions do matter at a general level, which can be included in the growth equation as follows.

$$\Delta Y = g = f(K, L, X)$$

in which, as in social economics, the distribution of capital matters: the more equal, the higher growth. But also the origin of K matters: the more domestic origin, the more stable capital, and the more stable private and public firms. This, we can indicate as the domestic/foreign capital ratio: K_{dom} / K_{for}.

For labour, what matters is not so much the quantity of labour but the quality of human resources. This is indicated through a new variable under X: H. The higher H, the higher growth. Finally, X includes developmental institutional variables. But, since there is much debate about their measurement and causality, these will not be specified here. The institutional growth equation, hence, is as follows:

$$\Delta Y = g = f(K, \text{equality of } K, L, H, \text{developmental institutions})$$

12.4 Post Keynesian growth theory

12.4.1 Demand-led growth

In Post Keynesian economics, growth is driven by the demand side. So, economic growth analysis focuses on AD: aggregate demand. Remember the macroeconomic equation, which defined AD as the aggregation of consumption, investment, government expenditures, and net exports:

$$AD = Y = C + I + G + EX - IM$$

This means that growth can be stimulated by four factors: more domestic consumer demand, more investment, more net government expenditures, and more export demand. So, growth is a matter of stimulating demand. How can this be done? Most of the mechanisms have already been discussed in earlier chapters. I will briefly review them here.

12.4.1.1 Stimulation of consumer demand: C

This can be done through lowering taxes for households. Think about income taxes and value added taxes. This leads to higher disposable income. With a stable propensity to consume, a higher disposable income translates into higher consumer demand, according to the consumption function:

$$Yd = Y - T$$

$$C = cYd + C^*$$

Let us assume that Y = €1,500 billion. The tax rate is 20 per cent, which makes disposable income €1,200 billion. When the propensity to consume is 80 per cent and autonomous consumption €140 billion, consumer demand can be calculated as follows (in billion euros):

$$C = 0.8Yd + 140$$

$$C = (0.8 \times 1,200) + 140$$

$$C = 960 + 140 = 1,100$$

Let us assume that the average tax rate is reduced from 20 per cent to 18 per cent. This increases disposable income:

$$Yd = Y - 0.18Y$$

$$Yd = 0.82Y$$

$$Yd = 0.82 \times 1,500 = 1,230$$

From this new disposable income we can recalculate consumer demand:

$$C = cYd + C^*$$

$$C = 0.8Yd + 140$$

$$C = (0.8 \times 1,230) + 140$$

$$C = 1,124$$

So, the new consumer demand has increased from €1,100 billion to €1,124 billion. With all other variables in the AD equation remaining constant (*ceteris paribus*), AD will increase directly by €24 billion. Assuming that AS will adjust to this higher demand by increasing domestic production, the economy will grow directly by €24 billion. This is 2 per cent economic growth. But there are also indirect effects, through the multiplier of the increased consumer expenditures, as we have seen in the chapter on macroeconomic flow.

Remember that the multiplier is the increased demand factor multiplied by $1/(1 - c)$. In this example, the stimulation of the economy through C is €24 billion. Hence, the multiplier of this stimulation of consumption with a tax reduction is:

$$\frac{24}{1-0.8} = \frac{24}{0.2} = €120 \text{ billion}$$

Hence, the total effect of the tax reduction on economic growth is not €24 billion but €120 billion. This is $(120/1,500) \times 100\% = 7.5\%$ economic growth.

12.4.1.2 Stimulation of investment: I

The second variable through which AD can be increased is investment. Limiting ourselves to domestic investment, the Post Keynesian perspective states that this can be increased by providing more stable financial markets with less uncertainty and lower risk, as we have seen in the chapters on financial markets and on money. A variety of policy measures can contribute to this. One example is to have a stable long-term industrial policy, in which a system of subsidies, fiscal advantages, and regional planning is set out clearly and implemented for at least 10 years. This may invite private investment into the economy, in particular in growth sectors selected by the state. The increased investment will directly increase AD (again, *ceteris paribus*), and with a response from AS, the economy will grow by the amount of the additional investment.

12.4.1.3 Stimulation through an increase in net government expenditures: G

The third pathway to Post Keynesian economic growth is through increasing G, without raising T (taxes) to the same extent. This is what is meant by an increase in net government expenditures, as the chapter on macroeconomic flow has already explained. Of course, the additional G should be spent in such a way that it stimulates growth. As we have seen earlier, Keynes argued that as long as it is spent productively, it does not matter how: any increase in G will increase national income, even a public work project digging holes one day and filling them up the next. But a more effective and lasting effect on growth would involve smarter policies. For example, extension and improvement of physical or social infrastructure: roads, public housing, sanitation, and education.

12.4.1.4 Stimulation through export demand: EX

The fourth and final pathway to stimulate AD is by exporting more goods and services to consumers abroad. This implies stimulating foreign demand. How to do this? We will see in more detail in the chapter on trade. One way to do this is through currency devaluation, which makes the exporting country's currency cheaper for foreign buyers. Hence, their export prices will be lower for foreign consumers, which is an incentive to buy more products from this country.

The four pathways to stimulate AD (through C, I, G, and EX) are not complete without a fifth policy measure that is key to Post Keynesian theory, namely redistribution. This source of demand relies on the differences between the capital and labour classes in their propensity to consume. This parameter, c, is higher for the labour class than for the capitalist class. Simply because the capitalist class has sufficient disposable income to satisfy its consumer needs, and therefore is able to save more money. The example below shows how a redistributive policy, through a progressive tax rate, shifts disposable income from capitalists to labourers, and thereby increases C, without changing anything in the other variables, such as taxation or government expenditures. The tax policy simply shifts tax burdens between the two classes but does not change the total tax burden, and hence, it will not change total tax revenue and net government expenditures.

Let us assume a flat tax rate of 30 per cent. A *flat tax* is the same tax rate for everyone, irrespective of their income level. For the average income of the capital class, €75,000 per year, this means a tax payment of:

€75,000 × 0.3 = €25,000 per year

For the average income of the labour class, €30,000 per year, this means a tax payment of:

€30,000× 0.3 = €9,000 per year

Let us now move to the case of a progressive tax. A *progressive tax* system has lower tax rates for low incomes and higher tax rates for higher incomes.

Let us go back to the example. Total tax revenue for the government is €25,000 from an average capitalist and €9,000 from an average labourer. Let us assume that a country has 80 per cent labourers and 20 per cent capitalists, and 1 million taxable inhabitants. Hence, total income (Y) is the sum of capitalist incomes and labourers' incomes:

Capitalist income Y^k = € 75,000 × 200,000 = €15 billion

Labour income Y^l = €30,000 × 800,000 = €24 billion

Total income Y = 15 + 24 = €39 billion

We can also calculate the total tax revenue for this country's government:

200,000 Capitalists × €25,000 = €5 billion

800,000 Labourers × €9,000 = €7.2 billion

Total tax revenue: €12.2 billion

Let us now assume a progressive tax system in which income is taxed at a rate of 28 per cent up to €30,000 of income per year. And for incomes above that threshold, the rate is 50 per cent. Do you think this is extremely high? The Netherlands has an even higher tax rate for incomes that are more than twice the mean income. As a consequence, I paid 52 per cent taxes on my last earned €10,000 of income in the year 2012. But it pays for a relatively extensive welfare state, which entitles me to €1,100 monthly income if I become unemployed and when I reach the age of 67 years, for the rest of my life.

Well, after this personal note, let us go back to the example of the effect of progressive taxation on economic growth. With the new, progressive tax system with two rates of 28 per cent for incomes up to €30,000 and 50 per cent for incomes above that threshold, we can now recalculate disposable incomes for the two classes.

For an average labourer, the tax to be paid is €30,000 × 0.28 tax rate = €8,400. This is a big advantage compared with the flat tax system, in which a labourer had to pay €9,000 per year: a benefit of €600 per year (€9,000 – €8,400), which is 7 per cent less than before. An average capitalist now needs to pay in two steps. The first step is the lower tariff. The first €30,000 is taxed at the rate of 28 per cent, as was the case for the labourer. Hence, the tax in the first step is the same as for the labourer, namely €8,400. The second step is for the remaining income: €75,000 – €30,000 = €45,000 × 0.5 tax rate = €22,500. So, the total tax to be paid by the average capitalist is €8,400 + €22,500 = €30,900. This is an increase of €5,900 in annual tax payment (€30,900 – €25,000 = €5,900).

In percentages, this is an increase in tax burden for the average capitalist of 24 per cent. So, the lower income households now pay 7 per cent less and the richer households now pay 24 per cent more taxes. As a percentage of their incomes, each class has the following tax burdens. An average labourer now pays €8,400 in taxes on a €30,000 income = 28 per cent. An average capitalist now pays €30,900 in taxes on a €75,000 income = 41 per cent. So, the progressive tax system requires capitalists to pay on average 41 per cent taxes and labourers 28 per cent taxes, rather than both a 30 per cent flat tax as in the earlier example. It is up to you to judge whether this is fair.

Before we end this example, we need to check whether the total tax revenue for the government has remained the same, as we promised for this tax reform. What is the total tax revenue for the government now? That is 800,000 labourers × €8,400 = €6,720 million. Plus 200,000 capitalists × €30,900 = €6,180 million. The total tax revenue, hence, is €6,720 million + €6,180 million = €1,290 million. When we round this off to €1.3 billion, we have the same amount as the €1.3 billion before the tax reform.

So, redistribution of household income increases the disposable income of the poor and reduces the disposable income of the rich. Let us now look at the effects on economic growth. Which type of tax stimulates economic growth more: a flat tax or a progressive tax? In order to compare these, I use a simpler example, starting at the individual level. Also, we assume an initial tax rate of 20 per cent. The flat tax is a 2 per cent reduction to 18 per cent. The progressive tax is an increase to 20 per cent for the rich (capitalists) and a reduction to 16 per cent for the poor (labourers).

12.4.1.5 Flat tax reduction example

The new tax for the capitalists will be 0.18 × €75,000 = €13,500 per person per year. This leaves as disposable income Yd^k: €75,000 − €13,500 = €61,500.

The new tax for the labourers will be 0.18 × €30,000 = €5,400 per person per year. This leaves as disposable income Yd^l: €30,000 − €5,400 = €24,600.

Now, we can calculate the effect on individual consumption because we know the disposable incomes for each class:

$C^k = 0.8 Yd^k + 140 =$

$C^k = (0.8 \times 61,500) + 140 =$

$C^k = 49,200 + 140 = 49,340$

$C^l = 0.8 Yd^l + 140 =$

$C^l = (0.8 \times 24,600) + 140 =$

$C^l = 19,680 + 140 = 19,820$

Now, we can multiply the consumption of each individual class by the number of people per class:

Aggregate C^k = €49,340 × 200,000 capitalists = €9.868 billion

Aggregate C^l = €19,820 × 800,000 labourers = €15.856 billion

Adding the two gives total consumer expenditures:

$C = C^k + C^l$ = €9.868 billion + €15.856 billion = €25.724 billion

12.4.1.6 Progressive tax example

The new tax for the capitalists will be 0.20 × €75,000 = €15,000 per person per year. This leaves as disposable income Yd^k: €75,000 − €15,000 = €60,000.

The new tax for the labourers will be 0.16 × €30,000 = €4,800 per person per year. This leaves as disposable income Yd^l: €30,000 − €4,800 = €25,200.

Now, we can calculate the effect on individual consumption because we know the disposable incomes for each class:

$C^k = 0.8d^k + 140 =$

$C^k = (0.8 \times 60{,}500) + 140 =$

$C^k = 48{,}000 + 140 = 48{,}140$

$C^l = 0.8d^l + 140 =$

$C^l = (0.8 \times 25{,}200) + 140 =$

$C^l = 20{,}140 + 140 = 20{,}300$

Now, we can multiply the consumption of each individual class by the number of people per class:

Aggregate C^k = 48,140 × 200,000 capitalists = €9.628 billion

Aggregate C^l = 20,300 × 800,000 labourers = €16.240 billion

Adding up the two gives total consumer expenditures:

$C = C^k + C^l$ = €9.628 billion + €16.240 billion = €25.868 billion

The aggregate consumer expenditures under the progressive tax system are slightly higher than under the flat tax system: the difference is:

€25.868 billion − €25.724 billion = €144 million

This allows us to calculate the difference in the multiplier:

144/ (1 − 0.8) = 144/0.2 = €720 million

The conclusion is that with the progressive tax reform of 2 per cent more for the rich and 2 per cent less for the poor, GDP will be €720 million higher than with the flat tax reduction of 2 per cent less for everyone. On the total income of Y = €39 billion, €720 million is 1.8 per cent, which means that economic growth, or g, is 1.8 percentage points higher with the redistributive tax.

With these five types of stimulus to AD, I have described the direct increase in AD, and with an immediate response by AS, in national income (or GDP). This, then, describes economic growth from the demand side of the economy. But these direct effects trigger indirect effects, leading to the multiplier effect. Again, we have discussed this earlier: the multiplier effect of a macroeconomic variable involves indirect effects, which together lead to the total effect on AD. Remember that the multiplier effects of C, I, G, and EX follow these processes:

- more demand allows for more product sales, which in turn increases the demand for labour to produce the additional goods and services;
- more production requires more investment, which in turn increases aggregate demand;

- more employment generates more income for households, which in turn increases consumer demand;
- more income generates higher tax revenue, which enables increases in government expenditures.

In conclusion, Post Keynesian growth theory understands economic growth as driven by the demand side of the economy, which has five sources: consumption, investment, government expenditures, exports, and redistribution of income from high- to low-income earners. The multiplier effect increases initial changes in demand, so that the total effect on economic growth is larger than the initial effect from the five sources of demand.

12.4.2 Endogenous growth

The Post Keynesian perspective understands economic growth as endogenous. Not driven by exogenous factors such as technological innovations or random shocks. But caused by the economic dynamics itself. The foundational equation for endogenous growth is the definition that investments equal savings. And savings are the residual from income minus consumption, as you will remember from Chapter 10. In equations this reads:

$$S = Y - C$$

and

$$S = I$$

So, investment is not determined by the level of the interest rate but by the level of savings available after consumer demand is met. Moreover, the class disaggregation typical for Post Keynesian economics explains that most, if not all, savings come from capitalist incomes and not from labour incomes. Simplified, all savings come from capitalist incomes, which are earned not from wages but from profits. In an equation:

$$I = sR$$

in which s = the propensity to save out of profit income and R = profit income.

When we divide both sides of the equation by the stock of capital, K, we arrive at the following equation:

$$I/K = sR/K$$

Remember that R/K is r, the profit rate. And I/K is the growth rate of the economy, g, when assuming that capital is the binding constraint, and not labour. Labour is assumed to be abundant in Post Keynesian economics, given a labour reserve and persistent unemployment in many real-world economies. So, we can re-write the equation as follows, which gives the Post Keynesian growth equation:

$$g = sr$$

This equation means that economic growth is the product of the propensity to save of the capitalists and the profit rate. This formulation of economic growth is endogenous. Why?

Because growth (g) and the profit rate (r) are determined at the same time. Profits in the Post Keynesian model are determined by the bargaining process between capital and labour, in which capital has more bargaining power when there is unemployment. Workers need to find a job and are dependent upon capitalists hiring them. While capitalists can choose among more labour than they need, either due to low aggregate demand or due to technological development substituting labour for machines.

So, when profit income is high and wage income low, savings will be high and hence, economic growth will be high through investments out of these savings. If, of course, savings don't leak away to the rest of the world or remain in financial assets in the FIRE sector . . . .

And there is another endogenous dynamic at play, namely the demand for goods and services as we have discussed in section 12.4.1. When wages are low, household consumption will be affected, because workers have low incomes with low wages, so their consumption will be constrained. And with low consumer demand, growth will be constrained (*ceteris paribus*). When more income flows to wages, incomes increase and hence consumer demand goes up. But the lower profit going to capitalists will reduce the growth rate. You can see that from the growth equation above: when r, the profit rate, declines, g, economic growth, will also reduce.

This endogeneity of growth implies that growth may be driven either by profits (but constrained by low consumer demand) or by wages (but constrained by investments, because sR = S = I, so lower profits generate lower investments). For some countries, growth is profit led, whereas for other countries, growth is wage led.

In the profit-led strategy, low consumer demand is the binding constraint due to low wages. The solution to this constraint is exports, which adds consumer demand from the RoW to the economy. The more exports, the more demand (EX), and hence, the higher AD. Hence, a profit-led growth strategy can continue to pay low wages, as long as foreign consumers are willing to buy the country's products. China is a good example of such a strategy. In the wage-led strategy, low investment is the binding constraint, due to low profits from which capitalists can save money to invest. Again, the RoW provides a solution. This through encouraging foreign investment to flow into the country. So, low domestic investment is compensated for by investment flows from abroad. This also stimulates AD, not through C, as in the wage-led strategy, but through I, in the profit-led strategy.

In conclusion, going back to the standard growth equation in section 12.1.3, growth in the Post Keynesian perspective is not a function of L or of any other 'X factor'. Growth only depends on capital, but thereby it depends on the distribution of income over capital (R) and labour (W) and on the profit rate obtained from product sales to consumers (C and EX). So, we can re-write the growth equation from a Post Keynesian perspective as follows:

$$\Delta Y = g = sr = I/K$$

in short:

$$\Delta Y = I/K$$

in which I is the complement of consumption (I = S) out of profit income (R): the higher R, the higher capitalist savings (S) and hence investment (I):

$$I = f(R)$$

and in turn profit depends on the distribution of income over profits and wages:

$R = Y - W$

Hence, economic growth, ΔY, partly depends on how Y is distributed. That is precisely what is meant by endogenous growth.

For China, with an average growth rate of 10 per cent over several decades, $g = \Delta Y = 0.10$. The investment rate (i) has been around 40 per cent since 2005. Hence, the capital/output ratio (k) is 4, using the Post Keynesian growth equation above:[4]

$\Delta Y = g = I/K$

$0.10 = 0.40/4$

Hence, China's growth is a combination of a high savings rate and a low capital/output ratio, indicating that the available stock of capital produces relatively high output per unit. Partly thanks to an educated and healthy labour force, generating high labour productivity.

Box 12.4 China's economic growth

From 1978 onwards, the Chinese economy grew on average by 10 per cent per year, until it reduced to around 7 per cent in 2012. What were the three main factors behind this growth miracle? First, a structurally strong investment in infrastructure in combination with high labour supply with increasing health and education levels. Second, a quick transition from a state-directed economy to a mixed market economy with sufficient public goods provided by the state. The stability thus provided allowed households to have high savings rates. Third, high trust and dense commercial ties within the country and with its neighbours.

Where did the growth start? In the rural areas where price controls were lifted, allowing farmers to earn higher incomes and to organize themselves in collectives. This resulted in food surpluses, allowing the rural population to start up manufacturing. In the 1990s this process was supported with central industrial planning, resulting in export growth higher than GDP growth. The combination of high domestic savings and incoming FDI from foreign multinationals increased the savings rate from 30 per cent in the 1970s to 40 per cent since 2005.

Source: Naughton, B. (2007) *The Chinese Economy, Transitions and Growth*. Cambridge, MA: The MIT Press.

12.5 Neoclassical growth theory

12.5.1 The supply side as driver of growth

Neoclassical growth theory focuses on the supply side of the economy. It is concerned with shifting out the aggregate supply curve (AS) rather than the aggregate demand curve (AD).

328   *Economic growth*

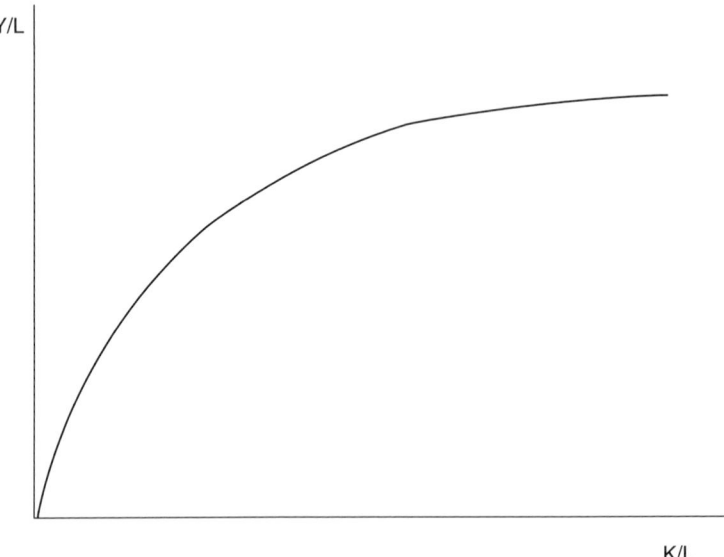

Diagram 12.4 Aggregate production function

Hence, the drivers of growth are incentives to produce and to invest, rather than to consume and to export. Of course, investment is part of the AD function, but in neoclassical economics investment is not determined by savings but by the interest rate. Hence, efficient capital markets and interest rates which increase investments are key drivers of economic growth.

Economic growth in the neoclassical perspective is explained with the help of the *aggregate production function*. This is the economy-wide production function, the aggregation of all individual production functions of firms in an economy. Diagram 12.4 shows the aggregate production function, with GDP per worker (Y/L) on the vertical axis and capital per worker (K/L) on the horizontal axis. The curve shows all possible combinations of capital and output per worker, moving from low capital input and low output to high capital input and high output. Along the production function, we assume a constant level of technology for capital and a constant level of human capital for labour.

Diagram 12.4 shows that the aggregate production function is positive, but with decreasing returns. This means that the more capital-intensive an economy, the less the additional benefits of capital investment for output. Decreasing returns of growth is an expression of the law of diminishing marginal returns that we have seen in Chapters 1, 3, and 4. The aggregate production function shows that the same law is applicable to the macro level, according to standard neoclassical theory. At low levels of capital, output increases quickly. But the higher the capital intensity of production, the slower output growth. In other words, the shape of the aggregate production function explains the growth rate as reducing over time: growth rates are high in the early stages of economic development but will decline in more advanced stages of development.

Movement along the production function indicates short-term economic growth: growth with given technology and human capital. This can be expressed with the standard growth equation from section 12.1.3, but without the additional 'X factor':

$$\Delta Y = f(K, L)$$

The neoclassical production function divides this equation by the number of workers, L, to obtain:

$$\Delta Y/L = f(K, L)$$

This neoclassical formulation of the growth equation defines growth relative to the number of workers, so, growth per worker (Y/L). This depends on capital per worker (K/L).

Will growth always decline over time? Perhaps become zero or even negative soon for the high-income countries of the world? No, not necessarily. In the long run, economic growth in neoclassical theory is influenced by technological change and improvements in the human capital of workers. The production function shifts entirely upwards when either technology improves, making capital more productive, or human capital increases, making labour more productive. The new curve, located above the old one, will also show diminishing marginal returns, but at a later stage of capital use per worker. This process of an economy moving from a lower production function to a higher production function is caused by exogenous change in neoclassical theory. So, with technological development or when labour becomes more efficient, the production function will shift upwards. Hence, neoclassical growth theory is an exogenous growth theory, depending on positive shocks to the economy: shocks of innovation and education. Diagram 12.5 shows long-term growth in neoclassical economics: a shift upwards of the aggregate production function due to shocks.

As a consequence of exogenous shocks to the economy, pushing up the production function, the growth rate will also be pushed up. Hence, the economy has a new chance to attain high growth rates. But again, these are subject to decreasing returns. So, in the long run,

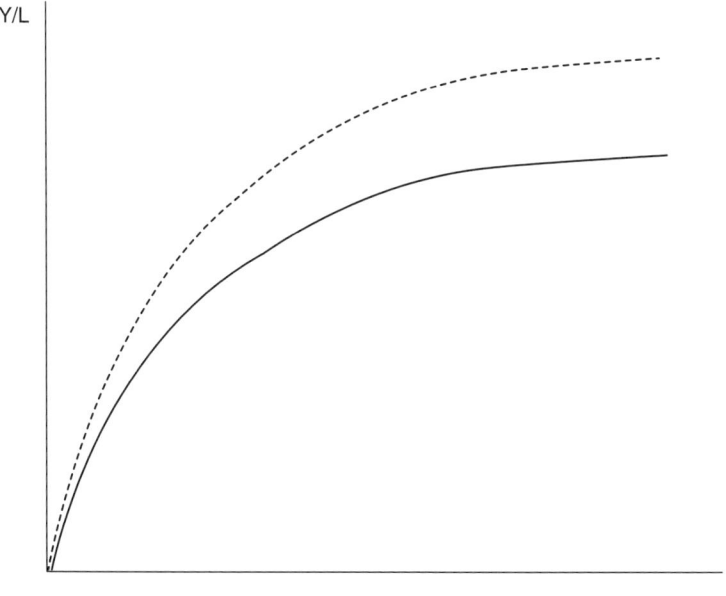

Diagram 12.5 Long run growth through shocks

330 *Economic growth*

economic growth makes jumps and then slides back to lower growth rates. This exogenous process is by definition erratic and beyond the control of firms or government policy. Long-term growth is not systematic, so the shifts from low to high growth rates and back cannot be caused by economic cycles, in neoclassical economics.

The major growth policy tools in the neoclassical perspective focus on the supply side and are also referred to as neoliberal policies. *Neoliberal policies* are economic policies increasing the role of the market and reducing the role of the state, assuming that free markets are the most efficient allocation mechanism and therefore stimulate economic growth. They are the opposite of the policy followed by developmental states as explained in section 12.3. In developing countries, neoliberal policies became known as *structural adjustment programmes*, or *SAPs* in the 1980s. These are macroeconomic reform programmes which reduce government expenditures and expand markets, through expenditure cuts, privatisation of public firms, and the liberalisation of several markets. And they have been called the *Washington Consensus* since the 1990s, which are SAPs with additional policy measures of good governance and some minimum of social protection. The name *Washington Consensus* refers to the location of the World Bank, the IMF, and the US Treasury Department, three institutions which together have strongly favoured neoliberal policy since the 1980s.

The neoliberal, or supply side, policy tools of neoclassical economics are listed below.

12.5.1.1 Lower taxes and lower government expenditures

Lower taxes, in particular for firms and capital owners (higher income households) would stimulate investment, because lower taxes raise net returns on investment. Moreover, less tax revenue for the government requires, as a consequence, lower government expenditures, in order to keep budgets balanced. This is also referred to as *fiscal discipline*: reduced taxes and reduced government expenditures towards lower and balanced budgets.

12.5.1.2 Flexible labour markets

Labour is assumed in the neoclassical perspective as abundant and fully employed. This can only be realised when labour markets are liberalised. This includes policy measures such as the abolition of minimum wages, lowering standards of labour protection, and lowering wage costs. But flexible labour markets also imply free immigration, which often is not allowed by the same governments following neoliberal policies.

12.5.1.3 Privatisation of public companies

More market and less state includes the *privatisation* of public firms (the sale of a public firm to market parties), from the assumption that market discipline will force them to become more efficient. This can only work when there is a competitive market, when corruption is effectively dealt with, and when the goods produced are not public goods.

12.5.1.4 Flexible exchange rates and open capital markets

When capital markets are liberalised to open exchange of currency and capital, they allow the inflow of foreign investment.

Image 12.3 Major currencies

12.5.1.5 Deregulation of domestic markets

Several domestic markets, such as food markets, transport markets, and energy markets, are deregulated on the assumption that this will enhance competition and thereby efficiency. This, in turn, would attract more investment to these sectors. The tools are the abolition of price controls (no prices set by the government anymore), the abolition of subsidies (to prevent dependence on the state), and the abolition of constraining regulations on products.

12.5.1.6 Trade liberalisation

The major policy tool for trade liberalisation is a reduction in import tariffs. This confronts domestic firms with competition from cheaper imported goods, and hence, an incentive to become more efficient. In the short run, some domestic firms may go bankrupt, but in the long run, this policy should benefit consumers with cheaper products, and firms with export capacity.

The era of neoliberal policies started at the beginning of the 1980s but was disrupted by the global financial crisis and the policies that Western governments undertook to fight the crisis. Since 2007, the developed countries have implemented stimulation policies, which are in many respects the opposite of neoliberalism. And the IMF has made a similar alteration in its advice to both developed and developing countries, cautioning now about too much and too fast deregulation and liberalisation. But it is unclear now, as I write this book in 2014, where the global policy trend will go in the short and medium term.

Were SAPs successful in stimulating economic growth? This question has dominated the development debate for at least 25 years. Statistics show that countries with SAP policies (the majority of developing countries) followed a wide variety of growth trajectories, but remained on average below their growth rates of the 1960s and 1970s. Moreover, the world's fastest growing countries like China and India did not follow SAP policies. Instead, they had a strong state role and they still control imports and foreign investments. Whereas numerous countries that have strictly followed SAPs since the 1980s have not benefitted from growth at all or have even experienced crises such as Mexico, Argentina, Russia, Turkey, and various sub-Saharan African countries.

The greatest criticism of SAPs does not refer to their disappointing growth performance. But to their destructive social effects. Already in the 1980s, the United Nations Children's Fund (UNICEF) showed that SAPs had negative effects on children. While in the new millennium, development economists generally agreed with the prominent African development expert Thandika Mkandawire that the 1980s and some of the 1990s have been a lost decade for Africa, with low growth and no poverty reduction, despite the widespread implementation of SAPs.

But high growth rates do not necessarily lead to poverty reduction. In China, the reduction in poverty only started after 1995, some 15 years after the high-growth episode began. The reduction in poverty in China since then can indeed be attributed to GDP growth, but only because of its enormous size and continuation over three decades since 1980. Not because of a trickle-down of growth to all low-income households across the country. Chinese government anti-poverty programmes in the cities have had little to no effect on urban poverty. So, economic growth can certainly trickle down to all agents in the economy, including socially disadvantaged groups, but will not necessarily do so, and may require extremely high growth rates over a long period of time as well as effective policies of redistribution.

12.5.2 New Growth Theory

The idea that growth is beyond the control of policy makers because it is exogenous is not very satisfactory from an economic policy perspective. Moreover, neoliberal policies, focusing on the supply side of the economy, assume that policies can influence growth, if only indirectly by creating the conditions for free markets. These considerations have led neoclassical economists to develop what is simply called New Growth Theory. This is not merely an addition to standard neoclassical growth theory, but a major shift in thinking about the causes of growth. It is no longer assumed that growth is exogenous, but that it is caused within the economic process in its particular context, and hence, endogenous. This shift acknowledges insights from institutional economics (context matters) and Post Keynesian economics (endogeneity).

New Growth Theory is concerned with the long run, and attributes growth to the same two factors of production as the standard growth theory: capital and labour. Growth occurs, according to the New Growth Theory, through increases in the productivity of each factor. Capital becomes more productive through technological change, while labour becomes more productive through a combination of education and on-the-job training. These productivity increases follow from the accumulated stock of physical and human capital, and hence, are not exogenous but endogenous to the economy. The more stimulation of R&D, higher education, scientific grants, technological incubators, and processes of workers' autonomy, the more an economy benefits from productivity increases. So, productivity increases are no longer regarded as static with sudden shocks, but as dynamic, continuously evolving.

Moreover, economic growth can now escape the law of diminishing marginal returns. It will no longer exhibit decreasing returns, with erratic shocks and then again back to better returns on a higher production function. But New Growth Theory acknowledges increasing returns on capital and labour inputs. Because it is no longer only the *quantity* of capital and labour which matters (and which are finite), but also the *quality* of capital and labour. This results in an upward sloping part of the production function, which postpones diminishing returns to the future. Of course, economic growth rates cannot go up forever. Statistics show they don't. Depletion of natural resources and economy-driven pollution are two important constraints which the natural system puts on economic growth. And also the social system forces constraints upon growth, in terms of human depletion due to stress, burn-out, and preference for more leisure time versus work time with growing incomes, as well as social conflict when economic growth is distributed very unevenly.

Diagram 12.6 shows the aggregate production function of the New Growth Theory, in which the major part shows increasing returns, from the origin up to point A. From A to B there are constant returns (more or less a straight line) and from point B onwards the standard growth theory kicks in with diminishing returns.

This leads to a re-formulation of the standard neoclassical growth equation. Again, it does not require an 'X factor', but it does include qualitative dimensions of K and L. For K, the qualitative dimension is symbolised with T for technology, the qualitative dimension of a stock of capital. The same stock of capital, say computers, trucks, and office buildings, can be low tech or high tech. The higher the value of T, the higher the level of technology embedded in a capital stock K. Similarly for L, the labour force: the qualitative dimensions of the labour force are symbolised with H, for human resources. The higher H, the better skilled and innovative and mutual-learning the labour force is.

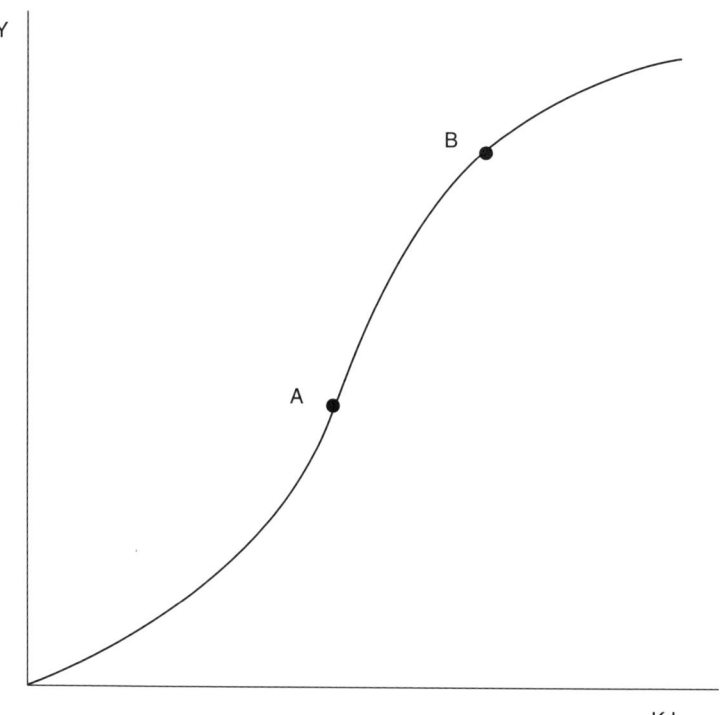

Diagram 12.6 New Growth production function

The New Growth Theory, hence, has the following preliminary growth equation:

$$\Delta Y = f(K, T, L, H)$$

The actual specification of the New Growth equation is more complex than the standard one, because we cannot treat K and T independently, and neither can we regard L and H independently: T and H are embedded in their respective production factors. So, the equation should be grouped into a function with two terms, each with their own functional form (f and g). This gives the New Growth equation:

$$\Delta Y = f(K, T) + g(L, H)$$

This specification shows that economic growth can be stimulated not only by increasing K per worker, as in the standard growth theory, but also by policies focusing on T and policies focusing on H. For T, the typical policies are related to innovation, knowledge, and transformation of how to produce. For H, the typical policies concern not just formal education, but also on-the-job training, and forms of teamwork which enable mutual learning.

12.6 Interesting sources

Chang, H.-J. (2007) *Bad Samaritans – Rich Nations, Poor Policies, and the Threat to the Developing World*. London: Bloomsbury Press.
Indices of Social Development database: www.IndSocDev.org
Tianyong, Z. (2014) *The China Dream and the China Path*. Singapore: World Scientific Publishing.

12.7 Glossary

Aggregate production function   The economy-wide production function as the aggregation of all individual production functions of firms in an economy

Dependency ratio   The ratio of people outside the labour force, over the working population, who earn the income to provide for both groups

Developmental state   A state which guides the market on a long-term economic development path with subsidies, investments, and risk absorption for firms

Economic growth   The increase in gross domestic product (GDP)

FIRE sector   The monetary sector of the economy consisting of Finance, Investment, and Real Estate

Fiscal discipline   Reduced taxes and reduced government expenditures towards balanced budgets

Flat tax   The same tax rate for everyone, irrespective of their income level

Growth equation   Equation which explains the determinants of economic growth

Inclusive growth   Economic growth of which the benefits extend to all social groups

Neoliberal policies   Economic policies increasing the role of the market and reducing the role of the state, assuming that free markets are the most efficient allocation mechanism and therefore stimulate economic growth

Privatisation   The sale of a public firm to market parties

Progressive tax system   Lower tax rates for low incomes and higher tax rates for higher incomes

Social cohesion   Connectedness in a society, which is valuable in itself and helps to overcome economic problems of transaction costs, free riding, and moral hazard

Structural adjustment programmes (SAPs)   Macroeconomic reform programmes, which reduce government expenditures and expand markets, through expenditure cuts, privatisation of public firms, and the liberalisation of several markets

Washington Consensus   SAPs with additional policy measures of good governance and some minimum of social protection

Notes

1 www.IndSocDev.org
2 Source for the figures for China: Naughton, B. (2007) *The Chinese Economy, Transitions and Growth*. Cambridge, MA: The MIT Press.
3 See for the full study on this example: Van den Brink, R., H. Binswanger, J. Bruce, G. Thomas and F. Byamugisha (2006) 'Consensus, Confusion and Controversy. Selected Land Reform Issues in Sub-Saharan Africa'. Working Paper no. 71. Washington, DC: World Bank.
4 See note 2.

13 Nature

13.1 The economics of nature

The impact of economic behaviour on the natural environment has been larger since the early 20th century than ever before in human history. There are two ways to roughly measure this impact. One focuses on material use in the economy, and the other on damage inflicted by economic behaviour on nature.

13.1.1 Material use

Material use by the world economy has increased eight-fold since 1900.[1] Material use can be divided into four categories: biomass, fossil energy, metal ores, and construction minerals. The largest increases were in construction minerals (34-fold increase) and mineral ores (27-fold increase), followed by fossil energy (12-fold increase) and biomass (4-fold increase). The use of these four categories has not only grown but also shifted from biomass toward the other three categories, as Diagram 13.1 shows.

Material use has grown faster than the global population, so that economic agents use on average more materials per person every year. In fact, material use per capita has doubled over the past century, increasing from 5 to 10 tonnes per capita per year. But material use has grown slower than GDP due to higher material productivity. For example, cars today use much less petrol per kilometre than cars 30 years ago and they weigh less. The newest generation of electric cars and hybrid cars (which have both fuel and electric motors) have much lower emission rates of CO_2 and other air pollutants. Many governments use fiscal incentives to stimulate the use of small and fuel-efficient cars.

Since 2006, the Dutch government has reduced sales tax and road tax for consumers buying such cars. These tax benefits have been effective, because between 2006 and 2012, fuel use and CO_2 emissions have been reduced by 2 per cent instead of increasing as was the case in previous years.[2] The 2015 EU norm of a maximum of 130 grams of CO_2 emissions per kilometre was achieved in the Netherlands in 2011, whereas the rest of Europe was still above this limit in 2013. However, the tax consequences were costly for the government, which was losing €2 million in tax revenue every year. The tax benefits have been reduced in 2014. As a consequence, the sales of fuel-efficient cars have plunged in the first quarter of the year. For example, 623 Opel/Vauxhall Ampera (also known as Chevrolet Volt) hybrid cars were sold in the first quarter of 2012 and 502 in the first quarter of 2013, but only nine in the first quarter of 2014.[3]

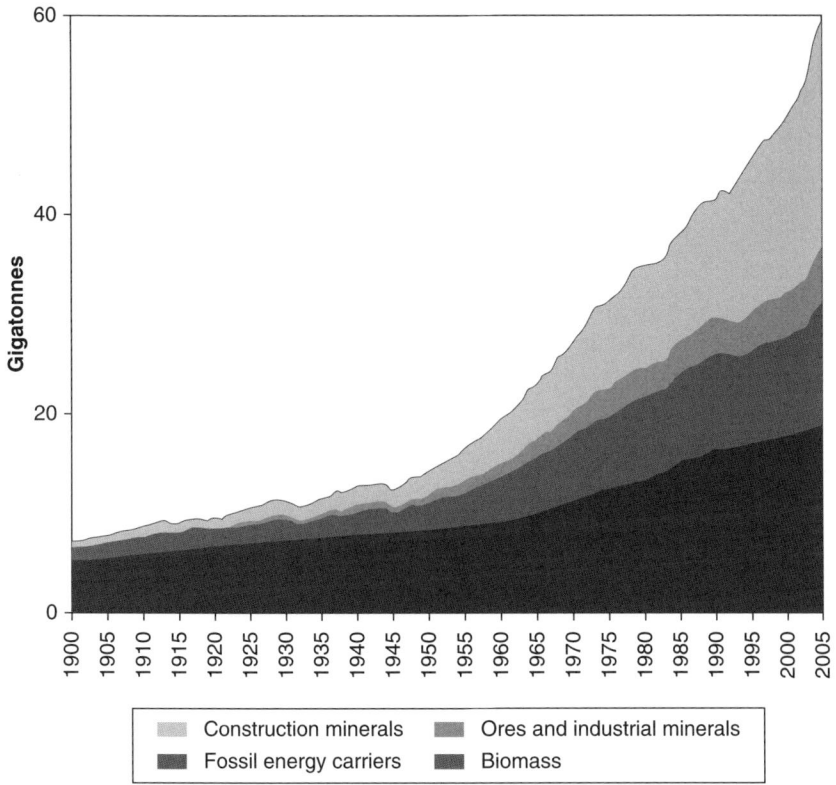

Diagram 13.1 Global material use, 1900–2005

Source: Krausmann, F., S. Gingrich, N. Eisenmenger, K. Erb, H. Haberl and M. Fischer-Kowalski (2009) 'Growth in Global Materials Use, GDP and Population during the 20th Century', *Ecological Economics*, (68)10, Figure 1a

13.1.2 Damage

The second way to measure the economy's impact on nature is through the damage inflicted by economic behaviour on nature. Such damage is varied and ranges from water pollution to garbage dumps and from a reduction in biodiversity to deforestation. Much of this damage to nature has a long-term impact and contributes to overall deterioration of the environmental conditions on our planet. One aggregate form that this damage takes is global warming. The Intergovernmental Panel on Climate Change (IPCC), already mentioned in Chapter 7 where I discussed an end to global warming as a global public good, has published an update with the most recent scientific insights on global warming. It concludes that since 1950, global warming is unequivocal: the atmosphere and ocean have warmed, the amount of snow and ice has diminished, the sea level has risen, and the concentration of greenhouse gases has increased.[4] The average temperature on Earth has increased by 0.85°C since 1880. As a consequence, the sea level has risen by 1.5 cm, as Diagram 13.2a shows, and CO_2 emissions have increased by a quarter, as shown in Diagram 13.2b.

Of course, for the Netherlands (whose very name derives from its location below sea level), global warming will have serious consequences. Dikes have gradually been raised and strengthened since the 1953 floods, but debate continues about how effective this will be. And also the relatively large rivers Rhine and Meuse end their journey in this small and water-rich country, causing regular floods, while population pressure has increased the construction of homes along the banks of these same rivers. . . .

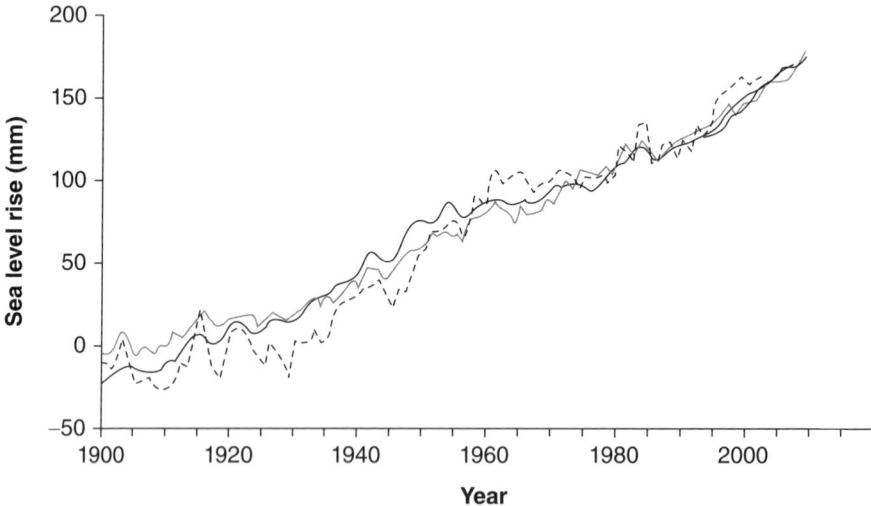

Diagram 13.2a Global sea level change

Note: The lines refer to different scenarios.

Source: Diagram SPM.3d in http://www.climatechange2013.org/images/report/WG1AR5_SPM_FINAL.pdf

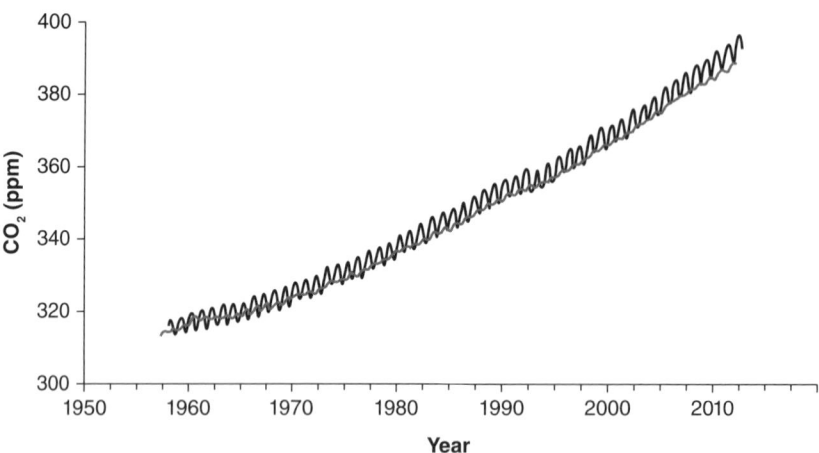

Diagram 13.2b Global CO_2 level change

Note: The lines refer to different scenarios.

Source: Diagram SPM.4a in http://www.climatechange2013.org/images/report/WG1AR5_SPM_FINAL.pdf

Each of the four economic theories has different explanations and different policy tools to address the increasing economic impact on nature. What they have in common is the understanding that this impact cannot and should not grow forever since we have only one planet Earth. This insight has led to the common notion of sustainable development in economics, defined in 1987 by the Brundtland Commission in its report *Our Common Future*. That report defines *sustainable development* as the kind of development that meets the needs of the present without compromising the ability of future generations to meet their own needs. Of course, this definition has been criticised and adapted over so many years. But the basic idea of a limit to the capacities of the earth to deal with present economic development remains the same.

13.2 Social economics of nature

13.2.1 Ecological economics

In social economics, the economy is understood as an open-system relationship with nature, or more broadly, the biosphere, which is a closed system. This recognition has led to the development of ecological economics, a field of study which in addition to social economic insights also covers inputs from institutional and Post Keynesian economics. The foundation of ecological economics was laid by the social economist Kenneth Boulding with his 1966 essay called 'The Economics of the Coming Spaceship Earth'.[5] He emphasised that without energy inputs to the earth, the economy would not be able to grow or even to continue at the same level, because fossil energy is non-renewable and we depend enormously on daily solar energy inputs. Before using the label, Boulding laid the foundation for *ecological economics*, which is defined as the study of the interdependence and co-evolution of the economy and natural ecosystems over time and space.

Energy is the most crucial factor in ecological economics, because in an open system, energy gets diffused over time, it leaks away. Think about a cuckoo clock: when you pull the chord in the morning, you have given it the energy to keep ticking all day long. But gradually, the energy dissipates away from the mechanics of the clock, until the little bird does not come out again and the ticking stops. Energy leaking is characteristic of an open system. If you could find a closed environment for your cuckoo clock, without any friction, you would only need to pull the chord once and it would give you the correct time and bird-calls for the rest of your life. The economy is an open system, like your home. Thus it also leaks energy, and in an irreversible way. You can never get the ticking of the clock back as energy into the chord, or the muscles in your hand and arm. Likewise, energy (labour power or petrol) dissipates in the economy over time and cannot be reversed to its original forms. In physics, this is known as the Second Law of Thermodynamics, or the *Entropy Law*: the capacity of energy to do useful work, as an input, is diminished over time. The economic consequence of this law is that without entropy, there would be no scarcity: every energy input could be used over-and-over-and-over again. But we live in an open system with finite energy sources and relying on inputs of energy from outside: the sun and the biosphere.

13.2.2 Limits to growth

In response to the environmental trends mentioned in section 13.1, and the recognition of entropy, ecological economists have argued for limits to economic growth. But there is disagreement about what this implies for economic policy. Should we have zero GDP growth? Or zero GDP *per capita* growth (allowing for economic growth to match population growth)? Or should we rather focus on reducing the growth of material use? Or, yet others argue, should we turn away from a focus on quantitative growth and concentrate on qualitative growth instead?

Ecological economics includes all these perspectives. They are expressed in three ways: a steady-state economy, green growth, and qualitative growth.

13.2.2.1 The steady-state economy: zero growth

The starting point of steady-state economists is that we have enough. 'We' refers to the affluent part of the world population, the majority of those living in the developed world, as well as the rich living in the developing world. A *steady-state economy* is an economy that aims to maintain a stable level of resource consumption and a stable population level. This implies that the objective is zero GDP growth with zero population growth, so that GDP per capita also remains constant over time. This objective has two major challenges: to end the increase in output and income as measured by GDP, and to end population growth, which is still relatively high although decreasing in the developing world. In the words of two proponents of a steady-state economy, Rob Dietz and Dan O'Neill:[6]

> A steady-state economy would require striking a balance between the stock of natural capital and the stock of built capital, with both remaining relatively constant over time. A constant stock of natural capital implies the preservation of wilderness areas and maintenance of important ecosystem services, such as climate regulation. A constant stock of built capital means maintaining and improving the quality of infrastructure, such as buildings and roads, but not constructing more and more of these over time.

Steady-state economists admit that zero population growth is a tricky issue. Partly because of the human rights to family life and bodily integrity. And partly because the environmental impact per person in countries with zero population growth is much higher than that in poor countries with much higher population growth. Moreover, it involves a gender issue because it is women who are child bearing, whereas they do not always have the freedom and means to choose if and when to become pregnant. Empirical research has shown that fertility decisions involve an economic power asymmetry between men and women, which needs to be addressed first before fertility rates start to decline. So, there is an enormous moral problem involved in the idea of a steady-state economy.

13.2.2.2 Green growth: reducing the impact of growth

Green growth is economic growth with a decreasing environmental impact. The proponents of green growth may be regarded as dreamers: how can you have GDP growth with less environmental impact? Well, the green growth economists are the first to admit that GDP is a very biased measure of well-being in the first place. We are in need of green measures of well-being, and using those that are already available. I will present such measures in section 13.2.3. For now, let us stick with GDP.

Image 13.1 Natural resource: wood

For green growth, we need to distinguish between four elements: environmental impact (I), population size (P), consumption per person (A for affluence), and technology (T). This results in the so-called I-PAT equation:

$$I = PAT$$

This equation explains environmental impact as the product of population size, consumption per capita, and the level of technology. If we take A and T together, we have the intensity of environmental impact: resource use and waste, for a particular level of technology. Now, green growth means that the change in I, the environmental impact of a certain level of GDP, should be smaller than the increase in GDP:

$$\Delta GDP < \Delta I$$

This equation makes green growth less problematic than steady-state growth, because it does not require zero population growth. The only thing that matters, is that ΔI should be smaller than ΔGDP, which can be achieved not only through lower P growth but also through lower A growth and more efficient T.

If ΔGDP is 3 per cent and I is 2 per cent, we can speak of green growth. But it still means that the environmental impact is increasing. Therefore, a more radical equation of green growth is possible:

$$\Delta I < 0, \textit{for any } \Delta GDP$$

This radical green growth equation indicates that whatever the level of GDP growth, the impact on the natural environment should be less than it was for the previous level of GDP.

13.2.2.3 Quality of life instead of growth

The proponents of this perspective analyse the dimensions of human well-being beyond material needs satisfaction (basic needs) and material wants satisfaction (luxuries). They point at three non-material intensive dimensions of well-being: (1) leisure time rather than income and material consumption; (2) social-psychological dimensions of well-being; and (3) engagement with nature as a well-being end in itself, rather than a means for material consumption.

On leisure time as a dimension of well-being, many empirical studies have shown that people value leisure time, and tend to value it increasingly more in developed countries, as compared to material consumption. In OECD countries, people reduced their paid work hours by 18 per cent between 1950 and 1980, and again by 7 per cent between 1980 and 2000.[7] The Netherlands is a leader in the substitution of paid work with leisure time. Dutch people reduced their paid work hours between 1950 and 1980 by 27 per cent, and between 1980 and 2000 by another 14 per cent. They did so not only through shorter working weeks and early retirement, but also through part-time jobs, particularly among women but increasingly also among fathers choosing to spend more time with their children. Such substitution of paid work with leisure time and unpaid caring implies a shift towards lower-impact growth by diversifying the sources of well-being. In other words, there is already a transition going on in the developed world from quantity of stuff to quality of life.

Engagement with nature through civic activism, recreation, and financial support, points at the third form of greening the quality of life. About 3.5 million Dutch people are members of environmental non-profit organisations, ranging from Greenpeace to provincial conservation associations and the Dutch branch of the World Wildlife Fund. There is even a political party called the 'Party for the Animals', which has two seats in parliament and one seat in the senate. For others, engagement with nature becomes a way of life, as for farmers and fishing-folk and those who leave urban life behind to find peace in a green environment which does not produce smoke or noise and does not talk back.

13.2.3 Green well-being measures

This section will present two green well-being measures, developed from a social economic perspective: (1) the ecological footprint and (2) the Happy Planet Index.

13.2.3.1 Ecological footprint

The *ecological footprint* is an index for how much nature we have, how much we use, and who uses what. The more we consume material goods, the bigger our ecological footprint. For example, the ecological data show that if the ecological footprint of everybody in the world were as large as that of an average American, we would need five planets Earth. The ecological footprint measure consists of six types of bio-capacity and their uses, all measured in global hectares:

- cropland
- grazing
- forest

- fishing grounds
- carbon
- built-up land.

The ecological footprint is measured as the difference between the use of these resources and their available capacity. Only for the least developed countries, is the difference more or less zero: they use what they have. For many high-income countries, however, the difference is large. In 2010, use is about 6 global hectares per capita, whereas the bio-capacity is only 3 global hectares per capita. This results in a deficit of 3 hectares per person in the developed world. In other words, producers and consumers in the developed world not only use all available capacity in their own country, they also import natural resources from developing countries, such as wood, food, oil, minerals, and fish, to serve their own wants.

Table 13.1 shows a few examples of ecological footprints. The top panel shows the countries with the largest deficit in bio-capacity, with the Netherlands ranking sixth. This may perhaps help explain the large numbers of Dutch people who are members of environmental organisations. A feeling of guilt? Or urgency?

The bottom panel of Table 13.1 shows the countries with the greatest bio-capacity surplus. As you will see in the column for total bio-capacity, this is due to the large capacity of the land available, not yet used for production and consumption. Gabon, the small West African country with its huge rainforest, is the top country for bio-capacity reserves.

13.2.3.2 Happy Planet Index

The Happy Planet Index combines ecological footprint data with two social economic measures of well-being: one concerning health (life expectancy) and the other happiness (life satisfaction). The *Happy Planet Index* measures how many long and happy lives countries produce per unit of environmental output. This makes the Happy Planet Index a richer well-being index than the ecological footprint measure, because it measures how much people get out of the environment they use, in terms of long and happy lives. The index ranks countries from 0 to 100, but the whole range is not used. The bottom country in 2012, Botswana, scores 22.6 (ranking country number 151), while Costa Rica tops the ranking with a score of 64.

If we now look at the same countries ranked top and bottom for their ecological footprints, we find quite different country rankings on the Happy Planet Index. Table 13.2 shows the top six and the bottom six on the Happy Planet Index.

The Happy Planet Index suffers from an important problem in its measurement of well-being. The problem is that it has only two well-being indicators, and the choice of happiness and life expectancy as capturing well-being is arbitrary. Why not a combination of health indicators, including child mortality? And why a subjective measure of well-being (happiness feelings) rather than an objective indicator?[8]

In order to address this problem, a green well-being indicator must have both sufficient detail about environmental impact, and also sufficient coverage of well-being. There are several proposals, one of them for a Genuine Progress Indicator.[9] It includes 26 measures: economic, environmental, and social. But data collection and calculation is quite complex, and therefore not available for many countries. This is precisely the trade-off for a green well-being measure: the more detailed it is, the less data will be available, so fewer countries can be ranked. . . .

Table 13.1 Ecological footprint: largest deficits and largest surpluses of bio-capacity

	Crop land	Grazing	Forest	Fishing ground	Carbon	Built-up land	Ecological footprint	Total bio-capacity	Ecological reserve
Top six countries									
Gabon	0.48	0.12	0.64	0.15	0.00	0.03	1.4	29.3	27.9
Paraguay	0.70	1.11	0.87	0.02	0.38	0.11	3.2	11.2	8.0
Mongolia	0.26	3.89	0.13	0.00	1.24	0.01	5.5	15.1	9.6
Congo	0.26	0.05	0.47	0.10	0.06	0.03	1.0	13.3	12.3
Bolivia	0.46	1.51	0.17	0.00	0.37	0.06	2.6	18.8	16.3
Canada	0.95	0.26	1.59	0.12	4.03	0.05	7.0	14.9	7.9
Bottom six countries									
The Netherlands	1.85	0.57	0.47	0.17	2.99	0.15	6.2	1.0	−5.2
Qatar	1.03	0.54	0.12	0.58	8.13	0.12	10.5	2.5	−8.0
Belgium	2.14	0.70	0.61	0.23	3.87	0.45	8.0	1.3	−6.7
Kuwait	0.75	0.38	0.25	0.34	4.53	0.08	6.3	0.4	−5.9
Singapore	0.68	0.42	0.30	0.25	3.69	0.00	5.3	0.0	−5.3
UAE	1.35	0.43	0.47	0.29	8.10	0.04	10.7	0.8	−9.8

Note: The units are global hectare capacity minus global hectares used; global hectares are measured using global average productivity.

Source: http://www.footprintnetwork.org/en/index.php/GFN/page/footprint_data_and_results/

Table 13.2 Top and bottom six countries on the Happy Planet Index, 2012

HPI rank	Country	Life expectancy	Well-being	Footprint	Happy Planet Index
Top six countries					
1	Costa Rica	79.3	7.3	2.5	64.0
2	Vietnam	75.2	5.8	1.4	60.4
3	Colombia	73.7	6.4	1.8	59.8
4	Belize	76.1	6.5	2.1	59.3
5	El Salvador	72.2	6.7	2.0	58.9
6	Jamaica	73.1	6.2	1.7	58.5
Bottom six countries					
146	Bahrain	75.1	4.5	6.6	26.6
147	Mali	51.4	3.8	1.9	26.0
148	Central African Rep.	48.4	3.6	1.4	25.3
149	Qatar	78.4	6.6	11.7	25.2
150	Chad	49.6	3.7	1.9	24.7
151	Botswana	53.2	3.6	2.8	22.6

Source: http://www.happyplanetindex.org/data/

13.3 Institutional economics of nature

13.3.1 Formal institutions mediating economy and nature

Since the *Our Common Future* report, there have been several intergovernmental meetings about the environment. This has resulted in various international agreements. For climate change, the most important is the Kyoto Protocol, signed in 1997 in the Japanese city of Kyoto, with country-level targets to reduce global warming. The Kyoto protocol went into force in 2005. The average target was a 5.2 per cent reduction in six greenhouse gases in 2012 as compared to 1990. Only a few countries have not signed the Kyoto Protocol, including that with one of the largest ecological footprints, the USA. Developing countries, including the biggest ones, India and China, did not have to achieve any targets, given their low ecological footprints up to 1997. As a consequence of these exceptions, the global objective of a significant decline in greenhouse gases has not been met. The USA and China increased their CO_2 emissions more between 1990 and 2012 than all the other countries have reduced theirs in line with the Kyoto Protocol. Therefore, the Intergovernmental Panel on Climate Change (IPCC) has urged governments to increase the reduction targets for the coming years.

How is a small but highly industrialised and densely populated country below sea level doing on achieving the reduction targets? Surprisingly bad, given its own high vulnerability to global warming. In 2014, only 4.5 per cent of energy use in the Netherlands was from renewable sources. This should rise to 16 per cent in 2023 according to the National Energy Agreement. The neighbouring country of Germany already met this target in 2013. In the first quarter of 2014, it even achieved 27 per cent renewable energy.[10]

What is worse in this comparison that the proportion of oil and coal used to produce Dutch energy is increasing compared to natural gas. This increases CO_2 emissions. Indeed some economic sectors, including transport and agriculture, receive a subsidy for fossil energy use. Kerosene for the aviation sector has zero taxation, which makes air tickets artificially cheap. Over the past 30 years, cars have become 90 per cent cleaner but the Dutch now drive twice as many kilometres in more luxurious (and hence heavier) cars, which has resulted in increased CO_2 emissions from private car use.

Image 13.2 Renewable energy production in Germany

The country is not only densely populated, ranking fifth among the world's most densely populated countries, but it is also densely populated with farm animals. The Netherlands has 12 million pigs, close to the number of people (17 million). This generates agricultural greenhouse emissions. Moreover, the pork industry relies on the import of soya to feed the pigs, which requires many hectares of land use in other countries, while many of the animals or their meat are exported because we grow more than we can eat ourselves. This whole process of intensive farming and trading generates much CO_2 in the country itself as well as abroad.

The Dutch economy is transport intensive because logistics is a key economic sector, with a major sea-port in the west and a major export partner in the east (Germany). This leads to high nitrogen dioxide (NO_2) emissions from road transport. The EU target for NO_2 for 2015 will not be met by the Netherlands.[11] Moreover, the country is performing well below the EU average in reducing CO_2 emissions. Whereas the EU28 decreased CO_2 emissions from 4,320 to 3,740 megatonnes between 1990 and 2012, the Netherlands only reached the 1990 level in 2012. In other words, the EU has achieved a decline in CO_2 emissions of 13 per cent in 22 years, while the Netherlands has not achieved any decline at all over the same period.[12]

Many political parties, labour unions, employers, housing corporations, consumer platforms, and environmental organisations in the Netherlands therefore feel Dutch policies on climate change must be urgently speeded up. In 2013, they reached an agreement through the acclaimed typical Dutch *poldermodel* of collective bargaining with all relevant social groups through consensus. This resulted in the National Energy Agreement. It includes a wide variety of policy measures on energy supply, energy transport, energy use in living, industry, and transport, and on employment in the energy sector. Box 13.1 provides an overview of the targets and policy measures agreed, most of them for a 10-year period. The energy agreement will be monitored by an independent committee. But, as for the international agreements, there are no sanctions involved. . . .

> **Box 13.1 The 2013 Dutch National Energy Agreement**
>
> - Target of 60% less greenhouse emissions in 2050 as compared to 1990
> - Target of 16% of energy use from renewable sources in 2023
> - Certified energy labels for houses and tools to reduce energy use in everyday life
> - Housing corporations will renovate 111,000 houses to high energy efficiency by 2018
> - Less bureaucracy and fewer constraints for citizens to generate their own energy, individually or in communities
> - Better facilities for commuters to travel by bike, for example the provision of bicycle fast-lanes
> - Projects and opportunities for training in green skills for employees who lose their jobs in fossil energy intensive sectors
> - Banks will set up a sustainable investment instrument in capital markets to fund sustainable development
> - The government will encourage green technology through its procurement policies
> - Firms will obtain an international competitive edge in smart solutions for sustainability
> - Tax reductions for business investments in clean technology
> - Lower subsidies for energy prices from 2015 onwards for the greenhouse agricultural sector if it does not meet the 2015 reduction targets it agreed to
> - 4450-megawatt wind energy production on the North Sea and 6000-megawatt production on land by 2020
>
> Source: http://www.energieakkoordser.nl/energieakkoord.aspx

The problem with formal agreements on targets for emission reductions is that when a country does not meet the agreed targets, there are no sanctions. So, these formal institutions – UN agreements, EU agreements, national agreements – are not very effective in reducing the environmental impact of the economy. As Diagram 13.3 shows, they clearly have not helped to reduce the trends in car use and CO_2 emissions in the Netherlands.

13.3.2 Self-regulation

Firms increasingly realise that reducing their environmental impact not only decreases costs in the long run but is also smart business. It projects a responsible brand image, attracts long-term investment, signals a willingness to embrace innovation, and reduces operational risk. This trend is observable among all types of businesses, small and big, and operating in competitive markets or in oligopolistic and monopolistic market structures.

For multinational companies, their dependence on raw materials and fuel makes them vulnerable to world market price fluctuations. While the growth in the world population and world GDP will put increasing pressure on input prices. This is the reason why worldwide, firms make an effort to reduce their material resource inputs and reduce their dependence on fossil energy. And that is precisely why those companies which perform best in reducing their environmental impact want to be listed on the Dow Jones Sustainability Index (DJSI). Ranking on the DJSI has a double impact. First, it enables investors to integrate sustainability

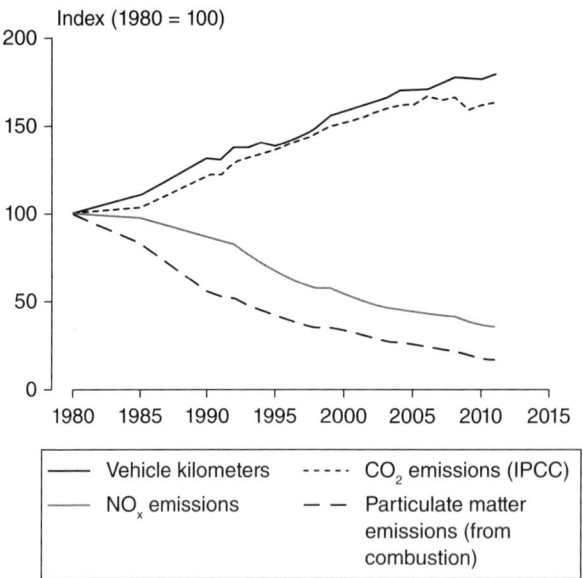

Diagram 13.3 Environmental pressure of road traffic in the Netherlands, 1980–2015

Source: *Changing Track, Changing Tack: Dutch Ideas for a Robust Environmental Policy for the 21st Century.* The Hague: PBL Netherlands Environmental Assessment Agency, 2013. Available at http://www.pbl.nl/sites/default/files/cms/publicaties/PBL_2013_Changing%20track,%20changing%20tack_1183.pdf

into their portfolios. Second, it provides an engagement platform that encourages companies to adopt sustainable best practices. Companies like to be the best, to beat the others – they generally thrive on competition. The DJSI provides them with a competitive platform to play precisely that game, which makes them sometimes more ambitious than national and international agreements. For the top firms on the DJSI, it is no longer the case that they follow government regulation. Instead, they demand more ambitious and consistent long-term regulation from governments to speed up the environmental performance of *all* firms.

Box 13.2 Dow Jones Sustainability Index

The Dow Jones Sustainability Index (DJSI) started in 1999. Today, over 3,000 firms worldwide are invited to participate. The ranking of firms is based on an elaborate corporate sustainability assessment, which provides an analysis of all company practices, such as innovation, supply chain management, climate strategy, and stakeholder engagement, with a focus on industry-specific environmental risks and opportunities. The assessment is not published; only the results are made public. The methodology consists of ranking companies in twenty four sectors and fifty nine industries based on benchmarks. Only the best companies in their industry and sector are listed on the DJSI.

Source: http://www.sustainability-indices.com/

13.3.3 Individual and household behavioural change

Environmental damage is caused by human behaviour. So, reductions in environmental impact depend on behavioural change. This is where informal institutions come in, because the slow progress in the reduction in greenhouse emissions can be attributed to slow behavioural change. People follow routines, adjust to group norms, and do not have a strong enough will to really change their behaviour on a structural basis. People in general, and economic agents in particular, have two parallel decision-making systems in their brains. The first is the rational, calculating system, which we use to make cost–benefit calculations and deliberate before coming to a decision. The second one is the automatic, intuitive system, in which we make decisions so fast that we are not even aware of it, based on habits, values, norms, and framing of information. The standard policy measures in any policy area are geared towards the first decision-making system. But they do not work very well when economic agents make decisions with their automatic decision-making system.

Here is where *nudging* comes in, the framing of choice situations towards a desirable default choice. Nudges work through the automatic decision-making system via three distinctive pathways: (1) default, (2) stimulus, and (3) feedback. Often, nudges are combined with traditional policy instruments (financial incentives, rules, and awareness campaigns) and can make these more effective.

13.3.3.1 Changing the default

Most people go with the default when offered a default and alternatives, because they assume the default will be good enough, or they see it as the social norm and do not want to deviate, or they think it should be the best tested on safety or economic benefit. A nudge directed at a default changes the default in order to change the behaviour of those who tend to follow the default.

An example of an environmental nudge in the Netherlands initiated by the private sector, based on a default change, is that shops which used to offer a free plastic bag to carry home one's shopping, changed to offering to help to put the goods into the customer's own bag and charging (€0.10) for a plastic bag. Whereas the old default of a free plastic bag stimulated the majority of consumers to thoughtlessly carry their shopping home in a plastic bag, the reversal of the default is expected to reduce the use of plastic bags by 50–75 per cent according to a Dutch pilot study by the packaging industry.[13]

13.3.3.2 Stimulus of a social norm

Economic agents are social animals and tend to follow group norms. Sometimes because they do not like to deviate or simply because they assume that the group knows best or they do not want to put in effort to make a deliberate decision, collecting the necessary information themselves. This habitual behaviour allows for policy measures which reinforce environmental behavioural norms. Such as the DJSI for firms. For example, energy suppliers can provide neighbourhoods with information about the average energy use per household. This will often be perceived as an acceptable and feasible social norm by the inhabitants of the neighbourhood. Moreover, this will stick in people's mind as a target to be achieved by themselves if they happen to be above the average level of energy use. Hence, the information about the average behaviour of others may stimulate others to behave accordingly, either because they like to follow the norm set by the average energy use score, or they like to compete with their neighbours and beat the average. In both cases, the average energy use score in the neighbourhood will improve. So, what works for firms in the DJSI, can also work for consumers: triggering their taste for competition to combine economic benefit and environmental improvement.

13.3.3.3 Personalised feedback

People find it difficult to change their habits if they have no idea what the consequences of their habits are. Often, people want to reduce energy use, for a mix of financial and environmental reasons, but have no idea which activity uses how many kilowatt hours. Smart energy use meters in homes give feedback on real-time energy use. Whereas normally one receives an energy bill after several weeks or months, smart meters provide direct feedback which can be related to particular behaviour. For example, it allows people to see how much energy their computer uses as they surf the internet for an hour, or it informs their teenage son how much his long shower costs in kilowatt hours as well as in euros. On an annual basis, such smart energy use meters have already saved Dutch households several hundreds of euros per year.

13.3.3.4 Dutch Disease and the resource curse

Economics has a term derived from a policy first applied on a large scale in the Netherlands: *Dutch Disease*. This refers to the negative economic consequences of the export of natural resources. In the Netherlands this was the case for natural gas, which was discovered in the 1960s. What are the two major negative consequences? First, a sudden increase in exports leads to an appreciation of the currency. There is a higher demand for a country's currency without an accompanying demand for foreign currency for intermediary goods for production or from added wage income (natural fossil resources are capital intensive and do not create many jobs). Currency appreciation disadvantages all other exports from the country, which will become relatively more expensive abroad. This negatively affects the private sector, such as agriculture and industry, while at the same time the public sector benefits from the export revenues of a natural resource (either because it is exploited by a public firm, or because the natural resources and their exports are highly taxed).

The second negative effect of high natural resource revenues is a fiscal effect. When a significant amount of government revenues is dependent upon windfall gains, as from the discovery of natural resources, this makes the government budget vulnerable to changes in the natural resource earnings, which are often dependent upon world market prices. When world market prices decline, the government budget will go down as well.

In the 1960s, a large natural gas field was discovered under the northern province of Groningen. The gas is extracted by a public company, Gasunie, and its export revenues go directly to the Treasury and are available for the current government budget. Natural gas is a major source of electricity production in the Netherlands, so that approximately 50 per cent of Dutch electricity is generated by gas-fired power stations, and close to 100 per cent of houses, firms, and greenhouses are heated by domestic natural gas.

Whereas in the past gas revenues contributed between 10 per cent and 40 per cent (the best year was 1985 when oil prices were very high, and gas prices were pegged to oil prices) to the government budget, today they have declined to 5–10 per cent. Other countries have much higher shares of natural resource revenues, indicating a move abroad of the Dutch Disease.

For example, Mexico relies on their oil exports for about 40 per cent of government revenues, and in some oil-rich Arab countries the share exceeds 80 per cent or even 90 per cent.

Perhaps out of pity for the Dutch, the economic term for the negative side effects of natural resource revenues has been replaced with a broader but equally negative one: the *natural resource curse*. This refers to the paradoxical effect of natural resources on economic growth and economic development. It consists of three dimensions (one extra in addition to the two Dutch Disease disadvantages):

1 Currency appreciation, and hence loss of competitiveness of other export sectors;
2 Volatility of government revenues due to volatile world market prices;
3 Risk of rent-seeking, corruption, and social conflict over the resource revenues in the case of weak governments, which leads to a leakage of revenues to a small elite group.

Luckily for the Dutch, the first disadvantage has disappeared in the Netherlands with the introduction of the euro: the Dutch guilder no longer exists, so there is no longer a negative effect on the exchange rate. The appreciation effect of Dutch gas exports on the euro is negligible, given the fact that the eurozone includes many more and bigger economies than the Dutch. Also the second disadvantage is diminishing, because natural gas prices in the Netherlands are increasingly determined by spot-market contracts, independent of the world price for oil. This happens through a so-called gas hub, an exchange market for Dutch natural gas. Even households can now choose to buy gas on a short- or long-term contract and at a fixed or flexible gas price. The risk of the third negative effect of the resource curse mentioned above, rent-seeking, corruption, and social conflict, is low in the Netherlands given its high ranking on transparency and anti-corruption indexes. But it is high in some developing countries suffering from a natural resources curse, for example Congo with its diverse and

Image 13.3 Earthquake damage in Groningen

scarce mineral resources. However, there is a distribution problem involved in gas extraction in the Netherlands, leading to increasing social tension.

This distribution problem concerns the negative externalities of gas extraction, causing harm to the environment and buildings in the province of Groningen. The environmental damage is relatively limited because most of the operations happen underground. But the economic damage to houses and other buildings has been increasing over recent years, due to earthquakes induced by gas extraction. In 2012, an earthquake of the magnitude of 3.6 on the Richter scale hit the province. The financial benefits move to the national budget, while the citizens of Groningen suffer from insecurity, damaged homes, and losses in the market value of their houses. The biggest fear is a high-impact earthquake with not only material damage but also human casualties.

Since 2012, the number and severity of earthquakes in the province of Groningen has increased. The inhabitants of the villages on the gas fields are worried and have demanded compensation from the Dutch state. After protests and negotiations in 2013, they have received €1.2 billion compensation for a 5-year period. But the bureaucracy involved has left many households with cracks in their walls, emergency rooms in cellars, sleeping problems, stress, and their houses held up inside and outside by structural supports. There is an urgent need for a new institutional setup to deal with fair compensation for households and to reduce gas extraction to lower the level of fear about future earthquakes. The national government has agreed to reduce the amount of gas extracted in one field. But according to experts, this small reduction is insufficient, while the government's revenues still depend significantly on gas revenues. . . .

The only way out of this dilemma of the resource curse is institutional change. How? By cutting the flow of gas revenues to the treasury and building a separate wealth fund from which compensation can be paid and a faster transition towards renewable energy sources can be financed. Is this fantasy? No. Norway did this two decades after it discovered oil. It set up a *sovereign wealth fund*, which is a public investment fund containing the revenues from natural resource exports and managed by the state, a tool also used by other countries. The Norwegian sovereign wealth fund, set up in 1990, appeared to be a vaccine against the Dutch Disease. The Norwegian fund is the world's biggest sovereign wealth fund, worth over €500 billion. The Treasury is allowed to use the investment revenues, estimated at around 4 per cent annually, but not the fund itself, as long as oil resources remain productive. The fund revenues largely pay for pensions, but also for education and green infrastructure, although the Norwegian green movement argues that the fund should invest much more in the transition towards a green economy.

13.4 Post Keynesian economics of nature

The Keynesian economic perspective on ecological economics starts with an essay written by Keynes himself, in 1930, in the middle of the Great Depression. The essay was called 'Economic Possibilities for our Grandchildren'. Keynes argued that in the distant future, capital will have replaced most labour, providing economic agents with more leisure time than they ever had before, but as a mixed blessing for their purpose in life:[14]

> to those who sweat for their daily bread leisure is a longed-for sweet – until they get it.

Keynes recognised the challenges of population growth for the well-being of all, but did not foresee the environmental problems of today.

13.4.1 Uncertainty and the precautionary principle

The Post Keynesian distinction between risk and uncertainty is crucial for ecological economics. Climate change, nuclear energy disasters, and resource extraction calamities are all in the realm of uncertainty – without any known or even near-known probabilities because we are not aware of all the possible future states to which probabilities should be attached. And since the economy is an open system, embedded in the closed system of the earth's biosphere, ecological uncertainties have direct and unknown effects on the economy.

Uncertainty has no probabilities, so how then can we protect our economies, and human life more generally, from the vulnerability to ecological disasters? Open systems theory, with its recognition of non-linear dynamic relationships between variables, provides an answer for this. The character of non-linear dynamics in open systems is that they move at two different scale levels. Around certain values, they are relatively stable. But beyond a threshold, open system dynamics become chaotic with amplified effects on other variables in the system, directly and through feedback loops. It is like a butterfly in Japan causing a hurricane in Canada. So, in order to prevent an open system descending into chaos, with uncontrollable effects, the critical values in the system need to remain below their threshold values. This is very similar to Minsky's recognition of financial fragility. Like financial markets, ecological systems are fragile and can cause harm to the economy.

For ecological economics, this reduces the complex analytical question of open system dynamics to a much simpler question of determining the relevant threshold variables and the critical values under which we should remain with our economies. The availability of data on resource use has led to the estimation of *planetary boundaries*, which are the thresholds beyond which there will be irreversible damage to ecological systems.[15] The starting point of this threshold analysis is the recognition that humans have lived for 10,000 years in an unusually stable natural environment. This has changed since the industrial revolution, when economic activities began to change this stability and may even push it towards an irreversible state in which human life and well-functioning economies are no longer possible. In order to remain in the stable state, we need to keep our economic activities within planetary boundaries dictated by our closed biosphere system. There are eight subsystems in the biosphere for which threshold values have been estimated and two more for which they have not yet been estimated:

- Climate change
- Rate of biodiversity loss
- Interference with the nitrogen cycle
- Interference with the phosphorous cycle
- Stratospheric ozone depletions
- Ocean acidification
- Global freshwater use
- Change in land use
- Chemical pollution
- Atmospheric aerosol loading.

Moreover, the boundaries are inter-related. For example, ozone depletions may speed up climate change. Irreversibility is a key element in the determination of planetary boundaries. For example, loss of biodiversity is not likely to be reversed, and certainly not with the same species. This recognition of uncertainty about possible damaging and irreversible effects leads to the *precautionary principle*. This is a decision rule to avoid ecological damage in the face of lack of scientific proof about the type, extent, and impact of economic behaviour on the ecological system. This principle puts the burden of proof on the proponents of such actions: they must convince policy makers not only that the expected benefits exceed the costs of an action, but also that there will not be any significant unanticipated damage. Applying the precautionary principle to the planetary boundaries, research has estimated most of the boundary values. The sobering message is that three thresholds have already been transgressed. These are the boundaries for climate change, biodiversity loss, and the nitrogen cycle. Hence, Post Keynesian ecological economics teaches us that there is no time to lose – not because we know what will happen and when, but because we do not know.

In Post Keynesian economics, uncertainty about possible events with severe damage, such as financial crises, leads to policy measures setting boundaries to the operating space of markets. For financial markets, these include capital reserve controls for banks and capital account controls on international capital flows, a limit on bonuses, and a financial transactions tax. For the planetary boundaries, parallel policy measures should be found to keep economic behaviour within the planetary boundaries. Post Keynesian economics suggests, just like it does for the prevention of severe financial crises, the scale of operations should be reduced. This is precisely what many concerned citizens do in the area of energy production: they shift towards local small-scale energy production and locally produced food. Other forms of localisation of economic behaviour are recycling of consumer goods, insulation of homes against cold and heat, and growing vegetables.

In the Netherlands localisation of energy production is done through a wide variety of initiatives at the level of individual households, farms, neighbourhoods, and virtual communities. A tax on new cars is used to finance the recycling of car parts, 95 per cent of which are now re-used. The city of Rotterdam has subsidised roof gardens by €25 per square metre, leading to citizens not only having roof gardens but also producing their own vegetables and fruit on the roofs of their homes. Wind co-operatives have become increasingly popular for community-level power production. Such co-operatives are groups of consumers who invest in a wind turbine to generate the power they use in their households. The surplus energy, produced when there are strong winds and at times of low energy use, is sold to regular energy firms. An example is the Dutch co-operative *de Windvogel*, which owns six wind turbines and has a membership of 3,300. Together, the six turbines produce 8,800 megawatt hours, supplying the electricity needs of 2,500 households.

13.4.2 Ecological stock-flow model

The previously mentioned I-PAT model is an ecological stock-flow model measuring the environmental impact of resource use. This model can be integrated into a Post Keynesian stock-flow model which was developed to analyse flows of money and stocks of debt in the economy. Both types of stock-flow models are integrated by incorporating GDP and the trade balance of material consumption into the model. This leads to change in two of the four I-PAT variables: I (impact) and T (technology). I is replaced with a new variable DMC, which stands for domestic material consumption:

$$DMC = DE - PTB$$

in which DE = domestic extraction of resources and PTB = the physical trade balance, consisting of net imports of material resources minus net exports of material resources. This allows us to define material intensity (MI), which is relative to GDP:

$$MI = DMC / GDP$$

and this is then the variable used for T. This gives the ecological stock-flow model:

$$DMC = P \times A \times MI$$

The model has been used to understand the trends in environmental damage in the fast-growing Asia-Pacific region.[16] Diagram 13.4 shows how the level of technology has lagged behind GDP since the 1990s. Whereas the material impact of economic growth is declining for the world as a whole, for the Asia-Pacific region MI is increasing. The next Diagram, 13.5, shows DMC. This shows, again, that the growth rate of environmental impact per capita for the Asia-Pacific region is higher than that of the rest of the world.

Interestingly, the increasing environmental impact values for Asia and the Pacific region can hardly be attributed to population growth (P). For the regional average, material intensity (18 per cent) contributes twice as much as population growth (9 per cent) to the increase in domestic material consumption. Moreover, it is affluence, the increased consumption level per capita (A), which contributes most (26 per cent increase over the 2000–2008 period). In China, population growth contributed 5 per cent, whereas consumption per capita growth contributed 107 per cent, slightly compensated for by a decline in material intensity of 8 per cent. See Table 13.3 for data on the top five largest consumer countries in the Asia-Pacific region.

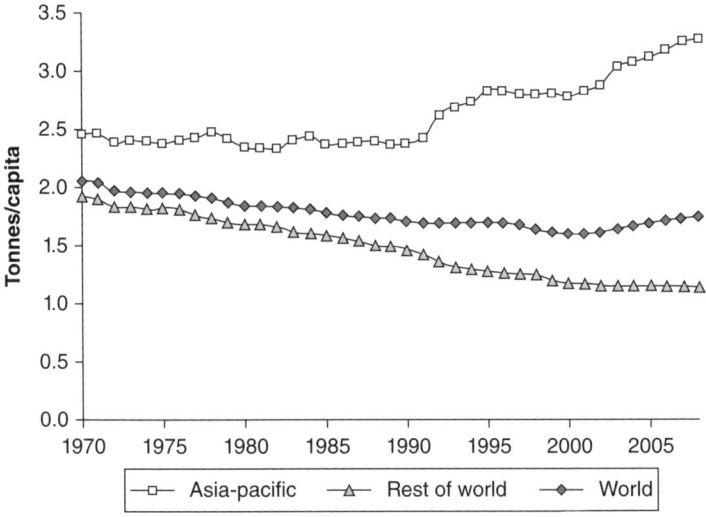

Diagram 13.4 Trends in material intensity (MI) in the Asia-Pacific region

Source: *Resource Trends in Material Flows and Resource Productivity in Asia and the Pacific*. Bangkok: UNEP, 2013.

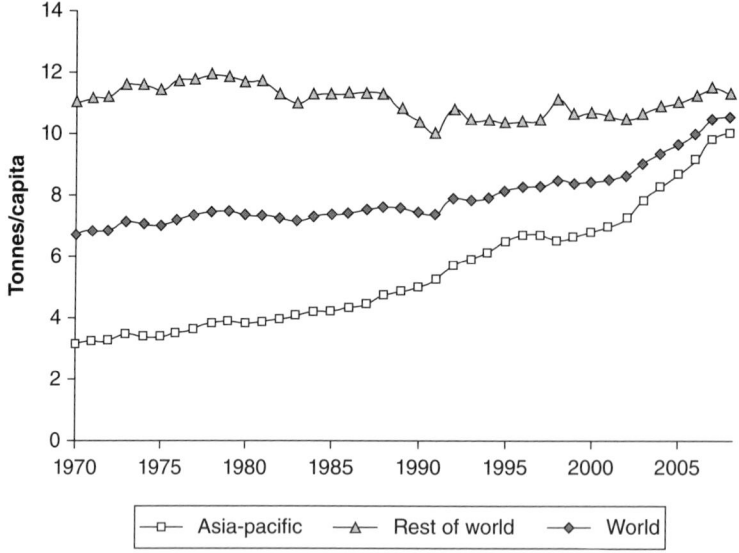

Diagram 13.5 Trends in domestic material consumption (DMC) in the Asia-Pacific region

Source: *Resource Trends in Material Flows and Resource Productivity in Asia and the Pacific.* Bangkok: UNEP, 2013.

Table 13.3 Drivers of change in domestic material consumption, Asia-Pacific region, 2000–2008 (%)

	DMC	P	A	MI
Australia	12	12	15	−13
China	100	5	107	−8
India	45	12	58	−18
Indonesia	27	11	35	−15
Japan	−19	1	10	−26

Source: *Recent Trends in Material Flows and Resource Productivity in Asia and the Pacific.* Bangkok: UNEP, 2013.

The table shows that China has doubled material consumption, while Japan has reduced it. And it points out that for all countries, the impact of population growth is smaller than the impact of affluence.

The ecological economic stock-flow model allows for the analysis of environmental impact per country, per capita, and relative to a country's level of economic development and material trade balance. The current version only addresses the planetary boundary on land use, which can function as a threshold variable in the model. The model needs extension to the other planetary boundaries, to include all relevant environmental thresholds within which the economy should remain in order to be sustainable.

13.5 Neoclassical economics of nature

Environmental economics is the field in neoclassical economics which studies the possibilities and constraints required so that economic growth will have less environmental impact. It understands the relationship between the economy and the natural environment in terms of inadequate pricing. This takes two forms. One is low or absent prices for natural resources, such as clean air, safe drinking water, forests, and biodiversity. Often these natural resources have no price at all, and hence, have no value in markets. The other form is inadequate low prices for products that have negative environmental externalities. The product prices are too low because the full costs, including pollution and resource depletion, are not taken into account in the market price at which the products are sold.

13.5.1 The environmental Kuznets curve

With economic growth, there is more resource use, and without policies to address the inadequate pricing of the natural environment, the negative impact of economic growth on the environment increases. But only up to a certain level of national income, according to neoclassical economics: after that income level, pollution decreases again. This is what is called the *environmental Kuznets curve* (EKC), an inverted U-shaped curve picturing the relationship between pollution on the one hand and a country's income level on the other hand. See Diagram 13.6. The turning point of the curve is argued to lie between US$5,000 and US$10,000 per capita per year. After that point, pollution is supposed to decline.

The EKC is empirically observed for selected types of local air and water pollutants, such as smoke in cities, nitrates, cadmium, and faecal coliform in rivers. For many other pollutants and damage, ranging from small particles in the air to dissolved oxygen in rivers, and from CO_2 in the atmosphere to loss of tropical rainforest, no decrease is observed with economic growth.

What explains the EKC for those pollutants where it can be observed to hold? There are basically three factors:

1. Environmental regulation (targets, prohibitions, taxes, subsidies);
2. New technology (filters, recycling);
3. Shift away from pollution-intensive economic activity (such as manufacturing) to labour-intensive economic activity (personal services sector).

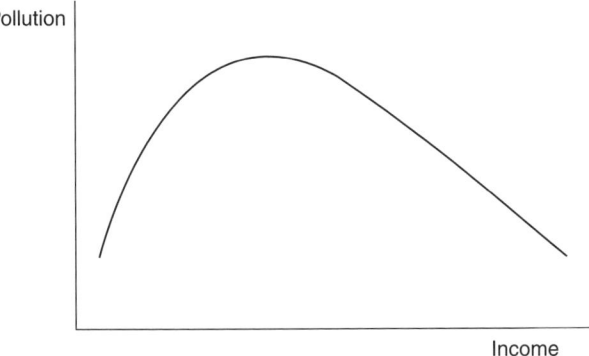

Diagram 13.6 Environmental Kuznets curve

The first and second factors behind the EKC are largely driven by public awareness and consumer demand for lower pollution and better environmental quality. The third factor is more problematic, because it indicates that the EKC may hold for developed countries, but not for developing countries or the world as a whole. Polluting industries shifting from the developed world to the developing world will only shift pollution globally, not reduce it. The trends in global environmental degradation as sketched in section 13.1 are not likely to reverse with economic growth, wherever this growth is concentrated. EKC seems empirically valid for developed countries only and for a limited number of local forms of air and water pollution.

13.5.2 Cost–benefit analysis

The inadequate pricing of productive activities in the economy can be addressed, according to neoclassical economists, by mechanisms that force the internalisation of the full costs of natural resources and externalities. At the micro level, this is done through cost–benefit analysis (CBA). For example, through willingness-to-pay surveys resulting in an estimate of the money value of natural resources by the economic agents directly affected by the degradation of the resource. This is what was explained in Chapter 7 with the example of a city park: as long as the collective monetary evaluation of an additional square metre of park exceeds the costs of building and maintaining it, the government should build a park because it is cost effective.

The same method can be used for the opposite, namely to estimate the money value of preventing pollution. In that case, a survey could ask how much money people would be willing to pay to save a nearby forest from destruction. When it is a private company planning to cut down the rainforest to plant oil palm trees, the local government may undertake a willingness-to-pay survey and demand an environmental tax from the private company equal to the sum of money that the people living in the area would be willing to pay to keep the forest (and not be employed by the firm). If the firm considers this tax too high relative to its expected profits, it will not start the palm oil project and the rainforest is saved. But if the palm oil is expected to be very profitable, the firm may choose to pay the tax.

In December 1991, the then chief economist of the World Bank, Larry Summers, wrote a memo to some colleagues arguing that shifting pollution from rich to poor countries would be beneficial from a CBA perspective. The memo was leaked to *The Economist*. It caused a scandal. Later, two economic philosophers used it as an example in their textbook on economics and ethics. They have quoted the memo, which is copied in Box 13.3.

CBA, in particular when it includes social and environmental criteria, can be a powerful tool for investment evaluations. But is should always be used with caution, because money units are always imperfect measures of complex reality. Perhaps that is what Larry Summers wanted to say to his colleagues.

Box 13.3 Pollution in poor countries is cheaper . . .

'Just between you and me, shouldn't the World Bank be encouraging more migration of the dirty industries to the LDCs [less developed countries]? I can think of three reasons: (1) The measurement of the costs of health-impairing pollution depends on the foregone earnings from increased morbidity and mortality. From this point of view a given amount of health-impairing pollution should be done in the country with the lowest cost, which will be the country with the lowest wages. I think the economic logic behind dumping a load of toxic waste in the lowest-wage country is impeccable and we should face up to that. (2) The costs of pollution are likely to be non-linear as the initial increments of pollution probably have very low cost.

I've always thought that under-populated countries in Africa are vastly under polluted. (. . . .) (3) The demand for a clean environment for aesthetic and health reasons is likely to have very high income-elasticity. The concern over an agent that causes a one-in-a-million change in the odds of prostate cancer is obviously going to be much higher in a country where people survive to get prostate cancer than in a county where under-5 mortality is 200 per thousand. Also, much of the concern over industrial atmospheric discharge is about visibility-impairing particulates. (. . . .) The problem with the arguments against all of these proposals for more pollution in LDCs (intrinsic rights to certain goods, moral reasons, social concerns, lack of adequate markets, etc.) could be turned around and used more or less effectively against every Bank proposal for liberalisation.'

Source: Hausman, D. and M. McPherson (1996) *Economic Analysis and Moral Philosophy*. Cambridge: Cambridge University Press, pp. 9–10.

13.5.3 Carbon dioxide trading market

At the macro level, inadequate pricing is solved, in the neoclassical perspective, by the creation of a market for the externality. In a way, this comes down to creating markets for the right to pollute, where increasing pollution and/or a reduction in permits to pollute, drive up the market price and hence stimulate cleaner production by firms in order to prevent increasing expenditures on pollution permits. The idea uses the market mechanism rather than the state or contingent valuation through surveys to affect the environmental impact of the economy.

The actual creation and monitoring of such a market is quite difficult if the initial objectives of a substantive reduction in greenhouse gases are to be achieved. It shows that markets need more institutions than only property rights. A good illustration of the workings, effects, and challenges of such a market is the European Union Emissions Trading System, in short: EU ETS.

The EU ETS is the world's first and largest trading market for carbon dioxide (CO_2). It was created by the European Commission in 2005 as the major European-wide mechanism for the implementation of the Kyoto Protocol, which required an average 5.2 per cent reduction in greenhouse gas emissions in the period 2008–2012 as compared to 1990 emission levels, for 38 industrialised countries. However, the European Commission (EC) has acknowledged that additional policy measures are necessary in order to achieve more ambitious reductions of 60–80 per cent by the year 2050, which the EC deems necessary to prevent the global average temperature from rising more than 2°C above pre-industrial levels. This has resulted in new reduction targets set by the EU, namely to reduce CO_2 emissions by 20 per cent on average by 2020, again as compared to 1990. The objective of the EU ETS is to help the 28 EU member states to achieve their commitments to the Kyoto Protocol and to the new EU emission target in a cost-effective way.

The EU ETS is a market in permits for the emission of CO_2 and equivalent greenhouse gases. One permit allows the emission of 1 tonne of CO_2. The market involves over 10,000 energy-intensive plants in the EU, mainly in the energy production sector, but also the steel, construction, and paper industries. It thereby covers about 45 per cent of all CO_2 emissions in the EU. The EU ETS determines the total number of permits in the market. In this way, it creates scarcity by putting a cap on the total number of permits available on the market. The cap on the trade pushes up the price of permits if it is set at an effective level. Experts have estimated that this is the case when prices move up to €20 or €30 for a permit (that is, per tonne CO_2).[17] Below that price, there is insufficient scarcity of permits, and hence, pollution remains relatively cheap so that the market will not lead to significant reductions in emissions.

How does it work? Firms have to keep an account of their CO_2 emissions and report annually how much they have emitted. When they emit more than their allowance, they have to buy additional permits. Firms which have emitted less than they were entitled to can either keep the surplus on their emissions account to be used in later years (called banking), or sell it to firms which have a deficit in permits. The extent of trading can be explained with a neoclassical marginal cost analysis. If the marginal cost for a firm of obtaining a permit exceeds the cost of reducing emissions by this firm (for example by using new filter technology), this leads to greener production. Similarly, when the marginal cost of a permit is relatively low (a low permit price), this will not stimulate the use of cleaner technologies or a shift to renewable energy sources: buying permits will be cheaper than investing in clean technology. As with CBA, a pollution trading system relies on prices, not regulation, taxation, or social norms.

Did it work? Not quite as expected. The EU ETS has three phases, the first (2005–2007) of which was a try-out phase. In the first phase, at least 95 per cent of the allowances were allocated freely, with a price of zero. The remaining permits were allowed to be sold by member state governments at a national CO_2 auction. Only four countries did so, with only Denmark selling its remaining 5 per cent for this purpose. The other 24 member states gave the remaining 5 per cent of permits away for free. In the second phase, which ran parallel to the Kyoto Protocol period (2008–2012), at least 90 per cent of permits were allocated freely, while again only a few permits were sold at auction. The caps set by the EU for the individual countries were lowered to create more scarcity. The third phase (2013–2020) started off with a very low permit price of €3–5 in the first few months of 2013. As a consequence, the EU has decided not to bring additional permits on to the market until 2016. The market has an oversupply of permits, which keeps the price very low. Much lower than the €20–30 per permit necessary for a strong financial incentive to shift to clean technologies.

Did the market lead to a reduction in CO_2 emissions? The first phase was not successful because the allowances exceeded the actual emissions by 5.6 per cent. So, the market did not push for reductions. Only three countries experienced a shortage and had to buy additional permits. Some countries had considerable surpluses, such as France (17 per cent) and the Netherlands (11 per cent), which they were allowed to bank, as assets on their emissions accounts. The second phase, although with a lower cap (2,083 million tonnes CO_2 per year), appeared hardly effective either. This was largely due to the financial crisis, which resulted in lower levels of production and construction and hence, lower levels of energy use. In 2009, actual emissions were 5 per cent below the allocation of permits. At the same time, the average CO_2 price decreased from €22 in 2008 to €14 in 2009. During 2010 it fluctuated around €15, with a small increase up to mid-2011 to €17. From mid-2011 onwards, the CO_2 price found itself in free-fall with prices stabilising at around €3–5 in 2013, when the third phase began. All three phases showed considerable price fluctuations. For example, in the first phase, the price peaked at more than €30 per tonne CO_2 in April 2006, whereas during the

Diagram 13.7 Price development in the EU ETS

Source: *Changing Track, Changing Tack: Dutch Ideas for a Robust Environmental Policy for the 21st Century.* The Hague: PBL Netherlands Environmental Assessment Agency, 2013, p. 32.
Available at http://www.pbl.nl/sites/default/files/cms/publicaties/PBL_2013_Changing%20track,%20changing%20tack_1183.pdf

first months of 2007 it fell to less than €1. Moreover, firms have banked large reserves. The accumulated surplus that firms hold in permits is similar to an entire year of CO_2 emissions of between 1.50 and 2 billion tonnes CO_2.[18] This banking of permits creates a disincentive to invest in clean technology and green energy.

In order to make the market for CO_2 permits more effective, the third phase has considerable changes. These include:[19]

1 An EU-wide cap of a 1.74 per cent reduction per year in relation to the cap in phase II. This should achieve a reduction of 21 per cent in greenhouse emissions as compared to 2005 by 2020 and a reduction of 43 per cent by 2030.
2 More industries and greenhouse gases will be included.
3 Phasing out of free allowances and an increase in auctioning at market prices.

The expected benefits of phase III include a fund from auction sales, at least 50 per cent of which will be invested in low-carbon technologies. And from 2021 onwards, the EU ETS will introduce a stabilisation fund, which reduces the number of surplus permits in the hands of the private sector, and enables stabilisation of price fluctuations by the European Commission. Whether phase III will be more effective than phases I and II remains to be seen. The empirical literature has recognised nine weaknesses in EU ETS phases I and II:

1 The global financial crisis which hit Europe in 2008 led to reduced demand for CO_2 and hence a reduction in the price of CO_2 permits. This event shows that the scarcity in the market is strongly influenced by the economic cycle, with ineffective caps during economic downturns.

2   The energy-intensive sector targeted by the EU ETS is operating in (regional) monopolies and oligopolies. Since such markets allow cost price increases to be transferred, at least in part, to consumers, the firms do not have the cost reduction incentive they would have if they operated in more competitive markets. The so-called pass-through rate for this sector is estimated to be 75–100 per cent of the cost price increase. So, consumers pay the CO_2 permit price, in particular low-income households and elderly people in Europe who spend a relatively large proportion of their household expenditures on energy, in particular during cold winters. It has been estimated that in the UK, at a pass-through rate of 80 per cent, consumers pay £117 extra for their energy bill each year because of the pass-through of permit costs by firms.[20]

3   Government capture by powerful energy companies and even fraud through the abuse of VAT rules in intra-European trade.

4   Rent-seeking by firms, in particular by energy companies who have received the largest free allowances in the system and hence have accumulated large surpluses of permits. Since the financial crisis, they have sold these unused surpluses to banks and hedge funds, which brought them windfall gains. While the financial trading companies use the permits for speculative purposes. This may lead to a carbon bubble, an inflated price for carbon-related assets on bank balances. It is estimated for the Netherlands that the windfall gains from selling unused permits were €3–5 per megawatt hour of energy produced.[21]

5   Permission to offset CO_2 emissions with investments in environmental protection in developing countries. This is facilitated through the UN's Clean Development Mechanism (CDM) whereby firms can compensate for pollution in their home countries by funding green projects in the developing world. Planting of trees in the Amazon region is often cheaper than installing new green technology in EU-based factories. Moreover, it allows them to invest in those green projects with the highest marginal benefits CO_2 equivalents, which gives them very high CO_2 reductions in their emission accounts. During phase II, firms were allowed to buy CDM credits worth 280 megatonnes of CO_2, which was 13 per cent of the total amount of the market cap. This shift away from reducing pollution in developed countries to reducing pollution in developing countries is the mirror image of what Larry Summers had proposed in his memo at the World Bank 20 years earlier (see Box 13.3).

6   Relatively warm winters and strong winds bring about falls in non-renewable energy prices, because of the EU rule that green energy must always have priority in energy distribution networks. This has resulted in the fact that in France nuclear energy plants, which cannot be switched off during off-peak hours, need to sell their energy at negative prices: they have to pay to get the necessary demand. And whereas energy demand used to peak around mid-day, it no longer necessarily does so, because daily solar energy production picks up right at that time and peaks later. In fact, hourly supply and demand is determined at the margin more by the weather than by energy supply and demand.

7   Cheaper CO_2 makes heavily polluting coal more attractive than cleaner gas for energy production in the EU. Moreover, cheaper gas in the USA has resulted in an oversupply of coal in the USA. The consequence is cheap imported coal from the USA to the EU. This leads electric power generators to switch from gas to coal in Europe. European countries are now planning several dozens of new coal-fired power plants. At the same time, they have ceased production in several gas-fired power plants, including four in the Netherlands.

8   The trading system is prone to so-called carbon leakage. This is similar to the leakage of macroeconomic stimulation through the multiplier effect of spending. When the price of permits becomes relatively high, firms may decide to relocate partially or completely outside Europe, to countries which are not signatories to the Kyoto Protocol. In this way, there will be a carbon permit surplus in the EU, so that both the departing company and those remaining in the EU have no incentive to use cleaner technologies.
9   The trading system does not address the systemic causes underlying global warming.[22] First, the prices fluctuate so strongly that firms do not receive the incentives for long-term green investments. They would rather make short-term decisions depending on the quickly changing and large differences in the marginal costs of permits. Second, even if prices were stabilised, fossil fuel technologies are so dominant in production and consumption structures that a shift to renewable energy involves large transaction costs. For example, the surplus solar energy produced in Spain's deserts cannot be sold to France because 'the wire between the two countries is too thin'.

In conclusion, the EU ETS appears to involve far more inflexibilities than the European Commission had expected of markets. After all, stricter annual caps on emissions per firm may not have been more costly and bureaucratic than the management and continuous adaptations of the EU ETS. . . .

13.6 Interesting sources

Documentary film about nature in the Netherlands: *The New Wilderness*: http://www.rewildingEurope.com/news/the-new-wilderness-coming-soon/
Personal footprint calculator: http://www.footprintnetwork.org/en/index.php/GFN/page/personal_footprint/
Video on 'stuff': http://storyofstuff.org/

13.7 Glossary

Dutch Disease   The negative economic consequences of the export of natural resources

Ecological economics   The study of the interdependence and co-evolution of the economy and natural ecosystems over time and space

Ecological footprint   A measure of how much nature we have, how much we use, and who uses what

Entropy Law   The capacity of energy to do useful work, as an input, is diminished over time

Environmental economics   The field in neoclassical economics which studies the possibilities and constraints required so that economic growth will have less environmental impact

Environmental Kuznets curve (EKC)   An inverted U-shaped curve picturing the relationship between pollution on the one hand and a country's income level on the other

Green growth   Economic growth with decreasing environmental impact

Happy Planet Index   A measure of how many long and happy lives countries produce per unit of environmental output

364 *Nature*

Natural resource curse   The paradoxical effect of natural resources on economic growth and economic development

Nudging   The framing of choice situations towards a desirable default choice

Planetary boundaries   The thresholds beyond which there will be irreversible damage to ecological systems

Poldermodel   Collective bargaining with all relevant social groups through consensus

Precautionary principle   Decision rule to avoid ecological damage in the face of lack of scientific proof about the type, extent, and impact of economic behaviour on the ecological system

Sovereign wealth fund   A public investment fund containing the revenues from natural resource exports managed by the state

Steady-state economy   An economy that aims to maintain a stable level of resource consumption and a stable population level

Sustainable development   Development that meets the needs of the present without compromising the ability of future generations to meet their own needs

Notes

1. Measured between 1900 and 2005, just before the global financial crisis. Source: Krausmann, F., S. Gingrich, N. Eisenmenger, K. Erb, H. Haberl and M. Fischer-Kowalski (2009) 'Growth in Global Materials Use, GDP and Population during the 20th Century', *Ecological Economics*, 68(10), pp. 2696–705.
2. van Meerkerk, J., G. Renes and G. Ridder (2014) 'Greening the Dutch Car Fleet: The Role of Differentiated Sales Taxes'. The Hague: Planbureau voor de Leefomgeving. PBL Working paper no. 18.
3. http://www.autozine.nl/overzicht/autoverkopen.php?mok=1666
4. http://www.climatechange2013.org/images/report/WG1AR5_SPM_FINAL.pdf
5. Boulding, K. (1996) 'The Economics of Coming Spaceship Earth', in: Jarrett, H. (ed.), *Environmental Quality in a Growing Economy: Essays from the Sixth RFF Forum*. Baltimore: Johns Hopkins Press, p. 3–14.
6. Dietz, R. and D. O'Neill (2013) *Enough is Enough - Building a Sustainable Economy in a World of Finite Resources*. San Francisco: Berrett-Koehler.
7. Schor, J. (2005) 'Sustainable Consumption and Worktime Reduction', *Journal of Industrial Economy*, 9(1–2), pp. 37–50.
8. Chapter 15 will discuss happiness as a well-being indicator. It will do so as part of neoclassical economics. In this chapter, as part of the Happy Planet Index, it is included in the social economics section. This is admittedly a bit arbitrary.
9. http://genuineprogress.net/about/
10. Source for the German data: http://www.bloomberg.com/news/2014-05-09/renewables-meet-record-27-percent-of-german-electricity-demand.html
11. http://www.pbl.nl/en/publications/exceedances-of-the-no2-limit-value-in-the-netherlands-partly-due-to-higher-than-expected-real-world-emissions
12. http://www.pbl.nl/sites/default/files/cms/publicaties/pbl-2013-trends-in-global-co2-emissions-2013-report-1148.pdf 8   http://www.kidv.nl/3174/kwantitatieve-resultaten-en-kwalitatieve-evaluatie-pilot-plastic-tasjes-doc.pdf
13. http://www.kidv.nl/3174/kwantitatieve-resultaten-en-kwalitatieve-evaluatie-pilot-plastic-tasjes-doc.pdf

14 Keynes, J. M. [1931], 'Economic Possibilities for our Grandchildren', in *Essays in Persuasion*, Part IV, Chapter 2. London: Rupert Hart-Davis, 1951, pp. 358–73. Quote on p. 363.
15 See, for example, a short article summarising our planetary boundaries and how the world economy functions relative to these: Rockström, J., W. Steffen, K. Noone *et al.* (2009), 'A Safe Operating Space for Humanity', *Nature* 461(24), pp. 472–5.
16 *Recent Trends in Material Flows and Resource Productivity in Asia and the Pacific.* Bangkok: UNEP, 2013.
17 Stephen Tindale of the independent European think tank Centre for European Reform, in May 2013: http://www.cer.org.uk/insights/commission-should-move-structural-reform-ets
18 'ETS RIP?', *The Economist*, 20 April 2013.
19 http://ec.Europa.eu/clima/policies/2030/index_en.htm
20 Sinclair, M. (2009) 'The Expensive Failure of the European Union Emissions Trading Scheme', www.taxpayersalliance.com/ets.pdf
21 Sijm, J. P. M., K. Neuhoff and Y. Chen (2006) 'CO_2 cost pass through and windfall profits in the power sector', *Climate Policy*, 6(1), pp. 49–72.
22 Vlachou, V. (2014) 'The European Union's Emissions Trading System', *Cambridge Journal of Economics*, 38, pp. 127–52.

14 International trade

14.1 Introduction

14.1.1 Globalisation and trade

Globalisation is the process through which the world becomes increasingly interconnected through the international expansion of markets. This happens along four axes:

1. International trade in goods and services: imports and exports;
2. International capital flows with foreign direct investments and portfolio investments;
3. International labour migration, for example within trade unions such as the European Union or through undocumented migrant workers without official residence permits;
4. Internationalisation of production processes in global value chains through the production facilities of multinational companies and subcontracting (outsourcing).

In our globalised world, these four axes are closely inter-related in global production networks producing for global value chains. *Global value chains* (GVCs) are the globally organised production activities for a final good driven by a lead firm. They organise production either through foreign subsidiaries of a single multinational company, or through outsourcing production activities to a variety of foreign firms. Lead firms in global value chains, often a well-known consumer brand such as Wall-Mart, IKEA, or Mitsubishi, break up their activities across the globe, sourcing inputs and organising production activities from a large number of low-cost suppliers. Some lead firms, such as Nike, are even 'fab-less firms': they are manufacturers without factories for fabrication (fab). Approximately 50 per cent of global trade occurs within multinational companies (MNCs).

International trade is key to globalisation. *Trade* is the international exchange of goods and services. It is the opposite of autarky, when a country is self-sufficient and produces everything that it consumes. Trade makes sense when it provides benefits as compared to autarky. These are called the *gains from trade*: the advantages of trade for both trading partners, as compared to autarky. What are these? We distinguish two types of gains from trade: static gains, which occur in the short term, and dynamic gains, which occur in the long term.

14.1.1.1 Static gains from trade

14.1.1.1.1 CONSUMER SURPLUS

Consumer surplus, which is the advantage for consumers due to the lower prices of imported goods as compared to domestically produced goods. When foreign firms sell goods similar to those produced by domestic firms but at lower prices, consumers benefit from trade, namely imports. Of course, this is only the case when the government does not have an *import tariff*, a tax on imported goods that compensates for the price advantage. For example, if imported jeans costs 75 per cent of domestically produced jeans and the import tariff applied is 10 per cent of the price of the imported good, then the consumer surplus can be calculated as follows. The gross price difference is:

$$P_{imp} = 0.75 P_{dom}$$

in which P_{imp} = the price of the imported good, and P_{dom} = the price of the domestically produced good, both expressed in the same currency.

The import tariff applied by the government is $0.10 P_{imp}$.

This makes the after-tariff price, or net price, of the imported good, the gross price plus the tariff:

$$P_{imp} net = P_{imp} + 0.10 P_{imp}$$

$$P_{imp} net = 1.10 P_{imp}$$

$$P_{imp} net = 1.10 (0.75 P_{dom})$$

$$P_{imp} net = 0.83 P_{dom}$$

Hence, consumers have a financial benefit of 17 per cent when buying imported jeans rather than domestically produced jeans, because the net price of imported jeans is only 83 per cent of the price of domestically produced jeans.

14.1.1.1.2 INCREASED SALES FOR DOMESTIC FIRMS FROM EXPORTING TO FOREIGN CONSUMERS

Domestic firms can enlarge their sales by selling not only to domestic consumers (through C) but also to foreign consumers (through EX), or more abstractly to the rest of the world (RoW). The additional sales will earn additional returns and add to profits. This will only occur, of course, when the sales prices (including a possible tariff by the importing country) is lower than the price demanded by the firms located in the importing country. In addition, the higher production implies more employment, which also benefits workers. But other firms, who face competition from higher imports of goods in their sector, will suffer: their sales will go down. The net effect of trade depends on the relative size of exports versus imports and the characteristics of the firms: if the exporting firms produce higher value added goods and the importing firms produce lower value added goods, the net effect is positive even when the volume of exports and imports is the same. That is precisely why for the UK economy as a whole, businesses benefit from the closing down of the textile industry and the expansion of higher value added manufacturing and the services industry.

14.1.1.2 Dynamic gains from trade

1   Economies of scale emerge when the size of the sales market increases, allowing for decreasing production costs per unit. If the limits of sales to the domestic markets have

been reached, exports allow firms to reap economies of scale beyond the national borders. The economies of scale enable a reduction in product prices, attracting more customers and increasing market share.

2   Access to foreign technology. Imported goods that are relatively high-tech include technologies that receiving country firms may want to copy. This has happened widely in the manufacturing sectors of Japan first and later China. Another pathway to acquiring foreign technology is through inviting multinational companies to produce in one's country and to require sharing of technology, for example after an initial period of protection of technology by patents.

If trade is so complex, then how do we measure trade? That is fortunately quite simple. The measure that we use for the extent of trade by a country is the combination of exports and imports as a share of GDP. We call a country relatively closed when this share is low, and relatively open when this share is high. *Trade openness* is the share of exports and imports of GDP calculated as: (EX + IM)/GDP). For an open economy engaging in a lot of trade, this share can exceed 100 per cent. This is because a country may import most of its consumer needs and export most of its production or natural resources. Diagram 14.1 shows a selection of the trade ratios of small and large countries from across the world.

The trade ratios in Diagram 14.1 show that the world has some very open countries. The most globalised economies of the world are small, developed countries. These include Singapore, Ireland and the Netherlands. At the bottom of the ranking we find countries which are relatively closed to trade. Of the big countries, China and India trade much more relative to their GDP than the USA and Brazil. On average, the trade openness of the least developed countries is 76 per cent, while for the EU it is around 40 per cent and for the USA it is 30 per cent. So, the low level of development of the poorest countries in the world is not caused by limited involvement in trade.

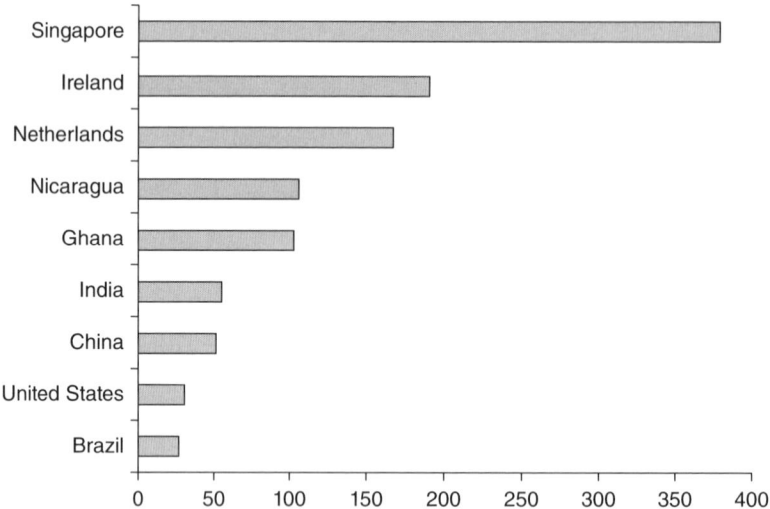

Diagram 14.1 Trade ratios (EX + IM)/GDP, selected countries (%), 2012

Source: Databank, World Bank.

Are you surprised to see such limited trade openness for the USA and the EU (for example, France is 57 per cent and the UK is 65 per cent)? You find American and European products everywhere around the world, from Pepsi Cola to Renault, and from computers to wine. The explanation is that the USA and the EU indeed export a lot, but have protected their own markets, in particular agricultural markets, from imports from other countries. This has developed historically and has not been sufficiently corrected with several rounds of world trade negotiations. The rest of the world does not have these privileges of market protection. As a consequence, developing countries have on average higher trade shares than some European countries and in particular the USA.

14.1.2 Balance of Payments and exchange rates

In this short subsection, I will briefly go over two key concepts in relation to trade analysis from Chapter 11. First, the *Balance of Payments* (BoP). This is the account of a country's transactions with the rest of the world. Its main components are the *current account* (for the trade in goods and services: EX and IM), and the *capital account* (for capital inflows and outflows). It is generally the case when a country has a surplus in one, it has a deficit in the other.

The *exchange rate* is the value of a country's currency expressed in a foreign currency. So, the exchange rate of the Brazilian real is US$0.44 or €0.32 (date: 4 April 2014). For regional trade, it is more relevant to know the exchange rate with close trading partners. The exchange rate of the real with the Argentinian peso stands at 3.51 peso. Every exchange rate can also be expressed in units of the foreign currency. This is useful when you want to know how much a foreign good or service will cost you, such as an item you want to buy on the internet from another country or the cost of your hotel stay abroad. If you are based in Brazil and want to buy on the internet an American baseball cap of the Chicago Bulls costing US$25, you first need to get the dollar exchange rate in reais. US$1 costs 2.27 reais. So, the Chicago Bulls cap will cost you (excluding transport and administration costs) US$25 × 2.27 = 56.75 reais.

We have already seen in the chapter on money that there are two possible exchange rate regimes: flexible, determined by the demand and supply for currency on international currency markets, and fixed, determined by a country's Central Bank. Brazil, the USA, and the eurozone all have flexible exchange rate systems. So, if you check the exchange rate of the real against the dollar and euro today, it is quite likely that it is different from the one I found on the day I wrote this section. You can find out very easily because there are a variety of currency converters freely available on internet. So, if you now look up the current exchange rate of the dollar in reais, how many reais do you need to pay for a US$25 Chicago Bulls cap today?

14.1.3 Leakage effect

The third concept, which changes when an economy is part of the globalised world, is the size of the multiplier. That is because any stimulation of the domestic economy, for example through government expenditures (G), will partly leak away to the RoW. We have seen this already in Chapter 10. This is because consumers not only buy domestically produced goods and services when their incomes rise, but they also go on holidays abroad, order goods through internet from other countries, and buy imported clothing or cars. Remember from the macroeconomic equation that imports (IM) are subtracted from the other variables: $Y = C + I + G + EX - IM$.

The proportion of their income that consumers spend on imports is called the *propensity to import*. The symbol is a small 'm'. Hence, we have the following import equation:

$$IM = mY$$

in which $0 < m < 1$

The propensity to import is smaller than the propensity to consume: you cannot consume more imported goods than you consume in total. As soon as a country is open, which means that it engages in trade, we have to correct any multiplier effect for leakages to the RoW. We do this by subtracting the propensity to import, m, in the denominator term of the multiplier. Remember from the chapter on macroeconomic flow, that the multiplier in a closed economy is the following:

$$\frac{1}{1-c}$$

So, when the propensity to consume is 0.8, the multiplier is:

$$\frac{1}{1-0.8} =$$

$$\frac{1}{0.2} = 5$$

In an open economy, part of the increase in consumption leaks away to other countries, so we must subtract the propensity to import from the propensity to consume to account for this:

$$\frac{1}{1-c-m}$$

Now, if we assume the propensity to import is 0.3, we have the following multiplier for an open economy:

$$\frac{1}{1-(0.8-0.3)} =$$

$$\frac{1}{1-0.5} =$$

$$\frac{1}{0.5} = 2$$

If we compare the multiplier in the situation of a closed economy (multiplier = 5) with the multiplier in the situation of an open economy (multiplier = 2), we see that government stimulation policy can suffer from a substantial leakage effect in an open economy: the multiplier effect has reduced significantly.

14.2 Social economics of trade

In social economics, the focus in trade analysis is on power asymmetries. Between stronger and weaker countries, between large and small firms, and between capital and labour. These power asymmetries explain, in social economics, why some countries benefit more from trade than others, and why world trade does not necessarily lead to narrowing gaps in economic development, incomes, and poverty. Two theoretical insights are relevant here, one from the history of economic development of Latin America, and the other related to the current era of globalisation through global value chains.

14.2.1 Dependency theory

The Latin American school of trade economics gave rise to the dependency theory. The Argentinian economist Raul Prebisch in particular led this school. His work is briefly described in the annex to this book. Dependency theory distinguishes between a central group of countries and a peripheral group of countries. The central group consists of industrialised countries, with high levels of savings, investment, and technological development. The peripheral countries consist of all the countries that have the opposite economic structure: low levels of savings and investments, low levels of technological advancement, and a high share of agriculture in their GDP. The dependency theorists observed that trade between the two country groups benefits the centre more than the periphery. Just as it did for several hundred years during colonialism. The peripheral countries export their natural resources and agricultural products to the centre, while the central countries export their manufactured products and high-tech capital goods to the periphery.

The dependency theory led to an important hypothesis that has since been supported by empirical evidence: the *Prebisch-Singer hypothesis*.[1] This hypothesis postulates that the terms of trade are decreasing for countries exporting primary goods to countries exporting manufactured goods. Hence, the periphery gains from trade with the central countries decreases over time. *Terms of trade* are defined as the ratio of the value of exports over the value of imports. Decreasing terms of trade imply that a country must export more and more of its primary goods in order to pay for the same amount of imported goods. Terms of trade have generally worsened for developing countries in the period 1970–2000. However, since 2000 terms of trade have been stable or have improved for developing countries, due to large increases in world market prices for resources and commodities.

The hypothesis was developed before the current era of globalisation. From the 1980s onwards, the structure of global trade quickly adjusted to globalisation. It moved away from specialisation on the basis of types of goods and rapidly shifted towards a global division of labour between low-skilled and high-skilled labour. With that shift also came a break with national firms as the major trading partners, towards global value chains (GVCs) and trade within the same multinational. So, the Prebisch-Singer hypothesis is now relevant for trade between countries supplying to global value chains on the basis of low-cost labour, and countries leading global value chains with their FDI flows and widespread global sourcing strategies.

14.2.2 Global value chains and the race to the bottom

The empirical evidence on decreasing terms of trade under globalisation has led social economists to re-evaluate gains from trade as a race to the bottom for some developing countries.

372 *International trade*

This implies that the gains from trade are distributed so unevenly that the stronger trading partner gains 100 per cent, while the weaker trading partner gains 0 per cent. The unevenness of gains for trade holds even for very large developing countries dominating world trade, such as China, which lost 20 per cent of its terms of trade between 1990 and 2010.[2]

What explains a global race to the bottom? There are three factors at play.

14.2.2.1 More complex goods require more imports

The more complex the manufactured goods that developing countries produce for GVCs, the more components they need to import for these. And the sourcing and accounting of these are often managed by the lead firm to its own cost advantage and fiscal advantage. For example, only 5 per cent of the value of the iPhone, which is produced in China and exported to the USA, is added in China. This is the low-wage labour that Chinese factory workers provide assembling iPhones. The other 95 per cent of the value added is accounted for by labour in other low-wage countries, such as mining for metal for components, and especially by marketing, development, and profits for the lead company, Apple, in the USA.

14.2.2.2 Lead firms in GVCs tend to be oligopolistic

The lead firms in GVCs are in the position of global buyers, forcing strong competition between a large number of suppliers at every stage of the GVC. The lead firms are often oligopolists. Remember from Chapter 5 that oligopolistic firms have a degree of freedom to determine their prices, through a mark-up, which allows for more profits than in firms operating in competitive markets. Moreover, the multinational buyers can quickly move their investments from one country to another. They use this mobility of their capital as bargaining power vis-à-vis labour in the countries they operate in and threaten local labour representatives that they will relocate to another country when labour demands wage rises or protests for better labour standards. The host countries of the subsidiaries of MNCs often feel forced to choose the side of the MNC to attract employment and new technology. So, MNCs have double bargaining power. First, from their oligopolistic sales market structure (allowing above-normal profits) combined with highly competitive suppliers' markets (pushing the prices of suppliers down), and, second, from the fact that capital is highly mobile, whereas labour is not, so labour is in a disadvantaged bargaining position vis-à-vis these MNCs which seek cheap labour inputs.

14.2.2.3 Oversupply in world markets of inputs to GVCs

The suppliers in GVCs find themselves in strong competition with each other for access to GVCs. Once access is obtained, the only strategy to increase earnings from being in a value chain is to expand production volumes. There is simply no room for increasing the prices they obtain for their sales in a GVC. As a consequence, all suppliers try to expand their production. This has the negative externality of over-supply of inputs and intermediary goods in the world market. This puts further downward pressure on the prices of suppliers, and hence, on the wages earned by the workers downstream in a GVC.

14.2.3 Fair trade

Trade policy in social economics focuses on *fair trade*. This is trade in which the gains are distributed more or less equally so that trade also contributes to development for the least developed trading partner. Fair trade policy may be at the firm level, government level, or the level of trading blocks and agreements. For example, The Body Shop has had fair trade as its key trade policy from the beginning. It buys ingredients for its cosmetics from community producers, often cooperatives, at reasonable prices, cutting out intermediaries so that much of the value added remains in the local communities. Moreover, it seeks to stimulate organic production to reduce environmental impact, and it draws on local knowledge about physical health and beauty. It thereby strengthens local knowledge to balance the expansion of western consumer products from the big-brand MNCs.

Fair trade policy in trade agreements is set out in *social clauses*. These are social conditions in trade agreements, often about labour standards. The best-known are the four core labour standards formulated by the *ILO (International Labour Organization)*:

1 Freedom from forced labour
2 Abolition of exploitative forms of child labour
3 Equal opportunity in employment
4 Freedom of association and collective bargaining.

Examples of trade agreements with social clauses are trade agreements between the European Union and external partners. For example, between the EU and Belarus. The trade agreement involves a preferential tariff for exports from Belarus to the EU, under the condition that the country respects the ILO's four core labour standards. Belarus, however, did not respect the fourth core labour standard mentioned above. Hence, in 2007, the EU implemented a sanction of a 3 per cent higher tariff for Belarus imports into the EU.

14.3 Institutional economics of trade

14.3.1 Trade agreements

There are two types of trade agreements: bilateral and multilateral. Bilateral trade agreements are between two parties, which may be two individual countries, or two trade unions, or one trade union with an individual country. For example the EU's EPAs: European Partnership Agreements. Multilateral trade agreements are within a group of countries rather than between two parties. The world's major trade agreement is a multilateral trade agreement under the coordination of the World Trade Organization (WTO). The agreement currently involves 159 member countries. The main policy of the WTO is tariff reduction to stimulate imports between countries. This covers manufactured goods, services, and investments. The WTO has its own court of justice, a settlement body, to handle trade disputes. It has the power to approve bilateral trade sanctions by one trading partner imposed on another as a result of dispute settlement. This judicial power makes the WTO unique among all the other economic and social UN organisations. For example, the ILO does not have the right to impose sanctions on countries which do not respect the agreed core labour standards.

On paper, the WTO uses a democratic one-country one-vote system. In the practice of trade negotiations, however, hierarchies of countries emerge. This happens through the so-called 'Friends of the Chair' who are allowed to coordination meetings, and side-talks in so-called 'Green Rooms' from which poor country delegations are effectively excluded because they are not invited and their delegations are too small to keep up with all the activities going on. Decisions generally are not made through voting (the developing countries have more than 75 per cent of all votes) but through consensus, achieved through a multiplicity of plenary and side negotiations, where the most powerful economies carry most weight.

Natural resources and agricultural commodities are largely excluded from WTO consideration. Hence, for these products we often see high import tariffs and quotas limiting the volume of imports, combined with subsidies to domestic producers. In particular, we see such trade protection by the developed world in order to safeguard food security (sometimes leading to over-production) and to protect their farmers' incomes. For example, in Japan, domestic rice production is heavily subsidised and on top of this the government has set an extremely high import tariff on rice (778 per cent), which keeps almost all foreign rice away from Japan.

Agricultural protection through farm subsidies consumes around 40 per cent of the total EU annual budget. The EU agricultural budget for support to EU farmers was €40 billion in 2012. That was €80 per inhabitant of the 28 European Union countries – the average price of a sheep. With 500 million inhabitants in the EU, this farm subsidy amounts to the value of 500 million sheep per year, or 40 million cows per year. Obviously such large subsidies affect market prices and supply. But they are excluded from WTO policy. EU import tariffs are zero only for imports of specified commodities from the 49 least developed countries of the world.

WTO negotiations occur in long rounds, named after the country or city where the round has opened. The previous trade negotiation round was the Uruguay round, which occurred from 1986 until 1994. Currently, the WTO is involved in the Doha round, named after the capital of Qatar, which started in 2001. The Doha round is also referred to as the development round, because after the Uruguay round the developing countries demanded that their interests should be taken much more seriously. The Doha round was planned to end in 2005 but the first stage of negotiations was only concluded in 2013. Why is this round of world trade negotiations moving so slowly?

First, because the largest and fast-growing developing countries no longer accept their subordinate role. In particular, China, India, Brazil, and South Africa have demanded structural changes in the world trade system, with not just preferential treatment for the poorest countries but with equal market access to all markets for all countries. This implies the abolition of the EU Common Agricultural Policy (CAP) with its farm subsidies, import quotas, and high import tariffs, and similarly, the agricultural protection policies of the USA, Japan, and other developed countries. Obviously, these countries have experienced strong resistance from their own agriculture lobbies, including agro-business, against this abolition of privileges.

The second reason for the slow movement of the Doha round is because developing countries experienced serious limitations in their technological development and production cost reduction as a result of previous WTO agreements. These include agreements concerning patents on genes, which require poor farmers to pay high prices for seeds, and to buy complementary pesticides and fertilisers for these seeds from the same firm in order to realise promises of high yields. The seed patents and the complementary goods are owned by western-based multinationals. Hence, there is frustration about the consequences of earlier rounds that were clearly in the interest of the developed countries. A sign of the increasing dependence of developing countries on multinational agro-businesses and the constraints from trade protection of agricultural markets by developed countries, is the increasing net food imports by developing countries. Around the mid-1990s, the developing countries became net food importers. Not because they don't have sufficient arable land to feed their own populations. On the contrary, the African continent has the most arable land in the world. And Thailand, like many other countries, was a food exporter until it became member of the WTO. Today, it is a net rice importer.

International trade 375

Taking a dispute to the dispute settlement body of the WTO is, just like the trade rounds, a long-term process. The result may be twofold: the dispute settlement body may dismiss the case or agree with the complainant and leave it to the parties to settle the case with trade retaliation measures. An example of the second result is the complaint by Brazil about US subsidies to its cotton farmers. This unfairly disadvantages Brazilian cotton farmers who do not receive subsidies from their government. Hence, Brazilian cotton farmers export less to the USA as well as to other cotton-importing counties as compared to the situation without American subsidies to US farmers. The dispute settlement body of the WTO decided that Brazil was right and therefore allowed Brazil to retaliate against the USA. Hence, Brazil could increase import tariffs for US products to Brazil, for example American cars or machines. In order to prevent such retaliation, the US government has offered Brazil a bilateral settlement: US$147 million in annual payment to Brazilian cotton farmers.[3] Brazil has accepted this arrangement. But this has not changed anything in the asymmetric trade conditions of cotton in the world. Other cotton producers, such as Benin, Burkina Faso, Chad, and Mali, are equally disadvantaged by the US cotton subsidies but have not received any compensation from the US government. In fact, the US subsidy program benefits around 25,000 US farmers. The number of cotton farmers disadvantaged in the developing world is a multiple of that number, probably close to 1 million.

14.3.2 Trade union

A *trade union* is a free trade agreement among a group of countries in a region. The European Union is a trade union. It developed from a custom union in the 1950s of just a few north-western European countries, into a common market, with, for a smaller number of members, a common currency in a currency union, the European Monetary Union (EMU). The EU now consists of 28 member states which have abolished most of their

Image 14.1 Containerships from the Netherlands to Germany

376 *International trade*

tariffs and harmonised most of their regulations around cross-border trade in goods, services, investment, and labour migration. This has further strengthened the historical trade integration of European countries. Today, around 80 per cent of the average trade of a EU member country is with another EU member country. This is very high given the fact that many European economic structures are quite similar. None of them grows kiwi fruit or produces microwaves, for example.

Part of intra-EU trade is simply the transport of intermediary or final goods from one EU country to another, in particular from those with deep sea ports receiving bulk goods and container goods from the rest of the world. This explains why Germany is the largest export trading partner of the Netherlands: not just because Germans are so fond of Dutch cheese, tulips, and butter (which they, in fact, are), but because the goods Germans import from the rest of the world are to a large extent shipped through the port of Rotterdam and then carried in smaller boats on the river Rhine to the major German industrial area, the Ruhr, and on to the rest of the country in trucks.

Intra-trade in the EU is also facilitated by the EMU, because it saves the transaction costs of currency exchange. So, German importers of Chinese goods no longer need to change German marks into Dutch guilders to get the goods from Rotterdam. They simply pay the Dutch cargo handlers and transporters in euros. But the advantage of a currency union should not be overstated. As we have seen in the chapter about money, upholding the euro is also costly due to serious imperfections in the euro system. EU members who do not participate in the euro, such as the UK, still engage in much trade with the EU.

14.3.3 Trade patterns

Institutional economics recognises patterns in trade. These patterns often have historical origins. Such patterns display what institutional economics calls *path dependency*: the behaviour of today is strongly guided by behaviour in the past. This should not be confused with the dependency trade theory discussed in section 14.2.1. Path dependency is the resilience of old norms and routines. Path dependency in trade often evolves from colonial ties and other historical, political, or economic relationships.

An example is the trade relationship between the EU and another trade union, Mercosur in Latin America. Mercosur is a custom union between Argentina, Brazil, Paraguay, and Uruguay (and more recently, Venezuela). It is the world's third largest trade union, after the EU and NAFTA (North Atlantic Free Trade Agreement, between Canada, the USA, and Mexico). Mercosur covers about 70 per cent of trade in Latin America, while the EU is Mercosur's most important trading partner, accounting for 20 per cent of its trade. For the EU, Mercosur ranks only eighth among its most important trading partners. Only 3 per cent of EU trade is with Mercosur.

When we look at the pattern of trade between Mercosur and the EU, we see a very traditional trade pattern, one that better fits the pre-globalisation era before the 1980s than the current globalisation period. As Table 14.1 shows, the major exports from Mercosur to the EU are still agricultural commodities (74 per cent of all exports to the EU). And the major imports from the EU consist predominantly of manufactured goods (89 per cent). This trade pattern between the EU, including two former colonial powers in Latin America, Spain and Portugal, and Mercosur, exhibits a clear path dependency. The former colonies in South America have been used as the grain and meat suppliers of Europe for a long time.

Table 14.1 Composition of trade between Mercosur and EU (2012)

	Exports from Mercosur to EU	Imports to Mercosur from EU
Agriculture	74%	11%
Manufacturing	26%	89%

Source: http://trade.ec.europa.eu/doclib/docs/2006/september/tradoc_111832.pdf

14.3.3.1 International distribution of gains from trade

Another pattern that institutional economists detect in trade is around the distribution of gains from trade. This includes the distribution of the costs of trade, because trade may not only include benefits but also costs. An example is NAFTA, which has very strong rules on free investment flows between the three member countries of Canada, the USA, and Mexico. As a consequence, a Canadian investor had to be financially compensated with millions of US dollars by the Mexican government when a Mexican municipality did not grant the Canadian company a permit to build a hazardous waste facility in 1997. Studies had demonstrated that this would endanger the drinking water supplies of the municipality. But NAFTA rules only allow federal governments to interfere with investments between the three trading partners and not municipal governments. Hence, the municipal rejection of the building permit was over-ruled by NAFTA rules on investor protection.

14.3.3.2 Asymmetric exceptions

A further asymmetry in the distribution of the gains from trade is seen in exceptions. Despite NAFTA, which came into being in 1994, US agriculture is still protected by subsidies, quota, and tariffs against Mexican imports. And another asymmetry in the distribution of gains from trade is seen in tax revenue. For developing countries, a large share of their tax revenue is collected through trade taxes, in particular import tariffs. These have relatively low transaction costs for the government because the taxable items can be easily located at the border, and custom procedures that are already in place can be used to impose the tax. Hence, lower import tariffs imply higher transaction costs for tax collection for developing countries. Researchers have calculated that the reduction in import tariffs for developing countries can be even higher than the consumer surplus gained from lower prices, so that the net gains from trade are negative for those countries. For Africa, the average import tax revenue makes up more than 5 per cent of GDP, whereas for the OECD, import taxes make up less than 0.5 per cent of GDP.

14.3.3.3 Transaction costs for the least developed trading partner

The 49 poorest countries in the world have not benefitted at all from the Uruguay round of the WTO. Even though they have been granted preferential access to the markets of developed countries, they experience a net loss of trade liberalisation. This is partially due to overly optimistic expectations of trade gains for these countries in the model calculations by the WTO and its most powerful members and advisors, used during the negotiations. These models did not sufficiently take into account the resistance of the developed countries to imports of key goods from the poorest countries, such as cotton and rice. But what also hurts the least

378 *International trade*

developed countries is the cost of implementing all the trade regulations around hygiene, transport, laboratories, quality controls, etc. These involve high transaction costs.

14.3.3.4 Domestic distribution of gains from trade

A final type of asymmetric distribution of gains from trade is seen within countries. This can be between high-skilled and low-skilled workers, for example. If one group systematically benefits and the other group systematically loses, the gains from trade are not equally distributed within a country or trade union. An example that I have analysed myself is the gender distribution of the gains from trade between Mercosur and the EU, which is explained in Box 14.1.

Box 14.1 More gender inequality through Mercosur–EU trade

The stable trade sector in Mercosur is agriculture, with continued demand from the EU (74% of exports), while the vulnerable trade sector in Mercosur is manufacturing, with much competition from imported goods from Europe (89% of imports). Given this traditional trade pattern, we see the following shifts occur since the trade agreement between Mercosur and the EU, analysed over the 10-year period of 1995–2004. First, men moved from manufacturing jobs to agricultural jobs, while women's employment in agriculture declined. Women found jobs in manufacturing, the more vulnerable sector. Women enjoyed equal wages to men in agriculture in 1995, but 10 years later they earned only 87% of what men earned. This loss was only partially compensated for by wages in manufacturing, where they earned only 57% of what men earned in 1995 and 61% 10 years later. So, women severely lost wages to men in the stable sector and gained a small amount of wages relative to men in the vulnerable sector, but the wage gap there is much bigger. Finally, women, in their role as providers for the household, had to spend 40% more money on food since the trade agreement with the EU.

In conclusion, it does not seem that the trade agreement between Mercosur and the EU has brought more gender equality to the women in South America or supported their role as food providers for the household.

Source: van Staveren, I. (2007) 'Gender Indicators for Monitoring Trade Agreements', in: van Staveren, I., D. Elson, C. Grown and N. Cagatay (eds), *The Feminist Economics of Trade*. London: Routledge, pp. 257–76.

14.3.4 Institutions enabling gains from trade

Because of the asymmetric institutions of trade embedded in trade agreements and trade patterns, institutional economists have analysed which institutions could prevent such asymmetries in the gains from trade. These are institutions enabling weaker trading partners to reap net gains from trade, leading to symmetric gains from trade. The key to such institutions is timing. Such enabling institutions rely on the *infant industry argument* that we have seen in Chapter 12. This is the argument that countries that have a weak trade position require trade protection until their industries are sufficiently equipped to become internationally competitive.

Trade protection was not an exception in the early days of the now developed countries, but rather the rule.[4] During the centuries up to the 1980s, the now developed countries used interventionist trade policy and industrial policy to protect, build, and promote their agriculture and manufacturing. There was only one short period in which trade protection in Europe was low, between 1860 and 1880. But these same European countries used their colonies to obtain resources without any trade restrictions, and forced many other nations, including China, Turkey, and Japan, into unequal trade treaties. Table 14.2 shows the tariffs in the countries for which data are available, for 1875 and 1931. They show that soon after the period of relatively free trade, the now developed countries made use of high import tariffs (the percentages in the table) or other trade restrictions (the R in the table).

The USA imposed an import tariff (of 5 per cent) back in 1789 as soon as federal tax collection started. This was soon raised to 12.5 per cent, and in 1820, the US import tariff was further raised to 40 per cent. It remained at that level until World War II, more than a century later. In addition to the tariff, and the naturally high transport costs for trade with Europe, the US government strongly subsidised education, infrastructure, and research and development. Even today, more than 25 per cent of the R&D of the US pharmaceutical industry is funded by the government.

The Netherlands has a somewhat different experience, because they enjoyed a very prosperous period in the 16th and in particular the 17th century, referred to as the Golden Age. That was not built on free trade but on power: naval power through its world dominating fleet, and commercial power due to its colonies and the monopoly granted to the East Indian Trading Company (VOC in Dutch). The decline came with the defeat in 1780 in the war with the British. After this, the Dutch state tried free trade, following *laissez-faire* advice of Adam Smith. Since then, the Dutch have brought tariffs down to less than 10 per cent. The country even abolished patent law in 1869. But patents were re-introduced in 1912 under international pressure.

The laissez-faire period did not bring back the golden days for the Dutch. Instead, economic growth remained slow for the next 200 years. Precisely because of this disappointment with a free trade regime and limited government intervention (apart from public education and public health), the Dutch government embarked upon an ambitious and costly industrial policy after World War II. This included subsidies to the steel industry, nationalisation of the newly discovered natural gas supply, and large transport (Schiphol airport, Rotterdam seaport) and other infrastructural projects (land reclamation in the Zuiderzee).

Table 14.2 Historical import tariffs of developed countries

	1875	1931
Austria	15–20%	24%
Belgium	9–10%	14%
France	12–15%	30%
Germany	4–6%	21%
Italy	8–10%	46%
Russia	15–20%	R
Spain	15–20%	63%
Sweden	3–5%	21%
Switzerland	4–6%	19%
USA	40–50%	48%

Source: Chang, H.-J. (2007) 'Kicking Away the Ladder: The "Real" History of Free Trade', in Shaikh, A. (ed.) *Globalization and the Myths of Free Trade - History, Theory, and Empirical Evidence*. London: Routledge, p. 26.

The core of the institutional theory of trade is asymmetric trade institutions. When in favour of the strongest trading partner, strong in terms of level of development and productivity, gains from trade are necessarily biased against the weaker trading partner. This can only be prevented by temporary trade protection and an industrial policy to protect and promote the infant industries of the weaker trading partner until they are internationally competitive. But even after infant industry protection, trade is never automatically equal, due to a variety of natural and strategic asymmetries in trade patterns.

14.4 Post Keynesian economics of trade

14.4.1 Absolute advantage

Post Keynesian theory recognises, as we have seen before, a general state of disequilibrium of markets, with unemployment, under-utilisation of production capacity, and insufficient aggregate demand. This is similar at the global level in Post Keynesian theory. Hence, free trade is not the magic bullet to compensate for the above-mentioned ills at the domestic level. Globalisation is not a solution to country-level lack of aggregate demand and it offers no escape from economic cycles for the world.

Because disequilibrium is the normal state of the economy, trade imbalances persist. Some countries have continuous surpluses on their current account, while others have continuous deficits on their current account. For example, the US economy has a persistent trade deficit, while China and the Netherlands have surpluses. They invest the surplus dollars they earn from exports to the USA back into that economy through private investments and US government bonds. One way in which the imbalance could theoretically adjust is through a depreciation of the US dollar vis-à-vis the euro and the Chinese renminbi. But the Fed cannot control this fully because the US exchange rate is flexible and not controlled by the government.

The Fed may buy dollars on the world market, but this is a costly operation for which it needs to sell gold and other currencies. But it needs the other currencies to pay for its imports. Hence, the US government is currently demanding that China, which has a fixed exchange rate, revaluates the renminbi, making it more expensive against the dollar. The Chinese, however, do not want to do this, because this would make their export goods more expensive everywhere around the world: if the renminbi's value is increased vis-à-vis the dollar, this would mean that it would become more expensive for those having euros, yens, pesos, pounds, and francs. . . . A managed exchange rate, which keeps the currency value relatively low, stimulates exports, which is a strategy to increase employment through producing for foreign demand.

In Post Keynesian economics, how could a trade imbalance be reversed? A trade deficit (IM > EX) implies that a country spends more on imports than it earns with its exports. Hence, money flows away abroad. This creates a smaller domestic money supply ($\downarrow$ M). As we have seen in the chapter on money, a tighter money supply (M) pushes up the interest rate ($\uparrow$ i). But the higher domestic interest rate is a double-edged sword. On the one hand, it may attract foreign investors who want to reap the higher returns on investment by investing in this country's assets, in particular in bonds and investment funds. This brings the domestic currency back into the country and lowers the interest rate again. The deficit on the current account is now balanced by a surplus on the capital account. On the other hand, the higher interest rate makes borrowing more expensive for domestic firms, which may discourage productive investment, and hence, employment. This brings the domestic economy further out-of-balance. Hence, the solution to a trade deficit through a compensating surplus on the capital account is not a sustainable solution to the trade imbalance, according to Post Keynesians.

What can then be done to address the trade imbalance itself? In the presence of unemployment, trade flows are determined by absolute trade advantages of countries. An *absolute advantage* is the cost advantage that a country has in a particular production factor. In Post Keynesian trade theory, for countries with relatively high unemployment among low-skilled labour, cheap labour is often the absolute advantage. Such countries will attract domestic and foreign investment in low-skilled labour production activities, such as agriculture, microelectronics assembly, and the textile and clothing industries.

Countries with an absolute advantage in a particular and scarce natural resource will specialise in that resource for exports. Think about oil-exporting countries and Mercosur's agricultural commodities. Other countries may have a technological advantage and a very high-skilled work force, so that they specialise in the production and export of goods and services that are capital intensive and high-skill intensive. For example Finland, which enjoyed over a decade of export success through exports of fancy mobile phones and related products from its firm Nokia. Or Luxembourg, which specialises in financial services and spin-off services to investors from all over the world. So, due to the normal conditions of unemployment and highly mobile capital, Post Keynesian economics explains trade flows and imbalances with absolute advantages.

14.4.2 Competitive advantage

The persistence over time of absolute advantages needs a bit more explanation. Why has China been able to keep the low-wage advantage for three decades? How does the German economy manage to remain one of the most competitive economies in high-tech industrial products? Why is Mercosur still exporting such high volumes of wheat and meat to Europe, even though it produces cars and airplanes? Why is Africa's export share in the world persistently less than 5 per cent? In other words, how do countries maintain absolute trade advantages or get stuck in absolute trade disadvantages, as fortunate or unfortunate path dependencies?

The answer to this lies in the Post Keynesian theory of *competitive advantage*. This is promoting and protecting trade advantages based on anything that matters. This may vary from employing child labour to women's wage discrimination, and from the exploitation of natural resources at a cost to nature, to protecting parts of one's market with high tariffs, and to patents on the genes of seeds of food products. Competitive advantage, just like oligopoly, makes use of entry barriers, not for firms but for whole sectors and countries. We can group the types of competitive advantage that countries make use of as follows:

1   Trade protection: limiting imports and protecting domestic production with tariffs, quotas, and specific product requirements;
2   Subsidies: making domestic products cheaper on world markets;
3   Patents and intellectual property rights: preventing other countries from using these technologies;
4   Discrimination and exploitation: keeping the costs of labour and/or natural resources below their level of productivity or replacement;
5   Ignoring negative environmental and social externalities: not including costs that can be shifted away to society and nature;
6   *Dumping*: temporarily selling products below cost price to price competitors out of the market.

382 *International trade*

You will recognise in this list that the first two are precisely those supporting the infant industry argument. But this is supposed to be a temporary strategy, until a country can engage in international competition. When countries still make use of these advantages after their industries have become internationally competitive, they become barriers of entry for foreign firms, resulting in unfair competition.

The current trade patterns in a globalised world can be explained with a combination of the theories of absolute advantage and competitive advantage. Many developing countries, in particular those in Asia with high supplies of low-skilled labour, specialise in labour-intensive manufactured exports, using low-wage labour. They have all established special zones, close to ports for shipping the final goods abroad on container ships, called *EPZs: Export Processing Zones*. These zones are set up by the governments of developing countries in order to attract the factories of multinational companies, with their FDI, and domestic producers with their factories and workshops and home workers, for global value chains. EPZs generally have low tax regimes, or even provide tax holidays to MNCs for 10 years or more. A *tax holiday* is a temporary period in which a company is exempt from paying profit taxes. Moreover, EPZs offer flexible labour regimes where some domestic labour laws do not apply or are not enforced by the labour inspectorate. EPZs are therefore genuinely free trade zones.

Finally, the EPZ labour force consists of large numbers of cheap workers, young, not members of trade unions (which are often kept out of EPZs anyway), and with supposedly nimble fingers for the assembly lines and delicate textile and clothing production jobs. As a consequence, the labour force in EPZs consists largely of young women, with good academic qualifications, often teachers or nurses, who can earn higher wages in the EPZs, thanks to over-time and cheap accommodation, than in public schools and hospitals operating on meagre government budgets. Not that the wages are absolutely high: they are not. And they are lower than the wages men earn in similar jobs. The trade-off for the relatively higher wages these women earn in EPZs is the lack of freedom and say over their labour power and working conditions, plus the practice of being fired as soon as they marry and have children. In countries as diverse as Bangladesh, Sri Lanka, El Salvador, Jamaica, and Nicaragua, more than 75 per cent of the manufacturing workforce consists of women.

Diagram 14.2 shows the empirical relationship between the growth of the cheap female share of manufacturing workers on the one hand and the growth in the value added per worker in manufacturing on the other in 16 developing countries specialising in labour-intensive manufacturing. The diagram shows that the higher the female share, the less value added a country generates. This is due to a combination of gender wage discrimination, low labour standards, and limited labour unionisation. Moreover, labour unions tend to be dominated by men who see their factory jobs go to women and are therefore not much interested in fighting for women's labour rights.

14.5 Neoclassical trade economics

Neoclassical trade economics expands the assumptions underlying perfectly competitive markets to the global level. It analyses the world as a single market where goods and services are exchanged relatively freely. Any trade barriers reduce the volume of trade, and hence, the gains from trade. The theory explains trade in the classical tradition going back to David Ricardo, who developed the theory of comparative advantage.

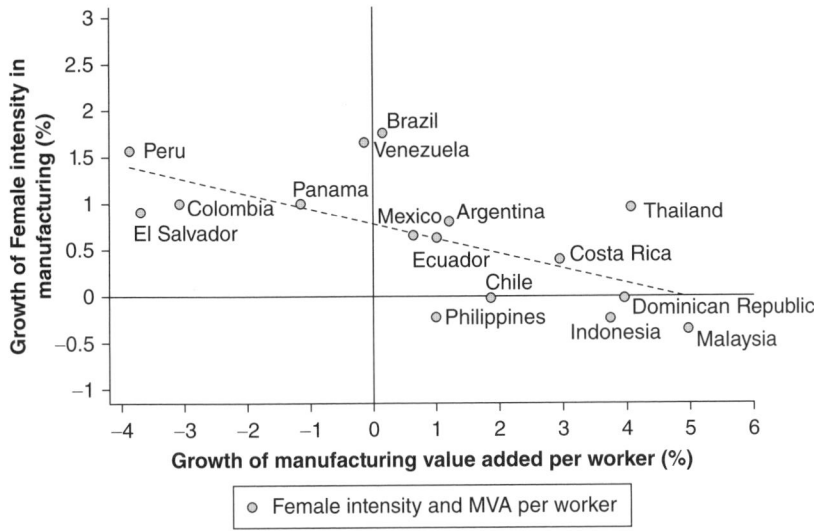

Diagram 14.2 Female labour share and manufacturing value added per worker

Note: MVA, manufacture value added.

Source: Tejani, S. (2011) 'The Gender Dimension of Special Economic Zones', in: Farole, T. and G. Akinci (eds), *Special Economic Zones: Progress, Emerging Challenges and Future Directions*. Washington, DC: The World Bank, p. 268.

14.5.1 Comparative advantage

David Ricardo's theory of comparative advantage was the successor of the theory of absolute advantage proposed by Adam Smith. Smith explained trade between two countries as arising from each trading partner having an *absolute advantage* in the production costs of a different product. This leads to each country specialising in the production of a different good. David Ricardo, an early 19th century British economist, discovered that trade would even be beneficial for both trading partners if one country has an absolute advantage in the production of both goods, but can produce one of these goods more cheaply. This sounds perhaps rather incredible. Why would country X import good A from country Y if it can produce it cheaper by itself? Well, Ricardo was a clever observer of actual trade patterns in 18th and 19th century Europe, and did the maths correctly to explain why this could happen. Ricardo was not only an economist, but also a businessman, speculator, and member of parliament.

Ricardo explained that even when country X has an absolute cost advantage in producing both good A and good B, trade can still be beneficial to both countries. This is the case when the comparative cost advantage of producing one of these goods, say A, is higher than the relative cost advantage of the other good. This can be shown by expressing the production costs of good A in terms of good B (rather than in money terms). And the other way around: expressing the production costs of good B in terms of good A. If country X now specialises in the production of good A and country Y in the production of good B, trade will still be beneficial for both countries. So, the theory of *comparative advantage* shows that specialisation on the basis of relative cost advantage uses less resources, as compared to no trade and both countries (X and Y) producing all the goods (A and B) they need in a situation of autarky.

Before we go through an example, let us make the assumptions underlying the theory of comparative advantage explicit. First, the assumption of full employment in both countries. This implies full flexibility of labour, so that those who lose their jobs in a sector where employment goes down, will easily find work in a sector where employment is expanding. Second, both countries are supposed to have a fixed amount of capital and land available for production, and the stock of capital and the amount of agricultural land are the same. Third, consumer preferences are assumed to be the same: consumers of both countries want to consume both goods and to an equal extent. Fourth, the goods are assumed to be of comparable quality in both countries.

Our example will take the above four assumptions to be true, although we do not find this very often in the real world. If only because trade agreements often also include free capital flows (foreign investment) and countries suffer from unemployment. The example concerns trade between two large middle-income countries, Argentina and Brazil. From the most recent trade statistics by UNCTAD, we find that the major goods in which these two countries trade are quite similar. For example, both countries have car manufacturing industries and exported around US$7 billion worth of cars to each other in 2012. Apparently, the South American consumers like the cars made in both countries. This is not unexpected, because in both countries a variety of well-known foreign brands are produced, such as Fiat, Volkswagen, Ford, and Toyota. At least the assumption of similar preferences seems satisfied. Now, what are the comparative production costs of the cars produced in each country?

We estimate the production costs of these goods, not in money terms but expressed in the other good. Assuming an average price per car of around US$20,000 and a commercial profit of 10 per cent, the production costs would be US$18,000 per car on average for both countries. In Argentina, the car industry produces on average 15 cars per hour. In Brazil, manufacturing productivity is slightly less, although reliable numbers are lacking in the statistics. Let us assume that Brazil produces 14 cars per hour. Assuming wage and capital costs are the same in the Mercosur trade union, it is clear that Argentinian cars are produced more cheaply than Brazilian cars, simply because Argentinians produce more cars per hour.

How can we explain the lack of specialisation on this comparative cost advantage of Argentina? There must be other reasons why Brazil holds on to its car industry. One is its domestic sales market for cars, which is growing quickly. Second, trade protection by the Brazilian government makes imported cars more expensive. Third, regional cooperation in the car supply industry in which Brazil supplies parts to Argentina and the other way around. And fourth, Brazil may have a comparative advantage vis-à-vis other countries in Latin America.

Let us now move to a clear example of specialisation between the two countries. The UNCTAD trade statistics include data on the following agricultural product categories: coffee and cereals. Brazil exports much more coffee to Argentina than the other way around, while Argentina exports far more cereals to Brazil than the other way around. Table 14.3 shows the trade data for 2012 in US dollars.

The table indicates that there is clear specialisation going on in these two food items. For coffee there is an absolute advantage because of the climate difference: it is too cold in Argentina to grow coffee. Brazil therefore exports a 15-fold higher volume of coffee to Argentina than the other way around (which is only tea). But the latter country exports a 34-fold higher volume of cereals to Brazil than it imports from that country. Cereals grow equally well under the climate conditions of Argentina and Brazil. There is no clear absolute advantage for either of these countries in producing cereals. So, apparently, there is a comparative advantage for Argentina to specialise in cereals.

Here follows a fictitious example of the relative production costs of cereals and coffee in both countries, although comparable to the real-world situation. First, we compare the yield per hectare (ha) of each commodity. Cereal production in Argentina would yield 6,000 kg/ha and in Brazil 7,000 kg/ha in our example. For coffee, the yield in Brazil would be 2,000 kg/ha, whereas in Argentina it is almost nothing, say 100 kg/ha, and could possibly grow in the north-east of the country which has a subtropical climate. Hence, Brazil has an absolute advantage in the production of both commodities: its yields of both coffee and cereals are higher than for its southern neighbour.

Table 14.3 Trade specialisation between Argentina and Brazil, 2012 (in US$ thousand)

	Exports from Argentina to Brazil	*Exports from Brazil to Argentina*
Coffee and tea	61,631	288,683
Cereals	2,108,105	19,496

Source: Compiled by the author from UNCTAD Trade Statistics.

Image 14.2 Trade in coffee beans and cereals

For Argentina, the production of 1,000 kg of coffee would cost 60,000 kg of cereals, the opportunity cost. As 100 kg of coffee takes 1 ha of land, so 1,000 kg of coffee takes 10 ha of land. On 1 ha of land, Argentina can grow 6,000 kg of cereals, so on 10 ha the country can grow 60,000 kg of cereals. For Brazil, the production of 1,000 kg coffee costs 0.5 ha, so, it would take the same as 3,500 kg of cereal production. Comparing these opportunity costs, it becomes clear that the opportunity costs of coffee production for Argentina are very high: 60,000 kg cereals for 1,000 kg coffee, whereas for Brazil, it only needs to give up 3,500 kg of cereal production to grow 1,000 kg coffee. Clearly, Argentina opts for specialisation not in coffee but in cereal production.

When we express cereal production in terms of coffee yields, we find that for 1,000 kg of cereal production, the opportunity costs in coffee for Argentina are only 17 kg of coffee (1,000 kg cereals are produced on 1/6 ha, and this involves 1/6 × 100 kg coffee = 16.67 = 17 kg coffee). For Brazil, 1,000 kg of cereal production implies giving up 286 kg of coffee (1,000 kg cereal uses 1/7 ha, and this involves 1/7 × 2,000 kg coffee = 286 kg coffee). Hence, Brazil will choose to specialise in coffee production, in which it is more efficient than in cereal production as compared to Argentina.

Hence, Argentina will specialise in cereal production and Brazil in coffee production. Even though Brazil has an absolute cost advantage in the production of both commodities. Tables 14.4a and 14.4b show the aggregate results of this specialisation and the gains from trade as compared to autarky.

Tables 14.4a and 14.4b show that total production of coffee increases from 107,500 kg to 200,000 kg with specialisation. And total production of cereals increases from 500,000 kg to 600,000 kg with specialisation. Now, of course, Brazil produces more coffee than it can consume, and Argentina produces more cereals than it can eat. So, the two countries will engage in trade. If Brazil exports 100,000 kg of coffee and Argentina exports 400,000 kg of cereals, the situation is as shown in Table 14.4c.

Table 14.4a Autarky: production in kilograms

	Argentina	Brazil	Total production and consumption
Coffee	7,500	100,000	107,500
Cereals	150,000	350,000	500,000

Table 14.4b Specialisation: production in kilograms

	Argentina	Brazil	Total production
Coffee	0	200,000	200,000
Cereals	600,000	0	600,000

Table 14.4c Specialisation on comparative advantage and trade: consumption in kilograms

	Argentina	Brazil	Total production	Consumer surplus Argentina	Consumer surplus Brazil
Coffee	100,000	100,000	200,000	92,500	0
Cereals	200,000	400,000	600,000	50,000	50,000

Comparing the situation with autarky (Table 14.4a), we see that both countries benefit from specialisation and trade. Argentina now consumes 92,500 kg more coffee and 50,000 kg more cereals than with autarky (compare with Table 14.4a). And Brazil consumes the same amount of coffee as before but more cereals, namely 50,000 kg more than with autarky (see Table 14.4a). So, the consumers in both countries reap gains from trade with specialisation on comparative advantage: the consumer surplus.

But, remember the assumptions of the theory of comparative advantage: the mutual gains from trade as shown in Table 14.4c will only occur if everything else remains unchanged: *ceteris paribus*. But this is not very likely. In the case of Argentina and Brazil, they are regularly involved in trade disputes, using suddenly imposed import licences (making imports from the other country more expensive) or exchange rate devaluations (making their own exports cheaper) as weapons. . . .

14.5.2 Global convergence

The theory of comparative advantage as developed by Ricardo was further refined in neoclassical economics with a trade theorem developed by two Swedish economists. This is the *Heckscher-Ohlin theorem* (H-O theorem): a country has a comparative advantage in the production of a good if that country is relatively well endowed with inputs used intensively in the production of that good.

The theorem has an important assumption about production factor mobility, namely, production factors (most importantly capital and labour) are mobile between sectors within an economy but not between countries. Of course, different sectors require different skills, so in the real world labour mobility between sectors is problematic even within countries. Even more so due to labour market segmentation which goes beyond skills and includes social segmentations along the lines of sex, age, and geographical origin. Moreover, the restrictive assumption that capital remains within the borders of each country is not realistic in today's globalised world with large international capital flows.

The H-O theorem explains why countries enjoy comparative advantages in the first place. It addresses the question of why in the era of globalisation, so many labour-intensive industries have moved away from the developed world to South Asia and Latin America. Not only because labour is cheaper but also because there is abundant labour supply of the type of labour in high demand: labour with low formal skills, high dexterity, and limited bargaining power.

A major prediction of the H-O theorem is *convergence*. This implies that the levels of economic development of countries involved in trade will converge with each other on the basis of their comparative advantage: countries with low levels of GDP per capita will grow faster than countries with higher levels of GDP, so that eventually, all countries will enjoy similarly high levels of GDP per capita. Why would convergence happen?

Neoclassical theory predicts that the specialisation of poor countries in labour-intensive production will raise the incomes of workers, and hence, GDP per capita. The low capital-intensity will enable widespread sharing in the economic growth, because most income is earned through labour in an employment-expanding economy, and not through capital ownership. In capital-intensive countries, there will be a decline in demand for labour, so that labour incomes will not increase much further in developed economies. In this way, the (labour) incomes in poor and rich countries will converge with each other, according to the Heckscher-Ohlin theorem.

But there are many exceptions to the H-O theorem. For example, the Netherlands is among the world's top 10 exporters of agricultural products. But it is also in the top 10 of the most densely populated countries in the world. Not really a comparative advantage for growing large surpluses of food, and the agricultural sector is strongly subsidised. And Argentina and Brazil export cars to each other, as we have seen above, more or less the same number annually. They are produced very much in the same way, capital intensively and increasingly with the help of robots. Again, not easily explained with the H-O theorem because neither of the countries specialises. Moreover, the theorem predicts that women's wages will increase relative to men's wages in developing countries, because their labour is in high demand in the labour-intensive export industries. But the gender wage gap has not declined since the 1970s in major exporting countries such as Taiwan, Korea, and Mexico.[5]

So, although the theory of comparative advantage finds some support in real-world trade patterns, the more restrictive Heckscher-Ohlin theorem does not. Simply because in the real word, the restrictive assumptions do not hold. As a consequence, there is only limited support for the global convergence hypothesis stemming from the H-O theorem. First, within Europe, there was convergence during the period of high tariff barriers (1870–1950) rather than during the period of globalisation after that. Second, Latin America experienced a decline in income inequality during its import substitution strategy from the beginning of the 20th century until the late 1980s. After that, with trade liberalisation, income inequality rose sharply. And also the Asian Tiger economies and China have experienced increasing income inequality since their new export strategies were implemented.[6]

14.6 Case study: NAFTA

Let us review the case of a north–south trade union to see what has happened and how the various theories explain this. The case study concerns NAFTA, the North American Free Trade Agreement, between Canada, the USA, and Mexico, which began in 1994. NAFTA involves a reduction in tariffs between the three trading partners and the abolition of other trade barriers (except for the US and Canadian agricultural markets). For Mexico, the import tariff declined from 10 per cent to 5 per cent, while its trade increased from 30 per cent of GDP to 60 per cent of GDP between 1994 and 2000.[7] NAFTA also includes free capital flows.

Mexico has gained employment for its largely low-skilled labour force in the newly built manufacturing region close to the US border, in the Mexican EPZs, called the *maquiladora* industry. An important part of this consists of the assembly of microelectronic products, other products, and garments, with a largely young female labour force. The USA and Canada have lost jobs in manufacturing, and have generally more jobs for higher skilled workers in the tradable sectors, with their remaining low-skilled jobs being in non-tradable sectors, such as restaurants, cleaning, security guards, shop assistants, and secretarial work.

Did wages for low-skilled labour increase in Mexico, as the H-O theorem predicts? No. Real wages (remember, these are nominal wages corrected for inflation) have remained almost stable since the beginning of NAFTA: they increased by between 2 and 2.5 per cent between 1994 and 2014.[8]

Did Mexico manage to keep its food security? No. The cheap food prices of its northern neighbours, due to their farmer subsidies and a lack of investment in the Mexican agricultural sector, have resulted in stagnation of food production and food productivity in Mexico. This has resulted in an increase in food imports from the USA and Canada to Mexico. US and Canadian consumers benefit from cheaper manufactured products, while investors in these countries benefit from relatively good returns on investment in the maquiladora industry. And the American and Canadian farmers export food thanks to subsidies and tariff protection. The Mexican labour force has gained manufacturing jobs but not wage increases and they have lost employment in agriculture. Obviously, US and Canadian factory workers have lost employment in manufacturing. Some of them have received compensation thanks to the bargaining power of their labour unions.

Another asymmetry in the gains from trade in NAFTA is dynamic. The technology of FDI is standard, and does not help to move Mexico up to higher levels of productivity in the future. And the jobs are moving on to even cheaper countries: the trade agreement does not bind the USA and Canada to trade only with Mexico. In fact, their trade with China has become larger.

Finally, what happened to poverty? NAFTA has not been able to reduce national poverty in Mexico.[9] The number of extremely poor people declined marginally from 23.6 million people in 1994 to 22.3 million in 2008. But the number of moderately poor increased from 29.1 million to 35.6 million. Income inequality remained almost stable at a high level of the Gini coefficient, decreasing slightly from 0.55 to 0.52 in Mexico. In Latin America as a whole, poverty declined over the same period from an average of 45 per cent to below 30 per cent.[10]

The NAFTA case study illustrates how real-world trade agreements do not necessarily fulfil their promises. The reasons for this can be found first in the neoclassical economics theory of comparative advantage, but are supported more thoroughly by a combination of institutional economics (asymmetric institutions in the trade agreement), social economics (dependency and race to the bottom), and Post Keynesian economics (short-term absolute advantages and long-term competitive advantages by the strongest trading partners).

14.7 Interesting sources

World Trade Game: http://www.oikoumene.org/en/resources/documents/wcc-programmes/ecumenical-movement-in-the-21st-century/youth/world-trade-game

14.8 Glossary

Absolute advantage Trade between two countries arising from each trading partner having an absolute cost advantage in the production of a different product

Balance of Payments (BoP) The account of a country's transactions with the rest of the world

Capital account Part of the Balance of Payments which registers capital inflows and outflows

Comparative advantage Specialisation in production on the basis of a relative cost advantage in the production of a good as compared to other goods

Competitive advantage Promoting and protecting trade advantages based on anything that matters

Consumer surplus The advantage for consumers due to lower prices of imported goods as compared to domestically produced goods

Convergence The levels of development of countries involved in trade will converge with each other on the basis of their comparative advantage

Current account Part of the Balance of Payments which registers trade in goods and services

Dumping Temporarily selling products below cost price to price competitors out of the market

Fair trade Trade in which the gains are distributed more or less equally so that trade contributes to development for the least developed trading partner

Foreign direct investment (FDI) Direct investment by firms in productive activities in other countries

Gains from trade The advantages of trade for both trading partners, as compared to autarky

Global value chains (GVCs) The globally organised production activities for a final good driven by a lead firm

Globalisation The process through which the world becomes increasingly interconnected through the international expansion of markets

Heckscher-Ohlin theorem A country has a comparative advantage in the production of a product if that country is relatively well endowed with inputs used intensively in the production of that product

Import tariff A tax on imported goods

Infant industry argument The argument that countries that have a weak trade position require trade protection until their industries are sufficiently equipped to become internationally competitive

International Labour Organization (ILO) The UN tri-partite organisation of governments, employer associations, and labour unions

Path dependency Behaviour of today is strongly guided by behaviour in the past

Portfolio investments Investments in financial funds and assets

Prebisch-Singer hypothesis Decreasing terms of trade for countries exporting primary goods to countries exporting manufactured goods

Propensity to import (m) The proportion of their income that consumers spend on imports

Social clauses Social conditions in trade agreements, often about labour standards

Subcontracting = outsourcing Externalising production activity to other firms, often in other countries with lower labour costs

Tax holiday A temporary period in which a company is exempt from paying profit taxes

Terms of trade The ratio of the value of the exports over the value of the imports

Trade The international exchange of goods and services

Trade openness The share of exports (EX) and imports (IM) of GDP: (EX + IM) / GDP

Trade union A free trade agreement among a group of countries in a region

Notes

1 Hans Singer, born German and later obtaining British nationality, was among the first development economists. He collaborated with dependency theorists to explain the gap between the developed and underdeveloped countries of the world.
2 UNCTAD data, available online: www.unctad.org
3 For an account of this settlement, see: http://www.fas.org/sgp/crs/row/R43336.pdf
4 For the full history, see Chang, H.-J. (2002) *Kicking Away the Ladder: The "Real" History of Free Trade*. London: Anthem.
5 Berik, G. (2011) 'Gender Aspects of Trade', Chapter 5 in: Jansen, M., R. Peters and J.-M. Salazar-Xirinachs (eds), *Trade and Employment: From Myths to Facts*. Geneva: ILO.
6 Rodrik, D., and F. Rodríguez (2001) 'Trade Policy and Economic Growth: A Skeptic's Guide to the Cross-National Evidence', in: Bernanke, B. and K.S. Rogoff (eds), *Macroeconomics Annual 2000*. Cambridge, MA: MIT Press for NBER.
7 Nicita, A. (2004) 'Who benefited from trade liberalization in Mexico? Measuring the effects on household welfare'. Policy Research WP series 3265. Washington, DC: The World Bank.
8 http://www.cepr.net/documents/nafta-20-years-2014-02.pdf
9 Iniguez-Montiel, A. J. (2014) 'Growth with Equity for the Development of Mexico: Poverty, Inequality, and Economic Growth (1992-2008)', *World Development* 59, pp. 313–26.
10 http://www.cepr.net/documents/nafta-20-years-2014-02.pdf

15 Well-being and poverty

15.1 Introduction: the biases of GDP

15.1.1 GDP biases

Gross domestic product (GDP) is the most widely used measure for the economy. As you will remember from Chapter 10, it can be measured by adding up the market value of all consumer expenditures (C), investments (I), net government expenditures (G − T), and net trade (EX − IM). And when divided by population size, we get GDP per capita (GDPpc), which allows us to compare well-being between countries. Net domestic product (NDP) subtracts depreciation from GDP, which is on average 10 per cent. Gross national product (GNP) only includes what is produced by nationals: it adds income earned by nationals abroad and subtracts income by foreigners earned in the country. By definition, domestic product equals domestic income, and national product equals national income. So you can use the labels 'product' and 'income' interchangeably.

Even though every economic theory acknowledges problems in this measure of well-being, they all make use of it because alternative measures lack sufficient data, are complex, or focus on other partial aspects of well-being. This chapter presents alternative well-being measures for every theory. Nevertheless GDP (and the variations mentioned above) remains dominant in economics. Let us therefore chart its major biases. Although it has more flaws, the three major biases of GDP as a measure of well-being are the following: GDP ignores distribution, counts damage as well-being, and excludes unpaid production. These three biases will be explained briefly.

15.1.1.1 Distribution

The level of a country's GDP says nothing about its distribution. Even GDP per capita (GDPpc) gives no information about the actual distribution of income in a country. It simply divides all the income by the number of inhabitants. This is the average income per person and not a measure of who actually gets what. As a consequence, we do not know how well-being is distributed in a country. How is it spread over urban and rural areas, over regions, over classes, or between men and women? If income is distributed relatively equally, and the average GDPpc makes it a middle-income country according to World Bank ranking, we may conclude that the majority of people are not poor. But when the same GDPpc income level is distributed very unequally, poverty will be much higher – perhaps even half of the population will live in poverty.

15.1.1.2 Damage

When an oil tanker spills oil, the clean-up activity is an economic service provided by firms and paid for by the oil company at market value, and therefore is part of GDP. Whether a country grows tobacco or wheat, both get included in GDP. And the higher the health care expenditures with an ageing population, the more GDP a nation will have. The more guns people buy to protect themselves, the bigger the GDP. GDP is morally neutral: it simply counts everything sold through the market or supplied as a public good. It would therefore be more accurate to refer to GDP as a measure of production exchanged through markets and supplied as public goods.

15.1.1.3 Unpaid production

Following from the conclusion of the previous point, GDP only counts paid production, not unpaid production. So, everything produced in an economy without money being received in return or paid by the state is excluded from GDP. But the overwhelming majority of unpaid production contributes to well-being, and often crucially so, through reproduction of the labour force and caring labour more generally. The tea I drink after teaching new members at the rowing club the basics of rowing is included in GDP, while my hour of providing training is not. The polite and friendly attitude of my daughter in her student job as a night nurse assistant is the result of her character, her own efforts, and her upbringing by her parents. But she is paid only for her services as an assistant nurse in the emergency room of the hospital, not for her good manners and spirit. And the long hours that a poor rural woman needs to walk for every day to fetch water and firewood to provide for her household in rural east India is not included in GDP – only the occasional sales of baskets she manages to produce in-between caring for her husband and children, and growing vegetables is part of GDP.

15.1.2 GDP adjustment and alternatives

Can these three biases be corrected when measuring GDP? The answer depends on your expectations. If you want to address all three biases mentioned above, you need alternative measures of well-being. But if you do not want to throw the baby (relatively wide data availability and high-quality measurement on an annual basis) out with the bathwater (the three biases), you can use corrections to GDP. Countries already make estimations of some unpaid production, namely the imputed market value of goods produced in family businesses by unpaid family members. This does not count all unpaid labour, and perhaps not even the majority, but it is a first step. Others compare GDP with ecological accounts to make the ecological footprint behind GDP visible. And yet others use measures of income inequality, such as the Gini coefficient, in their analysis of growth and well-being to study the inequality of income distribution.

Alternative well-being measures move away from counting what is produced with paid labour to measuring what total production (paid and unpaid) *does* for people. So, a focus on consumption, capabilities, and social, political, and environmental conditions. This is not easy because of a trade-off between completeness and how many items a well-being indicator measures. The longer and more complex the list of well-being components is, the more difficult it becomes to measure well-being.

The OECD has recently introduced such an alternative well-being measure, the Better Life Index (BLI). It is available for 36 high-income countries. It addresses inequalities, unpaid contributions to well-being, and ecology, along 11 dimensions of well-being. Some dimensions are measured with more than one indicator, so that the BLI includes 24 indicators. This explains why the BLI only covers a small group of countries, and the most developed ones: for other countries the data are insufficient. Box 15.1 provides an overview of the BLI indicators, which allows country-level scores on each of the 11 dimensions. Australia performs best on the BLI in 2014, but the BLI does not use country ranking, it only gives scores per country to each of the 11 dimensions. So, countries can only be compared per dimension.

Box 15.1 Better Life Index indicators

- Dwellings without basic facilities
- Housing expenditure
- Rooms per person
- Household net adjusted disposable income
- Household net financial wealth
- Employment rate
- Job security
- Long-term unemployment rate
- Personal earnings
- Quality of support network
- Educational attainment
- Student skills
- Years in education
- Air pollution
- Water quality
- Consultation on rule-making
- Voter turnout
- Life expectancy
- Self-reported health
- Life satisfaction
- Assault rate
- Homicide rate
- Employees working very long hours
- Time devoted to leisure and personal care

Source: http://www.oecdbetterlifeindex.org/

15.2 Social economics: multidimensional well-being and poverty

15.2.1 Multidimensional well-being

Social economics looks beyond income and regards well-being as multidimensional. But there is no agreement on which dimensions to include and how to measure them. It may sound trivial, but being alive is a precondition to achieving anything else in life . . . and we have a widely available indicator to measure this, namely life expectancy. In countries where average life expectancy is barely 60 years, well-being can be considered less than in countries where life expectancy exceeds 80 years. Not only because these people have the opportunity to live longer lives, but also because life expectancy is a measure of health: the more people die prematurely, the less healthy their lives will have been.

Amartya Sen was together with the Pakistani economist Mahbub ul Haq, founder of a simple and widely available alternative to GDP in 1990. It has only three dimensions: gross national income per capita (GNIpc), health (life expectancy), and education (school enrolment and literacy). This well-being measure has become the widely known Human Development Index (HDI), published annually by UNDP. It is an index with a value between 0 and 1. The higher the value, the higher human development. So, each country has an HDI value and each country is ranked according to its HDI value, from high (a HDI value close to 1) to low (a value close to 0). *Human development* is well-being in terms of basic capabilities such as health, education, and purchasing power.

The HDI allows for a comparison with GNI (which also is included in the HDI, so it can also be considered as an adaptation of GDP rather than an alternative) through ranking countries twice. First according to their GNIpc score, and second according to their HDI score. When the HDI rank is subtracted from the GNIpc rank, we can immediately see whether a country transforms its income effectively into human development or not. Negative outcomes (GNIpc rank − HDI rank <0) indicate that a country is wasting human development, because it is not investing its national income as efficiently as possible to increase human development. In contrast, countries which show positive outcomes (GNIpc rank − HDI rank >0) manage to translate their income quite effectively into human development. Table 15.1 shows the country scores for South Asia.

The table shows some interesting results about human development in South Asia. First, the countries are ranked in the table according to their HDI value, which shows that Sri Lanka has the highest level of human development. Even though its income is much lower than that of the Maldives: US$5,170 per year for Sri Lanka, versus US$7,478 per year for the Maldives. This results in a large positive score in the last column for Sri Lanka, the income rank minus the human development rank: +18. And a negative score for the Maldives of −9. This means that Sri Lanka is much more effective in translating national income into human development than the Maldives. A second interesting insight from Table 15.1 is that Pakistan

Table 15.1 Human Development Index and performance, South Asia, 2012

Country	GNIpc value (US$)	GNIpc rank	HDI value	HDI rank	GNIpc rank − HDI rank
Sri Lanka	5,170	110	0.715	92	18
Maldives	7,478	95	0.688	104	9
India	3,285	135	0.554	138	−3
Bhutan	5,246	110	0.538	141	−31
Pakistan	2,566	137	0.515	146	−9
Bangladesh	1,785	156	0.515	147	9
Nepal	1,137	168	0.463	157	11
Afghanistan	1,000	173	0.374	176	−3

Note: GNIpc, gross national income per capita.

Source: 'Human Development Report 2013'. New York: UNDP. Available at https://data.undp.org

and Bangladesh, with equal scores on human development, show very different efforts in translating their income into human development. Whereas Bangladesh does this quite efficiently, with a +9 score in the last column, Pakistan, with a higher income level, does not score so well: −9. Finally, we need to discuss the remarkable result for Bhutan. Remember from Chapter 1 that it has its own National Happiness Index as an alternative well-being measure to GDP. It is a multidimensional measure of well-being, which is broader than the HDI. It includes cultural and ecological dimensions of well-being.

But Bhutan scores very low on income rank minus human development rank: −31, as shown in Table 15.1. It is the worst scoring country in South Asia. How is this possible? The answer is related to the emphasis on 'national' in the Bhutanese policies supporting national happiness. It involves very strong protection of national identity, leading to the exclusion of immigrants and refugees with different religions and languages, such as the Nepalese minority in Bhutan.[1] Even though these minorities contribute to national income with their agricultural labour. Such social exclusion results in low scores of health and education for part of the population, lowering the average HDI score relative to income.

15.2.2 Multidimensional poverty

When we measure well-being in a multidimensional way, we also need to measure poverty as such. Of course, this can be done with the same measure, such as HDI: the lowest ranking countries can be considered poor, whereas the highest-ranking countries can be regarded as rich. But poverty requires more policy attention than richness: poverty is a priority economic problem. So, the more precisely we measure poverty, the better we can understand how it changes in response to economic development, crises, or macroeconomic policies. And good poverty indicators enable close monitoring of poverty. That is why the UNDP has developed, next to the HDI, the Multidimensional Poverty Index: the MPI.

The MPI covers the same three dimensions and has the same structure as the HDI but focuses on deprivation. According to the MPI, one third of the population of the 109 countries included in the MPI, 1.7 billion people, can be considered extremely poor. This number is higher than that calculated with the income measure of poverty, which counts the number of people living on less than US$1.25 per day. The MPI has two advantages over the income measure. First, it measures what people are able to do with their income in terms of health and education. Second, it reveals the most urgent needs that must be addressed in order to reduce poverty, based on the scores on nine indicators. The multidimensional poverty indicators are shown in Table 15.2.

Table 15.2 Multidimensional poverty indicators

Living standards	Assets
	Floor
	Electricity
	Water
	Cooking fuel
Education	Children enrolled
	Years of schooling
Health	Child mortality
	Nutrition

Source: 'Human Development Report 2013'. New York: UNDP. Available at https://data.undp.org

Table 15.3 Multidimensional Poverty Index and indicators, South Asia, 2012

Country	Data year	MPI value	Poverty (%)
Sri Lanka	2003	0.021	5.3
Maldives	2009	0.018	5.2
India	2006	0.283	53.7
Bhutan	2010	0.119	27.2
Pakistan	2007	0.264	49.4
Bangladesh	2007	0.292	57.8
Nepal	2011	0.217	44.2
Afghanistan	–	–	–

Source: 'Human Development Report 2013'. New York: UNDP. Available at https://data.undp.org

Table 15.3 shows the value of the MPI and the percentage of the population living in multidimensional poverty, for the same region as Table 15.2 did for the HDI: South Asia. It shows that, as for the HDI, Sri Lanka and the Maldives do quite well: these countries score low on the MPI, and have only 5 per cent of their population living in poverty. Bangladesh, India, and Pakistan have high MPI values and have poverty rates of around 50 per cent. The combination of the HDI and MPI measures gives a more complete indication of the extent of poverty in a country. When we look at Bangladesh, for example, which did quite well in transforming income into human development according to the HDI, it nevertheless has a poverty rate of almost 60 per cent when we use the MPI poverty measure. Nepal, with less income, has a much lower poverty rate.

What explains multidimensional poverty? In social economics, the explanation is social exclusion. There are basically three drivers of social exclusion, described below.

15.2.2.1 Market forces

Often, markets are not fully competitive. This results in market power by firms over consumers (driving up consumer prices) and suppliers (pushing down the sales prices for the products produced by small-scale entrepreneurs). And where labour unions are weak, firms have market power over labour, pushing wages down. But even when markets are fully competitive, some groups find themselves socially excluded from participation in markets on an equal basis. For example, labour markets may be in equilibrium with high levels of unemployment, discouraged workers, and underemployment. This weakens the bargaining power of those employed, resulting in low wages.

And land markets may be in equilibrium, but landless farmers have no access to land due to lack of purchasing power, lack of access to credit, lack of collateral to obtain credit, or no permission from husbands, brothers, or fathers to buy or sell property. Or their communal land may have been appropriated or informal land rights ignored by municipal governments seeking land to expand urban housing and industrial areas.

Finally, small-scale entrepreneurs may have no access to skills, tools, and sales markets, so that they are locked into low value added activities, competing with each other for a limited size and geographical spread of market demand. This often results in a local over-supply of the same types of medium quality goods.

15.2.2.2 Social norms

Social norms can discriminate against certain social groups: migrants, ethnic groups, women, or low caste people. This explains why poverty is also persistent in developed countries. In

Europe, the partially nomadic Roma and Sinti people are among the most deprived. In the Arab world, migrant workers from South Asia are the ones living in poverty. And in the world's largest cities, slums are populated by rural-urban migrants, who cannot find jobs and lack the skills and capital to set up a profitable business. While throughout the western world, women are less financially independent than men.

15.2.2.3 Social protection deficiencies

Even when people are not excluded from markets, do not suffer from disasters, and do not belong to a group discriminated against, they may find themselves poor. The reason is not only a low level of economic development, although this is obviously a major reason for widespread poverty. It is also because of a lack of social protection provided by communities and the state. Without any social protection, in the shape of relief by central government, foreign aid, or social security, external shocks and bad luck may drive people into poverty. Often, the extent of social protection in a country reflects power relations: elites often have organised state social protection for themselves, for example through pensions in the formal sector. Organisation of health care insurance, old-age pensions, and disability benefits can take many years, in particular in countries with high levels of inequality.

15.3 Institutional economics: relative well-being and poverty

15.3.1 Inequality and social norms

Relative well-being measures poverty not in absolute terms, such as the HDI and MPI, but as inequality. So, it does not measure how many children are out of school, or the extent of child mortality, but how unequally well-being is distributed. This can be done by measuring inequality in a vertical way, ranking individuals or households along a continuum, or in a horizontal way, grouping individuals or households along particular social stratifications. So, *vertical inequality* ranks people along a continuum of a single dimension, often income. It focuses on incomes, because income inequality cuts across social groups: there are poor and rich immigrants, poor and rich women, and poor and rich farmers. *Horizontal inequalities* are group inequalities along social dimensions, such as ethnicity, geography, and gender.

Institutional economics focuses on inequality rather than on absolute poverty, because it recognises the importance of social norms for well-being. Especially norms about status and fairness. These are particularly relevant for analysing poverty at the micro level: between individuals and households and social groups.

15.3.1.1 Status

People tend to strive for the levels of well-being of those above them in the income distribution: the grass-is-greener-at-the-Jones' effect. The economic benefit of this is that people are concerned with achievement, and hence, with investing in their skills in order to obtain higher incomes. The economic cost of this is that status and materialism result in high ecological footprints. And it may lead to a decline in social cohesion, in particular when social classes increasingly distinguish themselves from those below them. This may lead to segregated neighbourhoods, segregated education, and discrimination in the labour market.

15.3.1.2 Fairness

Who deserves what in the economy? This is the driving economic question of fairness. Societies differ in their average answer to this question. *Meritocratic societies* closely connect fairness with contribution: those who work hardest, have the most unique skills in demand, or make the most risky investments, are generally agreed to be most deserving of high income. A meritocratic view of fairness is not much concerned with inequality. Those at the top of the income distribution can earn extremely high salaries and bonuses, without much jealousy or criticism from the rest of society. Millionaires and billionaires rather evoke admiration in meritocratic societies. Those at the bottom of the income distribution in meritocratic societies are considered as deserving their status too: they are seen as not putting in enough effort to obtain economic success.

More *egalitarian societies*, such as social welfare states, connect economic fairness with the value of human dignity: nobody deserves to be poor. Such societies provide social protection for the poor, even when some of the receivers of welfare benefits are considered to be free riders or suckers who waste every opportunity provided to them to obtain a job or start a business. In fact, in such societies the majority of the population values equality as an intrinsic value, and hence, everyone also values suckers – because they're considered *our* suckers.

So, the likelihood that an individual will live in an unequal society and suffer from very low levels of well-being crucially depends, in institutional economics, on whether one lives in a society where meritocratic norms are dominant or in a society where egalitarian norms are dominant.

Image 15.1 Homeless man in Barcelona

15.3.2 Income inequality

Income inequality in developed and developing countries increased by 10 per cent between 1990 and 2010, according to the UN.[2] Income inequality has real effects. In developing countries we find that children in the poorest 20 per cent of households are up to three times more likely to die before their fifth birthday than children in the richest 20 per cent of households. And women in rural areas in developing countries are up to three times more likely to die while giving birth than women living in cities. In developed countries, data show that in the more equal countries, such as Germany, Italy, and Japan, less than 10 per cent of the population suffers from mental illness (in particular drug and alcohol addiction), whereas in the more unequal countries, such as the USA, UK, and Australia, the rate is around 25 per cent.[3]

Moreover, more unequal developed countries appear to have more social problems of all kinds, as compared to less unequal developed countries. The social problems include high mortality, obesity, low educational performance, high homicide rates, and high rates of imprisonment.[4] It also seems that more inequality makes the most disadvantaged in a society more concerned with social status, in particular in meritocratic societies. Box 15.2 illustrates the point for those at the bottom of the income distribution in the USA.

Box 15.2 Poverty in the USA

'Surveys of the 12.6 per cent of Americans living below the federal poverty line (an absolute income level rather than a relative standards such as half the average income) show that 80 per cent of them have air-conditioning, almost 75 per cent own at least one car or truck and around 33 per cent have a computer, a dishwasher or a second car. What this means is that when people lack money for essentials such as food, it is usually a reflection of the strength of their desire to live up to the prevailing standards. You may, for instance, feel it more important to maintain appearances by spending on clothes while stinting on food. We knew of a young man who was unemployed and had spent a month's income on a new mobile phone because he said girls ignored people who hadn't the right stuff. As Adam Smith emphasized, it is important to be able to present oneself creditably in society without the shame and stigma of apparent poverty.'

Source: Wilkinson, R. and K. Pickett (2009) *The Spirit Level*. New York: Bloomsbury Press, p. 25.

We have already seen that economists use the Gini coefficient to measure income inequality. Remember that the Gini coefficient is 0 for full equality and 1 for complete inequality. Over the period 1990–2010, the Gini coefficient for developed countries increased from 41.4 to 45.3, while for developing countries it increased from 38.5 to 41.5.[5] Regional averages reveal a more varied picture. Africa shows the largest decline in the Gini coefficient, from 48.0 to 44.4. Europe and the Commonwealth of Independent States show the largest increase, from 33.0 to 43.8. So, income inequality has gone down in Africa, but up all over Europe.

The Gini coefficient is a very crude measure of income inequality, because the biggest inequalities are found at the very top. That is why it is insightful to compare the income earned by the top 1 per cent of households with the other 99 per cent – just like the slogan of the Occupy movement, critiquing the power of the financial sector, the wealth of bankers, and their responsibility for causing the financial crisis: 'we are the 99%'.

The top 1 per cent earn 20 per cent of national income in Colombia, 17 per cent of national income in South Africa, and 13 per cent of national income in Singapore.[6] In Western countries, inequality is highest in the USA, where the top 1 per cent take home 20 per cent of national income.[7] What are the causes behind income inequality? There are three main categories of causes.

15.3.2.1 Globalisation

Globalisation concerns capital flows and trade in goods and services, while they are related in the so-called global assembly line, through which production is organised, and in global value chains. Financial globalisation has resulted in global investment flows to low-cost labour production sites and to emerging investment opportunities in a wide variety of assets. The first has created downward pressure on wages, due to the strong bargaining power of foot-loose companies vis-à-vis the weak bargaining power of immobile labour. This certainly has created more jobs in the Global South than it has destroyed in the Global North, but at much lower wages. The second has resulted in an increasing share of global investment going to the financial sector itself, creating high-risk-high-return assets with increasing volatility, instead of jobs in productive activities.

15.3.2.2 Technological change

Wages are theoretically related to productivity: the higher labour productivity, the higher wage incomes, because workers produce more output per hour and therefore can be paid more income per hour. If not, they may reduce their productivity out of frustration (slowdown or go-slow) or protest (strike). But in the context of globalisation, technological change has only increased capitalist earnings and not labour income. Since the 1980s, the labour share of income has declined steadily: technological change still translates into higher labour productivity, but no longer into relatively higher wages.

Moreover, technological change increases the demand for skilled labour and reduces the demand for unskilled labour, so that the wages of better educated workers are more likely to increase while the wages of less educated workers are likely to reduce. This is another driver of income inequality, in particular in developed counties.

15.3.2.3 Market liberalisation with reduced government protection

The liberalisation of markets since the 1980s has gone hand-in-hand with reductions in government expenditures and weaker social protection for the poor through social floors (minimum wages) and social safety nets (welfare benefits). Lower tax revenues constrain governments from implementing adequate social policies. In particular in developing countries, tax revenues as a percentage of GDP remain limited, ranging from 15 per cent in Asia to 21 per cent in transition economies. This is shown in Diagram 15.1.

Tax revenue is the input-side of social policy. What matters also is the output-side. When countries succeed in spending tax money effectively, including on social policy, the effects can be significant for the reduction in income inequality. An example is the improved taxation in Latin America and the conditional cash-transfer policies for the poor. *Conditional cash transfers* are a social policy of income support for poor households on the condition that they send their children to school or meet other social policy criteria. Diagram 15.2 shows the percentage decline in the Gini coefficient due to cash-transfer policies in Latin America.

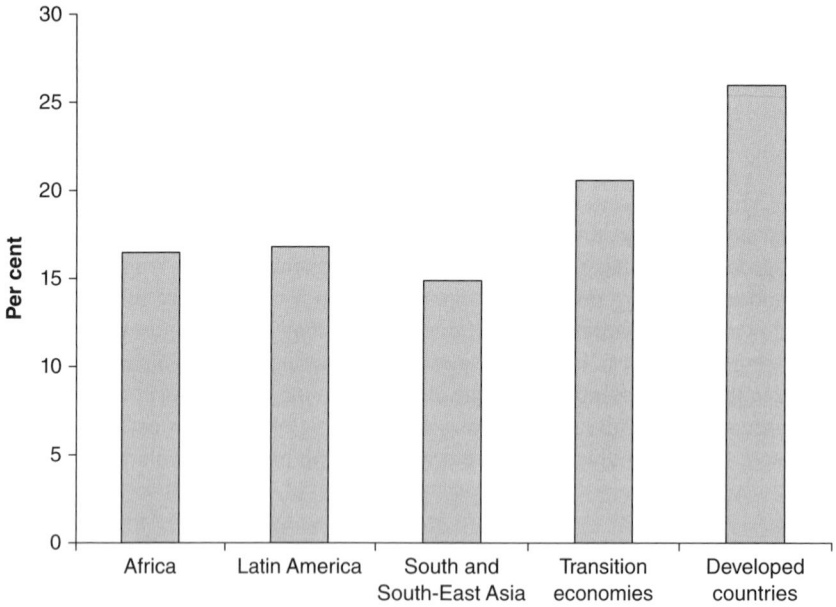

Diagram 15.1 Tax revenue % of gross domestic product (GDP), 2006–2010

Source: UNDP (2013) 'Humanity Divided: Confronting Inequality in Developing Countries', p. 245.

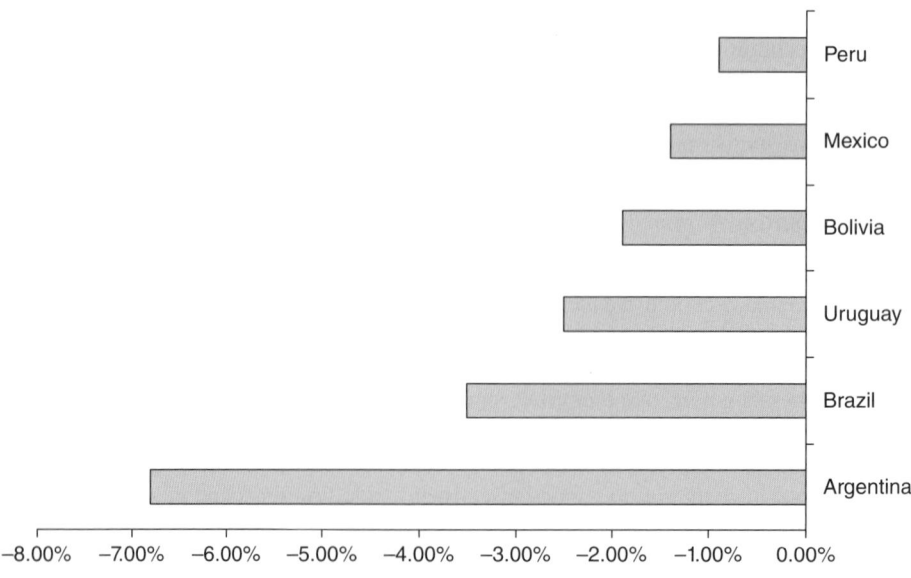

Diagram 15.2 Conditional cash transfers in Latin America: reductions in the Gini coefficient

Source: UNDP (2013) 'Humanity Divided: Confronting Inequality in Developing Countries', p. 92.

15.3.3 Horizontal inequality

Horizontal inequality was defined above as group inequalities along social stratifications, such as ethnicity, geography, gender, and caste. Its causes are a combination of social exclusion, as explained in the social economic theory of poverty, and social norms, which may legitimise inequality.

Horizontal inequalities can be large and persistent. In particular regional inequalities. Because they are often correlated with social divisions along the lines of ethnicity and concentration of economic activity. In Thailand, for example, regional inequalities are relatively large as compared to neighbouring countries. And the disparities have remained stable over the past 10 years. For example, household income in the richest province was five times that in the poorest. Table 15.4 shows a summary of the regional disparities in human development in the 76 provinces of Thailand. They are measured not with the HDI but with a Human Achievement Index (HAI), which the UNDP office in Thailand developed in 2003 in order to take more dimensions of well-being into account than the HDI. The HAI consist of eight dimensions, rather than three: health, education, employment, income, housing and living environment, family and community life, transport and communication, and participation. To put it simply, the HAI is an 'HDI-plus': it contains five more dimensions than the HDI.

Table 15.4 shows a summary of the human development scores of the top five and bottom five provinces. The three columns on the left-hand side show the top five provinces and the three columns on the right-hand side show the bottom five provinces. The province of Bangkok, containing the capital city, ranks top, while the province of Mae Hong Sun is at the very bottom. The human development value for Bangkok is 34 per cent higher than that for Mae Hong Sun. This is quite a large difference within a single country, indicating high regional inequality in multi-dimensional well-being.

One of the institutional policies which the Thai government has implemented to decrease regional inequalities, is to reduce the relative isolation of the poorer provinces. This is done through the development of so-called economic corridors which connect the various provinces within the country as well as with neighbouring countries and partners in the ASEAN trade union.

Another major form of horizontal inequality is gender inequality. This is a special type of horizontal inequality because it cuts right through households, unlike inequalities of ethnicity

Table 15.4 Regional disparities in human development in Thailand, 2014

Rank (top five)	Province	HAI value	Rank (bottom five)	Province	HAI value
1	Bangkok	0.697	76	Mae Hong Son	0.521
2	Phuket	0.691	75	Tak	0.565
3	Nontaburi	0.671	74	Si Sa Ket	0.571
4	Trang	0.666	73	Nakhon Phanom	0.578
5	Phayao	0.666	72	Surih	0.586

Note: HAI, Human Achievement Index.

Source: 'Advancing Human Development through the ASEAN Community. Thailand Human Development Report 2014'. Bangkok: UNDP. Available at http://hdr.undp.org/sites/default/files/thailand_nhdr_2014_0.pdf

or geography. That is why it is called an intra-household inequality. And it is caused, as we have seen in Chapter 2, by a combination of factors within and outside households. Institutions are a major driver of gender inequalities. This involves both formal institutions and informal institutions. Recent data even allow this to be measured. Not only the extent of gender inequality in a country, but also the various formal and informal asymmetric institutions that drive this type of horizontal inequality.

Table 15.5 shows the Gender Equality Index (GEI) and two indicators from the Social Institutions & Gender Index (SIGI) for the MENA region (Middle East and North Africa). The first SIGI indicator measures women's access to resources, and hence, formal gendered institutions. The second SIGI indicator measures women's civil liberties, and hence, informal gendered institutions. The GEI is measured positively: the higher the score, the more gender equality. The gendered institutions from SIGI are measured negatively: the higher the score, the more restrictive the gendered institutions are for women.

Table 15.5 ranks the MENA-region countries according to their level of gender equality (GEI). Oman and Lebanon top the ranking. Yemen and the United Arab Emirates (UAE) have the lowest GEI scores. Diagrams 15.3a and 15.3b show how the two types of gendered institutions correlate with gender equality. Remember that the GEI is measured positively: the higher the score, the more gender equality. While the two institutional measures are measured negatively: the higher the score, the more restrictive these institutions are for women.

The scatter plots show that there is a negative correlation between the GEI on the one hand and each of the two gendered institutions on the other. The more unequal the gendered institutions, the lower gender equality. The policy implication is that with more equal institutions, gender equality is likely to improve *ceteris paribus*. Moreover, the relationship between gender equality and informal gendered institutions is stronger. This implies that policies addressing people's attitudes may be even more urgent and effective for reducing gender inequality than changes in laws.

Table 15.5 Gender Equality Index (GEI) and gendered institutions in the Middle East and North Africa (MENA region), 2010–2012

Country	GEI	Formal gendered institutions (access to resources)	Informal gendered institutions (civil liberties)
Oman	0.70	0.51	0.96
Lebanon	0.69	0.51	0.78
Morocco	0.68	0.35	0.11
Tunisia	0.68	0.18	0.48
West Bank and Gaza	0.68	0.51	0.54
Libya	0.68	0.51	0.76
Bahrain	0.67	0.00	0.72
Iran	0.67	0.51	0.99
Jordan	0.67	0.51	0.11
Algeria	0.66	0.00	0.97
Syria	0.66	0.51	0.74
Egypt	0.65	0.30	0.79
Iraq	0.64	0.35	0.70
UAE	0.63	0.65	0.93
Yemen	0.59	0.51	1.00

Source: Author's calculations from OECD: Social Institutions & Gender Index, 2012. Available at http://genderindex.org/data

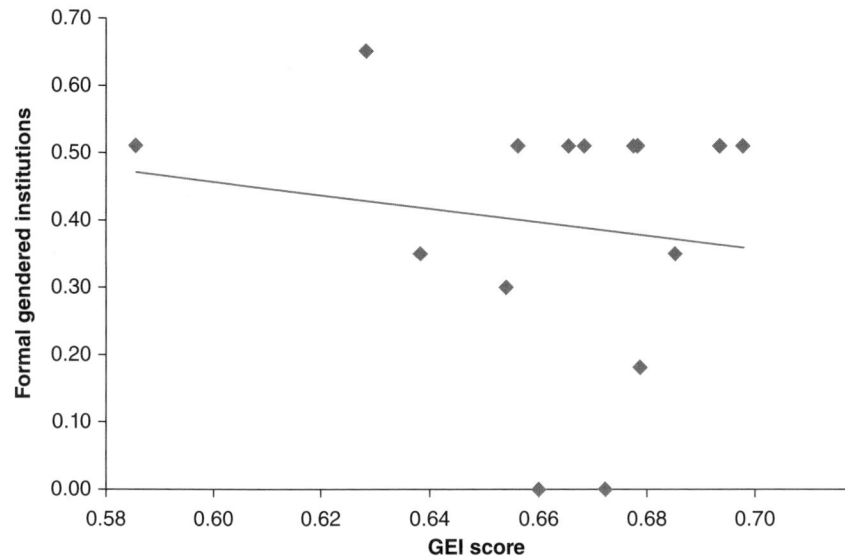

Diagram 15.3a Scatter plot of the Gender Equality Index (GEI) and formal gendered institutions in the Middle East and North Africa (MENA) region, 2010–2012

Source: Author's calculations from Indices of Social Development and OECD: Social Institutions & Gender Index, 2012.

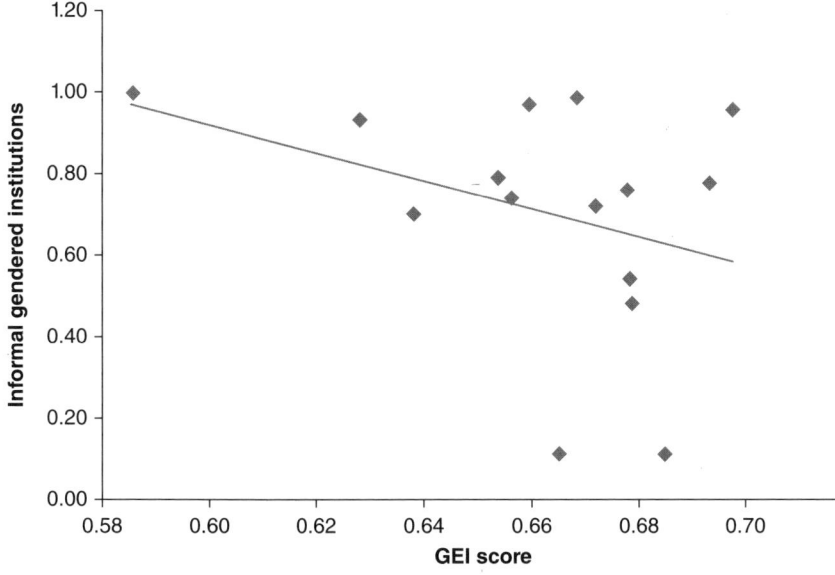

Diagram 15.3b Scatter plot of the Gender Equality Index (GEI) and informal gendered institutions in the Middle East and North Africa (MENA) region, 2010–2012

Source: Author's calculations from Indices of Social Development and OECD: Social Institutions & Gender Index, 2012.

15.4 Post Keynesian economics: the dynamics of wealth inequality

15.4.1 Wealth inequality

Wealth can be measured as the total stock of capital: cash and savings, financial assets, buildings, productive land, machines, techniques, brands, and copyrights. Wealth is more unequally distributed than income. The reason for this is accumulation, not only individually, over a lifetime, but also through inheritance over generations, reproducing the capitalist class. Capital income is accumulated through inheritance, profits, dividends, interests, rents, and royalties.

The French economist Thomas Piketty has recently carried out detailed historical research of wealth inequality in various countries. His research is helpful to explain the Post Keynesian theory of inequality, which is rooted in capital accumulation and the difference between capital income and labour income. I will use Piketty's two equations, which he refers to as the fundamental laws of capitalism, to present the Post Keynesian perspective of well-being and poverty. The first wealth equation describes that wealth accumulation is a product of the capital stock and the return on capital:

$$\alpha = r \times \beta$$

in which α = the share of national income from capital earnings, r = the return on capital, and β = the capital/income ratio, the value of the stock of capital expressed in the value of annual income of a country. This equation shows that the higher the return on capital, and the higher the stock of capital accumulated, the higher will be capital's share of a country's income. As a consequence, with an increasing value of capital income, α, the labour share of income (which can be calculated from the equation above as $1-\alpha$) will be lower. Capitalist economies will therefore increase the capital share of income vis-à-vis the labour share of income, unless returns on investment are very low or negative for a long period of time.

As Diagram 15.4 shows, the value of β, the capital/income ratio, was around 600–700 per cent of annual national income at the end of the 19th century. Hence, β is a ratio between six and seven to one, so, a number between 6 and 7. The return on capital was (and is) around 4–5 per cent. As a consequence, the value of α, the share of income going to capital, is approximately 5% × 6 = 30%. So, capital earned 30 per cent of national income and labour earned, as a consequence, 70 per cent of national income. This distribution of capital and labour income was common for a long period of time. Only in the period of the two world wars, was the stock of capita significantly lower.

The first wealth equation is also valid at the firm level: with a capital stock of, say, four times its annual returns (such as the total value of a factory), and a rate of return on capital of 6 per cent, the capital share of the firm's income will be 6% × 4 = 24%. Hence, the labour share of income in the firm will be 76 per cent. With investment in a new factory, the value of the capital/income ratio will increase, say, by 5. With the same rate of return on the investment, the capital share of the firm's earnings will now be 6% × 5 = 30%. As a consequence, the labour share will decline from 76 per cent to 70 per cent. Not because labour has become less productive. On the contrary, the new machines and logistics are likely to have made labour more productive than in the previous year. It is the capital accumulation process which is responsible for the higher share of capital earnings of the firm, as the first wealth equation explains.

This shows the Post Keynesian point that there is not a clear relationship between labour productivity and wages. The distribution of income between capital and labour, whether at

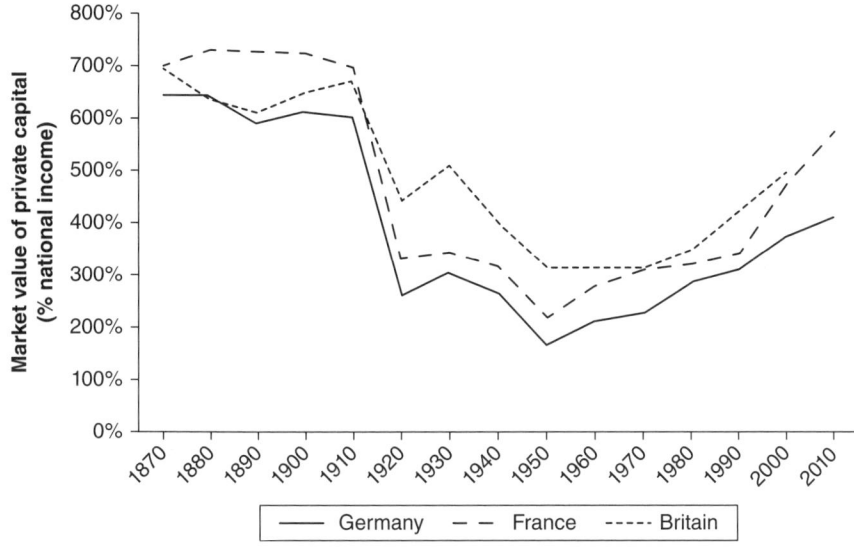

Diagram 15.4 Capital/income ratio in Germany, France, and Britain, 1870–2010

Note: Aggregate private wealth was worth about 6–7 years of national income in Europe in 1910, between 2 and 3 years in 1950, and between 4 and 6 years in 2010.

Source: http://piketty.pse.ens.fr/en/capital21c2

the macroeconomic level or firm level, is not derived from the level of labour productivity, but depends on the bargaining power of capital over labour, which is in favour of capital, and the capital stock. Unless labour markets are so tight during an economic boom that sufficient quality and numbers of workers can only be hired and retained by paying them higher wages.

The second equation of wealth accumulation is a dynamic one. It explains the capital/income ratio from the first equation as the ratio of the savings rate (s) over the per capita economic growth rate (g):

$$\beta = s/g$$

This equation explains long-term capital accumulation. The higher the savings rate and the lower the GDP per capita growth rate, the higher the capital/income ratio in a country. Remember from Chapter 10 that the savings rate, which is the same as the propensity to save, is the complement of the propensity to consume: s + c = 1. The more capitalist the country, the richer the capitalists, and the more very-high-wage earners, the higher the savings rate. Hence, also the second wealth equation shows an endogenous process of accumulation: the more income inequality, the more likely it is that the savings rate will be higher, and the higher the capital/income ratio in future.

For example, if the savings rate is 20 per cent, which is not unusual for a country, and the per capita economic growth rate is 3 per cent, which is the average for all developing countries over the past 20 years (1990–2010), we can calculate that β will be 20%/3% = 6.7. This was the value of β for developed countries during the 50 years before World War I. Historically, per capita economic growth rates have been much lower than 3 per cent. GDP growth was

0.1 per cent annually for the period since Roman times up to around 1700. With population growth also being 0.1 per cent, this resulted in a per capita GDP growth rate of 0.1% − 0.1% = 0.0%. Hence, despite some economic progress in technology and skills, economic growth was negligible for 17 centuries. The following century, of the Industrial Revolution, showed GDP per capita growth of 0.1 per cent up to 1820. From 1820 to 1913, world output grew by 0.9 per cent per capita. Only after World War I, did output grow at the unprecedented rate of 3 per cent. Corrected for the increased population growth rate of 1.4 per cent, due to better health care, GDP grew by 1.6 per cent per capita over the period 1913–2012. Only since the 1970s has the world known countries with higher per capita growth rates, such as Japan and China. But Japan is 'back to normal', and so are the USA and Europe. China's growth has also slowed down recently. Based on historical growth figures, GDP per capita growth is likely to be not more than 1.2 per cent annually in the long run over the 21st century.[8]

Going back to the example for the second wealth equation, the assumption of a 3 per cent per capita growth rate is very optimistic for the long run. So, let us replace it with the expected long-term growth rate of 1.2 per cent. In that case, keeping the savings rate at 20 per cent, β will be 20%/1.2% = 16.7. This is of course an enormous capital/income ratio: the value of the capital stock will be more than sixteen times annual income. The world has never seen this before, for not a single country. It took the USA, for example, several centuries to beat Europe's capital/income ratio. The actual numbers used in this example are quite realistic from a historical perspective. But the effect on β is alarming. And when we put its long-term value of 16.7 per cent in the first wealth equation, even when using a low return on investment of r = 3%, it results in a very high share of income going to capital, namely 50 per cent, implying very high inequality, with only 50 per cent of income going to labour:

$$\alpha = 3\% \times 16.7 = 50\%$$

In conclusion, the result of the ever-faster capital accumulation and relatively low long-term economic growth rate in capitalist economies is very high inequality. In the words of Thomas Piketty:

> in a quasi-stagnant society wealth accumulated in the past will inevitably acquire disproportionate importance.[9]

Like the first equation of wealth accumulation, the second can also be applied to the firm level. Remember from Chapter 4, that the Post Keynesian perspective explained that firms tend to grow until their return on investment gets close to their rate of growth, or equals it: $r \leq g$. So, a firm will invest in expansion until the rate of return on investment is no longer higher than the growth rate. This makes sense for a firm. Why invest more if it does not lead to more sales?

For countries, a similar rule of thumb may be reasonable. But there are no CEOs in charge of r and g. As the two equations of wealth accumulation demonstrate, it is the market that is driving the values of these two variables. So, it requires redistributive policies, preferably on a world scale, to reverse the trend towards further increasing inequality.

Now, suppose that a country ensures that r is not higher than g, as in $r \leq g$ at the firm level. This lower rate of return on capital can be enforced by wealth taxation, limiting after-tax returns on investment. Let us go back to the earlier example. Now if r is taxed so that net r = 2.5%, and we start from the current capital/income ratio of 6 (β), the first equation of wealth accumulation gives α, the capital/income share, of r × β = 2.5% × 6 = 15%. Hence, the labour share of income is quite high, namely 85 per cent. This does not reflect high inequality favouring capital owners. Hence, when the difference between r and g becomes smaller, through wealth taxation, inequality will be less. So, what was rational at the firm level seems good guidance for macroeconomic policy as well: bring r down closer to the long-term average of g so that the current accumulation trend of r > g will tend towards r ≤ g.

15.4.2 Economic drivers and effects of increasing inequality

There are two endogenous factors helping to reduce economic inequality (inequality in income, wealth, or human development): education and technology. Higher levels of technology generate higher labour productivity, which creates the space for wage increases for workers, in particular production workers. Steady technological advancement, and its wide spread across countries and sectors, will help to reduce labour income inequalities. Education is the other endogenous factor behind more equality. Over time, technological development requires higher skilled labour. When individuals therefore invest in higher levels of education, they will be able to obtain higher skilled jobs, and hence be able to earn higher wage incomes – although this is not automatic but depends on the bargaining power of labour. Even with good and accessible education, there remain winners and losers.

There are also endogenous counterforces at work. The major driver of more inequality is the level of economic growth, coupled with the rate of return of capital, as we have seen above. And this force was more powerful in history than the forces of technology and education. As a consequence, inequality was historically high between 1870 and 1914, declined with the capital destruction of the two world wars, and then has increased again since the

Image 15.2 We cannot all be winners

1980s with the current era of globalisation. Both periods of high inequality have shown low economic growth rates, so that the rate of return on capital was higher than the GDP growth rate. This has happened irrespective of economic cycles: it is a long-term phenomenon in which the accumulation of capital dominates the economic growth rate.

What is, in addition to the social problem, the economic problem of inequality? Post Keynesian economics provides four macroeconomic reasons why high inequality is bad for the economy: social conflict, low aggregate demand, under-investment, and increasing financial fragility. These will be explained briefly below.

15.4.2.1 Social conflict

High inequality may eventually result in social conflict. This may vary from relatively mild efficiency losses through labour strikes, to serious costs through political destabilisation and damage to physical capital stocks. This will, in turn, affect investment. Recent economic history has shown many examples of capital flight, when domestic investors move their capital abroad where it is more secure against damage and appropriation. Moreover, foreign investors are not willing to invest in a country with high social and political instability.

15.4.2.2 Low aggregate demand

High inequality implies high capital income and low labour income. Plus a very unequal distribution of labour income, where most of the income is earned by a small elite. This leads to a high savings rate for most of the income, and hence, a low propensity to consume. Overall, this leads to relatively low aggregate demand. And this implies that an economy gets stuck at a low level of capacity utilisation with high unemployment rates.

15.4.2.3 Under-investment

Lack of access to resources by the poor leads to *under-investment* in production. This is low investment in a resource, leading to low returns. Very unequal land distribution is inefficient, because it leads to lower levels of agricultural production than a more equal distribution of land. Large landowners do not work their land as intensively as small landowners. Moreover, insecurity of landownership prevents farmers from investing in improving the land, because they are not sure whether they can reap the returns on such investments. Child labour in households where parents earn below-living wages results in limited or no education at all for these children, which is an under-investment in human capabilities. Finally, large income inequalities negatively affect social cohesion. This, in turn, may make the poor distrustful of higher income groups and the government, which may be seen as representing the interests of the elites. The poor may decide to no longer vote, or they may expect hand-outs by political parties seeking votes rather than redistribution and jobs. Low social cohesion discourages long-term investment in any sector of the economy, including the public sector.

15.4.2.4 Increasing financial fragility

High income and wealth inequality, and the subsequent high propensity to save, result in increasing investments in the FIRE sector of the economy, where capital is accumulating steadily. Without much capital taxation and with continuously newly designed rent-seeking and moral hazard opportunities, the FIRE sector will attract more and more investments at a cost to the real economy. This growing imbalance towards the dominance of financial investments increases financial fragility in the economy. And through financial globalisation it also increases asset price volatility worldwide.

15.5 Neoclassical economics: head counts and happiness

15.5.1 Income poverty: head count ratio

The neoclassical economic theoretical measure for well-being is utility. But utility cannot be objectively measured, as we have already seen in Chapter 1. It has no empirical measure. Therefore, income is used to measure well-being levels, whether at the micro level or the macro level. Of course, neoclassical economists realise that this is a second-best measure. But it makes sense in capitalist economies, whether the market has a dominant role or the welfare state has a relatively large role: income is an important means to satisfy consumption, savings and insurance, and investment. Income, and to some extent wealth, is also important for the tax base for many types of tax revenue and the financing of public goods. Hence, the income measure of well-being, and of poverty, is not such an unrealistic measure for many modern economies of the world.

The income measure of poverty is an absolute poverty measure: it measures the number of poor people in a country living below a certain poverty threshold, and the percentage of that group of the whole population. That is why such a poverty measure is also referred to as the *headcount ratio*: the proportion of poor people in a population. The best-known absolute international poverty measure was developed by the World Bank. Currently, this international poverty line is set at US$1.25 per person per day. This is less than US$500 per year. Some people spend this amount just on a pair of shoes for a party. But in many countries, a substantial proportion of the population does not even have US$500 to spend in a whole year.

How is absolute poverty measured? First, minimum consumer baskets are defined, consisting of goods and services that are deemed basic necessities, minimally needed by individuals to be considered not poor. Second, national household surveys measure household income and the number of people per household. This allows the calculation of how many people cannot afford to buy the goods in the minimum consumer basket.

Third, an international price comparison is used to equalise purchasing power between countries. It uses *purchasing power parity*. This is an adjustment of income levels to differences in national prices to obtain the same level for the purchasing power of income. These three steps together allow the calculation of the number of poor per country and for the world as a whole, living under a certain income level expressed in US dollars.

Purchasing power parity is crucial. For example, a hamburger in Japan is more expensive than a hamburger in the USA. In fact, the British magazine *The Economist* every year publishes the Big Mac Index, comparing local prices of hamburgers.[10] This burgernomics shows that in Japan, on 1 January 2014, a Big Mac cost 310 yen, whereas in the USA it cost US$4.62. The official exchange rate of the yen to US dollar is 104.25, so the hamburger should cost US$4.62 × 104.25 = 482 yen. This implies that the exchange rate of the yen to the US dollar is overvalued by 36 per cent (482 − 310/482); hence, the purchasing power of the Japanese is lower than that of Americans: they can buy more hamburgers in the USA than at home at the official exchange rate.

The weakness of the purchasing power parity technique for a complete consumer basket is that it is a complex exercise, which is not done on an annual basis but only every 5–10 years.

Adjustment of price levels with a new estimate of price comparisons therefore can result in quite different levels of poverty. For example, using the 1993 purchasing power parity data, 29 per cent of the world population was considered poor in 1990. But using the 2005 price data, this increases the share of the poor in 1990 to 42 per cent of the world population.[11]

When we have a poverty line, what should be done about poverty reduction in the neoclassical perspective? Remember from Chapter 1, that there is a strict dichotomy between positive economics (understood as economic analysis without value judgments) and normative economics (understood as political, namely preferences about desired states of the economy). Poverty reduction is part of normative economics, in neoclassical theory. Hence, policy objectives can only come from outside economics, by political choices. Once a target is set, positive economics can analyse how this can be 'best' achieved, that is, in the most efficient way. The problem with the positive–normative dichotomy was already discussed in Chapter 2. So here, let us go straight to the politically set target and whether countries succeed in meeting the target.

15.5.2 Millennium Development Goal 1: poverty reduction target

In the year 2000, the international community agreed upon the so-called Millennium Development Goals, as already referred to in Chapter 7. MDG1 is a poverty reduction target of 50 per cent worldwide. The base year was 1990, and the target year 2015. By the end of this 25-year period, 50 per cent less people should be living below the US$1.25-a-day poverty line.[12]

This seems quite an ambitious target: it concerns millions and millions of people. However, the target was met in 2010. World poverty fell from 47 per cent in 1990 to 22 per cent in 2010. This was largely due to the world's largest economies, China and India, in particular China. There the poverty rate fell from 60 per cent in 1990 to 12 per cent in 2010. These are the most populous economies in the world, and have experienced above-average economic growth. So, the high economic growth in China and India, each having more than 1 billion inhabitants, has helped many poor people in these countries to move above the poverty line. This shows that in certain periods of high growth, poverty may reduce through a trickle-down mechanism. But growth is not at all an automatic poverty-reducing mechanism. By 2015, an estimated 1 billion people in the world will still live under the US$1.25/day poverty line. And one in eight people live in hunger. Moreover, not all countries will meet the target individually by 2015. In particular, sub-Sahara Africa lags behind: the poverty rate fell by only 8 per cent between 1990 and 2010. As a consequence of population growth, low GDP growth, weak public services, high debt, decreasing terms of trade, and government failures, the absolute number of poor did not fall but increased. The number of people living in poverty in sub-Sahara Africa went up from 290 million in 1990 to 410 million in 2010.

The head count ratio of poverty has the advantage of providing a clear, one-dimensional target for policy makers. Its disadvantages are imprecise measurement through complex and irregular price comparisons, and the use of consumer baskets for the country as a whole rather than for the goods consumed only by the poor, as well as the exclusion of other dimensions of poverty apart from income.

15.5.3 Welfare economics

Neoclassical analysis of well-being and poverty is called welfare economics. It is concerned with, among other things, *how* poverty can be reduced at the macro level. Here we need to distinguish between the long term and the short term.

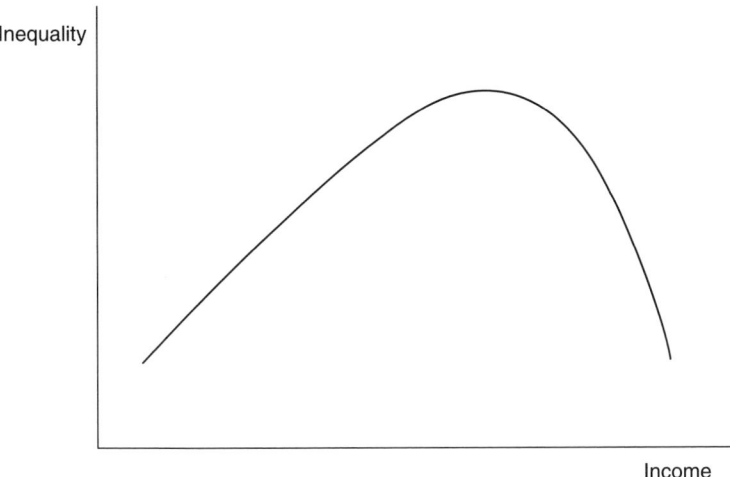

Diagram 15.5 The Kuznets curve

A major neoclassical thesis is that in the long run relative poverty decline is driven not so much by particular poverty-reduction policies but by the trickle-down mechanism. Relative poverty is concerned with inequality as we have seen in section 15.3. The Kuznets curve was developed by Simon Kuznets, whom we met earlier in this book. The Kuznets curve describes the relationship between GDP per capita and income inequality. The curve has a reversed U shape, indicating that at early stages of economic development, income inequality increases, while after some level of GDP per capita, it decreases, as shown in Diagram 15.5.

So, the *Kuznets curve* describes how relative poverty, measured as income inequality, declines with higher levels of economic development. The curve is based on the experiences of the developed countries, but has not yet been tested for developing countries. It may well be that the point of reversal, the top of the curve, differs widely between countries. It seems that the curve is flatter or steeper for some regions of the world. And that income inequality may reduce, but not wealth inequality, as we have seen in section 15.4. So, whether Kuznets was right only for developed countries or also for the world as a whole remains to be seen.

Welfare economic analysis is not concerned with the long term but with the short term. Its starting point is the *possibility frontier* at the macroeconomic level. This curve reflects all possible combinations of output at maximum capacity utilisation in an economy. Below the frontier, production is suboptimal, and outside the frontier, combinations of output are not feasible. The most efficient economy produces exactly on its frontier, irrespective of where.

An economy functions below its possibility frontier when it suffers from market failures. The major market failures behind poverty are threefold: (1) the need for public goods for the poor, (2) limited access for the poor to credit, and (3) rent-seeking and moral hazard by the economic and political elites. Removing these market failures will bring an economy up to its possibility frontier, thereby making it more efficient, and when poverty is reduced, also more equitable. How can this be done? Let me go briefly through each of the three market failures.

15.5.3.1 Public goods for the poor

Major causes of poverty in developing countries are bad health, low education, and lack of employment. Markets fail to provide these in sufficient quantity and quality, partly because poor countries have a low tax base: if not much income is earned, there is little to tax. This is precisely the reason for providing official development assistance (ODA) from rich to poor countries. The rich countries have agreed to give 0.7 per cent of their annual GDP as ODA, but very few rich countries meet this target, in particular not since the financial crisis. Moreover, much of the money is in loans, not grants, while some of the goods and services are provided by the origin country's firms, which make a business out of ODA. On the other hand, a relatively large share of ODA goes to public goods in developing countries, in particular those focusing on the poor. With more education and better health care, the poor will eventually become more productive in markets, which helps an economy to move in the direction of the possibility frontier.

15.5.3.2 Access to credit

Credit markets rely on available funds for lending out money. With limited savings available, capital flight by the rich, and banks targeting middle- and high-income groups, the poor in developing countries have limited access to credit. And when there are credit programmes available to them, they often lack the necessary collateral (land, house) to obtain a loan, or their illiteracy constrains them from going through the bureaucracy, or they are simply discriminated against because of their sex or ethnicity. This market failure is met by *microcredit* programmes. This is credit in small amounts lent out to groups with joint pay-back responsibility. Microcredit programmes target the poor and often women. Such group loans tend to be repaid very well, even by people living under the poverty line, because lack of repayment by one individual will exclude the whole group from future loans. Hence, group loans make use of social pressure. Not by the lender, but by the borrowers themselves, saving the costs of monitoring the loans by the lender. A famous example of microcredit is the Grameen Bank, which started in Bangladesh. The model has been copied thousands of times, all over the world, and indeed reaches the poorest of the poor, mainly women.

But empirical research has also pointed out the downsides of microcredit, precisely because they are so small scale and make use of the social norms present in a community. Small size implies that loans are often used to bridge liquidity problems in a household rather than for business investments. Or they are just enough to pay for the inputs in a local market, leading to an increase in the local production of the same product by everyone, without more sales per person. The social norms are not immune to the general asymmetries in norms and values at the community level. For example, married women obtaining credit are often expected by their husbands to hand the money over to them, while remaining responsible for paying it back from their own pocket. So, overcoming the market failure of credit markets for the poor appears more complex than it is often thought to be.

15.5.3.3 Rent-seeking and moral hazard

The political and economic elites of countries that are weak states often manage to extract rents from public resources, such as tax revenue, the profits of public companies, or procurement contracts. Moreover, they manage to keep control of major economic interests, such as

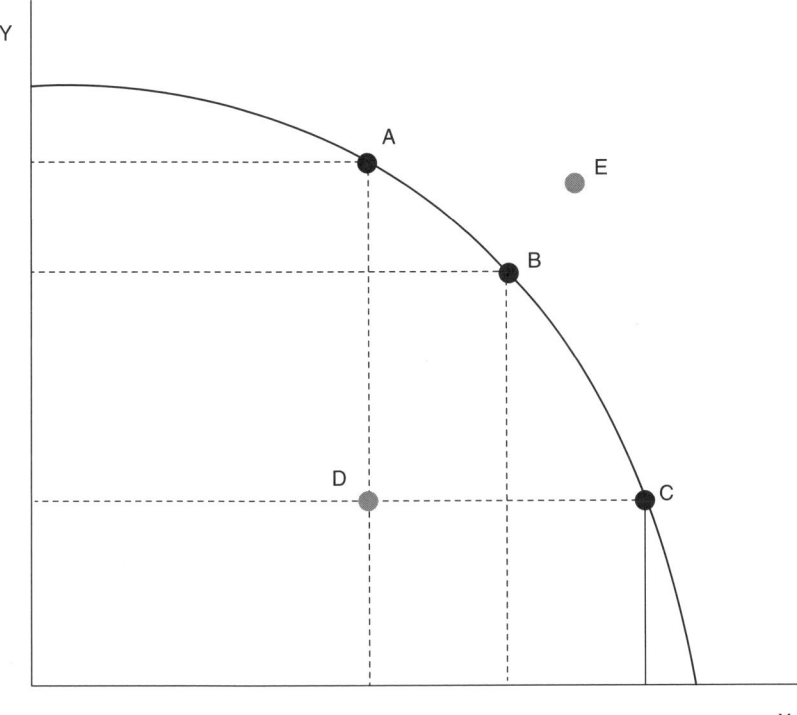

Diagram 15.6 Production possibility frontier

mining concessions and the public sector. This can only be addressed at the political level, and perhaps partly with international support. But when the developed countries benefit from the status quo, for example through access to oil, mining concessions, or export markets, political objectives of poverty reduction can become compromised by national and international economic interests. As a consequence, such market failures keep an economy functioning at low efficiency and low equity.

Diagram 15.6 shows the possibility frontier for all possible combinations of good X and good Y. It shows that the combinations AX and AY can be produced, but also BX and BY and CX and CY. Whereas DX–DY is not efficient: there are idle production factors that could produce more X and more Y. And EX–EY is not feasible: it is located outside the possibility frontier because it requires more production factors than are available in the economy.

Now, suppose that good X is food and good Y is cars. Poor households cannot afford cars. But the poorest households cannot afford sufficient food either. So, in order to reduce poverty, more X and less Y should be produced. This would make some rich people suffer, because they will no longer be able to buy a car, or they have to pay more to obtain one. While the poorest households now will have access to food, which is more readily available and cheaper, due to its increased supply. Is such redistribution from Y to X possible along the production possibility curve? In other words, is it efficient?

If it involves moving from point A to point B, it is feasible: less people and capital used in car factories and more people and capital employed in agriculture will realise the shift away from Y (cars) to X (food). But how can this be realised in a competitive, free market economy? If the poor lack the purchasing power to buy more food and the rich have sufficient purchasing power to buy the quantity A of cars, nothing will change. The only way to force the economy to move from point A to point B is government intervention. This would require taking away purchasing power from the rich and shifting it to the poor. The poor are not likely to buy cars with the additional purchasing power as long as they are hungry. Although in meritocratic societies, they may prefer to buy a mobile phone first. The rich will now buy fewer cars. This redistribution, for example through taxation, will reduce efficiency, according to welfare economics. It will not move the economy from A to B, but from A to D, well below the possibility frontier. Why?

Because taking away money from the rich will be a disincentive to produce as much as they did before, and giving money to the poor will be a disincentive to work: they get money anyway. So, rather than moving the economy from A to B, the redistributive policy moves the economy from A to D. There, it produces less cars and not more food . . . that is inefficient.

The conclusion from welfare economics is that redistribution creates a trade-off between equity and efficiency: the more equity (less poverty), the less efficiency (capacity utilisation). This conclusion depends, of course, on the rationality assumption of neoclassical economics, namely that people are utility maximisers, driven by their self-interest and asking every time *wiifm*? And self-interest is then expressed, at least with the above choice between two goods, as materialistic: preferring more goods over less and working less hours when more hours are taxed or when income is received without additional work.

But it may well be that some rich people are ashamed about the poverty in their country and are willing to redistribute some of their income to the poor. Perhaps not through taxation but through charity. And it may well be that poor people are just as willing as before to work and do not reduce their efforts to find and keep a job when they receive financial support. In fact, individual utility functions may include much more than income and material goods. But how can this be analysed when utility is a black box and we use income and physical goods as second-best measures of well-being? A way-out is measuring utility directly. By asking people how happy they feel. This is a new development in neoclassical economics, explained in the next subsection.

15.5.4 Well-being as happiness

Recent empirical research asks people about their utility through questions about life satisfaction and happiness in household surveys. The World Database of Happiness collects such survey data and allows economists to analyse well-being and poverty directly on a scale of 1–10.[13]

Happiness measurement solves the problem of the impossibility of interpersonal utility comparison, because utility is no longer an individual black box. When one person states that she is happy at a rate of 7.3 and another at a rate of 7.7, we can safely say that the second person is 0.4 points happier than the first one. Because the scale is the same: everyone is asked to rate their feeling on a scale of 1–10. So, this allows interpersonal utility comparison, averaging happiness levels per country, and monitoring country-level happiness scores over time. Diagram 15.7 shows a world map with happiness scores.

Average happines
2.6 ▨▨▨▨▨■ 8.5

Diagram 15.7 Happiness of nations, 2012

Source: Veenhoven, R. *Average Happiness in 148 Nations 2000–2009*, World Database of Happiness, Erasmus University Rotterdam, The Netherlands. Accessed on 20 June 2014 at: http://worlddatabaseofhappiness.eur.nl/hap_nat/findingreports/RankReport_AverageHappiness.php

Studies of happiness and economic growth have pointed out repeatedly that there is only a weak correlation between economic growth and happiness. When poor countries experience economic growth, this clearly improves the happiness feelings of its population. But for middle-income and high-income countries, economic growth does not seem to affect happiness anymore. One calculation suggests that it takes a country on average 60 years of economic growth of at least 5 per cent per year, to see its happiness rating go up by 1 point on a 10-point scale.[14] The weak long-term relationship between happiness and income, with increasing happiness at low income levels but no increase in happiness anymore after a middle-income level is reached, is called the *Easterlin paradox*, named after the economist Richard Easterlin, who described it first.

There are several explanations for the paradox. Here I will mention two of them. The first one comes from institutional economics and is the keeping-up-with-the-Jones' effect: people's perceived satisfaction with life significantly depends on how they do relative to others. Hence, when others are improving their position at the same pace, relative positions remain unchanged and people's reported happiness does not improve. The second explanation comes from neoclassical economics itself: the law of diminishing marginal returns. It may well be that once people and countries have reached a certain level of income, more of it does not add as much to their happiness. Instead, they may value having more leisure time, enjoying a clean environment, or seeking flow experiences in meaningful activities beyond paid employment.

Happiness studies provide a wealth of information about subjective well-being. The more contextualised the questions of life satisfaction are, the more detailed the well-being data become. This is valuable for the understanding of well-being beyond the Easterlin paradox. It helps, for example, to find out what types of policies contribute most to people's life satisfaction in a particular area of life, such as health, community life, or work life.

But this creates another paradox: whereas happiness measurement was created in order to have a *single* measure for utility, it seems to provide most value added for policy makers when disaggregated to *different* areas of life satisfaction. . . .

15.6 Interesting sources

Jolly R., G. A. Cornia, D. Elson *et al.* (2012) *Be Outraged – There Are Alternatives*. Richard Jolly.
Millennium Development Goals: http://www.un.org/millenniumgoals/
Piketty, T. (2014) *Capital in the Twenty-First Century*. Cambridge, MA: The Belknap Press of Harvard University Press.
The World Top Incomes Database: http://topincomes.g-mond.parisschoolofeconomics.eu/

15.7 Glossary

Conditional cash transfers   A social policy of income support to poor households on the condition that they send their children to school or other social policy criteria

Easterlin paradox   The weak long-term relationship between happiness and income, with increasing happiness at low-income levels but no increase in happiness anymore after a middle-income level is reached

Egalitarian societies   Societies in which fairness is defined by human dignity and which organise social protection

Headcount ratio   The proportion of poor people in a population

Horizontal inequality   Inequality along social dimensions, such as ethnicity, geography, gender, and caste

Human development   Well-being in terms of basic capabilities such as health, education, and purchasing power

Kuznets curve   Describes how relative poverty, measured as income inequality, declines with higher levels of economic development

Meritocratic societies   Societies in which fairness depends on contribution and where there is not much concern about inequality

Microcredit   Credit in small amounts lent out to groups with joint pay-back responsibility

Possibility frontier   A curve which reflects all possible combinations of output at maximum capacity utilisation in an economy

Purchasing power parity   Adjustment of income levels to differences in national prices to obtain the same level for the purchasing power of income

Under-investment   Low investment in a resource, leading to low returns

Vertical inequality   Inequality along a continuum of a single dimension, often income

Notes

1. Pellegrini, L. and L. Tasciotti (2014) 'Bhutan: between Happiness and Horror', *Capitalism Nature Socialism*. Online publication: http://dx.doi.org/10.1080/10455752.2014.898673
2. UNDP (2013) *Humanity Divided: Confronting Inequality in Developing Countries*. New York: UNDP.
3. Wilkinson, R. and K. Pickett (2009) *The Spirit Level*. New York: Bloomsbury Press, p. 67.
4. See note 3.
5. See note 3.
6. See note 3.
7. Piketty, T. (2014) *Capital in the Twenty-First Century*. Cambridge, MA: The Belknap Press of Harvard University Press, p. 249.
8. This is estimated by Thomas Piketty, see note 7.
9. See note 7, p. 166.
10. For the Big Mac Index, see: http://www.economist.com/content/big-mac-index
11. For this example and a thorough critique of the poverty line calculations, see Klasen, S. (2014) 'Measuring Levels and Trends in Absolute Poverty in the World - Open Questions and Possible Alternatives', in Betti, G. and A. Lemmi (eds), *Poverty and Social Exclusion - New Methods of Analysis*. London: Routledge, pp. 194–210.
12. For information about the MDGs, see: http://www.un.org/millenniumgoals
13. Website for the World Database of Happiness: http://www1.eur.nl/fsw/happiness//index.html
14. See for the result mentioned above: http://mpra.ub.uni-muenchen.de/43983/1/MPRA_paper_43983.pdf

Annex

History of economic thought

Family tree

Chapter 1 showed a timeline of nine key economists in the history of economic thought. This annex will briefly summarise the contribution of each economist on that strangely asymmetric family tree – from father Adam Smith, a Scottish philosopher at the beginning of the line, to mother Elinor Ostrom, an American political economist who brought society back into economics, at the end of the line. Whereas Smith recognised the economy to be more than the market, it was Ostrom who again demonstrated the important role of the community in today's economies. The timeline also shows a shift away from dominance by Western males, with Amartya Sen and Elinor Ostrom marking the first Nobel Prizes in economics for an Indian economist and a woman.

After the discussion of this timeline, three more economists will be introduced, who have provided important contributions to development economics, turning economics into a truly global science.

Image A1 Adam Smith

Adam Smith (1723–1790) was a philosopher and professor at the University of Glasgow, Scotland. Economists refer to his key book, *An Inquiry into the Nature and Causes of the Wealth of Nations*, as the foundation of economics. The book can be read as a lively description of production, markets, and international trade and their role in a country's economic development. Smith claimed that for a thriving economy, three economic values are necessary – liberty, justice, and benevolence: liberty through free exchange on markets, justice through the state ensuring rights and dignity, and benevolence through people's connectedness to each other in communities. But he forgot to mention the key role of households, probably because he was never married and lived for many years with his mother, disregarding housework, which in his days was exclusively the task of women.

Smith analysed the market as a *mechanism* rather than merely as a space of trading. He argued that the market allows for the provisioning of livelihoods not through giving and sharing, nor through stealing and exercise of power, but through voluntary exchange in the interest of both trading parties. Smith meant not that markets by themselves are benign, but that they imply a dissolution of feudalism, an unfree, exploitative, and inefficient economic system based on very unequal land ownership and class relations, and that free markets imply a move away from mercantilism, a Western policy that supported import protection (through high tariffs) while seeking opportunities, often through state power, to expand trade with the help of war, colonies, and slaves.

He foresaw the great power of markets and their potential as compared to feudalism and mercantilism. First, he pointed out that economic actors seek to invest in a resource (labour, land or a financial asset) to reap benefits. Markets stimulate this behaviour, because when one under-invests in a resource, it will be less productive than that of a competitor, and one will lose out in the competitive process. He predicted that the mechanism of the market will lead to an equalisation of the returns on investment everywhere, because competition urges everybody to reap the last potential benefit anywhere until there are no more benefits to be gained. Second, he described the gains from the division of labour. He used the example of a pin factory. He said that ten workers would produce only a few pins per person per day without any division of labour. But if the production process was cut into ten tasks, and each worker specialised in only one task, a total of 48,000 pins could be produced per day. So, Adam Smith showed how competitive markets enforce cost reduction and lead to a division of labour in firms, which increases productivity.

Next on the timeline we find the British economist David Ricardo (1772–1823). He was an active stock trader and accumulated considerable wealth, which allowed him the free time to study economics. His major contributions were on trade and labour. Like Smith he opposed the practice of mercantilism pursued by many 18th century European countries. David Ricardo argued that a system of free trade is more beneficial for all. He proposed an alternative to the then accepted trade theory of absolute advantage. That theory claimed mutual benefits of trade for two trading countries when they exchange goods in which they have an absolute cost advantage as compared to each other. So, when country A produces product X cheaper than country B, and when country B produces good Y cheaper than country A, exports of X by country A and of Y by country B generate mutual benefits of trade.

Ricardo instead proposed a more ingenious trade theory: the theory of comparative advantage. Ricardo explained that even when country A has an absolute cost advantage in producing both good X and good Y, trade can still be beneficial to both countries A and B. This is the case when the comparative cost advantage of producing one of these goods, say X, is

Image A2 David Ricardo

higher than the relative cost advantage of the other good. If country A now specialises in the production of good X and country B in the production of good Y, trade will still be beneficial for both countries. So, the theory of comparative advantage shows that specialisation on the basis of relative cost advantage uses less resources as compared to no trade and both countries (A and B) producing all the goods (X and Y) they need.

The second major contribution by David Ricardo was the labour theory of value. He argued that the value of a good can be determined through accounting for the labour time that went into producing it, including the labour included in the production of the intermediate goods. When we subtract the raw material inputs from the exchange value, any additional returns reflect the rents earned by capital. Hence, Ricardo argued that basically, the value of a good comes down to the quantity of the labour time that went into producing it, in addition to the raw materials.

The third and last classical economist on our time line is Karl Marx (1818–1883), born and educated in Germany and exiled in Paris, Brussels, and London. He was also a philosopher, a journalist and, most importantly, a socialist revolutionary. His main economic book was called *Das Kapital* in the original German version. Marx's first economic contribution is a sharp analysis of capitalism, an economic system which came to full development in his day, with great potential for wealth creation but also ugly side effects for those people who could only rely on their labour power and had no assets. Marx criticised the inhumane working conditions in which workers were reduced to extensions of machines. He analysed this as a process of alienation of workers from their labour power. Economists today, left and right, largely agree that Marx's analysis of capitalism, as a system with internal weaknesses and systemic crises, is still adequate.

The second major contribution of Marx to economics is his class theory in which he recognised that under capitalism, there is an inherent asymmetry between the two classes in the economy, capital, and labour: capital hires labour for production and not the other way around. This inherent inequality of power leads to alienation and exploitation and, Marx claimed,

Image A3 Karl Marx

should not be accepted but replaced by a socialist system through a revolution of the labour class. This class theory led to his political views inspiring the foundation of the Soviet Union in 1922 and the People's Republic of China in 1949, as well as other communist economies.

The next economist on the timeline is generally considered to be the first neoclassical economist: Alfred Marshall (1842–1924). He was British and Professor of Political Economy at the University of Cambridge, where he established the first degree in economics in the world. He wrote some of his work with his wife Mary Paley. He had strong mathematical skills and was a follower of the theory of utilitarianism. This is a major ethical theory that was developed by Jeremy Bentham, who characterised utilitarianism as 'the greatest happiness

Image A4 Alfred Marshall

for the greatest number'. It was Marshall who succeeded in technically integrating this ethical perspective into economics and thereby making economics much more mathematical. His major achievement was the development of the concept of marginal utility, and related notions such as marginal cost and marginal revenue. Marginal utility is the extra utility gained from adding one unit of a resource to production or consumption. However, the concept implies strong assumptions that often do not hold in the real world, like perfect information and maximisation.

Alfred Marshall's book *Principles of Economics*, published in 1890, became the first textbook of the discipline and was widely used for several decades. In the book, Marshall demonstrated in diagrams the law of supply (when prices rise, producers will produce and offer more of a good) and the law of demand (when prices go down, consumers will demand more of a good). The intersection of the two curves expresses the equilibrium quantity sold (on the x-axis) at the equilibrium price (on the y-axis). These diagrams are still central in the economic textbooks of today.

The fifth founder of the economics discipline on our timeline, Thorstein Veblen (1857–1929), did not follow the neoclassical path but established, like Marx, one of his own. He is also the first American on the timeline, an early herald of the dominance of the USA in economics in the 20th century. But he was also a heterodox economist. Veblen was the son of Norwegian immigrants and remained in a way a stranger. He was inspired by evolution theory as well as by sociology, and developed institutionalism as a new approach in economics. He was co-founder of the New School in New York, which still is among the few graduate schools in economics in the world that is not dominated by neoclassical economics. At the same time, he did not hold a university position for long, having a difficult character and not being valued by his students who left his classes in great numbers.

His most influential book was *The Theory of the Leisure Class*. The book argued that economic agents often are not interested in enhancing productivity and spreading higher standards of living across society. He regarded most firms as simply interested in making money and protecting their interests at the cost of free markets and societal interests. On consumption

Image A5 Thorstein Veblen

Image A6 Joseph Schumpeter

he argued that economic actors are much concerned with power, status, and leisure, which he brought together under the label of 'conspicuous consumption'. Veblen argued that such behaviour results in inefficiencies and does not change because of the social norms, habits, beliefs, and enabling rules and regulations which allow and reward this behaviour. The well-known concept of 'the Veblen effect' stems from this theory and refers to the situation in which consumers buy Gucci handbags or Armani sunglasses, even though lower priced substitutes are available at more or less similar levels of quality.

Veblen laid the foundations of the institutional school in economics, in which institutions are social regularities which guide economic behaviour and are in turn shaped by economic processes. Veblen was also among the very few economists in his day who acknowledged the marginalised role of women in the economy, with a wife being a housewife seen as a status symbol for the higher classes. Later, feminist economists would recognise the importance of this insight for the development of feminist economic theory.

We enter the 20th century with Joseph Schumpeter (1883–1950). He was an Austrian economist who began his career in Austrian universities. Before his appointment at Harvard University, USA, he was briefly Minister of Finance in Austria but rather unsuccessful. He had also led a bank which went into bankruptcy. Schumpeter's comparative advantage was clearly in thinking about the economy, rather than taking a leading role in it. He was inspired by evolution theory and sociology, just like Veblen. But where Veblen criticised businessmen for their lack of concern with productivity-enhancing innovation, Schumpeter saw the entrepreneur as the motor of economic dynamics, both of innovation and of business cycles with their 'creative destruction'. This concept means that markets both stimulate creativity, through innovation and investment, and stimulate destruction, through shifts of finance between and within industries. For Schumpeter, an entrepreneur is in the first place a risk-taker, rather than a capitalist hiring labour to produce at the lowest possible cost. His most influential work was *The Theory of Economic Development*. Its major message was that economies are not stable but highly dynamic, driven by innovation and entrepreneurship, with the collateral damage

Image A7 John Maynard Keynes

of take-overs and bankruptcies. He recognised three parallel business cycles: a short term, a medium term, and a long term business cycle, attributing the last one (Kondratieff cycle, lasting 45–60 years) to innovation.

John Maynard Keynes (1883–1946), a contemporary of Schumpeter, was a British economist and the founder of macroeconomics. He was in the first place an intellectual, often seen in art circles, an investor on the stock exchange, a civil servant, government adviser on finance, and director of the Bank of England. He was born in Cambridge, studied economics under Marshall, lectured for a short period and remained affiliated with Cambridge University as a fellow. He founded the school of thought that most strongly challenged neo-classical economics, namely Keynesianism. His major contribution was the idea that markets are not self-adjusting and tending towards equilibrium, with full employment and sales of all goods produced. He focused not on the supply side of the economy, as Schumpeter did, but on the demand side, with the notion of aggregate demand. This is the total of demand in an economy, by consumers, the state, investors, and foreign buyers. Instead of seeing markets as being in equilibrium, Keynes argued in his major work, *The General Theory of Employment, Interest and Money*, that a lack of aggregate demand keeps the economy in a state of unemployment and depression. He argued that even when the unemployed are prepared to work below market wages, they will not find work because firms are not willing to hire in times when the demand for their products is low. This insight was the result of Keynes' analysis of the 1929 Great Depression in the USA. His policy advice was aimed at an increase in aggregate demand through government expenditures because he recognised that households reduce their consumer demand in times of crisis and that owners of capital are hesitant to invest. Increased government spending should lead the economy out of a crisis. Hence, like Schumpeter, Keynes had a dynamic view of the economy, although more in the short term, stating that 'in the long run, we are all dead'.

Another insight he gained from the 1929 crisis was that financial markets are uncertain and therefore volatile and prone to crises. That is because of speculation (to which, ironically, he himself contributed as an investor) and herd behaviour, when due to lack of information about

Image A8 Amartya Sen

future asset prices, investors follow each other in buying and selling assets. Keynes concluded that it is the combination of speculation and herd behaviour which leads to severe cycles in financial markets.

The first non-Western economist on the timeline is Amartya Sen (born in 1933). He was born in India and later moved between professorial appointments in Britain (Oxford University) and the USA (Harvard University), and won the Nobel Prize in 1998. His work has been greatly influenced by his witness of famine as a child in India. His work can be read as an eloquent and forceful critique of neoclassical economics and its underlying utilitarianism. He also has a strong political engagement and has influenced the *Human Development Report*, published annually by the UNDP (United Nations Development Programme), and IAFFE (International Association for Feminist Economics). And he is founder of the capability approach. This argues that the end of economic behaviour should not be understood as utility maximisation, but as the achievement of people's capabilities to function in life. Capabilities are skills and opportunities, such as being literate or having the opportunity to engage with nature. The actual functionings based on these capabilities may be unequal because some people choose to spend more time and effort turning their talents and assets into goods and services than others, but capabilities should be equal, according to Sen.

Sen developed several concepts that evolved from this theoretical approach. One is adaptive preferences, which are individual preferences that are determined by repressive social norms, and hence, negatively affect one's ability to function. An example is the habit of poor Indian women to eat less meat than male family members because women would be less deserving of protein-rich food, even when in practice they burn just as many calories as men with farm work, housework, child bearing, and lactation.

428 *Annex: history of economic thought*

Image A9 Elinor Ostrom

At the other end of the timeline we find the American political economist Elinor Ostrom (1933–2012), recipient of the Nobel Prize in economics in 2009.

She specialised in the study of economic governance at Indiana University and Arizona State University, both in the USA. Even though there are more than two centuries between her and Adam Smith, she may well be regarded as the mother of economics. She brought the enabling role of the state back into the discipline and recognised the role of communities again, as Smith had done before her. She can therefore be considered as the economist who brought the balance back in economics, between market, state, and community. One way she has done this is by clearly distinguishing four types of goods: private goods, public goods, club goods, and common-pool resources.

Another way in which she is clearly different from most economists mentioned above is through her extensive field research all over the world. This has demonstrated how market failures and fundamental failures of markets are being resolved by economic actors in real-world situations. She discovered, acting as an economic anthropologist, how communities solve collective action problems, which are problems faced by groups which cannot be solved through markets without costs to individuals. Ostrom showed that communities across the world solve these problems by relying on communities' social resources, like trust and bottom-up rules. And she has used a wider variety of empirical methods, from interviews to games, to study collective action problems and solutions, as compared to most economists. Ostrom sought to explain complex real-world situations and to develop policy advice on the basis of her empirical findings. That is why the following quote from her work has become famous:

> The power of a theory is exactly proportional to the diversity of situations it can explain.[1]

Image A10 Thandika Mkandawire

Such a renewed attention to the economic role of communities was shown to be relevant in the 2007 financial crisis, with various innovative economic responses stemming from civil society, such as cooperative banking, alternative currencies, and crowd funding.

Contributions to economics from the Global South

In addition to Nobel Prize winner Amartya Sen, other economists from the Global South have been significant for the development of economics over the past few decades. They have largely been influential in development economics, trade, and macroeconomics. This section will briefly review the contributions of three major development economists from Africa, Asia, and Latin America.

Thandika Mkandawire (born in 1940), from Malawi, is a major contributor to social policy theory, working in the tradition of social economics. He served as director of UNRISD (United Nations Research Institute for Social Development). He has been a major critic of the World Bank structural adjustment policies implemented in Africa in the 1980s and 1990s. He has argued that the unbalanced focus in these policies on low inflation, urging high interest rates to discourage borrowing by firms, has constrained investment, and thereby limited employment growth in Africa. He has argued that the 1980s and part of the 1990s have been a lost decade for African development, with low economic growth and little advancement in human development. Later modifications in World Bank policies as well as more opportunities for African countries to control their own progress have helped to overcome this experience. But other problems have remained, such as civil war and corruption, problems which Mkandawire does not hesitate to address in his academic work and policy advice.

Raul Prebisch (1901–1986) was an Argentinian economist and co-founder of the structuralist school which integrated Marxist thought and political science and sociology in modern economics. He was professor at the University of Buenos Aires and has led ECLAC (Economic Commission for Latin America) and UNCTAD (United Nations Conference of Trade and Development). He became well known for his inter-related contributions to trade theory and dependence theory. Dependence theory was developed by several Latin American economists as a response to the portrayal of countries of the South as 'underdeveloped'.

Image A11 Raul Prebisch

Dependency theorists state that this disadvantaged position was a result of the inclusion of former colonies on the terms of the countries of the North in the world economy. In particular, Prebisch argued that the core countries of the North rely on the periphery countries of the South for food and raw materials. But Prebisch calculated that the compensation for these raw materials is very limited and worsening over time. He developed, with Hans Singer, the Prebisch–Singer hypothesis, which claims that the terms of trade deteriorate over time for countries of the South: they will have to export more and more raw materials in order to be able to import the same quantity of manufactured products. This thesis has found empirical support and is partly explained through high import tariffs and import quotas by countries in the North for processed primary goods, for example processed coffee (high tariff) rather than the raw coffee beans (low tariff).

Gita Sen (born in 1948) is an Indian economist affiliated with the Indian Institute of Management in Bangalore, India, and Harvard University, USA. Although much in demand

Image A12 Gita Sen

as a policy advisor in the international arena, Gita Sen combines her academic work first and foremost with activism to influence policy agendas. She has been a major critic of development economics because of its dominance by economists and policy makers from the developed world, and the marginalisation of women from economic policy making. Being a feminist herself, she has also criticised feminist movements from the North, which were more concerned with critiquing policies in and on the South rather than challenging policies in the North that negatively affect the lives of the poor and women in the Global South. Both her concerns, the dominance of the North and of men in development policy, led her to found DAWN (Development Alternatives with Women for a New era) in the 1980s, an influential network of women, mostly from the Global South, working in the area of development, as academics, policy advisors, and activists. Her major contribution to development economics, therefore, was in shifting the debate towards more inclusion and agenda setting by men and women from the Global South, precisely what was needed to challenge the dependency described so well by Prebisch.

Note

1 Elinor Ostrom (1990) *Governing the Commons. The Evolution of Institutions for Collective Action.* New York: Cambridge University Press, p. 24.

Index

accumulation 13, 28, 31–3, 134, 151, 157, 277, 279; capital 406–8, 410, 422; wealth 406–9
adverse selection 139
Africa: North Africa 313; sub-Sahara Africa 39, 45, 129, 157, 307, 332, 412; West Africa 121, 128, 343
African Americans 198–9; *see also* Blacks
agency 12, 19, 36–7, 54, 64, 100–1, 139; collective agency 36, 52, 100
agent *see* agency
Akerlof, George 139
America 5, 14, 16, 29, 87, 375; Latin America: and inequality 146, 147, 152, 162, 388–9; and the state 152, 156–7, 161, 163, 401; North America 161, 202, 388; South America 53, 152, 376, 378, 384
ANC 215
Angola 191, 318
animal spirits 28, 241
anti-trust 54
Antoncic, Madelyn 234, 239
appreciation 288, 297, 350–1
Arab countries 193, 351
Argentina 69, 146–8, 281–2, 287–8, 332, 376; and the Central Bank 287–8; and the state 161–2; and trade 384–8
Arrow, Kenneth 25
ASEAN 403
Asia: Asia-Pacific 355–6; South Asia 299, 313, 316, 387, 395–8
asymmetric information 29, 33, 55, 138–9, 280; in credit markets 225, 229, 247–8; in labour markets 201; in the household 39
Australia 5, 30, 43, 180, 234, 356, 394, 400
Austria 160, 180, 379, 425
Austrian economics 8, 425
automatic stabiliser 154, 177, 261; automatic green stabiliser 177
autonomous consumption 253, 266, 319

Bair, Sheila 234
Baker, Dean 5, 234
Balance of Payments 237, 270, 297, 302–3, 369
Bangladesh 160, 382, 395–7, 414
Bank for International Settlements 227
bargaining power: in the household 46–8, 58, 60; of firms 93, 372; in the labour market 203, 214, 256
Basel Committee on Banking Supervision 181, 227; Basel II 227; Basel III 227, 289
basic needs 72, 180, 282, 342
behavioural economics 8, 15, 67–8, 101, 186, 239, 241
Belarus 373
Belgium 180, 298, 344, 379
benchmarking 122–3, 173
Benin 129, 375
Bentham, Jeremy 423
Bhutan 12, 395–7
BIS *see* Bank for International Settlements
Blacks; 199 *see also* African Americans
Bolivia 54, 147, 150, 160, 244, 402
Born, Brooksely 234, 239
Boulding, Kenneth 339
Bounded rationality 53
Bowles, Samuel 18
brain drain 178
Brazil 7, 43, 69, 146, 153, 181, 281, 315; and inequality 147, 151, 312; and the state 152, 155–6, 160–4; and trade 368–9, 374–6, 383–8
Britain 314–5, 407
Brundtland Commission 339
bubbles 232, 242, 362, 282, 289; housing 5, 234, 241; financial 235, 238–9, 243, 260, 293, 303; carbon 362
budget: anti-cyclical 153–4; balanced 159, 330; deficit 6, 27, 153–4, 181, 251, 268, 301; and public finance 159, 163, 166, 280, 287; surplus 153, 159

Burkina Faso 121–2, 128–30, 375
business cycle 425–6; *see also* economic cycle

Cambodia 69
Cameroon 83
Canada 47, 160, 180, 344; and NAFTA 376–7, 388–9
capital account 297, 302–3, 369, 380; controls 287, 299, 302, 316, 354
capitalism 223, 406, 422; economy 64, 99, 107, 279; firm 107, 247,
care 41–4, 190, 193, 306; and community 25, 141; ethics of 15, 46; gender and 28; and giving 18, 38, 45, 192, 209; home 38, 45, 66; unpaid 38, 41, 306
cartel 26, 29, 126
Cayman Islands 315
CBA 358, 360; *see* cost benefit analysis
Chad 129, 345, 375
Chavez, Hugo 148
children 12, 39, 46, 72, 135–6, 147, 201, 306; as agents 36–7; and gender 42, 50, 342; and labour 37, 68, 117, 142, 179, 189, 410; and policy 208, 332, 400; and reproduction 38, 190, 393; and school 66, 100, 172, 190–2, 281, 398, 401, 410
childcare 18, 52, 66; and gender 50; and the labour market 58–60, 179, 196–8, 200; and reproduction 38, 41, 43, 45–6.
Chile 54, 147, 152, 161, 383
China: and the environment 345, 356; and finance 237, 299; and growth 71, 308, 310–11, 326–7, 408; and the labour market 307, 316; and poverty and inequality 388, 412; and production 67, 105–6, 156, 312, 368; and the state 156, 160, 315, 317–8, 332; trade 368, 372, 374, 379–80
circular economic flow 281, 290; economic flow 236, 251, 255–64, 268–75, 308, 320–1, 370
class 22, 68–9, 190–3, 198, 282, 321–5, 422–4; and land 312, 421; middle 64, 80, 118, 137, 161, 176,
club good 171, 184
CO_2 71, 83, 135, 172, 336, 338, 357–62; emissions 12, 178, 308, 336–7, 345–7, 359–61
collusion 22, 126
Colombia 147, 151, 345, 401
commons 169, 183–4, 186–7; common-pool resources 169, 183–4, 185–7, 428
comparative advantage 382–4, 387–9, 421–2, 425

compensating wage differentials 208;
competition: competition policy 29, 54, 123, 173; monopolistic competition 130–1; perfect competition 130–4
competitive advantage 382–4, 386–9, 421–2, 425
conditional cash-transfers 66, 401–2
Congo 344, 351
consumer: good 54, 64, 74; durable consumer good 39, 64, 68, 72, 291; sovereignty 66–7, 84; surplus 366, 377, 386–7
consumer price index 284
cooperative firm 92–3, 256
cost: average cost 104, 111, 126, 128, 137; of consumers 173; of firms 88–9, 105, 222; fixed cost 97–9, 104, 110–3, 124, 204; marginal cost 98, 110–3, 124–5, 132, 174–5, 204, 360, 363; in markets 151, 363, 376–8; social 257, 309; sunk cost 98; total cost 98–9, 104, 110–13, 125, 183, 204; transaction cost 17, 173, 257, 309; variable 97–8, 108, 111
cost benefit analysis, 174, 358, 360, 345
Costa Rica 147, 152, 161, 343
CPI *see* Consumer Price Index
CPR *see* common-pool resources
crisis *see* financial crisis
crowd funding 96, 429
currency: currency devaluation 121, 280, 303, 321, 387; currency revaluation 281
current account 237, 302–3, 369, 380
Cyprus 280, 289

Debreu, Gerard 25
debt: ratio 164; service 162; public 159–62, 164–6, 181, 280
deflation 282, 286, 300
demand: aggregate 21–2, 141, 251–3, 264–6, 426; and credit 291; derived demand 202–3, 210; effective demand 21, 264–6; and labour 203, 205, 211–4; and policy 154, 262–3, 267–71, 319, 324, 326, 410; and trade 281, 380;
depreciation 288, 297, 303, 380, 392
deprivation 68, 141
derivatives 219–20, 224, 229–41, 247–8, 289, 298
developmental state 153–6, 314–5, 330, 334
discrimination 118–20, 137, 257, 310; ethnicity and race 8, 31, 146; gender 42, 146, 313, 381–2; in financial markets 223; in labour markets 8, 199–209, 256, 398; statistical discrimination 201, 223

Dodd-Frank Act 228, 234
Dow Jones 239, 244, 246; Dow Jones Sustainability Index 347–8
dumping 122, 149, 381
duopoly 124
Dutch Disease 350–2

Easterlin paradox 417
Easterlin, Richard 417
EC *see* European Commission
ECB *see* European Central Bank
ECLAC 429
ecological economics 8, 184, 339–40, 352–4
ecological footprint 84, 99, 342–4, 393
economic agent 20, 25, 36, 87, 169–70, 174, 256, 301; *see also* agency
economic cycle 107, 253, 262; *see also* business cycle; in labour markets 193, 202–3, 207, 214, 256; in financial markets 22, 291, 361; and policy 153–4;
economic growth *see* growth
economies of scale 39, 50, 88, 98, 124, 159, 367–8
economies of scope 39
efficiency wages 209–11, 217
efficient market hypothesis 231–2, 237, 243–8, 289
El Salvador 345, 382
EMH *see* Efficient Market Hypothesis
EMU *see* European Monetary Union
Engel curve 72–3
Engel, Ernst 72
entry barriers 29, 122, 124, 128, 130–2, 381
environmental economics 357
EPA *see* European Partnership Agreement
EPZ *see* Export Processing Zone
equilibrium: general market equilibrium 25; market equilibrium 5, 25–6, 121, 213, 215–16
equity capital 220, 227, 260, 279
ethics: deontological ethics 19–20; virtue ethics 16–18
Ethiopia 47, 160, 308
EU *see* European Union
EU ETS *see* European Union Emissions Trading System
European Union 6, 89, 182, 230, 366; environmental policy 336, 346–7, 359–62; external trade 373, 368–9; policy 4, 29, 165, 181–2, 248, 374–5
European Central Bank 280, 289
European Commission 29, 230, 359, 361, 363

European Monetary Union 227, 280, 289, 375–6
European Partnership Agreement 373
European Unions Emissions Trading System 359–63
exchange rate: fixed exchange rate 287–8, 303, 380; flexible exchange rate 288, 369
export processing zone 96, 316, 382
externality 81, 83, 136, 177–9, 183, 359; negative externality 135, 172–3, 179, 372; positive externality 135

failure of markets 140–141
fallacy of composition 262–3, 270
Fama, Eugene 231–2, 243
Fannie Mae *see* Federal National Mortgage Association
FDI *see* Foreign Direct Investment
feasible no-trade option 118–20, 146
Fed *see* Federal Reserve Bank
Federal Deposit Insurance Corporation 234
Federal Home Loan Mortgage Corporation 224–5
Federal National Mortgage Association 224–5
Federal Reserve Bank 4, 224, 227–8, 232, 237, 380
female 28, 151, 191; leadership 16–7, 92; and the labour market 62, 195–7, 199, 208, 382, 388
feminism 1, 431; femininity 16–7, 41; masculinity 16–7, 41, 130, 199–200
feminist economics 8, 425, 427
finance frontier 104–6
financial crisis: year 1929 15, 227, 263; Asian 232, 299, 303–4, 316; global financial crisis 331, 360–2
financial fragility 22, 236–8, 243, 353, 410–11
financial transactions tax 182–3, 354
financialisation 223, 224, 226, 236, 238, 243
Finland 89, 98, 180, 381
FIRE sector 235, 238, 269, 274, 326, 410–1
fiscal policy 152, 159
fiscal discipline 330
Fisher, Irvin 231
foreign direct investment 297–302, 316, 366, 371, 382, 389
France 30, 180, 228, 261, 298, 360–3, 369, 379
Freddie Mac *see* Federal Home Loan Mortgage Corporation
free riding 17, 40, 162, 173, 309; and common pool resources 186–7; and public goods 149, 158, 170, 174
FTT *see* Financial Transactions Tax
futures 219, 234

GEI *see* Gender Equality Index
gender: gender division of labour 1, 41–5, 50, 61–2, 256; in the household 192, 195, 197, 209; gender inequality 313, 378, 403–5
Germany 317, 400; firms 89, 100, 228, 298; policy 280, 345; trade 346, 376, 379, 381
Giffen good 69, 75
Giffen, Robert 69
Gini coefficient 146–7, 389, 393, 400–2
Gini, Corrado 146
Gintis, Herbert 18
Glass-Steagall Act 227–8
globalisation 80, 410–11; financial 223, 228, 236, 238, 302, 401; firms 91; trade 366, 371, 376, 380, 387–8
gold standard 277
good: global public 177, 181, 183, 337; heterogeneous 124, 128, 130; homogeneous 124, 128, 132; inferior 69; merit 147, 169–71, 174, 185; normal 69, 131, 253; public 96, 134–5, 170–6, 180–3, 187, 307, 315, 393; status 71
government: government capture 152, 362; government consumption 65–6, 160–1; government failure 145, 149, 152, 187; government investment 161, 169, 177
Grameen Bank 414
Great Depression 241, 263, 352, 426
Greece 280, 286, 289, 315
Greenspan, Alan 4–5, 7, 228, 232
growth: equation 309, 313, 319, 325–9, 333–4, 341; green 340–1; inclusive 310–12
Guatemala 147, 151

happiness 12–3, 24, 67, 76, 343, 411, 416–7, 423; Global Happiness Index 396
Haq, Mahbub ul 395
HDI *see* Human Development Index
Heckscher-Ohlin theorem 387–8
herd behaviour 22, 27, 235, 238, 241, 262, 426–7
household: household bargaining 46–8, 56–61; household functions 37
human capability 38, 47, 189, 190, 199, 208, 410
human capital 38, 189, 311, 332; in the labour market 31, 36, 178, 208, 258, 329–32
human development 13, 145, 308, 395–7, 403, 409, 429; Human Development Index 395–8, 403

IAD *see* Institutional Analysis and Development framework
Iceland 5, 180, 228–9, 289

ILO *see* International Labour Organization
IMF *see* International Monetary Fund
import tariff 314–6, 331, 367, 374–7, 379, 388, 430
income: disposable 154, 159, 260, 268, 319–24; effect 75, 196, 198, 395
India 6–7, 47, 345, 356; economist 427, 430; and financial regulation 289, 299; and firms, 128, 295, 297; and monetary policy 284–9; and poverty 395, 397; and the state 160, 317–18, 332; and trade 302, 368, 374
Indonesia 1, 160, 316, 318, 356
inequality: horizontal 312–3, 403–4; vertical 312, 398
infant industry 378, 380, 382
inflation 27, 153, 211, 274, 282–5; and the Central Bank 280, 286, 293–4, 299–301, 429; and cost price 295–6, 388; and debt 165–6, 283; and pensions 172; hyper- 286
informal economy 162, 194, 198, 201–2
institutions: asymmetric institutions 19, 31, 39, 47, 120, 378, 389, 404; Institutional Analysis and Development framework 185; institutionalism 19, 424; monetary institutions 279
interest rate: conventional interest rate 293–4
Intergovernmental Panel on Climate Change 177, 337, 345
International Labour Organization 202, 373
International Monetary Fund 5–6, 165, 180–1, 286, 303–4, 316, 330–1
Investment: portfolio investment 298, 366; return on investment 97–8, 103, 408; under-investment 410
IPCC *see* Intergovernmental Panel on Climate Change
Ireland 318, 368
Islamic banking 95
Italy 160, 180, 379, 400
Ivory Coast 90

Jamaica 345, 382
Japan 263, 356, 400; and firms 106, 368; and growth 252, 314, 408; and the macro economy 254, 269, 411; and the state 180, 374, 379
junk bonds 164

Keen, Steve 5, 234, 239
Kenya 54, 136, 160
Keynes, John Maynard: and macroeconomics 8, 121, 153–4, 262, 321; and behaviour 28, 72, 241, 298; and uncertainty 21–2; and money 290; biography and work 12, 163, 352, 426–7

Kuznets curve 413; Environmental Kuznets Curve 357
Kuznets, Simon 308, 413
Kyoto Protocol 345, 259–60, 363

labour: division of 38, 41, 46, 60, 109, 371, 421; and governance 100, 146, 202; and inflation 148, 285, 295; and power 18, 100, 198, 389, 397; and rights 200–2, 382; unions and collective agency 52, 208, 215, 346, 382
labour market: internal 101, 200–2; segmentation 198, 208–9, 387 *see also* segmentation
Laffer, Arthur 176
Laffer curve 176
Latino 223, 225
Latvia 90
law of diminishing marginal utility or returns 25, 76, 215, 328, 332, 417; *see also* marginal utility
leadership 16–7, 44, 92, 101, 187, 199
Lebanon 404
Lesotho 190–1
leverage ratio 219, 227, 232
Libor 230
London Interbank Offered Rate *see* Libor
Long-Term Capital Management 232
LTCM *see* Long-Term Capital Management
Luxemburg 228

macroeconomic: equation 252–3, 268, 273, 291, 319, 369; equilibrium 251, 253, 263–4, 269–74; injection 268; leakage 267–8
Malawi 429
Maldives 395, 397
male 16–7, 19, 28, 58, 191, 196–9, 427
Mali 129, 345, 375
marginal rate of substitution 79
market: failure 134–8, 187, 246–8, 414; static 120
market power 66, 158; and accumulation 33, 88, 146, 157; and competition 22–3, 28–9, 67, 111, 397; and firm strategy 89, 98–9, 106, 124, 224–5; and market types 29, 107, 124, 128, 130–1;
Marshall, Alfred 23, 423–4, 426
Marx, Karl 1, 134, 223, 279, 422–4
Marxism 8, 22, 107, 429
Mauritius 315–6
MBS *see* Mortgage Backed Securities
MDG *see* Millennium Development Goals
Médecins sans Frontières 93–94
MENA *see* Middle East and North Africa 404–5

Mercosur 376–8, 381, 384
Mexico: and crisis 164–5, 332; and exports 351, 388; and NAFTA 376–7, 388–9; and the state 147, 160–1
microcredit 137–8, 414
Middle East 126; Middle East and North Africa 157, 313, 316, 404–5
Mill, John Stuart 1
Millennium Development Goals 180, 182, 412
Minsky, Hyman 235–6
Mishkin, Frederic 5
Mkandawire, Thandika 332, 429
MNC *see* multinational corporation
Mondragon 93–4
monetarism 299–300
money: fiat money 280–3, 286, 292; liquid money 279
monopoly 29, 121–5, 128, 130, 173, 292, 379
monopsony 22, 128–30
moral hazard 17, 139–40, 152–7, 247, 309, 411–14
mortgage backed securities 3–5, 220, 229, 234–41, 245, 248, 271
MPI *see* Multidimensional Poverty Index 396–8
MSF *see* Médecins sans Frontières
multinational company *see also* multinational corporation
multinational corporation 315, 347, 366; and investment 368, 372, 382; power of 130, 374; and tax evasion 149, 156; and trade 200, 371; Unilever 29, 87, 92, 105–6
multinational firm *see also* multinational corporation
multiplier 154, 266–9, 320, 324–5, 363, 369–70

NAFTA 376–7, 388–9
natural resource curse 351
neoliberal policies 1, 80, 162, 223, 228, 316, 330–2
Nepal 187, 395, 397
Netherlands 7, 40, 298; and the environment 336–7, 343–52, 354, 360–2; and the financial crisis 228, 234, 289; and governance 100, 160, 379; and public finance 280, 322; and time allocation 18, 189, 432; trade 237, 368, 376, 380;
New Growth Theory 332–4
New York Stock Exchange 231, 239
Nicaragua 382
Nigeria 3, 127, 135, 160
Nobel Prize 10, 93, 139, 184, 231–4, 304, 420, 427–8

Norway 147–8, 352
nudging 69, 34
NYSE *see* New York Stock Exchange

Occupy 400
ODA *see* Official Development Assistance
OECD 156, 163, 180, 182, 342, 377, 393
official development assistance 180, 183, 414
oligopoly 29, 126, 381
Oman 404
OMO *see* open market operations
OPEC 26, 29, 126
open market operations 286–7, 296–7
open system economics 262–4, 269, 272, 339, 353
opportunity cost 118, 214, 301, 312; of consumption 64–5; of production 82, 98; of public goods 174–5, 177, 183; of trade 386; of work 59–61, 159, 195–6, 211–2
options 219–20; stock options 103, 248
Ostrom, Elinor 183–6, 420, 428

Pakistan 7, 170, 307, 395–7
Paley, Mary 423
paradox of thrift 262, 264
Paraguay 54, 147, 152, 344, 376
path dependency 376
Penrose effect 106
Penrose, Edith 106
Philippines 315
Piketty, Thomas 406–8
pluralism 2, 7, 11, 14–15
Portugal 280, 289, 376
possibility frontier 48, 59, 413–16
poverty: reduction 159, 180, 286, 307–8, 332, 412–15; trap 192
power: and competition 128, 130, 134; in financial markets 222–5; in trade 387, 401; of capital over labour 107, 326, 389, 397, 407, 409
Prebisch-Singer hypothesis 371
Prebisch, Raul 371, 429–31
precautionary motive 291–4
precautionary principle 353–4
price: controls, 148, 149, 327, 331; elasticity 74–5; leader 124; taker 132
principal-agent problem 102–3, 248
private equity fund 95
privatisation 118, 122–3, 130, 147, 158, 162, 165, 330
pro-social norms 52, 100, 119–20, 141, 257, 309, 318

production function 108–10; aggregate 328–9, 333
production possibility frontier 48, 415
profit: business 99; capitalist 107; commercial 99, 384; gross 98, 105; net 96, 98, 129; normal 107; profit and loss account 97–8; rate 99, 105, 107, 325–6;
propensity to consume 72–3, 253–4, 260–9, 319–21, 370, 407, 410
propensity to save 73, 254, 260, 264, 325, 407, 410
property rights: as institution 119–20, 150–2, 318, 359; intellectual 381; policy 182, 268; as rules 19, 185; and the state 145, 157–8
public finance 159–60, 169, 268
purchasing power: and demand 22, 25, 64, 141, 157; and income 49, 75, 195, 205, 211, 395, 397; and inflation 172, 285; and markets 118, 134; and prices 121–2, 225, 273, 282; purchasing power parity 411–2; and segmentation 137–8, 170

quantitative easing 228

RBI *see* Reserve Bank of India
redistribution: of income 149, 315; of land 146, 313
rent-seeking 142, 152, 156–7, 351, 362, 410, 413–14
repo *see* repurchase agreement
reproduction 37–8, 190–1, 258, 393
repurchase agreement 220
Reserve Bank of India 277–8, 285–8, 299, 302
revenue: average 112, 124; marginal 112–13, 124, 128, 130, 132, 204, 424
Ricardo, David 382–3, 387, 421–2
rights, human 142, 179, 310, 340
risk: principle of increasing 104; pooling 37, 41; systemic 3–4, 8, 237–8
Robinson, Joan 11, 21–2, 157
ROI *see* return on investment
Roubini, Nouriel 5, 234
Russia 7, 46, 50, 56, 61, 71, 332, 379

SAP *see* Structural Adjustment Programme
satisficing 54, 56, 100
Say, Jean Baptiste 84
Say's Law 84
Scandinavia 317
Schumpeter, Joseph 425–6
securities 219–20, 224, 228–9, 232, 237–8, 247–8, 298, 302
securitization 220, 228, 237

social security 146, 161–3, 172, 255–6, 260, 398; food security 122, 151, 374, 388; job security 201, 217
segmentation 69–72, 134–8, 198–9, 206–10, 222–4, 387; horizontal 72, 198; vertical 198
self-interest 3–5, 23, 174, 187, 416
Sen, Amartya 1, 10, 395, 420, 427
Sen, Gita 430–1
shareholder interest 93, 103
Shiller, Robert 6, 231–2, 234, 239–41
Singapore 318, 344, 368, 401
Singer, Hans 430
small and medium sized enterprise 89
SME *see* Small and medium sized enterprises
Smith, Adam 15, 68, 120, 145, 208, 379, 383, 420–1
social capital 16–18, 47, 132, 149; bonding 17, 256, 318; bridging 17
social clauses 373
social cohesion 16–19, 45–6, 138, 142, 175, 309–13, 398, 410
social contract 256–7
social safety net 65–6, 161, 255, 401
South Africa 7–8, 191, 193–4, 198, 202, 206, 209, 215, 312, 374, 401
South-Korea 127, 314–16, 388
sovereign wealth fund 352
Spain 93, 280, 289, 363, 376, 379
speculation 180; financial 22, 140, 219, 254, 426–7; commodity 298; currency 287, 298, 299
speculative motive 291–4, 300–01
Sri Lanka 382, 395, 397
stakeholders 88–9, 96, 98–9, 103, 174, 233, 248
Stiglitz, Joseph 304
stock exchange 3, 91, 96, 103, 230, 299; Amsterdam 91–2; London 90, 92, 163; Paris 91; New York 92, 231, 239; and Keynes 426
Structural Adjustment Programme 165, 330–2, 429
subprime loans 219, 225, 229, 234, 241, 248, 289
subprime mortgages *see* subprime loans
substitution effect 75, 196, 198, 203
Summers, Larry 358, 362
supply: aggregate 251–2, 263–4, 267, 271, 327; labour 152, 190–9, 205, 211–16, 255–8, 264, 387
sustainable development 258, 339, 347
swap 219–20
Sweden 10, 379
Switzerland 30, 181, 227, 317, 379

Taiwan 314–5, 388
Tanzania 54, 136, 139
tax: base 149, 172, 175, 411, 414; holiday 382; flat 321–4; progressive 149, 321–4; regressive 149; value added 21, 93, 162–3, 172, 319, 362
Thailand 160, 318, 374, 403
tiger economies 156, 316–18, 388; Asian tigers 156, 316, 388; baby tiger 318; Celtic tiger 318
toxic assets 3, 181, 237, 241, 280, 289
trade: fair 83, 84, 136, 372–3; gains from 18, 118, 138, 366–7, 371, 377–89; openness 368–9; terms of 371, 412, 430
trade union (labour) 19, 100, 121, 215; *see also* labour union
trade union (trade) 366, 373–8, 382, 384, 388, 403
transfer payments 160–2, 255, 257
Tunisia 181, 404
Turkey 332, 379

UAE *see* United Arab Emirates
Uganda 136
UK *see* United Kingdom
UN *see* United Nations
uncertainty 33, 36; of climate change 177, 353–4; in consumption 64, 70; of demand 21–3, 141, 262–3, 320; in financial markets 4, 233, 236, 291; fundamental 5, 7, 28, 238, 243; versus risk 23, 236, 246, 248
UNCTAD *see* United Nations Conference on Trade and Development
UNDP *see* United Nations Development Programme
underemployment 193–5, 198, 211, 397
unemployment: structural 206–7; temporary 206–7
UNICEF *see* United Nations Children Fund
United Arab Emirates 160, 193, 307, 344, 404
United Kingdom 7, 400; and consumption 69, 362; and the financial crisis 228, 289, 298; and firms 89–90, 94, 297; and trade 261, 367, 369, 376
United Nations 45, 180, 182, 258, 308, 310, 347
United Nations Children Fund 332
United Nations Conference on Trade and Development 384, 429
United Nations Development Programme 395–6, 403, 427
United Nations Research Institute for Social Development 429
United States: and banks 229, 234–5, 228–9, 280; and the Central Bank 4, 224, 227, 277,

289, 411; and consumer markets 151–2; and economics 2, 7, 14, 424, 426; and the environment 345, 362; and the financial crisis 4–6, 8, 22, 181, 280, 227–8; and financial markets 5, 214, 219, 225, 234, 237, 289; and financial policy 6, 224–5, 228, 232, 234, 263; and firms 92, 102, 122, 223, 247; and growth 408; and housing markets 5, 239, 241; and inequality 47, 223–5, 248, 400–1; and the state 155–6, 160, 162, 314, 330; and trade 237, 302, 368–9, 372, 374–80, 388–9

unpaid labour 28, 47, 64, 66, 142, 258, 393

unpaid work 13, 15, 42, 46, 256–8; and children 37, 179; and the division of labour 38, 61, 192; and gender 41, 44–5, 47, 209; and production 66; and time-use 48–51, 59, 195–8, 213–14

UNRISD *see* United Nations Research Institute for Social Development

Uruguay 90, 147, 152, 374, 376–

US *see* United States

USA *see* United States

utilitarianism 423, 427

utility 24, 174, 411, 417; marginal 25, 76–7, 332, 424; function 23–4, 28, 76; maximization 14, 20, 25, 28, 77–9, 416, 427

value chain 152, 366, 371–2, 382, 401

VAT *see* value added tax

Veblen effect 70–1, 84

Veblen, Thorstein 19

Venezuela 147–8, 158, 376

wage: indexation 285; inequality 206, 208; discrimination 202, 208–9, 381–2; gender gap 338

Weber, Max 317

white Americans 198

WHO *see* World Health Organization

worker effect: added 41, 113, 193, 195, 211, 256; discouraged 193–5, 198, 272, 397

World Bank: criticism of 6, 181, 429; lending by 162, 165; as an organisation 31, 304, 358, 362; policy 316, 330; and poverty 180, 411

World Economic Forum 181–2

World Health Organization 68

World Social Forum 181–2

World Trade Organization 316, 373–5, 377

World Wildlife Fund 342

WTO *see* World Trade Organization

WWF *see* World Wildlife Fund

Yemen 404

Zambia 191, 307

Zhang Xin 31–2

Zimbabwe 54, 191, 286

eBooks
from Taylor & Francis

Helping you to choose the right eBooks for your Library

Add to your library's digital collection today with Taylor & Francis eBooks. We have over 50,000 eBooks in the Humanities, Social Sciences, Behavioural Sciences, Built Environment and Law, from leading imprints, including Routledge, Focal Press and Psychology Press.

Choose from a range of subject packages or create your own!

Benefits for you
- Free MARC records
- COUNTER-compliant usage statistics
- Flexible purchase and pricing options
- 70% approx of our eBooks are now DRM-free.

Benefits for your user
- Off-site, anytime access via Athens or referring URL
- Print or copy pages or chapters
- Full content search
- Bookmark, highlight and annotate text
- Access to thousands of pages of quality research at the click of a button.

Free Trials Available

We offer free trials to qualifying academic, corporate and government customers.

eCollections

Choose from 20 different subject eCollections, including:

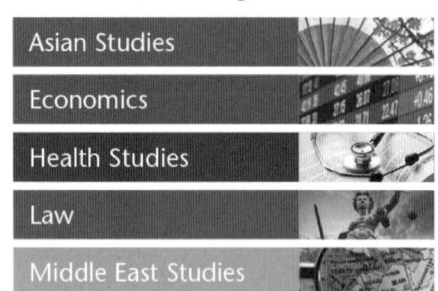

- Asian Studies
- Economics
- Health Studies
- Law
- Middle East Studies

eFocus

We have 16 cutting-edge interdisciplinary collections, including:

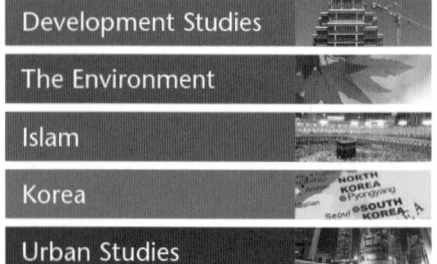

- Development Studies
- The Environment
- Islam
- Korea
- Urban Studies

For more information, pricing enquiries or to order a free trial, please contact your local sales team:

UK/Rest of World: **online.sales@tandf.co.uk**
USA/Canada/Latin America: **e-reference@taylorandfrancis.com**
East/Southeast Asia: **martin.jack@tandf.com.sg**
India: **journalsales@tandfindia.com**

www.tandfebooks.com